AFRICA 2011

by
Les de Villiers

A publication of
The Corporate Council on Africa
and
Business Books International

Copyright © 2011 by Business Books International, P O Box 1587, New Canaan, Connecticut 06840, USA. All rights reserved. No part of this book may be reproduced, stored in a retrieval system, or transmitted, in any form or by any means, electronic, mechanical, photocopying, recording, or otherwise, without the prior written permission of Business Books International, except for quotations embodied in critical articles and reviews. Manufactured in the United States.

AFRICA 2011
Africa - Reference

ISBN-13: 978-0-916673-32-1
ISBN-10: 0-916673-32-4
ISSN 1536-1454

The information in this book is furnished for informational use only and should not be construed as recommendations on investment and business transactions. It was developed on the basis of review of both secondary resources and first-hand advice and contains subjective opinion. While efforts were made to include the most recent and reliable sources of information, the accuracy of the content cannot be guaranteed. Investment and business decisions should only be made after proper further investigation and due diligence on the part of the reader.

Size	11,709,908 sq miles/30,328,662 sq. km	Island nations	Six, with Equatorial Guinea part landbased
	Second largest continent after Asia		Madagascar is world's 4th largest island
Distance	North-South 5,000 miles/8,000 km	Population	At 1 billion 13% of world total
	East-West 4,700 miles/7,560 km		Speak more than 1,000 languages
Mountains	Highest: Mt. Kilimanjaro 19,340 ft/5,895 m	Density	Average of 65 people per sq. mile
	Ranks sixteenth worldwide		Well below world average of 105 and Asia's 203
Lakes	Lake Victoria is world's 3rd largest	Resources	9.6 % of world's oil, 7.9% of its natural gas
	Lake Tanganyika is 7th largest		11% to 45% of world's strategic minerals
Rivers	Longest: Nile is 4,180 miles/6,690 km	Economy	Average GDP growth of 5.3% from 2001 to 2009
	World's longest river		Per capita GDP in 2008 was $2,876
Countries	53 countries of which 15 landlocked	Investment	Returns on investment rarely dips below 10%
	Largest: Sudan, Algeria & DR of Congo		Highest returns in the world according to OPIC

africa's bridges

expand - relationships - trust - prosperity - trade - investments - business - understanding

that bring us together

Creating Engineered Solutions Worldwide®

Acrow Corporation of America 181 New Road | Parsippany, New Jersey USA 07054-5625
Tel: +1-973-244-0080 Fax: +1-973-244-0085 Email: sales@acrowusa.com | www.acrowusa.com

CONTENTS

	AFRICA TODAY (POLITICAL MAP)	3
FOREWORD	STEPHEN HAYES	11
EDITORIAL	LES DE VILLIERS	13
	THE YEAR IN REVIEW	15
	AFRICAN MILESTONES	25
	DID YOU KNOW	30
	AFRICA'S NOBEL LAUREATES	31
	HOW AFRICA MEASURES UP	32

CHAPTER 1—THE AFRICAN CONTINENT 33

TOPOGRAPHY	34
VEGETATION, PEOPLES AND LANGUAGES	35
RELIGIONS, EARLY HISTORY	36
FIRST EUROPEANS, SLAVERY, FIRST SETTLEMENT	37
COLONIALISM, DECOLONIZATION	38
RECENT DEVELOPMENTS	39
RIVERS, LAKES AND MOUNTAINS	40
THE NILE RIVER	41
THE CONGO RIVER	42
THE NIGER RIVER	43
THE ZAMBEZI RIVER	44
AFRICAN UNION	46

CHAPTER 2—THE ECONOMY OF AFRICA 47

SAFER ENVIRONMENT, GLOBAL CRISIS	48
INFLATION, DEBT	49
AGRICULTURE, MANUFACTURING, SERVICES	50
URBAN POPULATION	51
INTERNATIONAL LINKS	52
UNITED NATIONS SYSTEM	52
UN, ECA, FAO, IAEA, IDA	52
IFC, IFAD, ILO, IMO, IMF, ITU	53
UNCTAD, UNESCO, UNHCR, UNIDO, UPU, IBRD	54
WHO, WIPO, WMO, WTO	55
OTHER WORLD & REGIONAL	55
AFRICAN, CARIBBEAN & PACIFIC (ACP)	55
ADB, AU, ABEDA, AMU, BDEAC	56
COMMONWEALTH, COMESA, CEMAC	57
CCC, EAC, EADB, CEEAC, CEPGL, ECOWAS, CFA	58
ICC, ICFTU, INTERPOL, IGAD, IOM	59
INMARSAT, IOC, ISO, INTELSAT, IOR-ARC, ICRM	60
OPEC, SACU, SADC	61
WADB, WAEMU	62

CHAPTER 3—TRADE AND INVESTMENT 63

US TRADE	64
AFRICAN TRADE STATISTICS	65
DIRECT INVESTMENT	67
INDIRECT INVESTMENT	69
PRIVATIZATION	72
CHINA SYNDROME	76

www.ge.com/africa

1,500 EMPLOYEES ACROSS 17 COUNTRIES

MAKING AFRICA CLEANER,

HEALTHIER AND BETTER

NOW.

GE imagination at work

CHAPTER 4—KEY SECTORS IN AFRICA 77

PETROLEUM & ENERGY 78
- RESERVES AND PRODUCTION (TABLE) 78
- RESERVES AND PRODUCTION (MAP) 79

ELECTRICITY 89
- AFRICA'S ELECTRICITY (TABLE) 88

MINERALS & MINING 93
- STRATEGIC MINERALS 92
- AFRICA MINERALS PRODUCTION MAP 94
- PRODUCTION SELECTED MINERALS (TABLE) 95

TELECOMMUNICATIONS 97
- MILLENNIUM GOALS, FIXED LINES 97
- MOBILE SERVICES, DISPARITY 98
- TELECOMMUNICATIONS IN AFRICA (TABLE) 99
- REGIONAL INITIATIVES, COMPETITION, RATES 100
- MEGADEALS, BUSINESS POTENTIAL 101

INTERNET 103
- INTERNET USE IN AFRICA (TABLE) 102
- AFRICA & THE WORLD (TABLE) 104
- COMPUTER USE IN AFRICA (TABLE) 105

TRANSPORT 107
- TRANSPORT FACILITIES IN AFRICA (TABLE) 106
- RAILROADS AND HARBORS MAP 107
- MAJOR AIRPORTS MAP 108

AGRICULTURE 112
- FOOD SHORTAGES, EXPORTS 113
- SECTORAL SHARE OF GDP IN AFRICA (TABLE) 114

MANUFACTURING 115
- GOING GLOBAL 116
- INDUSTRY AS PERCENTAGE OF GDP (MAP) 116

BANKING 118
- REFORMS, ELECTRONIC, RANKINGS 118
- TOP FIFTY BANKS IN AFRICA 119

TOURISM 121
- INTERNATIONAL ARRIVALS (TABLE) 121
- CULTURES OF AFRICA 122
- SAFARI 126

CHAPTER 5—DOING BUSINESS WITH AFRICA 133
- PAYING TAXES 132
- SETTING UP 134
- STARTING A BUSINESS (CHART) 136
- TAX RATES IN AFRICAN COUNTRIES 138
- SOVEREIGN CREDIT RATINGS 143
- ADVICE AND ASSISTANCE 145

CHAPTER 6—CHALLENGES OF AFRICA 151
- WARS AND REFUGEES 152
- PEACEKEEPING 153
- FAMINE IN AFRICA 154
- TROPICAL DISEASES 156
- HIV/AIDS 158

CHALLENGES OF AFRICA (CONTINUED)

WATER WARS	161
AFRICA'S CHALLENGES (TABLE)	166
CORRUPTION	167
ILLITERACY	169
DEBT BURDEN	170
AFRICAN HUMAN INDICATORS (TABLE)	172

CHAPTER 7—THE NATIONS OF AFRICA   173

HUMAN DEVELOPMENT INDICATORS (TABLE)	172
THE 53 NATIONS OF AFRICA (MAP)	174
ECONOMIC DEVELOPMENT INDICATORS (TABLE)	176
ALGERIA	177
ANGOLA	181
BENIN	185
BOTSWANA	189
BURKINA FASO	193
BURUNDI	197
CAMEROON	200
CAPE VERDE	206
CENTRAL AFRICAN REP.	210
CHAD	213
COMOROS	217
CONGO, DEM, REP.	220
CONGO, REP. OF	224
CÔTE D'IVOIRE	227
DJIBOUTI	231
EGYPT	234
EQUATORIAL GUINEA	238
ERITREA	242
ETHIOPIA	246
GABON	250
GAMBIA, THE	254
GHANA	257
GUINEA	261
GUINEA-BISSAU	265
KENYA	268
LESOTHO	272
LIBERIA	276
LIBYA	280
MADAGASCAR	284
MALAWI	288
MALI	292
MAURITANIA	296
MAURITIUS	300
MOROCCO	304
MOZAMBIQUE	308
NAMIBIA	312
NIGER	316
NIGERIA	320
RWANDA	324
SÃO TOMÉ & PRÍNCIPE	327
SENEGAL	330
SEYCHELLES	334
SIERRA LEONE	337
SOMALIA	340
SOUTH AFRICA	343
SUDAN	350
SWAZILAND	353
TANZANIA	357
TOGO	361
TUNISIA	365
UGANDA	369
ZAMBIA	373
ZIMBABWE	377
WESTERN SAHARA	381

CHAPTER 8—TRAVEL TIPS & TRIVIA   383

TRAVEL TIPS	382
EXCHANGE RATES	387
COUNTRY CALL CODES, TIME ZONES	388
AFRICAN WEATHER CHART	389
DR. LIVINGSTONE, I PRESUME	390
DIPLOMATIC ADDRESSES	391

INDEX	395

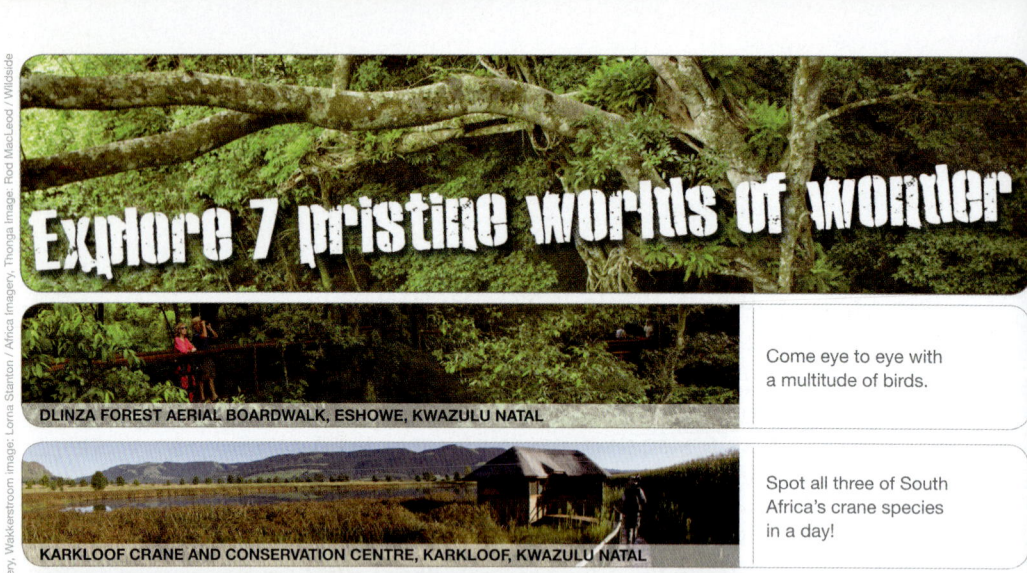

Explore 7 pristine worlds of wonder

DLINZA FOREST AERIAL BOARDWALK, ESHOWE, KWAZULU NATAL

Come eye to eye with a multitude of birds.

KARKLOOF CRANE AND CONSERVATION CENTRE, KARKLOOF, KWAZULU NATAL

Spot all three of South Africa's crane species in a day!

ONGOYE FOREST BIRDING CAMP, MTUNZINI, KWAZULU NATAL

"Tick off" the highly localised Green Barbet.

THONGA BEACH LODGE AND MABIBI CAMPSITE, MABIBI, KWAZULU NATAL

Experience the pristine beauty of this coastal World Heritage site.

WAKKERSTROOM BIRDING CENTRE, WAKERSTROOM, MPUMALANGA

Visit the home of the largest populations of threatened bird species in South Africa.

MARUTSWA FOREST TRAIL AND BOARDWALK, BULWER, KWAZULU NATAL

See rare Cape Parrots in their own home.

THE SOUTHERN KWAZULU NATAL BIRDING ROUTE, KWAZULU NATAL

Enjoy over 550 bird species in diverse habitats.

Intelligent conservation - caring communities

Over the years, we have enthusiastically supported and partnered with WWF South Africa, demonstrating our commitment to preserving some of South Africa's pristine natural habitats.

The SappiWWF TreeRoutes Partnership focuses on the sustainable conservation of threatened wetlands and forests in Mpumalanga and KwaZulu Natal, by empowering local communities in these areas through the development of sustainable community-based eco-tourism projects.

For more information about these initiatives, contact Celia Bayley on +27 (0)11 407 8430 or visit **www.treeroutes.co.za** to plan your trip.

FOREWORD

For more than a decade, the Corporate Council on Africa has worked closely with its member and partner Business Books International to create what we believe is one of the best primers on today's Africa for those interested in not only visiting but also investing in Africa. The countries of Africa are experiencing the greatest boom in business in the history of the continent. Global investment is beginning to pour into parts of Africa in amounts unimagined a decade ago when we started publishing this book. Each year, we have attempted to adjust the information on each country so that it contains some of the most up-to-date basic information on Africa that can be found.

It is not always easy to do, as the changes taking place in some countries is indeed rapid. Countries like Ghana are booming, and this is to be expected, as Ghana has long been an economic leader in Africa. But so too are countries like Mozambique, Namibia and Ethiopia, none of which had been known as the great investment destinations that they have become. Said simply, Africa is changing at a rate not easily comprehended in the United States.

We still see Africa in outdated terms, as if its development is still dependent upon traditional aid models, and upon the international non-governmental charity organizations. The truth is that the future of Africa is tied to the level of investment going into Africa, the last great frontier in the world for new investment and development. In this edition of Africa 2011 we have tried to provide more economic information, and we encourage you to see Africa not only as a fabulous travel destination, but as an opportunity for investment and business as well. Africa truly offers both these opportunities as few other locations in the world does. The future and the past is all in Africa.

Stephen Hayes
President and CEO
Corporate Council on Africa

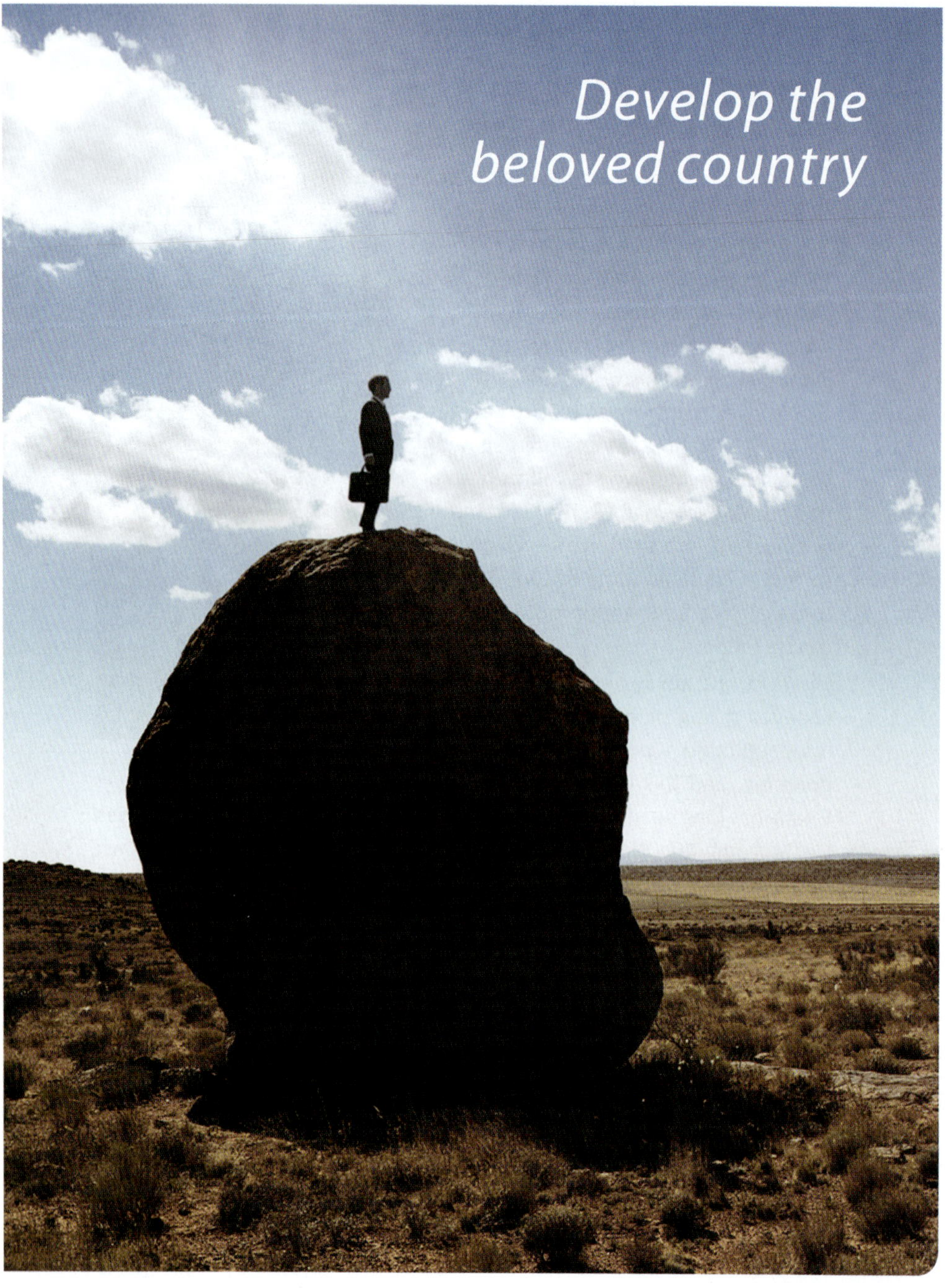

Develop the beloved country

The IDC is committed to the creation of a modern, dynamic economy, characterised by shared and sustainable economic growth for the prosperity and wellbeing of South Africa and the African continent.

IDC
Industrial Development Corporation

Your partner in development finance

The IDC provides finance for industrial and enterprise development.
To discuss funding of **R1 million or more**, please call 053 807 1050 or visit www.idc.co.za

PUBLISHER'S NOTE

The September 2005 issue of *National Geographic* was devoted in its entirety to Africa. Instead of a picture the cover simply carried the following message against a white background: *AFRICA: WHATEVER YOU THOUGHT, THINK AGAIN*.

I was tempted to do the same after South Africa (and Africa) showed the world that they can stage the world's premier sport event with as great, if not greater, flair and efficiency than any nation or region. Concensus is that FIFA's 2010 Soccer World Cup—the first in Africa—compares favorably with the best ever staged elsewhere.

Hopefully it prompted those among the billions abroad who followed the spectacle on their TV screens and still entertained visions of Africa as a Dark Continent, to think again.

In this, the eleventh edition of our Africa Yearbook we are once again trying to remain objective in our assessment of the potential (and pitfalls) of Africa as a business partner, a source for materials and manufactures, and a tourist destination. Africa does not need any embroidering on our part to make it worthy of serious consideration.

Having been associated with the Washington-based Corporate Council on Africa over the past eleven years in the production of this annual account, I can attest to the crucial role that the Council plays not only in promoting knowledge of Africa but in facilitating real results on the business front. A special word of gratitude goes to the president of the Corporate Council, Steve Hayes, and his colleagues for their help and support.

A special word of thanks also to our advertisers. It is only with their support that we can produce, in the words of the American Library Association, an "excellent reference work" inexpensively.

Dr. Les de Villiers
Publisher/Editor
lesdv@businessbooksusa.com

13

The PricewaterhouseCoopers African Footprint

The biggest tax network in Africa

PWC has an extensive network of offices in most countries of the African continent

More than 57 permanent offices located in 31 countries across the continent and employing more than 7,500 professional staff

Three lines of services everywhere (Assurance, Tax and Advisory) and some offices also provide legal assistance

- PricewaterhouseCoopers Member Firms in Africa
- Services provided by other PricewaterhouseCoopers Member Firms in neighboring countries
- Embargoed countries or no presence

For further information contact:
gilles.j.de.vignemont@us.pwc.com

THE YEAR IN REVIEW

Even though Africa's economies are less linked than many other parts of the world to global financial markets, the region has not been spared the fallout of a crisis that originated in the sophisticated financial markets of the industrialized world. Real GDP growth across the continent declined to 2.5% in 2009, compared to 5.6% a year before and an average of 5.9% during the period 2000-2008. However, 2010 will not be remembered for its economic setbacks but the successful staging of the first Soccer World Cup in Africa that finally dispelled the myth of Africa as a Dark Continent.

For a month an accumulated worldwide audience of some 40 billion people watched the world's premier sport event unfold in ten venues across South Africa. What they saw on their television screens was nothing remotely close to the stereotypical Dark Continent fit only for missionaries and hunters. Instead they were treated to images of state-of-the-art stadiums, airports, rapid transit systems, and modern skyscrapers. No only South Africa as the host country but all of Africa benefited from the new branding of a continent that has for too long been painted in terms of the past. Resources such as oil, gold, diamonds, chrome and other strategic minerals, and spectacular sights, beaches and safari destinations promoted by tourist operators, will continue to be important generators of foreign revenues. But this should not obscure the potential of Africa as both a supplier of and a market for sophisticated goods. UN Secretary-General Ban Ki-moon hailed South Africa and the entire African continent as the real winners of the 2010 FIFA World Cup. As the Soccer World

FIFA President Sepp Blatter welcomes former South African President Nelson Mandela and his wife Gracia to the 2010 Soccer World Cup Final between Netherlands and Spain at Soccer City Stadium in Johannesburg, South Africa. (Picture: Getty Images)

Wise investment or white elephant? The $600 million GreenPoint stadium constructed against the backdrop of Cape Town's famous Table Mountain is going begging for sport events after the Soccer World Cup. So far both the rugby and cricket administrators have turned down invitations. (Photo: Media Club)

Cup concluded on 11 July 2010 with Spain's victory in the final against The Netherlands, Ban described the month-long tournament as a success for South Africa and an opportunity towards development for the African continent.

"It is my hope that this renewed focus on Africa will lead to an African renaissance and I call upon all parties to focus on ensuring that the success is sustained," Ban said.

Former South African President Thabo Mbeki, who first pushed the idea of an African Renaissance, concurred. Africans have made an important statement that they are as capable as any in the world, Mbeki said. According to him success in hosting the World Cup meant that "Africa is well poised to continue its advance towards its renaissance, hopefully supported by the rest of humanity, acting as partners for Africa's renewal."

Madiba Magic

Would the World Cup have taken place in Africa if it weren't for Madiba Magic? FIFA President Sepp Blatter didn't seem to think so when he read out the name of South Africa as the winning bidder in Zurich May 15, 2004.

"You are the true architect of this FIFA World Cup. Your presence and commitment made it happen," Blatter said as he handed over the trophy to Nelson Mandela after announcing that South Africa had secured the event on its second attempt. For Mandela (affectionately referred to as Madiba), who had stepped down as president five years earlier, FIFA's decision was a ringing endorsement of his leadership.

"I feel like a young man of 15," exclaimed a delighted Mandela, who was 85 at the time.

He had campaigned vigorously for the tournament, believing that the key to reconciling blacks and whites in South Africa lays in forging a common identity—a goal that could be advanced by creating shared moments in sport. It was a formula that he had applied with great success when South African rugby under the leadership of its president, Dr. Louis Luyt, hosted the Rugby World Cup in 1995. Despite opposition from within his own party, then President Mandela prevailed in rallying South Africans of all races behind a largely white South African team that triumphed against the world's best.

Bafana Bafana

Even though South Africa's predominantly black soccer team, Bafana Bafana (the Boys), narrowly missed making it into the second stage of the 2010 World Cup tournament, all races in the country once again pulled together as one behind their team. Before it lost narrowly in overtime against Uruguay in the quarterfinals, Ghana was adopted by all of South Africa and the rest of the continent as the "home team."

Illness, compounded by the death of his great-granddaughter in a car crash, prevented Nelson Mandela from making an appearance at the glittering opening ceremony and witnessing the host nation's gutsy 1-1 draw against Mexico. But he and his wife Gracia did attend the final day on 11 July 2010 when Spain beat the The Netherlands for the championship.

Biggest event

The *Fédération Internationale de Football Association* (FIFA) Soccer World Cup is the world's biggest sport tournament. More than a billion people in some 200 countries tuned into the final match on 11 July in Johannesburg's Soccer City stadium. The four weeks of play that preceded it attracted an estimated cumulative TV audience of 40 billion. More than 30,000 print and electronic journalists followed and reported on the action. According to FIFA, a total of 3.1 million spectators attended the 64 matches of the tournament—close to 400,000 came from abroad.

Value for money?

In the five years since it was selected as the venue for the 2010 Soccer World Cup the South African government spent R33 billion on projects with most of the monies going into stadium, precinct and transport projects. There are those who question the wisdom of investing billions in stadiums that could become white elephants. With the exception, however, of Soccer City and the existing Coca-Cola Park (formerly Ellis Park) in Johannesburg, Green Point stadium in Cape Town and Moses Madiba stadium in Durban, all the stadiums have a seating capacity of below 50,000 that could be filled to capacity for many regional sport and social events in future. Few questioned the much-needed improvements to the country's major airports and transportation systems and

Ghana (in white) against Germany in the 2010 World Cup. Ghana reached the quarterfinal to the delight of millions in across the African continent who rooted for their "home team." (Picture: Coca-Cola Africa)

17

Vuvuzela blower at Soccer City stadium

beefing up of security. For years to come South Africa will be better equipped to handle the surge in tourism expected as the world became familiar with its beauty, wildlife and diverse cultures. Bordering countries and nations further north are bound to reap the benefits as well.

Sponsors

Coca-Cola that had stadium advertising at every World Cup since 1950 and has been an official World Cup partner since 1978 was once again prominent among the sponsors. Fittingly so, as this company is Africa's largest job provider and active in promoting and funding life-style enhancements ranging from water supplies to education and recreational facilities. Coca-Cola's World Cup 2010 campaign reached across 170 countries. Other major sponsors included McDonalds and Adidas.

Vuvuzela

Soccer World Cup 2010 will also be known as the occasion when the word Vuvuzela made its noisy entrance into the world's vocabulary. Likened to the sound of a multitude of angry bees or snorting wildebeest, the sound of tens of thousands of fans blowing their vuvuzelas amused some and irritated others. Attempts by the organizers to ban the use of this plastic trumpet, manufactured by an enterprising entrepreneur in Cape Town, failed. So the vuvuzela made its lasting impact as part of the African experience—ripping like a buzz-saw from the spectator seats at every game. The vuvuzela has made an indelible, lasting impression as it is unlikely that sound technicians will manage to remove the humming background from their recordings.

Elections

In 2010 citizens of 21 African countries went to the polls. Elections ranged from local councils to legislatures and the selection of heads of state. Elections were held in Burkina Faso, Burundi, Central African Republic, Chad, Côte d'Ivoire, Egypt, Ethiopia, Equatorial Guinea, Ghana, Guinea, Guinea-Bissau, Lesotho, Mauritania, Mauritius, Namibia, Rwanda, São Tomé and Príncipe, Sudan, Tanzania, and Togo as well as the semi-autonomous region of Somaliland. With few exceptions these elections were for the most part conducted peacefully and orderly. There were claims of voter intimidation and other irregularities—issues with which other parts of the world, including the United States, are not unfamiliar.

Côte d'Ivoire

After numerous postponements Côte d'Ivoire finally held presidential elections in October 2010. In the first round the incumbent, Laurent Gbagbo of the FPI, garnered 38.06% of the popular vote against 32.26% for Alassane Ouattara of the RDR. Henri Konan Bédié was third with 25.01%. All three candidates featured in the turbulent decade that followed more than thirty years of religious and ethnic harmony under President Felix Houphouet-Boigny. In 1999, Henri Bédié, who succeeded Houphouet-Boigny, was toppled in a coup led by Robert Guei. Bédié fled after having been charged of stoking up ethnic discord by stirring up xenophobia against Muslim

Alassane Dramane Ouattara casts his ballot in Côte d'Ivoire's long-awaited presidential elections at a polling station in Abidjan on 31 October 2010 (UN Photo).

northerners, including his main rival, Alassane Ouattara. Laurent Gbagbo replaced Robert Guei after he was deposed in a popular uprising in 2000. Violence erupted as Ouattara's supporters took to the streets demanding new elections. In September 2002 troop mutiny escalated into a full-scale rebellion by northern Muslims. Thousands on both sides were killed in the conflict. Although the fighting has stopped, the country is still tense and divided and French and UN peacekeepers patrol the buffer zone separating the north, held by rebels known as the New Forces, and the government-controlled south. The presidential election, originally scheduled for 2005, had been delayed several times by the ongoing civil strife. A peace agreement between the government and the New Forces was signed in March 2007 and elections—scheduled and rescheduled numerous times since—eventually held on 31 October 2010. As none of the three candidates emerged with an outright plurality a second round was held and Ouattara declared the winner by the electoral commission with 54 percent of the vote. On appeal from Gbagbo, who alleged fraud in the northern region of the country where most of his Quattara's support is based, the country's Constitutional Council overturned the results and reaffirmed the incumbent. As the year drew to a close considerable diplomatic pressure were brought to bear on Gbagbo to step down. "There was only one winner—with a clear margin," Mr Choi Young-Jin, special representative of the UN Secretary General in Côte d'Ivoire, told the Security Council. Mediation attempts by the African Union through its envoy, former South African President Thabo Mbeki, and threats of sanctions by the European Union and the United States, followed by pressures from the 15-member Economic Community of West African States (ECOWAS), all failed to show results by mid-December. The standoff continued as the year came to a close and Pres. Gbagbo proceeded with the appointment of a new government, rivalling the one declared by Mr Ouattara in the wake of election.

Alpha Condé (Photo:Conde.flickr)

Guinea

In Guinea, Alpha Condé emerged the surprise winner of what is considered to have been this country's first free presidential election since its independence from France in 1958. After placing second with a mere 18.2% to Cellou Dalein Diallo's 43.7% in the first round, Condé turned the tables in the final round by winning 52.5% of the popular vote against Diallo's 47.5%—thus becoming Guinea's first freely elected president. As Diallo's supporters clashed with police in the streets UN Secretary General Ban Ki-moon appealed to them to accept the result and resolve any differences by peaceful means. In this instance the Supreme Court of the country affirmed Condé as the winner and allowed him to form a new government and start Guinea out on the difficult road to recovery. Educated in France, the 72-year old Condé has had more than his fair share of adversity on the road to the presidency. During the long dictatorial rule of Sekou Touré, lasting from 1958 until 1984, Condé was sentenced to death in absentia. In the subsequent 24-year rule by General Lansane Conté, Condé was arrested several times and jailed for two years. His role model is Nelson Mandela.

Choi Young-Jin (right), Special Representative of the Secretary-General for Côte d'Ivoire, meets with Simone Ehivet Gbagbo, First Lady of Côte d'Ivoire, in Abidjan on 27 November 2010, ahead of presidential run-off elections.

19

Sudan

Under the 2005 Comprehensive Peace Agreement (CPA) ending the fighting between the two warring parties, a power-sharing Government of National Unity (GNU) was formed between the Khartoum-based National Congress Party (NCP) in the north and southern Sudan People's Liberation Movement (SPLM). Parliamentary and presidential elections were held in April 2010. Despite a warrant for his arrest by the International Criminal Court to stand trial on charges of war crimes, incumbent President Omar al-Bashir captured 68 percent of 10 million valid ballots to win another five year term. In southern Sudan another incumbent Salva Kiir of the SLPM also prevailed, winning 93 percent of the vote to remain president of the semi-autonomous region. He also serves as Vice-President in the national government.

Referendum

If the authorities keep to the current schedule the Southern Sudanese will be given the opportunity in January 2011 to vote in a referendum for or against secession from Sudan. The referendum is part of the 2005 peace agreements that created a power-sharing government with Kiir as vice president to Sudanese President Omar al-Bashir. It is viewed as a gateway to total independence and freedom from Khartoum rule. Voter registration started in October 2010 in close to three thousand centers in Southern Sudan. Southern President Salva Kiir kicked off the process in symbolic fashion at a booth in Juba close to a memorial to John Garang, who led the mostly Christian south to a 2005 peace deal that ended a 22-year war with the north before dying in a helicopter crash. About five million South Sudanese are eligible to vote, including between 500,000 to two million living abroad, according to UN estimates. The vote is to be held on the same day as a referendum in the oil-rich Abyei region, with voters there choosing whether to stay with the north or go with the south. In an agreement signed in October 2009, the central government of Sudan and the South Sudanese authorities agreed that the turnout would have to be 60% for the vote to be valid, and that as long as turnout is 60% or higher, a simple majority vote in favour of independence will result in independence for South Sudan. The proposed date for the referendum is 9 January 2011. Should the turnout be insufficient in the first referendum, a second one will be held within sixty days. Not all of Africa is in favor of this development as they fear that this might set a precedent for disgruntled factions and regions within their own borders. Egypt has been historically opposed to South Sudan's secession for fear that it would affect its share of the Nile waters.

A woman in Zam Zam Internally Displaced Persons Camp, North Darfur, submits her ballot in Sudan's national elections on 11 April 2010. (UN Photo/Albert Gonzalez Farran)

Sudan and Darfir

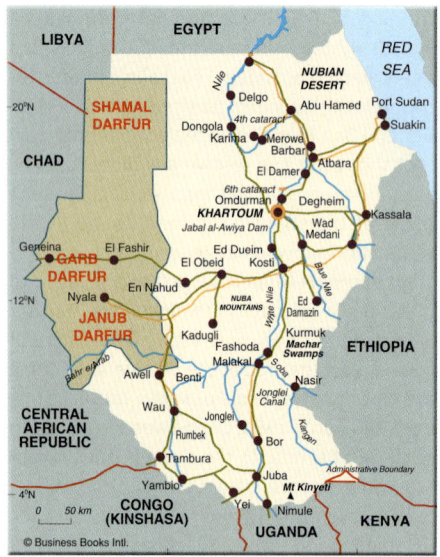

Darfur

In the midst of all these developments between the south and the north the plight

George Clooney, actor and UN Messenger of Peace, visits with children in the El Sheriff Internally Displaced Persons Camp (IDP) in South Darfur. (UN Photo)

of Darfur in western Sudan seemed to have slipped off the radar screen. This is not for lack of trying on the part of American film star George Clooney who has gone way beyond being a mere honorary celebrity UN Ambassador for Peace into becoming an ardent activist on behalf of this region. Between meetings with Congress and President Barack Obama he produced a documentary together with his father Nick depicting the ongoing plight of Darfur's population. The fighting in Darfur began in February 2003 when the region's ethnic African population revolted against what they saw as decades of neglect and discrimination by the Arab-dominated government in Khartoum. The government launched a counterinsurgency in which the Janjaweed, an Arab militia, committed widespread atrocities. An estimated 200,000 lost their lives and some 2.5 million people were forced from their homes in what has been declared a genocide by the UN and most of its member states, including the US.

African seat

At the September 2010 session of the General Assembly several African leaders once again called on the United Nations to grant the Continent a permanent seat on the Security Council. Senegalese President Abdoulaye Wade noted that the current makeup of the UN Security Council does not reflect the "collective will" of a body that has grown from 51 Member States in 1945 to its current 192. The Council has increased its membership only once, in 1965, from 11 to 15. At present only the five permanent members—China, France, Russia, United Kingdom and United States—have veto rights. All five were victorious allies in the Second World War, part of what Mr. Wade called the legacy of a closed historical period.

Uganda's Permanent Representative to the UN, Ruhakana Rugunda, takes the rotating presidential seat in the Security Council on 29 October 2010 with his delegation posing for a picture prior to the Council's meeting on post-conflict peacebuilding. Pressure is still on to have a permanent seat established for Africa. (UN Photo)

Mohammed Al Amoudi   Nicky Oppenheimer   Patrice Motsepe   Aliko Dangote

Africa is not alone in its calls for permanent membership. The so-called Group of Four—India, Japan, Germany and Brazil—have also pressed their case for permanent seats. Both Japan and India enjoy US support in their bid. There still is uncertainty over which nation in Africa will represent it should it be afforded a permanent seat. In the foreseeable future it seems likely that Africa's nations will have to be content with temporary representation on a rotation basis and largely ceremonial honors in chairing meetings when they get their turn.

Afro-Optimism

Apart from pressing the UN for two permanent and five non-permanent seats on the Security Council in his capacity as chairman of the African Union, Malawian President Bingu wa Mutharika spoke about Afro-optimism and a continent poised for new beginnings. "This is the Africa of new hopes and new possibilities; Africa of industrial, mineral, and agro-processing opportunities; Africa with new jobs creation prospects; and an Africa that can produce enough food to feed its people," Mutharika said. "The media has long portrayed Africa as a region of conflicts, diseases, poverty and despair, ignoring any positive developments on good governance, peaceful multi-party elections and strong microeconomic growth."

The new head of Barclays Bank echoed similar sentiments in an appearance at the Clinton Global Initiative by calling the continent an "incredible" opportunity. Citing high growth rates and rapid expansion of consumer spending as driving Barclays' presence in a dozen African countries, CEO Bob Diamond pointed out that this decade Africa had the third highest rate of GDP growth behind emerging Asia and the Middle East. "African countries' $1,600 billion GDP is equal to that of Brazil and Russia," he reminded his audience.

Africa's Richest Ten

In 2010 Ethiopian-born Mohammed Al Amoudi was, according to *Forbes* magazine, Africa's richest man. In its March 2010 listing the magazine placed Al Amoudi, who is based in Saudi Arabia, tops on the Continent with a fortune of $9 billion. He is a self-made mogul with interests spread across Sweden, the Middle East and Ethiopia. Al Amoudi owns a broad portfolio of businesses not only in oil but also in mining, agriculture, hotels, hospitals, finance, operations and maintenance. Nicky Oppenheimer, who controls the family's wealth of some $5 billion in diamonds and mining, placed second, followed by Nassef and Naguib Sawiris, each with some $3 billion in assets. Aliko Dangote of Nigeria comes next in line also in the $3 billion range and, more significantly, is now reputed to be the single largest foreign investor in South Africa. After Dangote ranks Mo Ibrahim of the Sudan who made most his US$2 billion from a sale of his Celtel mobile phone empire to Kuwaiti investors. He is better known for establishing the Mo Ibrahim Foundation that awards an annual US$5 million prize for outstanding African leadership and sponsors studies on governance. Another member of the Egyptian Sawiris family, Onil, stayed in the top ten with $1.7 billion despite setbacks as a result of the global crises. Rounding out the list from South Africa are Patrice Motsepe who made it from rags to riches in mining and minerals and Johann Rupert who diversified and expanded the family interests in tobacco, liquor and luxury goods.

African Milestones[1]

BC

5,000,000	Australapithecus africanus—fossils found in eastern and southern Africa.
2,200,000	Homo habilis (emergent man and first toolmaker)—fossils found in East Africa.
1,600,000	Homo erectus (middle-period man)—expansion into Eurasia.
500,000	Homo sapiens.
100,000	Middle Stone Age (Neolithic era).
20,000	Late stone age and early agriculture.
4000	Stone and copper age. Settlement of the Nile Valley. Settlements in the Sahara.
3200	King Menes unites the kingdoms of the Delta and the Nile. Egypt invades Nubia.
2700	King Zoser, Imhotep and Step Pyramid at Sakara.
2600	Khufu (Cheops) and Great Pyramid at Giza.
2500	Egypt sends expeditions to land of Punt and into Sahara area.
2280	Old Kingdom ends. First Intermediate Period in Egypt.
2100	Middle Kingdom begins with Mentuhotep. Egypt expands southward into Nubia.
2000	Amenemhet I, founder of new Dynasty.
1780	Second Intermediate Period; Egypt has fifty rulers in slightly over a century.
1660	Asiatic invaders (Hyksos) conquer Lower and Middle Egypt.
1557	Ahmose I drives Hyksos out of Egypt and establishes XVIII Dynasty.
1511	Thutmose I reconquers Nubia. Egypt expands into Asia and Kush area.
1400	Amenophis III. Queen Tiy.
1360	Amarna Period in Egypt. Akhnaten, the heretic Pharaoh.
1340	Pharaoh Tutankhamen.
1300	Time of Moses. First horses in Africa.
1230	Exodus of Israelites from Egypt.
1000	Makeda of Axum (Queen of Sheba) visits Solomon.
751	Kush King Kashta conquers Upper Egypt. Piankhi conquers all of Egypt.
690	Pharaoh Taharqa.
650	Assyrians under Assurbanipal conquer Egypt. Capital of Kush moved to Meroë.
600	Greeks establish colony at Cyrene.
525	Persians, under Cambyses, conquer Egypt.
500	Axum begins to develop.
450	Herodotus visits Egypt and Kush. Earliest construction at Zimbabwe.
332	Alexander the Great conquers Egypt.
304	Ptolemy I establishes dynasty.
200	Height of Nok culture.
150	Cities of Zanj established.
100	Bantu introduce iron working into the area south of the Sudan.
146	Carthage conquered and razed by Rome.
31	Augustus Caesar conquers Egypt.

AD

1	Beginning of east African city states.
30	Lion Temple built in Kush.
100	Axum becomes capital of the major state of Eritrea.
200	Nok culture fades away; Ghana begins.
200	Roman Emperor Septimus Severus fortifies frontier in North Africa.
238	Revolt in Africa against Roman rule.
300-400	Bantu cereal cultivators begin to herd cattle.
333	King Ezana of Axum becomes a Christian.
350	Kingdom of Axum supercedes Kush.
354	St. Augustine born at Carthage.
429	Vandals invade North Africa.
534	Justinian's Byzantine expedition conquers North Africa.
571	Yoruba migration from Upper Egypt.

1. Some dates and events in the early years remain in dispute among scholars.

African Milestones (CTD)

550	Nubians in Sudan become Christian.
600	Muslims start conquering North Africa.
640	Caliph Omar, successor to Mohammed as Islamic leader, conquers Egypt.
652	Christian Nubians and Arabs agree on Aswan as border on Nile.
700	So tribes settle Kanem (Lake Chad). Bantu peoples spread out.
788	Idris, Arab chief, ruler in Morocco.
790	First dynasty established in Benin. Ghana at its peak.
800s	Christian empire in Ethiopia continues after decline of Aksum.
800s	Arabs and Persians establish trading posts in East Africa.
950	Kilwa established. University of Cairo founded.
1000	Igbo-Ukwu culture thrives in Nigeria.
1100	Bantu-speaking peoples move into Southern Africa.
1054	Almoravid Moslems invade Ghana.
1061	Beni Halil Moslems invade North Africa.
1173	Muslim warrior Saladin becomes sultan of Egypt.
1200	King Lalibela of Ethiopia establishes churches cut from rock.
1220	City state of Kilwa in Tanzania prospers.
1235	Warrior Sun Diata founds Mali empire.
1250	Kanem kingdom in Lake Chad disintegrates; Mamelukes seize power in Egypt.
1300	Ife culture of West Africa produces famous brass objects.
1324	Emperor Mansa Musa of Mali travels on pilgrimage from Timbuktu to Mecca.
1348	Egypt devastated by Black Death plague.
1380	Kongo kingdom at river mouth.
1400	Mombasa becomes Swahili city state.
1445	Portuguese start slave trade on West Coast of Africa.
1450	Great Zimbabwe at its height; Oyo Empire is created.
1460	Songhai Empire established.
1479	Portuguese build Elmina Castle on West African coast.
1482	Portuguese explore Congo river estuary.
1488	Portuguese explorer Bartholomeu Dias sails around the southern tip of Africa.
1491	Ruler of Kongo kingdom baptized as Christian by Portuguese.
1497	Portuguese explorer Vasco da Gama sails around Africa to India.
1500	Songhai empire expands in West Africa. Hausa states grow through trade.
1502	First African slaves sent to the New World.
1505	Portuguese capture Sofala and settle in Mozambique on east coast.
1517	Ottomans defeat Mamelukes in Egypt.
1528	Portuguese capture Mombasa.
1529	Muslims defeat Ethiopian Christians.
1530	Beginning of trans-Atlantic slave trade by Portuguese.
1543	Portuguese help Christian Ethiopians to defeat Muslims.
1562	Sir John Hawkins starts English slave trade from West Africa to Americas.
1575	Portuguese start colonizing Angola.
1598	First Dutch trade posts on Guinea coast.
1619	First slaves arrive in colony of Virginia.
1640	Beginning of large-scale selling of slaves to Caribbean and Americas.
1650	Ethiopian ruler expels Portuguese missionaries.
1652	Dutch establish a settlement at the Cape of Good Hope.
1670	French settle in Senegal.
1680	Ashanti Kingdom is formed.
1686	Louis XIV of France officially annexes Madagascar.
1689	French Huguenots arrive at the Cape.
1701	Osei Tutu creates free Ashanti nation in West Africa.
1705	Bey Husain ibn Ali founds Tunis dynasty.
1727	Death of Mulai Ismail followed by 30 years of anarchy in Morocco.
1740	The Lunda create new kingdom.
1746	Mazrui dynasty in Mombasa becomes independent from Oman.
1750	Buganda becomes the leading Lake Kingdom.
1755	First outbreak of smallpox at Cape by sailors, decimating Khoisan tribesmen.
1768	Scottish explorer James Bruce travels to Ethiopia.

African Milestones (ctd)

1770	Tukulor kingdom emerges in former Songhai region of West Africa.
1777	Sidi Mohammed, ruler of Morocco, abolishes slavery of Christians.
1779	First war between the Bantu and Boers in Cape border areas
1784	Yoruba civil wars.
1785	Omani rulers reassert rule over Zanzibar.
1787	British settlers, including slaves, establish colony at Sierra Leone.
1789	Spain opens slave trade to Cuba.
1794	French National Convention emancipates French colonial slaves.
1795	British occupy Dutch Cape Colony to preempt French until 1803.
1796	Scottish explorer Mungo Park reaches Niger.
1798	Napoleon takes Egypt.
1801	French troops withdraw after defeat by British at Alexandria.
1805	Mohammad Ali conquers Egypt.
1806	British wrest Cape Colony from Dutch.
1807	British parliament bans slave trade.
1807	Britain converts Sierra Leone into a crown colony.
1810	British negotiate elimination of slave trade in South Atlantic with Portugal.
1814	Cape colony finally ceded to Britain by Netherlands.
1815	British pressure Netherlands, Spain, Portugal and France to end slavery.
1816	Gambia occupied by British after French withdrawal.
1816-28	Shaka Zulu dominates eastern part of South Africa.
1817	American Colonization Society encourages return of slaves to Africa.
1820	Mohammad Ali captures Sudan in search of slaves and gold.
1820	British settlers land at Cape Colony.
1821	American Colonization Society establishes colony at Cape Mesurado—Liberia.
1822	Ex-slaves from America settle in Liberia.
1828	Egyptians found city of Khartoum in Sudan.
1830	French capture Algiers.
1832-47	Abd-al-Kadir directs resistance against French in Algeria.
1834-36	Great Trek begins in Cape as Boers migrate north away from British authority.
1838	Boers defeat Zulu leader Dingaan at Blood River in Natal.
1845	British annex Natal.
1847	Liberia declares itself an independent state.
1852	Independent Boer Transvaal Republic established.
1854	Independent Boer Republic of Orange Free State founded.
1852	Tukolor leader al-Hajj Umar launches Jihad along Niger and Senegal rivers.
1853-56	Livingstone discovers Victoria Falls.
1858-59	Burton and Speke discover Lake Tanganyika and Speke, Lake Victoria.
1858-61	Livingstone discovers Lake Nyasa.
1860	Speke identifies Lake Victoria as source of the White Nile.
1861	US recognizes the new state of Liberia founded by freed American slaves.
1862	US President Lincoln grants freedom to slaves after rebellion in the South.
1863	Al Hajj Umar captures Timbuktu.
1863	French establish protectorate over Porto Novo on coast of Dahomey.
1865-68	Wars between Orange Free State Republic and Basuto people.
1866	French establish posts on Guinea coast.
1867	Diamonds discovered at Hopetown in Cape colony of South Africa.
1868	French sign protectorate treaties for Ivory Coast.
1868	Britain annexes Basutoland at request of Basuto King Mosweshwe.
1870	Diamond rush starts at Kimberley South Africa.
1871	Stanley meets Livingstone at Ujiji and resupplies him.
1873	Livingstone dies at Chitambo's village, Ilala.
1879	Stanley begins operations in Congo on behalf of King Leopold.
1879	British defeated by Zulu at Ulundi in Natal.
1874	Britain occupies former Dutch colony of Gold Coast.
1880	Brazza signs treaty with King Makoko and establishes Brazzaville.
1881	Transvaal Republic defeats British in First Boer War.
1881-7	Stanley signs treaties with Congo chiefs and founds Leopoldville.
1881	French army invades Tunisia from Algeria and imposes protectorate.
1883	French establish protectorate over Dahomey.

African Milestones (ctd)

1883	Paul Kruger elected president of Transvaal.
1884	Nachtigal takes over Togo on behalf of Bismarck.
1884	Carl Peters signs treaties with mainland chiefs in Zanzibar region.
1884	Britain signs protectorate treaties with Niger and Oil River chiefs.
1884	With assistance from Bismarck, Leopold gets recognition for Congo claims.
1885	Mahdi captures Khartoum and massacres Gordon and the British garrison.
1885	Bismarck declares German protectorate over part of East Africa.
1885	European powers divide Africa at the Berlin Conference.
1886	Gold discovered in the Transvaal.
1887	Britain signs conditional agreement with Turkey to withdraw from Egypt.
1887	British incorporate Zululand into Natal.
1888	Cecil Rhodes gets mining rights from Lobenguela north of Transvaal.
1888	Britain gives royal charter to Rhodes' British South Africa (BSA) in new region.
1889	France declares protectorate over Ivory Coast.
1889	Emperor Yohannes of Ethiopia killed by Menelik—supported by Italy.
1890	British-French agreement recognizes their respective interests in West Africa.
1890	Peters extends German influence in Uganda by treaty with Kabaka Mwanga.
1891	British recognize Italian protectorate over Ethiopia.
1891	Britain recognizes Rhodes BSA Company's control over Rhodesia.
1892	French defeat King Behanzin of Dahomey and extend protectorate.
1891-2	Harry Johnston secures British influence over Nyasaland.
1893	Guinea and Ivory Coast colonies established by France.
1894	French set up protectorate in Dahomey (Benin).
1895	Britain secures control over Uganda.
1895	Italians start invasion of Ethiopia from Eritrea.
1896-8	Kitchener and Anglo-Egyptian army recapture Sudan.
1896	Menelik defeats Italians but allows them to keep Eritrea.
1897	Britain signs treaty with Ethiopia and concedes part of Somaliland.
1897	Slavery is banned in Zanzibar.
1899	British and Egyptian governments create condominium rule over Sudan.
1899	Anglo-Boer War ends in British supremacy in South Africa
1901-1902	British add Ashanti to Gold Coast.
1902	In treaty with Anglo-Egyptian authority Menelik abandons claims to Upper Nile.
1903-1905	Exposure of atrocities in the Belgian and French Congo by Morel and Brazza.
1904	France creates the Federation of French West Africa.
1910	Union of South Africa granted independence by Britain.
1922	Egypt gains sovereignty from British under King Fuad.
1930	Ras Tafari crowned emperor of Ethiopia as Haile Selassie.
1931	First trans-African railroad from Angola to Mozambique completed.
1935-36	Italians under Mussolini invade and annex Ethiopia.
1936	Native Representation Act denies black South Africans chance of equality.
1939	South Africa under Smuts declares war against Germany.
1941	German army under Rommel campaigns in North Africa.
1941	Ethiopia liberated from Italy by South African and British troops.
1942	British Commonwealth troops defeat German army at El Alamein in Egypt.
1942	Germany and Italy driven from North Africa.
1948	National Party comes to power in South Africa and adopts apartheid.
1951	Libya gains independence under King Idris.
1952-59	Mau-Mau guerillas led by Kenyatta fight British in Kenya.
1952	King Farouk forced to abdicate by Colonel Naguib.
1954-62	War for independence in Algeria.
1954	Colonel Abdul Nasser succeeds Naguib and exiles King Farouk.
1956	Sudan receives independence from Egypt.
1956	Suez crisis erupts and British and French lose control of the canal.
1956	Morocco gains freedom from France and additional territory from Spain.
1956	Tunisia gains freedom from France.
1957	Ghana (former Gold Coast) granted independence by Britain.
1958	Guinea gains freedom from France.
1960	Civil war starts in South Sudan.
1960	Independence for Benin (former Dahomey), Burkina Faso (former Upper Volta).

African Milestones (Ctd)

1960	Central African Republic, Chad, Congo (Brazzaville), Côte d'Ivoire independent.
1960	Gabon, Madagascar, Mali, Mauritania, Niger, Senegal, and Togo independent.
1960	French Cameroon and part of British Cameroon form new nation of Cameroon.
1960	Belgian Congo becomes independent and civil war starts.
1960	Colonel Mobutu establishes rule over Zaire (former Belgian Congo).
1960	Nigeria gains independence from Britain.
1960	Former British and Italian Somaliland form independent Somalia.
1961	Sharpeville uprising in South Africa results in death of 69 black protesters.
1961	Sierra Leone independent from Britain.
1961	Tanzania (Tanganyika) gains independence from Britain.
1962	Algeria gains independence from France.
1962	Rwanda and Burundi (former Ruanda-Urundi) gain freedom from Belgium.
1962	Uganda becomes independent from Britain.
1963	Kenya gains independence from Britain.
1963	Organization of African Unity formed.
1964	Malawi (former Nyasaland) gains independence from Britain.
1964	United Republic of Tanzania and Zanzibar established.
1964	Zambia (Northern Rhodesia) gains independence from Britain.
1965	The Gambia granted independence by Britain.
1965	White-ruled Rhodesia declares unilateral independence from Britain.
1964	Nelson Mandela and other ANC leaders jailed at Robben Island, South Africa.
1966	Botswana (Bechuanaland) and Lesotho (Basutoland) independent from Britain.
1967-70	Biafran War in Nigeria.
1968	Equatorial Guinea granted independence by Spain.
1968	Mauritius gains freedom from Britain.
1968	Kingdom of Swaziland gains independence from Britain.
1968	Cape Town surgeon Christiaan Barnard performs world's first heart transplant.
1969	Muammar Qaddafi seizes power after coup in Libya.
1973	Guinea-Bissau granted freedom by Portugal.
1975	Angola, Mozambique, and Cape Verde independent from Portugal.
1975	São Tomé & Príncipe granted independence by Portugal.
1975	Comoros receives independence from France.
1976	Seychelles gains independence from Britain.
1976	Soweto uprising results in calls for further sanctions against South Africa.
1977	Former French Somaliland becomes independent Djibouti.
1980	Zimbabwe (Rhodesia) gains independence from Britain under Robert Mugabe.
1986	US Congress passes law requiring sanctions against South Africa.
1990	Nelson Mandela freed from jail.
1990	Namibia (former South West Africa) gains freedom from South Africa.
1991	Eritrea wins freedom from Ethiopia.
1994	ANC wins first multiracial election in South Africa.
1994	Nelson Mandela sworn in as president of South Africa.
1995	South Africa's Springboks win Rugby World Cup in South Africa
1997	Democratic Republic of Congo replaces Zaire.
1997	Ghanaian diplomat Kofi Annan elected UN Secretary General.
2001	Organization of Africa Union disbanded in favor of new African Union.
2001	New Partnership for Africa's Development (NEPAD) launched.
2001	Kofi Annan reelected UN Secretary General.
2002	African Union inaugurated in Durban, South Africa.
2004	First meeting of the Pan African Parliament in South Africa.
2004	South African Charlize Theron becomes first African to win Oscar for best actress
2004	Ms. Wangari Maathai of Kenya awarded Nobel Peace Prize.
2005	G8 nations write of $40 billion in debt owed by 18 African nations
2005	Egypt's Mohamed ElBaradei receives Nobel Peace Prize
2005	Liberian Pres. Ellen Johnson-Sirleaf becomes Africa's first female head of state
2006	South African film Tsotsi is first African film to win Oscar for best foreign film
2007	South Africa's Springboks win Rugby World Cup in France
2008	Barack Obama, son of a Kenyan citizen, elected president of the United States
2009	First state visit of US African-American President Barack Obama to Africa
2010	FIFA Soccer World Cup tournament held in Africa for the first time

Did you know?

- Since the mid 1990s oil-exporting countries in Africa have grown more than three times faster than non-oil-exporting countries.
- In Madagascar, 30.6% of crop land is irrigated; in Central African Republic, Democratic Republic of Congo and Uganda the figure is less than 0.1%. On average, only 4.7% of the arable land in Africa is irrigated.
- Mauritius has the highest life expectancy (74 years); Swaziland has the lowest (47.9 years). Since 2000 Rwanda has made the greatest gains in life expectancy—about 5 years; in Lesotho life expectancy has decreased by about 6 years.
- The highest numbers of clinical malaria cases reported between 2007 and 2008 were in Malawi (4.9 million); Mozambique (4.8 million); and Zambia (3.0 million).
- The economies of South Africa and Nigeria comprise almost 60% of the GDP of Sub-Saharan Africa (SSA).
- In Sierra Leone 2,000 women die for every 100,000 live births; in Mauritius 15 die per 100,000 live births.
- Equatorial Guinea has the highest GDP per capita income ($27,000); Malawi the lowest ($212).
- In 2005 SSA was a net food importer with a negative balance of $4.6 billion; Angola (–$805 million), Nigeria (–$1.7 billion) and Senegal (–$700 million) were among those with the highest food trade deficits, while Côte d'Ivoire ($1.9 billion) and South Africa ($935 million) were among those with the highest food trade surplus.
- South Africa has the largest GDP ($260 billion); São Tomé and Principe has the smallest ($160 million).
- In 2000–2006 the electric power consumption per capita (KWh per capita) of South Africa was 4,847; Ethiopia's was 34.4.
- Nigeria with 154 million has the largest population in Africa; Seychelles has the smallest with 84,000.
- For the period 2000–06, Seychelles had the highest adult literacy rate (92%); Mali and Burkina Faso had the lowest (24%).
- 65% of SSA's population lives in rural areas; Burundi has the highest rural share (90%), while Djibouti has the lowest (13.5%).
- South Africa has 87 mobile phones per 100 people; Ethiopia has 1.45 per 100 people.
- 43.3% of SSA's population are between the ages of 0 and 14; Uganda has the highest share at this age range (49.3%) and Mauritius the lowest (24%).
- In Eritrea, 5% of the population has access to improved sanitation facilities; in Mauritius, 94% has access.
- Burundi has the highest participation rate of women in the labor force (93.0%); Sudan has the lowest (24.1%).
- It takes 7 days to start a business in Madagascar and Mauritius, and 233 days in Guinea Bissau.
- Youth make up 36.9% of the working-age population, but 59.5% of the total unemployed, which is much higher than the world's average for 2005 (43.7%).
- Parenthood starts very early. In Mozambique, 58% of females in the age range of 15–24 had already given birth at least once, and 18% of males at this age were fathers. These figures are respectively 57% and 17% in Malawi (2004); 57% and 7% in Niger (2006); 53% and 10% in Chad (2004); 47% and 15% in Uganda (2006); and 47% and 17% in Gabon (2000).
- Africa was the first region in the world to offer free, mobile roaming services across several countries. Today, 45 out of 100 Africans have mobile phones.
- In more than half of African countries, tax revenue represents less than 20 per cent of GDP as compared to 36 per cent in OECD countries.
- The rate of return on FDI is higher in Africa than any other part of the developing world.

Africa's Nobel Laureates

Africa had a total of twelve Nobel laureates since 1901 when this prize was first awarded in the name of Sweden's dynamite magnate, Alfred Nobel. In 2005, Egyptian **Dr. Mohamed ElBaradei**, head of the International Atomic Energy Agency (IAEA), and the agency jointly received the Nobel peace prize for their efforts to prevent nuclear energy from being used for military purposes. A year earlier Kenya's **Wangari Maathai** was awarded the peace prize for her contribution to sustainable development, democracy and peace. In 2001, Secretary General **Kofi Annan** received the Nobel Peace Prize for his own and the UN's endeavors to promote world peace. In 1993, **Nelson Mandela** and **FW de Klerk** were joint recipients for their role in terminating apartheid and laying the foundation for a new nonracial South Africa. In 1984, Bishop **Desmond Tutu** was honored in his capacity as General Secretary of the South African Council of Churches for his role in the struggle against apartheid. In 1978, Egyptian President **Anwar Sadat** was recognized, together with Israeli Prime Minister Menachem Begin, for his contribution to peace in the Middle East. The first African recipient of the Nobel Peace Prize in 1960 was **Albert John Luthuli**, who led the non-violent campaign for civil rights in South Africa.

Four Africans won the Nobel prize for literature. Nigerian playwright, **Wole Soyinka**, was honored in 1986 for his poetical plays written in English. In 1988 Egyptian novelist **Naguib Mahfouz** won the prize for his short stories and novels and in 1991 South Africa's **Nadine Gordimer** received recognition for her novels and short stories. In 2003, another South African, **John Maxwell (JM) Coetzee** was the recipient of the literary prize.

Desmond Tutu

Albert Luthuli

Nelson Mandela

Anwar Sadat

FW de Klerk

Kofi Annan

Nadine Gordimer

Wole Soyinka

Courtesy: Nobel Museum

Mohamed ElBaradei

Wangari Maathai

Naquib Mahfouz

JM Coetzee

How Africa Measures Up

SEVEN BIGGEST ISLANDS

	Sq. miles	Sq. km.
Greenland	839,000	2,175,597
New Guinea	316,515	820,033
Borneo	286,914	743,107
Madagascar	226,657	476,068
Baffin (Canada)	183,810	476,068
Honshu (Japan)	88,925	230,316
Great Britain	88,758	229,883

THE SEVEN LONGEST RIVERS

	Miles	Km
Nile (Africa)	4,180	6,690
Amazon (South America)	3.912	6,296
Mississippi (USA)	3,170	5.970
Yangtze Kiang (China)	3,602	5,797
Ob (Russia)	3,459	5,567
Huang Ho (China)	2.900	4,667
Yenisei (Russia)	2,800	4,506

THE SEVEN SUMMITS[1]

	Feet	Meters
Mt. Everest (Asia)	29,035	8,850
Mt. Aconcagua (Sth.Am.)	22,834	6,960
Mt. McKinley (Nth. Am.)	20,320	6,194
Mt Kilimanjaro (Africa)[2]	19,340	5,895
Mt. Elbrus (Europe)	18,510	5,642
Vinson Massif (Antarctica)	16,066	4,897
Kosciusko (Australia)	7,316	2,230

1. Highest peaks on each of the 7 continents.
2. The world's highest "free standing" mountain.

THE SEVEN BIGGEST LAKES

	Sq. miles	Sq. km
Caspian Sea (Russia etc)[1]	152,239	394,299
Superior (US-Canada)	31,820	82,414
Victoria (Tanz.-Uganda)	26,828	69,485
Huron (US-Canada)	23,010	59,596
Michigan (USA)	22,400	58,016
Aral (Kazakhstan-Uzbeki.)	13,000	33,800
Tanganyika (Tanz.-Congo)	12,700	32,893

1. Considered landlocked lake even though Romans called Mare Caspian a sea because of its saltiness.

THE SEVEN CONTINENTS

	Sq. miles	Sq. km
Asia[1]	17,212,041	44,579,000
Africa	11,065,000	30,065,000
North America	9,465,290	24,256,000
South America[2]	6,879,952	17,819,000
Antarctica	5,100,021	13,209,000
Europe[3]	3,837,082	9,938,000
Australia[4]	2,967,966	7,687,000

1. Includes the Middle East.
2. Includes Central America and the Caribbean.
3. Includes the recently-independent states of the former Soviet Union.
4. Includes Oceania.

THE SEVEN LARGEST DESERTS[1]

	Sq. miles	Sq. km
Sahara (Africa)[2]	3,500,000	9,065,000
Arabian (M. East)	1,000,000	2,590,000
Gt.Victoria (Australia)	250,000	647,500
Kalahari (Africa)[3]	220,000	569,800
Gt. Sandy (Australia)[4]	150,000	388,500
Gibson (Australia)	120,000	310,800
Simpson (Australia)	56,000	145,040

1. Subtropical deserts are the hottest, consisting of parched terrain with rapid evaporation. The Namib in Namibia (13,000 sq. miles/33,600 sq. km) is a cool coastal desert region).
2. Covers parts of Algeria, Chad, Egypt, Eritrea, Ethiopia, Libya, Mali, Mauritania, Morocco & Western Sahara, Niger, Somalia and Tunisia.
3. Spans parts of Botswana, Namibia and South Africa.
4. Also known as The Outback.

Sources: Columbia Encyclopedia, Time Almanac and Internet.

Chapter 1
The African Continent

Africa is the second largest continent. Ras ben Sekka in the north near Bizerte in Tunisia, and Cape Agulhas in South Africa, are 5,000 miles (8,000 km) apart. The farthest eastern extremity, Ras Hafun Peninsula in Somalia, and the westernmost point, Cape Verde in Senegal—are about 4,700 miles (7,560 km) apart. The Sahara Desert is the world's largest and Mt. Kilimanjaro in Tanzania is Africa's highest peak. The Nile river flowing northwards to the Mediterranean sea, is the world's longest.

Okavango Delta, Botswana
Photo: Wilderness Safaris

Topography

Africa is basically one enormous plateau modified in part by erosion and earth movements. It resembles, in the words of explorer David Livingstone, "a wide awake hat with the crown a little depressed." Another explorer, John Speke, described it as "a dish turned upside down." Africa consists of three major regions: the Northern Plateau, the Central and Southern Plateau, and the Eastern Highlands. Elevation increases across the continent from the northwest to southeast reaching an average of 1,900 ft (600 m). The main feature of the Northern Plateau is the Sahara desert, occupying more than one-quarter of the continent. At the fringes of the Northern Plateau are the Atlas Mountains, which extend from Morocco into Tunisia. The higher Central and Southern Plateaus contain several major depressions, notably the Congo River Basin and the Kalahari Desert, as well as the peaks of the Drakensberg mountains. The Eastern Highlands, extending from the Red Sea to the Zambezi River, averages more than 5,000 ft (2,000 m) and reaches 15,157 ft (4,620 m) at Ras Dashen in northern Ethiopia. South of the Ethiopian Plateau are a number of towering volcanic peaks, including Kilimanjaro, Mount Kenya, and Mount Elgon. A distinctive feature of the Eastern Highlands is the Great Rift Valley—a vast geological fault system. With three-quarters of its landmass situated between the Tropic of Cancer and Cap-

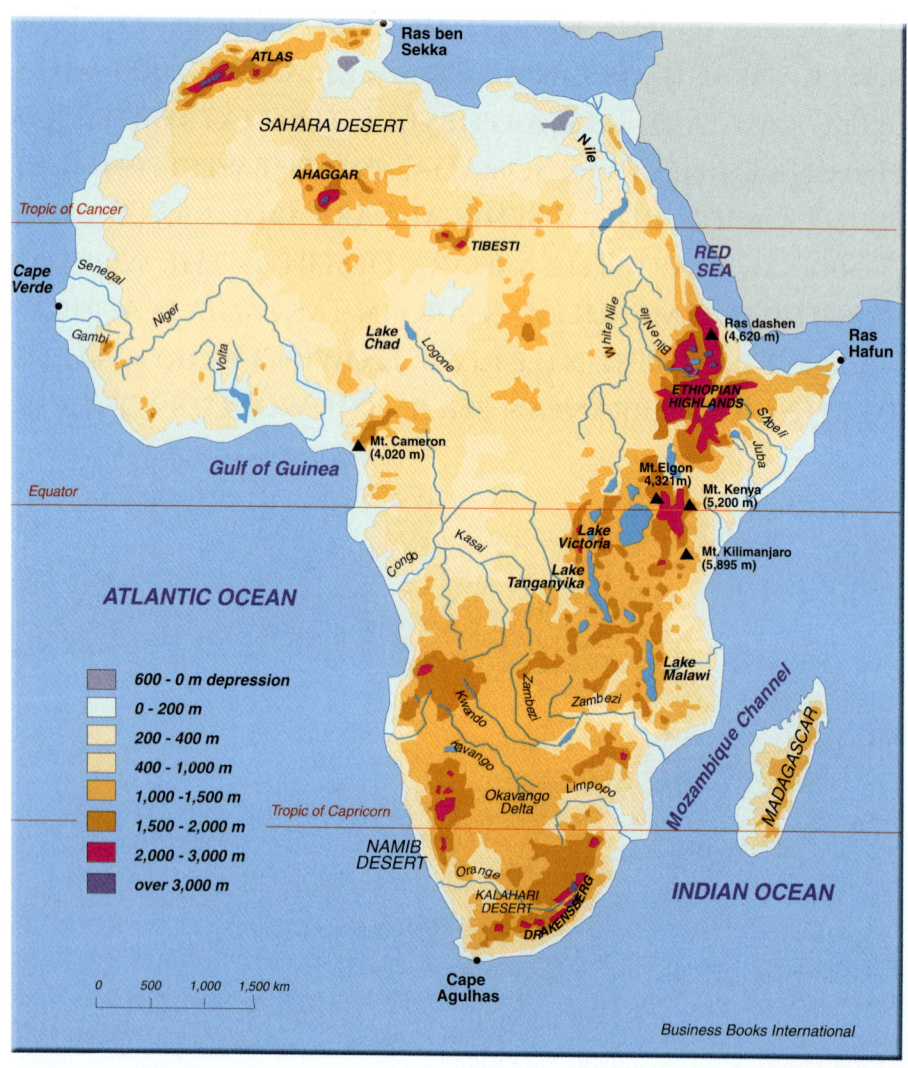

34

ricorn Africa is mostly tropical—hot summers and brief, mild winters. In some regions altitude has a moderating influence, and mountains near the equator such as Mt. Kilimanjaro and Mt. Kenya are covered with snow. Beyond the equatorial zone rainfall is unreliable and large parts of the continent are prone to droughts. Some 40% of Africa is desert or semi-desert. Even in high rainfall areas, downpours are strictly seasonal and unpredictable in both volume and timing, making farming a gamble. The Namib and Sahara Desert get less than 2 inches (50 mm) of rain per year.

Vegetation

With its average annual rainfall of more than 50 inches (1,300 mm), Africa's tropical rain forest is densely covered tropical hardwood trees, oil palms and a thick undergrowth of shrubs, ferns, and mosses. In the mountain forest zones of Cameroon, Angola, eastern Africa, and parts of Ethiopia, where the rainfall average is only slightly less, a ground covering of shrubs gives way to oil palms, hardwood trees, and primitive conifers. The savanna woodland zone, with an annual rainfall of 35 to 55 inches (900 to 1,400 mm), consists of deciduous and leguminous fire-resistant trees and undergrowth of grass and shrubs. The savanna grassland zone, with an annual rainfall of 20 to 35 inches (500 to 900 mm), is covered with low grass and shrubs and widely spaced, small deciduous trees. The so-called thornbush zone with its annual rainfall of 12 to 20 inches (300 to 500 mm), has a sparser grass covering and scattered succulent and semi-succulent trees. The sub-desert scrub zone, with an annual rainfall of 5 to 12 inches (130 to 300 mm) is covered with grasses and scattered low shrubs. In the desert zones, with an annual rainfall of less than 5 inches (130 mm), vegetation varies from sparse to none.

Peoples & Languages

In 2000, some 13% of the world's population lived in 53 African countries. Africa tops the world not only with the number of countries within one continent but also the diversity of its 800 million peoples and the number of languages spoken. Rural cultures where foods, religions, life-styles, dress and daily life have remained unchanged for hundreds of years, continue to thrive despite the rapid intrusion of bustling modern cities. More than 1,000 languages and dialects are spoken. Arabic in northern Africa, Mandinke, Igbo, Yoruba and Hausa in western Africa, Swahili in eastern Africa, Amharic and Oromo in the Horn of Africa, and Zulu, Sotho and Xhosa in southern Africa, are spoken by millions. Most of Africa's languages are, however, spoken by less than a million people and some, such as Kw'adza in Tanzania used by only a few older people, are close to extinction. Many countries have selected the languages of former colonial powers

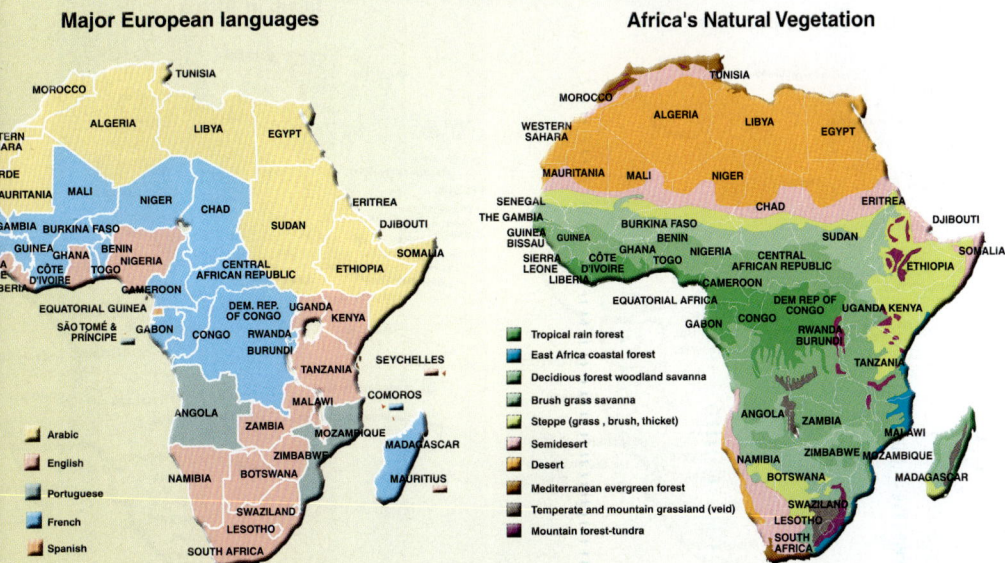

for official and business purposes. Arabic is the official language in 12 countries, English in 20, and French in 21. Cameroon and Mauritius have both English and French as official languages. Portuguese is official in five countries and Spanish and French enjoy equal status in Equatorial Guinea. Spanish is spoken in Morocco and some Italian in Libya, Eritrea and Somalia.

Religions

Christianity at its very beginning spread from the north to Nubia (northern Sudan) and Ethiopia. Much later it was introduced elsewhere by Portuguese and other seafarers, early Dutch settlers at the Cape and 19th Century missionaries. Islam spread from the Arabian Peninsula through Northern Africa in the course of the 17th Century. Today, Christianity dominates in 19 countries, Islam in 13 countries, and the Hindu faith in one (Mauritius). In the rest, ethnic beliefs still largely prevail and other faiths remain in the minority. Even though there is no single unifying and distinct religious code set out in a Koran or a Bible, indigenous religions continue to exert a strong influence on family life, rulers and the justice system in parts of the continent. What ethnologists refer to as Naturism, Animism, and Fetishism are all aspects of a deep-seated belief in a Creator that defies definition. Indigenous African religions—practiced under the guidance of priests, elders, rainmakers, diviners and prophets—are concerned with the origin of tribes and their cultures, the nature of society, the relationship of men and women and of the living and dead. Social values are frequently expounded in myths, legends, folktales, and riddles are passed along by word-of-mouth. Voodoo (juju) and other forms of witchcraft have mistakenly come to represent foreigners the essence of African religion.

Early history

Several scientific discoveries of the remains of what seems to be early man in South Africa's Sterkfontein area and Tanzania's Olduvai Gorge lend strong support to Africa's claim of being the cradle of mankind. Less contentious is Egypt's claim to be among the world's first civilizations. A number of city states in the lower Nile Valley were united some 5,000 years ago under Menes, the first pharaoh. To the south in the Nubian desert (today's northern Sudan) another kingdom developed some 3,000 years ago that equalled Egypt in both splendor and achievement. The Semitic Phoenicians became the first colonizers of Africa when they set out from today's Lebanon to establish the city state of Carthage along the Mediterranean in what eventually became Tunis. Centuries of struggle in North Africa involving Romans and Germanic Vandals,

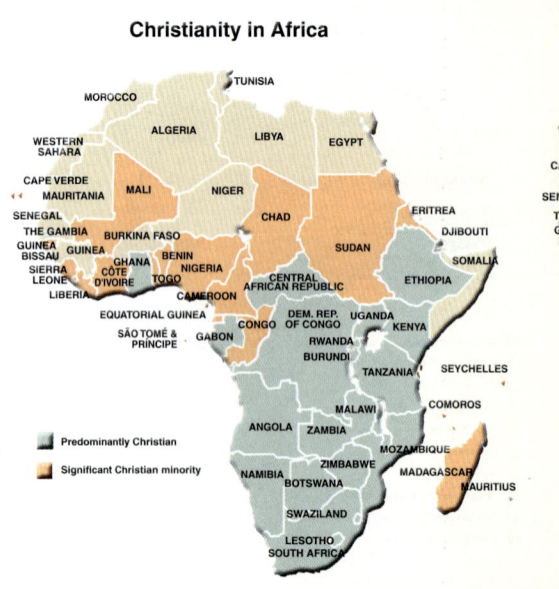

and Christians and Muslims, left the rest of the continent largely free from outside influences. It was only about 1,000 AD that black Africans from the Sahel region first entered the North African theater—even though the kingdoms of Ghana, Mali, and Kanem (on the shores of Lake Chad) had existed for centuries. Inhabitants of the tropical forest regions originated in the north and were exclusively Negroid. More than 2,000 years ago some of them migrated from West Africa to settle around the great lakes and on the savannah plains in East Africa and the Congo Basin. Bantu-speaking, they were crop cultivators and livestock breeders. To the north of Lake Victoria (in today's Uganda) the Nilotes (or Nilotic people), migrating from the north, ruled for centuries over various Bantu-speaking groups. Some Bantu-speakers moved south and reached South Africa about 1,500 years ago.

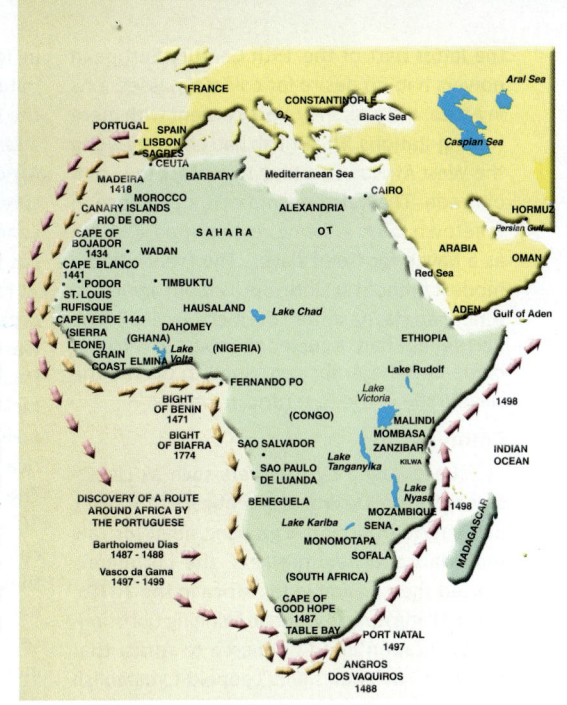

First Europeans

At the end of the 15th Century Portugal had established trade relations with the kingdoms of Benin and Kongo and built a fort at Elmina (Ghana). Barter items included gold, palm oil, cocoa, ivory and slaves supplied by African kingdoms to a ready market. In their search for a sea route to the Far East, Portuguese explorers rounded the Cape and extended trade to the east coast where the Arabs were already active. The Dutch, English, French and Spanish soon followed and for the next four centuries established spheres of influence along the coast of Africa.

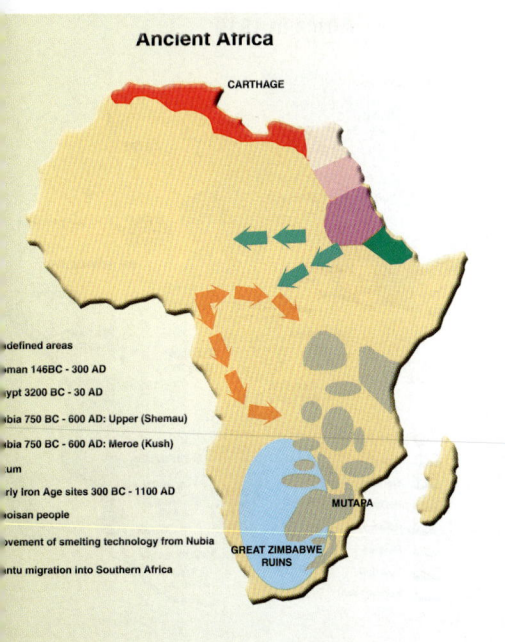

Slavery

For most of the 18th Century the relationship between Europe and Africa was dominated by the slave trade. Before the middle of the 19th Century, it was declared illegal in the northern hemisphere by all the former European and North American slave-trading nations. That did not completely deter profit seekers from moving human cargo in bondage wherever the opportunity presented itself, and at towards the end of the 19th Century explorer David Livingstone still encountered a flourishing slave trade on his exploration routes.

First settlement

In 1652 the Dutch established a small settlement at the southern tip of the African continent. Originally intended as a supply station for its ships en route to the Far East, the Cape settlement soon developed into a full-fledged colony. After the British took over, the Dutch descendants (Boers) trekked north to establish independent republics in the 1850s. The Cape was, however, the exception. Until the latter part of the 19th Century European powers had no desire for colonial possessions in Africa. Instead, they were content with mere trading stations. The British had enclaves along the West African coastline to protect the palm oil trade. They also maintained a presence in Freetown, Sierra Leone, established in 1787 as a haven for freed slaves. The French had a modest toehold in Libreville (Gabon) and freed American slaves settled in Liberia in 1822. The Portuguese had occupied the coast of Mozambique and the Arabs continued to pursue the slave trade in the East African interior.

Colonialism

Encouraged by explorers such as Livingstone, Burton, De Brazza, Nachtigal and Stanley, and spurred on by the growing need for raw materials and new markets, the Europeans started their scramble for Africa in the 1870s. It was Livingstone's vision of bringing Christianity, Civilization and Commerce to Africa that prompted Belgium's King Leopold to establish a personal colony in the Congo basin. Soon the European superpowers were tripping over each other in their quest for colonies all over Africa. The Berlin Conference of 1884-1885, convened by the German government to determine the fate of Leopold's Congo and to set the rules of the game, further turned up the heat. The Germans established enclaves in Togo, Cameroon, German West Africa (Namibia) and German East Africa (Tanzania) while the French expanded their territorial holdings inland from Senegal and Gabon across West Africa and parts of Equatorial Africa. Britain spread its rule over Nigeria, Ghana and Sierra Leone and retained The Gambia. Its major focus was, however, on Egypt and South Africa. At the turn of the century, Cecil John Rhodes' dream of a British Africa from the Cape to Cairo was well underway with Rhodesia, Nyasaland (Malawi), Kenya, and Uganda flying the Union Jack. Portugal acquired two major overseas possessions, Angola and Portuguese East Africa (Mozambique), which it ran as provinces. The scramble for Africa—completed in under 30 years—repainted the continent in bright colonial colors without any consideration for the peoples or their homelands. Italy and Spain had their own designs in North Africa. In one celebrated instance Queen Victoria decided to indent the straight border drawn between British East Africa and German East Africa (today's Kenya and Tanzania) to make a detour around Mt. Kilimanjaro so her German cousin King Wilhelm could have the mountain. "Willie likes big things," she explained.

Decolonization

After the First World War Germany's possessions were confiscated and passed along to

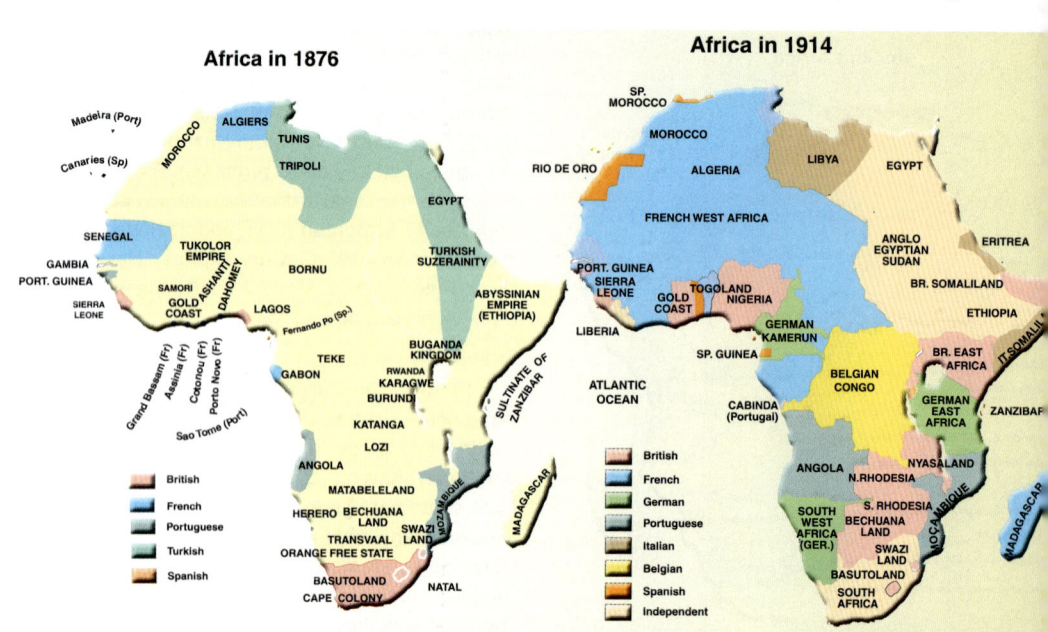

Africa in 1876

Africa in 1914

African Independence

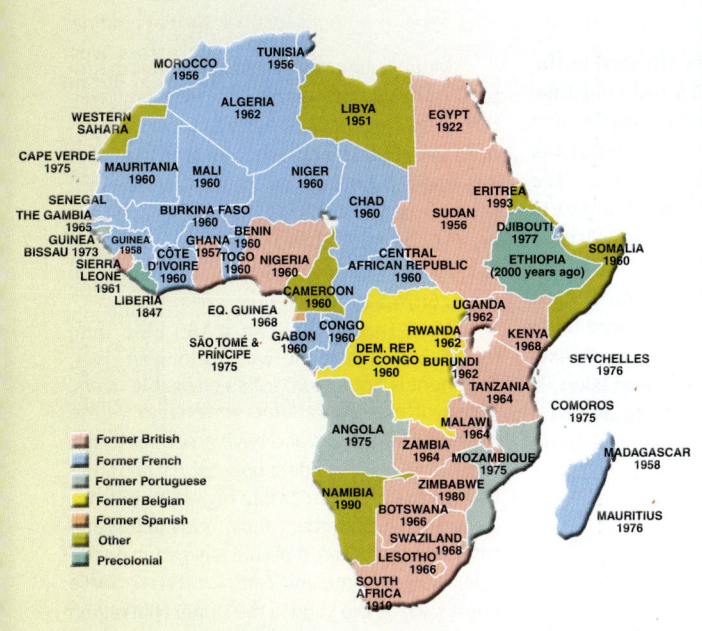

In 1951, Libya was granted independence by France and Britain which were in joint control after Italy's defeat during World War II; in 1960, when the French (former German) Cameroon received its independence, part of British Cameroon joined in while the rest merged with Nigeria; in 1960, the former Italian (then under French control) and British Somalia joined to become independent Somalia; incorporated into Ethiopia after World War II, the former Italian colony of Eritrea gained its freedom in 1991; a mandate under South African control since the end of World War I, the former German colony of South West Africa gained its independence as Namibia in 1990; administered by Morocco since 1976, Western Sahara is still an area under dispute, awaiting a final UN referendum.

the victors. In the wake of a Second World War (fought with the help of thousands of African soldiers in colonial armies) came a revulsion against colonial rule that led to armed uprisings in many of the colonies. This "wind of change" swept across Africa, forcing first Belgium and Britain, then France, and eventually Portugal to grant freedom to all their former colonies. In some cases the departure of the former colonial rulers had some dignity and style while in others it was a frantic scramble to escape the consequences of mismanagement. The initial euphoria of the 1960s soon made way for pessimism and despair as military rulers and despots took the place of former colonial rulers. In many instances, the root of the problem was the artificially drawn colonial borders grouping together diverse peoples. By using Africa as a surrogate battleground the new superpowers, the United States and the Soviet Union added fuel to the fire. Oppressive dictatorships were tolerated and supported from both sides in a struggle for ideological supremacy in Africa. For many years, South Africa, despite its apartheid policies, received the support of the US and its allies because of its strategic importance at the tip of the continent and supplies of strategic minerals.

Reform & Hope

Coinciding with the collapse of the Soviet bloc and the end of the Cold War, a wave of democratic reform swept over Africa in the early 1990s. Coming to the fore were a new breed of leaders who are no longer driven by ideological conflict at the behest of outside powers but by the imperatives set by internal economic and social conditions. Despite ongoing unrest and frequent warfare between ethnic groups boxed into entities created in 19th Century Europe, corruption, the occasional coup, and a few remaining dictatorships, there has been enough stability, growth and development in recent years to raise hopes of a resurgent Africa in the new millennium.

Recent developments

There has been some measure of success on the part of Africa's diverse 53 nations to follow in the footsteps of the European Union. The African Union (replacing the Organization of African Unity) has established a secretariat that oversees many issues of common concern. The AU has also been instrumental in solving some disputes on the continent and participates in UN peacekeeping operations. A Pan African Parliament, styled after the European Parliament, has been established, Africa is, however, a long way off from accomplishing the same unity of purpose and cohesion that typify the European model. Still, observers see great promise in these recent developments.

Rivers, Lakes and Mountains

Several major lakes are situated in the Great Rift region of East Africa, including Lake Turkana, Lake Albert, Lake Tanganyika, and Lake Malawi. Although it forms part of the so-called Great lakes region Lake Victoria—the largest lake in Africa and the third largest in the world—is not part of this system. (Victoria is sometimes ranked second only after Lake Superior in North America but purists put the Caspian Sea first as it is considered land-locked despite its saltiness). Lake Tanganyika, the least accessible of Africa's great lakes, is Africa's deepest with depths up to almost a mile (1.5 km) and ranks second in the world in depth after Lake Baikal in Russia.

While fish life at Lake Victoria is under threat of pollution from motorized vehicles, fertilizers and pesticides, water hyacinths, and algae blooms, early intervention has provided protection for the natural wealth in Lake Malawi. With between 500 and 1,00 species of the family Cichlidae and a multitude of other species, the lake is the source of over 70 percent of animal protein in Malawi.

Mount Kilimanjaro is Africa's highest mountain—ranking 16th worldwide. It is, however, the world's highest freestanding mountain. Africa's five highest mountains are all in the Great Rift Region: Kilimanjaro (19,340ft/5,895m); Mt.Kenya (17,057ft/5,199m); Mt. Stanley (16,765ft/5,110m); Ras Dashen Terara (15,157ft/4,620m); and Volcan Karisimbi (14,826ft/4,519m).

Even though Africa's 4,160 mile long (6,695 km) Nile is the world's longest river, continent is not known for its navigable rivers. Africa offers few reliable waterways. Some rivers are very short and have no outlet to the sea. Many are dependent on seasonal rains that transform dry riverbeds into raging torrents for a short while. Sandbars and muddy deltas and cataracts and falls complicate navigation on the Nile, Congo, Niger, and Zambezi rivers. Some rivers such as the Sudd in the Upper Nile region disappear in swamps while others terminate in enclosed pools. Still these major rivers as well as the Senegal, Gambia and others serve not only as important water sources for communities along their banks but as local traffic routes.

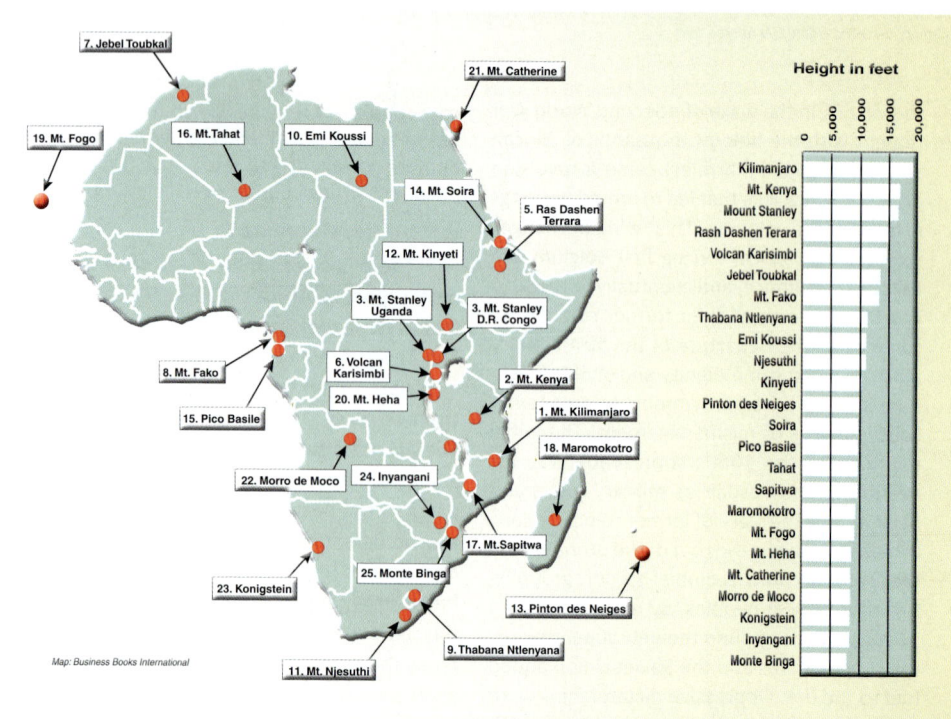

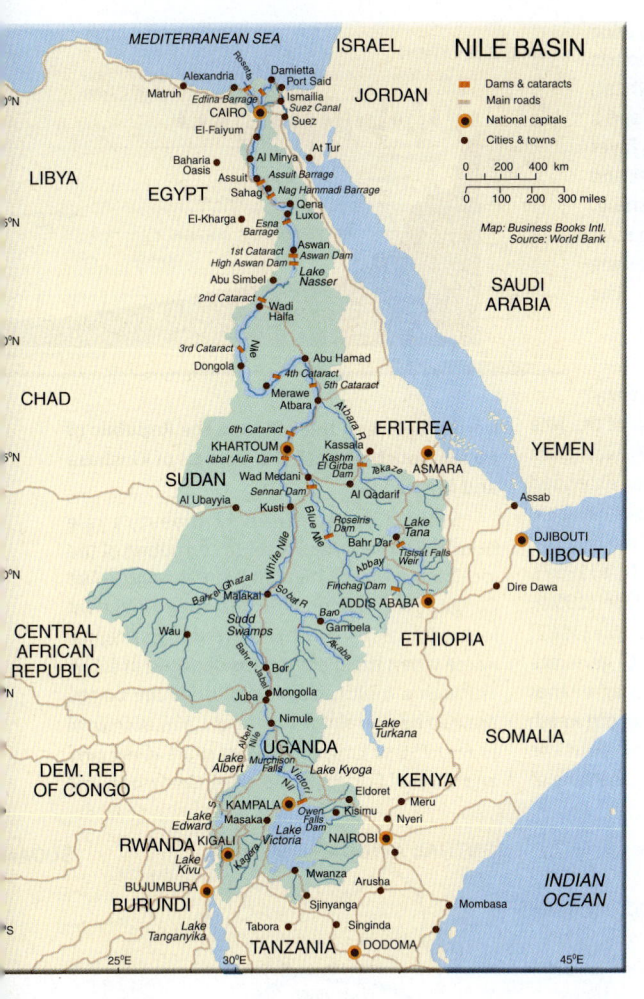

Nile River

The Nile is the world's longest river and its fertile basin covers one-tenth of the African continent. It is the umbilical cord to world's oldest civilization. Starting at about 5,000 BC, the Egyptian pharaohs spread their influence south along the river as far as northern Sudan, leaving along its banks magnificent pyramids, temples and burial sites.

Greek historian Herodotus saw Egypt as "the gift of the River Nile." The Nile derives its current name from the Greek word Neilos (valley or river) but originally the Egyptians called it Ar or Aur (black) after the seasonal deposits of fertile black sediment along its banks. This is where the art of agriculture was perfected in ancient times with the first use of the hand plow.

Length

The actual length of the Nile remains in dispute, depending on where the starting point is drawn. It measures 3,470 miles (5,584 km) from its principal source, Lake Victoria, and 4,160 miles (6,695 km) from its remotest headstream in Burundi—a branch of the Kagera River that feeds into the lake. Indeed, it was the search for the origin of the Nile that lured 19th Century explorers such as Baker, Speke, Burton, Livingstone and Stanley, who in turn wetted the appetite of European powers for acquisitions in the region. Much of the tumultuous colonial period involved the independent nations that today feed off the Nile and its tributaries—Tanzania, Burundi, Rwanda, Democratic Republic of Congo, Kenya, Uganda, Ethiopia, Sudan, and Egypt. The terrain along the Nile and its tributaries changes from rain forests and mountains in the south to savanna and swamps halfway, and ultimately to desert along its northern section.

Origin

Starting in the mountains of Burundi, the waters flow via Lake Victoria into the Victoria Nile in Uganda and follow a northwest course for about 300 miles (500 km) through Lake Kyoga and across rapids and the famous Murchison Falls before entering Lake Albert. Continuing northwards as the Albert Nile, it becomes the Bahr al Jabal in Sudan and slows down in the As Sudd swamps, changing its name once again to the White Nile. At Sudan's capital, Khartoum, the White Nile is joined by the Blue Nile that originates 850 miles (1,370 km) southeast at Lake Tana in the Ethiopian highlands. Now known as the Nile, this river is joined further north by the Atbara River before it takes an S-shape turn through the Nubian desert. After passing through five cataracts in Sudan and one in Egypt, near Aswan, the Nile takes a course past Cairo, splitting into the Rosetta and Dalmietta branches before entering the Mediterranean Sea along a 160 mile (250 km) wide delta. Irrigation from the river supports large-scale cultivation of cotton, wheat, sorghum, citrus fruit, sugar, dates and a variety of legumes along the Nile River Basin. An abundance of Nile perch and tilapia underpins commercial fishing. Tourism, concentrated around the river with its historical sites and interesting wildlife, is a major revenue source. The river is navigable in parts.

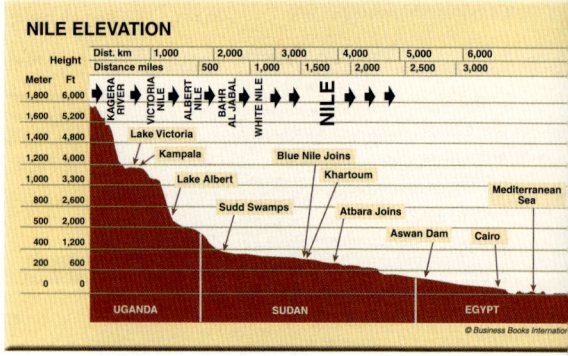

Dams

During the 20th Century several dams were built to control the flow of the Nile and to generate power. Egypt's Aswan Dam was completed in 1902 and further extended in 1936. In 1919, Sudan built the Sennar Dam to supply water for its cotton industry. The Jabal Aulia Dam on Sudan's White Nile (1937), Owen Falls on Uganda's Victoria Nile (1954), Roseires Dam on the Sudanese Blue Nile (1962) and Egypt's High Aswan Dam (1970) generate hydroelectricity. While most experts agree that the pros of these dam projects far outweigh the cons, critics are not slow to point out the negatives. Controlling and reducing the flow of the river deny farmers deposits of fertile sediment along the river banks that came with summer floods. A decrease in flow towards the ocean has caused a greater salt content in the delta region. Lake Nasser, formed upstream from High Aswan Dam, submerged several once thriving communities and historical sites.

Congo River

The 2,900 mi (4,667 km) Congo River is Africa's second longest, flowing in a northern and western direction from the interior plains of the Democratic Republic of Congo (DRC) towards Moanda where spills into the Atlantic Ocean with such force that its murky waters can be detected 100 miles offshore. For several hundred miles it serves as the border between the DRC and the Republic of Congo, touching both the capitals of Kinshasa and Brazzaville.

Known during President Mobutu's rule from 1971 as the Zaïre River (a corruption of the local name Mzadi, meaning "great water") the Congo River (named after the Kongo kingdom located near its mouth) reverted to its original name when the dictator was deposed in 1997. Through a multitude of tributaries the Congo drains a heavy rainfall region of 1,425,000 sq mi (3,690,750 sq km), comprising most of the DRC and parts of Congo (Brazzaville), Cameroon, the

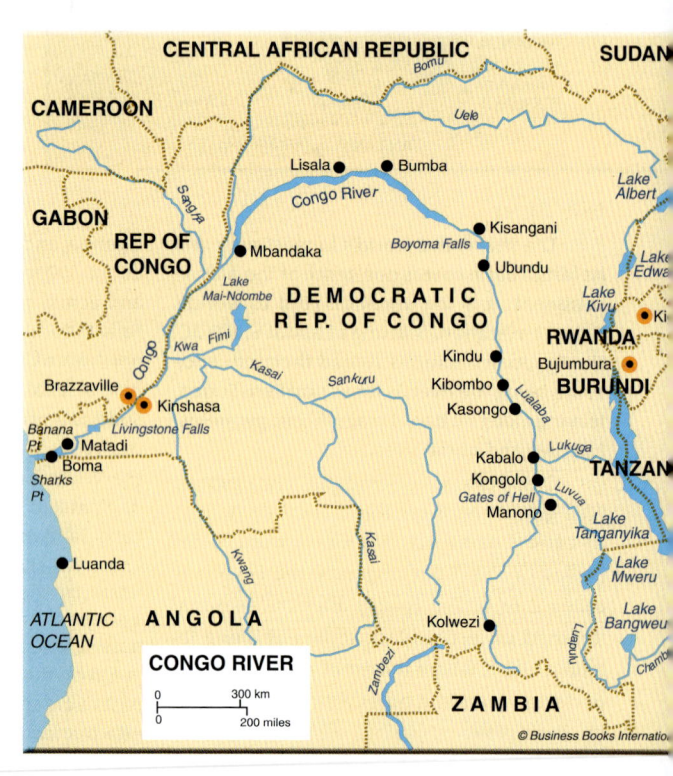

42

Central African Republic, Burundi, Tanzania, Zambia, and Angola. However, its main source is Lake Mweru, situated on the DRC's border with Zambia, which serves as a receptacle for the waters of the Chambeshi River. First the Luvua and subsequently the Lualaba River carry water northwards from Lake Mweru to Kisangani, where they join the Congo River. The Lualaba River, regarded as the upper Congo River, forms a deep and narrow gorge (the Gates of Hell) below Kongolo. A short navigable stretch from Kasongo to Kibombo switches to rapids and falls from Kibombo to Kindu, before reaching a shallow but navigable section from Kindu to Ubundu. The final section between Ubundu and Kisangani contains seven cataracts—known as Boyoma Falls.

Lifeline

The Congo River serves as a lifeline for humans, animals, and plant life along its banks. It has great potential for hydroelectric power but aside from the partly completed Inga Power Project at Livingstone Falls little has been done. In the 1870s, explorers David Livingstone and Henry M. Stanley travelled throughout the Congo basin. Joseph Conrad sailed along the Congo and immortalized the river in his novel, Heart of Darkness. The river was heavily used by Belgian King Leopold II to move tons of rubber, ivory, gold and other treasures to Europe in an era of unbridled colonial exploitation.

Today, utilizing railroads to bypass major falls such as Matadi-Kinshasa, Kisangani-Ubundu and Kindu-Kongolo, the Congo River and its tributaries offer a 9,000 mi (14,480 km) transport system to move central Africa's copper, palm-oil kernels, cotton, sugar, and coffee to the coast. Below Matadi (83 mi/134 km inland) the Congo accommodates oceangoing vessels. Despite the hazardous whirlpools of the Devil's Cauldron, shifting sandbars, and sharp bends in the river, Matadi offers one of the largest natural harbors in Africa. Dredging is, however, necessary to preserve a 4,000 ft (1,220 m) deep, 500-mi-long (800-km) navigation channel in the Atlantic Ocean at the mouth of the Congo near Moanda, between Banana Point in the DRC and Sharks Point, in Angola.

Niger River

The 2,504 m. (4,030 km) Niger River is Africa's third longest and impacts four West African nations—Guinea, Mali, Niger and Nigeria. More than twenty tribes rely on it for their livelihood. It is a major source of fish such as Nile perch, carp and tiger fish. Below Lokoja in Nigeria it is navigable year round. Its vast oil-rich delta region on the Nigerian Atlantic coastline has yielded billions of dollars in foreign exchange earnings. Wildlife includes crocodiles, hippos and a wide variety of exotic birds.

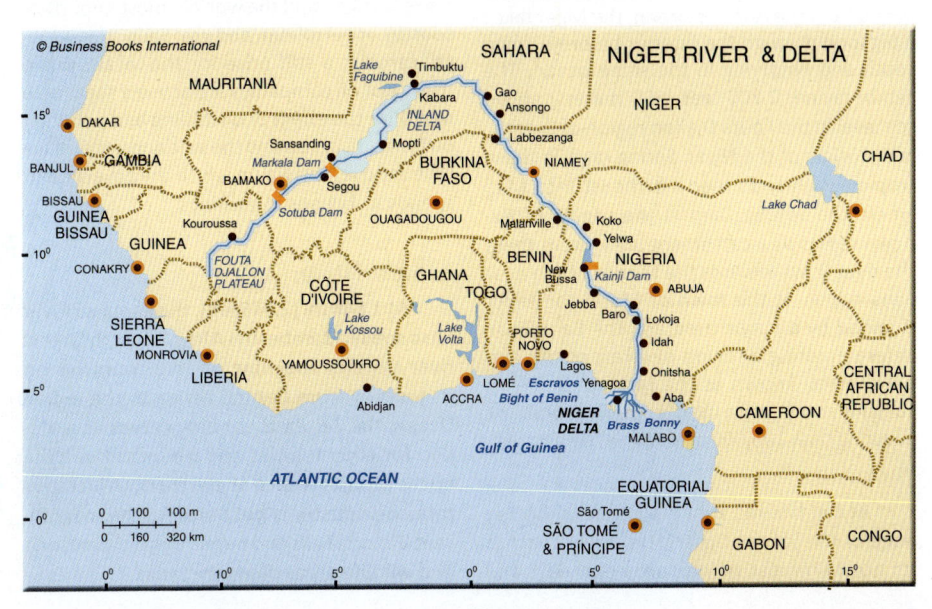

NIGER DELTA

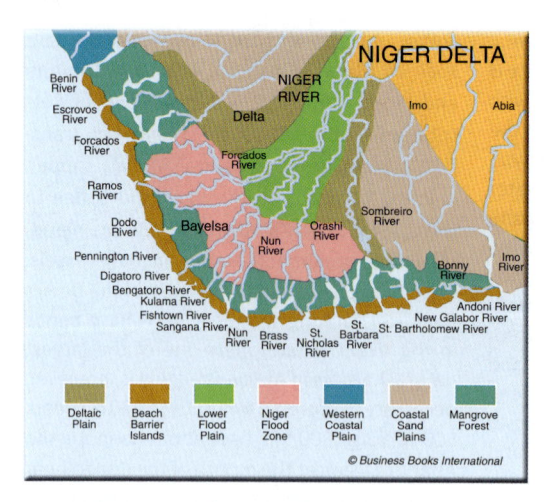

Map legend: Deltaic Plain, Beach Barrier Islands, Lower Flood Plain, Niger Flood Zone, Western Coastal Plain, Coastal Sand Plains, Mangrove Forest

© Business Books International

The horseshoe-shaped Niger River originates on the Fouta Djallon plateau in Guinea and flows in a northeasterly direction to Timbuktu in Mali before swinging in a southeastern direction through Niger and Nigeria, where it spills into the ocean in the vast Niger Delta region. At one time the main artery for the ancient Malian empire, the Niger is believed to have been named by the Greeks. The Malinke tribe calls it Joliba, meaning Great River, while others have come up with names such as Mayo Balleo, Isa Eghirren, Kwarra, Kworra and Quorra.

It is not surprising that early inhabitants and explorers searching for the source of the Niger, were baffled. Starting barely 150 miles inland from the Atlantic Ocean, the Niger takes a big loop through the interior before turning south and emptying in the same ocean. The Tembi ravine, 2,800 feet (850 meters) above sea level in the Fouta Djallon region of Guinea, is the origin of the Niger. Spring rains in these tropical highlands feed northeast into Mali where the Sotuba Dam at the capital of Bamako serves as a catchment area. From there the river flows towards the Markala Dam near Sansanding. At the town of Mopti the Niger is joined by a major tributary, the Bani River, before entering a region of lakes, creeks and backwaters, known as the Internal Delta. It sustains a vast crops, mostly rice and sorghum, covering than 100,000 acres (40,470 hectares).

Timbuktu

At the historic Timbuktu, nestled on the edge of the Sahara Desert, the Niger reaches its northernmost point, turns due east and continues for 250 miles through rocky ridges and a narrow gorge. At Gao it once again widens into a floodplain between three to six miles wide. The River Niger enters the country Niger at Labbezanga, taking a southeasterly course past capital Niamey before pressing on to Jebba where it is joined by the Kaduna River. It is, however, at Lokoja where the Niger River links with its greatest tributary, the Benue River—more than doubling its water capacity in the process. (The Niger is estimated to drain a total of more than 730,000 sq. miles). Together the Niger and the Benue form a lake-sized slow-moving body of water flowing towards Idah through a restricted valley, flanked by sandstone cliffs that flatten out at Onitsha.

Niger Delta

South of Onitsha the river empties through the vast Niger Delta—the largest of its kind in the world—into the Atlantic Ocean at the Gulf of Guinea, splitting into a vein-like network of channels and rivers. The Nun River is considered to be a direct continuation of the Niger. Other major offsprings include the Forcados river, the Brass, the Sombreiro and the Bonny. Many of these channels and rivers are obstructed by sandbars fed continually by silt and sediment carried from the interior. Once a major supplier of palm oil the 14,000 sq. m. (36,260 sq. km) Niger Delta has since become one of Africa's and the world's most important sources of petroleum and gas. Sadly, this windfall came at a stiff price for the locals. While the major oil companies are actively seeking to minimise the effect of oil drilling and pollution on farms, fisheries and the wetlands, they have little say over the way in which the government spends its billions in earnings.

Zambezi River

At 1,646 mi (2,649 km), the Zambezi River (also spelled Zambesi) is Africa's fourth largest river system. Touching on five countries on its journey from Central Africa to the Indian Ocean, the Zambezi not only serves as a lifeline for communities and abundant wildlife but as a major source of electricity. A lucrative tourism industry is built around the magnificent Victoria Falls and numerous water resorts and wildlife areas along its banks.

ZAMBEZI RIVER

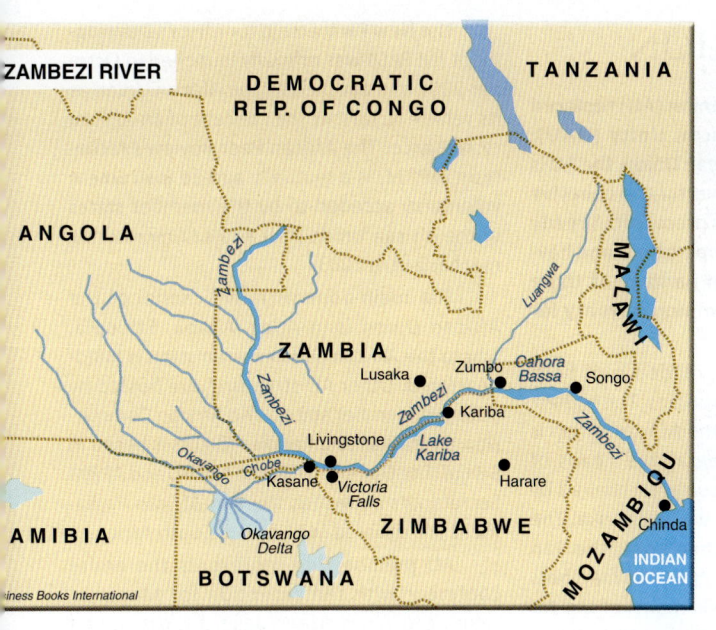

Livingstone, "discovered" the falls on November 16, 1855, and named it Victoria in deference to his queen, the Batonga people had dubbed it, perhaps more appropriately, Mosi-Oa-Tunya—"the smoke that thunders". The Kariba Dam offers the single most important navigable stretch along the Zambezi. Completed in 1959 with a surface area of 2,124 sq mi (5,500 sq km), Kariba is one of the largest human-made lakes in the world with an installed generation capacity of 1300 megawatts.

Named Zambezi ("great river) by the Batonka tribe it has a modest beginning in the northwest corner of Zambia, gaining strength in its southward course through Angola before re-entering Zambia where it turns east to form the border between Zambia and Namibia. It joins up with the Chobe River in the Caprivi Swamps, to briefly form a border with Botswana. For the next 310 mi (500 km) the Zambezi serves as a border between Zambia and Zimbabwe, thundering over the Victoria Falls and through the narrow, steadily deepening Batoka Gorge that flattens out at the broad Gwembe Valley.

Kariba Dam

From here it flows into the Kariba dam for 175 mi (281 km)—reaching a width of 25 mi (40 km). From Kariba the river travels due north, heading east again at Chirundu where it is flanked by the Lower Zambezi National Park on the Zambian side and Mana Pools National Park on the Zimbabwean side. Strengthened by the Luangwa confluence, the Zambezi flows into Mozambique where it is slowed down once again by the Cahora Bassa dam before emptying into the Indian Ocean at Chinde.

Victoria Falls

Rapids interrupt the river's flow, including the world-renowned Victoria Falls, making it unsuited for continuous navigation. Long before Scottish missionary and explorer, Dr. David

Kafue

After Zambia gained independence in 1964 and relations soured with the white government of Rhodesia (today's Zimbabwe), Zambia built two dams of its own near Kafue. Today these two, together Kariba, provide 50 per cent of the two nations' total electricity need. In the 1970s when the Portuguese colonial rulers and South Africa jointly constructed the Cahora Bassa Dam it won accolades for bringing the world's fifth largest hydroelectric power installation to a backward corner of Mozambique. The dam was intended as a source of additional electricity for power-hungry industrial South Africa, and much-needed hard currency for impoverished Mozambique. However, continuing rebel wars have rendered Cahora Bassa inoperative and it is only after the departure of the Portuguese rulers that the project was restored and fulfilled its initial promise.

Criticism

As with Aswan and other major dams along the Nile, both the Kariba and Cahora Bassa dams have attracted criticism from environmentalists for their displacement of small farmers and intrusion on wildlife and nature in general. While conceding their important contribution to the economies of Zambia, Zimbabwe and Mozambique, purists maintain that these projects came at too heavy a price. Kariba alone, they pointed out, displaced a tribe of more than 50,000 along the Zambezi shores.

AFRICAN UNION

In 2002, the African Union (AU) replaced the Organization of African Unity (OAU). Styled in part on the European Union, the AU is intended to be a more powerful and cohesive and effective body than its precursor. Already involved in peacekeeping operations and having established an African parliament there has even been talk of a common currency for the continent.

The African Union is made up of both political and administrative bodies. The highest decision-making organ of the African Union is the Assembly, representing all the heads of member states. The AU is currently chaired by Malawian President Bingu wa Mutharika. The AU also has a representative body, the Pan African Parliament, consisting of 265 members elected by the national parliaments of the AU member states. Other political institutions of the AU include the Executive Council, made up of foreign ministers, to prepare decisions for the Assembly; the Permanent Representatives Committee, made up of the African ambassadors at AU headquarters in Addis Ababa; and the Economic Social and Cultural Council (ECOSOCC), a civil society consultative body.

The AU Commission or Authority, the secretariat to the political structures, is chaired by Jean Ping of Gabon.

The New Partnership for Africa's Development (NEPAD) was officially launched in October 2001 and adopted by the African Union as its vehicle to further the concept of an African renaissance. The African Peer Review Mechanism (APRM) is a mutually agreed instrument voluntarily acceded to by the member states of the African Union (AU) as a self-monitoring mechanism in 2003.

The main administrative capital of the African Union is in Addis Ababa, Ethiopia, where the African Union Commission is headquartered. Other AU structures are hosted by different member states. The African Commission on Human and Peoples' Rights is based in Banjul, The Gambia while the NEPAD and APRM Secretariats as well as the Pan-African Parliament are situated in Midrand, South Africa.

AU membership represents the entire continent with the exception for Morocco, refusing to join in protest against the membership of Western Sahara as the Sahrawi Arab Democratic Republic. Morocco has, however, a special status within the AU and benefits from the services available from AU-related institutions such as the African Development Bank. Moroccan delegates also participate in important events.

The AU's first military intervention in a member state was the May 2003 deployment of a peacekeeping force of soldiers from South Africa, Ethiopia, and Mozambique to Burundi to oversee the implementation of the various agreements. AU troops are also deployed in Sudan for peacekeeping in the Darfur conflict as part of UNAMID. The AU has had a peacekeeping role in Somalia with troops from Uganda and Burundi.

The AU has adopted a number of important resolutions establishing rules of conduct at continental level and established mechanisms to implement its decisions. Since its establishment it has shown willingness to step in when it felt that certain states were stepping out of line. Even though this met with mixed results it augurs well for the future of the African Continent.

UN Secretary-General Ban Ki-moon (right) meets with Jean Ping, Chairperson of the African Union (AU) Commission at the United Nations

UN Photo/: Eskinder Debebe

Chapter 2
The Economy of Africa

Agriculture accounts for one third of the Continent's GDP and almost half of its export revenues but most foreign economic activity is in the exploitation of Africa's abundant mineral resources. Multinationals are prominent in petroleum, gas and minerals ranging from gold to copper, uranium, manganese and phosphate rock to platinum and bauxite. Increasingly, however, foreign investors are engaging in manufacturing and infrastructure development.

Economy

Africa was among the fastest-growing regions of the world between 2001 and 2008, averaging an annual 5.9 percent growth. While the commodity boom played a major role in this growth, stable macroeconomic conditions and structural reforms—including the privatization of state-owned enterprises and lowered barriers to competition—contributed largely. Foreign direct investment more than tripled during these years and included substantial inflows from the Gulf countries, China and India. While Africa's resource-rich countries received most of the foreign direct investment during the decade, there has been a shift into other areas in the last three to four years. New investment has been flowing into non-resource sectors such as tourism, manufacturing, financial services, telecommunications, and construction.

In *A Continent on the Move* issued in June 2010, McKinsey points out that growth acceleration was widespread across most countries and sectors, including 27 out of 30 of the continent's largest economies. Resources accounted for 32 percent of the acceleration since 2000 with non-resource exporters recording similar growth rates. After declining for two decades, productivity has accelerated, reflecting growing economies of scale, increased competition, and the greater use of mobile phones and other modern technologies. Underlying Africa's growth acceleration are two main factors: first, the emergence of a domestic economy based on rising incomes, consumption, employment, and productivity growth and, second, the boom in resource prices.

Safer environment

Gross corruption, constant wars, and irrational economics long made Africa a poor, troubled continent where natural-resource companies were almost the only multinationals that dared or cared to do business. But in the 1990s, the picture improved. This, according to McKinsey's assessment in August 2010, has changed. "Wars started subsiding. Many governments balanced their budgets and created a better, safer environment for companies, both foreign and domestic." The number of African countries that achieved an internationally-recognized "good performance" benchmark in macro-economic management and trade policy has risen from 5 to 15 in the past eight years—and 27 of 36 countries evaluated have improved their performance.

Consumers

Today 80 million households earn at least the equivalent of $5,000 annually, the point where discretionary spending commences—representing an increase of 80 percent in the past eight years.

Global Crisis

It is true that Africa's economies are less linked than many other parts of the world to global financial markets. But the region has not been spared the fallout of a crisis that originated in the sophisticated financial markets of the industrialized world. Starting in 2009 the majority of Africa's economies weakened. Real GDP growth across the continent declined to only 2.5% in 2009, compared to 5.6% a year before and an average of 5.9% during the period 2000-2008. Southern Africa was the subregion most severely affected, with the GDP in the region recording a negative growth of 1.1%. This was largely due to the technical recession that affected South Africa during the first half of the year, reducing the positive average growth of 3.7% achieved in 2008 to a negative 1.8% for the 2009. According to McKinsey the slowdown was less severe in East Africa, with growth in the region falling to 5.8%, butressed by a modest recovery of 2.5% of the Kenyan economy and sustained growth of 5.5% in Tanzania and 9.9% in Ethiopia. Still, the slowdown in all of Africa was less severe than predicted as a growth in domestic demand compensated in part for the decline in export of goods and services. An analysis by the World Economic Forum concluded that some African countries—including South Africa, Algeria, Nigeria, and Egypt—are well poised to bounce back from the crisis. These large economies enjoy competitive banking systems and have functional regulatory systems as a result of financial-sector reforms adopted since the early 1990s. However, according to the World Bank more than 40 percent of the people in Sub-Saharan Africa still exist on less than $1 a day, while life expectancy gains have stalled in some countries and retreated in others.

Inflation

On the other hand, in 2009 inflation decreased in the majority of African countries, after rising to critical levels in 2008. The median inflation rate for the continent as a whole almost halved over the twelve-month period, to 5.9% in 2009 from 10.5% in 2008. The spike in the price of petroleum and of foodstuffs in 2008 pushed inflation to high levels in many African countries but this rate started to fall in the second half of the year. This downward trend continued during 2009. The average inflation rate for Africa is estimated at 9.9% in 2009, compared to 10.6% in 2008. Average inflation was lower in all subregions, except for Central Africa, where it increased by 2.3 percentage points to reach 10%, and in to a lesser extent for North Africa that recorded an inflation rate of 9.2% in 2009 compared with 8.5% in 2008.

Structural Adjustment

During the 1970s and 1980s, the IMF and the World Bank extended loans in terms of structural adjustment programs (SAPs) conditioned on balanced budgets, devaluation of currencies, a cutback in state employment and privatization of state enterprises. In most cases these programs played a positive role arresting economic decline and increasing economic growth. In some, however, they had negative side effects on the population. Even though countries with structural adjustment programs showed growth rates double those of nonparticipants, the austere and at times harsh, conditions remain contentious.

Debt

Equally heated has been the debate on foreign debt and aid. Little of the borrowed money found its way into real development and productive programs. The bulk was used to cover budget deficits and imports, quite often from the lending countries. An undetermined amount found its way into the private foreign bank accounts. According to a recent estimate by the UN Industrial Development Organization (UNIDO) about $107 billion of Nigeria's money is held in private accounts in Europe and the US while the country's foreign debt stands at $35 billion.

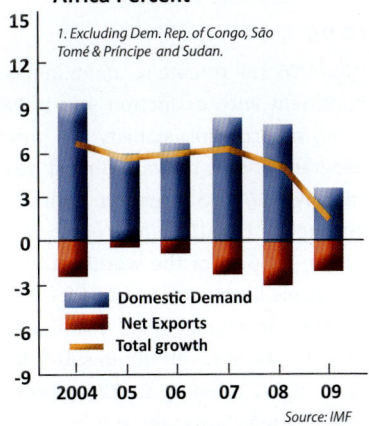

Aid

During the Cold War, aid to Africa was quite often based on development considerations but ideology. Today aid is by and large driven by a genuine effort to stimulate real growth instead of buying favors from rulers. The consensus is that Africa will still need significant aid until at least 2015 in its efforts to attain preset UN Millennium Development Goals (MDGs).

Debt Relief

In 2005 the Group of Eight Industrialized Nations gathering in Gleneagles, Scotland, agreed to full cancellation of the $40 billion debt of 18 African Heavily Indebted Poor Countries (HIPCs). There was also an agreement to boost aid for developing countries by $50 billion over the next ten years. Relief under two international initiatives has also helped reduce significantly the debt burden of heavily indebted poor countries in Africa and freed up additional resources for poverty-reducing and social expenditures. The Heavily Indebted Poor Countries Initiative (HIPC Initiative) was launched by the IMF and the World Bank in 1996 to ensure that poor countries do not face a debt burden they could not manage. In 2005, the HIPC Initiative was supplemented by the Multilateral Debt Relief Initiative (MDRI) to help accelerate countries' progress toward the Millennium Development Goals.

HIV/AIDS

HIV/AIDS still threatens communities on the continent with extinction and impacts negatively on economic stability and growth. Sub-Saharan Africa is the region most heavily affected by HIV/AIDS infection. In its most recent report UNAIDS shows the region accounting for 67% of the world total of 33 million people living with HIV and for 75% of AIDS deaths. An estimated 1.9 million people were newly infected with HIV in sub-Saharan Africa in 2007, bringing to 22 million the number of people living with HIV.

FDI

Foreign Direct Investment (FDI) inflows in Africa topped $87 billion in 2008, setting a new record. Returns on investments in Africa were the highest among developing regions. Factors that boosted FDI inflows were a booming commodity market and investor friendly reforms. Most of the investments were linked to the extraction of natural resources. The commodity price boom also helped Africa to maintain the relatively high level of outward FDI, amounting to $9 billion in 2008. Africa's share of the total global FDI, however, remained at about 3%.

Agriculture

Despite the importance of minerals, Africa's people remain largely dependent on farming for jobs and survival. Today agriculture accounts for 14.0 percent of Africa's total output—slightly below its 17.2 percent share during the period from 1998-2000. The share of agriculture in individual economies range from a mere 2.6 percent in Botswana to 58.7 percent in the Democratic Republic of Congo. Major food crops include cassava, maze, millet, rice and sorghum. Prime exports are cocoa and coffee beans, palm oil, ground nuts, cotton, tea, sisal and tobacco. With food production falling steadily behind population growth, Africa has become a net importer of food.

Manufacturing

Apart from South Africa, which ranks among the world's industrialized nations, manufacturing in Africa is underdeveloped. However, it contributes significantly to the overall economic activity of countries such as Zimbabwe, Morocco, Algeria and Egypt. In 2007 Industry accounted for slightly more than 40% of Africa's GDP with manufacturing a mere 11% of this share. Oil is currently the major foreign exchange earner.

Services

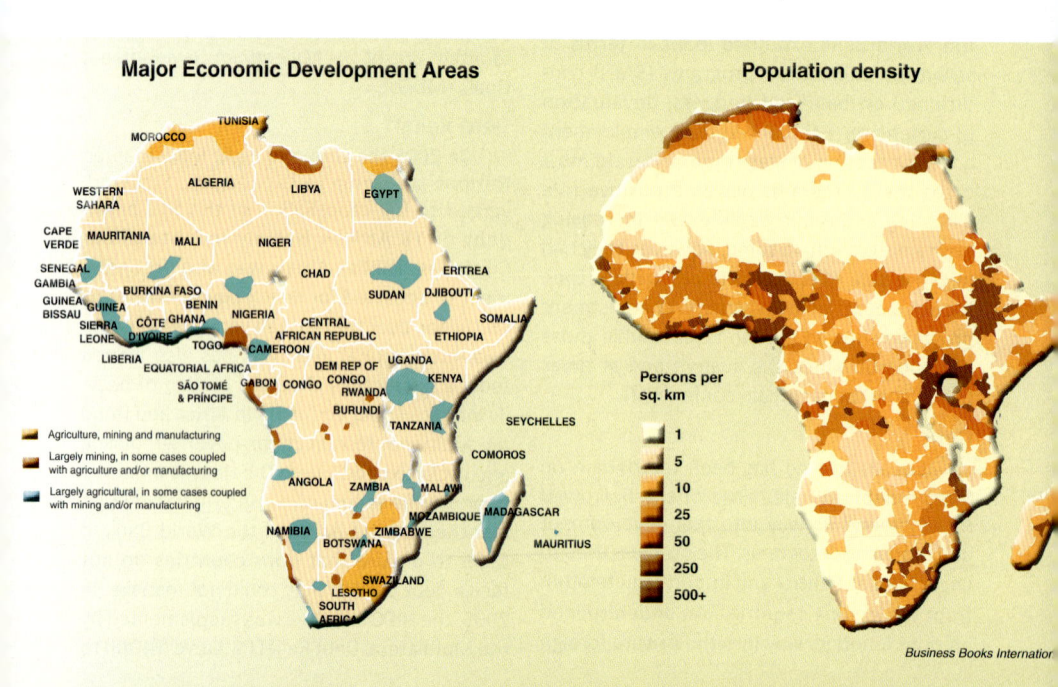

The service sector—banking, insurance and other financial services, wholesale and retail trade, tourism, transport and communications—is the single largest contributor to the African economy. Foreign financial institutions have been particularly active in recent times. Reforms continue, opening up not only state utilities in telecommunications and power generation but making it possible for local and foreign entrepreneurs to become partners in air, road and rail transport and shipping.

Population

In 2009 Africa's total population stood at 1 billion. The continent's population is expected to double every 25 years. There are indications, however, that growth might have peaked. The high incidence of HIV/AIDS may also prompt futurists to revise their forecasts. Still, the US Census Bureau projects a population of 1.34 billion on the African continent in 2025. The African Development Bank's *Population Clock* reveals the following dynamics of demographic change in Africa: an average of 4,125 people born per hour, 69 per minute, 1.1 persons per second. At the same time 235 infants die every hour, 4 every minute. At an average of 65 persons per sq. mile Africa has a population density well below the world average of 105 people per sq. mile. . In Asia population density runs as high as 203 and in Europe tit is 134. The United States has a density of 76 people per square mile—slightly higher than Africa.

The Ten Largest Economies in Africa
GDP at Current Market Prices 2008
(US$ Billion)

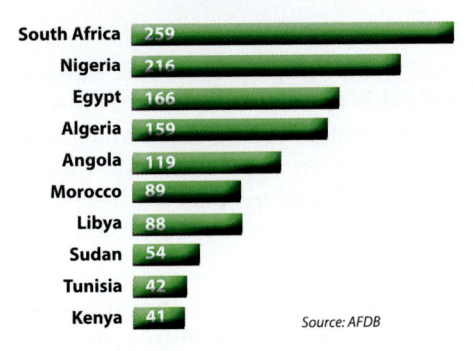

South Africa	259
Nigeria	216
Egypt	166
Algeria	159
Angola	119
Morocco	89
Libya	88
Sudan	54
Tunisia	42
Kenya	41

Source: AFDB

Urban population

Africa is the world's least urbanized continent with more than 60 percent of its population living in rural areas. At latest count there were more than 60 urban areas with a population of more than a half a million, including 30 cities with more than one million. The largest metropolitan center in Africa is Lagos at 15 million. Cairo is second with more than 12 million inhabitants in its metropolitan area. Africa's most affluent urban area is, the Pretoria/Witwatersrand/Vereeniging or PWV complex around Johannesburg, South Africa, with some 7 million people.

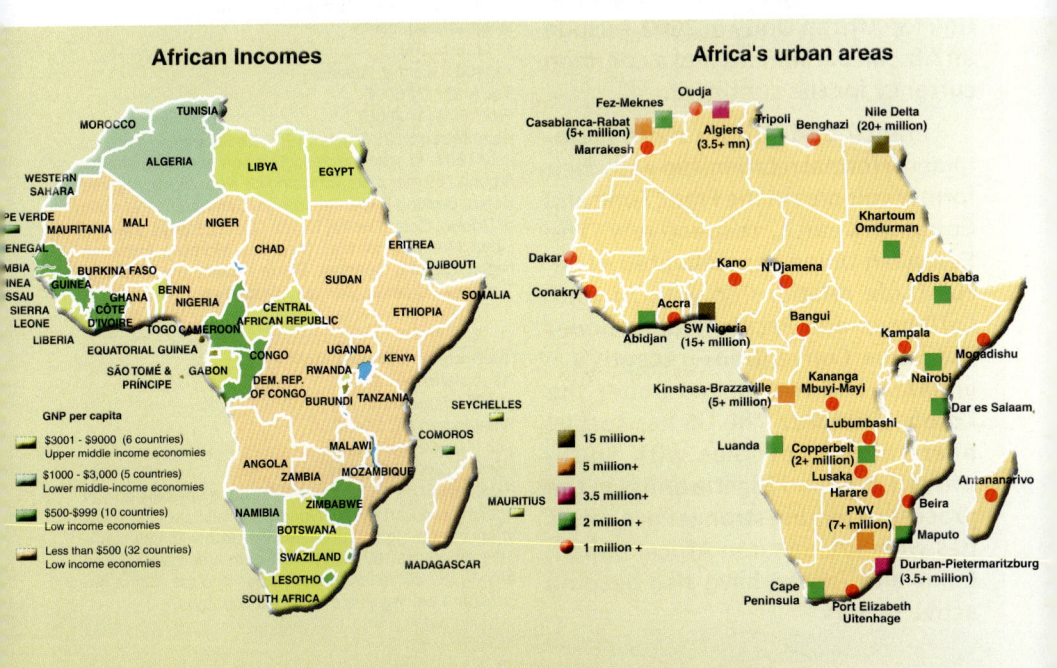

INTERNATIONAL & REGIONAL LINKS

The United Nations has been a valuable forum for African nations in their struggle to end colonialism and apartheid on the continent. Today, Africa's 53 nations play a strong role in the world organization itself and its agencies.

There has been a concerted effort in Africa to establish economic regions able to compete more effectively in world markets. While groupings such as ECOWAS, COMESA, SADC, UDEAC, UAM and SACU are determined by geographical factors, common currency and historical ties, there has been a tendency of late to be more pragmatic. One recently formed grouping, IOARC, aims at promoting trade and economic cooperation among African, Arab, Asian and Australasian nations along the rim of the Indian Ocean.

Ambitious plans for the African Union which replaced the Organization for African Unity in 2002 include an African parliament and a common currency for the continent.

France and Britain have maintained a formal relationship with their former colonies in the Franc Zone and Commonwealth, respectively. The European Union has cultivated a special trade relationship with African, Caribbean and Pacific nations under the Lomé Convention—recently revitalized and rearranged under the Cotonou accord. The US has special bilateral relationships with South Africa, Egypt and Nigeria and is in the process of forging stronger economic ties with Sub-Saharan Africa. Japan, China and Taiwan have also become active suitors.

UN SYSTEM

United Nations (UN)
United Nations
New York NY 10017, USA
Tel: [1] (212) 963 1234
Fax: [1] (212) 963 4879
Established on 26 June 1945, and starting operations on October 1945, the United Nations has witnessed the growth of a formidable and active African bloc since the sixties.

Economic Commission for Africa (ECA)
P. O. Box 3001-3005
Addis Ababa, Ethiopia
Tel: [251] (1) 51 72 00 Fax: [251] (1) 51 44 16
Web: *www.un.org/depts/eca/*
Established on 29 April 1958 to promote economic development as a regional commission of the UN's Economic and Social Council. All African nations are members. France and Britain serve as associate members.

Food and Agriculture Organization (FAO)
Viale delle Terme di Caracalla
00100 Rome, Italy
Tel: [39] (6) 57051 Fax:[39] (6) 5705 3152
Web: *www.fao.org*
Established on 16 October 1945 to raise living standards and increase availability of agricultural products.

International Atomic Energy Agency (IAEA)
Wagramerstrasse 5
P. O. Box 100
A-1400 , Vienna, Austria
Tel: [43] (1) 26000
Fax: [43] (1) 26007
Established on 26 October 1956, and operating since 29 July 1957, to promote peaceful uses of atomic energy among 129 members, including 25 from Africa: Algeria, Benin, Burkina Faso, Cameroon, Democratic Republic of Congo, Cote d'Ivoire, Egypt, Gabon, Kenya, Liberia, Libya, Madagascar, Mali, Mauritius, Morocco, Namibia, Niger, Nigeria, Senegal, Sierra Leone, South Africa, Tanzania, Uganda, Zambia, Zimbabwe.

International Development Association (IDA)
1818 H Street NW
Washington DC 20433
Tel: [1] (202) 477 1234
Fax: [1] (202) 477 6391
Established on 26 January 1960, as a specialized UN agency and part of the World Bank affiliate to provide financing on highly concessional terms to low countries among its 160 members. South Africa is classified among the 26 developed countries and the rest of the continent among less developed countries.

International Finance Corporation (IFC)
2121 Pennsylvania Avenue NW
Washington, DC 20433, USA
Tel: [1] (202) 477 1234
Fax: [1] (202) 974 4384
Established on 25 May 1955, and starting operations on 24 July 1956, as a support mechanism for private enterprise in international economic development. It is a UN specialized agency and World Bank affiliate. All African countries are members by virtue of their Wolrd Bank membership.

International Fund for Agricultural Development (IFAD)
Via del Serafico 107
I-00142 Rome
Italy
Tel: [39] (6) 54591 Fax:[39] (6) 5043463
Web: www.ifad.org
Established in December 1977 to promote agricultural development.

International Labour Organization (ILO)
4 route des Morillons
CH-1211 Geneva 22
Switzerland
Tel: [41] (22) 799 61 11
Fax: [41] (22) 798 86 85
Web: www.ilo.org
The ILO was founded in 1919 and is the only surviving major creation of the Treaty of Versailles which brought the League of Nations into being and became the first specialized agency of the UN in 1946. The ILO formulates international labor standards and set minimum standards of basic labor rights: freedom of association, the right to organize, collective bargaining, abolition of forced labour, equality of opportunity and treatment, and other standards regulating conditions across the entire field of work-related issues. The ILO has a unique tripartite structure with workers and employers participating as equal partners with governments. All African nations and other UN members belong.

International Maritime Organization (IMO)
4 Albert Embankment
London SE1 7SR, UK
Tel: [44] (171) 735 7611
Fax: [44] (171) 587 3210
Web: www.imo.org
Established on 6 March 1948, as the Intergovernmental Maritime Consultative Organization (IMCO) and changed to the IMO on 22 May 1982, this specialized UN agency deals with international maritime affairs. Its 157 members include 39 African countries: Algeria, Angola, Benin, Cameroon, Cape Verde, Democratic Republic of Congo, Republic of the Congo, Côte d'Ivoire, Djibouti, Egypt, Equatorial Guinea, Eritrea, Ethiopia, Gabon, The Gambia, Ghana, Guinea, Guinea-Bissau, Kenya, Liberia, Libya, Madagascar, Malawi, Mauritania, Mauritius, Morocco, Mozambique, Namibia, Nigeria, São Tomé & Príncipe, Senegal, Seychelles, Sierra Leone, Somalia, South Africa, Sudan, Tanzania, Togo, Tunisia.

International Monetary Fund (IMF)
700 19th Street NW
Washington DC 20431, USA
Tel: [1] (202) 623 7000 Fax: [1] (202) 623 4661
Web: www.imf.org
Established on 22 July 1944, and operative since 27 December 1945, the IMF, a specialized UN agency, works towards world monetary stability and economic development. All African countries are represented in the 182-member organization.

International Telecommunication Union (ITU)
Place des Nations
CH-1211 Geneva 20, Switzerland
Tel: [41] (22) 730 5111
Fax: [41] (22) 733 7256
Web: www.itu.int
Established on17 May 1865 and affiliated with the UN since 1947, the ITU handles world telecommunications issues among members.

Maite Nkoana-Mashabane, Foreign Affairs Minister of South Africa, addresses the General Assembly in September 2010.
UN Photo: Devra Berkowitz

United Nations Conference on Trade and Development (UNCTAD)
Palais des Nations
CH-1211 Geneva 10, Switzerland
Tel: [41] (22) 907 12 34 Fax: [41] (22) 907 00 57
Web: www.unctad.org
Established on 30 December 1964 to facilitate the integration of developing countries into the world economy and international trading system.

United Nations Educational, Scientific, and Cultural Organization (UNESCO)
7 place de Fontenoy
F-75352 Paris 07SP, France
Tel: [33] (1) 45 68 10 00
Fax: [33] (1) 45 67 16 90
Web: www.unseco.org
Established on in 1946 to promote cooperation in education, science, and culture among UN members.

United Nations High Commissioner for Refugees (UNHCR)
Case Postale 2500 Depot
CH-1211 Geneva 2, Switzerland
Tel: [41] (22) 739 81 11
Fax: [41] (22) 731 95 46
Web: www.unhcr.ch
Established on in1951, UNHCR seeks to ensure the humanitarian treatment of refugees and to find permanent solutions to refugee problems. A significant part of its operations, which now aid internally-displaced persons as well as cross-border refugees, are geared to Africa.

United Nations Industrial Development Organization (UNIDO)
Vienna International Center
PO Box 300
A-1400 Vienna, Austria
Tel: [43] (1) 260 260 Fax:[43] (1) 269 2669
Web: www.unido.org
This United States agency was established in 1966, to promote industrial development among UN member nations. All African nations are members.

Universal Postal Union (UPU)
Bureau International de l'UPU
Weltpoststrasse 4
CH-3000 Berne 15
Switzerland
Tel: [41] (31) 350 31 11
Fax: [41] (31) 350 31 10
Established in 1874, and became a UN specialized agency in 1948, Its role is to promote international postal cooperation among UN member states. All African states are members.

World Bank
The International Bank for Reconstruction and Development or IBRD
1818 H Street NW
Washington DC 20433
Tel: [1] (202) 477 1234
Fax: [1] (202) 477 6391

Malawi President Bingu Wa Mutharika meets with US President Barack Obama at the UN in September 2010

UN Photo:Eskinder Debebe

Web: www.worldbank.org
Established on 22 July 1944 and operative since 27 December 1945, this UN specialized agency provides economic development loans to its membership of 181 members, including all 53 African countries. It is an

World Health Organization (WHO)
20, Avenue Appia
CH-1211 , Geneva 27, Switzerland
Tel: [41] (22) 791 21 11 Fax: [41] (22) 791 07 46
Web: www.who.org
The World Health Organization was established on 22 July 1946, as a specialized UN agency and started on 7 April 1948. It deals with health matters worldwide. All African states are members.

World Intellectual Property Organization (WIPO)
34 Chemin des Colombettes
CH-1211 Geneva 20, Switzerland
Tel: [41] (22) 338 9111
Fax: [41] (22) 733 5428
Web: www.wipo.int
Established on 14 July 1967 and operative since 26 April 1970, WIPO as a specialized UN agency furnishes protection for literary, artistic, and scientific works. Its 171 members include all 53 African countries.

World Meteorological Organization (WMO)
41 Avenue Giuseppe-Motta
CH-1211 Geneva 2, Switzerland
Tel: [41] (22) 730 81 11
Fax: [41] (22) 734 23 26
Web: www.wmo.ch
Established in 1947 and became a UN specialized agency in 1951. Its aims at providing authoritative scientific meterological information on a global basis. All African nations are members.

World Tourism Organization (UNWTO)
Calle Capitan Haya 42
28020 Madrid, Spain
Tel: [34] (1) 567 81 00
Fax: [34] (1) 571 37 33
Established on 2 January 1975, to promote tourism as a means of contributing to economic development, international understanding, and peace. Its 131 members include 47 African countries: Algeria, Angola, Benin, Botswana, Burkina Faso, Burundi, Cameroon, Central African Republic, Chad, Democratic Republic of the Congo, Republic of Congo, Côte d'Ivoire, Djibouti, Egypt, Equatorial Guinea, Ethiopia, Gabon, The Gambia, Ghana, Guinea, Guinea-Bissau, Kenya, Lesotho, Libya, Madagascar, Malawi, Mali, Mauritania, Mauritius, Morocco,Mozambique, Namibia, Niger, Nigeria, Rwanda, São Tomé & Príncipe, Senegal, Seychelles, Sierra Leone, South Africa, Sudan, Tanzania, Togo, Tunisia, Uganda, Zambia, Zimbabwe.

World Trade Organization (WTO)
Centre William Rappard
154 Rue de Lausanne
CH-1211 Geneva 21, Switzerland
Tel:[41](22)7395111
Fax:[41](22)73954 58
Web: www.wto.org

Established on 15 April 1994, and operating since 1 January 1995, as a successor to the General Agreement on Tariff and Trade (GATT), the WTO provides the mechanism to resolve trade conflicts between members and to carry on negotiations with the goal of further lowering and/or eliminating tariffs and other trade barriers. Its 140 members include 41 African members: Angola, Benin, Botswana, Burkina Faso, Burundi, Cameroon, Central African Republic, Chad, Democratic Republic of the Congo, Republic of Congo, Côte d'Ivoire, Djibouti, Egypt, Gabon, The Gambia, Ghana, Guinea, Guinea-Bissau, Kenya, Lesotho, Madagascar, Malawi, Mali, Mauritania, Mauritius, Morocco, Mozambique, Namibia, Niger, Nigeria, Rwanda, Senegal, Sierra Leone, South Africa, Swaziland, Tanzania, Togo, Tunisia, Uganda, Zambia, Zimbabwe. Two African nations have observer status: Somalia, Sudan. Another five have applications pending: Cape Verde, Comoros, Equatorial Guinea, São Tomé & Príncipe, and Seychelles.

OTHER ORGANIZATIONS

Following are other significant world and regional organizations to which all or some of Africa's nations belong:

African, Caribbean, and Pacific Group of States (ACP Group)
Avenue Georges Henri 451
B-1200 Brussels, Belgium
Tel: [32] (2) 743 06 00
Fax [32] (2) 735 55 73
Established on 6 June 1975 to manage preferential economic and aid relationships with the EU. All Sub-Saharan African countries belong to the group of 71 less-developed African, Caribbean and Pacific (ACP) countries associated with the European Union (EU) under the Lomé Convention. Under this treaty the EU grants ACP exports access to its markets on either a low or zero tariff basis. The EU also provides financial and technical aid to Lomé signatories, including the Stabex and Sysmin stabilization funds. The Stabex scheme was designed to compensate the ACP countries for fluctuations in the price of their agricultural exports. Similarly, Sysmin safeguards exports of minerals. Four Conventions have been concluded since 1975 when the first treaty was signed in Lomé, the capital of Togo. When it became a signatory in 1997, South Africa did not qualify for all the provisions of the convention as it was considered too highly developed for full membership. Other African member states are Angola, Benin, Botswana, Burkina Faso, Burundi, Cameroon, Cape Verde, Central African Republic, Chad, Comoros, Democratic Republic of the Congo, Republic of the Congo, Côte d'Ivoire, Djibouti, Equatorial Guinea, Eritrea, Ethiopia, Gabon, The Gambia, Ghana, Guinea, Guinea-Bissau, Kenya, Lesotho, Liberia, Madagascar, Malawi, Mali, Mauritania, Mauritius, Mozambique, Namibia, Niger, Nigeria,

Rwanda, São Tomé & Príncipe, Senegal, Seychelles, Sierra Leone, Somalia, Sudan, Swaziland, Tanzania, Togo, Uganda, Zambia, Zimbabwe. The Cotonou Agreement, signed in Benin in June 2000, replaces the Lomé agreement. Discussions are underway to thrash out details among the 15 European signatories and the African and other ACP member nations. Considered are not only changed circumstances in Europe and Africa but WTO requirements.

African Development Bank (ADB)
Banque Africaine de Developpement
01 BP 1387
Abidjan 01
Côte d'Ivoire
Tel: [225] 20 44 44
Fax: [225] 21 77 53
Established on 4 August 1963 to promote economic and social development in Africa. All African countries are are regional members regional members. There are 25 non-regional members: Argentina, Austria, Belgium, Brazil, Canada, China, Denmark, Finland, France, Germany, India, Italy, Japan, South Korea, Kuwait, Netherlands, Norway, Portugal, Saudi Arabia, Spain, Sweden, Switzerland, UAE, UK, US.

African Union (AU)
PO Box 3243
Addis Ababa, Ethiopia
Tel: [251] (1) 517700
Fax: [251] (1) 512622, 517844
On 2 March 2001 the African Union was approved by a required two-thirds of Africa's 53 nations as a successor to the Organization of African Unity. Until its inauguration on 8 July 2002 at a special ceremony in Durban, South Africa, the African Union (AU) was given the opportunity to phase itself into OAU headquarters, which it inherited together with other assets and liabilities—including arrears of $42 million in membership dues. It was felt that the OAU, established on 25 May 1963, to promote unity and cooperation among African states in their fight against colonialism and apartheid had served its purpose and needed to be replaced. As in the case of the OAU, all 53 African nations are members of the AU. The general consensus among is that the African Union should be different from its predecessor to be able to meet new and changed circumstances. Priorities have changed from pure political activism to closer economic cooperation, globalization and peacekeeping in Africa. The aim is to eventually duplicate and adapt the European Union model, replete with a common parliament, monetary system and currency. The ultimate goal is to enhance the economic and political future of the continent and find African solutions to local problems. The African Union's economic revival mandate is closely linked to the so-called New African Initiative and the New Partnership for Africa's Development (NEPAD) plan.

Arab Bank for Economic Development in Africa (ABEDA)
[A.k.a. Banque Arabe de Developpement Economique en Afrique or BADEA]
Abdel Rahman El Mahdi Avenue
P. O. Box 2640

UN Photo:Devra Berkow
Senegal's President Abdoulaye Wade addresses the UN General Assembly, September 2010

Khartoum, Sudan
Tel: [249] (11) 770498
Fax: [249] (11) 770600
Established on 18 February 1974, and started operations on 16 September 1974, to promote economic development. Its 17 members include: Algeria, Egypt, Libya, Mauritania, Morocco, Sudan, Tunisia. Other Arab members: Bahrain, Iraq, Jordan, Kuwait, Lebanon, Oman, Qatar, Saudi Arabia, Syria, UAE.

Arab Maghreb Union (AMU)
27 Avenue Okba Agdal
Rabat, Morocco
Tel: [212] (7) 77 26 82
Fax: [212] (7) 77 26 93
Established on 17 February 1989, to promote cooperation and integration among the Arab states of northern Africa. The Union du Maghreb Arabe (UMA), aims at safeguarding the region's economic interests, fostering and promoting economic and cultural cooperation, and intensifying mutual commercial exchanges as a precursor for integration and the creation of a North African Common Market. The secretariat is based in Rabat, Morocco. It has a membership of 5: Algeria, Libya, Mauritania, Morocco, Tunisia.

Central African States Development Bank (BDEAC)
[Acronym for *Banque de Developpement des Etats de l'Afrique Centrale*]
Place du Gouvernement

Ethiopia's Prime Minister Meles Zenawi speaks at UN Summit on the Millennium Development Goals, September 2010
Photo: John McIlwane

BP 1177, Brazzaville
Republic of the Congo
Tel: [242] 81 18 85
Fax: [242] 81 18 80
Established on 3 December 1975, to provide loans for economic development in African countries. The BDEAC's African members are Cameroon, Central African Republic, Chad, Republic of Congo, Equatorial Guinea, and Gabon. Other members are France, Germany, and Kuwait.

Commonwealth (CWLTH)
[A.k.a. Commonwealth of Nations]
Commonwealth Secretariat
Marlborough House
London SW1Y 5HX
United Kingdom
Tel: [44] (171) 839 3411, 747 6535
Fax: [44] (171) 930 0827, 839 9081
The Commonwealth was established on 31 December 1931 as a voluntary association evolving from the British Empire, to foster multinational cooperation and provide assistance to members where needed. The Commonwealth functions as an association of independent states—most of them, but not all, former British colonies. More affluent members such as Australia, Canada, New Zealand and the United Kingdom channel a substantial portion of their foreign aid into less developed fellow Commonwealth nations. There are also special trade and investment agreements. Links between governments are complemented by the activities of a large number of non-governmental Commonwealth organizations active in a variety of community building projects. Its current membership of 54 includes 18 from Africa: Botswana, Cameroon, The Gambia, Ghana, Kenya, Lesotho, Malawi, Mauritius, Mozambique, Namibia, Nigeria, Rwanda, Seychelles, Sierra Leone, South Africa, Swaziland, Tanzania, Uganda, Zambia, Zimbabwe. The other members are: Antigua and Barbuda, Australia, The Bahamas, Bangladesh, Barbados, Belize, Brunei, Canada, Cyprus, Dominica, Fiji, Grenada, Guyana, India, Jamaica, Kiribati, Malaysia, Maldives, Malta, Nauru, New Zealand, Pakistan, Papua New Guinea, Saint Kitts and Nevis, Saint Lucia, Saint Vincent and the Grenadines, Samoa, Singapore, Solomon Islands, Tonga, Trinidad and Tobago, Sri Lanka, United Kingdom, Vanuatu.

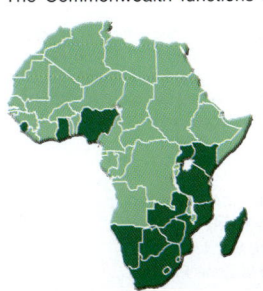

Common Market for Eastern and Southern Africa (COMESA)
Tel: [260] 1 229-726
Fax: [260] 1 225-107
PO Box 30051
Lusaka 10101, Zambia
In November 1993, the member states of the Preferential Trade Area for Eastern and Southern Africa (PTA) signed a treaty transforming the PTA into the Common Market for Eastern and Southern Africa (COMESA). It aims at a fully integrated free trade area, a customs union with a common external tariff, free movement of capital and finance, a payments union, and free movement of people. It aims at promoting cooperation in the development and rationalization of basic and strategic industries, agricultural development, the improvement of transport links, and the development of technical and professional skills. COMESA has 21 members: Angola, Burundi, Comoros, Djibouti, Eritrea, Ethiopia, Kenya, Madagascar, Ma-lawi, Mauritius, Namibia, Rwanda, Seychelles, Somalia, Sudan, Swaziland, Tanzania, Uganda, Democratic Republic of Congo, Zambia and Zimbabwe.

Customs and Economic Union of Central Africa (CEMAC)
[Acronym for *Communauté économique et monétaire en Afrique Centrale*].
Bangui, Central African Republic
Tel: [237] 21 44 15
Fax: [237] 21 44 88
Established in 1966 under the Brazzaville Treaty of 1964 as a customs union, the *Union douanière et économique de l'Afnique Centrale* (UDEAC) allowed duty-free trade between French- and Spanish-speaking countries in Central Africa. A common external tariff applied to imports from third countries. In 1994 the members of UDEAC entered into a second agreement, the Economic and Monetary Community in Central Africa or *Commu-*

nauté économique et monétaire en Afrique Centrale (CEMAC), replacing the UDEAC. Members are: Cameroon, Central African Republic, Chad, Congo, Equatorial Guinea and Gabon. CEMAC's secretariat is in Bangui, Central African Republic. CEMAC members share as a central bank the *Banque des états de l'Afrique centrale (BEAC)* in Yaoundé, Cameroon.

Customs Cooperation Council (CCC)
[World Customs Organization (WCO)]
Rue du Marche 30
B-1210, Brussels, Belgium
Tel: [32] (2) 209 92 11
Fax: [32] (2) 109 92 92
Established on15 December 1950 to promote international cooperation in customs matters. Its 145 signatories include 44 African nations: Algeria, Angola, Botswana, Burkina Faso, Burundi, Cameroon, Cape Verde, Central African Republic, Comoros, Democratic Republic of Congo, Republic of the Congo, Côte d'Ivoire, Egypt, Eritrea, Ethiopia, Gabon, The Gambia, Ghana, Guinea, Kenya, Lesotho, Liberia, Libya, Madagascar, Malawi, Mali, Mauritania, Mauritius, Morocco, Mozambique, Namibia, Niger, Nigeria, Rwanda, Senegal, Sierra Leone, South Africa, Sudan, Swaziland, Tanzania, Togo, Tunisia, Zambia, Zimbabwe.

Commission for East African Co-operation (EAC)
P.O. Box 1096
Arusha, Tanzania
Tel: [225] 57 4253/8
Fax: [225] 57 4255
The Tripartite Commission for East African Cooperation (EAC) was formed by Kenya, Tanzania and Uganda in July 1999. It aims at eliminating all tariff rates between the member states and issuing a single passport for the region. Both Rwanda and Burundi are expected to join.

East African Development Bank (EADB)
4 Nile Avenue
P. O. Box 7128
Kampala
Uganda
Tel: [256] (41) 230021, 230825
Fax: [256] (41) 259763
Established on 6 June 1967, and started operations on 1 December 1967, promoting economic development among its members—Kenya, Tanzania, and Uganda.

Economic Community of Central African States (CEEAC)
[Acronym derived from *Communaute Economique des Etats de l'Afrique Centrale*]
BP 2112
Libreville
Gabon
Tel: [241] 73 35 47, 73 35 48
Established on 18 October 1983, to promote regional economic cooperation and develop a Central African Common Market. Its eleven members are: Angola, Burundi, Cameroon, Central African Republic, Chad, Democratic Republic of Congo, Republic of the Congo, Equatorial Guinea, Gabon, Rwanda, São Tomé & Príncipe.

Economic Community of the Great Lakes Countries (CEPGL)
[Acronym—CEPGL—derived from *Communaute Economique des Pays des Grands Lacs*]
BP 91, Gitega
Burundi
Established on 20 September 1976, to promote regional economic cooperation and integration of its 3 members: Burundi, Democratic Republic of Congo, Rwanda.

Economic Community of West African States (ECOWAS)
6 King George V Road
PMB 12745, Lagos, Nigeria
Tel: [234] (1) 636839, 636841, 636064, 630398
Fax: [234] (1) 636822
Established in May 1975, the Economic Community of West African States (ECOWAS) is a common market striving towards uniform lower tariff rates. Poorer members are to be compensated from a common fund. ECOWAS also promotes the free movement of people, services and capital, harmonization of agricultural policies, joint development of economic and industrial policies, common monetary policies, and the elimination of disparities in levels of development. It has a membership of 16: Benin, Burkina Faso, Cape Verde, Côte d'Ivoire, The Gambia, Ghana, Guinea, Guinea-Bissau, Liberia, Mali, Mauritania, Niger, Nigeria, Senegal, Sierra Leone and Togo.

Franc Zone (CFA)
[Officially known as the *Communauté Financière Africaine or CFA*]
Direction Generale des Service
Etrangers (Service de la Zone Franc)
Banque de France
Paris, France
Tel: [33] 42 92 31 26
Established in December 1945, the Franc Zone is a union of African countries with currencies linked to the

French franc at a fixed rate of exchange. The *Communauté Financière Africaine* (CFA) franc is ensured by the French Treasury, and remains readily convertible. In 1994, the exchange rate parity was reduced by 50 percent to a fixed parity of 100 CFA francs to one French franc. Under mutual agreement members hold their reserves mainly in French francs and undertake to exchange them on the French market. With the exception of Guinea and Mauritania, all former members of French West Africa and French Equatorial Africa joined this monetary union. So did the former French island possession of Comoros. Equatorial Guinea, a former Spanish colony, joined in 1985, and in 1997, Guinea Bissau, a former Portuguese Guinea, in 1997. There are two Franc Zone groupings, one in Western and one in Central Africa. A separate agreement applies to Comoros. Apart from Guinea and Mauritania, other African francophone nations who opted not to join the monetary union are Madagascar, Djibouti, the Democratic Republic of Congo, Rwanda and Burundi. The CFA franc has been useful in facilitating international payments and foreign trade. Francophone countries received assistance from France in the form of development and technical, budget and military support, as well as subsidies on commodity exports.

International Chamber of Commerce (ICC)
38 Cours Albert 1st
F-75008 Paris, France
Tel: [33] (1) 49 53 28 28
Fax: [33] (1) 49 53 29 42
Established in 1919 to promote free trade and private enterprise and to represent business interests at national and international levels. Its 62 national councils represented include 11 from African countries: Burkina Faso, Cameroon, Côte d'Ivoire, Egypt, Madagascar, Morocco, Nigeria, Senegal, South Africa, Togo, Tunisia.

International Confederation of Free Trade Unions (ICFTU)
International Trade Union House
Boulevard Emile Jacqmain 155
B-1210 , Brussels, Belgium
Tel: [32] (2) 224 02 11
Established in December 1949, to promote trade union movements. More than 200 organizations representing 141 countries, are affiliated. Movements from 38 African countries are represented: Algeria, Benin, Botswana, Burkina Faso, Cameroon, Cape Verde, Central African Republic, Chad, Democratic Republic of the Congo, Republic of Congo, Côte d'Ivoire, Djibouti, Eritrea, Gabon, The Gambia, Ghana, Guinea, Guinea-Bissau, Kenya, Liberia, Madagascar, Malawi, Mali, Mauritius, Morocco, Mozambique, Rwanda, Senegal, Seychelles, Sierra Leone, South Africa, Swaziland, Tanzania, Togo, Tunisia, Uganda, Zambia, Zimbabwe.

International Criminal Police Organization (Interpol)
BP 6041, F-69411
Lyon CEDEX 06, France
Tel: [33] (4) 72 44 70 00
Fax: [33] (4) 72 44 71 63
Established in 1923 as the International Criminal Police Commission and modified on 13 June 1956, under its current name to promote international cooperation among police authorities in combating crime. Among its 177 members, 51 African countries are represented: Algeria, Angola, Benin, Botswana, Burkina Faso, Burundi, Cameroon, Cape Verde, Central African Republic, Chad, Democratic Republic of the Congo, Republic of the Congo, Côte d'Ivoire, Djibouti, Egypt, Equatorial Guinea, Ethiopia, Gabon, The Gambia, Ghana, Guinea, Guinea-Bissau, Kenya, Lesotho, Liberia, Libya, Madagascar, Malawi, Mali, Mauritania, Mauritius, Morocco, Mozambique, Namibia, Niger, Nigeria, Rwanda, São Tomé & Príncipe, Senegal, Seychelles, Sierra Leone, Somalia, South Africa, Sudan, Swaziland, Tanzania, Togo, Tunisia, Uganda, Zambia, Zimbabwe.

Intergovernmental Authority for Development (IGAD)
BP 2653, Djibouti
Djibouti
Tel : [253] 354050, (253) 352880
Fax : [253] 356994
Signatories to the Intergovernmental Authority on Development (IGAD) are Djibouti, Eritrea, Ethiopia, Kenya, Somalia and Uganda. The group focuses on economic cooperation and regional integration to combat the effects of drought and to help solve regional conflicts. The focus has also been on transportation and communications infrastructure building. There is a possibility that in the long term, the membership could increase as countries such as Egypt might join.

International Organization for Migration (IOM)
17 route des Morillons CP 71
CH-1211 Geneva 19, Switzerland
Tel: [41] (22) 717 91 11
Fax: [41] (22) 798 61 50
Established on 5 December 1951, to facilitate orderly international emigration and immigration. Among its 69 members are the following 13 African countries: Angola, Egypt, Guinea-Bissau, Kenya, Mali, Morocco, Senegal, South Africa, Sudan, Tanzania, Tunisia, Uganda, Zambia. Fourteen African countries are among the 47 hat have observer status: Algeria, Cape Verde, Democratic Republic of Congo, Republic of the Congo, Ethiopia, Ghana, Guinea, Madagascar, Mozambique, Namibia, Rwanda, São Tomé & Príncipe, Somalia, Zimbabwe.

International Mobile Satellite Organization (Inmarsat)
99 City Road
London EC1Y 1AX, UK
Tel: [44] (171) 728 1000 Fax: [44] (171) 728 1044
Established on 3 September 1976 as the International Maritime Satellite Organization, the renamed Inmarsat, it promotes cooperation in worldwide communications for commercial, distress, and safety applications at sea, in the air, and on land. Its membership of 86 includes 12 from Africa: Algeria, Egypt, Gabon, Ghana, Kenya, Liberia, Mauritius, Mozambique, Nigeria, Senegal, South Africa, Tanzania.

Indian Ocean Commission (IOC)
Commission de l'Océan Indien
Q4 Avenue Sir Guy Forget
Quatre Bornes
Ile Maurice
Fax: [230] 425.12.09
The Indian Ocean Commission (IOC) was formed by Comoros, Madagascar, Mauritius, Seychelles and France (Reunion), in 1999 to represent members' interests in other regional and international organizations. It also aims at tariff reduction among members and joint trade promotion.

International Organization for Standardization (ISO)
CP 56, 1 Rue de Varembe
CH-1211 Geneva 20
Switzerland
Tel: [41] (22) 749 01 11
Fax:- [41] (22) 733 34 30
Established in February 1947, to further the development of international standards in the exchange of goods and services and to develop cooperation in the sphere of intellectual, scientific, technological and economic activity among members. There are 14 African countries among the 88 members: Algeria, Botswana, Egypt, Ethiopia, Ghana, Kenya, Libya, Mauritius, Morocco, Nigeria, South Africa, Tanzania, Tunisia, Zimbabwe. Eleven African nations are among the 44 correspondent and subscriber members: Benin, Democratic Republic of Congo, Côte d'Ivoire, Guinea, Madagascar, Malawi, Mozambique, Namibia, Seychelles, Sudan, Uganda.

International Telecommunications Satellite Organization (Intelsat)
3400 International Drive NW
Washington
DC 20008-3098
Tel: [1] (202) 944 7500
Fax: [1] (202) 944 7890
Esyablished on 20 August 1964, as the Telecommunications Satellite Consortium and changed to Intelsat on 12 February 1973, the International Telecommunications Satellite Organization aims at developing and operating a global commercial telecommunications satellite system. Forty- three of its 143 members are African: Algeria, Angola, Benin, Botswana, Burkina Faso, Cameroon, Cape Verde, Central African Republic, Chad, Comoros, Democratic Republic of Congo, Republic of the Congo, Côte d'Ivoire, Egypt, Equatorial Guinea, Ethiopia, Gabon, Ghana, Guinea, Kenya, Libya, Madagascar, Malawi, Mali, Mauritania, Mauritius, Morocco, Mozambique, Namibia, Niger, Nigeria, Rwanda, Senegal, Somalia, South Africa, Sudan, Swaziland, Tanzania, Togo, Tunisia, Uganda, Zambia, Zimbabwe. A further 10 African countries are among the non-signatory users: Burundi, Djibouti, Eritrea, The Gambia, Guinea-Bissau, Lesotho, Liberia, São Tomé & Príncipe, Seychelles, Sierra Leone.

Indian Ocean Rim Association for Regional Cooperation (IOR-ARC)
Port Louis, Mauritius
Launched in Mauritius in March 1997, the Indian Ocean Rim Organization for Regional Cooperation aspires to be a regional economic grouping such as ASEAN and APEC. It involves the business community, academia and governments in the promotion of wide-ranging co-operation among member states. Similar trading blocs elsewhere prompted a movement towards closer economic ties among the countries bordering the Indian Ocean. The focus is on trade and investment and the exchange of technical know-how, research and training. The following 18 countries are signatories: Australia, Bangladesh, India, Indonesia, Iran, Kenya, Madagascar, Malaysia, Mauritius, Mozambique, Oman, Singapore, South Africa, Sri Lanka, Tanzania, Thailand, UAE and Yemen. Seychelles withdrew as a member in July 2003. The nations of the IOR-ARC have a combined population of more than 1.3 billion or 23% of the world's population—with India and Indonesia accounting for 85% of the Association's total population. The Association represents a GNP of $1,184 billion or 4% of the world total. The GNP per capita for the region as a whole amounted to about $892 in 1995, which qualified it as lower middle income area in terms of the World Bank's classification. At the beginning of 2000 a Working Group on Trade and Investment (WGTI) met formally for the first time in Muscat to formulate formulate an Action Plan to liberalize trade and promote investment in the Indian Ocean Rim Region. Egypt, Japan, China, France and the United Kingdom are "dialogue partners."

International Red Cross and Red Crescent Movement (ICRM)
International Conference of the Red Cross
19 Avenue de la Paix
CH-1202 Geneva
Switzerland
Tel: [41] (22) 734 60 01
Fax: [41] (22) 733 20 57
Established in 1928 to promote worldwide humanitarian aid through the International Committee of the Red Cross (ICRC) in wartime, and in peacetime through the International Federation of Red Cross and Red Crescent Societies (IFRCS). Of the 175 national societies 50 African: Algeria, Angola, Benin, Botswana, Burkina Faso, Burundi, Cameroon, Cape Verde, Central African Republic, Chad, Democratic Republic of the Congo, Republic of Congo, Côte d'Ivoire, Djibouti, Egypt, Equatorial Guinea, Ethiopia, The Gambia, Ghana, Guinea, Guinea-Bissau, Kenya, Lesotho, Liberia, Libya, Madagascar, Malawi, Mali, Mauritania, Mauritius, Morocco, Mozambique, Namibia, Niger, Nigeria, Rwanda, São Tomé & Príncipe, Senegal, Seychelles, Sierra Leone, Somalia, South Africa, Sudan, Swaziland, Tanzania, Togo, Tunisia, Uganda, Zambia, Zimbabwe.

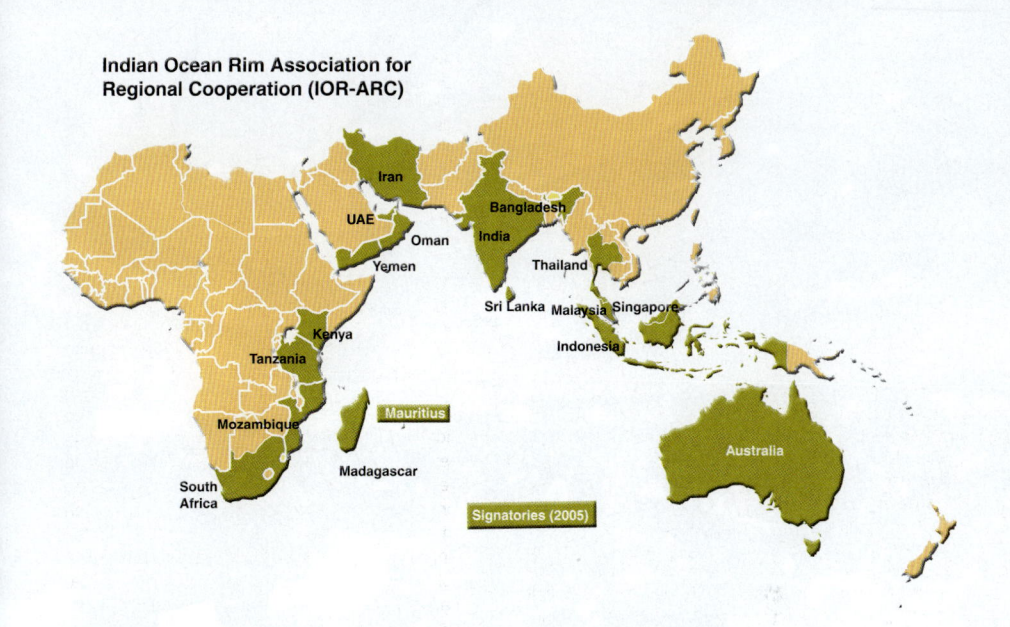

Indian Ocean Rim Association for Regional Cooperation (IOR-ARC)

Signatories (2005): Iran, UAE, Oman, Yemen, Bangladesh, India, Thailand, Sri Lanka, Malaysia, Singapore, Indonesia, Kenya, Tanzania, Mozambique, Mauritius, Madagascar, South Africa, Australia

Organization of Petroleum Exporting Countries (OPEC)
Obere Donaustrasse 93
A-1020 Vienna
Austria
Tel: [43] (1) 21 11 20
Fax: [43] (1) 216 43 20

Established on 14 September 1960 to coordinate petroleum policies among major oil producers. Algeria, Libya and Nigeria are members of the eleven-member body. Other members include Indonesia, Iran, Iraq, Kuwait, Qatar, Saudi Arabia, UAE, Venezuela.

Southern African Customs Union (SACU)
Director of Customs and Excise
Ministry of Finance
Private Bag 13295
Windhoek
Namibia

A Southern African Customs Union (SACU) was established in 1969 between South Africa, Botswana, Lesotho and Swaziland. Namibia became a member in 1990. Goods move freely between members, unhampered by tariffs or quantitative constraints, and there is a common customs tariff on goods imported from outside. All duties are paid into a common pool administered and disbursed annually by the South African Reserve Bank. Smaller countries receive a 42 percent allowance to compensate for the disadvantage of sharing with the much larger South Africa. Except for Botswana, all members of the Southern African Customs Union are also in a common monetary area arrangement (CMA), under which the currencies of Lesotho, Namibia and Swaziland are backed by the South African rand.

Southern African Development Community (SADC)
Private Bag 0095
Gaborone
Botswana
Tel: [267] (31) 351863
Fax: [267] (31) 372848

The Southern African Development Community (SADC) is an outgrowth of the Southern African Development Coordination Conference (SADCC). It was established in July 1979 by 11 nations in an effort to reduce the region's economic dependence on apartheid-ruled South Africa. On 17 August 1992, ten SADCC member states signed a treaty establishing the Southern African Development Community (SADC) with South Africa as the eleventh member. Mauritius joined in 1995, followed by the Democratic Republic of Congo and the Seychelles in 1997. All the members of the SADC—with the exception of Botswana, South Africa, Lesotho and Mozambique—are also members of COMESA. The Southern African Development Community promotes cross-border economic cooperation, investment and trade, and freer movement of goods and services, free enterprise, competitiveness, democracy and good governance, respect for the rule of law and human rights, popular participation and the alleviation of poverty. A tribunal was established to arbitrate disputes between member states arising from the treaty. To avoid an unwieldy bureaucracy at the SADC secretariat in Gaborone, Botswana, organizational responsibilities are shared by the various member states: Angola—energy; Botswana—economic affairs, agricultural research, animal disease control and livestock production;

61

UN Secretary-General Ban Ki-moon addresses the opening of the African Union Summit in Addis Ababa in January 2010. (UN Photo)

Lesotho— tourism, environment and land management; Malawi—inland fisheries, wildlife and forestry; Mozambique—transport and communication, culture and information; Namibia—marine fisheries and resources; Swaziland—human resources development; Tanzania—trade and industry; Zambia—mining; Zimbabwe—food security. When South Africa became the eleventh member in August 1994, it was given responsibility for finance and investment. The sector for tourism was allocated to Mauritius after the island nation it joined the Southern African Development Community in August 1995.

West African Development Bank (WADB)
[A.k.a. Banque Ouest-Africaine de Developpement or BOAD]
68 Avenue de la Liberation
BP 1172 Lome
Togo
Tel: [228] 21 59 06, 21 42 44
Fax: [228] 21 52 67, 21 72 69
Established on 14 November 1973, as a financial institution of WAEMU, the WADB promotes regional economic development and integration among its 8 regional members: Benin, Burkina Faso, Cote d'Ivoire, Guinea-Bissau, Mali, Niger, Senegal, and Togo. Also represented are 5 international/nonregional members: African Development Bank, Belgium, European Investment Bank, France, and Germany.

West African Economic and Monetary Union (WAEMU)
[A.k.a. Union Economique et Monetaire Ouest Africaine or UEMOA]
01 BP 543
Ouadgadougou
Burkina Faso
Tel: [226] 31 88 73 
Established on 1 August 1994, to increase the competitiveness of its 8 members' economic markets. The West African Economic and Monetary Union (WAEMU) promotes closer cooperation between West African states, the establishment of a common market and coordination of monetary policies. Tariff reduction is high on the priority list. Members are: Benin, Burkina Faso, Côte d'Ivoire, Guinea Bissau, Mali, Niger, Senegal and Togo. A secretariat is planned at Bamako in Mali.

Chapter 3
Trade and Investment

Africa relies heavily on the export of petroleum and other natural resources such as gold, diamonds and other strategically important minerals, including chrome, platinum and manganese. The trend is towards diversification Although oil exploration remains the primary target of foreign investors, telecommunications and infrastructure development in transport, health services, energy and manufacturing are also attracting sizeable capital inflows.

TRADE

Over the past ten years Africa's share of global exports and imports ranged between 2% and 3%. In 2005 China passed several of Africa's long-standing principal trading partners to take second place after the United States as an importer of African goods and top the list as an exporter to the Continent. Africa's merchandise exports increased by more than almost 42 percent in 2008 to $567 billion, showing a trade surplus of $97 billion—only to drop by 33 percent to $383 billion in 2009 in the wake of the global financial crisis. In 2009 Africa recorded its first trade deficit in recent times, amounting to $30 billion.

While the continent still relies heavily on its rich natural resources, including gold, diamonds, petroleum and a whole range of strategic minerals, foreign firms have found that trade preferences for African-made products and a growing number of export free zones on the continent make it profitable to move factories there. However, primary products and raw materials still account for about seventy five percent of Africa's total merchandise exports. South Africa is a notable exception. As an exporter of sophisticated manufactured products South Africa has not only made inroads overseas but became one of the rest of Africa's major trading partners.

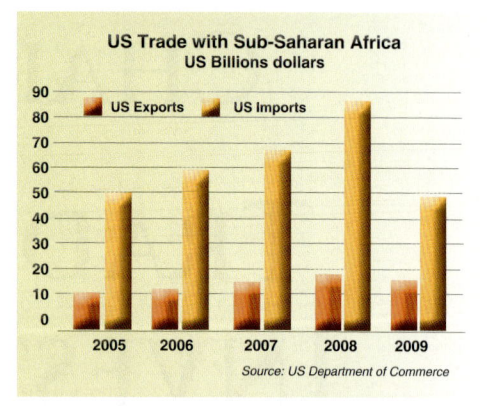

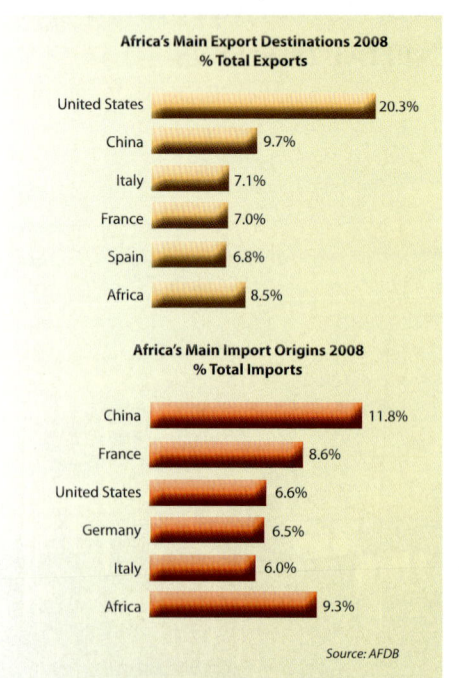

US trade

United States imports from Sub-Saharan Africa increased from $67 billion in 2007 to a record $86 billion in 2008 before dropping by 45.5 percent to $46.9 billion as a result of the global financial crisis and a shrinking demand for raw materials. US exports to Africa reached a record 18 billion in 2008 before falling back by 18 percent to $15.1 billion in 2009. The decline in US imports from Africa was largely due to a 47.3 percent fall in crude oil imports (accounting for 95.8 percent of total imports from Sub-Saharan Africa) with both price and quantity declining. Oil imports from Nigeria decreased by 50 percent, from Angola by 50.6 percent, from the Republic of Congo by 38.8 percent, from Chad by 40.5 percent, and from Gabon by 46 percent. US imports from South Africa continued to show a sharp decline of 40.9 percent, driven mainly by declines in the import of platinum, diamonds, passenger vehicles, and ferroalloys. US exports decreased in a variety of sectors including machinery, vehicles and parts, wheat and other grains, non-crude oil, and aircraft. Of the top five African destinations for US products, exports to Kenya rose by 47.9 percent (due to an increase of aircraft, fertilizers, and cereals exports) and to Ghana by 4.3 percent. Exports to South Africa decreased by 31.3 percent, to Nigeria by 10.9 percent, and to Angola by 29.6 percent.

AGOA

The US African Growth and Opportunity Act (AGOA), introduced in 2000 and renewed in 2004, has served to boost trade with Africa. AGOA covers over 6000 product items, after the extension of GSP preferences to a further 1,800 product lines (including numerous food products, handbags, gloves, footwear, iron and steel items, automotive components and vehicles). Countries meeting the 'Apparel Provisions' further qualify for duty-free access for apparel. U.S. imports under AGOA are becoming increasingly diversified. Products include: jewelry and jewelry parts; fruit and nut products; fruit juices; leather products; plastic products; and cocoa paste. In 2009, US imports under AGOA were $33.7 billion, 49 percent down from 2008. This figure includes duty-free imports from AGOA-eligible countries under both the pre-existing US Generalized System of Preferences (GSP) and the expanded AGOA GSP, plus textile and apparel imported duty-free and quota-free under AGOA provisions. Petroleum and energy products with a 93 percent share of overall AGOA imports continue to account for the largest portion of imports under AGOA and GSP privileges.

Demand

Agricultural products find a ready market in most of Africa, with Egypt, Algeria, Morocco, Nigeria, South Africa and Ghana among the biggest buyers. The market for forest products is limited. The sale of chemicals and related products averages a billion dollars per year, consisting primarily of miscellaneous organic chemicals used as feedstock, downstream specialty chemicals and pharmaceuticals, plastics in primary and semi-primary forms, and various finished

AFRICAN MERCHANDISE TRADE

	2008 Exports US$m	2008 Imports US$m	2009 Exports US$m	2009 Imports US$m
Algeria	79,297.59	39,474.72	45,193.92	39,258.33
Angola	72,179.00	20,982.00	40,985.00	15,737.00
Benin	1,150.05	1,973.01	1,005.74	2,007.73
Botswana	4,838.11	5,210.50	3,415.00	4,704.74
Burkina Faso	693.16	2,041.07	746.31	2,047.10
Burundi	54.10	402.34	65.00	402.23
Cameroon	4,350.00	4,360.00	3,600.60	4,262.30
Cape Verde	35.44	826.15	37.11	708.19
Central African Republic	150.29	300.35	118.17	259.20
Chad	4,328.22	1,678.63	2,650.40	1,946.40
Comoros	9.23	175.67	11.80	155.40
Congo, Rep.	8,359.22	3,052.89	6,520.30	2,899.90
Congo, Dem. Rep. of	3,950.00	4,100.00	3,200.00	3,300.00
Cote d'Ivoire	10,090.55	7,883.68	8,820.60	7,079.50
Djibouti	68.82	574.14	75.00	410.00
Egypt	26,246.30	48,774.60	23,061.90	44,946.10
Equatorial Guinea	14,930.38	3,745.83	8,842.20	5,197.10
Eritrea	15.00	548.90	15.00	515.00
Ethiopia	1,601.83	8,680.33	1,618.17	7,973.88
Gabon	8,350.00	2,550.00	5,218.00	2,022.80
Gambia, The	13.92	329.40	15.00	303.94
Ghana	5,650.00	10,400.00	5,839.70	8,046.26
Guinea	1,300.00	1,600.00	916.00	1,127.60
Guinea-Bissau	125.05	196.29	115.63	203.31
Kenya	4,972.17	11,074.40	4,463.42	10,206.80
Lesotho	900.00	2,030.00	650.00	1,900.00
Liberia	242.40	813.50	148.00	565.20
Libya	62,782.00	21,949.00	32,976.00	23,462.00
Madagascar	1,666.54	3,845.89	1,095.90	3,159.33
Malawi	879.00	1,700.00	912.20	1,845.00
Mali	2,097.18	3,338.93	1,978.00	3,065.00
Mauritania	1,750.91	1,726.00	1,370.10	1,429.80
Mauritius	2,399.46	4,665.87	1,940.51	3,709.10
Morocco	18,525.30	40,566.40	13,680.60	32,776.80
Mozambique	2,653.26	4,007.76	2,147.17	3,764.21
Namibia	3,166.08	4,520.00	3,470.59	5,202.70
Niger	903.96	1,574.50	911.07	1,646.04
Nigeria	80,615.30	42,378.10	49,937.46	33,906.28
Rwanda	256.36	1,177.70	191.83	1,203.93
Sao Tome and Principe	10.63	114.05	8.12	103.28
Senegal	2,005.94	6,527.60	2,017.39	4,712.90
Seychelles	491.16	1,099.10	427.26	796.33
Sierra Leone	215.26	533.40	205.00	505.00
Somalia	456.00	1,131.00	439.00	931.00
South Africa	86,118.00	96,168.70	66,542.20	74,746.40
Sudan	11,670.50	9,351.54	7,400.00	8,300.00
Swaziland	1,790.00	2,200.00	1,450.00	1,940.00
Tanzania	3,040.00	7,081.13	2,621.00	6,296.31
Togo	836.08	1,540.00	796.50	1,566.60
Tunisia	19,318.80	24,611.80	14,449.40	19,099.60
Uganda	2,703.46	4,525.86	2,700.36	4,307.43
Zambia	5,098.69	5,060.45	4,312.05	3,792.64
Zimbabwe	1,693.89	2,831.81	2,268.90	3,526.78
AFRICA	567,044.61	478,005.03	383,596.57	413,980.46

Source: UNCTAD

Exports as Percentage of GDP - 2008

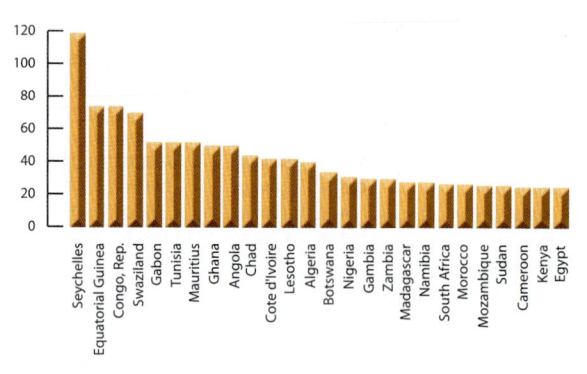

Bar chart showing exports as percentage of GDP for: Seychelles, Equatorial Guinea, Congo Rep., Swaziland, Gabon, Tunisia, Mauritius, Ghana, Angola, Chad, Cote d'Ivoire, Lesotho, Algeria, Botswana, Nigeria, Gambia, Zambia, Madagascar, Namibia, South Africa, Morocco, Mozambique, Sudan, Cameroon, Kenya, Egypt.

Source: AFDB

chemical products such as soaps, detergents, and cosmetics and toiletries. Imports of chemicals and related products from Africa consist largely of miscellaneous organic and inorganic chemicals. In recent times the strongest growth in exports to Africa was in electronic products as improvement of telecommunications and computer networks created an ongoing need for a whole range of sophisticated equipment. There is also a growing demand for transportation equipment, consisting of construction and mining equipment, general aviation aircraft, motor vehicles, and automotive parts. With the emphasis on infrastructure development there will be a steadily increasing demand for construction equipment.

Tariffs

High tariffs and duties on imports aimed at protecting domestic industry, corrupt practices, inadequate transport and marketing facilities, relatively small markets and low consumer bases have hampered trade in some parts of the continent. Lack of infrastructure left valuable mineral and other natural resources untouched in countries that are in great need of additional revenues. Fifteen countries are landlocked, paying a premium on transport.

Reforms

Duty reduction and other reforms, a move towards greater transparency, the creation of free trade zones and the formation of regional trade groupings have addressed some of these concerns. Infrastructural projects including road, rail and pipeline construction, airport improvement and the expansion of air links and telecommunications, widening use of radio and television and the Internet, and the refurbishing of harbors, and expansion of shipping links should place Africa closer to the trading lanes of the world.

Liberalization

Until 1990, when reforms started, much of Africa was closed to trade except in minerals, oil and other natural resource exports. In the past decade, however, Africa has become part of the process of globalization, offering ample opportunity for both exporters of products ranging from consumer goods to high technology equipment and importers not only of minerals, oil and raw materials, but food, textiles and other manufactures. A variety of tax incentives and lowered tariffs encourage both trade and investment. Export Processing Zones (EPZs) have become a convenient springboard for foreign manufacturers taking advantage of special trade quotas and privileges for African goods in the US, Europe and other parts of the world.

Regional markets

Africa is bolstering markets by combining individual countries into regional groupings. By lowering or eliminating tariffs among the member states, these economic groupings facilitate cross border marketing to an extended market. The Southern African Development Community (SADC), the Common Market for Eastern and Southern Africa (COMESA), and the Economic Community of West African States (ECOWAS) are all becoming common markets.

European Market

Several African nations have signed Interim Economic Partnership Agreements (IEPAs) while others opted for the less generous General System of Preferences while trade agreements between the European Union and Africa are under review.

Global crisis

The global crisis and drastic decrease ion demand for raw materials has affected the continent mainly through trade. Exporters of oil, mining products and agricultural raw materials have been hard hit by the drop in the prices of primary commodities.

Direct Investment

Foreign Direct Investment (FDI) inflows in Africa topped $87 billion in 2008, setting a new record. Returns on investments in Africa were the highest among developing regions. Factors that boosted FDI inflows were a booming commodity market and investor friendly reforms. Most of the investments were linked to the extraction of natural resources. The commodity price boom also helped Africa to maintain the relatively high level of outward FDI, amounting to $9 billion in 2008. Africa's share of the total global FDI, however, remained at about 3%.

The United States and Europe were the main investors in the region, followed by African investments, mostly from South Africa. Investment from Asia, notably China, concentrated mainly on oil and gas extraction and infrastructure. The positive trend in FDI flows to Africa was reversed in 2009 as a result of the global financial and economic crisis. Even though Africa is not well integrated in global financial markets, it was severely impacted by the crisis, with a substantial reduction in FDI. UNCTAD estimated inward FDI to Africa in 2009 has fallen by 36.2 per cent compared to 2008. Currently, developed countries account for the bulk of FDI flows. In 2008, they accounted for 91.6 per cent of total inward FDI stock in the region but in recent years FDI from developing countries has increased—with Asia the most important source.

Downturn

In Africa where FDI's share of the region's total gross fixed capital formation stood at 21% in 2008 the downturn in 2009 seriously impacted on growth. Furthermore, despite the adoption of new policy measures to reduce red tape for business start-ups, the privatization of more state-owned firms and encouragement of foreign participation in public projects, the United Nations Conference on Trade and Development (UNCTAD) contends that greater policy changes are needed to enhance national productive capacities in Africa..

Top Ten

According to UNCTAD, African countries receiving more than a billion dollars in FDI increased from eight in 2006 to eleven in 2008. Nigeria topped the list with $20 billion, followed by Angola with $15.5 billion, Egypt with 9.5 billion and South Africa with $9 billion. Other nations in the top ten included Tunisia, Sudan Congo, Morocco, and Ghana.

Global ranking

FDI flows into sub-Saharan Africa (SSA) during the first half of this decade have nearly doubled. The increase has been primarily in the extractive industries (oil, gas and mining) and the service sector, primarily in telecommunications, finance and transportation. However, in relation to global FDI flows or even to flows to emerging markets SSA's standing is low and that is unlikely to change. Furthermore, sub-Saharan countries without significant natural resources or with small domestic markets, lack of infrastructure or skills and more difficult business environments are unlikely to be significant beneficiaries of the growing FDI trend. In general, FDI into South Africa is more diversified than in other resource-rich countries in Africa.

China

China, India, and increasingly Middle Eastern Gulf states, have made significant investments in SSA in sectors such as natural resources, infrastructure, and tourism. Companies from Brazil, Malaysia, and Russia are actively investing

Rates of Return on inward FDI in developing regions 1995-2007

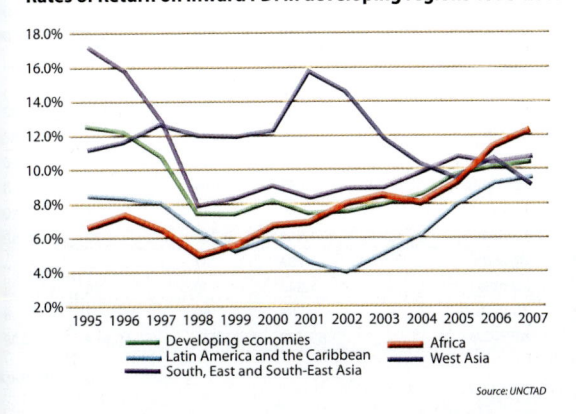

Developing economies
Latin America and the Caribbean
South, East and South-East Asia
Africa
West Asia

Source: UNCTAD

in the region as well. The Chinese Ministry of Commerce estimates that Chinese direct investment into Africa during 2000-2006 was US$6.6 billion. It is estimated that over 800 state-owned Chinese companies are engaged in Africa today.

North Africa: FDI in Egypt was more than $9 billion in 2008, followed by Libya with $4 billion and Morocco $2.3 billion..

West Africa: Nigeria benefited from a $20 billion infusion of foreign capital, followed by Egypt with $9 billion. Apart from oil, privatization schemes of telecommunications companies attracted considerable inflows.

East Africa: In East Africa FDI was more modest. The United Republic of Tanzania had an increase in FDI in several natural resource exploitation projects already in operation. There were also significantly higher inflows to Djibouti, Madagascar, Mauritius, Uganda and Seychelles.

Central Africa: In the Central African subregion, Asian transnational corporations (TNCs) largely contributed to the increase in FDI inflows.

Southern Africa: FDI inflows to Southern Africa grew dramatically, largely as a result of almost a twofold increase in South Africa from $5.6 in 2007 to $9 billion in 2008.

Outflows

FDI outflows from Africa remained large in 2008 at $9 billion. Libya with 5.8 billion replaced South Africa at the top of the list. The other top contributors were Egypt, Angola, Morocco, Nigeria and Algeria.

Sectors

Manufacturing continued to lag behind natural resources in attracting FDI to Africa. Significant FDI inflows from the United States, China, India and Malaysia in oil exploration and other primary resources are continuing to bolster resource-rich countries on the continent. Higher labor costs relative to other developing regions, especially Asia, and increasing costs of production in manufacturing, are, however, a deterrent to foreign investment in manufacturing.

FOREIGN DIRECT INVESTMENT

	FDI Inflows 2007 US$m	FDI Inflows 2008 US$m	FDI Outflows 2007 US$m	FDI Outflows 2008 US$m
Algeria	16,62	2,646	295	318
Angola	9,796	15,548	912	2,570
Benin	255	120	-6	-3
Botswana	495	-4	51	3
Burkina Faso	344	137	0	0
Burundi	1	1	0	..
Cameroon	284	260	-2	2
Cape Verde	190	209	0	2
Central African Republic	57	121	...	..
Chad	718	834	...	..
Comoros	8	8	...	..
Congo	1,816	2,622	...	..
Congo Dem. Rep.	720	1,000	...	..
Cote d'Ivoire	427	353	0	8
Djibouti	195	234	...	..
Egypt	11,578	9,495	665	1,920
Equatorial Guinea	1,726	1,290	...	..
Eritrea	0	0	...	..
Ethiopia	222	93	...	..
Gabon	269	20	59	96
Gambia	76	63	...	..
Ghana	855	2,120	...	4
Guinea	386	1,350	...	694
Guinea Bissau	19	15	0	0
Kenya	728	96	36	44
Lesotho	106	199	...	..
Liberia	132	144	363	382
Libya	4,689	4,111	3,933	5,888
Madagascar	777	1477	...	..
Malawi	55	37	1	1
Mali	73	127	7	3
Mauritania	153	103	4	4
Mauritius	339	383	58	52
Morocco	2,803	2,388	621	369
Mozambique	427	587	0	0
Namibia	733	746	3	5
Niger	129	147	8	1
Nigeria	12,454	20,279	468	299
Rwanda	67	103	13	14
São Tomé & Príncipe	35	33	3	7
Senegal	297	706	25	9
Seychelles	238	364	9	10
Sierra Leone	94	30	...	...
Somalia	141	87	...	..
South Africa	5,687	9,009	2,962	-3,533
Sudan	2,436	2,601	11	98
Swaziland	37	10	3	-5
Tanzania	647	744	5	8
Togo	49	68	-1	-10
Tunisia	1,618	2,761	20	42
Uganda	733	787	...	..
Zambia	1,324	939	86	..
Zimbabwe	69	52	3	8
AFRICA	**69,170**	**87,647**	**10,614**	**9,309**

Source: UNCTAD

Indirect Investment

In recent years a number of new exchanges have sprung up in Africa to join well established bourses in South Africa, Egypt and Zimbabwe. The Cairo Exchange (today known as the Egyptian Exchange or EGX)was founded in 1883, the Johannesburg Securities Exchange (JSE Ltd) in 1887 and Zimbabwe's exchange in 1896. Newcomers include Botswana Ghana, Kenya, Libya, Malawi, Mauritius, Côte d'Ivoire, Morocco, Namibia, Nigeria, Sudan, Tanzania, Tunisia, Uganda and Zambia.

Over the past decade eleven new exchanges have been created on the continent, bringing the total to 19—including one regional bourse and the South African Futures Exchange. The Johannesburg Securities Exchange (JSE Ltd) tops Africa in trade volume, measured by value but the Nigerian Stock Exchange leads by sheer volume. The JSE also leads Africa in number of listings with 425 companies, followed by the Egyptian Stock Exchange (EGX) with 373 and the Nigerian Stock Exchange with 213. Most of Africa's exchanges still remain severely restricted by lack of liquidity and have been further impacted by the ripple effect of the uncertainty and turmoil on the leading exchanges towards the end of 2008. With the exception of Ghana (+58%), Malawi (+26%) and Dar es Salaam (+21%) all other African exchanges suffered losses in 2008. With the decline of the Zimbabwean economy, the stock exchange remained closed for a while, only reopening on February 2009.

Global crisis

Even though Africa has been less exposed to the financial crisis in the United States its ripple effect did impact negatively on the continent's stock markets.

ASEA

The African Stock Exchange Association (ASEA) was formed in the early nineties to provide a formal framework for cooperation between all African stock exchanges. It has concentrated its efforts on four main regions: East Africa, including Kenya, Tanzania and Uganda; Southern Africa, led by the world-ranking JSE in South Africa, and including Namibia, Botswana, Zambia and Zimbabwe; North Africa, led by the Cairo and Alexandria Exchanges; and West Africa, including Nigeria, Ghana and the Francophone countries.

Regional

Apart from introducing economic reforms and seeking credit rating certification to reassure and attract investors, smaller countries

AFRICAN STOCK EXCHANGES

COUNTRY	EXCHANGE	CITY	Website
BOTSWANA	Botswana Stock Exchange	GABERONE	www.bse.co.bw
WEST AFRICA	BRVM (REGIONAL)[1]	ABIDJAN	www.brvm.org
EGYPT	Egyptian Exchange (EGX)	CAIRO	www.egyptse.com
GHANA	Ghana Stock Exchange	ACCRA	www.gse.com.gh
KENYA	Nairobi Stock Exchange	NAIROBI	www.nse.co.ke
LIBYA	Libya Stock Market	Tripoli	www.libyastockmarket.com
MALAWI	Malawi Stock Exchange	BLANTYRE	www.mse.co.m
MAURITIUS	Mauritius Stock Exchange	PORT LOUIS	www.semdex.c
MOROCCO	Casablanca Stock Exchange	CASABLANCA	www.casablanca-bourse.c
NAMIBIA	Namibian Stock Exchange	WINDHOEK	www.nsx.co
NIGERIA	Nigerian Stock Exchange	LAGOS	www.stockmarketnigeria
SOUTH AFRICA	JSE Securities Exchange (JSE)	SANDTON, JNB	www.jse
SOUTH AFRICA	SA Futures Exchange	SANDTON, JNB	www.safe
SUDAN	Khartoum Stock Exchange	KHARTOUM	www.kse
SWAZILAND	Swaziland Stock Exchange	MBABANE	www.s
TANZANIA	Dar es Salaam Exchange	DAR ES SALAAM	www.darstockexch
TUNISIA	Tunis Stock Exchange	TUNIS	www.b
UGANDA	Uganda Securities Exchange	KAMPALA	www.use.or.u

1. Bourse Régionale des Valuers Mo

Gains and Losses at Selected African Exchanges during 2008

Ghana	+58%
Malawi SE	+26%
Dar es Salaam SE	+21%
Khartoum SE	-9%
Botswana SE	-16%
Uganda SE	-21%
JSE Ltd	-26%
Lusaka SE	-29%
Nairobi SE	-35%
Mauritius SE	-36%
Namibian SE	-40%
Nigerian SE	-46%
EGX	-56%

Source: ASEA

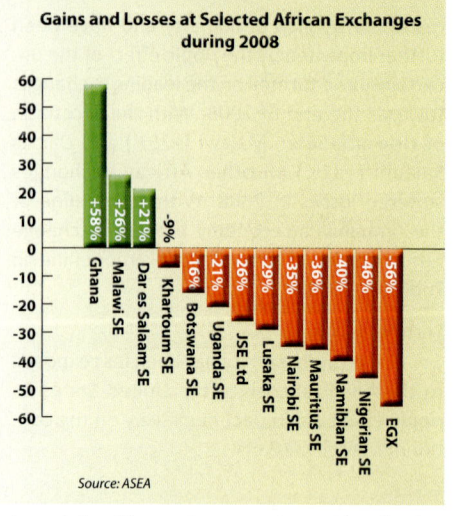

have joined forces to present a more cohesive and attractive equity market to outsiders. In the late nineties the Abidjan Stock Exchange in Côte d'Ivoire was replaced by the first regional exchange, *Bourse Régionale des Valeurs Mobilières (BRVM)*, serving the members of the West African Economic and Monetary Union (WAEMU)—Benin, Burkina Faso, Côte d'Ivoire, Guinea Bissau, Mali, Niger, Senegal and Togo. It opened with a listing of 35 companies. The SADC Committee of Stock Exchanges was formed in January 1997 with South Africa, Namibia, Botswana, Mauritius, Swaziland, Tanzania, Malawi, Zambia and Zimbabwe as members. These exchanges have agreed to adopt the JSE Securities Exchange's (JSE) listing requirements. An integrated real-time network among all the exchanges in the region has been developed, each offering automated trading in a wide range of financial instruments from a single desktop workstation with settlement and central depository facilities conforming to international standards.

Market Capitalization of Africa's Stock Exhanges - 2008
US$ billion

- Other 26
- Nigeria 80
- Nairobi 10
- Ghana 15
- EGX 85
- Namibia 79
- JSE Ltd 549

JSE

As Africa's premier stock market, the Johannesburg Securities Exchange (JSE Ltd) ranks with the world's major bourses in both volume and sophistication. Its open-outcry trading floor gave way to fully electronic trading. Listing requirements and the trading system are similar to those of the London Stock Exchange. The JSE's Single Stock Futures (SSF) market is the world leader in terms of contracts traded according to the WFE/IOMA Derivatives Market Survey. Statistics for the first quarter 2007 show that the JSE traded 44 million contracts surpassing the National Stock Exchange of India, until then the world's leader SSF trading, with its 30 million contracts traded during the same period. According to the ASEA the JSE had a market capitalization of $549 billion in 2008, placing it among the top twenty in the world. Liquidity, measured by the ratio of trading volume to market capitalization, has risen to 36.6%. The Johannesburg Securities Exchange, which accounts for most of the region's market capitalization, has not only helped financial markets in Southern Africa but the rest of the continent. Although the South African securities exchange encourages dual listings, it is not trying to lure companies away from their home exchanges. In November 2005, Oando, a Nigerian energy group listed in Lagos, became the first company from another African country to be listed on the JSE as well. This foreign listing has helped boost Oando's credibility with international investors and gave it access to a deeper pool of money. With 25 foreign companies already listed on the JSE it is actively pursuing listings from companies beyond Africa. The Johannesburg Securities Exchange offers screen trading through its Johannesburg Equities Trading (JET) system. Its Share Transactions Totally Electronic (STRATE) system eliminates paper transactions by making settlement and the transfer of ownership of scrip possible through electronic book entry. In June 2007 JSE's interest rate exchange, Yield-X, expanded its futures trading in Euro/Rand and Sterling/Rand currency to Dollar/Rand Currency Futures.

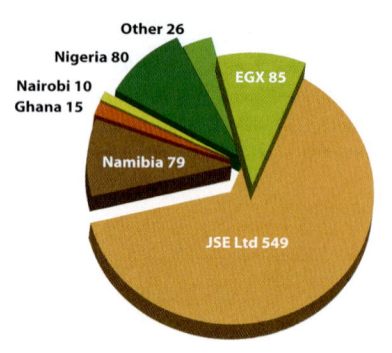

Performance of Selected African Stock Exchanges - 2008

Exchanges	Value Traded US$	Volume Traded	Market Cap US$	Turnover Ratio %	# Listed Co's
Botswana SE	155,060,000	192,710,000	3,680,000,000	0.00%	31
Dar-Es Salam SE	25,730,000	26,980,000	3,800,000,000	0.68%	14
EGX	96,825,000,000	25,489,630,000	85,840,000,000	70.30%	373
Ghana SE	316,690,000	545,790,000	14,910,000,000	2.10%	35
JSE Ltd.	394,560,000,000	83,780,000,000	549,200,000,000	71.84%	425
Khartoum SE	939,590,000	289,010,000	4,170,000,000	5.00%	53
Lusaka SE	167,956,100	1,585,765,172	4,106,000,000	1.14%	19
Malawi SE	60,700,000	607,527,000	1,788,390,000	3.34%	15
Mozambique SE	9,540,000	3,430,000	288,790,000	3.30%	6
Nairobi SE	1,250,000,000	5,860,000,000	10,980,000,000	11.42%	56
Namibian SE	1,080,000,000	291,760,000	78,980,000,000	1.38%	29
Nigerian SE	20,100,000,000	193,140,000,000	80,600,000,000	21.86%	213
SE of Mauritius	437,420,000	318,680,000	4,530,000,000	9.66%	93
Uganda SE	51,920,000	216,930,000	2,870,000,000	1.81%	13

Source: ASEA

Africa Index

The FTSE/JSE Africa Index Series together with Britain's FTSE (Footsie) followed shortly after the implementation of the JSE's new trading system, JSE SETS, and its new information dissemination system, InfoWiz. This move made the JSE more transparent to investors and particularly to foreigners who are able to track the movement of the JSE's market using indices with which they are familiar. In October 2007 the Johannesburg Securities Exchange launched a new fundamentally weighted index, FTSE/JSE RAFI 40, to extend the FTSE/JSE Africa index range and create new investment opportunities. The FTSE/JSE RAFI 40 will contain the top 40 companies selected and weighted by four fundamental factors—sales, cash flow, book value and dividends—from the FTSE/JSE All-Share index.

Capital growth

Both foreign and local capital market experts are advocating better utilization of the continent's exchanges to attract overseas funds for industrial and social projects. The JSE has for many years been successful in attracting huge foreign involvement through the issuance of bonds in state and semi-government expansion projects.

ADRs

American Depositary Receipts (ADRs) and Global Depositary Receipts (GDRs) offer a convenient way for Americans who wish to invest in about 100 African companies listed by major US banks and institutions. All but four—Ashanti Goldfields of Ghana, Botswana RST Ltd., Mangura Copper Mines and Nigeria's United Bank for Africa PLC—are South African companies. South African companies are active participants in the global markets, including assets and corporations listed on various overseas exchanges, including London and New York. The NYSE lists six companies from South Africa with a total global market capitalization of more than $70 billion.

Johannesburg Securities Exchange

Privatization

Privatization, which first gained acceptance and popularity in conservative Britain in the early 1980s, became an inextricable part of the economic development plans of most African nations. Although still a mere mantra for some, most of them are set on selling off or liquidating state assets in a variety of sectors ranging from power utilities to railroads, telecoms, hotels and factories. Privatization comes in a variety of configurations, ranging from outright sales to partial minority shareholdings and joint venture ownership. In some countries, including South Africa, the government sets aside at least part of the ownership for locals.

The World Bank defines privatization as *"a transaction or transactions utilizing one or more of the methods resulting in either the sale to private parties of a controlling interest in the share capital of a public enterprise or of a substantial part of its assets"*, or *"the transfer to private parties of operational control of a public enterprise or a substantial part of its assets"*. Some African governments still seem reluctant to release control altogether, while others find it politically expedient to restructure in stages. In South Africa, where the government is committed to rectify the racial injustices of the past, a certain percentage of the shareholding in restructured state-owned enterprises is usually reserved for black investors and employees.

Sectors

Favorite sectors in the privatization process are manufacturing, services and agricultural products and processing. To date the financial sector has been the least targeted sector. Recent privatization deals include water distribution in Angola; agro-industries, transport, mining, beverages, and tourism in Cameroon; more than a hundred private firms established in the two Congos; palm oil industries in Côte d'Ivoire: electricity and water in Gabon; breweries, mines, resorts, and land in Mozambique; game reserves, breweries, tour operations, and hotels in Tanzania; retail stores, flour mills and pharmaceutical companies in Lesotho; and telecommunications, hotels, airlines, banks, and coffee marketing in Uganda. Although the term 'privatization' is widely bandied about in discussions about sea and airport reforms, it is the privatization of services rather than infrastructure. Major multi-million dollar deals in the past include South Africa's sale of a 30 percent share in its huge telecommunications monopoly, Telkom, to US and Malaysian investors; Morocco's sale of a 30 percent stake in its state refinery, SAMIR, to Swedish investors and a 35% share in Maroc-Telecom to the French; Ghana's sale of its gold mining company, Ashanti Goldfields, through an international placement of shares; and Kenya and South Africa's partial sale of their respective national airlines.

Objectives

The **objectives** are usually one or more of the following: 1) raising revenue for the state; 2) raising investment capital for the industry or company being privatized; 3) reducing government's role in the economy; 4) promoting wider share ownership; 5) increasing efficiency; 6) introducing greater competition; and 7) exposing firms to market discipline.

African Privatization by sector

- Other 13%
- Trade 9%
- Agricultural 21%
- Financial 4%
- Services 22%
- Manufacturing 31%

Sources: IMF, ADB, UNCTAD

South Africa

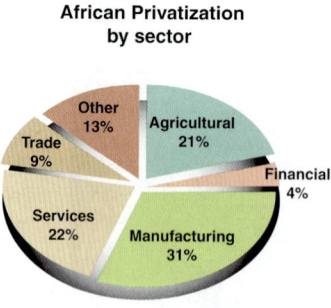

Privatization came to South Africa first. It started in the eighties with the highly successful sale of Sasol's assets on the Johannesburg Stock Exchange and broadened in the post-apartheid era to include state-owned iron, steel industries, toll roads, agricultural marketing, transport, broadcasting and telecommunications. The process continues despite continued fierce opposition from powerful trade union groupings. Not only South Africa but other governments in Africa frequently experience opposition from some quarters who see it simply as the transfer of state monopolies to private conglomerates, thereby enriching a small elite class at the expense of the masses. Another recurring concern on the part of organized labor is that it will result in job retrenchment as the private sector tries to accomplish greater efficiency and profitability with fewer people. Still the trend towards privatization continues across Africa. Apart from South Africa, Algeria, Angola, Comoros, Congo, Côte d'Ivoire, Kenya, Libya, Mauritius, Morocco, Nigeria, Sierra Leone and Tunisia are among those who took significant steps towards privatization. The industries affected included utilities, telecommunications and tourism.

Methods

"Privatization" has been defined in a number of ways. Most see it simply as the reduction of the role of government or increasing the role of the private sector through the sale of part or all of a state enterprise. As such "privatization" is the opposite of "nationalization." Other terms often found in the privatization stable are devolution, corporatization, commercialization, deregulation and restructuring of state assets. The removal of a state subsidy can also be viewed as a form of privatization. Privatization can be implemented in varying degrees. It could be comprehensive—with the private investors taking over a major portion of the state entity—or partial. Private participation comes in many forms: the purchase of a shareholding, directly or in a competitive bid, or via preemptory rights or a public offering; the purchase of assets, directly or through a competitive bid or in a liquidation procedure; through a debt/equity swap; leasing; joint venture; a management or employee buyout; management contract; or a trusteeship arrangement. It can be a combination of several of these.

BOOT

One innovative financing method growing in popularity in Africa involves a foreign investor who builds and operates a plant for a prescribed period, and then transfers it to the host company or country (BOOT). This has been a popular means of encouraging foreign investment in power projects. In some African countries foreign investment commitments have been restricted to a joint venture with a domestic company, especially in strategic industries. Africa has utilized most of these methods.

Recent trends

World Bank Group's Privatization Database shows that in 2007 privatizations in developing countries amounted to $133 billion—a record in nominal terms. In 2007, 51 developing countries carried out 236 privatization transactions, valued at $132.6 billion. Total transaction value was up 26% from 2006 and 150% from 2005. East Asia led in privatization value, followed by Europe and Central Asia. Value increased in Latin America and Sub-Saharan Africa, declined in the Middle East and North Africa, and held steady in South Asia. In the Middle East and North Africa value dropped by nearly 70% to $3.4 billion, while the number of transactions declined from 33 in 2006 to twenty. Libya was a newcomer with its $205 million sale of Sahara Bank while Morocco continued its program with a secondary offering of 4% of Maroc Telecom and the sale of a container shipping company for a combined value of $800 million. Egypt, the main contributor in the region 2006, saw its privatization value plummet from $7.6 billion to just $310 million in 2007 as public opposition brought its program to a virtual halt. In Sub-Saharan Africa telecoms led as the value of privatization increased by 26% to $2.4 billion. Two-thirds came from 12 telecommunications transactions in 11 countries. The rest came from a railway concession in Tanzania and sales in Nigeria in mining, oil and gas, electricity, manufacturing, and real estate (in addition to telecommunications).

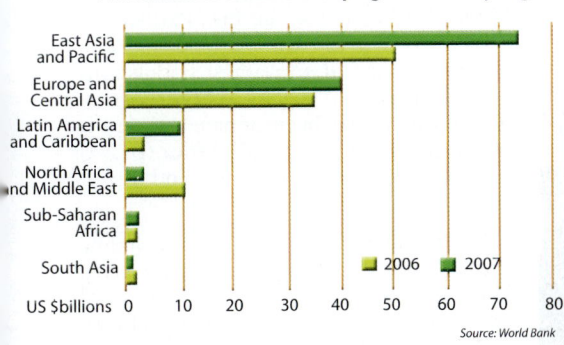

SappiWWF Tree Routes Partnership and eco-tourism

Sappi committed to eco-tourism in South Africa as far back as 1998, when it gave WWF SA a grant of R10 million to set up the SappiWWF TreeRoutes Partnership. The Partnership was based on the understanding that environmentally-sensitive wetlands and indigenous forest suited to eco-tourism are often situated in remote parts of South Africa where there is little formal employment and levels of education are low. The local inhabitants are impacting the environment in order to feed themselves and because they don't understand the long-term consequences of their actions.

The Partnership promotes eco-tourism while giving rural communities an understanding of the natural environment by involving them in programs. Development and operational management of projects was contracted to the Wildlands Conservation Trust.

Funding of projects by the Partnership targets community-based, inclusive and economically sustainable projects serving as catalysts for further eco-friendly development. Communities benefit in the broadest sense through direct and indirect employment, skills training, community ownership and infrastructure.

The staff and community shareholders of the Thonga Beach Lodge. (Photo: Rod Macleod)

The SappiWWF TreeRoutes Partnership projects are situated in KwaZulu Natal and Mpumalanga, mostly in areas where Sappi has operating units. These are home to many unique and endangered species, such as the Karkloof Butterfly, the Blue Swallow and the Oribi. In some instances, the land also encompasses rare habitats, such as the Coastal Dune Forests of Maputaland.

Wetland Reserve

The creation of the Wakkerstroom Wetland Reserve was the first Partnership project. It was chosen as Wakkerstroom is home to one of the largest populations of threatened bird species in South Africa. The property has been donated to and is managed by BirdLife South Africa (BLSA) as a bird guide training center and visitor facility.

There are six other projects, including the 250 hectare Dlinza Forest and Aerial Boardwalk that are home to rare bird species such as the Spotted Ground Thrush and Eastern Bronze-naped Pigeon, as well 85 butterfly species. The Marutswa Forest Trail and Boardwalk also incorporates lookout jetties, decks and viewing points, allowing visitors to observe the various layers of the forest, including the canopy. Here birders look out for Cape Parrots, the Orange Ground-thrush, the Green Twinspot and shy KwaZulu-Natal mistbelt forest bird species. Managed by BirdLife South Africa, Ongonye Forest Reserve comprises over 3,000 hectare of rolling grasslands and Coastal Scarp Forest, recognized for high biodiversity value. Until the Partnership opened the Ongonye Forest Birders' Camp (now refurbished) the forest was largely ignored by tourists.

Opened in 2007, the Southern KwaZulu-Natal Birding Route takes visitors from the golden beaches and dense lush forests of the North and South coasts through the Lowveld to the heights of the Drakensberg Mountains. Its 500 bird species include many rare and endemic species such as Blue Swallow, Cape Parrot, Drakensberg Rock-jumper, Eurasian Bittern, all three of Southern Africa's Crane species and Bearded Vulture.

The Blue Crane—South Africa's national bird—the Grey-Crowned Crane and the Wattled Crane can all be seen in the Karkloof Valley in the Natal midlands. Visitors to the Karkloof Crane and Conservation Centre, established by the Partnership, can learn more about the valley's natural beauty and assets and also wander through the farmlands to two strategically positioned bird hides that provide visitors with intimate insight into the lives of the many bird species that frequent the valley.

Greater St Lucia

The Isimangaliso Wetland Reserve World Heritage Site is situated on the spectacular Zululand north coast. The Partnership was involved in the establishment of the 22-bed luxury Thonga Beach Lodge – the first tourism concession in the reserve. The Lodge is tucked into the dune forest right on the Beach at Mabibi, just north of the world-famous Sodwana dive site. The Mabibi Development Trust, comprising the Mabibi community, 68% of the development, was financed through grant funding from the Partnership and low-interest loan funding from the Wildlands Conservation Trust and Ithala Development Finance Corporation Ltd.

"It was natural for Sappi, a company that is synonymous with sustainable forestry management in South Africa, to focus on a project that would protect endangered indigenous forests and wetlands," says André Oberholzer, Sappi's Group Head, Corporate Affairs. "The projects show that eco-tourism can be a key driver of sustainable development. The community-owned and -run eco-tourism projects developed under the auspices of the Partnership have demonstrated tangible conservation benefits and created long-term socio-economic benefits for the communities in which they are situated."

Detail about Sappi and its educational and conservation programs can be found on our website at www.sappi.com and information on SappiWWF TreeRoutes Parttnership at www.treeroutes.co.za.

sappi

The Crowned-Crane bird-hide at the Karkloof Crane and Conservation Center.

CHINA SYNDROME

China's rise as a global economic power has had serious implications for trade and development in Africa. Its total trade with the continent has grown by an average of 30 percent per year from a mere $10 billion in 2000 to $107 billion in 2008, making it Africa's second largest trading partner after the United States. China's growing presence in Africa is largely fueled by the need to secure essential raw materials, particularly oil. China also views African countries as strategic markets for lower-end manufactured goods and apparel and textiles exports—often threatening domestic African manufacturers.

The composition of the goods traded between Africa and China mirrors that of the trade between Africa and its other major trading partners. On an average oil and gas account for over 60 percent of Africa's exports to China, followed by nonpetroleum minerals and metals at 13 percent. Africa's imports from China are largely manufactured products, machinery and transport equipment—accounting for about three-fourths of all imports.

Oil Appetite

China, with nearly $1 trillion in reserves and a voracious appetite for natural resources, has decided to spend some of its billions of dollars in savings to secure access to the oil, gas, copper, coal and other mineral riches in African countries. In 2003, it surpassed Japan as the world's second-largest oil consumer after the US. Currently China gets 25 percent of its oil supplies from Africa.

Benefits

Africa is second to Asia as the major destination of Chinese FDI. Today, about 700 Chinese enterprises are operating in Africa. The Continet's recent impressive growth is in considerable part due to Chinese investment. Experts say the roads, bridges, and dams built by Chinese firms are low cost, good quality, and completed swiftly. China also contributes peacekeepers to UN missions across Africa, including Liberia and Darfur. It has cancelled $10 billion in bilateral debt from African countries, sends doctors to treat Africans across the continent, and hosts thousands of African workers and students in Chinese universities and training centers. This recent strengthening of China–Africa relations is not accidental. It simply reflects the reality that Africa needs China, while China needs Africa even more.

Tantalizing threat

Moeletsi Mbeki, the deputy chairman of the South African Institute of International Affairs, sees China as representing "both a tantalizing opportunity and a terrifying threat." It is a familiar story, he says. "We sell them raw materials and they sell us manufactured goods with a predictable result—an unfavorable trade balance against us." Critics in the United States and Europe are not slow in pointing out that China is putting profit before principle by legitimizing dictatorships and repressive regimes in Africa through trade and economic relations. Sudan, where China has almost a monopoly, is often cited. Objections are also voiced against China's thriving arms sales to unsavory warlords.

China - Africa Trade

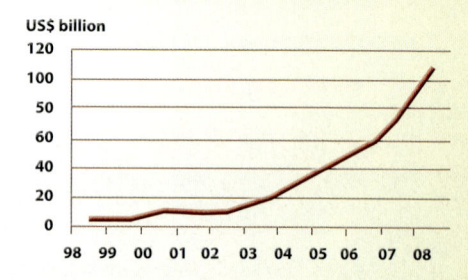

US$ billion

(Chart showing China-Africa trade growth from 1998 to 2008, rising from near 0 to over 100 billion US$)

Growing presence

China is serving notice to both Europe and North America to increase their stake on the continent or lose out in the long run. Farah Arbab of the Institute of Strategic Studies at Islamabad concludes: "While many in the West now consider China as a threat, Africans see China mostly as an opportunity. If the West wants to have increased leverage in Africa, the business investment will have to be much more visible and aggressive across the continent."

Chapter 4
Key Sectors in Africa

In the past, coffee, cocoa, cotton and a whole range of other cash crops from the continent attracted foreign investors and traders. Then came gold and diamonds and a slew of high priced strategic minerals. This was followed by major oil discoveries. In recent times restructuring and reform have opened up lucrative new avenues for entrepreneurs in telecommunications, transport, tourism, health services and banking.

Sasol, Secunda, South Africa

Petroleum & Energy

Africa's abundant energy products are major sources of export revenues and the engine for local development and growth in a number of countries. With 9.6% of the world's proven oil reserves, 7.9% of its natural gas reserves and 3.9% of its coal supply, the continent is a significant player in the field of energy exports. Participation of major overseas firms in partnership with governments and domestic firms in the exploration and exploitation of these assets has had considerable spin-offs aside from earning much-needed foreign reserves.

The African continent produces an average of almost 10 million barrels per day and is currently the third largest crude oil exporter to the United States. African countries with the largest proven crude oil reserves are Libya with 44.3 billion barrels, Nigeria with 37.2, Angola with 13.5, Algeria with 12.2, and Egypt with 4.4 billion barrels.

Nigeria is the continent's largest producer at 2.06 million barrels per day (bbl/d), followed by Algeria and Angola each with 1.8 million, Libya with 1.6 million, and Egypt with 742,000 bbl/d. Other significant producers are Sudan with 480,000, Equatorial Guinea with 490,000, the Republic of Congo with 274,000 and Gabon with 229,000 bbl/d.

Nigeria leads Africa in natural gas reserves with 5.25 trillion cubic meters (Tcm), followed by Algeria (4.5), Egypt (2.19), and Libya (1.54). Algeria accounts for the major share of Africa's total gas production with Egypt second and Nigeria third. Ghana, with substantial recent offshore finds, and Tunisia, have the potential to become significant producers in the foreseeable future. Proven coal reserves of more than 30 billion tons in South Africa compensate in part for its lack of oil. With 3.7% of the world's total coal reserves, South Africa, accounting for 4.1% of the world's total production, has become the third largest exporter of this solid fuel. Coal is also used by South Africa's Sasol to manufacture oil with a locally developed process based on the Kellogg system that is also utilized elsewhere.

Rising demand

The demand for Africa's natural resources, particularly oil, is rising. The United States aims at reducing its dependence on Middle Eastern oil by 75 per cent through increased supplies from Africa. Petroleum from Libya (light with low sulphur content and cheap to produce) has become attractive to Europe after sanctions against this North African nation were lifted. Transnational companies from China, India

Africa's Share

Oil - end 2009

Country	Reserves Barrels billion	Reserves Share world total	Production Barrels thousand per day	Production Share world total
Algeria	12.2	0.9%	1,811	2.3%
Angola	13.5	1.0%	1,784	2.0%
Cameroon	#	#	73	0.1%
Chad	0.9	0.1%	118	0.2%
Congo Rep. of	1.9	0.1%	274	0.4%
Egypt	4.4	0.3%	742	0.9%
Equatorial Guinea	1.7	0.1%	307	0.4%
Gabon	3.2	0.3%	229	0.3%
Libya	44.3	3.3%	1,652	2.0%
Nigeria	37.2	2.8%	2,061	2.6%
Sudan	6.7	0.5%	490	0.6%
Tunisia	0.6	#	86	0.1%
Other Africa	0.6	#	79	0.1%
AFRICA TOTAL	127.7	9.6%	9,705	12.0%

Natural Gas - end 2009

Country	Reserves Trillion cubic meters	Reserves Share world total	Production Billion cubic meters	Production Share world total
Algeria	4.50	2.4%	81.4	2.7%
Egypt	2.19	1.2%	62.7	2.1%
Libya	1.54	0.8%	15.3	0.5%
Nigeria	5.25	2.8%	24.9	0.8%
Other Africa	1.27	0.7%	19.5	0.7%
AFRICA TOTAL	14.76	7.9%	203.8	6.9%

Coal - end 2009

Country	Reserves Million tonnes	Reserves Share world total	Production Million tonnes	Production Share world total
South Africa	30,408	3.7%	140.94	4.1%
Zimbabwe	502	0.1%	1.1	#
Other Africa	1,103	0.1%	1.0	#
AFRICA	32,013	3.9%	143.0	4.2%

Less than 0.05

Source: BP Statistical Review 2009

and Malaysia have also joined the search for oil (and other primary resources) to sustain their rapidly growing economies. As a result nearly every subregion in Africa has attracted new foreign direct investment flows into petroleum projects. China's energy companies announced plans to spend at least $16 billion on oil and gas fields on the continent.

Regions

North Africa is the continent's most developed oil region. It contains close to 50% of Africa's proven reserves, has 54% of its refining capacity and represents 44% of its total production. Algeria, Libya and Egypt dominate the region's oil sector while Morocco and Tunisia are actively seeking to expand their upstream facilities.

West Africa is Africa's second largest oil producing region and ranks third in terms of oil consumption. Nigeria, with more than 90 percent of West Africa's proven oil reserves, is the continent's largest oil producer. Benin produces a small amount. Togo, Gambia, Ghana, Mauritania and Senegal have granted offshore exploration rights to foreign firms. Recent impressive finds in Ghana has the potential of making this nation one of Africa's significant oil producers. West Africa is also the second largest gas producer and consumer in Africa.

Central Africa has seen has seen crude oil production rise considerably in recent years. Largest increases were in Equatorial Guinea, the Congo and Gabon. Equatorial Guinea has become the focus of many multinationals and is referred to as Africa's Kuwait. Production from Chad's Doba Basin fields has reached 127,000

Sub-Saharan Africa: Oil-Exporting Countries
Revenues, Expenditures and Fiscal Balance

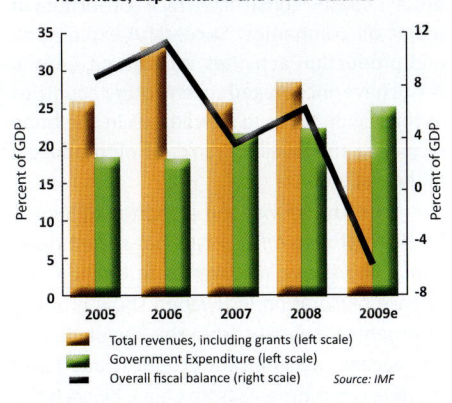

- Total revenues, including grants (left scale)
- Government Expenditure (left scale)
- Overall fiscal balance (right scale)

Source: IMF

ved reserves at the end of 2009

North America (incl. Mexico)
Oil 73.3 (5.5%)
Gas 9.16 (4.9%)
Coal 246 (29.8%)

South & Central America
Oil 198.9 (14.9%)
Gas 8.06 (4.3%)
Coal 15 (1.8%)

Europe & Eurasia
Oil 136.9 (10.3%)
Gas 63.09 (33.7%)
Coal 272 (33.0%)

Middle East
Oil 754.2 (56.6%)
Gas 76.18 (40.6%)

Africa
Oil 127.7 (9.6%)
Gas 14.76 (7.9%)
Coal 33 (4.0%)

Asia/Pacific
Oil 42.2 (3.2%)
Gas 16.24 (8.7%)
Coal 259 (31.4%)

urement
Billions barrels (% of world total)
Gas - Trillion cubic meters (% of world total)
Billions tons (% of world total)

Map: Business Books Intl.

bbl/d after the completion of a pipeline to Cameroon's coast—constructed by a consortium of major oil companies. Successful exploration and production activities throughout Central Africa have encouraged several other countries in the region to issue new leases in the hope of joining the swelling ranks of oil producers in the region.

East Africa, with the exception of Sudan, has little proven oil reserves but recent news about impressive discoveries in Uganda and intense exploration in Rwanda show promise of expanded supplies from this region. Sudan has become a significant producer and lured massive commitments from China. Kenya is the region's largest oil consumer (overall, Africa's 9th largest) and net importer.

Southern Africa's oil production is dominated by Angola while most of the refineries are situated in South Africa. As Africa's second largest oil consumer, South Africa is also the continent's largest oil importer. It manages only in part to fill its own need with synthetic oil from coal and natural gas.

MAJOR PRODUCERS

Petroleum and other energy products make a major contribution to the economies of several African nations. Algeria's oil and gas export revenues account for almost 90% of its total export revenues, and more than half of total fiscal revenues. Oil export revenues account for about 98% of Libya's hard currency earnings and half its fiscal receipts. Crude oil exports generate over 90% of Nigeria's foreign exchange earnings. Recently Chad joined the list of major producers after the completion of the Chad-Cameroon pipeline. Of special significance is South Africa which has developed into a major player in the energy field despite its hitherto limited proven reserves of oil. Aside from the processing of recent impressive discoveries of offshore gas, South Africa became the first country to commercially extract oil-from-coal in with a state-run operation established in the fifties. Privatized since, Sasol is not only a significant producer of synfuels but a major producer and exporter of chemicals, polymers and plastics.

Algeria

Algeria is a member of OPEC and an important oil and natural gas for Europe. It accounts for forty percent of Africa's total gas production and close to 20 percent of its oil. Crude oil exports rose as the country shifted towards domestic natural gas consumption and increased the oil production by the state-

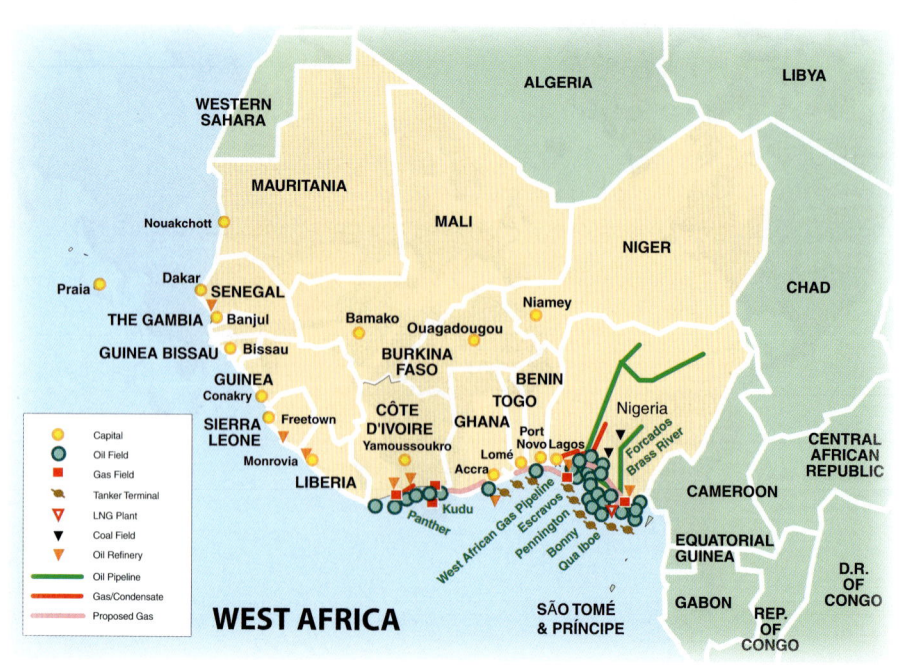

WEST AFRICA

80

NORTH AFRICA

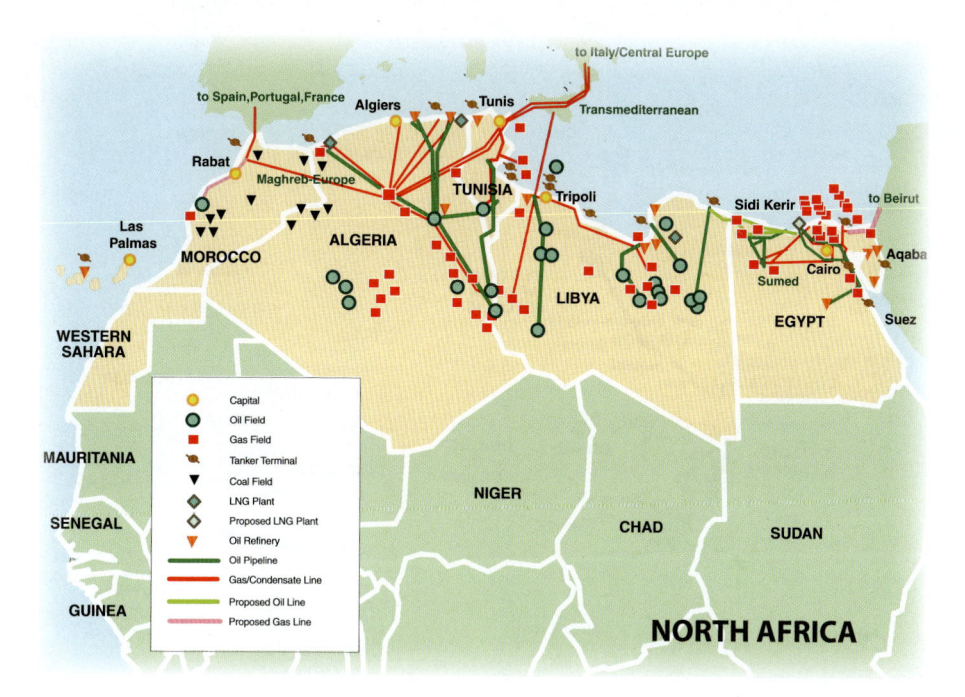

Map Legend:
- Capital
- Oil Field
- Gas Field
- Tanker Terminal
- Coal Field
- LNG Plant
- Proposed LNG Plant
- Oil Refinery
- Oil Pipeline
- Gas/Condensate Line
- Proposed Oil Line
- Proposed Gas Line

owned Sonatrach and its foreign partners. Approximately 90% of Algeria's crude oil exports go to Western Europe. Algeria's Saharan Blend oil—45% API with 0.05% sulfur and negligible metal content—is among the best in the world. Algeria opened its oil sector to foreign investment more than a decade ago. There are 25 foreign firms from 19 countries operating in Algeria including ConocoPhillips, ExxonMobil, Anadarko, BP, Lasmo, Burlington Resources and Occidental Petroleum Corporation. Algeria's 4.50 trillion cubic meters (Tcm) of proven natural gas reserves place it among the top ten countries worldwide. It provides more than 25% of Europe's needs. Algeria is the world's first producer of liquefied natural gas (LNG).

Angola

Angola is Sub-Saharan Africa's third largest oil producer after Nigeria and Algeria. It is seen as having the potential in Africa for the greatest increase in production capacity over the next 10 years. Tens of billions of dollars have been invested by major oil companies in deepwater and ultra deepwater projects along the shores of Angola. China's growing demand for Angolan crude is driven by its adoption of stricter environmental standards that place a premium on lower-sulfur West African crudes. Although reserves have been located north of Luanda, most of its crude production is in the Cabinda exclave. Crude reserves are also located onshore around the city of Soyo, offshore in the Kwanza Basin north of Luanda, and offshore along the northern coast. The oil sector accounts for almost half of GDP and four-fifths of the country's revenues. Arrangements between the state-owned Sonangol and foreign companies are either joint ventures (JVs) with investment costs and production divided according to shareholding in the venture, or production-sharing agreements (PSAs) with the foreign partners acting as contractors who finance all investment costs, to be recovered when production begins. Foreign companies involved in Angola include Chevron, ConocoPhillips, ExxonMobil, Shell and Elf Aquitane. Angola is not a member of OPEC.

Cameroon

Despite rapidly declining reserves, Cameroon is still one of sub-Saharan Africa's significant oil producers. Its refinery capacity and its role as the terminal for the 127,000 barrels-per-day export pipeline from Chad make up in part for the decline in oil reserves. In 2004 a 650 mile (1,050 km) oil pipeline from the Doba oil fields in landlocked neighboring Chad to Kribi in Cameroon was completed by a consortium including Chevron, EssoMobil and

CENTRAL AFRICA

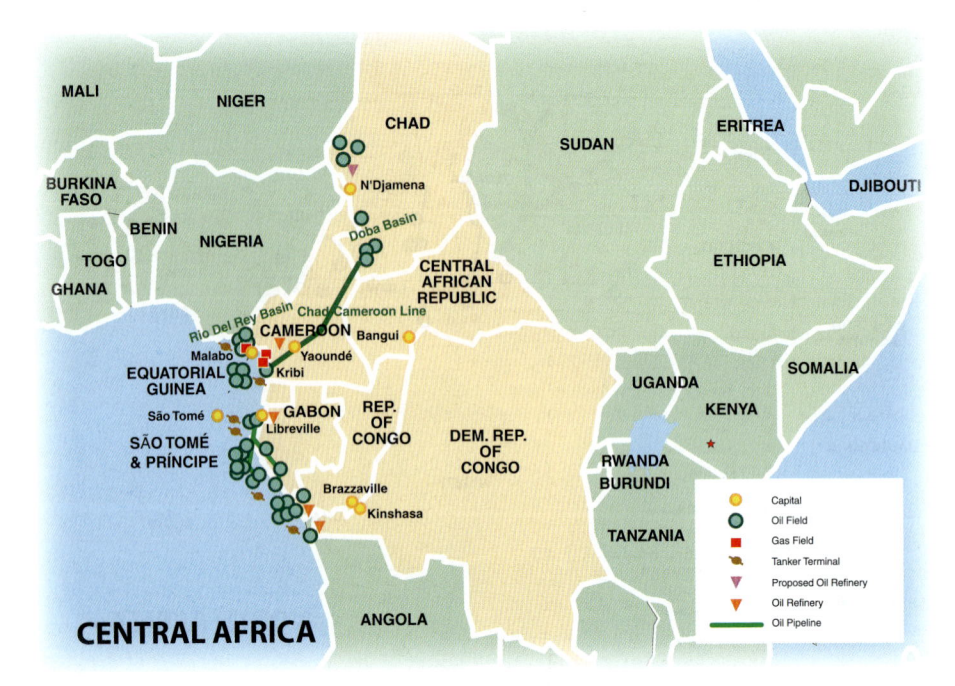

Malaysia's Petronas. Cameroon and Nigeria have both laid claims to the 1,000 sq km oil-rich Bakassi Peninsula in the Gulf of Guinea. In 2002, the International Court of Justice (ICJ) ruled in favor of Cameroon. Both countries will, however, continue to have a stake in these resources and they have agreed to work together to survey the offshore oil reserves that remained largely untapped because of the dispute. Petroleum products constitute more than half of Cameroon's exports. Elf Aquitaine, Chevron, Phillips Petroleum, ExxonMobil, Shell are active in the country.

Chad

In 2004 a 650 mile/1,070 km pipeline to Kribi in Cameroon was completed by a World Bank supported consortium including Chevron, EssoMobil and Petronas to transport oil from Chad's dormant Doba fields. The transportation of 127,000 barrels-per-day along this pipeline to Cameroon's Kribi port boosted Chad's revenues by between about 50% per year.

Congo

Most of the crude in Republic of Congo (Brazzaville) is located offshore. The state-owned *Société Nationale des Pétroles du Congo* (SNPC) prefers production-sharing agreements (PSAs) with foreign firms that carry out exploration and development within a pre-determined time (usually three years for each phase) and finance all investment costs. These investments are recovered when production starts. Congo's gas reserves are mostly found with oil and vented or flared. TotalFinaElf operates the majority of Congo's crude oil producing fields. Also involved are Chevron and Marathon. Most of Congo's crude oil exports go to Western Europe and the United States.

Côte d'Ivoire

Offshore oil discoveries in the Gulf of Guinea as well as gas finds in its territorial waters, make Côte d'Ivoire a popular area for hydrocarbon exploration in Sub-Saharan Africa. This renewed interest followed almost a decade of relative inactivity. From 1970 to 1990 over 100 wells were drilled offshore Côte d'Ivoire, and several commercial oil and gas fields developed.

Egypt

Egyptian crude oil production peaked in 1996. Since then there has been a rapid rise in domestic consumption due to strong economic growth. Currently oil is produced in four main areas: the Gulf of Suez (about 70%), the Western Desert, the Eastern Desert, and the Sinai Peninsula. A discovery in 2001 by East Zeit Petroleum Company (Zeitco) in the Gulf of Suez concession doubled reserves from that province. The company is also active in several other concession blocks. Other major foreign companies involved in gas exploration and production include British Gas, BP and Shell. Egypt also serves as a conduit for oil supplies from other Middle Eastern producers to Europe. The 200 mile Sumed pipeline carries 2.2 million barrels-per-day from the Persian Gulf region to the Mediterranean.

Equatorial Guinea

Referred to as the "Kuwait of Africa," Equatorial Guinea became the seventh largest oil producing country in Africa. Production from Equatorial Guinea averaged 361,000 bbl/day in 2008—a twenty-fold increase since 1996. Production comes from offshore fields located off the shore of Bioko island and the mainland enclave of Rio Muni. Equatorial Guinea's recent emergence as an important oil producer has not been without controversy. Regional relations between Equatorial Guinea, Cameroon, São Tomé & Príncipe and Nigeria have been strained over maritime border demarcation in the Gulf of Guinea. Equatorial Guinea and Nigeria have signed a treaty for joint exploration of crude oil at the Zafiro-Ekanga oil field located at the maritime boundary between the two. The state-owned Petroguinea, created in 2000, plays an important role in the upstream hydrocarbon sector. Among the foreign participants are ExxonMobil, Marathon and Energy Africa.

Gabon

Crude oil accounts for about 80% of Gabon's total export revenues, 60% of its revenues, and over 40% of its GDP. Even though Gabon's proven oil reserves have nearly doubled since 1996, its government has expressed fears about a longer-term trend of diminishing oil reserves. In an effort to boost reserves and production, Gabon's oil ministry has revised its production-sharing contracts to attract new investors. Oil exploration and production are undertaken by Shell, Elf, Kerr McGee and several others.

Ghana

Off-shore discoveries have led to large overseas investments. Underscoring a growing interest in West Africa by the oil majors ExxonMobil paid $4 billion for its stake in the Jubilee oil field, mooted to be one of the most lucrative finds in recent years. China's CNOOC was listed among the bidders. Ghana's recoverable oil reserves are located in five sedimentary basins. The Ghana National Petroleum Company (GNPC) currently produces about 6,000 bbl/d. The Tema Oil Refinery (TOR) near Accra primarily processes imported Bonny Light/Brass River crude from Nigeria for domestic use and export. Ghana is the terminal of the West African Gas Pipeline.

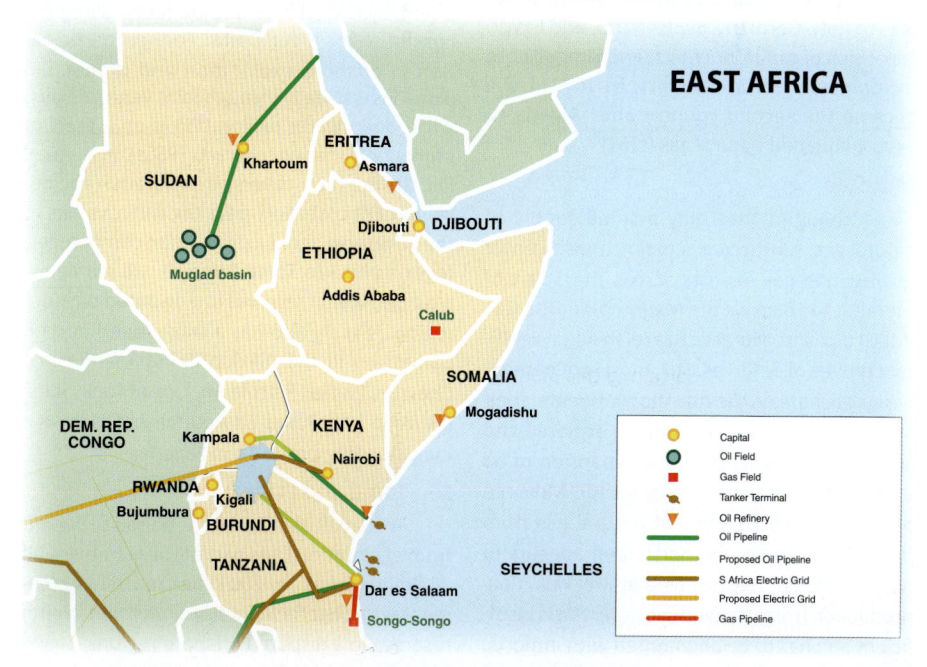

Libya

With 43.7 billion barrels of oil in reserve, Libya, an OPEC member, has Africa's largest proven oil reserves. It is a major exporter of high-quality, low-sulphur crude. Oil revenues account for about 95% of Libya's hard currency earnings but declined during sanctions. Two US oil companies (Exxon and Mobil) withdrew from Libya in 1982 following a US trade embargo but five others (Amarada Hess, Conoco, Grace Petroleum, Marathon, and Occidental) remained until 1986, when President Reagan ordered them to cease all activity. After the 1988 bombing of Pan Am flight 103 over Lockerbie, Scotland, by Libyan nationals, the UN Security Council also adopted sanctions. While UN sanctions were suspended after the extradition of two suspects United States sanctions remained in place until April 2004 when the Bush administration lifted most of the trade restrictions, allowing American firms to re-establish relations. Since 1968, Libya's oil industry has been run by the state-owned National Oil Corporation (NOC) together with several foreign firms, including Italy's Agip-ENI, which has been operating in the country since 1959. There are three refineries with a combined capacity nearly twice domestic oil consumption. Libya distributes refined products to Italy, Germany, Switzerland, and Egypt. Expansion of gas production is encouraged both for domestic use and export. In 1971, Libya became the second country after Algeria to export liquefied natural gas (LNG).

Morocco

Although it has only a small supply of natural gas, Morocco is a major transit center for Algerian gas exports across the Strait of Gibraltar to Spain via the Maghreb-Europe Gas (MEG) pipeline. Morocco has relatively insignificant proven oil reserves. Still, most sedimentary basins offshore on the Atlantic continental shelf or in deep waters have not been explored and Morocco is actively pursuing expansion of its upstream oil and natural gas sector. Morocco produces small volumes of natural gas from the Gharb Basin in the north, and appears to have a considerable gas field at Meskala. Coal production from its one mine at Jerada is insufficient and has to be augmented with imports.

Mozambique

South African synthetic fuels and chemicals producer, Sasol, purchased the Pande gas exploration and production rights and a 373-mile (610-km) and earmarked $1.2 billion to develop an extensive pipeline network to its plants in South Africa and the Maputo Iron and Steel Project. This agreement with Mozambique's state oil firm, *Empresa Nacional Hydrocarbonetos* (ENH), gave Sasol operating control of both the onshore Pande and Temane blocks, as well as the offshore M10 and Sofala blocks. Two small power stations, utilizing gas from the Pande gas field, came online and in October 2000, Sasol signed the first of several agreements with the governments of Mozambique and South Africa outlining a timetable for the further development of the Temane and Pande fields. A gas pipeline stretching from Mozambique's southern Inhambane province to Secunda in South Africa has been completed.

Nigeria

Nigeria, a member of OPEC, is one of the world's largest oil exporters. It is a major seller to Western Europe and the fifth largest supplier of crude oil to the US. Oil accounts for nearly 50% of its GDP and 95% of the country's foreign exchange earnings. Nigeria's proven oil reserves of 36.2 billion barrels place it second in Africa after Libya. Most reserves are found along the coastal Niger River Delta. Foreign participation in offshore exploration and production activities is usually through joint ventures (JVs) while deep water exploration is on a basis of production-sharing contracts (PSCs). In a typical PSC the operator covers all exploration and development costs and pays tax and royalties to the government once production commences. Nigeria and São Tomé Príncipe will jointly exploit petroleum reserves in a disputed offshore region. Nigeria also has a stake together with Cameroon in the oil-rich Bakassi Peninsula. Chevron, Phillips Petroleum, ExxonMobil, Shell, ENI/Agip (Agip) and Elf Aquitaine (Elf) have a long-standing presence in Nigeria.

São Tomé and Príncipe

This small island nation is poised to benefit from exploration in its part of the lucrative Gulf of Guinea basin. In 2001, has reached agreement with Nigeria to jointly exploit petroleum reserves in a disputed offshore region.

South Africa

With the exception of meaningful offshore gas reserves at Mossel Bay and the Kudu field off the west coast, South Africa has yet to show economically viable reserves of oil. Exploration continues on South Africa's West and South coasts. The Oribi gas field 87 miles (140 km) off the Mossel Bay coast produces 25,000 bbl/d through a liquefaction process run by Mossgas. This operation and most of the exploration is under control of the national oil company, Petroleum Oil and Gas Corporation of SA (Pty) Limited (PetroSA). Operating as a non-listed commercial entity, PetroSA owns, operates and manages the South African government's commercial assets in the petroleum industry as a subsidiary of the Central Energy Fund (CEF). The first privatization in South Africa's gas distribution sector was completed in December 1999, when a consortium led by the US-based Cinergy acquired Johannesburg's Metro Gas Company. South Africa is one of the major oil refining nations in Africa with a total refining capacity (excluding synfuel) of around 500,000 bbl/d. Multinational companies (including BP, Shell, Caltex, and Total) are major participants in South Africa's downstream petroleum markets. With proven coal reserves of more than 30.8 billion tons, South Africa compensates for the lack of oil and gas with this commodity. It is the third biggest coal exporter in the world and uses substantial quantities to produce synfuel. In the fifties the government established the South African Coal, Oil and Gas Corporation Limited (Sasol) to develop the world's first and largest commercially viable oil-from-coal extraction operation.

Sudan

Sudan has 6.7 billion barrels of oil in reserve and exports 480,000 bbl/day through a terminal in the Red Sea along a 930 mile (1,500 km) pipeline from the oil fields of the Muglad Basin. The pipeline is an undertaking of the Greater Nile Petroleum Operating Company (GNPOC), consisting of the China National Petroleum Corporation (CNPC)(40%), Petronas of Malaysia (30%), the Sudanese national firm Sudapet (5%), and Canadian-based Arakis (25%)..

Tunisia

Tunisia has over 600 million barrels of proven oil reserves and produces modest volumes of oil and gas. The state-owned oil company, *Enterprises Tunisienne d'Activites Petrolieres* (ETAP) encourages foreign exploration, especially in the northern region. Tunisia has 2.8 trillion cubic feet (Tcf) of proven natural gas reserves and British Gas engineered a $450 million expansion in the southeastern region.

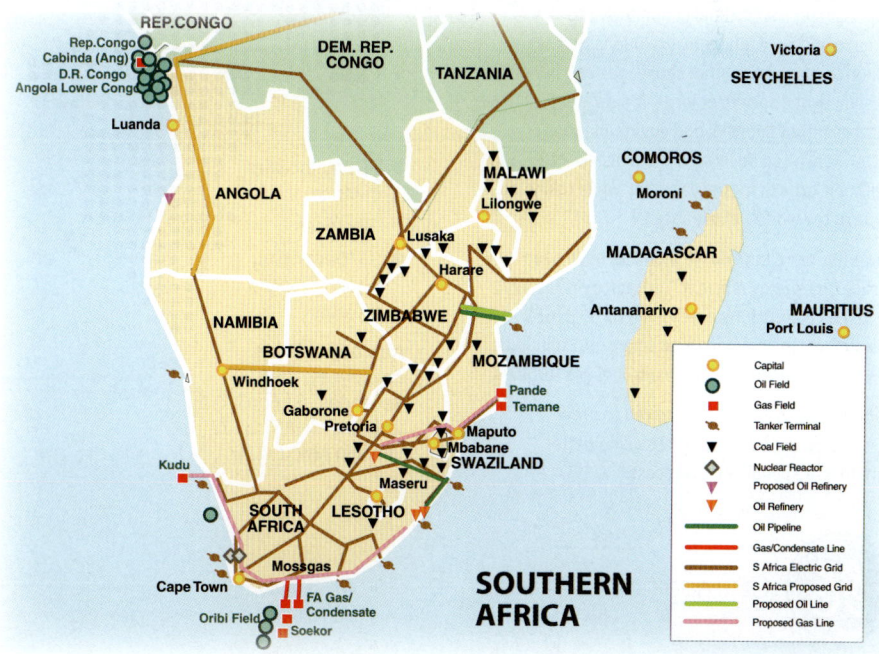

General Electric – Invested in Africa

For more than a century, General Electric (GE) has been committed to a vision for Africa as an emerging market driven by innovation. This deeply-rooted understanding contributes to the continent's economic rise and ability to positively impact on its various socio-economic challenges.

Africa faces substantial issues including the lack of adequate power supply and rising tariffs; inadequate clean water; rapid population growth and urbanisation; climate change and its impact on water and energy availability and access to affordable, modern healthcare.

As one of the world's most respected and admired innovative technology companies, GE is taking on the world's toughest challenges. The company is aligned with the major opportunities of the next decade including the demand for clean energy and water; transportation and healthcare.

This places GE in a position to use the breadth and depth of its businesses to build longterm partnerships; share its knowledge and provide Africa with the innovative solutions it requires.

GE has driven its business through two infrastructural growth initiatives, namely ecomagination and healthymagination, as the means by which to address the stubborn problems of energy efficiency and affordable healthcare. Ecomagination is the bold commitment to imagine and build innovative solutions that solve tomorrow's environmental challenges and benefit customers and society at large. It puts into practice GE's belief that financial and environmental performance can be integrated to accelerate profitable growth for the company while taking on some of the world's challenges.

Currently, more than 80 GE products have been certified as energy efficient. Technology is the key to a clean energy future, achieved through GE's investments to commercialise smart grid solutions, wind, smart appliances and multi-fuel gas turbines.

Healthymagination was conceived to grow GE's healthcare business by providing better care to more people at lower cost.

Building Partnerships with Government and Enterprise

GE believes Africa's solutions must emanate from Africa and has expanded its continental presence through partnerships with governments and private enterprises to deliver African-inspired answers. The company combines its technological capabilities and financial strength with local knowledge to capitalise on opportunities and foster sustained growth.

In Nigeria GE signed a landmark agreement with the federal government to promote collaboration between the company and Nigerian public and private sector organisations that are driving critical infrastructure projects across the country.

The agreement encourages active collaboration to use advanced technologies and solutions to enhance economic development and competitiveness.

- GE Key facilities in Africa
- GE offices
- GE 'Developing Health Globally' projects

Africa Fast Facts
Employees: 1500
Revenues: $3.6bn (2009)
Countries in Africa: 17
Years in Africa: 110

GE imagination at work

Providing innovative solutions

Energy

In South Africa, GE Energy concluded a half a billion rand contract to supply switchgear critical to the development of energy provider, Eskom's new generation Medupi Thermal Power Station. This will assist the state-owned enterprise to meet the growing power needs of the country. GE will supply low-voltage arc proof switchgear in line with Eskom's requirements. The switchgear, tested to global specifications, is in wide use in industrial and commercial applications around the world.

Transportation infrastructure

In South Africa GE recently won a contract to supply 100 locomotives to rail operator Transnet and has committed to locally developing 90 of these locomotives. By committing to the long-term localisation of GE innovations, the company ensures the best minds create the right solutions for Africa and share in GE's culture of creativity and development.

Over the past two decades, the quality of service on the Tanzania-Zambia Railway Authority (TAZARA) has declined due to aging locomotives, wagons and infrastructure. In a bid to improve this service and reconnect people and cargo between the two east African countries, GE Transportation will modernise 18 locomotives. TAZARA will also install the GE Bright Star control system that will improve fuel consumption and fault detection.

In Nigeria GE will deliver 25 locomotives to assist the government in reviving its railway system into an enabling engine of the economy.

Healthcare

In recognising the efforts of Cairo University's Cairo Foetal Medicine Units to raise awareness around maternal-infant care, GE Healthcare donated a Volusion E8 ultrasound imaging system with early diagnostic tools for women's healthcare.

This technology has enhanced the unit's ability to detect and aid foetal heart abnormalities and acquire volume images of the foetal heart. The university hospital aims to build on an existing sub-specialised programme; raise training standards and establish a global network around foetal medicine.

The Children's Cancer Hospital Egypt (CCHE), the largest paediatric oncology centre in the Middle East and Africa, has installed the GE Healthcare generation cyclotron production facility. This move is in line with a key healthymagination theme – accessibility. Currently the survival rate for children with cancer in Egypt is just 40%, but in using the cyclotron, the hospital will be able to produce fluorodeoxyglucose (FDG), essential for cancer detection and treatment in children and adults Six years ago GE launched the Developing Health Globally programme in Africa with the first site in Asesewa, Ghana. Since then the programme has expanded to 30 hospitals in 10 countries and donated more than 2500 products to improve the quality of care to 2.7m people.

The latest installations in Kenya and Rwanda have upgraded five major hospitals as part of a plan to upgrade 30 facilities in these countries ranging from rural clinics to regional referral hospitals.

Aviation

In the aviation sector, GE Commercial Aviation Services (GECAS) and GE Aviation have a strong presence among leading African airlines, especially in Nigeria. GECAS has seven aircraft on lease to Virgin Nigerian airlines and Bellview and since 2006, GE has sold about 95 engines worth $1bn in Nigeria.

Being Responsible – GE Volunteers

GE employees support their communities through GE Volunteers, an initiative that enables employees to donate their time and efforts to society. In 2008, 20 Kenyan volunteers donated 800 hours towards their communities in education, environment, healthcare and community development. They adopted the Emmanuel's Children Centre, a home for orphans and destitute children on the outskirts of Nairobi and have donated more than $13000 to support the facility.

The GE citizenship framework – "make money, make it ethically and make a difference" – enables the company to contribute and create value for society in ways aligned with its business strategy.

GE recognises that success in tomorrow's markets means working with Africa's stakeholders to understand, predict and shape our future environment and ways of living. This requires bold initiatives that can help drive Africa's socio-economic development. GE is committed to tackling important problems together in the spirit of partnership and respect.

Electricity Production by Type

Country	Electricity Gross Production million kw/hrs 2006	2007	Total Hydro Production million kw/hours 2006	2007	Total Thermal Production million kw/hours 2006	2007
Algeria	35,226	37,196	218	226	35,008	36,970
Angola	2,959	3,171	2,665	2,583	294	588
Benin	128	132	1	1	127	131
Botswana	1,042	1,119		1,114	1,119	
BurkinaFaso	548	612	80	111	468	501
Burundi	95	119	93	117	2	2
Cameroon	5,106	5,753	3,892	3,847	1,214	1,906
CapeVerde	252	269		139	263	
CentralAfricanRepublic	139	160	110	130	29	30
Chad	102	105		92	105	
Comoros	51	50	5	2	46	48
Congo	453	407	372	335	81	72
CongoDemRep	7,886	8,302	7,862	8,276	24	26
Côte d'Ivoire	5,535	5,631	1,510	1,797	4,025	3,834
Djibouti	280	292		180	292	
Egypt	118,407	128,129	12,925	15,510	104,866	111,788
EquatorialGuinea	95	95	7	2	88	93
Eritrea	269	288		209	286	
Ethiopia	3,270	3,503	3,259	3,369	10	133
Gabon	1,732	1,844	945	801	787	1,043
Gambia	216	229		90	229	
Ghana	8,435	6,984	5,619	3,727	2,816	3,257
Guinea	872	973	461	538	411	435
Guinea-Bissau	66	70		58	70	
Kenya	7,323	6,773	3,025	3,592	3,252	2,192
Lesotho	200	200	200	200		
Liberia	351	353			351	353
Libya	23,992	25,694		15,496	25,694	
Madagascar	990	935	600	540	390	395
Malawi	1,580	1,637	1,354	1,403	226	234
Mali	489	495	266	271	223	224
Mauritania	569	587		234	587	
Mauritius	2,350	2,465	77	84	2,273	2,381
Morocco	23,192	22,858	1,601	1,331	21,408	21,248
Mozambique	14,737	16,076	14,717	16,063	20	13
Namibia	1,491	1,694	1,385	1,564	106	130
Niger	179	197		190	197	
Nigeria	23,110	22,978	7,714	6,406	15,396	16,572
Rwanda	171	169	41	34	129	135
SaoTomePrincipe	42	43	8	10	34	33
Senegal	1,962	2,124		1,669	2,124	
Seychelles	252	271		188	271	
SierraLeone	41	60	4	18	37	42
Somalia	307	326	15	250	311	
SouthAfrica	253,798	263,479	5,581	3,908	236,384	248,201
Sudan	4,209	4,541	1,370	1,451	2,839	3,090
Swaziland	436	454	156	173	280	281
Tanzania	2,776	4,175	1,436	2,511	1,340	1,664
Togo	221	196	91	92	130	104
Tunisia	14,122	14,060	92	49	13,992	13,968
Uganda	1,615	1,952	1,239	1,412	376	540
Zambia	9,385	9,853	9,329	9,796	56	57
Zimbabwe	9,776	9,180	5,552	5,213	4,224	3,967
Africa	592,830	619,258	95,875	97,508	483,224	508,228

Source: African Development Bank

Electricity

North and Southern Africa account for more than 80 percent of total power generating capacity on the continent. The Democratic Republic of Congo (Central), Kenya (East), and Nigeria (West) are leading in power generation on the rest of the continent. South Africa's utility, Eskom, is not only Africa's biggest, but the world's fifth largest both in terms of electricity sales and generating capacity. Eskom also operates Africa's only two nuclear power generation facilities at Koeberg, near Cape Town. South Africa, Zambia and Ghana are the three largest net exporters of electricity in Africa.

Globally Africa lags far behind both in terms of production and consumption of electricity. Even though commercial energy production in Africa has nearly doubled since 1970 and is expected to increase by another 68% by 2020, its share of the world's total remains only 7%. The continent's share of world commercial energy consumption is also small due to low incomes, low levels of industrialization and ownership of electric appliances. Rural populations rely heavily on biomass and firewood and charcoal—environmentally detrimental energy sources. Deforestation is one of the most pressing environmental problems faced by African nations. In many countries three-quarters of the forest cover has already been depleted.

Eskom's Kendall Power plant

Investment

Interest is growing in new construction projects and a number of privatization prospects. International agencies are helping to accelerate the privatization process. Amog major players in various energy projects is GE, the second-largest company in the United States by market capitalization. It has a presence in 16 African countries ranging from interests in transport, energy, to oil and gas, security and healthcare, stretching from Cape Town to Algiers.

Projects

Among recent major projects is the Lesotho Highlands Water Project that provides additional power to the Witwatersrand complex around Johannesburg and the Inga project in the Congo River that will provide enough energy to power most of Africa's industrial areas and still have a lot left over to sell to Europe via a proposed Mediterranean connector. Several African state utilities have been targeted for overhaul with the help of private expertise. After recurring power shortages that reached critical dimensions in 2008, South Africa's Eskom has embarked on an expansion program at the cost of several billion dollars.

OVERVIEW

In its overview, the US Energy Information Administration (EIA) summarizes electricity generation in Africa as follows:

North Africa

A newly constructed Hamma 450-megawatt (MW) natural gas-fired facility provides power to **Algeria**'s capital city, Algiers. New projects include a 1,200-MW plant near Tipasa, the 2X600-MW Terga plant near Oran Tipasa

AES: Energizing Africa

The AES Corporation has 10 years experience providing reliable, affordable and sustainable energy while also promoting community development in Africa.

AES is a global power company with generation and distribution businesses. Through a diverse portfolio of thermal and renewable fuel sources, AES provides affordable and sustainable electricity to people on 5 continents in 29 countries.

AES brings global expertise and a long-standing commitment to Africa. We have been investing in Africa since 2001 and currently have operations in Cameroon and Nigeria, employing over 3,600 people and providing safe and reliable power to communities, improving their quality of life.

For more information, please visit www.aes.com

AES — *the power of being global*

---

and a 2X600-MW plant near Annaba. **Egypt**'s first Build Own Operate Transfer (BOOT) power project became operational in 2002. The complex, Sidi Kerir 3 and 4, consists of two 325-MW gas-fired units which and forms the largest private power station in North Africa and the Middle East. The Egyptian Electric Authority (EEA) has entered into two additional BOOT agreements for 650-MW gas-fired facilities at each end of Egypt's Suez Canal at an estimated total cost of $900 million. **Morocco**'s state-owned *Office Nationale d'Electricite* (ONE) is a major investor in the country's power generation sector. Additions to generating capacity include the Kouida al Baida 50-MW wind farm overlooking the Strait of Gibraltar, a 470-MW station located near Tangiers at Tahaddart, a 200-MW hydroelectric facility at Dchar el Oued, and a 300-MW pumped storage hydroelectric facility near Afourar. Morocco also added two 330-MW units on a build-operate-transfer (BOT) basis to the Jorf Lasfar plant. A US-based consortium developed **Tunisia**'s first privately-run generating facility. The 470-MW combined cycle gas-fired plant, Rades II, is located outside the capital of Tunis. More than 94 percent of the population has access to electricity.

Central Africa

AES has been present in Africa since 2001 and currently has operations in Cameroon and Nigeria, employing over 3,600 people. AES' integrated utility in **Cameroon**, AES SONEL, is the 5th largest company in the country with a total installed capacity of 1,017 MW (720MW Hydro, 297 MW Thermal) serving over 570,000 customers. The **Democratic Republic of Congo** undertook expansion at the Inga hydroelectric facility on the Congo River. The combined capacity of the 2,000-MW Inga II plant and the 40,000-MW Grand Inga facility will be almost as large as all of Southern Africa's current installed capacity and be able to provide enough power to export to Europe after servicing the region's industrial needs. EEF (Switzerland), Infra-Consult (Germany) and Medis (Belgium) have signed an agreement to rehabilitate the DRC's *Societe Nationale d'Electricite* (SNEL) electricity system, including work on generating facilities in, Kinshasa, and production and distribution in the North and South Kivu provinces.

East Africa

Electricite de Djibouti (EDD) increased its generating capacity by 20 MW with the purchase of four 5-MW diesel-powered generators. EDD also constructed an 18-MW facility in Marabout. Studies to evaluate the geothermal potential of **Eritrea**'s Alid region indicated that temperature and permeability conditions were favorable for an electrical-grade geothermal resource. **Djibouti** and **Uganda** are also exploring the possibility of utilizing geothermal resources for power generation. The Ethiopian Electric Power Corporation (EEPC) increased the country's electric generating capacity with the upgrading of facilities on the Koka and Tis Abay rivers and the completion of a 34-MW hydroelectric plant on the Fincha river in its western region. The EEPC is also constructing hydroelectric facilities on Ethiopia's Gilgel-Gibe (184 MW) and Blue Nile (73 MW) rivers. Additional hydroelectric facilities are envisaged on the Tekeze, Tana, Beles, and Halele Werabisa rivers. **Kenya** has several independent power projects (IPPs) underway. Recently completed are coal-fired plants at Nairobi South and the 75-MW Kipevu II. Kenya already has the highest penetration rate of photo voltaic systems in the world, with over 100,000 systems in place and annual sales of 20,000. Two Chinese firms financed 75% of the Kajbar hydroelectric facility in northern **Sudan**. The $200 million project is located on the Nile and have a generating capacity of 300 MW. US-based AES developed a 250-MW Bujagali Falls hydroelectric facility on the Nile at $450-$500 million. Norway's Norpak headed a consortium in the construction of the 180-MW Karuma Falls hydroelectric project in northwestern Uganda.

West Africa

With the help of US firms **Benin** developed an 80-MW power generation facility. The project included building a 20-mile (30-km) pipeline to feed natural gas to a plant south of Porto Novo. In **Côte d'Ivoire** a 210 MW gas-fired plant is a joint development of French firms. The government of **Burkina Faso** plans to provide electricity to 48 of its 350 communities in the country by 2010. **Ghana** has developed plans for an additional hydroelectric facility to be located on the Black Volta River at Bui with a generating capacity of 400 MW for exporting to **Burkina Faso, Côte d'Ivoire** and **Mali**. A consortium of American and Japanese firms participated in the construction of a 220-MW power station in Tema, Ghana. The 75-MW Garafi hydroelectric facility was inaugurated in **Guinea** seven years ago. It is the country's largest hydroelectric facility and will supply power to Conakry. **Nigeria** developed several IPP projects. Nigeria also rehabilitated six generating facilities in an effort to meet the rapidly expanding need for power. Less than half of the population have access to electricity. AES Ebute in Nigeria, is a natural gas-fired generation plant that generates approximately 8% of the country's electricity and is one of the largest employers in the local community. **Senegal**'s SENELEC plans to electrify over 150 rural towns, bringing electricity to all villages with a population of 3,000 or more. Currently only 30 percent of the population have access to electricity.

AFRICA'S ELECTRICITY BY TYPE

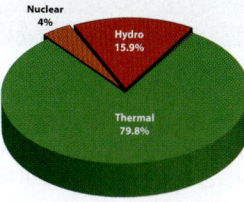

Installed Electricity Capacity
- Nuclear 1.7%
- Geothermal 0.2%
- Hydro 20.9%
- Thermal 77.2%

Electricity Production
- Nuclear 4%
- Hydro 15.9%
- Thermal 79.8%

Southern Africa

The Southern African Power Pool (SAPP) was created in the nineties by the 12 countries in the Southern African Development Community (SADC). Participating utilities include Angola's ENE, the Botswana Power Corporation (BPC), the Democratic Republic of Congo's SNEL, Lesotho Electricity Corporation (LEC), Malawi's Electricity Supply Commission, Mozambique's EDM, Namibia's Nampower, South Africa's Eskom, Swaziland Electricity Board (SEB), Tanzania Electric Supply Company (TANESCO), Zambia's ZESCO and Zimbabwe's ZESA. **Angola**'s generating capacity doubled with the completion of the 520-MW Capanda hydroelectric facility. Its state-owned utility, Empresa Nacional de Electricidade (ENE), plans to construct an oil-fired power plant in the city of Lubango. On completion the **Lesotho** Highlands Water Project, involving the

SYMBION
SYMBION-POWER.COM

ENGINEERING PROCUREMENT & CONSTRUCTION

Contact us: +1 703 621 0815 for more information   www.symbion-power.com

Victoria Falls. National Power of Britain, in conjunction with the **Zimbabwe** Electricity Supply Authority (ZESA), developed a 1,400-MW coal-fired plant at Gowke North to supply one-third of Zimbabwe's electricity requirements. **South Africa**'s state utility, Eskom—the world's fifth largest—used to supply over 95% of the country's electricity needs as well as 60% of the electricity needs of the continent. However, since 2006 Eskom experienced problems meeting demands due to lack of capacity and maintenance shortcomings. Electricity exports were curtailed and power-shedding introduced. By mid-2008 revenue loss due to the outages were estimated in terms of hundreds of millions rand— approximately half in mining production losses. Eskom has embarked on a multi-billion dollar program to upgrade and expand the country's electricity infrastructure. The building of new capacity in the form of reopening 3 power stations that were mothballed in the 1990s and the building of 2 open-cycle gas turbines and co-generation with business added 2,400 MW to its total capacity by the end of 2009. Plans envisage the building a new generation of power stations, including another nuclear power plant. Currently Eskom's 35,060 megawatts (MW) of nominal generating capacity—primarily coal-fired (34,532 MW)—includes one nuclear power station with two reactors at Koeberg (1,930 MW) producing 6% of the country's total electricity, two gas turbine facilities (342 MW), six conventional hydroelectric plants (600 MW), and two hydroelectric pumped-storage stations (1,400 MW). On completion nuclear contribution to power would rise from 6% to more than 25% and coal's contribution would fall from 87% now to below 70%. South African municipalities own and operate 2,436 MW of generating capacity and an additional 836 MW of generating capacity is privately held by mines and factories.

construction of dams, tunnels and pipelines, will have a power generating capacity of 274 MW. The Compagnie Thermique de Belle Vue (CTBV), a joint-venture between Harel Freres (51%) of **Mauritius**, France's Cidec (27%), the Sugar Investment Trust of Mauritius (14%) and the State Investment Fund (8%), constructed a 70-MW IPP facility north of the Mauritian capital of Port Louis. The CTBV plant utilizes bagasse (biomass refuse from the processing of sugar cane) as its primary fuel. *Electricidade de Mocambique*, **Mozambiqu**e's state utility, and *Hidro-electrica de Cahora Bassa* (HCB)—a joint venture involving Portugal—have restored the link between the Cahora Bassa dam and South Africa, replacing over 2,000 pylons that were damaged during the civil war. Cahora Bassa, with a nominal capacity of 2,000 MW, also supplies power to neighboring Zimbabwe. There are plans for a second dam on the Zambezi River, with capacity of 2,000 to 2,500 MW. The **Zambia** Electricity Supply Corporation (ZESCO) rehabilitated generating facilities at

Minerals & Mining

Africa is not only one of the world's major sources of hydrocarbon fuels but also of hard minerals. It ranks first or second in the world in terms of reserves of gold, antimony, bauxite, chromite, cobalt, diamonds, fluorspar, hafnium, manganese, phosphate rock, the platinum group, titanium, vanadium, vermiculite, and zirconium.

The continent accounts for between 1% to 6% of the world's supplies of aluminum, cement, coal, copper, graphite, iron ore, lead, steel, and zinc; from 11% to 31% of the global supplies of bauxite, cobalt, gold, manganese, phosphate, and uranium; and from 50% to 57% of the world's chromium and diamonds.

South Africa

South Africa alone accounts for 76% of the world supply of vermiculite, 62% of vanadium, 59% of its alumino–silicates, 43% of its platinum-group of metals, 26% of all zirconium minerals, and 23% of the world's titanium. South Africa's position as the world's largest gold producer—a position it held for over a century—was usurped by China in 2007. In that year China's gold production was 276 metric tons, surpassing the 254 tons produced by South African mines.

Vital

Natural resources continue to be vital to the economies of African nations as earners of foreign exchange, providers of employment and stimulants for the development of transportation, energy and other infrastructure projects. Trade in fuel and hard minerals in countries such as Algeria, Angola, Botswana, Gabon, Guinea, Libya, Namibia, Niger, Nigeria, and Zambia accounts for between 50% and 95% of their export earnings, and represents between 50% and 66% of the export earnings of South Africa, Ghana and Egypt. West and North Africa dominate in oil and gas and subequatorial Africa (especially the southern portion) leads in the production of hard minerals.

Anglogold Mine, South Africa

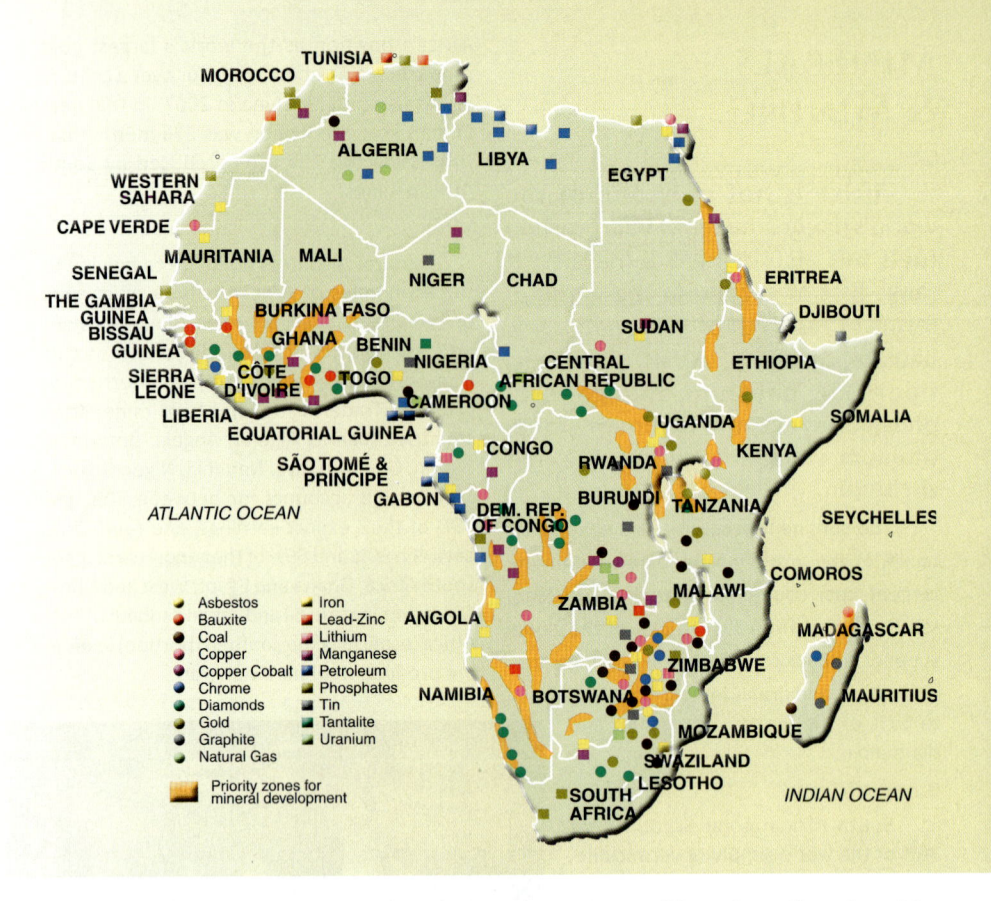

☑ Africa is a major supplier of strategic minerals to the United States and other world markets.

☑ There has been a resurgence in mineral exploration in Africa in recent years involving major and US, Canadian and South African mining companies. For the period 2000 to 2007 more than $26 billion was spent on mining and mineral processing projects on the continent—including nonferrous metals investments of $9.55 billion; ferrous metals, $4.82 billion; gold, $4.55 billion; and PGM, $3.7 billion.

☑ The Multilateral Investment Guarantee Agency (MIGA) has worked with many African countries to develop more progressive mining and foreign investment laws and reforms have been implemented.

☑ Changes in the political climate made it possible to resume exploration in countries such as Mozambique, Angola and the Democratic Republic of Congo.

☑ With the lifting of sanctions the mining giants of post-apartheid South Africa have been able to explore and develop mining elsewhere in the Continent. Target areas include Angola, Tanzania, Mauritania, Mozambique, Burkina Faso, Niger, Nigeria and Gabon. South Africa has become a major player not only in mining in Africa but worldwide.

☑ Economic reforms in several African countries have widened the scope for private enterprise and led to greater efficiency and profitability in privatized former state mining enterprises. These reforms have led to greater efficiency and profitability in the mining sector.

☑ There is a high probability that much of Africa's mineral wealth still lies hidden in the remote and high risk regions. As infrastructure improves and governments stabilize, these new opportunities are bound to attract mineral seekers from abroad.

AFRICAN PRODUCTION OF SELECTED MINERAL COMMODITIES
(THOUSAND METRIC TONS GROSS WEIGHT UNLESS OTHERWISE SPECIFIED - 2008)

	Aluminum Bauxite	Aluminum Metal	Chromite output gross wt	Cobalt output m. tons	Copper, output Cu content	Gold output kilogram	Iron & Steel ore gross wt	Iron & St. crude gross wt	Manganese-ore gross wt
Algeria	--	--	--	--	--	647	2,077	646	--
Angola	--	--	--	--	--	--	--	--	--
Benin	--	--	--	--	--	20	--	--	--
Botswana	--	--	--	--	22	3,176	--	--	--
Burkina Faso	--	--	--	--	--	7,633	--	--	--
Burundi	--	--	--	--	--	750	--	--	--
Cameroon	--	91	--	--	--	1,800	--	--	--
Cape Verde	--	--	--	--	--	--	--	--	--
Central African Republic	--	--	--	--	--	10	--	--	--
Chad	--	--	--	--	--	150	--	--	--
Comoros	--	--	--	--	--	--	--	--	--
Congo, Rep. of	--	--	--	--	--	100	--	--	--
Congo, Dem. Rep.	--	--	--	31,000	243	3,300	--	113	--
Côte d'Ivoire	--	--	--	--	--	4,205	--	--	76
Djibouti	--	--	--	--	--	--	--	--	--
Egypt	--	260	--	--	--	--	1,811	6,198	3
Equatorial Guinea	--	--	--	--	--	200	--	--	--
Eritrea	--	--	--	--	--	32	--	--	--
Ethiopia	--	--	--	--	--	3,465	--	110	--
Gabon	--	--	--	--	--	300	--	--	1,549
Gambia, The	--	--	--	--	--	--	--	--	--
Ghana	738	--	--	--	--	80,503	--	--	380
Guinea	17,200	--	--	--	--	19,945	--	--	--
Guinea-Bissau	--	--	--	--	--	--	--	--	--
Kenya	--	2	--	--	--	340	(5)	--	--
Lesotho	--	--	--	--	--	--	--	--	--
Liberia	--	--	--	--	--	624	--	--	--
Libya	--	--	--	--	--	--	--	1,137	--
Madagascar	--	--	84	--	--	72	--	--	--
Malawi	--	--	--	--	--	--	--	--	--
Mali	--	--	--	--	--	41,160	--	--	--
Mauritania	--	--	--	--	33	6,254	10,950	1,598	--
Mauritius	--	--	--	--	--	--	--	--	--
Morocco & W. Sahara	--	--	--	1,000	6	1,600	9	478	3
Mozambique	5	536	--	--	--	298	--	--	--
Namibia	--	--	--	--	7	2,126	--	--	10
Niger	--	--	--	--	--	2,314	--	--	--
Nigeria	--	20	--	--	--	200	62	500	--
Rwanda	--	--	--	--	--	20	--	--	--
Sao Tome e Principe	--	--	--	--	--	--	--	--	--
Senegal	--	--	--	--	--	600	--	--	--
Seychelles	--	--	--	--	--	--	--	--	--
Sierra Leone	954	--	--	--	--	196	--	--	--
Somalia	--	--	--	--	--	--	--	--	--
South Africa	--	811	9,682	400	109	212,744	48,983	8,550	2,900
Sudan	--	--	15	--	--	2,276	--	--	(5)
Swaziland	--	--	--	--	--	--	--	--	--
Tanzania	5	--	--	--	3	36,000	--	--	--
Togo	--	--	--	--	--	--	--	--	--
Tunisia	--	--	--	--	--	--	211	82	--
Uganda	--	--	--	--	--	20	(5)	30	--
Zambia	--	--	--	6,900	583	1,930	--	--	1
Zimbabwe	--	--	650	50	2	3,600	50	60	--
AFRICA TOTAL	18,900	1,720	10,400	39,400	1,010	439,000	64,200	19,500	4,920
% OF WORD TOTAL	9%	4%	37%	52%	6%	22%	3%	1%	35%

continued on next page

AFRICAN PRODUCTION—SELECTED MINERALs 2008

Country	Zinc m. tons	Diamonds '000 carats	Phosphate rock, gross wt	Uranium, U_3O_8 content m. tons
Algeria	--	--	1,805	--
Angola	--	8,907	--	--
Benin	--	--	--	--
Botswana	--	32,595	--	--
Burkina Faso	--	--	2	--
Burundi	--	--	--	--
Cameroon	--	12	--	--
Cape Verde	--	--	--	--
Central African Republic	--	377	--	--
Chad	--	--	--	--
Comoros	--	--	--	--
Congo, Rep. of	--	110	--	--
Congo, Dem. Rep.	18,000	20,947	--	--
Côte d'Ivoire	--	300	--	--
Djibouti	--	--	--	--
Egypt	--	--	5,523	--
Equatorial Guinea	--	--	--	--
Eritrea	--	--	--	--
Ethiopia	--	--	--	--
Gabon	--	1	--	--
Gambia, The	--	--	--	--
Ghana	--	643	--	--
Guinea	--	3,098	--	--
Guinea-Bissau	--	--	--	--
Kenya	--	--	--	--
Lesotho	--	450	--	--
Liberia	--	61	--	--
Libya	--	--	--	--
Madagascar	--	--	--	--
Malawi	--	--	--	--
Mali	--	--	--	--
Mauritania	--	--	--	--
Mauritius	--	--	--	--
Morocco & W. Sahara	96,900	--	25,000	--
Mozambique	--	--	--	--
Namibia	38,319	2,435	--	5,074
Niger	--	--	--	3,575
Nigeria	--	--	--	--
Rwanda	--	--	--	--
Sao Tome e Principe	--	--	--	--
Senegal	--	--	645	--
Seychelles	--	--	--	--
Sierra Leone	--	371	--	--
Somalia	--	--	--	--
South Africa	29,002	12,901	2,287	654
Sudan	--	--	--	--
Swaziland	--	--	--	--
Tanzania	--	180	8	--
Togo	--	9	842	--
Tunisia	--	--	7,692	--
Uganda	--	--	--	--
Zambiae	--	--	--	--
Zimbabwe	--	797	30	--
AFRICA TOTAL	182,000	84,200	43,800	9,300
% WORLD TOTAL	2%	55%	27%	19%

Source: US Geological Survey 2010

Key sector

Mining is seen as key to economic development in Africa. Mining operators, who are often pioneer foreign investors in African countries, generate substantial amounts of foreign exchange that significantly boost government revenues. Unlike other infrastructural projects, the immediate foreign exchange earnings of mines minimize currency risk—one of the main bugbears of investment in Africa.

Exploration

Exploration activity in Africa increased by 19% to $1.9 billion in 2008 from about $1.6 billion in 2007—representing 15% of the world's total. The principal mineral commodities of interest for exploration in Africa were base metals, diamond, gold, PGM and uranium, and focused primarily on South Africa, Zambia, Namibia, Tanzania, Dem. Rep. of Congo, Ghana, Burkina Faso, and Mali. Gold targets accounted for approximately 33% of reported African exploration projects; PGM made up about 15%; copper and diamond each represented about 13%; uranium represented about 12% and base metals about 7%.

Leaders

Two of the world's biggest mining companies originated in South Africa: BHP Billiton, the world's largest mining company, formed as a merger between South African company Billiton and Australian firm BHP; and Anglo American Plc, with its primary listing in London and a secondary listing in Johannesburg. Anglo owns many major subsidiaries, such as Anglo Platinum, Anglo Coal, Impala Platinum and Kumba Iron Ore. Diamond giant De Beers, also a South African company, is owned by Anglo American and a consortium led by the Botswana government. As the world's top diamond producer De Beers churned out about 51.1-million carats in 2007.

Reforms

Reforms to mining legislation have been introduced in many African countries but, unfortunately, development in some mineral-rich regions continues to be hampered by regional strife and ongoing civil wars.

TELECOMMUNICATIONS

Over the past decade there has been a continuing strong growth in Information and Communication Technology (ICT) in Africa. Particularly impressive has been the surge in mobile cellular subscriptions. The number of Internet users has also grown strongly, although penetration rates remain relatively low. In 2009, according to the International Telecommunications Union (ITU) the region recorded more than 440 million mobile cellular subscriptions, showing a penetration rate of more than 40 percent, and 110 million Internet users, showing a penetration rate of almost 11 percent.

Millennium Goals

The Millennium Declaration, adopted by 189 member states at the UN General Assembly in September 2000 acknowledged Information and Communication Technology (ICT) as an important tool to alleviate poverty, improve the delivery of education and health care and making government services accessible. It called on the private sector to make available to developing countries the benefits of new technologies, specifically information and communications. The International Telecommunications Union (ITU) was assigned to measure progress. Three indicators were chosen as yardsticks for ICT availability in countries: total number of telephone subscribers per 100 inhabitants, personal computers per 100 inhabitants and Internet users per 100 inhabitants.

Progress

Over the last decade, Information and Communication Technologies (ICT) have been growing at great speed, always exceeding global economic growth and changing the way people work, entertain, shop, communicate and organize their live. This growth has been driven by demand-side factors such as the increasing popularity of mobile phones and the Internet and by supply-side factors such as regulatory reforms, falling costs, and technological innovation. By the end of 2009, there were 110 million Internet users in Africa, and 440 million mobile cellular subscriptions. The annual growth between 2003 and 2008 in both services in Africa has been twice that of the world. Over the same period, fixed line growth in the region has been similar to that of the world—much lower compared to that of mobile cellular subscriptions and Internet users.

Penetration

Notwithstanding the emergence of Africa as one of the most dynamic regions in terms of Information Technology and Communications growth, the ITU noted in its 2009 report that the region's absolute figures as well as penetration rates remained low. Two decades ago achieving a teledensity of one per one hundred inhabitants represented a major milestone but today the benchmark

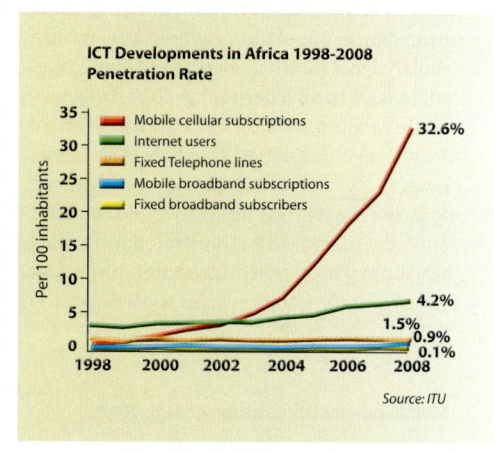

ICT Developments in Africa 1998-2008
Penetration Rate

- Mobile cellular subscriptions: 32.6%
- Internet users: 4.2%
- Fixed Telephone lines: 1.5%
- Mobile broadband subscriptions: 0.9%
- Fixed broadband subscribers: 0.1%

Source: ITU

is much higher. Although Africa has made impressive gains, it remains behind the ICT penetration levels of the world, and even those of developing countries elsewhere. There is also considerable disparity between countries and regions on the continent.

Fixed Lines

Between 1998 and 2008, Africa added only 2.4 million telephone lines—less than 1 per cent the total number of telephone lines added worldwide during the same period. As a result, fixed telephone line penetration remained stagnant and fell far behind other regions where increases were recorded. In 2008 in only Mauritius and Seychelles fixed telephone line penetration on a country level was above that of the developing world average (13.6 per cent). Both, however, cover a small land area and have a modest population base.

Mobile

At the same time mobile telephony in Africa has shown remarkable growth. In 2000, the number of mobile cellular subscriptions surpassed that of fixed telephone lines on the continent—two years before this happened globally. In 2009 according to the ITU, mobile telephone subscriptions in Africa reached a total of more than 440 million. Africa might lag in other areas but it has undoubtedly been a leader in the shift from fixed to mobile telephony. Between 2000 and 2009, mobile cellular penetration has risen from less than two in 100 inhabitants to 44 out of 100. Although this is significant in terms of growth rates, penetration rates are still considerably lower in Africa than in other regions. Overall, however, the population covered by a mobile cellular signal in Africa increased from 25 per cent in 2000 to 58.5 per cent in 2008. Originally mobile services were concentrated in a few of Africa's most developed countries. Over time, however, cellular subscriptions have become more evenly distributed between countries across the region. This is illustrated by the fact that South Africa which accounted for 74 per cent of Africa's mobile cellular subscriptions in 200 represented only 19 per cent of the total in 2008. The growth in Nigeria is most notable, but other countries including Kenya, Ghana, Tanzania and Côte d'Ivoire have also greatly contributed to the change in the distribution of mobile cellular subscriptions in the region.

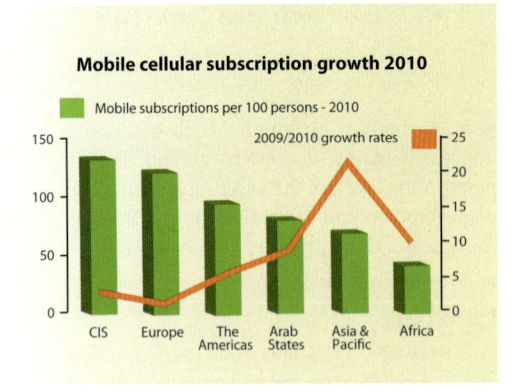

Disparity

Nevertheless, today there is still considerable disparity in mobile penetration among African countries. While the regional average number of mobile subscriptions per 100 inhabitants had grown to 45 in 2009, penetration rates ranged from more 131 in the Seychelles and above 90 in Gabon and South Africa to less than five in Eritrea and Ethiopia. Not surprisingly the level of development still correlates with the spread of mobile telephony, and more than twenty out of 30 African LDCs have a mobile cellular penetration rate below that of the regional average

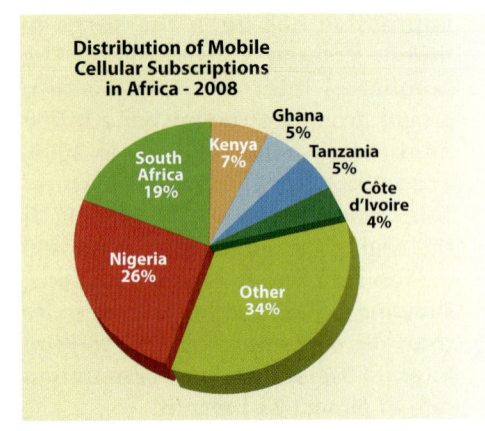

Mobile PCs

The technology revolution is coming to developing countries via the mobile phone, not the personal computer as it did in the developed world. In fact, before the rest of the world transformed phones into handheld computer devices they have served as Africa's affordable PCs. Problems related to web connectivity in developing countries such as low bandwidth, poverty, the technology learning curve, and access to software and hardware, are solved with this device. Just as the internet encouraged an entrepreneurial ethos and dotcom firms, Africa's surge in mobile-phone use may unleash the same sort of business energy tailored to local needs. In Ghana, for example, TradeNet unveiled a simple sort of eBay for agricultural products across a dozen West African countries. It lets buyers and sellers indicate what they are after and their contact information, which is sent to all relevant subscribers as an SMS text

TELECOMMUNICATIONS IN AFRICA - 2009

	Pop. Total million	Pop. Density per km²	GDP US$ per capita	Fixed-line Subscribers Total '000	Fixed-line Per 100 pers.	Mobile Phone Subscribers Total '000	Mobile Per 100 pers.	Ratio Mobile/Fixed
Algeria	34.9	15	4,885	2,576.20	7.38	32,730	93.79	12.7 : 1
Angola	18.5	15	4,592	303.2	1.64	8,109	43.84	26.7 : 1
Benin	8.93	79	748	127.1	1.42	5,033	56.33	39.6 : 1
Botswana	1.95	3	6,885	137.4	7.05	1,874	96.12	13.6 : 1
Burkina Faso	15.76	57	511	152.5	0.97	3,824	24.27	25.1 : 1
Burundi	8.3	298	140	31.5	0.38	838	10.1	26.6 : 1
Cameroon	19.52	41	1,191	435.4	2.23	8,004	41	18.4 : 1
Cape Verde	0.51	125	3,391	71.9	14.22	291	57.48	4.0 : 1
Central African Rep.	4.42	7	450	12	0.27	600	13.57	50.0 : 1
Chad	11.21	9	772	58.3	0.52	2,281	20.36	39.2 : 1
Comoros	0.68	363	784	21.5	3.18	125	18.49	5.8 : 1
Congo	3.68	11	3,402	24.3	0.66	2,171	58.94	89.3 : 1
Congo (Dem. Rep.)	66.02	28	177	42.3	0.06	9,459	14.33	223.5 : 1
Côte d'Ivoire	21.08	65	1,111	282.1	1.34	13,184	62.56	46.7 : 1
Djibouti	0.86	39	1,126	16.8	1.95	129	14.9	7.6 : 1
Egypt	83	83	1,988	10,312.60	12.42	55,352	66.69	5.4 : 1
Equatorial Guinea	0.68	24	27,393	10	1.48	200	29.57	20.0 : 1
Eritrea	5.07	54	291	48.5	0.96	141	2.78	2.9 : 1
Ethiopia	82.82	68	313	915.1	1.1	4,052	4.89	4.4 : 1
Gabon	1.47	6	9,846	26.5	1.8	1,373	93.11	51.8 : 1
Gambia	1.71	160	600	49	2.87	1,433	84.04	29.2 : 1
Ghana	23.84	100	1534	267.4	1.12	15,109	63.38	56.5 : 1
Guinea	10.07	41	377	22	0.22	3,489	34.65	158.6 : 1
Guinea-Bissau	1.61	45	523	4.8	0.3	560	34.79	115.7 : 1
Kenya	39.8	68	763	664.1	1.67	19,365	48.65	29.2 : 1
Lesotho	2.07	68	782	40	1.94	661	31.98	16.5 : 1
Liberia	3.95	36	211	2	0.05	842	21.29	421.0 : 1
Libya	6.42	4	14,843	1,100.70	17.15	5,004	77.94	4.5 : 1
Madagascar	19.63	33	480	186.2	0.95	6,284	32.02	33.8 : 1
Malawi	15.26	162	280	175	1.15	2,400	15.72	13.7 : 1
Mali	13.01	10	672	84.8	0.65	4,446	34.17	52.4 : 1
Mauritania	3.29	3	1,090	74.5	2.26	2,182	66.32	29.3 : 1
Mauritius	1.29	691	7,235	381.7	29.63	1,087	84.36	2.8 : 1
Morocco	31.99	48	2,778	3,516.30	10.99	25,311	79.11	7.2 : 1
Mozambique	22.89	29	421	74.1	0.32	5,971	26.08	80.5 : 1
Namibia	2.17	3	3,884	142.1	6.54	1,217	56.05	8.6 : 1
Niger	15.29	13	351	65	0.43	2,599	17	40.0 : 1
Nigeria	154.73	167	1,300	1,419.00	0.92	74,518	48.16	52.5 : 1
Rwanda	10	380	469	33.5	0.33	2,429	24.3	72.6 : 1
S. Tomé & Principe	0.16	169	1,074	7.8	4.79	64	39.32	8.2 : 1
Senegal	12.53	64	1,057	278.8	2.22	6,902	55.06	24.8 : 1
Seychelles	0.08	209	9,947	26.1	30.95	111	131.36	4.2 : 1
Sierra Leone	5.7	79	343	32.8	0.58	1,160	20.36	35.4 : 1
Somalia	9.13	14	...	100	1.09	641	7.02	6.4 : 1
South Africa	50.11	42	5,517	4,319.80	8.62	46,436	92.67	10.7 : 1
Sudan	42.27	17	144,593	370.4	0.88	15,340	36.29	41.4 : 1
Swaziland	1.18	68	2,393	44	3.71	656	55.36	14.9 : 1
Tanzania	43.74	47	474	172.9	0.4	17,470	39.94	101.0 : 1
Togo	6.62	117	435	178.7	2.7	2,187	33.05	12.2 : 1
Tunisia	10.27	63	3,986	1,278.50	12.45	9,797	95.38	7.7 : 1
Uganda	32.71	138	504	233.5	0.71	9,384	28.69	40.2 : 1
Zambia	12.94	17	1,137	90.3	0.7	4,407	34.07	48.8 : 1
Zimbabwe	12.52	32	175	385.1	3.08	2,991	23.88	7.8 : 1
AFRICA TOTAL	1008.34	33	2,802	31,426.10	4.03	442,221	45.20	

Source: ITU

message in one of four languages. Interested parties can then each other directly to do a deal. In several countries mobile phones are used to transfer money between bank accounts while connectivity to the Internet on mobile phones is growing.

Competition

The International Telecommunications Union (ITU) points out that the majority of the countries on the African continent are allowing competition in mobile cellular networks. Growth in the number of mobile operators on the continent has been impressive. Today there are more than 100 mobile networks in operation compared to only 33 in 1995. With few exceptions these are not state-owned entities, multilateral donors or multinational giants but homegrown private telecommunication networks—often with overseas partners. By restructuring former monopolistic and inefficient state-owned telecommunications companies, entering into strategic partnerships with foreign entrepreneurs, and allowing others to compete, several African governments have succeeded in narrowing the gap.

Rates

Competition has been key to reducing mobile pricing across the region. As networks expanded and operators started competing for less affluent customers, tariffs dropped. The ITU cites the example of Kenya where Safaricom responded to increased competition by reducing call charges by up to 70 per cent for intra-Safaricom calls and up to 40 per cent for calls to other networks. Still, in 2008, according to the ITU's computation, the average monthly cost of a mobile cellular basket in Africa corresponded to 23 per cent of monthly Gross National Income (GNI) per capita. It ranged from a mere 1.0 per cent in Mauritius to as high as 60 per cent in Togo. A reduction in the price of handsets could further stimulate the market among low-income groups where the cost of the device is frequently the main entry barrier. Mobile component manufacturers, such as Texas Instruments, Motorola, and Philips, have started to develop less costly chips and other electronic components to replace those used in full-featured phones. Another strategy to reduce the price of handsets is through subsidies.

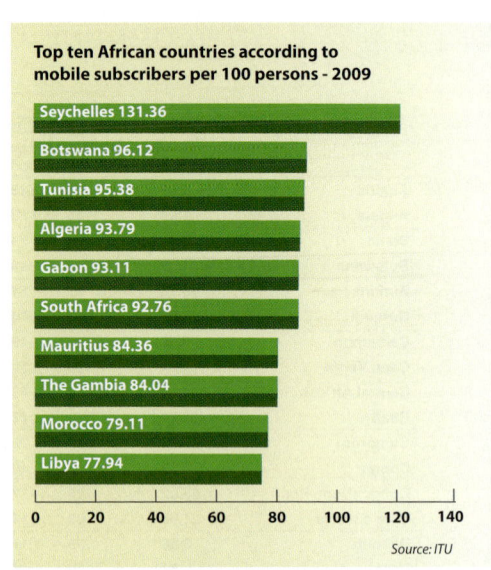

Top ten African countries according to mobile subscribers per 100 persons - 2009

Seychelles	131.36
Botswana	96.12
Tunisia	95.38
Algeria	93.79
Gabon	93.11
South Africa	92.76
Mauritius	84.36
The Gambia	84.04
Morocco	79.11
Libya	77.94

Source: ITU

Organizations

International organizations involved in the coordination and promotion of telecommunications development in Africa range from the International Telecommunications Union (ITU) and the African Telecommunications Union (ATU) to the African Connection Program. The ATU was created in December 1999 by the Organization of African Unity as a successor to the Pan African Telecommunications Union (PATU) to coordinate African telecommunications policy, establish a regulatory framework, and help arrange the financing of development programs. It has since transitioned into the African Union. The African Connection Program (ACP) was launched by African Ministers of Communication in October 2000 to fill the need for an African-led, regionally-focused, unified program. The Connect Africa Summit held in Kigali, Rwanda, in October 2007 underlined the importance of this sector.

Regional initiatives

Regional initiatives such as Pan-African Telecommunications (Panaftel)—covering some 39,000 kilometers of radio-relay systems, about 39 international telephone switches and 8,000 kilometers of submarine cable—aim at eliminating crossborder interconnection problems, such as those experienced between Kenya and Malawi; Kenya, Ethiopia and Djibouti; and Cameroon and Chad. The Regional African Satellite Communications (RASCOM) project

Top ten African countries according to total fixed line subscribers per 100 persons - 2009

- Seychelles 30.95
- Mauritius 29.63
- Libya 17.15
- Cape Verde 14.22
- Tunisia 12.45
- Egypt 12.42
- Morocco 10.99
- S. Africa 8.62
- Algeria 7.38
- Botsw. 7.05

Source: ITU

envisaged the creation of a regional satellite system that will be cheaper than the existing International Telecommunications Satellite Organization circuits. A major breakthrough came in July 2009 with the completion by Seacom of a 17,000 km (10,600 mile) submarine fiber optic cable system linking south and east Africa to global networks via India and Europe. Backhauls linking Johannesburg, Nairobi and Kampala with the coastal landing stations have been established and Seacom is also working with its partners to commission the final links to Kigali in Rwanda and Addis Ababa in Ethiopia.

Privatization

More than 35 countries in Africa are in the process of privatizing telecommunications services. Deregulation, privatization, and regulatory reform are creating a robust telecommunications environment that stimulates demand. Ten countries have indicated plans to sell off part of their state telecommunications corporations to the private sector: Benin, Burundi, Cameroon, Egypt, Kenya, Mauritius, Nigeria, Senegal, Seychelles, and Tunisia. Seventeen countries licensed cellular service providers on a wholly-owned private basis or in partnership with state telecoms: Benin, Botswana, Burundi, Central African Republic, the Republic of Congo (Brazzaville), Egypt, Ghana, Madagascar, Malawi, Mauritius, Mozambique, Rwanda, South Africa, Tanzania, Uganda, Zambia, and Zimbabwe.

Megadeals

For a while the single biggest privatization deal involving an African telecom was the purchase in 1997 of a 30% share in South Africa's Telkom by the American giant SBC and Telekom Malaysia for $1,260 million. In 2003 Telkom made an initial public offering on both the Johannesburg and New York Stock Exchanges. That same year the sale of a 35% share in Morocco's Maroc-Telecom to France's Vivendi Universal for $2.3 billion topped the Telkom deal by a billion.

Business potential

Foreign telecommunications firms are not only involved as partners in privatized former state telecoms but as independent new operators and suppliers of hardware, software, services and expertise. In many instances, the operation of cellular networks is licensed to local private operators with overseas partners. The United Nations Conference on Trade and Development (UNCTAD) cited telecommunications as one of the sectors in Africa with the greatest potential for foreigners. ITU estimates that this sector will grow by 40 percent over the next ten years. The recent growth in the African telecom market hasn't only benefited local economies—it has also generated significant amounts of revenue for mobile giants. In the past few years, MTN, a South African mobile-phone operator, with networks in Nigeria, Cameroon, Uganda, Rwanda and Swaziland had an operating margin of averaging 50%. Other major mobile service providers are Click-Afrique, Maroc Telecom, Safaricom, Vodacom, Vodafone, Mobine and Globacom.

BPO

Business process outsourcing (BPO) in telecommunications providing technical call centers and customer service for major corporations is still relatively underdeveloped in Africa. South Africa launched a financial incentive program to entice big foreign BPO clients to come and set up shop in the country. One of the most cited successful African competitors with India and Bangladesh is Egypt which has impressed western firms with its mix of savvy and linguistically talented agents at low costs. Not only South Africa but countries like Kenya and Ghana are now trying to follow Egypt's lead in the lucrative BPO field.

AFRICA ON THE INTERNET 2010

	Population 2008 Est.	Users Dec 2000	Users Oct 2010	% of Total Pop.	% of Africa	% Growth 2000-2010
Algeria	34,586,184	50,000	4,700,000	13.60%	4.30%	9300.00%
Angola	13,068,161	30,000	607,400	4.60%	0.50%	1924.70%
Benin	9,056,010	15,000	200,000	2.20%	0.20%	1233.30%
Botswana	2,029,307	15,000	120,000	5.90%	0.10%	700.00%
Burkina Faso	16,241,811	10,000	178,200	1.10%	0.20%	1682.00%
Burundi	9,863,117	3,000	65,000	0.70%	0.10%	2066.70%
Cameroon	19,294,149	20,000	750,000	3.90%	0.70%	3650.00%
Cape Verde	508,659	8,000	150,000	29.50%	0.10%	1775.00%
Central African Rep.	4,844,927	1,500	22,600	0.50%	0.00%	1406.70%
Chad	10,543,464	1,000	187,800	1.80%	0.20%	18680.00%
Comoros	773,407	1,500	24,300	3.10%	0.00%	1520.00%
Congo	4,125,916	500	245,200	5.90%	0.20%	48940.00%
Congo, Dem. Rep.	70,916,439	500	365,000	0.50%	0.30%	72900.00%
Cote d'Ivoire	21,058,798	40,000	968,000	4.60%	0.90%	2320.00%
Djibouti	740,528	1,400	25,900	3.50%	0.00%	1750.00%
Egypt	80,471,869	450,000	17,060,000	21.20%	15.40%	3691.10%
Equatorial Guinea	650,702	500	14,400	2.20%	0.00%	2780.00%
Eritrea	5,792,984	5,000	250,000	4.30%	0.20%	4900.00%
Ethiopia	88,013,491	10,000	445,400	0.50%	0.40%	4354.00%
Gabon	1,545,255	15,000	98,800	6.40%	0.10%	558.70%
Gambia	1,824,158	4,000	130,100	7.10%	0.10%	3152.50%
Ghana	24,339,838	30,000	1,297,000	5.30%	1.20%	4223.30%
Guinea	10,324,025	8,000	95,000	0.90%	0.10%	1087.50%
Guinea-Bissau	1,565,126	1,500	37,100	2.40%	0.00%	2373.30%
Kenya	40,046,566	200,000	3,995,500	10.00%	3.60%	1897.80%
Lesotho	1,919,552	4,000	76,800	4.00%	0.10%	1820.00%
Liberia	3,685,076	500	20,000	0.50%	0.00%	3900.00%
Libya	6,461,454	10,000	353,900	5.50%	0.30%	3439.00%
Madagascar	21,281,844	30,000	320,000	1.50%	0.30%	966.70%
Malawi	15,447,500	15,000	716,400	4.60%	0.60%	4676.00%
Mali	13,796,354	18,800	250,000	1.80%	0.20%	1229.80%
Mauritania	3,205,060	5,000	75,000	2.30%	0.10%	1400.00%
Mauritius	1,294,104	87,000	290,000	22.40%	0.30%	233.30%
Morocco	31,627,428	100,000	10,442,500	33.00%	9.40%	10342.50%
Mozambique	22,061,451	30,000	612,500	2.80%	0.60%	1941.70%
Namibia	2,128,471	30,000	127,500	6.00%	0.10%	325.00%
Niger	15,878,271	5,000	115,900	0.70%	0.10%	2218.00%
Nigeria	152,217,341	200,000	43,982,200	28.90%	39.60%	21891.10%
Rwanda	11,055,976	5,000	450,000	4.10%	0.40%	8900.00%
Sao Tome & Principe	175,808	6,500	26,700	15.20%	0.00%	310.80%
Senegal	14,086,103	40,000	923,000	6.60%	0.80%	2207.50%
Seychelles	88,340	6,000	33,900	38.40%	0.00%	465.00%
Sierra Leone	5,245,695	5,000	14,900	0.30%	0.00%	198.00%
Somalia	10,112,453	200	106,000	1.00%	0.10%	52900.00%
South Africa	49,109,107	2,400,000	5,300,000	10.80%	4.80%	120.80%
Sudan	41,980,182	30,000	4,200,000	10.00%	3.80%	13900.00%
Swaziland	1,354,051	10,000	90,000	6.60%	0.10%	800.00%
Tanzania	41,892,895	115,000	676,000	1.60%	0.60%	487.80%
Togo	6,199,841	100,000	356,300	5.70%	0.30%	256.30%
Tunisia	10,589,025	100,000	3,600,000	34.00%	3.20%	3500.00%
Uganda	33,398,682	40,000	3,200,000	9.60%	2.90%	7900.00%
Zambia	12,056,923	20,000	816,700	6.80%	0.70%	3983.50%
Zimbabwe	11,651,858	50,000	1,422,000	12.20%	1.30%	2744.00%
TOTAL AFRICA	1,013,779,050	4,514,400	110,931,700	10.90%	100.00%	2357.30%

© Miniwatts Marketing Group—www.internetworldstats.com

Internet

The number of Internet users in Africa has increased from 4.5 million in 2000 to 110 million in 2010, representing a growth of more than 2,350%. However, Internet penetration in Africa at 10.9% is well below the world average of 28.7%. Africa still has a long way to go before it can cross the digital divide as far as Internet connectivity is concerned.

Digital divide

The full extent of this digital divide becomes evident when Africa's Internet connectivity and usage are compared not only with the industrialized world but other developing regions. This is entirely consistent with the limited availability of fixed telephone networks in the region necessary for Internet dial-up and fixed broadband access. Indeed, in more than half of all African countries less than five per cent of the population use the Internet. Africa's 10.9% share of the world's total users is topped by North America (with about one third of Africa's population) with its 15% and Latin America's 10.5% (with about half Africa's population).

Broadband

Fixed broadband Internet services were first launched in Africa in 2000, and, by 2008, the region had 635,000 fixed broadband subscribers—less than a tenth of the population of the city of Lagos in Nigeria. Fixed broadband penetration therefore remained low in Africa (0.1 per cent), and much lower than in the developing countries (2.9 per cent) and the rest of the world (6 per cent). This is changing. A major breakthrough came in July 2009 with the completion by Seacom of a 17,000 km (10,600 mile) submarine fiber optic cable system linking south and east Africa to global networks via India and Europe. Backhauls linking Johannesburg, Nairobi and Kampala with the coastal landing stations have been established and Seacom is also working with its partners to commission the final links to Kigali in Rwanda and Addis Ababa in Ethiopia.

Disparity

There is a wide disparity among the nations of Africa as far as Internet usage goes. In 2010, not surprisingly, small island nations such as Seychelles with 38.40% Internet penetration, Cape Verde with 29.50% and Mauritius with 22.40% feature among the top ten. The task of providing connectivity on these islands is much less formidable than in Sudan, Africa's largest country (one-quarter the total size of the USA) with a population of 42 million. In 2010 Tunisia with led Africa's larger land-based nations with an impressive 34.0% penetration, followed by Morocco with 33.0%. In sheer numbers Nigeria topped the chart with almost 44 million, followed by Egypt's 17 million, Morocco's 10.4 million and South Africa's 5.3 million. Most promising is the rate at which Internet connectivity is spreading across certain parts of the continent.

Importance

The importance of greater connectivity to the Internet in Africa has frequently been emphasized by both its own leaders and international organizations. It goes beyond faster and more convenient personal and business connections by e-mail. E-commerce.

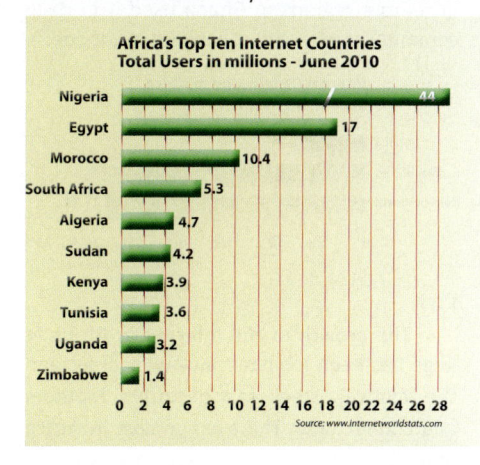

**Africa's Top Ten Internet Countries
Total Users in millions - June 2010**

Country	Users (millions)
Nigeria	44
Egypt	17
Morocco	10.4
South Africa	5.3
Algeria	4.7
Sudan	4.2
Kenya	3.9
Tunisia	3.6
Uganda	3.2
Zimbabwe	1.4

Source: www.internetworldstats.com

The availability of data and instant exchanges between African and overseas government policy makers, academicians, and medical and other professionals, are vital in the promotion of trade, investment, good governance, better education and health services. The Small Islands Developing States Network, or SIDSNet, enables 42 countries from Malta to Mauritius to Cuba and the Comoros to share

INTERNET USAGE AND POPULATION 2010

AFRICA REGION	Population (2010 Est.)	Pop. % in World	Internet Users, Latest Data	Penetration (% Population)	Use Growth (2000-2010)	% Users in World
Total for Africa	1,013,779,050	14.80%	110,931,700	10.90%	2357.30%	5.60%
Rest of World	5,831,830,910	85.20%	1,855,583,116	31.80%	420.50%	94.40%
WORLD TOTAL	6,845,609,960	100.00%	1,966,514,816	28.70%	444.60%	100.00%

Source: Miniwatts Marketing Group—www.internetworldstats.com

data on common concerns ranging from energy options and sustainable tourism to coastal and marine resources and biodiversity. PEOPLink, for example, links more than 130,000 artisans selling crafts across 14 countries in Africa, Asia and Latin America. As an example of the value of networking in the medical field, UNDP cites HealthNet which supports health care workers in more than 30 developing countries, including 22 in Africa. Using radio and telephone-based computer networks, this network provides summaries of the latest medical research, e-mail connectivity and access to medical libraries. It was, for example, used in 1995 to share information on the outbreak of the Ebola virus. Burn surgeons in Mozambique, Tanzania and Uganda utilized the network for consultation on reconstructive surgery techniques while malaria researchers in remote regions in Ghana used it in daily communications with colleagues in London.

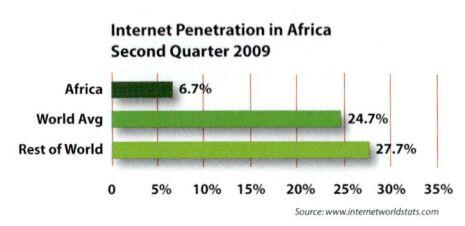

Internet Penetration in Africa Second Quarter 2009

- Africa: 6.7%
- World Avg: 24.7%
- Rest of World: 27.7%

Source: www.internetworldstats.com

Cost

The growth of the Internet in Africa at large has been inhibited by low incomes and the relatively steep cost of both computers and connectivity. The average cost in Africa of using a local dialup Internet account for 20 hours per month (including usage fees and local telephone time but not telephone line rental) is about $60. ISP subscriptions vary substantially between $10 and $80 a month, depending on the sophistication and level of maturity of the market. By comparison figures recently released by the Organization for Economic Cooperation and Development (OECD), show 20 hours of Internet access per month at an average of $22, across the European Union, with Germany at the higher end with $33. All of these countries have per capita incomes at least 10 times the African average. Actually, $60 per month is more than the average African monthly salary. In his study Olof Hesselmark of Sweden points out that the nominal cost of Internet services varies from $158 per year in Mauritius to $1,000 in Uganda. The purchase value of one dollar varies a great deal between countries and the affordability of Internet services varies even more when the income level in different countries is taken into account. Uganda is poorer than Mauritius but pays more than five times as much for Internet connectivity. Calculated as the share of the average income in the countries, a Ugandan pays 77 times as much as the Mauritian. In about half the countries in Africa, one year of Internet service will cost more than the average annual income, Hesselmark found. The promise of cheaper and faster international bandwidth for Africa has become a reality with the completion of the undersea Seacom cable. The $600m cable originally promised to slash South Africa's bandwidth costs by 80% and the mere threat of its entry has prompted incumbent operators such as Telkom to lower data tariffs by up to 80%. Even so, Seacom indicated that it would charge at least 50% less for its bandwidth.

E-mail

In response to the high cost of full Internet-based services lower-cost e-mail only services have been launched by many African ISPs. A large number of African e-mail users have resorted to free US and other overseas services such as Hotmail and Yahoo. There is also a rapidly-growing market for Internet kiosks, cyber cafés and other forms of public access. PCs have been installed for public use in phone shops, schools, police stations and clinics. Most hotels and business centers across the continent provide convenient Internet access for visitors.

Computers per 1,000 Population

	2001	2006	Avg. Growth
Algeria	7.1	10.5	8.3
Angola	1.2	6.7	51.6
Benin	1.5	5.7	28.7
Botswana	37.1	46.3	5
Burkina	1.4	2.2	10.1
Burundi	0.6	6.7	67.1
Cameroon	3.7	11	24.1
Cape Verde	65.1	106	11.6
Central African Rep.	1.8	2.8	10.7
Chad	1.4	1.5	2.8
Comoros	5.6	6.6	7.9
Congo	3.7	5.2	7.1
Congo Dem. Rep.	0.1	0.2	6.5
Côte d'Ivoire	6.8	17.1	22.2
Djibouti	9.4	23.2	18.5
Egypt	14.8	42.6	25.2
Equatorial Guinea	5.7	18.1	26.4
Eritrea	1.8	6.4	26.2
Ethiopia	1.1	3.7	28.6
Gabon	16.6	35.9	24.8
Gambia	11.9	18.9	9.9
Ghana	3.4	5.6	11.1
Guinea	3.8	4.9	6.1
Guinea Bissau	1.8	1.8	...
Kenya	5.5	13.5	19.6
Lesotho	0.6	0.7	3
Liberia	...	...	...
Libya	23.8	21.5	-2
Madagascar	2.4	5.3	18.2
Malawi	1.1	1.8	10.6
Mali	1.4	3.8	21.4
Mauritania	10.2	25.8	20.4
Mauritius	108.6	167.7	9.4
Morocco	13.7	29.8	16.4
Mozambique	3.8	13.5	33.5
Namibia	53.7	121.6	21.3
Niger	0.5	0.7	8.5
Nigeria	6.2	8.3	6.2
Rwanda	1.2	2	9.5
São Tome & Principe	9.8	38.7	27.8
Senegal	17	20.7	5.1
Seychelles	146.3	186	5.4
Sierra Leone	...	...	...
Somalia	0.7	8.9	...
South Africa	67.4	82.1	4.3
Sudan	...	3.4	112.4
Swaziland	14.9	37	22.9
Tanzania	3.5	9	21.2
Togo	21.5	28.9	8
Tunisia	26.4	62.1	19.3
Uganda	2.7	16.7	44
Zambia	7	11.2	9.2
Zimbabwe	15.7	65.4	39.3
AFRICA	9.5	21.4	16.4

Source: ADB

Computers

Cellular phones with internet connectivity compensates in part for the low average computer ownership. Long before the rest of the world transformed phones into handheld computer devices they have served as Africa's affordable PCs. Problems related to web connectivity and access to software and hardware, are solved in part by this device.

Circuits

ITU points out that apart from fixed broadband third-generation (3G) mobile cellular networks seem to be holding great potential for many countries in the region. In November 2004, EMTEL in Mauritius was the first operator to launch mobile broadband. By the end of 2008, there were twelve countries in the region with commercially available mobile broadband networks, and a total of seven million mobile broadband subscriptions. Although penetration levels in Africa (0.9%) remain below those of developing countries (1.5%), and that of the world (6%), mobile broadband growth has been much stronger than fixed broadband. An increasing number of countries in Africa are deploying IMT-2000/3G networks.

User Profiles

A recent survey showed a preponderance of non-governmental organizations (NGOs), private companies and universities among users in Africa while the ratio of nationals to non-nationals varied between different countries. In Zambia, for example, only 44% of the users surveyed were nationals compared to 90% in Ghana. Most users are male—86% in Ethiopia, 83% in Senegal, and 64% in Zambia. The large majority of users are well educated—87% in Zambia and 98% of the respondents in Ethiopia had university degrees. Another recent survey limited to South Africa showed similar results: an average user that is male, between 26 and 30 years, speaking English with a high-school or university-level education.

Development

The UN Economic Commission for Africa has launched several initiatives to upgrade Africa's information and communication technology (ICT) capability. The African Information Society Initiative (AISI) is working towards a common National Information and Communication Infrastructure (NICI) plan.

TRANSPORT FACILITIES IN AFRICA

	Total Area (sq km)	Coastline (km)	Railroads (km) - total	Highways (km) Total	Paved Road	Unpaved or Gravel	Inland Waterways (km)	Marine Ports	Runway
Total									
ALGERIA	2,381,740	998	4,733	95,576	57,346	38,230		13	139
ANGOLA	1,246,700	1,600	3,189	73,828	8,577	65,251	1,295	8	289
BENIN	112,620	121	578	8,432	1,038	7,397		2	7
BOTSWANA	600,370	LL	888	11,514	1,600	9,914		0	100
BURKINA FASO	274,200	LL	620	16,500	1,300	15,200		0	48
BURUNDI	27,830	LL	0	5,900	640	5,260		1	4
CAMEROON	475,440	402	1,111	65,000	2,682	60,318	2,090	5	60
CAPE VERDE	4,030	965	0	1,100	680	420		3	6
CENTRAL AFRICAN REP.	622,980	LL	0	22,000	458	21,542	800	2	61
CHAD	1,284,000	LL	0	31,322	263	31,059	2,000	0	66
COMOROS	2,545	525	0	792	228	564		4	5
CONGO (BRAZZAVILLE)	342,000	169	797	11,960	560	11,400	1,120	5	41
CONGO (KINSHASA)	2,345,410	37	5,138	146,500	2,800	143,700	15,000	11	270
CÔTE D'IVOIRE	322,460	515	660	46,600	3,600	43,300	980	4	40
DJIBOUTI	22,000	314	97	2,900	280	2,620		1	13
EGYPT	1,001,450	2,450	4,895	47,387	34,593	12,794	3,500	9	91
EQUATORIAL GUINEA	28,050	296	0	2,760	NA	NA		3	3
ERITREA	121,320	2,234	307	3,845	807	1,796		2	20
ETHIOPIA	1,127,127	LL	681	24,127	3,289	20,838		0	98
GABON	267,670	885	649	7,500	560	6,940	1,600	6	69
GAMBIA, THE	11,300	80	0	3,083	431	2,652	400	1	1
GHANA	238,540	539	953	32,250	6,084	26,166	1,293	2	12
GUINEA	245,860	320	1,048	30,100	1,145	23,455	1,295	3	15
GUINEA-BISSAU	36,120	350	0	3,218	2,698	520		1	32
KENYA	582,650	536	2,650	64,540	7,000	4,150		3	246
LESOTHO	30,350	LL	2.6	7,215	572	6,643		0	29
LIBERIA	111,370	579	490	10,087	603	9,484		4	59
LIBYA	1,759,540	1,770	0	19,300	10,800	8,500	0	9	146
MADAGASCAR	587,040	4,828	1,020	40,000	4,694	35,306		5	138
MALAWI	118,480	LL	789	13,135	2,364	10,771	144	4	47
MALI	1,240,000	LL	642	15,700	1,670	14,030	1,815	1	33
MAURITANIA	1,030,700	754	690	7,525	1,685	5,840		5	28
MAURITIUS	1,860	177	0	1,800	1,640	160		1	5
MOROCCO	446,550	1,835	1,893	59,474	29,440	30,034		12	74
MOZAMBIQUE	801,590	2,470	3,288	26,498	4,593	21,905	3,750	5	192
NAMIBIA	825,418	1,572	2,341	54,500	4,080	50,420		2	135
NIGER	1,267,000	LL	0	39,970	3,170	36,800	300	0	29
NIGERIA	923,770	853	3,567	107,990	30,019	77,971	8,575	6	80
RWANDA	26,340	LL	0	4,885	880	4,005		3	7
SÃO TOMÉ & PRÍNCIPE	960	209	0	300	200	100		2	2
SENEGAL	196,190	531	905	14,007	3,777	10,230	897	7	24
SEYCHELLES	455	491	0	260	160	100		1	14
SIERRA LEONE	71,740	402	84	7,400	1,150	6,250	800	3	11
SOMALIA	637,660	3,025	0	22,500	2,700	19,800		5	76
SOUTH AFRICA	1,219,912	2,798	20,638	188,309	54,013	134,296		7	853
SUDAN	2,505,810	853	5,516	20,703	2,000	18,703	5,310	7	70
SWAZILAND	17,360	LL	297	2,853	510	2,343		0	18
TANZANIA	945,090	1,424	2,600	81,900	3,600	78,300		11	108
TOGO	56,790	56	532	6,462	1,762	4,700	50	2	9
TUNISIA	163,610	1,148	2,260	29,183	17,510	11,673		7	31
UGANDA	236,040	LL	1,300	26,200	1,970	24,230		3	29
ZAMBIA	752,610	LL	1,273	36,370	6,500	29,870	2,250	1	113
ZIMBABWE	390,580	LL	2,745	85,237	15,800	69,437		2	471

LL: Landlocked

Source: US Department of Transport - World Directory of Transport

TRANSPORT

Africa is a vast, sparsely populated continent with only 19% of its people within 100 kilometers of the coast. With the exception of the Nile, Niger and a few others, most of Africa's rivers are seasonal or not navigable. There are few natural harbors. Rough terrain, varying from deserts to mountain ranges pose special challenges in rail and road construction. Fiscal shortfalls and other priorities have led to the decay of existing roads and railways. Lack of proper infrastructure has hampered trade and economic development and has become a priority.

Rail & Road

Sub-Saharan Africa accounts for only 3 per cent of the rail transport of developing countries, but has 17 per cent of its population and 7 per cent of its GDP. The OECD reports that less than a fifth of Africa's road network is paved compared to over a quarter in Latin America and over two fifths in South Asia. Even the paved roads are severely affected by overloading of trucks and poor drainage, posing special hazards. Only 16% of all roads are paved. While more than 80% of the unpaved roads are in fair condition, 85% of rural feed roads are in a poor state. Although Africa fares better than East or South Asia in the length of roads per capita, it is worse off in terms of road density per square kilometer of land. Poor transport in many areas is considered one of the main reasons for Africa's low competitiveness. Road and maritime transport costs top those of other parts of the

Africa's Railroads, Harbors and Rivers

107

world. In recent years, for example, freight costs for imported goods shipped to West and East Africa were 70% higher and to landlocked countries in Africa twice as high as to Asian destinations. The cost of air freight between destinations in Africa (where such services are available) often runs as much as two to four times the rate for equivalent distances across the Atlantic. Experts have concluded that in many parts of Africa, transport costs are more of a barrier to free trade than tariffs.

Modes

Roads remain Africa's principal mode of moving people and freight—accounting for 80% of the total in almost every country. After major construction projects in the 1960s and 1970s on top of networks left by former colonial powers, Africa had nearly 2 million km of roads in the early 1990s, much of it in a state of neglect due to shortages in budgets for post-construction maintenance. Railroads, harbors and airports suffered the same fate. With few exceptions—notably South Africa where links are well maintained—large sections of Africa's rail transport needs upgrading. Many harbors and airports need to be enlarged and modernized to cope with larger freight demands.

Southern Africa—where a sophisticated network of railroads and highways as well as efficient harbors and state-of-the-art airports support a rapidly expanding trade that benefits both South Africa and its neighbors—serves as a model for the continent.

Sea ports

One of the few exceptions to the historically poor state of African port facilities is South Africa. Its developed port infrastructure includes the largest container terminal in Africa, at Durban, plus the biggest dedicated coal terminal in the world, at Richards Bay. The nation's ports handle cargo for domestic traders but they are also important gateways for cargo bound for or exported from the rest of Southern Africa. More than $10 billion is earmarked for improvements at South African harbors over the next five years as part of an effort to increase capacity and reduce freight costs. Other terminals in the region are also being developed to provide a level of competition.

Air Transport

While the global airline industry collectively lost $16 billion in 2008 and $10 billion in 2009, Africa's aviation market has been

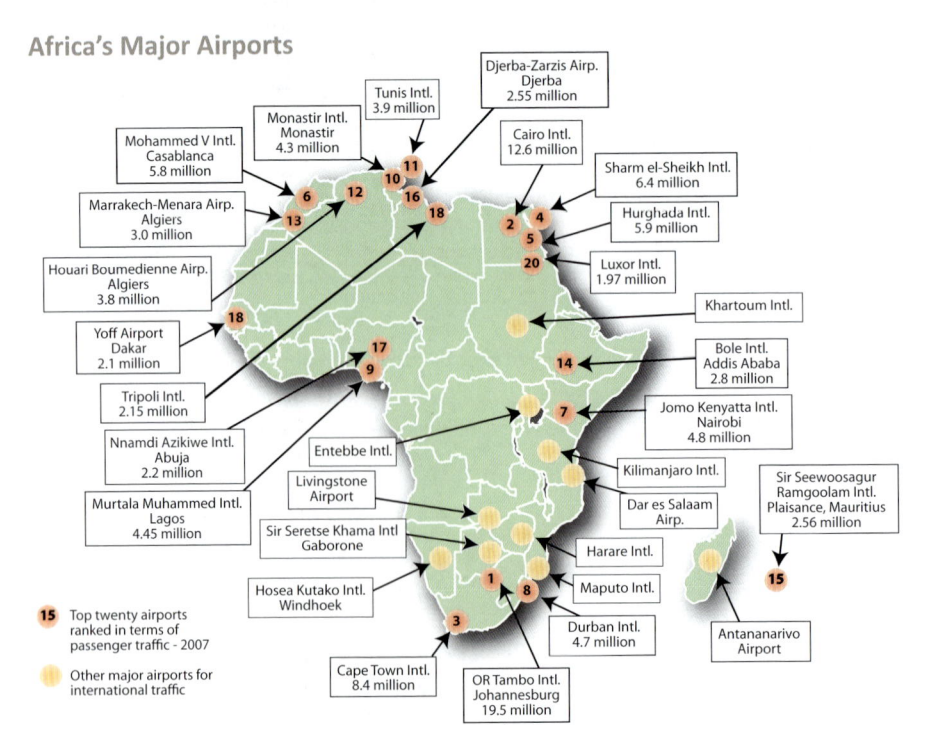

Africa's Major Airports

Djerba-Zarzis Airp. Djerba
2.55 million

Tunis Intl.
3.9 million

Monastir Intl. Monastir
4.3 million

Cairo Intl.
12.6 million

Mohammed V Intl. Casablanca
5.8 million

Sharm el-Sheikh Intl.
6.4 million

Marrakech-Menara Airp. Algiers
3.0 million

Hurghada Intl.
5.9 million

Houari Boumedienne Airp. Algiers
3.8 million

Luxor Intl.
1.97 million

Khartoum Intl.

Yoff Airport Dakar
2.1 million

Bole Intl. Addis Ababa
2.8 million

Tripoli Intl.
2.15 million

Jomo Kenyatta Intl. Nairobi
4.8 million

Nnamdi Azikiwe Intl. Abuja
2.2 million

Entebbe Intl.

Kilimanjaro Intl.

Sir Seewoosagur Ramgoolam Intl. Plaisance, Mauritius
2.56 million

Murtala Muhammed Intl. Lagos
4.45 million

Livingstone Airport

Dar es Salaam Airp.

Sir Seretse Khama Intl Gaborone

Harare Intl.

Hosea Kutako Intl. Windhoek

Maputo Intl.

15 Top twenty airports ranked in terms of passenger traffic - 2007

Durban Intl.
4.7 million

Antananarivo Airport

Other major airports for international traffic

Cape Town Intl.
8.4 million

OR Tambo Intl. Johannesburg
19.5 million

108

OR Tambo Airport   Photo: Les de Villiers

growing. The future projections are impressive. Experts predict that passenger volume in and to and from the African continent will increase by 6 percent per year until 2025. The largest growth is expected to be in Asian-African air traffic at a rate of 9 percent a year for the next decade. Air traffic between the U.S. and Africa has been growing at more than 5 percent annually. This growth potential has caught the attention of leading airlines across the globe and led to an infusion of services and resources. According to the International Air Transport Association, airlines increased the amount of flying capacity to and from Africa by 8.6 percent over the year ending in June 2010—outstripping all other regions in the world with the exception of the Middle East.

Future development

The World Bank estimates that African countries will need to spend the equivalent of 4 per cent of their GDP every year for the coming decade just on roads. There have been some modest gains in infrastructure construction and repair recent years in several countries where road and rail building and repair, harbor refurbishing and streamlining of air connections and airport facilities were undertaken. This is a costly affair. (For example, putting an all-weather road within 20 km reach of most of Ethiopia's population, will cost an estimated $4 billion). In the first twelve years since its inception in 1990 the *UN Transport and Communications Decade for Africa* (UNCTADA) raised almost $13 billion for projects. These included construction on the Trans-African Highway, railways in East and West Africa and liberalization of air transport. The Sub-Saharan African Transport Program (SSATP), administered by the World Bank, involves countries ranging from Burkina Faso in the northwest to Malawi in the East and Zimbabwe in the south. The US Overseas Private Investment Corporation (OPIC) underwrote an infrastructure fund to promote development in Africa, contributing together with other private equity funds towards an estimated $100 billion required for African infrastructural development over the next twenty years. These funds targeting Africa's infrastructural needs offer investors long-term appreciation in equity and overseas engineering and construction firms with plenty of work opportunities in Africa.

Building Bridges

The business opportunities presented by new construction and road repair have not been lost on contractors and suppliers in the United States and elsewhere. US-based Acrow Bridges (*www.acrowusa.com*) has provided solutions for bridge crossings across the world. In Africa it has been involved in the design and construction of some 140 bridges to reopen the lines of communication between villages and communities after devastating civil wars. In Sierra Leone, Liberia, and the Democratic Republic of Congo Acrow partnered with the UN by installing bridges to assist communities and to support UN peacekeeping. In Sudan an Acrow Bridge enabled the World Food Program to reach refugees with vital food supplies.

ACROW: BUILDING BRIDGES BETWEEN COMMUNITIES

During the past sixty years Acrow has provided solutions for bridge crossings across the world. The projects of Acrow cover a wide spectrum of types ranging from building urban bridges, feeder farm road bridges, railway bridges and the restoration of bridge crossings in disaster areas. On the African continent Acrow has been involved in the design, supply and construction of 450 bridges to reopen or reconnect the lines of communication between villages and communities. Acrow has worked for many years in Africa and we have found that simple bridges installed on rural feeder roads have the greatest impact for the expansion of individual prosperity. While Acrow has completed many urban projects, a company goal is to be the champion of improving bridge crossings in rural Africa, which is where more than 80% of the continent's population resides. In some countries Acrow partnered with the United Nations by supplying 60 bridges to assist communities by reopening river crossings so food and essential humanitarian items can be delivered to those in need and to also open the flow of commerce in countries such as South Sudan, Sierra Leone, Liberia, and the Democratic Republic of Congo.

Acrow Corporation is a US designer and manufacturer of prefabricated modular steel Acrow Bridges. The corporation's headquarters is based in Parsippany, New Jersey and the manufacturing facility is in Milton, Pennsylvania. Acrow Corporation also has offices in Lafayette, New Jersey—Mobile, Alabama—Denver, Colorado—and Saint Louis, Missouri. Our wholly owned subsidiary, Acrow Limited, has its headquarters near Toronto, Canada and a sales and engineering office in Vancouver, British Colombia.

Six decades

Throughout the past six decades Acrow has been called upon to provide solutions for bridge crossings and to design, fabricate, and mobilize bridges quickly, efficiently, and economically. On a number of occasions over the past ten years the company has been contracted to design and supply permanent Acrow Bridges for the purposes of development, attraction of foreign investment, expansion of prosperity, and to support previously established peace agreements. At other times the efforts of Acrow assisted with rebuilding bridge crossings following destruction by natural events such as the earthquake in Concepcion, Chile; the Christmas Tsunami in Aceh, Indonesia; Hurricane Ivan in Florida, USA; Hurricane Rita, in Florida, USA; and Hurricane Katrina, in Louisiana, USA. Acrow was also contracted to supply bridges following man made destructive events such as the war in Angola, the terrorist attack at Ground Zero in New York City, or when trucks carrying highly flammable fuel accidentally rolled over and exploded destroying bridges and closing Interstate Highways 95 in Connecticut and 80 in New Jersey. Another facet of Acrow's experience is supplying permanent bridges in North America, some of which are simple one span structures and others that are immensely complex because they open to allow the passage of ships.

Earthquake

An interesting project for Acrow was the emergency design and supply of a steel Acrow Bridge to the Army of Chile following the devastating earthquake

Acrow bridges span the world from Quincy, Massachu

that struck the City of Concepcion during February 2010. The bridge supplied is 1.44 kilometers long comprised of many 39 meter spans and providing a 7.35 meter wide roadway. The Army of Chile anticipates that bridge will be complete and commissioned by the end of the year of 2010.

Challenges

One complex permanent bridge project we designed and supplied was the Acrow Bridge across the Fore River in Massachusetts. Upon receipt of the Fore River contract our engineering team, which is comprised of civil, electrical, mechanical, and structural engineers, established what the existing field conditions were and proceeded to configure twin bridges that were comprised of 0.4 kilometers each (total of 0.8 km) and that included vertical lift bridge spans of 64 meters. When the movable spans are open they provide ships with more than 60 meters of clearance off of the water. Many obstacles were overcome to achieve the construction of these side by side bridges. Most of the obstacles were of a natural origin, such as the extremely harsh winter weather conditions and the highly soft soil conditions. Construction had to continue through the winter to achieve the specified opening dates even though winter snow and rain from the Atlantic Ocean impeded construction. At the end the project was delivered on time.

African Projects

Another set of remarkable projects that were on the African continent are: 1) In the Republic of Ghana we have an ongoing rural road development project where 100 Acrow Bridges will be installed over an 18 month period of time. These bridges will immensely improve the rural infrastructure so that farmers can efficiently ship their produce to the markets, attract foreign investment into regions that were once inaccessible, make it possible for citizens in the villages to have access to medical clinics, schools, and jobs, all of this resulting in an expansion of prosperity at both the personal and business levels. 2) The design and supply of approximately 290 Acrow Bridges to Angola. The projects took place in two phases. The first phase was from 2002 to 2004 and the second phase was during 2008. The bridges were installed by INEA to reopen the lines of communication between villages and communities that had been severed during the civil war. 3) In South Sudan west of Juba, a long Acrow Bridge was installed by the United Nations to support efforts for shipping food to western and northwestern Sudan to feed the refugees. 4) In The Gambia an Acrow Bridge with a length of 121 meters and a road width of 7.35 meters was constructed over the Gambia River creating a link that had not existed in the past. For the very first time, this region in The Gambia is able to transport goods and supplies with ease.

Katrina

Concluding with a fascinating project takes us to August 2005 when the City of New Orleans and the State of Louisiana were devastated by the effects of Hurricane Katrina. Acrow engineers were in Louisiana within 48 hours after the hurricane passed. We were faced with simple logistical problems as basic as where our engineers would sleep and eat. Cars became the home base and office. The Louisiana Department of Transportation and Development (LDoTD) was faced with a major Interstate Highway 10 link between the Cities of New Orleans and Slidell that was significantly destroyed and trying to solve how to reopen it quickly. LDoTD learned the procedures used by Florida following a hurricane for reopening Interstate Highway 10 by using Acrow spans. LDoTD worked closely with the Acrow engineers and engineers from a contractor to configure and plan the installation of 1.3 kilometers of Acrow Bridge on the westbound Interstate 10 bridge. 75 days later and after countless hours of work on everyone's part, the Acrow portions of the I-10 bridge were opened to traffic.

Acrow Corporation of America
181 New Road
Parsippany, New Jersey, 07054-5625
United States
Telephone: ++ 1-973-244-0080
Website: www.acrowusa.com
Email: sales@acrowusa.com

---

remote road in Liberia

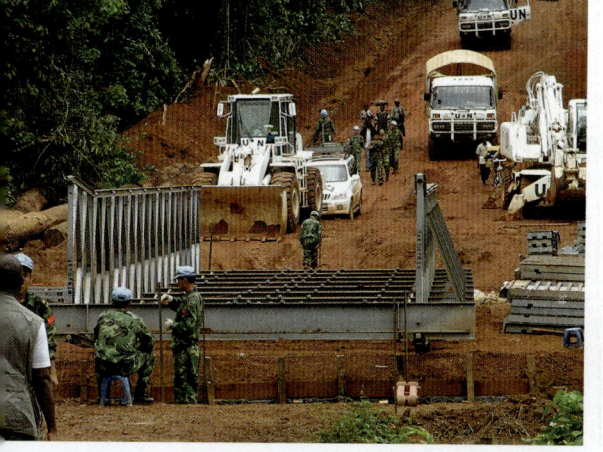

Agriculture

Africa has traditionally been seen as the continent of coffee, cocoa and cotton. Commercial and subsistence farming contribute between 30 and 40 percent of Africa's GDP. It provides employment for about 70% of the Continent's work force and is the primary source of livelihood for 65 percent of all Africans. In recent years, despite its importance as a job provider, agriculture has been allowed to slip far below its potential. Less than 7% of the crop-growing areas are irrigated, inputs are limited and mechanization often lacking. Most of the continent is vulnerable to droughts and there is little access to irrigation. Six countries—Egypt, Madagascar, Morocco, Nigeria, South Africa and Sudan—account for nearly 75 percent of the total irrigated land in Africa.

HIV/AIDS further undermines agricultural systems and threatens the food security of rural families. Global projections of food production show that even though the world population growth rate will be matched by a similar growth in food production and that food prices will continue to decline, Africa as a region will continue to be unable to meet its own food demand. The total annual shortfall is estimated to reach 150 million tons of grain by 2020. With some notable exceptions where nations actually manage not only to feed themselves but earn valuable foreign exchange through exports, agriculture in Africa at large has long been plagued by poor policies and institutional failures. Stringent state control, under-capitalization, inadequate rural infrastructures and antiquated farming methods coupled with low land productivity, vulnerability to natural disasters, and high levels of insecurity, have inhibited growth.

Potential

The UN Food and Agriculture Organization (FAO) maintains, however, that sub-Saharan Africa has the potential to increase agricultural production and become self-reliant. World Bank and IMF-inspired programs encourage research and new strategies to raise productivity. In its analysis of the agricultural crisis in Sub-Saharan Africa, the FAO identified arable land expansion, higher yields and increased cropping intensity as potential sources of boosting production. Biotechnology has shown that it can increase crop yields but research to date has been largely geared to reduce input and labor costs for large scale production systems in developed nations. There have been no serious investments in sorghum, groundnuts, peas and other crops that are important to large areas in Africa and other less developed semi-arid tropical regions.

NEPAD

The New Partnership for African Development (NEPAD) initiated the Comprehensive Africa Agriculture Development Program (CAADP) in conjunction with the African Development Bank, the UN Economic Commission for Africa and experts from UN Food and Agriculture Organization (FAO). The plan aims at boosting agricultural output to reduce hunger and to lower the cost of food imports. Improved agricultural yields will also have wider economic benefits, stimulating rural incomes and providing raw materials for African industry.

African Agriculture

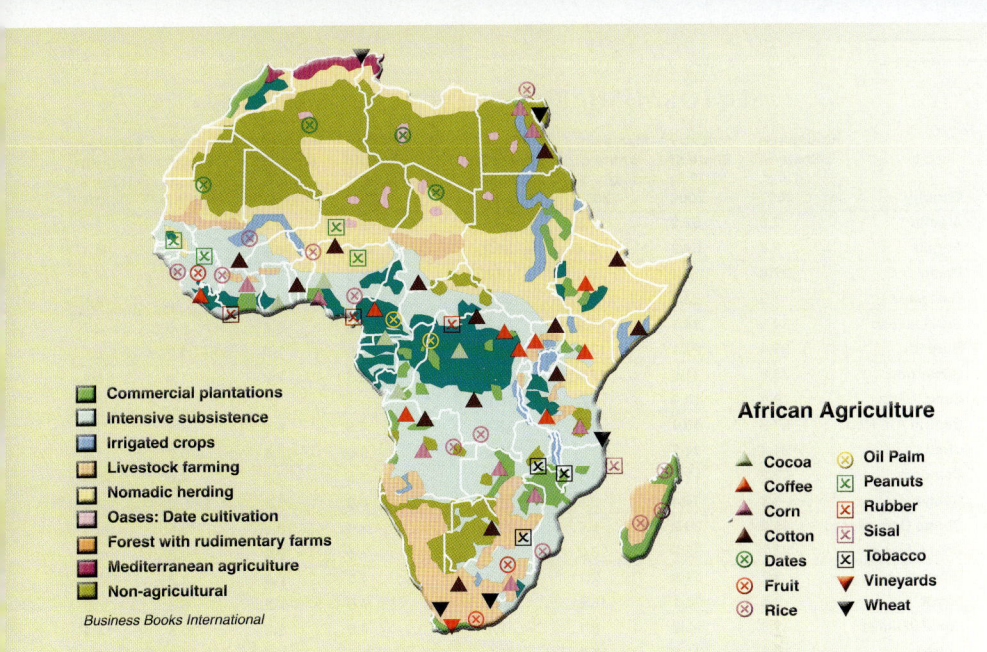

- Commercial plantations
- Intensive subsistence
- Irrigated crops
- Livestock farming
- Nomadic herding
- Oases: Date cultivation
- Forest with rudimentary farms
- Mediterranean agriculture
- Non-agricultural

Business Books International

- Cocoa
- Coffee
- Corn
- Cotton
- Dates
- Fruit
- Rice
- Oil Palm
- Peanuts
- Rubber
- Sisal
- Tobacco
- Vineyards
- Wheat

Food shortages

In March 2008 the FAO listed 44 African countries (out of a world total of 82) as low-income food-deficit countries (LIFDC). In East Africa millions of people faced serious food difficulties due to drought and conflict. In Sudan, insecurity remained a major factor in inhibiting access to food—especially in the troubled Darfur region. In Southern Africa, severe droughts, floods, economic constraints led to a sharp decline in harvests of maize in Zimbabwe, Swaziland, and Lesotho. The staple food for the region, maize, is particularly susceptible to drought. East and Central Africa are also expected see their agricultural capacity decline.

Exports

These crises tend to obscure Africa's importance as a supplier of cocoa, cotton and coffee, tobacco, tea, sisal, sugar cane, fresh fruit, palm oil, wines and meat to the world market. There is foreign investment in agricultural production and processing across the continent. As more countries are opening up their agricultural sectors to private entrepreneurs this involvement is bound to grow. With improved air links foreign firms have branched out from processing pyrethrum in Kenya to producing fresh cut flowers in Africa for the European and North American markets. Several overseas companies are involved in irrigation systems, pesticides and solar power.

Sorghum harvesting in Sudan and mango processing in South Africa

SECTORAL SHARE OF GDP & GROWTH

Country	Agriculture Share of GDP % 2007	Industry Share of GDP % 2007	Manufact. share of Industry % 2007	Services Share of GDP % 2007	Agriculture Growth Rate % 2007	Industry Growth Rate % 2007	Manufact. Growth % Indust. 2007	Services Growth Rate % 2007
Algeria	7.5	57.2	4.8	35.3	5.9	2.3	1.1	3.8
Angola	6.6	54.2	3.4	39.2	13.2	20.0	15.0	21.1
Benin	37.0	15.1	8.9	47.8	5.3	7.8	8.3	4.6
Botswana	1.9	53.5	3.4	44.5	2.0	5.6	...	6.8
BurkinaFaso	34.5	24.1	14.9	41.3	3.6	6.4	6.5	2.7
Burundi	35.4	21.1	13.5	43.5	5.0	7.5	5.0	0.0
Cameroon	20.6	31.8	17.9	47.6	3.3	2.2	1.8	5.4
Cape Verde	8.5	16.0	4.8	75.5	...	...	...	8.9
Central Afr. Rep.	57.8	16.1	2.6	26.1	4.5	6.0	8.1	1.0
Chad	21.4	44.7	1.7	33.9	3.0	-10.6	5.7	1.3
Comoros	52.2	11.1	4.5	36.7	3.5	2.0	3.0	-2.6
Congo	4.3	64.4	3.6	31.3	4.0	-3.2	5.0	4.2
Congo Dem. Rep.	43.2	26.2	5.9	30.6	2.0	10.0	9.5	8.4
Côte d'Ivoire	23.1	25.8	16.2	51.1	2.5	5.0	4.0	-0.6
Djibouti	3.7	17.9	2.7	78.4	4.5	6.0	4.2	3.3
Egypt	13.8	38.1	16.8	48.0	4.0	7.9	6.0	7.5
Equat. Guinea	1.8	95.6	0.1	2.7	4.0	9.9	20.6	13.4
Eritrea	18.6	31.6	15.4	49.8	1.0	3.0	3.0	0.7
Ethiopia	51.9	13.1	4.9	35.0	9.0	7.5	6.0	7.6
Gabon	5.5	62.9	5.4	31.5	3.1	5.2	3.7	6.6
Gambia	31.4	12.7	4.9	55.9	6.5	5.1	4.0	7.8
Ghana	36.6	23.8	8.2	39.6	6.7	6.0	5.0	5.3
Guinea	15.6	24.0	2.6	60.5	2.5	4.0	1.0	-0.7
GuineaBissau	44.2	16.6	12.4	39.2	2.5	2.5	2.5	2.5
Kenya	26.2	17.6	10.5	56.2	5.0	5.5	5.0	8.0
Lesotho	14.6	38.2	13.4	47.2	1.0	1.5	-2.0	9.3
Liberia	63.5	15.7	12.4	20.7	5.0	8.0	...	7.8
Libya	2.5	86.4	1.2	11.1	2.0	7.8	3.0	6.5
Madagascar	27.0	16.0	12.7	57.0	4.0	5.0	5.0	7.7
Malawi	35.2	18.6	11.6	46.2	5.0	6.0	5.0	8.4
Mali	36.9	23.7	8.4	39.4	3.3	1.1	-6.5	4.7
Mauritania	19.9	47.0	4.4	33.1	3.0	20.0	5.0	-11.3
Mauritius	4.7	28.1	19.9	67.1	0.5	4.8	3.5	6.2
Morocco	15.0	28.6	17.1	56.3	-2.0	5.0	4.0	2.2
Mozambique	28.8	25.8	15.6	45.4	8.7	7.0	8.0	6.5
Namibia	11.5	33.2	12.1	55.3	4.5	3.5	-5.0	3.7
Niger	45.4	11.2	5.6	43.4	6.9	4.0	2.7	2.9
Nigeria	23.2	55.5	3.8	21.2	4.5	3.2	3.5	2.0
Rwanda	43.8	14.2	6.3	42.0	5.0	5.5	5.0	4.6
Sao T.& Principe	11.6	14.5	3.1	73.8	3.0	10.0	3.5	7.3
Senegal	15.6	21.7	13.6	62.7	4.5	4.3	2.5	1.8
Seychelles	2.5	28.1	14.4	69.4	2.0	3.5	3.5	6.8
Sierra Leone	52.5	13.8	2.3	33.7	10.8	10.4	6.8	3.7
Somalia	...	...	...	...	...	...	...	...
South Africa	2.8	31.6	18.5	65.6	5.0	5.1	5.0	4.9
Sudan	25.9	34.2	6.4	39.9	5.0	20.0	3.0	10.3
Swaziland	9.2	50.3	35.3	40.5	1.9	1.6	1.8	2.7
Tanzania	33.2	23.9	9.7	42.8	5.5	9.9	9.1	5.7
Togo	43.0	23.1	10.8	33.8	3.5	2.5	6.5	1.1
Tunisia	12.1	32.1	18.5	55.8	5.0	4.3	5.5	7.7
Uganda	29.2	21.7	8.9	49.2	1.9	7.4	2.9	8.4
Zambia	21.3	35.3	11.0	43.4	4.0	9.5	5.2	4.2
Zimbabwe	40.0	40.4	33.7	19.5	-5.0	-5.0	-4.0	-6.7
AFRICA	14.0	41.7	10.9	44.3	4.4	6.2	3.9	4.5

Source: African Development Bank

Manufacturing

Africa's share of global manufactured products is minimal. With the exception of South Africa, which offers a broad range of manufactured goods, most other African countries are currently relying largely on the export of raw materials and agricultural products for more than one third of their GDP and are in urgent need of diversification. In many instances industrial activity is based on the extraction of a single product such as oil or diamonds or, as one economist put it, industrialization is likely to be linked to natural resource endowments rather than "foot loose" industries. That is bound to change as countries court foreign manufacturers with new incentives.

There is a concerted effort on the part of African nations to attract expertise and funding from abroad. The emphasis is on labor-intensive activity in rural regions and export-oriented manufacturing in free trade zones. Incentives range from tax holidays to subsidized training programs and facilities on government-sponsored sites and in state-owned buildings. In resource-rich countries there is increasingly an insistence on local beneficiation of minerals and fuels to create jobs and much-needed value-added income.

Southern Africa

Southern Africa—with South Africa at its hub—has the continent's strongest industrial base. Also in countries such as Mauritius, Swaziland, Zambia and Zimbabwe, manufacturing accounts for a substantial share of GDP. The sophistication of South Africa's manufacturing industry places it in the company of the world's 26 top industrial nations. Manufacturing, electricity, gas, water and construction constitute well over a third of this nation's total GDP compared to agriculture's 2.8% and mining's 7.8%. Some import substitution industries that were started during the apartheid era when South Africa was subjected to sanctions, grew rapidly with the help of large infusions of foreign capital and the opening up of foreign markets since 1994. Manufacturing and assembly in South Africa involve most of the larger multinationals in North America, Europe and the Far East and products range from autos and parts, to chemicals, textiles, machinery and pulp and paper. South African-made foreign brand cars and trucks are exported to South America, Australasia and China. Automotive parts from Johannesburg are sold to Detroit.

Flying geese

Africa has begun to experience what became known in the Far East as the "flying geese" phenomenon, with some of its more advanced countries opting for manufacturing in neighboring countries where wages are lower and incentives higher. Not only South Africa but even smaller nations such as Mauritius have, for economic reasons, shifted their manufacturing of garments and other textiles, handmade

Workers at an automotive plant in South Africa

toys and other labor-intensive operations to less developed nations in Africa, thus duplicating the process with which Asia has become so familiar in recent years.

Development Bank

The African Development Bank (ADB), the International Finance Corporation (IFC), the United Nations Development Programme (UNDP) and 15 other donor countries jointly established the Africa Project Development Facility (APDF) to assist African entrepreneurs. The Africa Project Development objective is to accelerate the development of productive private enterprises sponsored and owned by African entrepreneurs as a means of stimulating sustainable economic growth and productive employment in Sub-Saharan Africa.

Opportunities

Foreign direct investment in Africa is no longer solely concentrated in the traditional natural resources sector. Manufacturing and the service industries have received considerable amounts of foreign capital in recent years. Multinational textile and apparel manufacturers have established themselves in African countries to take advantage of trade preferences and quotas in European and North American markets. Products range from soft drinks to soap, leather goods to fashion clothing, cellphones to computers and automobiles to audio equipment. Foreign industries are setting up plants in free trade zones across the continent from Mauritius to Cape Verde.

Going global

Unleashed in the early 1990s when sanctions were scrapped, several of post-apartheid's South Africa's industrial giants have gone global, controlling markets abroad with their manufactures and buying out competitors. Starting with a dramatic takeover of the US-based Warren in the nineties, South Africa's Sappi has grown into the world's largest producer of coated fine paper and dissolving pulp.

Sectorial Composition of Africa's GDP - 2007

- Industry 41.7%
- Services 44.3%
- Agriculture 14.0%

Headquartered in Johannesburg, with manufacturing operations on four continents and in nine countries, and customers in more than a hundred countries, the company employs over 16,000 people. The group now produces over 15% of the world's coated fine paper, used in high quality publications. South Africa has long been a supplier of automobile and automotive parts to the rest of the world, including Detroit. Volkswagen, BMW and Mercedes Benz all manufacture in South Africa for export to other right-hand drive countries. The South African Motor Corporation (Samcor) exports locally assembled Mazdas to Britain. Vehicles are primarily manufactured in the industrial area around Johannesburg, in Mpumalanga, and in the Eastern and Western Cape provinces, using parts manufactured locally at more than 150 plants as well as some imported parts. Also Nissan and Toyota in manufacture automobiles and trucks in South Africa for export across the continent and overseas. The local market amounts to sales of more than 600,000 vehicles every year. The De Beers company has long been dominating the global diamond market while mining giants such as Anglogold and Billiton are rapidly taking over operations in

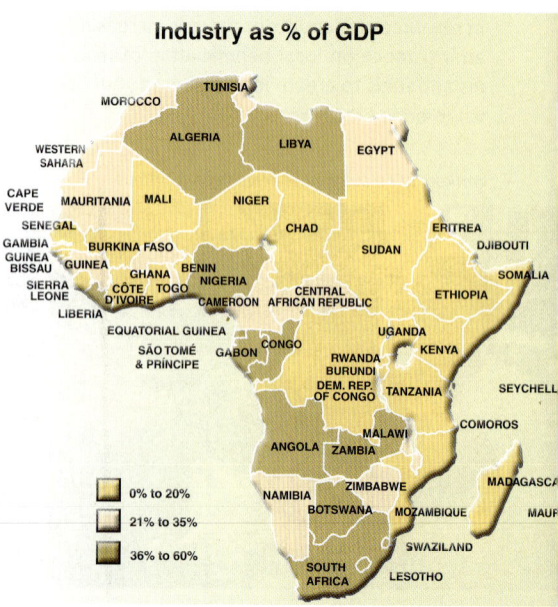

Industry as % of GDP

- 0% to 20%
- 21% to 35%
- 36% to 60%

other parts of the world. South African Breweries has established itself as one of the world's leading beer giants with acquisitions in Europe and the United States. Today the list of exports from South Africa runs the whole gamut from beer to barley, wines to windmills, chemicals to computers, textiles to titanium, and artifacts to automobiles—setting an example for the rest of the continent in its desire to diversify. In recent years South Africa has taken the lead in the industrial development of neighboring African countries as evidenced by the establishment of Mosal, a giant aluminum smelter in Mozambique, and numerous major mining and manufacturing projects elsewhere on the continent.

Low Share

However, overall, Africa has been lagging far behind other developing regions in taking advantage of opportunities to manufacture on an outsource basis for major corporations in the industrialized world. The United Nation's report on Economic Development in Africa 2008 found that in Sub-Saharan Africa exports from the manufacturing sector amounted to only 26% of total exports. This was the lowest proportion of all regions. Only eight African countries—including Botswana, South Africa, and Namibia—had manufacturing exports making up more than 10% of their GDP. The report contended that if Africa wished to increase its industrial output and exports, governments would have to take steps to deal with several key issues, including poor infrastructure, high entry costs for businesses, low investor protection, and cumbersome tax systems. The UN experts argue that many African manufacturers are too small to benefit from the efficiencies achieved by larger firms and suggested that governments should enact measures to help expand these firms to international standards. According to the report only a few African countries have taken the initiative to produce value-added products—and where they did, their share was very low. Africa's exports of manufactured goods represent only 0.82% of the world total.

Asia Factor

The intensification of ties with Asia in terms of aid, trade and FDI holds both benefits and challenges for Africa. African exports, mostly raw materials, to China have more than quadrupled between 2000 and 2008. A growing demand in Asian offers greater export opportunities for African manufactures and creates new opportunities for employment. The massive export of South African-made Volkswagens to China and other Far-Eastern markets is a good example of how Africa may benefit. However, smaller African manufacturing firms also face the risk of loosing their own domestic markets as they find themselves unable to compete with an increased flow of cheap imports from Asia.

World slump

As elsewhere in the world the current economic slump has impacted negatively on manufacturing industries in Africa. In South Africa, the leading industrial nation on the continent, insufficient power supplies and the high cost of fuel have put expansion plans and new developments on hold.

South African-manufactured Volkswagens for China

Banking

In recent years banking has been strengthened most parts of the Africa through financial liberalization, restructuring, and other reforms, and became more competitive and transparent. There is an ongoing process of consolidation through mergers, privatization and liquidations. Foreign banks are today allowed in countries where until recently banking was tightly controlled and overseas competition excluded. In countries where public sector institutions are the largest users of banking services, reforms are allowing them to decide whether to bank with public, local private or foreign banks.

In the immediate post-colonial era most African governments interfered in their financial sectors by nationalizing existing institutions and creating state-owned banks. Credit was curtailed and strict exchange controls introduced. In the 1980s when it finally became apparent that this approach failed miserably, a wave of reform spread across Africa. The transformation to freer financial markets did not happen without cost. In many instances the larger spread between lending and deposit rates led to higher local interest rates. Some governments still cling to failing state banks and a number of undercapitalized institutions spawned in the process of reform are experiencing problems. In general, however, the freer financial environment has been a boon to both domestic and foreign investors. In the process financial products have become increasingly sophisticated and widely available.

Electronic

African banks are making moving towards electronic banking. While South Africa with its ample landlines compete with the best in the world in the sophistication of its electronic services other countries, including the continent's most populous Nigeria, are facing challenges. Due to a shortage of landline connectivity Nigeria had to resort to an off-line smartcard payment system. In Ghana electronic banking relies on a satellite service company. Internet banking has been introduced to more than 15 African countries. In emerging markets such as Nigeria, Ivory Coast and Senegal where the majority of merchants are still off-line, magnetic stripe cards are often still rendered useless.

Rankings

In its October 2009 issue *African Business* notes that for the first time the joint assets region's top 100 banks exceeded one trillion US dollars. North Africa with 40 formed the largest grouping of top 100 banks, followed by West Africa with 26, Southern Africa with 20 and East Africa with 12. Only 2 banks in central Africa made it to the list. On soundness, measured in terms of the ratio between average capital and assets, Nigerian lenders topped the magazine's rankings with 16.13%—ahead of Kenya (15.45%), South Africa (12.89%) and Egypt (12.32%). Banks in the smaller and emerging markets recorded the strongest return on equity with Botswana leading the way (53.14%), followed by Angola and Mozambique (40%) and Mauritius (31%). South Africa at 27% and Egypt (22.81%) were above average with Nigeria (15.43%) and Morocco (14.14%), below.

Africa's top 100 Banks by region
- Central Africa 2
- East Africa 12
- West Africa 26
- Southern Africa 20
- North Africa 40

Source: African Business

Financial hub

South African banks continue to overshadow the rest of the region. The capabilities of the South African financial groups compare favorably with those of the best in the developed world. In recent years they have contributed largely to the upgrading of banking systems and the financial infrastructure in other parts of the African continent.

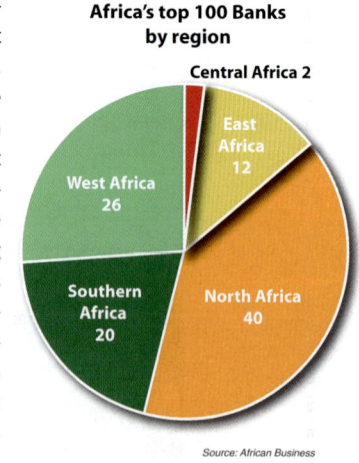

TOP FIFTY BANKS IN AFRICA

	Bank	Country	Capital US$m	Assets US$m	Profits US$m	Return on Investment
1	Standard Bank Group (Stanbank)	South Africa	7,275	162,133	2,155	29.6
2	FirstRand Banking Group	South Africa	6,303	106,156	1,968	31.2
3	Absa Group	South Africa	4,742	83,110	1,634	34.4
4	Investec Bank	South Africa	4,324	55,679	473	10.9
5	Nedbank Group	South Africa	3,594	60,905	953	26.5
6	Zenith International Bank	Nigeria	2,935	15,155	476	16.2
7	First Bank of Nigeria	Nigeria	2,808	13,339	101	3.6
8	Attijariwafa Bank	Morocco	2,637	32,362	454	17.2
9	Groupe Banques Populaires	Morocco	2,606	23,370	356	13.7
10	Oceanic Bank	Nigeria	1,750	8,265	183	10.4
11	EFG-Hermes	Egypt	1,715	2,439	274	15.9
12	Intercontinental Bank	Nigeria	1,699	11,801	387	22.7
13	Libyan Arab Foreign Bank	Libya	1,614	16,560	113	7
14	Banque Extèrieur d'Algerie	Algeria	1,605	33,424	314	19.6
15	United Bank for Africa	Nigeria	1,541	14,181	407	26.4
16	Access Bank	Nigeria	1,431	10,055	160	11.2
17	Bank PHB	Nigeria	1,421	8,798	165	11.6
18	Guaranty Trust Bank	Nigeria	1,382	6,225	232	16.8
19	National Bank of Egypt	Egypt	1,374	41,180	70	5.1
20	Fidelity Bank	Nigeria	1,163	4,539	138	11.8
21	Ecobank Transnational	Togo	1,158	5,306	111	9.6
22	First City Monument Bank	Nigeria	1,121	3,949	116	10.3
23	Banque Marocaine du Com. Ext. (BMCE)	Morocco	1,032	18,807	179	17.3
24	Diamond Bank	Nigeria	993	5,122	100	10.1
25	Credit Populaire d'Algerie	Algeria	980	9,925	139	14.2
26	Commercial International Bank (CIB)	Egypt	950	10,413	338	35.6
27	Banque Misr	Egypt	941	24,209	32	3.4
28	Union Bank of Nigeria	Nigeria	931	8,819	136	14.6
29	African Bank	South Africa	922	3,805	323	35
30	Ban. Marocaine pour le Comm. (BMCI)	Morocco	864	7,431	91	10.5
31	Skye Bank	Nigeria	776	6,703	184	23.7
32	National Sociête Gendrale Bank	Egypt	615	8,393	236	38.4
33	Stanbic IBTC Bank	Nigeria	613	2,766	74	12
34	Banque Nationale d'Algerie	Algeria	599	13,796	101	16.9
35	The Mauritius Commercial Bank	Mauritius	566	5,118	172	30.4
36	Banco de Foment° Angola	Angola	544	6,306	251	46.1
37	Arab International Bank	Egypt	534	4,200	48	9
38	Banco Africano de Investimentos (BAI)	Angola	526	7,625	166	31.6
39	Societe Generale Marocaine de Banques	Morocco	485	6,230	97	20
40	Commercial Bank of Ethiopia	Ethiopia	473	5,221	141	29.8
41	Arab African International Bank	Egypt	472	7,695	167	35.4
42	Banque du Caire	Egypt	455	8,876	9	2
43	Banque Internationale Arabe de Tunisie	Tunisia	446	5,574	25	5.6
44	HSBC Bank Egypt	Egypt	420	6,207	239	56.9
45	Credit du Maroc	Morocco	405	4,766	45	11.1
46	CNEP Banque	Algeria	405	9,416	n/a	n/a
47	BGFI Bank	Gabon	399	1,815	56	14
48	Societe Tunisienne de Banque (STB)	Tunisia	364	4,307	24	6.6
49	BNP Egypt	Egypt	352	3,267	45	12.7
50	Bank of Alexandria	Egypt	350	5,728	75	21.4

Source: African Business, October 2009 issue

Reforms

In North Africa countries such as Egypt, Morocco, Tunisia and Algeria have gone through major structural adjustments. In Morocco, which has led the way in both reform and privatization in the region, Wafa Bank, with 12 per cent of total Moroccan deposits, is a prime example of successful diversification. The same trend is evident in Tunisia, albeit at a slower pace due to a higher degree of state ownership of banks and a paternalistic political system. Challenges in both Morocco and Tunisia are much less severe than those faced in Algeria where the state-run banking sector has had a difficult time adapting to economic reforms. Egyptian banking has undergone substantial liberalization in the past decade. Even though the privatization of Egypt's "big four" state banks was delayed, private banks such as Commercial International Bank (CIB), Misr International Bank (MIBank) and Egyptian American Bank (EAB) have made great strides in gaining market share. Today the private sector accounts for some 20% of the total and is by far the most profitable with a return on equity (ROE).

Foreign Banks

Foreign banks have provided know-how and much-needed support for African financial systems in need of a fresh inflow of capital to buttress economic reforms. They have been useful catalysts for inward investment and trading by offering financing and expertise and, in some cases, acting as go-betweens to clinch deals. Often foreigners prefer the comfort zone of a familiar bank when dealing with remote and unfamiliar countries. US, French and British banks have a presence across the continent. In fact, in its review of the world banking scene, the World Bank concluded that Africa had the world's highest penetration of foreign banks.

Starting point

Most foreign banking institutions setting their sights on Africa start in South Africa where a sophisticated financial market presents no surprises and minimum risk. However, to make serious inroads in this market foreign enterprises have to spend substantial sums as opposed to relatively small outlays elsewhere on the continent. Competition is fierce among 30 local banking institutions—five of them rank among the top 300 worldwide—and 24 foreign-controlled banks. Another 30 foreign banking institutions have representatives stationed in the country. The largest South African banks not only have branch operations in neighboring countries but further afield in Africa.

Regional

Cross border cooperation and greater cohesiveness in banking, insurance and stock market activity within groupings such as the Southern African Development Community, the Common Market for Eastern and Southern Africa (COMESA) and the Economic Community of West African States (ECOWAS) should make the market more attractive for prospective foreign participants.

ADB

The African Development Bank, headquartered in Abidjan, focus on rural development, human capital development and the private sector. Its shareholders are the 53 countries in Africa as well as 24 countries in the Americas, Europe and Asia. The financial resources of the Bank comprises subscribed capital, reserves, funds raised through borrowings, and accumulated net income.

Wireless

Wireless and smart card technologies have been useful in the development of services in previously un-banked areas. South African banks and a local mobile phone companies joined forces to help the poor in remote areas who have never had access to banks, cash machines or credit cards.

Profitability contributors in African banking

Southern Africa, West Africa, Central Africa, East Africa

Source: KPMG Banking Survey 2004

TOURISM

In Henry IV Shakespeare spoke of "Africa and golden joys" and two thousand years ago Pliney the Elder coined the phrase "Out of Africa always something new." Foreigners who travel to the continent to go on safari or to get a close-up look at tribal life or the antiquities of Egypt find much else that is new in Africa's golden joys. There are breathtaking scenes, vast deserts, rainforests, savannah plains, pristine beaches, gracious wine estates, world class hotels, elegant restaurants, challenging golf courses, white water rafting, fishing and other recreational pursuits.

Tourism is the single biggest industry in the world. Considering its wealth of wildlife, ancient civilizations, cultural diversity, superb scenery, magnificent beaches, and sunny climate, Africa should be getting a lion's share of the world's growing tourist traffic. However, recent figures still show Africa with only 5.2% of the world total.

The continent's apparent inability to pull in larger numbers of visitors has been ascribed to a variety of factors including lack of promotion, insufficient infrastructure, remoteness and widely held perceptions of a continent plagued by disease, war and crime. Sophisticated and discerning tourists who will never entertain the thought of cancelling a visit to France or Germany because of a war in the Balkans eschew all of Africa when war breaks out in an area thousands of miles removed from the country on their itinerary. At the same time there are encouraging signs of increased investment from abroad in infrastructure and other tourist-related amenities that should increase Africa's competitiveness. It is slowly gaining on the rest of the world.

Statistics released by the UN World Tourism Organization (UNWTO) showed Africa recording the best growth in arrivals in 2008 (+3.6%) after the Middle East (18.2%) and

INTERNATIONAL ARRIVALS

	Arrivals million 2009	Share % 2009	Growth % 2008/9
WORLD	880	100	-4.2
EUROPE	392.2	52.2	-5.6
Northern Europe	53.4	6.1	-5.5
Western Europe	146.0	16.6	-4.7
Central/Eastern Europe	89.9	10.2	10.1
Southern/Mediter. Eu.	170.0	19.3	-3.8
ASIA & PACIFIC	181.2	20.6	-1.5
North-East Asia	98.1	11.1	-2.9
South-East Asia	62.2	7.1	0.65
Oceania	10.9	1.2	-1.7
South Asia	10.1	1.1	-1.5
AMERICAS	140.6	16.0	-4.9
North America	92.1	10.5	-5.8
Caribbean	19.6	2.2	-2.3
Central America	7.6	0.9	-7.4
South America	21.3	2.4	-2.1
AFRICA	46.0	5.2	3.3
North Africa	17.6	2.0	2.5
Sub-Saharan Africa	28.4	3.2	3.8
MIDDLE EAST	53.0	6.0	-5.1

Source: World Tourism Organization

Philae Temple, Aswan, Egypt

CULTURES OF AFRICA

In Long Walk to Freedom Nelson Mandela vividly recalls the Xhosa circumcision ceremony at age sixteen that signalled his entry into manhood. Even though this *abakwetha*, performed by an elder (*ingcibi*) with a spear or assegai and without any anaesthetic, caused excruciating pain, no one was to show any outward emotion. "A boy may cry; a man conceals pain," Mandela explains. "I had now taken the essential step in the life of every Xhosa man. Now I might marry, set up my own home and plough my own field."

Until this day the *abakwetha* is performed in the Xhosa region of South Africa. So are numerous other unique ceremonies across the face of Africa, designed to build character and honor, solidify marriages and strengthen family and community ties. Everyone of these ceremonies—even those that might seem as bizarre to foreigners as certain customs in their world might appear to the Africans—have a definite purpose and a deeper meaning.

Today much of the travel to Africa is inspired by a desire to learn more about the cultures and customs of this continent with its diverse peoples. African-American author Henry Louis Gates has done much to educate the outside world about the hidden Wonders of Africa in a television series, revealing its rich cultures and ancient civilizations unknown to many in the Western world.

In Delgo, Gates was invited to participate in a traditional Nubian wedding, in Ethiopia he mingled with Christians whose faith predated that of England by several hundred years and whose icons were all in black, and in Dogon he was allowed a glimpse of the circumcision cave with its fascinating wall paintings—an area totally closed to women.

But it took two enterprising women to produce what could arguably be described as the most extensive and impressive photographic record of Africa's ceremonies. Accomplished Africanists and photographers Carol Beckwith and Angela Fisher collaborated in the production of a dramatic two volume presentation of African Ceremonies, published by Henry M. Abrams Inc., New York. (www.abramsbooks.com).

"Living in traditional African societies has made us aware of the value that rites of passage have for the individual and the community. Ceremonies that mark the stages of life from birth to death provide clear definitions of what is expected of the individual and give him or her a sense of identity and belonging," write Beckwith and Fisher. "Each rite begins with a gift or an offering and nothing is taken from the land without giving something back to it. Survival depends on this basic principle."

While no one can truly expect to experience more than a fraction of the magnificent rites, rituals and ceremonies which took Beckwith and Fisher ten years to record, a mere sampling of these magnificent color photographs is bound to wet the appetite to know more through travel.

Himba, Namibia   Masaai, Kenya    Fulani, Mali    Ashanti, Ghana

© Carol Beckwith & Angela Fisher

ahead of the Americas (+2.9%), Asia and Pacific (1.2%) and Europe (+0.4%). In sheer numbers, however, Europe with 392 million, Asia and the Pacific with 181 million and the Americas with 140 million dwarfed both the Middle East (53 million) and Africa (46 million). Still, in 2008 international tourism earned $30 billion for Africa.

Economic crisis

Worldwide international tourist arrivals declined by 4.2 percent in 2009 as the global economic crisis deepened. The meltdown that began in September 2008 caused a decline in tourism to all parts of the world during 2009, with the notable exception of Africa. While Europe (-5.6%), Asia and the Pacific (-1.5%), the Americas (-4.9%) and the Middle East (-5.1%) all showed a negative growth in 2009, Africa managed to post an overall increase of 9%, helped in part by the buildup in worldwide publicity generated by the upcoming FIFA Soccer World Cup in South Africa.

World Cup

As was expected the staging of the Soccer World Cup in South Africa during June and July 2010 spiked tourist arrivals in the Sub-Saharan region. Statistics released by the World Tourism Organization showed Sub-Saharan Africa recording a growth of 13.1 percent in arrivals from January until October 2010. For a month an accumulated worldwide audience of some 40 billion people watched the world's premier sport event unfold in ten venues across South Africa. What they saw on their television screens was nothing remotely close to the stereotypical Dark Continent fit only for missionaries and hunters. Instead they were treated to images of state-of-the-art stadiums, airports, rapid transit systems, and modern skyscrapers. It stands to reason that only South Africa as the host country but all of Africa will benefit in the long-term from the new branding of a continent that has for too long been painted in terms of the past. It will no doubt inspire some of those who could not join the almost half a million overseas fans who converged on South Africa to see the drama unfold before their very own eyes, to visit in future.

Future growth

There is little doubt on the part of both economists and travel experts that with the proper planning and promotion Africa is bound to reap as much benefit from tourism as it has in the past from minerals. The UNWTO envisages Southern Africa within the next two decades outstripping the rest of the continent in the number of tourists it attracts. The world organization forecasts that in 2020 the number of travelers to Southern Africa alone will increase to 36 million in comparison with a total of 19 million for North Africa. East Africa is projected to be third with 17 million.

Boeing 777-200LR Worldliner™

GO THE DISTANCE

Distance runnig is synonymous with the Ethiopian culture. starting from Abebe Bikila, the winner of the Olympic Marathon gold medal in Rome and Tokyo in 1960 and 1964 respectively, to the living legend Haile Gebrselassie, one of the greatest distance runners in history. with 22 world records so far and many more to come, Ethiopians dominate all major long distance competitions in the world. In line with this tradition, Ethiopian Airlines is about to establish itself in the ultra-long distance arena as well.

Ethiopian Airlines will be the only airline to offer a direct, non-stop service from Washington DC to Addis Ababa. It will also be the first airline in Africa to operate the B777-200LR; the longest range airplane in the world. Unrivaled range of the B777-200LR, our extensive network in Africa and our modern hub in Addis Ababa will enable Ethiopian Airlines to offer the most convenient service to Sub-Saharan Africa. Come with us and see why we are the New Spirit of Africa.

Haile Gebrsela

FLY GREENER with
Ethiopian
WWW.ETHIOPIANAIRLINES.COM

Ethiopian
የኢትዮጵያ
THE NEW SPIRIT OF AFRICA

Discovery

Ancient Egypt and other exotic North African destinations have long intrigued the European traveler. The discovery of Sub-Saharan Africa came much later. It was only through the personal accounts of Livingstone, Stanley and others that Europe and North America became aware of the unique attractions of this part of the continent. Tourists followed in the footsteps of adventurers and hunters to the untamed hinterland in search of something new. They came from all corners of the world—the writers and the visionaries, the presidents and the princes, the rich and the regulars, the famous and the not so familiar.

Under-Traveled

Still, Africa remains surprisingly under-travelled for a continent with all its offerings and charm. According to the experts, it should be getting a much larger chunk of the world's tourist traffic. Many countries on the continent stand to gain almost as much from tourism as they did in past years from the exploitation of other natural resources such as oil, gas, gold, platinum and other precious and strategic minerals. At a total of $30 billion in revenues tourism is already second only to oil as a source of revenue for Africa.

Features

In the far north there is the mighty Nile, quietly flowing through the world's oldest civilization and at the southern tip majestic Table Mountain that impressed the world's seafarers since the days of Vasco da Gama and Francis Drake. And in-between there are the likes of Lake Victoria, Lake Tanganyika, Victoria Falls, Mt. Kilimanjaro and the Ngorongoro Crater. There are the Atlas mountains in the northeast, bordering the Sahara Desert, and there is a strip on the southwest coast aptly called the Skeleton Coast. There are tens of major animal kingdoms and literally hundreds of smaller wildlife estates where the exotic animals of the ark roam free for all to see. Africa offers visitors the treasures of Ancient Egypt and the throbbing excitement of the modern world.

Glimpse of Eden

In *A Glimpse of Eden*, Evelyn James declares: "Nothing can really prepare you for Africa. It is too full of extremes and contrasts, too immense, a spectrum of creation so much wider and more vivid than anywhere else that it seems to require a new set of senses, or the rediscovery of lost ones." Pres. Theodore Roosevelt, who spent considerable time on the continent, wrote from Khartoum on March 15, 1910: "There are no words that can tell the hidden spirit of the wilderness, that can reveal its mystery, its melancholy, and its charm."

Cultures

Egypt has long fascinated travelers from abroad with its rich offerings in ancient architecture and artifacts. More recently other parts of Africa have also become choice destinations for foreigners in search of history and culture. Gorée Island draws hundreds of thousands of visitors who wish to step back into the days when millions of slaves were sorted and shipped like cargo from this little island near Dakar in Senegal to the New World. While Afri-

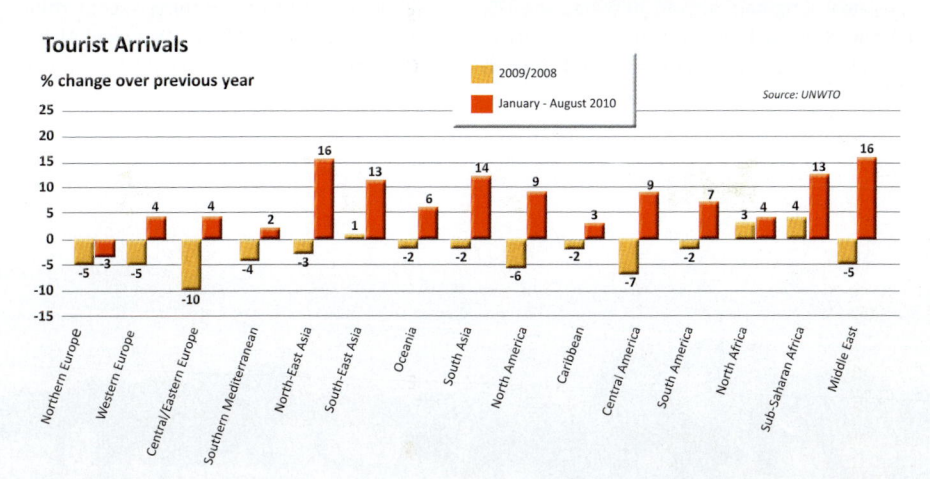

Tourist Arrivals
% change over previous year
Source: UNWTO

Region	2009/2008	January - August 2010
Northern Europe	-5	-3
Western Europe	-5	4
Central/Eastern Europe	-10	4
Southern Mediterranean	-4	2
North-East Asia	-3	16
South-East Asia	1	13
Oceania	-2	6
South Asia	-2	14
North America	-6	9
Caribbean	-2	3
Central America	-7	9
South America	-2	7
North Africa	3	4
Sub-Saharan Africa	4	13
Middle East	-5	16

Durban beach, South Africa

can Americans travel to Africa in search of their ancestral roots many more go simply to witness and experience the rich and diverse cultures of the continent. It comes replete with an array of local cuisines that appeals to every palate from mild to fiery spicy. Even though much of the continent's charm is in unspoiled nature, travelers are always assured of comfortable accommodation within easy distance from the most exotic parts.

Going there

Air services are provided by a number of international and domestic airlines utilizing the latest long-haul aircraft between the US, Europe, the Far East, Australasia and Africa. Two of Africa's leading airlines, South African Airways and Ethiopian Airlines, provide direct links between the continent and US, Europe and other parts of the world.

Safari

Major safari destinations in Southern and East Africa lure visitors from all parts of the world. National and private parks offer a wide variety of accommodations and services ranging from super de luxe to less extravagant. Regardless of the price tag the experience is guaranteed to be exquisite for all those who wish to view Africa's wildlife in their natural habitat.

"We couldn't do anything except think about getting back to Africa. We talked Africa, we dreamed Africa, we even held African par-

Katavi Plains (Photo: Les de Villiers)

ties. It's something in your blood. A combination of the climate, the landscape, the wildlife, the whole atmosphere. You somehow feel that you're missing everything when you're not there."

This passage in *The White Lions of Timbavati*, by American wildlife expert Chris McBride, neatly encapsulates the experience. Going on safari is addictive and few people stop at one trip.

There are those who contend that promoting Africa on the basis of its wildlife is perpetuating the misconception that it is a jungle. These are the same critics who are also opposed to the idea of showing off Africa's rich tribal culture in fear that the world might think that it is not fit for Western-style business. Africa tourist promoters, however, maintain that there is nothing wrong in luring tourists to the Continent on the basis of these two unique selling propositions. While other parts of the world also offer pristine beaches, spectacular scenery, bustling city life, and good restaurants, none can compete with Africa in wildlife and a wealth of culture, with more than a thousand languages and dialects spoken.

Side benefits

Foreign visitors usually overnight in cities before they are transported by bushplane to lion country. Many take side trips to meet the locals, eat in good restaurants, taste the wines and get a feel for the country. They buy local products

AFRICA'S NATIONAL PARKS

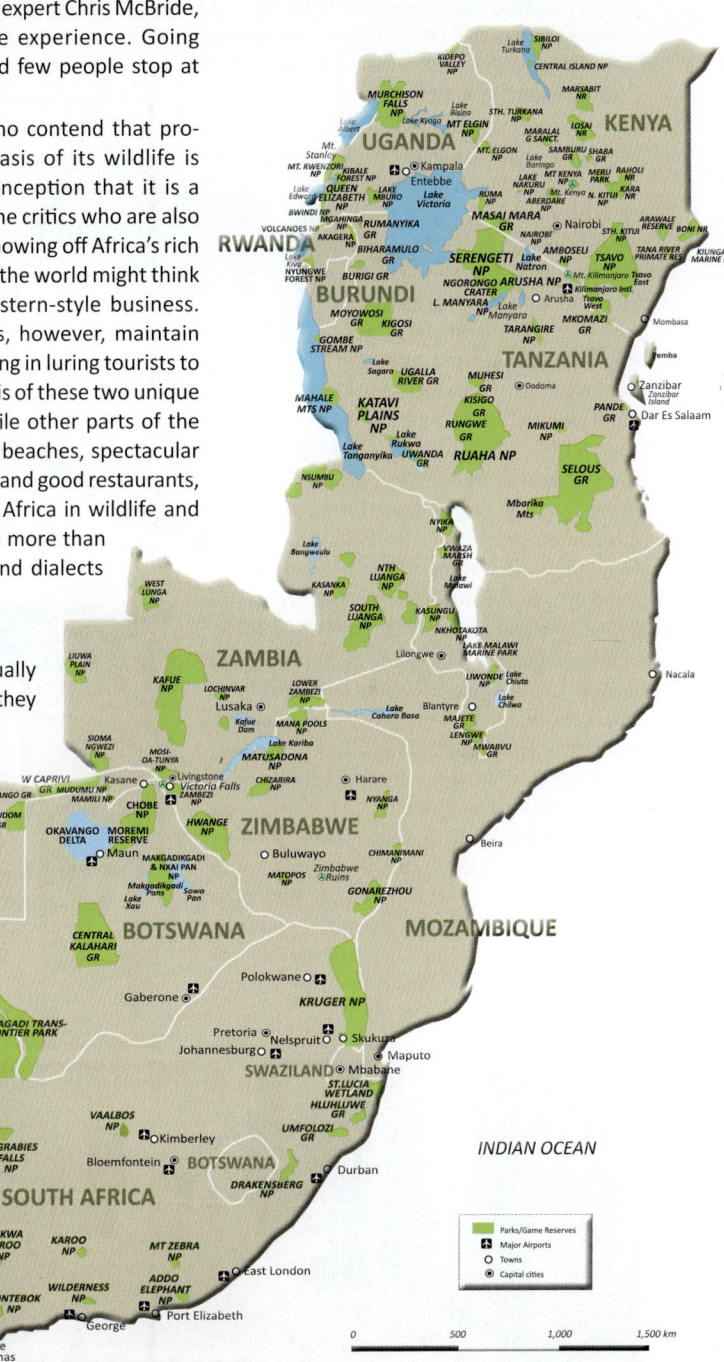

Safari Chic

Safari has become synonymous with travel to Africa, fittingly so because that is what the word means in Swahili. In the old days the journey comprised a few men with guns, a string of carriers and a tent or two. Since then a few enterprising entrepreneurs have turned it into a luxurious experience.

President Teddy Roosevelt gave new meaning to the word *safari* when he embarked on a major expedition to East Africa with shipload of supplies sufficient for an army. He proudly sent out a card to friends showing his tent under the American flag with the inscription: "My boma where I was camped alone."

While author-hunter Ernest Hemingway did much of his writing in a tent in Africa actor William Holden and a friend bought a hotel in the shadow of Mount Kenya and turned it into an exotic Safari Club—complete with a bowling green and a nine hole golf course frequented by wildlife.

Proceeding on the principle that to enjoy animals in their natural habitat you don't have to live like them, entrepreneurs in southern Africa started developing private game reserves. There is certainly nothing unecological about the sumptious luxury lodges that blend in so well with the bush that they keep winning accolades from both conservationists and comfort seekers. Several of these game lodges have been voted best hotesl in the world by Condé Nast, Tatler and Travel Leisure readers and there is a stampede of other private game reserves vying for the top spot.

Ivory Lodge bathroom, Lion Sands

Safari in today's world means waking up to the sound of drums in a luxurious private lodge in the wild; enjoying game tracking under the supervision of knowledgeable game rangers; feasting around a campfire in the boma on venison and other local dishes prepared by culinary wizards; sipping the local wines while watching wildlife from the soft comfort of a lounge chair on a private veranda; or soaking in the plunge pool or your bathtub to the amusement of the monkeys and the ever-present flocks of exotic birds.

Incidentally, President Teddy Roosevelt had it wrong. *Boma* simply means a roofless brush enclosure, not a tent. Today some private game reserves provide luxury tented accommodation as well— the kind that puts Roosevelt's to shame with their finely appointed interiors and hot and cold showers.

Ebony Lodge bedroom, Singita

and on their return they go to their local wine store shopping for African wines and SEARCH online to find out where they can buy objects to furnish their newly-established Africa or safari room. They become Africa promoters. Some get involved in community development programs spearheaded by owners of lodges and other game reserve operators in southern and eastern Africa. They make donations and send books, computers, and sporting equipment after their return to the United States. Their kids establish a lasting link with the young Africans that they have met on these trips. The late actor Paul Newman inspired his safari hosts in Botswana to start a program for children styled after his famous Hole-in-the- Wall program. For two weeks every year Wilderness Safaris opens up its luxury lodges in the Okavango Delta to HIV/AIDS orphans and other needy children from the region, giving them a true wildlife experience. But Newman is just one of a long list of notable Americans who were drawn to Africa's wildlife and ended up serving it in one way or another. Ernest Hemingway and Robert Ruark romanticized and immortalized safari life in their writings while George Eastman, of Eastman-Kodak fame, sponsored the first wildlife documentaries and U.S. President Teddy Roosevelt promoted knowledge of Africa through several well-publicized safaris and books. In Kenya, the William Holden Wildlife Foundation continues the work of the late actor and his companion, television star Stephanie Powers. The movie industry contributed largely to the promotion of Africa with films based on safari adventures. Among the first to be shot on locale in East Africa was The *Macomber Affair*, based on a Hemingway short story, starring Gregory Peck. Next came The *Snows of Kilimanjaro*, with Susan Hayward and Ava Gardner, followed by *Born Free* and the blockbuster *Out of Afric*a, co-starring Meryl Streep and Robert Redford. The rates at game reserves and lodges normally include sizeable levies to promote not only conservation but education and development in the local neighborhoods.

Foreign capital

In 2002 American billionaire commodities trader Paul Tudor Jones embarked on one of the most ambitious conservation projects in Africa when he leased 340,000 acres of Tanzania's western Serengeti— along with its abundant wildlife—for $70 million. Since then, two lavish lodges at Sasakwa and Faru Faru as well as a tented camp at Sabora under the design and management of Singita—one of South Africa's premier safari companies—were established in the eco-reserve, offering guests 21st-century service in a sumptuous bush-chic setting. This is only one example of foreign capital not only stimulating growth in the tourist industry, but promoting conservation of natural resources and community development. At latest count the Singita Grumeti Reserve is providing jobs for 800 locals and schooling, medical and other services for their relatives in adjoining villages. Tourism based on wildlife and game reserves is the largest single source of foreign exchange for both Tanzania and neighboring Kenya. It also accounts for a major portion of the earnings in Botswana, Namibia, Uganda, Malawi, Zambia and Zimbabwe and contributes largely to South Africa's overseas tourist traffic. Countries like Ghana and Gabon are in the process of updating existing and constructing new facilities in their national parks and reserves to take advantage of the outside world's hunger for wildlife in their natural surroundings.

Serengeti Plains (Photo: Nomad)

MORE THAN SEVENTY-FIVE YEARS OF EXCELLENCE IN THE SKIES

South African Airways celebrated its 75th Anniversary in 2009, commemorating a long and storied history of excellence over African skies. Founded in 1934 with a small fleet made up of only one Puss Moth, two Gypsy Moths, three Junker F-13s and one Junker W-34 in operation, South African Airways has gone on to become one of the world's premier carriers and is poised to carry on its tradition of excellence through 2010 and beyond.

The airline flew its first international flight in 1944 aboard a converted bomber that carried 14 passengers to Blackbushe, England, over a span of three days. Over seven decades more than 95 million passengers have traveled on South African Airways.

Service from the U.S.

South African Airways features nonstop service from the U.S. to South Africa with daily departures from New York and Washington DC, offering travel convenience and award-winning service. Flights from New York and Washington DC to Johannesburg, at just over 15.5 or 17 hours, respectively, are the quickest and most direct routes from the U.S. to South Africa.

Africa network

South African Airways' unrivaled African network features connections to more than 20 destinations within South Africa and more than 25 destinations across the rest of the continent, making SAA the savvy traveler's "gateway to Africa." Now that SAA's flight from New York departs in the morning, travelers can access same-day connections to key cities such as Gabarone, Botswana; Windhoek, Namibia; and Dar es Salaam, Tanzania.

Star Alliance

As a Star Alliance member, South African Airways is able to offer its customers 1,172 destinations in 181 countries and more than 21,200 flights daily, including convenient connections from more than 25 cities in the U.S. through code share service with Star Alliance member United Airlines. Members of United's Mileage Plus, US Airways' Dividend Miles and Air Canada's Aeroplan programs are able to earn and redeem miles on all South African Airways flights.

Comfort

Customers in premium class enjoy 180° flat-bed seats with individual entertainment systems, and customers in economy class enjoy the most legroom versus competitors and individual on-demand entertainment systems.

Newest and Most Advanced Aircraft to Africa

SAA has one of the youngest fleets in the sky, featuring the latest generation of 4-engine Airbus A340 series for intercontinental flights, as well as Boeing 737-800 and Airbus A-319 aircraft for internal segments.

For more information about South African Airways and its services please call 800-722-9675 or visit *www.flysaa.com*.

SOUTH AFRICAN AIRWAYS
A STAR ALLIANCE MEMBER

RECENT AWARDS WON BY SOUTH AFRICAN AIRWAYS

- ⇨ Winner of "Best Airline in Africa" and "Best Cabin Crew in Africa"– Skytrax World Airline Awards (2010)
- ⇨ Winner of "Best Airline to Africa" – Executive Travel Magazine Leading Edge Awards (2010)
- ⇨ Winner of "Africa's Leading Airline" – World Travel Awards (2010)
- ⇨ Winner of "Best in Africa" and "Best Cabin Crew" – Skytrax Best in Region Awards (2010)
- ⇨ Voted "Best Airline to Africa" for the 12th time – Business Traveler Magazine (2009)
- ⇨ Voted "Best Airline in Africa" for the 6th consecutive year – Global Traveler Magazine (2009)
- ⇨ Winner of "Best Airline to Africa" – Weekly Globe Awards (2007)
- ⇨ Winner "Best Airline Based in Africa" – OAG (2008)
- ⇨ Winner of "Best Scheduled Airline to Africa" – Weekly Globe Awards (2008)
- ⇨ Winner of "Best African Airline" – ASATA (2007)
- ⇨ Voted "Africa's Leading Airline," "Africa's Leading Business Class Airline," "Africa's Leading First Class Airline," and "Africa's Leading Airline Website" – 14th World Travel Awards (2007)

PAYING TAXES

Produced by PricewaterhouseCoopers (PwC), *Paying Taxes 2011* provides entrepreneurs with insight into the impact of taxes on doing business worldwide and in all parts of Africa. This is the fifth in the series produced in partnership with the World Bank and the International Finance Corporation (IFCC) and is downloadable in its entirety at *www.pwc.com*.

The *Paying Taxes* project covers 183 economies and enables an assessment of tax systems around the world from the point of view of business over a six year period. The data presented and the methodology used are unique to the project. The study looks beyond corporate income tax at all of the taxes and contributions mandated by government and considers their full impact on business in terms of both the tax cost and the compliance burden in every country.

TTR

In terms of Total Tax Rate (TTR)—the tax cost borne by the company expressed as a percentage of its gross profit—Africa's average of 66.4% is the highest in the world. The Asia Pacific region (36.9%) has the lowest TTR, followed by Latin America, and the Caribbean (48.0%), and the G20 (50.0%).

In Africa, however, five countries with TTRs over 100% as a result of cascading sales taxes, add considerably to its average. If Burundi, Comoros, Congo Democratic Republic, The Gambia, and Sierra Leone with TTRs over 100% are excluded, the average for the region drops to 43.2%, which is below the world's and EU's average.

Easing

Sub-Saharan African economies continue to focus on easing tax compliance. In 2010 Sierra Leone introduced administrative reforms at the tax authority and replaced four different sales taxes with a value added tax. Seven other economies—Burkina Faso, Cameroon, Cape Verde, Ghana, Madagascar, South Africa and Sudan—reduced the number of payments by eliminating, merging or reducing the frequency of filings and payments. Mozambique, São Tomé and Principe, Sierra Leone, Sudan and Zambia revamped existing tax codes or enacted new ones in the past six years.

During the past year, economies in Sub-Saharan Africa implemented a quarter of all the world's reforms affecting the paying taxes indicators—a record for the region compared with previous years. In the past six years the most popular feature in the region was reducing profit tax rates (28 reforms). The reductions lowered the average TTR for the region by 2.7 percentage points. Profit tax, just one of many taxes for businesses in Africa, accounts for only a third of the total tax paid. However, firms in the region still face the highest average TTR in the world, 68% of profit.

Time

In the African Union, the average compliance time of 313 hours is 31 hours above the world average, largely due to more time needed on consumption taxes. Twenty-seven economies in Africa need more time than the global average to comply with these taxes. The economies where the most time is needed are Mauritania (480 hours), Senegal (450 hours), Cameroon (300 hours), Namibia (288 hours) and Kenya (276 hours)—all have VAT.

Bottom line: Africa offers great opportunities to those who do due diligence with the assistance of expert tax consultants.

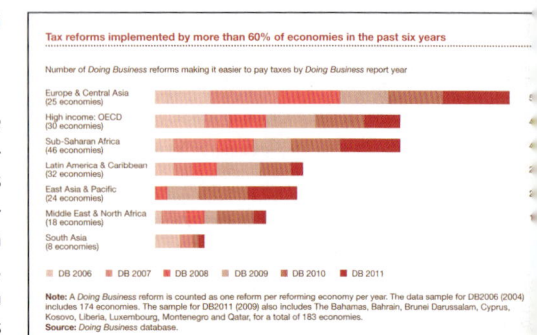

Chapter 5
Doing Business with Africa

Massive inflows of capital into the extraction of oil, gas and minerals tend to obscure significant foreign involvement in Africa's telecommunications, energy, banking, infrastructure and manufacturing sectors. While multinationals such as Barclays, General Motors, GE, Unilever, Proctor-Gamble, 3M and Coca-Cola have been household names in Africa for many decades, smaller and lesser known enterprises are becoming involved in increasing numbers.

...nk call center, Johannesburg

Setting Up

A growing number of consumers in Africa with dispensible income for luxury items—at latest count at least 80 million—makes it an increasingly attractive market for manufacturers. As the region becomes increasingly intent on manufacturing on its own soil instead of importing, foreign firms are increasingly looking at establising local plants, with or without local partnerships. (There are some countries where local shareholding is mandatory and others where part ownership by locals qualify for tax breaks and other incentives).

In their annual *Doing Business* reports the World Bank and the International Finance Corporation continue to rate Africa worst in the world in regard to roadblocks for setting up new businesses. Also as far as business taxes are concerned, Sub-Saharan Africa has been rated the highest.

In the past year, however, much has changed. In *Doing Business 2011* African countries topped five categories as having showed the best progress worldwide. In this latest assessment by the World Bank and the International Finance Corporation the Democratic Republic of Congo is listed as having shown the best progress in facilitating construction permits while Ghana topped the list in the "getting credit" column. Swaziland's improvements in "protection for investors" earned it first place in this category while Tunisia topped the list for tax improvementss and Malawi in improved enforcement of contracts. The 2011 report also notes that over the past five years since the iannual rankings were first issued, Sub-Saharan Africa has been more active than any other region in the introduction of reforms to facilitate easier business startups.

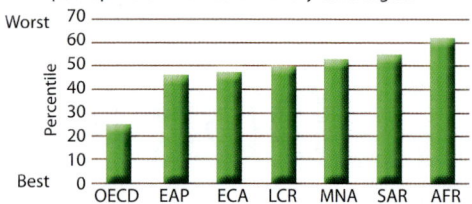

According to the report about half of all trade facilitation reforms in 2009/10 took place in Sub-Saharan Africa (with 9) and the Middle East and North Africa (6). It cautions, however, that despite these encouraging signs there is still considerable room for improvement. Exporting, for example, requires 11 documents in the Republic of Congo but only 2 in France. Starting a business still costs 18 times as much in Sub-Saharan Africa as in OECD high-income economies (relative to income per capita).

Rankings

In its rankings to determine the ease of doing business around the world the World Bank and IFC use the following nine criteria: (1) Starting a business; (2) Dealing with constriction permits; (3) Registerting property; (4) Getting credit' (5) Protecting investors; (6) Paying taxes; (7) Trading across borders; (8) Enforcing contracts; and (9) Closing a business.

In 2011 Singapore ranked number 1, Hong Kong second, New Zealand third, the United Kingdom fourth and the United States fifth. The five highest ranking African countries were Mauritius (20), South Africa (34),

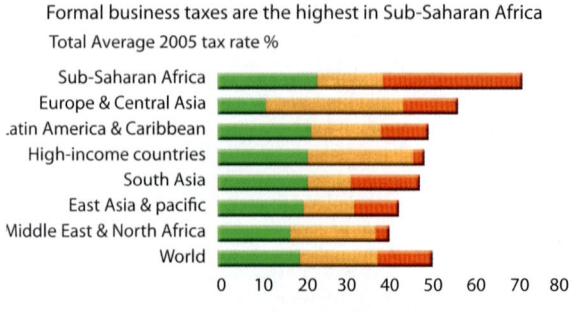

Botswana (52), Tunisia (55) and Rwanda (58). The following African nations occupied the five bottom positions from 179 to 183: Guinea (179), Eritrea (180), Burundi (181), Central African Republic (182), and Chad (183).

Largest strides

Doing Business 2011 lists Rwanda, Burkina Faso, Mali and Ghana among the 10 economies that made the largest strides in making their regulatory environment more favorable to business in the previous year. All implemented more than a dozen *Doing Business* reforms over the 5 years. Since 2005 Rwanda has implemented 22 business regulation reforms in the areas measured by *Doing Business*. In

Sub-Saharan Africa is most active in business start-up reforms
Source: World Bank & IFC Doing Business Database

Region	Value
Sub-Saharan Africa (46 economies)	65
Eastern Europe & Central Asia (25 economies)	64
OECD high income (30 economies)	49
Latin America & Caribbean (32 economies)	43
Middle East & North Africa (18 economies)	35
East Asia & Pacific (24 economies)	29

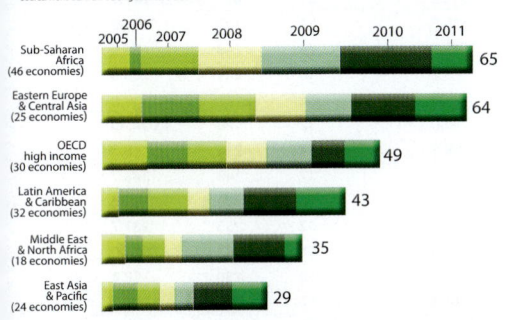

2005, starting a business in Rwanda required 9 procedures and cost 223% of income per capita. Today entrepreneurs can register a new business in 3 days, paying official fees that equals 8.9% of income per capita. Registering property in 2005 took more than a year (371 days), and the transfer fees amounted to 9.8% of the property value. Today the process takes 2 months and costs 0.4% of the value. More than 3,000 entrepreneurs entered after these reforms in 2008, up from an average of 700 annually in previous years. A new company law adopted in Rwanda in 2009 strengthened investor protections by requiring greater corporate disclosure, increasing the liability of directors and improving shareholders' access to information. Other nations such as Ghana and Mali, took a steady approach, improving their business environments over several years. Ghana implemented measures in 6 areas. It created its first credit bureau, computerized the company registry and overhauled its property

EASE OF DOING BUSINESS RANK

Country	2010	2011
Mauritius	20	20
South Africa	32	34
Botswana	50	52
Tunisia	58	55
Rwanda	70	58
Ghana	77	67
Namibia	68	69
Zambia	84	76
Egypt	99	94
Seychelles	92	95
Kenya	94	98
Ethiopia	103	104
Morocco	114	114
Swaziland	126	118
Uganda	129	122
Mozambique	130	126
Tanzania	125	128
Cape Verde	142	132
Malawi	132	133
Algeria	136	136
Nigeria	134	137
Lesotho	137	138
Madagascar	138	140
Sierra Leone	143	143
Gambia, The	141	146
Burkina Faso	154	151
Senegal	151	152
Mali	155	155
Sudan	153	154
Liberia	152	155
Gabon	158	156
Zimbabwe	156	157
Djibouti	157	158
Comoros	159	159
Togo	162	160
Angola	164	163
Equatorial Guinea	161	164
Mauritania	167	165
Cameroon	173	168
Côte d'Ivoire	168	169
Benin	172	170
Niger	171	173
Congo, Dem. Rep.	179	175
Guinea-Bissau	175	176
Congo, Rep.	177	177
São Tome & Principe	176	178
Guinea	178	179
Eritrea	180	180
Burundi	181	181
Central African Republic	182	182
Chad	183	183

Rankings out of 183 countries. Singapore ranked first, Hong Kong second, New Zeland third, United Kingdom fourth and the US fifth.

Source: World Bank & IFC Doing Business data

Starting a Business and Dealing with Licences

Country	Number of Procedures	Time Required	Cost as % of per capita income	Min. capital as % of per capita income	Number of Procedures	Time Days	Cost as % of per capita income
Algeria	14	24	13.2	45.2	22	240	57.8
Angola	12	119	343.7	50.5	14	337	1,109.70
Benin	7	31	195	354.2	15	332	316.6
Botswana	11	108	9.9	...	24	167	322.3
Burkina Faso	6	34	82.1	415.7	32	226	701.2
Burundi	11	43	251	...	20	384	9,939.00
Cameroon	13	44	129.2	177.1	15	426	1,202.90
Cape Verde	12	52	40.1	53.4	18	120	718.3
Cent. Afr. Republic	10	14	205.4	531.2	21	239	288.3
Chad	19	75	188.8	398.4	9	181	1,063.80
Comoros	11	23	188.4	280.3	18	164	77.8
Congo	10	37	150.1	206.3	14	169	565.9
Congo Dem. Rep.	13	155	487.2	...	14	322	2,112.60
Côte d'Ivoire	10	45	135.8	219.8	21	628	247.7
Djibouti	11	37	206.6	530.8	14	195	1,010.60
Egypt	7	19	28.6	12.9	28	249	474.9
Equatorial Guinea	20	136	105.1	23.2	18	201	239.9
Eritrea	13	84	125.8	488	...	...	...
Ethiopia	7	16	41.3	960	12	128	1,094.40
Gabon	9	58	164	38.2	14	210	48.3
Gambia	9	27	279	...	17	146	363.7
Ghana	11	81	41.4	20.9	18	220	1,498.30
Guinea	13	41	138.3	466.5	32	255	237.7
Guinea Bissau	17	233	255.5	1006.6	15	167	2,607.00
Kenya	12	54	46.1	...	10	100	58.8
Lesotho	8	73	37.4	14.3	15	601	805.3
Liberia	12	...	493.3	...	25	398	61,049.30
Libya	...	...	...	...	...	...	...
Madagascar	5	21	22.7	333.4	16	268	880
Malawi	10	37	188.7	...	21	213	189.2
Mali	11	42	132.1	434.6	14	208	1,320.70
Mauritania	11	82	56.2	503.1	25	201	565.5
Mauritius	6	46	5.3	...	18	107	43.3
Morocco	6	12	11.5	59.8	19	163	334.7
Mozambique	10	113	21.6	115.8	17	361	705
Namibia	10	95	22.3	...	12	139	156.7
Niger	11	24	174.8	735.6	16	293	2,823.60
Nigeria	9	43	56.6	...	18	350	1,016.00
Rwanda	9	16	171.5	...	16	227	822.1
São T. & Principe	10	144	94.5	...	13	255	825.9
Senegal	10	58	107	255	14	217	176.9
Seychelles	9	38	8.7	...	19	144	46.5
SierraLeone	9	26	1075.2	...	47	235	191.7
Somalia	...	...	...	...	...	...	...
South Africa	8	35	7.1	...	17	174	30.4
Sudan	10	39	57.9	...	19	271	296
Swaziland	13	61	38.7	0.6	13	93	94
Tanzania	12	30	47.1	...	21	308	2,365.50
Togo	13	53	245.7	546.4	15	277	1,366.30
Tunisia	10	11	8.3	25.3	20	93	922.1
Uganda	18	28	92	...	16	143	811.8
Zambia	6	35	30.5	2.2	17	254	1,518.00
Zimbabwe	10	96	21.3	54.6	19	952	11,799.00

Source: AFDB

registration system, moving from a deed to a title registration system. The multiyear reform reduced the time to transfer property from 24 weeks to 5. The state now guarantees the title and its authenticity. Regulatory reforms also picked up in Mali in recent years. Key achievements include customs reforms, a new one-stop shop for business start-up and amendments to the civil procedure code in 2009 that strengthened protections for minority shareholders and improved the (still lengthy) court procedures to resolve commercial disputes.

AFDB Ratings

Two years ago the African Development Bank issued its own data on procedures involved in various African countries, reproduced on the opposite page. As in the case of the reports issued by the World Bank and IFC this is not an exact science and subject to a margin of error. Nonetheless, it gives the entrepreneur who contemplates setting up a business entity in any part of the African continent an idea of the roadblocks and delays that he or she might encounter along the way.

Ibrahim Index

Every year the Africa-based Mo Ibrahim Foundation, launched in 2006, offers a comprehensive ranking of African countries according to governance quality. The index was designed as a tool to help monitor progress. The premise behind our work is an acute awareness of Africa's potential: a youthful population, 30 percent of the world's mineral reserves, and a wealth of renewable-energy sources continuing to underperform and failing to realize their full potential. This lack of progress during the past 50 years, the Foundation contends, can be attributed to a failure of governance and leadership. The goal is to promote a broader conception of good governance, which moves beyond the traditional emphasis on elections and legitimacy to an understanding of the components of a wellgoverned society. The index currently aggregates more than 80 outcome-oriented indicators. The foundation looks at the on-the-ground reality for citizens rather than at governments' claims, intentions, or spending. Moreover, citizens' experiences are assessed across the fullest range of public goods and services—from human development (poverty, health, education) to the rule of law and from economic opportunity to physical security. In measuring outcomes for citizens no distinction is made between services delivered by governments, the private sector, or nongovernmental organizations (NGOs). Its definition of good governance comprises the successful delivery, by government or nonstate actors of public goods and services that citizens have a right to expect. According to the Foundation this index has shown a broad upward trend and it "confidently" asserts that governance in Africa is improving—making it better for business.

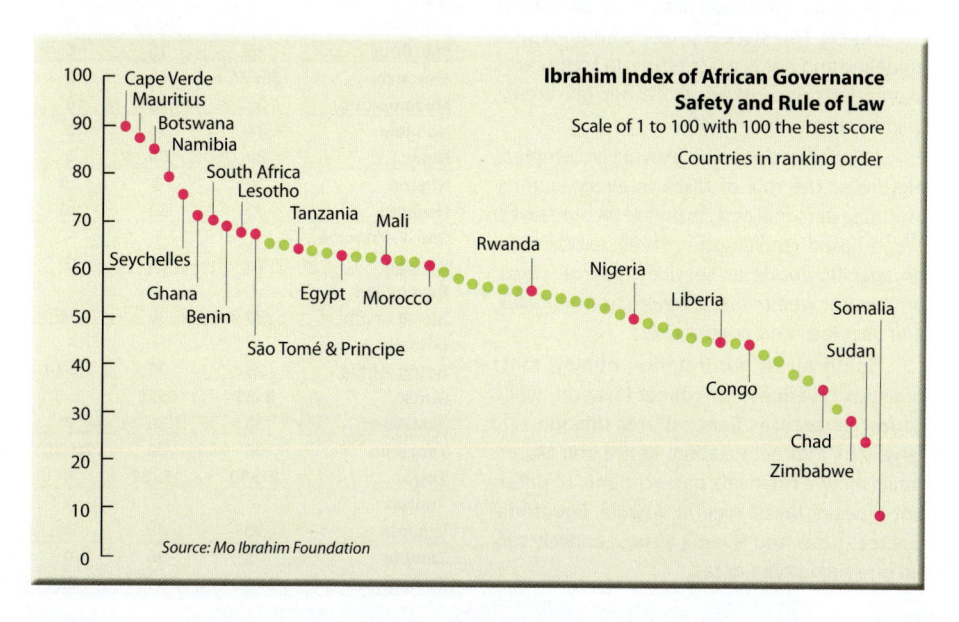

Ibrahim Index of African Governance
Safety and Rule of Law
Scale of 1 to 100 with 100 the best score
Countries in ranking order

Source: Mo Ibrahim Foundation

Taxes

Ultimately taxes are a very important consideration in deciding whether it is worthwhile for any business to move into another country. With constant legislative, regulatory and judicial changes, companies operating across borders are severely challenged in following and comprehending the impact of these ever-changing developments on their business.

Similarly, globalization, economic realities, operational adjustments, and corporate mandates require tax departments to follow and comprehend internal initiatives. As elsewhere understanding the tax impact on business operations and transactions in multiple jurisdictions across Africa is vital for success.

This table is based on information supplied by PricewaterhouseCoopers (www.pwc.com) that offers arguably the most extensive network of offices in the countries of the African continent. It has more than than 57 permanent offices located in 31 countries across the continent and employs more than 7,000 professional staff. Three lines of services are offered—Assurance, Tax and Advisory—with some offices also providing legal assistance.

It should be noted that as in any other region or country, tax rates in Africa and its 53 nations change frequently and the best way to verify the latest data is by contacting the source. This data is provided merely as a guideline and not in exact terms. In some cases exemptions, incentives and other tax breaks might apply.

Our table does not provide a complete picture of the mix of taxes in every country including personal and corporate income taxes, broad-based consumption taxes, excise taxes on specific goods or services, payroll taxes, property or wealth taxes, wealth transfer taxes, and user fees and benefit taxes.

South Africa, for instance, obtains most of its tax revenues from direct taxation, while countries such as Senegal and Uganda rely largely on indirect taxation. Kenya and Mauritania show a relatively balanced mix of different types of taxes. Algeria, Angola, Equatorial Guinea, Libya and Nigeria almost entirely rely on one single type of tax.

	COMPANIES			
	Company Taxes %		Capital Gains Tax %	
Country	Res	Non	Res	Non
Algeria	25	24	15	20
Angola	35	35	35	35
Benin	30	30	30	30
Botswana	15>25	25	18.75>25	18.75
BurkinaFaso	10>30	10>30	10	10
Burundi	-	-	-	-
Cameroon	38.5	38.5	38.5	38
CapeVerde	25	25	0	0
Cent. Afr. Rep.	20>30	20>30	0	0
Chad	40	25	25>40	25>
Comoros	-	-	-	-
Congo Rep.	36	20>35	0	0
Congo D. R.	30>40	NA	0	0
Côte d'Ivoire	25	25	25	25
Djibouti	-	-	-	-
Egypt	20	20	20	20
Equat. Guinea	-	-	-	-
Eritrea	34>38	10	0	10
Ethiopia	30	30	15>30	15>
Gabon	20>35	35	0	0
Gambia, The	35	35	10>25	10>
Ghana	25	25	5	5
Guinea	35	35	NA	NA
Guinea Bissau	-	-	-	-
Kenya	30	37.5	NA	NA
Lesotho	25	25	0	0
Liberia	35	35	10	10
Libya	15>40	15>40	15>40	15>
Madagascar	23	10>23	0	0
Malawi	30	15>35	30	15
Mali	-	-	-	-
Mauritania	25>30	25>30	25	25
Mauritius	15	15	0	0
Morocco	30>37	10	0	30
Mozambique	32	32	0	0
Namibia	34	34	0	0
Niger	30	30	0	0
Nigeria	30	6	10	10
Rwanda	30	30	30	30
São T. Principe	-	-	-	-
Senegal	25	25	0	0
Seychelles	-	-	-	-
Sierra Leone	30	30	30	30
Somalia	-	-	-	-
South Africa	28	33	10>14	10>
Sudan	0>35	0>35	2>5	2>
Swaziland	30	30	0	0
Tanzania	30	30	10>30	20>
Togo	27>30	15>30	0	0
Tunisia	-	-	-	-
Uganda	30	30	30	30
Zambia	35	35	0	0
Zimbabwe	25.75	25.75	20	20

VAT % / Sales Tax*	INDIVIDUALS Marginal Max % Res	Non	Dividends % Res	Non	Interest % Res	Non	Royalties % Res	Non	Management Fees % Res	Non	Exhange Control
17	35	35	10	15	10>50	10>50	24	24	24	24	YES
0	17	17	10	10	15	15	10	10	5.25	5.25	YES
18	35	35	10	9	15	15	1>5	25>30			YES
10	25	25	15	15	10	10	NA	15	NA	15	NO
18	10>30	10>30	12.5	12.5	6>25	6>25	5	20	5	20	YES
-	-	-	-	-	-	-	-	-	-	-	---
19.25	35	35	16.5	16.5	16.5	0	0	15	0	15	YES
6>15	35	35	0	0	15	20	15	20	NA	20	YES
0>19	50	50	15	15	15	15	NA	15	NA	15	YES
18	60	25	NA	20	NA	20	NA	20	-	-	YES
-	-	-	-	-	-	-	-	-	-	-	---
18	45	20	20	20	20	20	20	20	20	20	YES
NA	30	NA	10>20	10>20	0>20	0>20	14	14	-	-	YES
15	2.8	12	12	12	18	18	0	20	0	20	YES
-	-	-	-	-	-	-	-	-	-	-	---
0	20	10	NA	NA	NA	20	NA	20	-	-	NO
-	-	-	-	-	-	-	-	-	-	-	---
5>12*	20>30	20>30	0	0	NA	10	NA	10	NA	10	YES
15	35	35	10	10	5	5	5	5	10	10	YES
18>18	35	35	15>20	15	10>20	10.20	NA	10	NA	10	YES
10>18*	35	35	15	15	15	15	0	15	10	15	YES
15	25	15	8	8	8	8	5	10	5	15	YES
18	30	NA	10	10	5	NA	10	10	10	10	YES
-	-	-	-	-	-	-	-	-	-	-	---
16	30	30	0>5	10	15>25	15>25	5	20	5	20	NO
0>15	35	35	0	0>25	10	0>25	0	0>25	5	0>25	YES
0	35	35	10	15	10	15	10	15	10	20	YES
0	15>30	15>30	0	0	5	5	0	0	-	-	YES
20	23	23	0	0	23	23	0	10	0	10	YES
16.5	30	30	10	10	20	15	15	15>20	10	15	YES
-	-	-	-	-	-	-	-	-	-	-	---
14>18	35	35	10	10	10	10	0	0	-	-	YES
15	15	15	0	0	15	0	15	0	-	-	NO
20	38	38	10	10	20>30	10	0	10	0	10	YES
17	32	32	20	20	20	20	20	20	20	20	YES
15	37	37	0	10	10	10	0	30	0	0	YES
19	35	35	10	7.5	13>25	13>25	0	16	0	16	YES
5	20	20	10	10	10	10	5>10	5>10	10	10	YES
18	30	30	15	15	15	15	15	15	15	15	NO
-	-	-	-	-	-	-	-	-	-	-	---
18	50	50	0>10	10	6>16	6>16	NA	20	NA	20	YES
-	-	-	-	-	-	-	-	-	-	-	---
0	0>30	25	10	10	15	15	25	25	5	10	YES
-	-	-	-	-	-	-	-	-	-	-	---
14	40	40	NA	NA	NA	NA	0	12	-	-	YES
15>20	15	15	0	0	0	0	15	15	15	15	YES
0	33	33	0	15	0	15	0	15	0	15	YES
18	30	30	10	10	10	10	15	15	NA	15	YES
18	40	40	20	20	15	15	5>10	15	5>10	15	YES
-	-	-	-	-	-	-	-	-	-	-	---
18	30	30	15	15	15	15	0	15	6	15	NO
16	35	35	15	15	15	15	15	15	0	15	NO
15	36.05	36.05	10>15	10>15	15	0	0	15	0	15	YES

We Cover the Continent

PricewaterhouseCoopers (PwC) is one of the largest professional services firms in the world and our presence in Africa is no less impressive – and growing. As the African continent continues to enjoy impressive levels of economic growth, fuelled by the development of its abundant natural resources and the expansion of domestic infrastructure and consumer markets, so the scope of our service offerings is expanding to proactively meet our clients' immediate and emerging needs.

PwC member firms are present in 29 countries across Africa with more than 7 500 professional staff on the ground to meet the requirements of our diverse client base. Our network structure provides PwC firms with the flexibility to operate simultaneously as a local and a global business, creating a platform on which member firms share knowledge, skills and resources to deliver services of consistently high quality to international and local clients.

In sub-Saharan Africa, PwC is led by the Africa Leadership Team, which comprises the Territory Senior Partners:

- Southern Africa – Suresh Kana, who is also the Africa Region Senior Partner;
- Africa Central – Philip Kinisu; and
- Francophone Africa – Edouard Messou
- They are joined by the PwC Africa Assurance Leader, Brendan Deegan, from Southern Africa.

The Africa Leadership Team is committed to a shared vision with a common purpose of meeting client needs through seamless service delivery.

The breadth and depth of our skills base gives us unrivalled knowledge of African business and the regulations governing it in countries across sub-Saharan Africa. This allows us to work to the benefit of our clients in every jurisdiction in which they operate.

For further information contact:
gilles.j.de.vignemont@us.pwc.com

Regional staff complement

Territory	Partners*	Staff*	Total*
Southern Africa	288	4879	5167
Francophone Africa	18	524	542
Africa Central	66	1,818	1,884

* As at 30 June 2010

Regional organisation

PwC member firms in sub-Saharan Africa are organised into three operational territories: Africa Central, Francophone Africa and Southern Africa, which together make up the PwC Africa Region. In North Africa, member firms in Egypt and Libya form part of PwC's Middle East regional organisation, while PwC in Algeria, Morocco and Tunisia, as well as the island of Réunion, are aligned with PwC France.

PwC is already the leading audit firm in over 90% of territories in our region and in all industries. In proactively seeking to meet the growing needs of PwC clients in all sectors, we have taken a number of steps to extend our level of specialist support across the region.

To assist foreign companies wanting to explore the abundant investment opportunities Africa has to offer, we have dedicated Africa Tax Desks in New York and in Johannesburg.

The African Tax Desk:

- Provides quick responses to preliminary and generic questions that companies would like answered when considering investment in Africa;

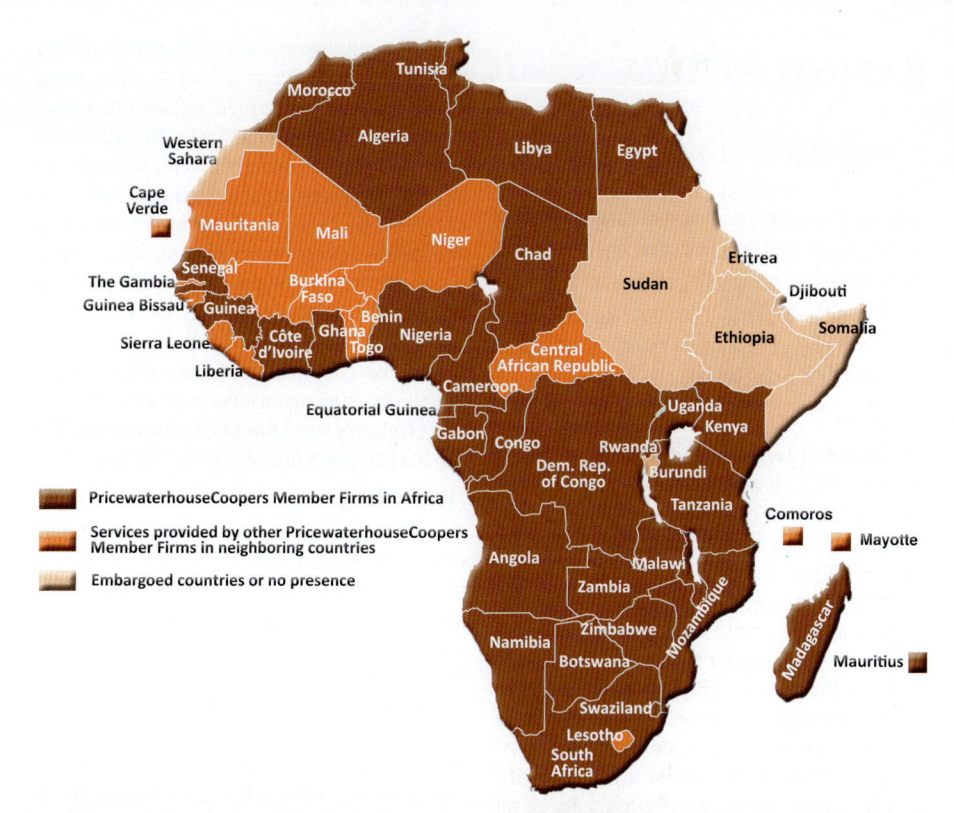

- PricewaterhouseCoopers Member Firms in Africa
- Services provided by other PricewaterhouseCoopers Member Firms in neighboring countries
- Embargoed countries or no presence

Africa Region industry groups

Industry practice	Leader	Resident office
Financial Services	Tom Winterboer	Johannesburg
Oil and Gas	Elias Pungong	Libreville
Technology, Information, Communication and Entertainment	Berno Niebuhr	Johannesburg
Mining	Hein Boegman	Johannesburg

- Facilitates investments and business operations by providing access to the right contacts for tax and legal advisory services to investors in Africa; and
- Can coordinate between companies investing into Africa and respective PwC offices in other countries.

The Africa Tax Desk is staffed by tax specialists from various African countries, including Kenya, Nigeria, Uganda and South Africa. The team works closely with colleagues in PwC offices in other African countries and the Africa Tax Desk in Johannesburg to help clients find solutions to challenges facing their commercial ambitions in Africa.

Economic activity in Africa is increasingly dominated by the exploitation of natural resources, the development of consumer markets and the penetration of communication technologies. In response to this, PwC Africa has appointed leaders to co-ordinate the work of our industry groups in key industries in the region.

pwc

Rating Africa

Mindful of the important role that credit ratings play in the global capital markets, an increasing number of African countries are subjecting themselves to assessments by the world's leading rating agencies. Currently twenty-two African economies are rated.

Moodys

Moody's (www.moodys.com) concedes that credit ratings are by their very nature subjective as they rely on the judgment of a diverse group of credit risk professionals weighing a number of pertinent factors. Moody's issues country ceiling ratings for foreign-currency bonds and notes (both long- and short-term), and country ceilings for foreign currency bank deposits (both long- and short-term). Using an Aaa-through-C rating, an Aaa signifies the best quality with the smallest degree of investment risk and is generally referred to as "gilt edged." Aa signifies high quality by all standards while A implies favorable investment at an upper-medium-grade level. Baa is considered as medium-grade, Ba has speculative elements, B generally lacks the characteristics of the desirable investment, Caa denotes poor standing, Ca is speculative to a high degree, and C shows extremely poor prospects of ever attaining investment grading. Moody's applies numerical modifiers 1, 2, and 3 in each generic rating classification from Aa through Caa. The modifier 1 indicates that the obligation ranks in the higher end of its generic rating category; a 2 indicates a mid-range ranking; and a 3 stipulates a ranking in the lower end of a specific category.

Standard & Poor's

Standard & Poor's (www.standardpoor.com) cautions against interpretation of its sovereign ratings as "country ratings." Instead, it suggests that a sovereign credit rating should be seen as an assessment of a government's capacity and willingness to repay debt according to its terms. Sovereign ratings address the credit risks of national governments and is not a recommendation to invest, according to S&P. An AAA rating, the highest assigned by Standard & Poor's, indicates an extremely strong capacity to meet financial commitments. An AA shows a very strong capacity to meet obligations and an A rating a strong capacity to meet financial commitments. A BBB is assigned to those judged to have an adequate capacity to meet their commitments but with a greater likelihood being affected by adverse economic conditions. BBB- is considered the lowest investment grade by market participants. Sovereign debt rated BB, B, CCC, and CC are all seen as having significant speculative characteristics—with BB less and B more vulnerable to adverse business, financial and economic conditions but currently has the capacity to meet financial commitments.

Fitch Ratings

Fitch (www.fitchratings.com) draws for its sovereign rating on recent instances of default and near-default to establish a range of key leading indicators of distress. This information is incorporated in a risk model that gives a percentage score to sovereign borrowers, which is used in turn to determine the long-term rating. Sovereign borrowers usually enjoy the highest credit standing for obligations in their own currency. There is the risk, however, that a country may service its debt through excessive money creation, effectively eroding the value of its obligations through inflation. On the other hand, when a sovereign nation borrows in a foreign currency there is the even more serious risk of outright default since the sovereign borrower cannot print the means of servicing the debt. In long-term obligations, an AAA rating indicates the highest credit quality and lowest expectation of credit risk and is highly unlikely to be adversely affected by foreseeable events. AA denotes very high credit quality and very low expectation of credit risk. An A rating indicates high credit quality and a low expectation of credit risk. BBB assigns good credit quality and low expectation of credit risk. This is the lowest investment-grade category. For its short-term ratings F1 is the highest credit quality and the strongest capacity for timely payment of financial commitments. A plus sign may be added to denote exceptionally strong credit. of financial commitments with the possibility that near-term adverse changes could result in downgrading to below investment grade. While a B rating is speculative, C indicates high default risk.

African Sovereign Credit Ratings – Nov. 2010

ANGOLA

Moody's Investors Service

Bond rating—local currency	B1/POS
Bond rating—foreign currency	B1/POS

Fitch Ratings

Foreign currency long-term	B+/Positive
Domestic currency long-term	B+/Positive

BENIN

Standard & Poor's

Domestic rating	B
Foreign rating	B

Fitch ratings

Foreign currency long-term	B/Stable
Domestic currency long-term	B/Stable

BOTSWANA

Moody's Investors Service

Bond rating—local currency	A2/NEG
Bond rating—foreign currency	A2/NEG

Standard & Poor's

Domestic rating	A
Foreign rating	A-

BURKINA FASO

Standard & Poor's

Domestic rating	B
Foreign rating	B

CAMEROON

Standard & Poor's

Domestic rating	B
Foreign rating	B

Fitch ratings

Foreign currency long-term	B/Stable
Domestic currency long-term	B-/Stable

CAPE VERDE

Standard & Poor's

Domestic rating	B+
Foreign rating	B+

Fitch ratings

Foreign currency long-term	B+/Stable
Domestic currency long-term	BB-/Stable

EGYPT

Moody's Investors Service

Bond rating—local currency	Ba1/STA
Bond rating—foreign currency	Ba1/STA

Standard & Poor's

Domestic rating	BBB-
Foreign rating	BB+

Fitch Ratings

Foreign currency long-term	BB+/Stable
Domestic currency long-term	BB-/Stable

GABON

Standard & Poor's

Domestic rating	BB-
Foreign rating	BB-

Fitch Ratings

Foreign currency long-term	BB-/Stable
Domestic currency long-term	BB-/Stable

GHANA

Standard & Poor's

Domestic rating	B
Foreign rating	B

Fitch Ratings

Foreign currency long-term	B+/Stable
Domestic currency long-term	B+/Stable

KENYA

Standard & Poor's

Domestic rating	B+
Foreign rating	B+

Fitch Ratings

Foreign currency long-term	B+/Stable
Domestic currency long-term	BB-/Stable

LESOTHO

Fitch Ratings

Foreign currency long-term	BB-/Stable
Domestic currency long-term	BB/Negative

LIBYA

Fitch Ratings

Foreign currency long-term	BBB+/Stable
Domestic currency long-term	BBB+/Stable

MAURITIUS

Moody's Investors Service

Bond rating—local currency	Baa2/STA
Bond rating—foreign currency	Baa2/STA

MOROCCO

Moody's Investors Service

Bond rating—local currency	Ba1/STA
Bond rating—foreign currency	Ba1/STA

Standard & Poor's

Domestic rating	BBB+
Foreign rating	BBB-

Fitch ratings

Foreign currency long-term	BBB-/Stable
Domestic currency long-term	BBB/Stable

MOZAMBIQUE

Standard & Poor's

Domestic rating	B+
Foreign rating	B+

Fitch Ratings

Foreign currency long-term	B/Stable
Domestic currency long-term	B+/Stable

NAMIBIA

Fitch Ratings

Foreign currency long-term	BBB-/Stable
Domestic currency long-term	BBB/Stable

NIGERIA

Standard & Poor's

Domestic rating	B+
Foreign rating	B+

Fitch Ratings

Foreign currency long-term	BB-/Negative
Domestic currency long-term	BB/Negative

RWANDA

Fitch Ratings

Foreign currency long-term	B-/Stable
Domestic currency long-term	B/Positive

SENEGAL

Standard & Poor's

Domestic rating	B+
Foreign rating	B+

SEYCHELLES

Fitch Ratings

Foreign currency long-term	B-/Positive
Domestic currency long-term	BBB/Stable

SOUTH AFRICA

Moody's Investors Service

Bond rating—local currency	A3/STA
Bond rating—foreign currency	A3/STA

Standard & Poor's

Domestic rating	A+
Foreign rating	BBB+

Fitch Ratings

Foreign currency long-term	BBB+/Negative
Domestic currency long-term	A/Negative

TUNISIA

Moody's Investors Service

Bond rating—local currency	Baa2/STA
Bond rating—foreign currency	Baa2/STA

Standard & Poor's

Domestic rating	A-
Foreign rating	BBB

Fitch Ratings

Foreign currency long-term	BBB/Stable
Domestic currency long-term	A-/Stable

UGANDA

Standard & Poor's

Domestic rating	B+
Foreign rating	B+

Fitch Ratings

Foreign currency long-term	B/Positive
Domestic currency long-term	B/Positive

IDC allocates R3.1 billion to distressed companies

At the onset of the economic crisis in 2008, the Industrial Development Corporation (IDC) realised that South Africa would not be spared the effects of the recession. Proactively, it formed a response to assist companies that were impacted negatively by the recession. As a result, the IDC announced that it had set aside R6.1 billion to support companies in distress.

One of the main aims of this fund is to assist companies that were successful before the onset of the economic crisis to withstand the impact of the recession and have the ability to continue growing once economic conditions improve. Divisional Executive Industrial Sectors Shakeel Meer comments: "Our focus is on businesses that have the potential to emerge from the crisis. One of our primary objectives is to create and preserve permanent jobs as efficiently as possible."

To date, approximately R3.1 billion has been committed to distressed businesses in 53 transactions. Meer adds: "Approximately 70% of the disbursed funding has been allocated to companies in the metals fabrication, motor, clothing and textiles, mining and forestry sectors. We estimate that over 17 500 jobs will be created and saved as a result of this assistance."

Thus far, the fund has mainly assisted the mining and primary metals industry as these sectors were highly affected by the decline in commodity prices. The fabricated metals, machinery and motor vehicle industries received the third-largest portion of funding to date as these were impacted by the slowdown in consumer spending on luxury goods. Other industries that received a large portion of distress funding were the forestry, sawmilling and transport industries. The fund is, however, committed to assisting most businesses that fit the criteria, not only those in specific sectors.

The role that IDC plays in these transactions goes beyond that of a financier. IDC's participation in the process frequently involves intense negotiations, thus giving comfort to other partners in the business. Recent amendments to the Distress Fund guidelines make assistance to businesses in need even more accessible. These amendments include the waiving of internal fees (e.g. raising-, holding-, commitment- and internal legal fees) by the IDC and reduced capital security requirements. The fund also enables the business to repay banks' funding first, once it has turned around, and does not insist on sureties from the shareholders, although these are a requirement. The Distress Fund will also be implemented alongside other initiatives e.g. the Training Lay-off scheme and other dti incentives, which will result in a full solution for the distressed business.

Throughout this economic downturn, the IDC continues to provide support for existing clients through advice and restructuring of funding facilities. "Furthermore, we are hosting various workshops and other forums throughout the country in an attempt to advise and partner with businesses in distress. These will afford entrepreneurs the opportunity to assess their options and understand how the funding works," concludes Meer.

IDC
Industrial Development Corporation
Your partner in development finance

For further information please contact:
IDC Call Centre – 086 069 3888
Email: distressfunding@idc.co.za
Website: www.idc.co.za

Advice & Assistance

There was a time when the outside world could blame its ignorance about the real Africa on a lack of solid sources. That is no longer the case. Students, investors, entrepreneurs and travelers looking for data and detail on all aspects of the continent have a wealth of information at their disposal on the Internet. The problem is to sort out the corn from the chaff.

There are numerous non-governmental organizations (NGOs) in Washington and other world capitals that are dedicated to African causes and countries and able to assist members in their search for information. Several universities have developed Africa-related databases. World organizations such as the United Nations and its specialized agencies, including the UN Development Program (UNDP) and the Inter-national Monetary Fund (IMF), all maintain databases on Africa.

Advice

Business executives who are seriously considering investment or dealings with any of Africa's 53 diverse and often complex nations, usually seek advice from experienced and trustworthy consultants to help analyze and evaluate prospects. When sorting through the many investment and trade advisors that specialize in Africa it is prudent to ask for referrals and to take a close look at past performance, as well as the personnel.

Corporate Council

A good starting point is the Washington-based The Corporate Council on Africa (CCA) (*www.africacncl.org*)—the premier business-related non-governmental organization for US and other multinational and medium-sized corporations. With a membership of more than 250 representing some 87 percent of all US investment in Africa, the Council acts as a catalyst for business by introducing American firms not only to potential top-level partners in Africa but to like-minded firms in the United States that might become partners in new ventures. The CCA's biennial Africa summits are the occasion where several thousand business leaders and Africa experts rub shoulders with a host of African heads of state and key members of their government. The 2009 Summit in Washington DC was attended by more than a dozen African heads of state and two thousand government and business executives. Among the speakers were US Secretary of State, Hillary Clinton, shortly after her return from an extensive Africa tour.

Business Center

In 2010 the Corporate Council has established a U.S.-Africa Business Center (USABC) with a grant from the US Agency for International Development (USAID). The USABC aims at increasing two-way trade and investment between the US and sub-Saharan Africa, with its focus on small and medium-sized enterprises. The USABC serves as a one-stop shop for information and technical assistance to American and African companies interested in regional and international trade and investment. It also focuses on a searchable database of American and African businesses seeking to do business with each other with a special focus on Africa's largest and most dynamic economies and organizing seminars in the U.S. to examine opportunities in Africa's most promising business sectors.

Corporate Council on Africa President Stephen Hayes introduces guest speaker US Secretary of State Hillary Clinton at the Council's 2009 Biennial Summit in Washington DC

Assistance

Within the World Bank Group there are several divisions that have aid and loan programs specifically for Africa, while in the United States Eximbank, OPIC, USAID, FAS and TDA are among the agencies that offer programs aimed at expanding US business involvement on the continent. Several infrastructural and other development projects of interest to US contractors are funded by the African Development Bank, the World Bank or country donors. These programs provide opportunities not only for multinational or transnational giants but also small and medium-sized firms looking for the first time at the possibility of doing business with Africa.

Africa has claimed an increasing share of funds allocated for special programs by major World Bank and United Nations development agencies. International agencies involved in funding and underwriting African projects include IDA, UNIDO and UNDP. MIGA helps to minimize risk by providing investment guarantees and technical assistance in member African countries. Especially in countries where foreigners are uncertain about their legal rights reliance on the ICSIP arbitration center is a good option.

No project is too big or too small to run by these agencies. In fact, the Small Business Administration has been an active promoter of business between small and medium-sized US enterprises and their counterparts in Africa. Even though the Trade and Development Agency works on a small budget, its impact on expansion of business in Africa has been significant. Several of the feasibility studies which it funded eventually led to major projects financed by other agencies.

Following are some of the key international and US agencies involved in Africa:

INTERNATIONAL

The African Development Bank (ADB)
01 BP 1387 Abidjan 01
Côte d'Ivoire
Tel: (225) 20.20.44.44
Fax: (225) 20.20.40.06
Website: www.afdb.org
The ADB was established in the 1960s to make loans and equity investments for economic and social advancement in its 53 member countries.

WORLD BANK GROUP

International Development Association (IDA)
1818 H Street NW
Washington DC 20433
Tel: 202-477-1234
Fax: 202-477-6391
Website: www.worldbank.org/ida
The International Development Association (IDA) is the World Bank Group's concessional lending window. Half of its active projects are in Africa amounting to over $1 billion a year.

International Finance Corporation (IFC)
2121 Pennsylvania Avenue NW
Washington DC 20433
Tel: 202-473-7711
Fax: 202-974-4384
Website: www.if.org
Since its creation in 1989, the IFC's African Enterprise Fund (AEF) has provided a total of $206 million for 309 projects in 30 African countries. Projects are appraised, processed, and supervised by IFC representatives in Africa.

Multilateral Insurance Guarantee Agency (MIGA)
1800 K Street NW (Suite 1200)
Washington DC 20433
Tel: 202-473-6167
Fax: 202-522-2630
Website: www.miga.org
MIGA's mandate is to encourage the flow of foreign direct investment to developing and other member countries. Through its guarantee program it offers insurance to mitigate political risk and provides promotional and advisory services to member countries to help attract and retain direct investment.

International Center for Settlement of Investment Disputes (ICSID)
1818 H Street N W
Washington DC 20433
Tel: 202-458-1534
Fax: 202-522-2615
Website: www.worldbank.org/icsid
ICSID was established in 1966 as an autonomous international organization but maintains close links with the World Bank. All its members are also members of the Bank. It provides facilities for the conciliation and arbitration of disputes between member countries and foreign investors. Recourse to ICSID arbitration is voluntary.

UNITED NATIONS

UN Industrial Development Organization (UNIDO)
Vienna International Center
A-1400 Vienna
Austria
Tel: (43) 1-26026
Fax: (43) 1-269-2269
Website: www.unido.org
UNIDO promotes and accelerates industrialization in developing countries by contracting with international

consultants to provide technical assistance to local companies and organizations. Consultancy projects range from general surveys to transfer of manufacturing technology and the establishment of pilot plants.

UN Development Program (UNDP)
Bureau for Development Policy
United Nations, New York
Tel: 212-906-5200
Fax: 212-906-5857
Website: www.undp.org
The UNDP is the world's largest multilateral grant development and assistance organization with offices in 124 countries and drawing on the expertise of 40 specialized and technical UN agencies. It also works extensively with non-governmental organizations and the business sector.

US AGENCIES

Export-Import Bank of the US (Eximbank)
811 Vermont Ave NW
Washington DC 20571T
Toll free: 800-565-3946
Tel: 202-565-3946
Fax: 202-565-3380
Website: www.exim.gov
The Eximbank is an independent government agency that assists in the sale of US goods and services overseas by providing loans and other credit measures. Eximbank's loans, guarantees and insurance supported more than $150 million in US exports to Sub-Saharan Africa in the first half of 1999. The bank is open to consider project finance business in every African country with the exclusion of Sudan and Libya. Financing is available for projects that do not rely on typical export credit security but need long-term cash flow financing.

Foreign Agricultural Service (FAS)
Department of Agriculture, Africa & Middle East
Washington DC 20250-1000
Tel: 202-720-3222
Website: www.fas.usda.gov
FAS assists in the development and expansion of US agricultural exports to Africa and other regions. Assistance includes Export Credit Guarantee Programs (GSM-102 and GSM-103) to underwrite private bank credit for three or ten years, a Supplier Credit Guarantee Program (SCGP) that extends short term guarantees up to 180 days, and the Facility Guarantee Program (FGP) that provides payment guarantees to improve or establish agriculture-related facilities in emerging markets.

Overseas Private Investment Corporation (OPIC)
1100 New York Avenue
Washington DC 20527
Tel: 202-336-8799
Website: www.opic.gov
OPIC is a self-sustaining government agency that provides investment information, financing, and political risk insurance for US investors in African and other developing countries. It currently has four privately managed funds that support investment in Sub-Saharan Africa: the New Africa Opportunity Fund for Southern Africa, the Modern Africa Growth and Investment Fund, the Global Environment Emerging Markets Fund II, and the Aqua International Partners Fund.

Trade Information Center (TIC)
International Trade Administration
US Department of Commerce
Washington DC 20230
Tel: 1-800-USA-TRADE
Fax: 202-482-4473
Website: www.ita.doc.gov
The TIC, operated by the International Trade Administration of the US Department of Commerce for the 20 federal agencies comprising the Trade Promotion Coordinating Committee (TPCC), is the first stop for US exporters seeking government advice and assistance. It provides country-specific export counseling and assistance for Africa, including trade leads and suggestions on potential sources for export financing.

US Agency for International Aid and Development (USAID)
Ronald Reagan Building
Washington DC 20523-0016
Tel: 202-712-4320
Fax: 202-216-3524
Website: www.usaid.gov
USAID implements government foreign economic assistance programs ranging from health, education, economic growth, population, democracy, environment, and crisis prevention. In most of these programs the US private sector has an opportunity to participate. Regional programs offered by USAID include the following: the Leland Initiative, the Greater Horn of Africa Initiative (GHAI), the Initiative for Southern Africa (ISA), the Africa Food Security Initiative (AFSI), and the Africa Trade and Investment Policy (ATRIP). The Leland Initiative seeks to bring the benefits of the global information revolution to the people of Africa.

US Small Business Administration (SBA)
409 3rd Street SW
Washington DC 20416
Tel: 800-U-ASK-SBA
Website: www.sba.gov
The SBA has taken an active role in promoting American small business ventures in Africa. SBA's Export Working Capital Program (EWCP) provides short-term loans to small businesses for export-related transactions. Its International Trade (IT) Loan Program offers a combination of working capital and fixed asset financing to help small businesses compete more effectively in the export markets. The Small Business Administration can guarantee up to $1 million for fixed assets and $750,000 for working capital.

US Trade and Development Agency (TDA)
1621 North Kent Street
Arlington VA 22209
Tel: 703-875-4357
Fax: 703-875-4009
Website: www.tda.gov
The TDA helps US businesses by funding feasibility studies, orientation visits, specialized training grants, business workshops, and various forms of technical assistance, enabling them to compete for infrastructure and industrial projects in Africa and other middle-income and developing regions. Overall TDA funding for projects related to the Africa/Middle East was $8.2 million out of a total budget of $41 million in 1998.

COMMITTED TO AFRICA

The Coca-Cola Company (TCCC) has a well-established and far reaching footprint across the African continent. Its success is related to its straightforward approach to business — sustainable, local, long term and community-focused.

In a business context, sustainability typically refers to the economic, social and environmental performance of a company. At TCCC, sustainability is defined as creating meaningful benefits for society as the company manages and grows its business – in effect, an inclusive business model.

"We're working to embed sustainability into every aspect of our business, beginning with our business planning process. In addition, we are committed to developing the capabilities of our people, and ensuring that our system associates, stakeholders, customers and consumers are engaged," says Muhtar Kent, Chairman and CEO, The Coca-Cola Company.

A local partner

The Coca-Cola Company has an 82 year history on the African continent and, today, operates in all countries and territories, has more than 160 plants and 68,000 direct system employees. It has invested heavily in Africa over the past few years and will continue to do so.

"We have always known that continued investment is required for the success of our business and the success of the community. That's why our system has invested $5.6-billion in Africa over the past 10 years. And by 2020, our system (which includes our Bottling partners) plans to invest an additional $12-billion in the continent," says Kent.

In Africa, the community investments of the Coca-Cola System are managed through The Coca-Cola Africa Foundation. The Foundation's mission is to enable African communities to improve the quality of their lives and fulfill their potential. It focuses on four key areas of community investment – water, preventive health, education and entrepreneurship. The Foundation is also involved in humanitarian assistance in Africa, for disaster relief and emergency aid.

Water Stewardship

Water is integral to The Coca-Cola Company – it is an essential ingredient in all of its products and production processes, and it is needed to produce the agricultural ingredients in these products.

TCCC has made a commitment as a water user, to return to communities and nature an amount of water equivalent to what it uses in its beverages and their production by 2020 – effectively committing to water balance.

The rationale behind this commitment is simple. Says Ahmet C Bozer, President, Eurasia & Africa Group: "To ensure that we have a sustainable business in the future, we need the communities we serve to be sustainable. Water is critical to the health and economic prosperity of these communities and thus, water is key for us too."

While no one company or organisation can solve the world's water problems alone, Coca-Cola has quantified and made its commitments public and is working to assist where it can. Its water stewardship goal is focused on three areas – Reduce, Recycle, Replenish.

On the ground

In Africa, The Coca-Cola Company has been running its RAIN – Replenish Africa Initiative – for just over a year now. While it has been involved with water projects across the continent

---

Well balanced

The Coca-Cola Company has set an aspirational goal to safely return to communities and nature an amount of water equivalent to what is used in all of its beverages and their production.

It has set global, time-bound, measurable targets in three areas related to water stewardship:

- **Reduce** the Company's water use ratio while growing the unit case volume, with a target to improve water efficiency by 20 percent over 2004 levels by 2012. By 2009, the Company had achieved a 12.6 percent improvement over the 2004 baseline.

- **Recycle** the water used in operations by returning treated water to the environment at a level that supports aquatic life by the end of 2010. In 2009, all plants system-wide complied with local standards, and 89 percent of Coca-Cola system facilities (approximately 95 percent of reported volume) were in compliance with the Company's generally more stringent global wastewater treatment standards.

- **Replenish** the water used in finished beverages by participating in locally relevant projects that support communities and nature and meet and maintain this goal by 2020. Estimates are that by the end of 2009, the Company was replenishing approximately 22 percent of the water used in finished beverages through the support of some 250 community water programs in approximately 70 countries.

for many years, the announcement of RAIN came with a defined set of goals and a financial commitment.

By leveraging a $30-million commitment, by 2015, RAIN seeks to:

- Provide over 2 million people with access to clean water
- Launch over 100 healthy watershed and sustainable community water access, sanitation and hygiene programs across Africa
- Contribute to the sustainability of water resources for communities across Africa
- Provide people with sanitation and hygiene education
- Leverage co-funding through partnerships.

Since the announcement in 2009, The Coca-Cola Africa Foundation, custodian of the RAIN initiative, has launched 12 projects in 11 different countries which will be completed between 2011 and 2013. It is expected that 5 projects in Kenya (2 projects), Mozambique, South Africa, and Zambia will close out in 2010.

It has also committed $6-million in 2010 to support water projects in Angola, Burundi, Cameroon, DRC, Egypt, Ghana, Liberia, Malawi, Morocco, Mozambique, Nigeria, Senegal, South Africa, Swaziland, Tanzania, Tunisia, Uganda, and Zimbabwe. Additional matched funding for these projects has been provided by USAID and other partners.

"For The Coca-Cola Company, leaving a lasting legacy is not about one project. It's an ongoing commitment. Helping African communities tackle their water challenges is an important priority for our Company and our Bottling partners and is an area where we can make a positive and lasting impact," says William Asiko, President of the Foundation and Group Public Affairs and Communications Director.

Community focused

The Coca-Cola Africa Foundation is also supporting communities through its other focus areas. In the Preventive Health space the Foundation runs programs related to the prevention of HIV/Aids and malaria. It runs three types of Education programs through partnerships with the Discovery Channel Global Education Partnership, the Zawadi Africa Education Fund and the Africa America Institute and provides Entrepreneurial skills-training

Finding new local solutions: a quick look at Micro Distribution Centers

In Ethiopia 10 years ago, Coca-Cola's local bottler was finding it difficult to distribute its products effectively to small shops in densely populated parts of Addis Ababa. Traditional methods using large trucks were proving ineffective – the small shops could only handle small drop sizes, and the roads were not suitable for large trucks.

To address this, a model was designed that made use of local entrepreneurs acting as distribution 'hub points', while allowing Coca-Cola to focus its efforts on growing the market. After an initial pilot, this challenge became an opportunity – both for the company and for the community as a new, innovative distribution approach spread quickly across East Africa and beyond.

A network of over 3,000 independently-owned micro-distribution centers can now be found across 15 (and growing) African countries. These in turn provide direct employment to over 13,500 people, together generate in excess of $550-million in revenue for local economies, and provide a close proximity service to over 400,000 small retail outlets. In some countries, this model accounts for the majority of sales volumes. Similar models are now being replicated in other comparable markets in Coca-Cola's business worldwide.

through partnerships with Students in Free Enterprise and Junior Achievement Worldwide.

Through these programs, The Coca-Cola Africa Foundation has touched the lives of over 500,000 people with an investment of over US$47.7-million (up to 2009). A further US$12.8-million has been invested in 2010.

For information about The Coca-Cola Company visit *www.thecoca-colacompany.com*. For further information about RAIN and The Coca-Cola Africa Foundation, please visit *www.tccaf.org*.

The Coca-Cola Company

Connected.
Trained.
Prepared.

In Africa, International Relief & Development is improving water security. From emergency response to irrigation to latrines to safe drinking water, our teams work with communities to ensure the long-term sustainability of their infrastructure development and rehabilitation activities.

The case of Mozambique. When the Zambezi river flooded in 2008, IRD constructed water supply points, distributed hygiene supplies, rehabilitated boreholes, and constructed new latrines. Then we focused on improving water and sanitation conditions for internally displaced persons, targeting behavior changes crucial to maintaining their health.

In Mozambique, Sudan, Swaziland, Zimbabwe, and a dozen other African countries, IRD is giving the most vulnerable people a strong voice in their development and the tools they need for self-sufficiency. Today we are training masons to install wells, construct rainwater harvesting systems, and bio-sand filters. We are also teaching conservation agriculture methods to farmers and establishing local risk-management committees to help communities prepare for the next event.

Since 1998, IRD has been giving the world's most vulnerable people a strong voice in their development and the tools they need for self-sufficiency.

Learn more at www.ird.org/infrastructure

INTERNATIONAL RELIEF & DEVELOPMENT
1621 N. KENT ST., 4TH FLOOR | ARLINGTON, VA 22209 | 703.248.0161

IRD

Chapter 6
Challenges of Africa

Reed-thin refugees from fierce fighting are real in Africa. So are the millions of HIV/AIDS infected Africans and the wars and corruption that persist despite admirable efforts by a new leadership to establish peace, democracy and responsible and transparent governance across the Continent. While some see these challenges as insurmountable others are making great progress in finding solutions.

A member of the UN Mission for the Referendum in Western Sahara (MINURSO)'s Military Liaison Office communicates with a family in Western Sahara. (UN Photo)

WARS & REFUGEES

According to the United Nations more than 30 wars have been fought in Africa since 1970—most of them internal struggles. In 1996, the worst single year, 14 of the continent's 53 countries were affected by armed conflict, accounting for more than half of all war-related deaths worldwide and resulting in more than 8 million refugees, returnees and displaced persons. A recent study shows that conflicts in Africa cost the continent over 300 billion U.S. dollars between 1990 and 2005—an amount equivalent to all the international aid received by sub-Saharan Africa in the same period.

Deaths as the result of a 17-year civil war in the Sudan are estimated at 2 million while 500,000 have died in Angola over the past 25 years and a million in Rwanda over a six year period. Almost all of these conflicts involve power struggles within countries. The IMF points out that while armed conflicts and political instability continue to undermine prospects in a number of countries, the frequency of such events in the region as a whole has declined over the past decade.

UNHCR

According to the UN High Commissioner for Refugees (UNHCR) there are 21.8 million refugees worldwide (1 out of every 275 persons) and 25 million internally displaced people. Africa at 4.17 million refugees is second to Asia with 8.8 million.

Main Causes

The legacy left by the Berlin Conference in 1885 when Africa was partitioned by European colonial powers without any regard for populations is undoubtedly a contributing factor. Some states, however, accomplished a remarkable degree of peace and national unity among diverse peoples within their arbitrary borders. Others, however, are having a hard time to cope with these divisions and attempts from split tribes to reunite.

Other reasons

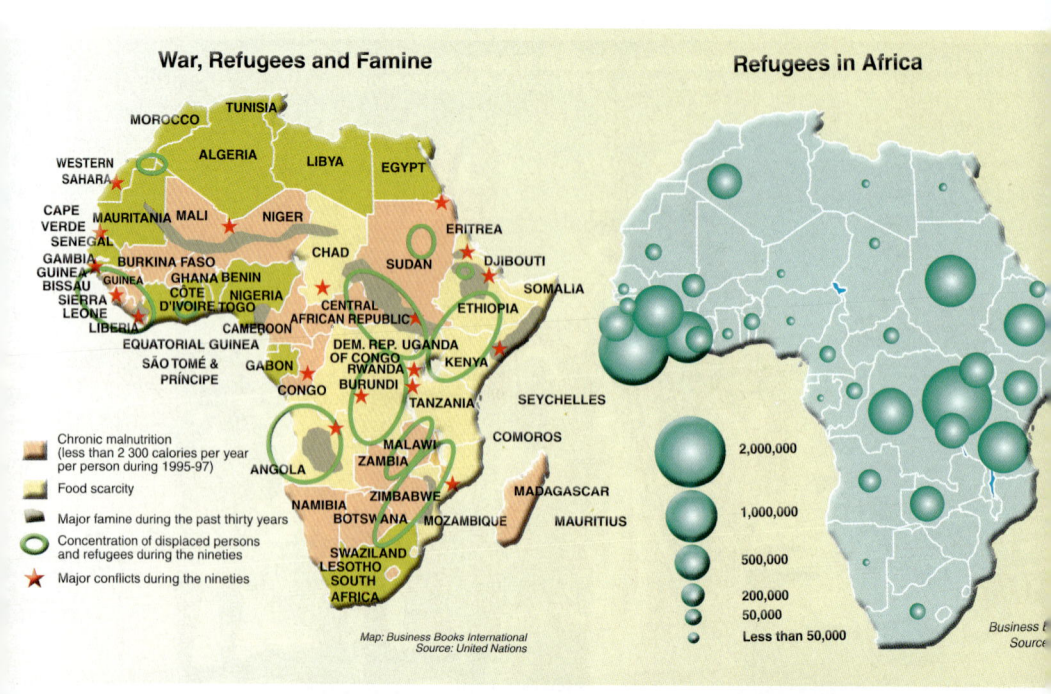

Other reasons are greed, grievance against leadership, and desperation born out of poverty and hunger. One cynical view is that rebellion and war might in some instances be the only job opportunity. The warlords and the international arms merchants who gain handsomely from these small but devastating wars-for-profit have little interest in stopping the conflict.

Peacekeeping

Despite criticism that the UN has been derelict in its peacekeeping duty in Africa, 7 out of 16 current operations are in Africa. It has met with mixed success. While strife continues in Somalia, Sudan and the Democratic Republic of Congo several operations were brought to a successful conclusion. In Sierra Leone, Burundi and Liberia the UN managed to oversee elections and restore a measure of stability. In the Democratic Republic of Congo, howver, UN-supervised elections failed to stop the fighting.

UN Patrol in Western Sahara

Africans themselves are becoming more active in finding solutions. The African Union has peacekeepers in the DRC and the Darfur region of Sudan. The Economic Community for West African States (ECOWAS) participated in peace efforts in Liberia, Sierra Leone and more recently in Côte d'Ivoire. The most recently implemented missions are in Darfur, Chad and the Central African Republic in an effort to meet the challenges posed by the spillover effect of the situation in Sudan. UN Peacekeeping missions currently undertaken in Africa are as follows:

UN Peacekeeping Operations

Business Books International
Source: United Nations

CURRENT OPERATIONS

UNAMID	UN/AU Mission in Darfur	Started April 2007
MINURCAT	UN Mission in Chad/CAR	Started Sept. 2007
MINURSO	UN Msn. Referendum (Western Sahara)	Started Apr. 1991
MONUC	UN Mission in Dem. Rep. of Congo	Started Dec. 1999
UNMIL	UN Mission in Liberia	Started Sep. 2003
UNMIS	UN Mission in Sudan	Started Mar. 2005
UNOCI	UN Operation in Côte d'Ivoire	Started Apr. 2004

COMPLETED OPERATIONS

ONUB	UN Operation in Burundi	May 2004-Dec. 2006
UNAVEM I	UN Angola Verification Mission	Dec.1988-Feb.1991
UNAVEM II	UN Angola Verification Mission	May 1991-Feb.1995
UNAVEM III	UN Angola Verification Mission	Feb. 1995-Jun.1997
MONUA	UN Observer Mission in Angola	Jun.1997-Feb. 1999
MINURCA	UN Mission in the CAR	Apr. 1998-Feb. 2000
UNASOG	UN Aouzou Observer (Chad/Libya)	May 1994-Jun. 1994
ONUC	UN Operation in the Congo	Jul. 1960-Jun. 1964
UNOMIL	UN Observer Mission in Liberia	Sep. 1993-Sep.1997
ONUMOZ	UN Operation in Mozambique	Dec. 1992-Dec. 1994
UNTAG	UN Trans. Asst. Gr. (Namibia)	Apr. 1989-Mar. 1990
UNAMIR	UN Assistance Miss. for Rwanda	Oct. 1993-Mar. 1996
UNOMUR	UN Observer Msn. Uganda/Rwanda	Jun. 1993-Sep. 1994
UNOMSIL	UN Observer Msn. (Sierra Leone)	Jul. 1998-Oct. 1999
UNOSOM I	UN Operations in Somalia I	Apr. 1992-Mar. 1993
UNOSOM II	UN Operations in Somalia I	Mar. 1993-Mar. 1995
MINUCI	UN Mission in Côte d'Ivoire	May 2003-Apr. 2004
UNMEE	UN Mission in Ethiopia and Eritrea	Jul. 2000-Jul. 2008

United Nations Organization Mission in the Democratic Republic of the Congo (MONUC)
Established in November 1999 to liaise with the signatories to the cease-fire agreement enforce the observation of the cease-fire.

United Nations Mission in Sudan (UNMIS)
EUNMIS supports the Comprehensive Peace Agreement signed by the Government of Sudan and the Sudan People's Liberation Movement/Army in Nairobi on 9 January 2005. It also provides support to the African Union Mission in Sudan (AMIS) which is operating in Darfur.

United Nations Operation in Côte d'Ivoire (UNOCI)
In April 2004 MINUCI was replaced by UNOCI after the UN determined that the situation in Côte d'Ivoire continued to pose a threat to international peace and security in the region. Its mandate is implement the peace agreement signed by the Ivorian warring parties in January 2003.

United Nations Mission in Liberia (UNMIL)
Established on 19 September 2003 to support the implementation of the ceasefire agreement and the peace process; protect United Nations staff, facilities and civilians; support humanitarian and human rights activities; as well as assist in national security reform.

United Nations Integrated Office in Burundi (BINUB)
The United Nations Integrated Office in Burundi (BINUB), established by Security Council on 25 October 2006, will be monitoring the situation as Burundi prepares for new elections in 2010.

Undernourished people
Millions - 2009

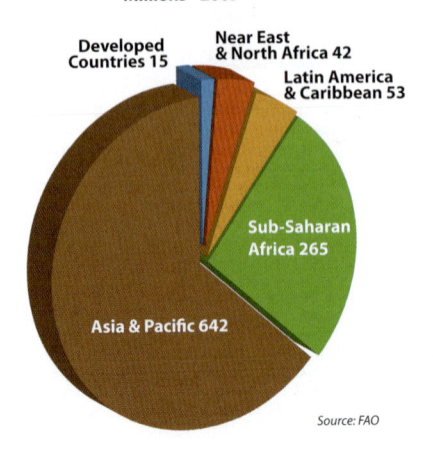

- Developed Countries 15
- Near East & North Africa 42
- Latin America & Caribbean 53
- Sub-Saharan Africa 265
- Asia & Pacific 642

Source: FAO

FAMINE

Famine is not a problem peculiar to Africa. In 1958, between 20 and 30 million Chinese died in the worst famine of the twentieth century. Famine and malnutrition, however, present major challenges in Africa with its large expanse of arid land. Drought, conflict, natural disasters, overpopulation, overgrazing and inadequate farming methods have all been identified as contributing factors to recurring famine in Africa. Famine is the result of both warfare and weather.

The Brussels-based *Center for Research on Epidemiology of Disasters* (CRED) that does research in cooperation with the WHO, put the number of people affected by drought and famine in Africa since 1960 at over 245 million.

Drought

At the beginning of the new millennium 36 African countries were affected by drought. Sometimes prolonged and extreme droughts are followed by equally devastating floods, as witnessed in Mozambique in recent times. Roughly 2 billion hectares or 65 percent of Africa's total land area, inhabited by more than half of the continent's total population, is arid land—one third of it hyper arid and the rest consisting of arid, semi-arid and dry land. Nineteen African countries are among 25 in the world identified as having the highest percentage of their population without access to drinking water. Precipitation ranges from almost zero over the Horn of Africa and the Namibian Desert to more than 158 inches (4,000 mm). Most of Africa's semi-arid landmass depends on between 8 and 16 inches (200-800 mm) per year. Due to inadequate infrastructure, only 4% of an estimated 5.2 trillion cubic yards (4 trillion cubic m) of Africa's renewable water is exploited. There is a lack of regional cooperation between countries in the development and exploitation of water resources offered by the Nile, Zambezi, Volta, and Niger rivers and Lake Victoria. Several new large dam projects have been launched with world organizations and multinational corporations.

UN Photo

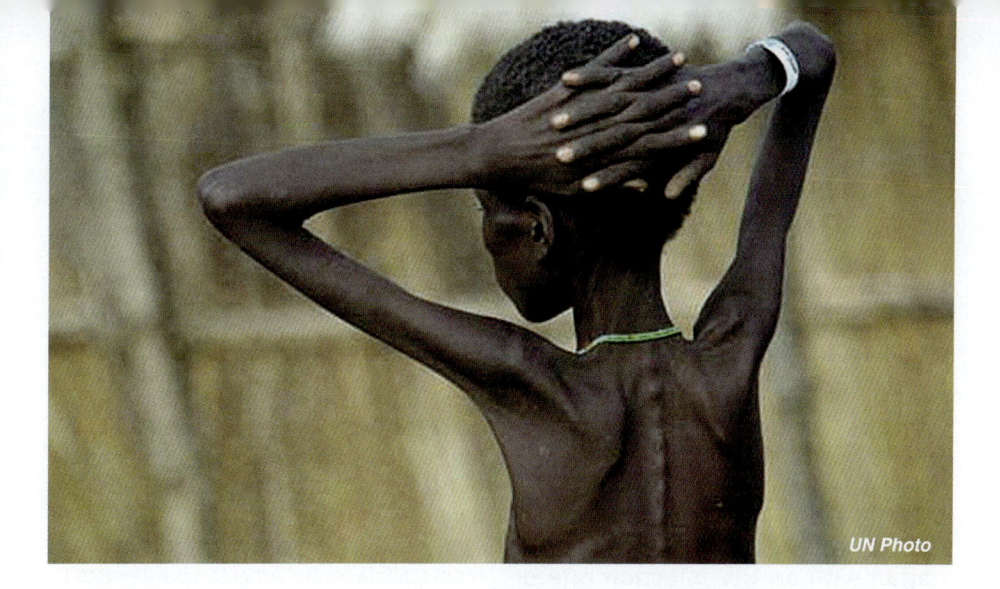

Overgrazing

Vegetation and soil degradation as a result of overgrazing, deforestation, and overcultivation, coupled with inappropriate agricultural technology, have been identified as major problems. About 90 percent of Africa's soils are deficient in phosphorus and low in organic matter. There is low water infiltration and retention due to surface crusting.

Rain forests

Between 1980 and 1990 Africa's rain forests shrunk from 569 million to 530 million hectares—averaging an annual deforestation rate of 0.7 percent. Commercial logging, clearance for agricultural reasons and wood fuel are all contributing to the problem. In Sub-Saharan Africa, 70 percent of the total consumed and 90 percent of household energy are derived from wood fuel. The average African family uses an estimated 7 metric tons of wood per year.

Conflict

There is the fear that unless properly developed and managed on a regional basis, Africa's available water resources might trigger conflicts at local, national and regional levels as the demand increases.

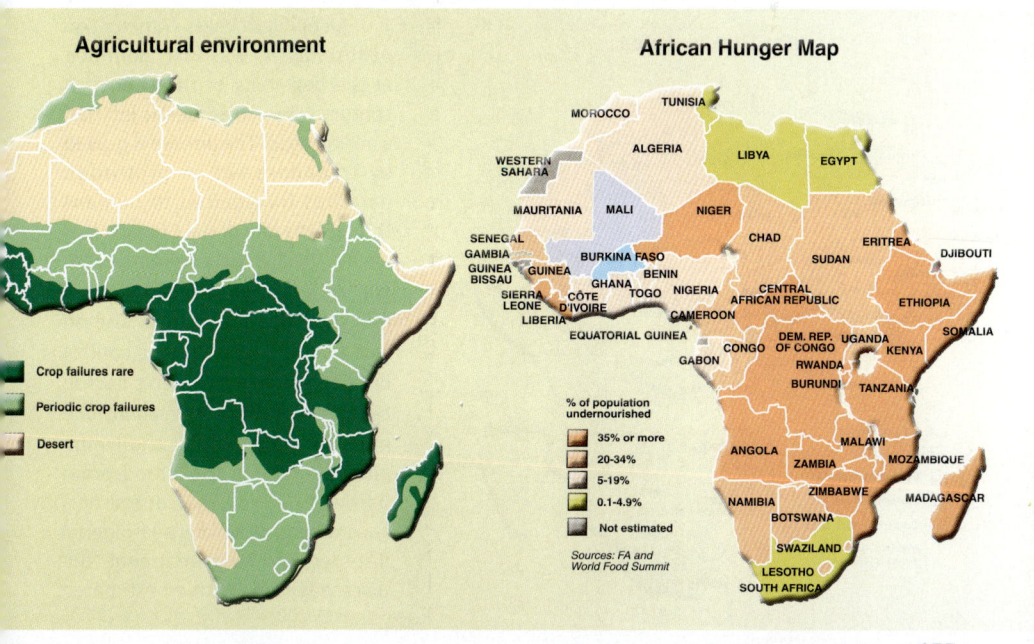

Agricultural environment

- Crop failures rare
- Periodic crop failures
- Desert

African Hunger Map

% of population undernourished
- 35% or more
- 20-34%
- 5-19%
- 0.1-4.9%
- Not estimated

Sources: FA and World Food Summit

TROPICAL DISEASES

HIV/AIDS, TB and malaria are the leading killer diseases in developing regions, including Africa. Between them these three affect 300 million people and each year cause some 5 million deaths worldwide. Apart from human suffering the affected countries pay a heavy economic toll. Some experts claim that Africa would have been $100 billion better off today if malaria had been eliminated years ago. Others claim that any African nation with an HIV infection rate of more than 20% could expect a GDP decline of 1% per year.

With the public focus on HIV/AIDS not only malaria and an alarming resurgence of tuberculosis, but also a host of other deadly and costly tropics-related diseases have been largely ignored in recent years. While Africans are less prone to heart disease and cancer than the inhabitants of Europe and North America they are exposed to a number of deadly and crippling tropical and subtropical diseases.

Malaria

Malaria is endemic in 101 countries and regions. Africa is most seriously affected with more than 90 percent of all malaria cases. Many millions on the African continent have this debilitating disease, transmitted by the Anopheles mosquito. Malaria kills more people worldwide than any other communicable disease with the exception of tuberculosis. Deaths as a result of malaria are estimated at over 1 million per year, mostly among African youth. The disease also exacts an enormous toll in medical costs and in labor days. The geographical area affected by malaria has shrunk considerably over the past fifty years but control is becoming more difficult with the emergence of multi-drug resistant strains of the parasite and increased international travel. According to UNICEF, the average cost for each nation in Africa to implement malaria control programs is estimated to be at least $300,000 a year. Mapping Malaria Risk in Africa (MARA) in conjunction with Atlas du Risque de la Malaria en Afrique (ARMA) undertook extensive studies on the incidence of malaria in Africa. Our map n the opposite page is based on MARA/ARMA data in which endemic regions are defined as "areas with significant annual transmission, be it seasonal or perennial" and epidemic regions as "areas prone to distinct inter-annual variation, in some years with no transmission taking place at all." The Multilateral Initiative on Malaria (MIM) was launched in Dakar in the nineties by public and private sectors and the WHO.

Sleeping sickness

Sleeping sickness *(African trypanosomiasis)* was first identified at the beginning of the twentieth century when an epidemic left half a million dead. The disease is caused by *trypanosomes* or protozoan parasites transmitted to humans through the bite of the Glossina tsetse fly. Through persistent research and with new tools and improved field strategies, the endemic disease was slowly brought under control but not eradicated. When a person becomes infected, the *trypanosome* multiplies in the blood and lymph glands, crossing the blood-brain barrier to invade the central nervous system, provoking neurological disorders. Without treatment, the disease is fatal. With an estimated

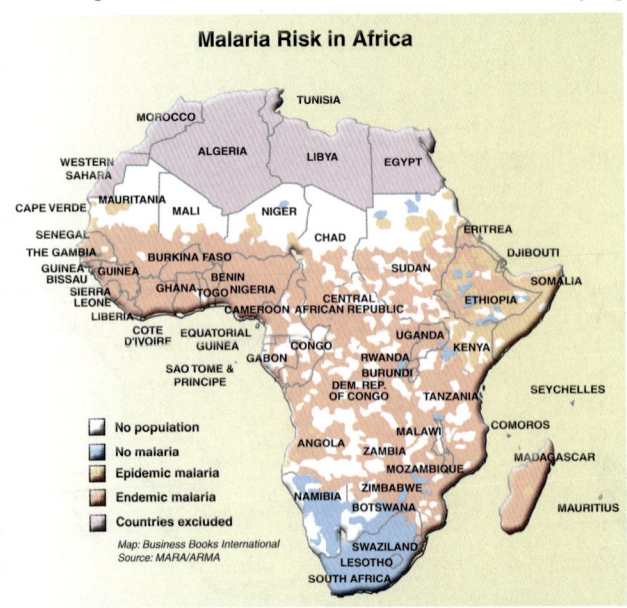

300,000 to 500,000 people infected the disease has a major impact on the labor force.

Ebola

Originating in the jungles of Africa and Asia, Ebola Haemorrhagic Fever (EHF) is one of the most virulent viral diseases known to humankind, causing death in 50% to 90% of all reported cases. The Ebola virus is transmitted by direct contact with the blood, secretions, and organs or semen of infected persons. Transmission of the Ebola virus has also occurred by handling sick or dead infected chimpanzees. Health care workers have frequently been infected while attending patients. The Ebola virus was first identified in 1976 after significant epidemics in northern Zaire (Democratic Republic of Congo) and Nzara, in southern Sudan. Ebola-related filoviruses were also isolated from *cynomolgus* monkeys (*Macacca fascicularis*), imported into the United States from the Philippines in 1989.

Yellow fever

Though largely associated with the tropics of Africa and South America, Yellow Fever has, until the beginning of the 20th Century, occurred in Europe and North America. The "yellow" in the name denotes jaundice that affects some patients. Although a safe and effective vaccine has been available for 60 years, the virus is still present with low levels of infection (i.e. endemic) in the African and South American tropical areas. In Africa thirty-three countries within a band from 15°N to 10°S of the equator and a combined population of 468 million are at risk. The virus is spread among animals and humans by mosquitos and to their offspring through infected eggs.

Dengue

Dengue is endemic in more than 100 countries in Africa, the Americas, the Eastern Mediterranean, South-East Asia and the Western Pacific. WHO estimates there may be as many as 50 million cases of dengue infection worldwide every year. The Dengue virus is transmitted by infected female *Aedes* mosquitoes. It causes a flu-like illness, which affects infants, young children and adults, but rarely causes death. At present the only method of controlling or preventing Dengue and DHF is to combat the vector mosquitoes.

River blindness

Although also present in the Arabian Peninsula and South America, river blindness (*Onchocerciasis*) is mostly associated with Africa where it has become a serious public health problem. Of the 36 countries where the disease is endemic, 30 are in Sub-Saharan Africa and six are in the Americas. Close to 99 percent of the 18 million people infected are in Africa. Among those infected 6.5 million suffer from severe *dermatitis* and 270,000 are blind. *Onchocerciasis* is caused by *Onchocerca volvulus*, a parasitic worm that lives in the human body for up to 14 years. Each adult female worm, thin but more than 1/2 meter in length, produces millions of *microfilariae* (microscopic larvae) carried from one human to another by the blackfly (*Simulium damnosum*).

Bilharziasis

Among human parasitic diseases, *schistosomiasis* (a.k.a. *bilharziasis*) is second only to malaria as a public health threat in the world's tropical and subtropical areas. The disease is endemic in 74 developing countries, infecting more than 200 million people in rural agricultural and peri-urban areas. *Schistosomes* enter the body through contact with infested surface water. Three drugs—*praziquantel, oxamniquine* and *metrifonate*—are used to treat the disease.

Secretary-General Ban Ki-moon (left) inspects a mosquito net, a key malaria preventer, at Mwandama Millennium Village, Malawi. (UN Photo)

HIV/AIDS

HIV/AIDS (human immunodeficiency virus/acquired immune deficiency syndrome) is the leading cause of death in Africa and among the greatest threats to the continent's social and economic development. The epidemic threatens the future of a continent, where in hard-hit countries up to a quarter of all adults are infected.

The most recent statistics jointly published by UNAIDS and the World Health Organization (WHO) put the number of people living with the virus in 2008 at 33.4 million or between 31.1 and 35.8 million—a significant decrease from the 2006 estimate of 39.5 million. (Applying an "improved methodology" UNAIDS has also revised its 2006 figure to 32.7 million). Based on "improvements in country data collection and analysis, as well as a better understanding of the natural history and distribution of HIV infection" the 2009 report puts the number of new infections in 2008 at 2.7 million, down from a peak of over 3 million a year in the late nineties. About 1.9 million of these new infections occurred in Sub-Saharan Africa. The estimated total number of deaths due to AIDS in 2008 was 2.0 million worldwide of which 1.4 million occurred in Sub-Saharan Africa.

Sub-Saharan Africa

Sub-Saharan Africa remains the region most heavily affected by HIV. In 2008, the region accounted for 67% of HIV infections worldwide, 68% of new HIV infections among adults and 91% of new HIV infections among children. It represented 72% of the world's AIDS-related deaths in 2008. An estimated 1.9 million [1.6 million–2.2 million] people living in sub-Saharan Africa became newly infected with HIV, bringing the total number of people living with HIV in Africa to 22.4 million [20.8 million– 24.1 million]. While the rate of new HIV infections in sub-Saharan Africa has slowly declined—with the number of new infections in 2008 approximately 25% lower than at the epidemic's peak in the region in 1995—the number of people living with HIV in sub-Saharan Africa increased slightly in 2008, in part due to increased longevity stemming from improved access to HIV treatment. Adult (15–49) HIV prevalence declined from 5.8% [5.5–6.0%] in 2001 to 5.2% [4.9–5.4%] in 2008. An estimated 1.4 million [1.1 million–1.7 million] AIDS-related deaths occurred in sub-Saharan Africa. This number represents an 18% decline in annual HIV-related mortality in the region since 2004. However, the epidemic continues to have an enormous impact on households, communities, businesses, public services and national economies in the region. In Swaziland, average life expectancy fell by half between 1990 and 2007, to 37 years. In 2008, more than 14.1 million [11.5 million–17.1 million] children in sub-Saharan Africa were estimated to have lost one or both parents to AIDS. Women and girls continue to be affected disproportionately by HIV in sub-Saharan Africa. For example, in Côte d'Ivoire, home to the most serious epidemic in West Africa, HIV prevalence among females (6.4%) was more than twice as high as among males (2.9%) in 2005. In sub-Saharan Africa as a whole, women account for 60% of all HIV infections.

Aids orphans in Tanzania (UN Photo)

Global HIV infection - 33.4 million people [31.1-35.8 million] living with HIV in 2008

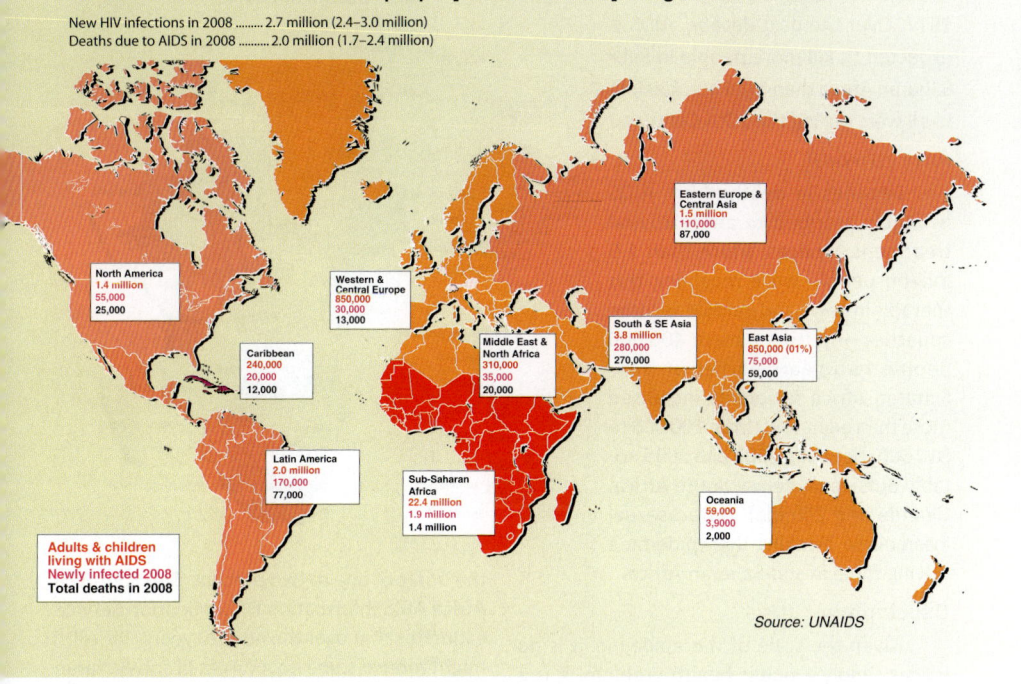

New HIV infections in 2008 .... 2.7 million (2.4–3.0 million)
Deaths due to AIDS in 2008 .... 2.0 million (1.7–2.4 million)

Region	Adults & children living with AIDS	Newly infected 2008	Total deaths in 2008
North America	1.4 million	55,000	25,000
Caribbean	240,000	20,000	12,000
Latin America	2.0 million	170,000	77,000
Western & Central Europe	850,000	30,000	13,000
Eastern Europe & Central Asia	1.5 million	110,000	87,000
Middle East & North Africa	310,000	35,000	20,000
Sub-Saharan Africa	22.4 million	1.9 million	1.4 million
South & SE Asia	3.8 million	280,000	270,000
East Asia	850,000 (01%)	75,000	59,000
Oceania	59,000	3,9000	2,000

Source: UNAIDS

Economic factor

HIV affects all social and economic groups in sub-Saharan Africa. Surveys in different settings in sub-Saharan Africa have detected a wide variation in the relationship between HIV and income. In eight African countries where surveys have been conducted (Burkina Faso, Cameroon, Ghana, Kenya, Lesotho, Malawi, Uganda and the United Republic of Tanzania), HIV prevalence is higher among wealthier adults. HIV prevalence tends to be higher in urban settings than in rural areas.

Southern Africa

Southern Africa Southern Africa remains the area most heavily affected by the epidemic. The nine countries with the highest HIV prevalence worldwide are all located in the subregion, with each of these countries experiencing adult HIV prevalence higher than 10%. With an estimated adult HIV prevalence of 26% in 2007, Swaziland has the most severe level of infection in the world. Botswana has an adult HIV prevalence of 24%, with some evidence of a decline in prevalence in urban areas. Lesotho's epidemic also appears to have stabilized, with an adult HIV prevalence of 23.2% in 2008. South Africa is home to the world's largest population of people living with HIV (5.7 million). For southern Africa as a whole, HIV incidence appears to have peaked in the mid-1990s. In most countries, HIV prevalence has stabilized at extremely high levels, although evidence indicates that HIV incidence continues to rise in rural Angola. However, antenatal surveillance in Swaziland found an increase in HIV prevalence, from 39.2% in 2006 to 42% in 2008, among female clinic attendees. There is also still no evidence of a decline in infections among pregnant women in South Africa, where more than 29% of women accessing public health services tested HIV-positive in 2008. While national adult HIV prevalence in South Africa has stabilized, prevalence among young people (aged 15–24) started to decline in 2005, from about 25% in 2004–2005 to 21.7% in 2008.

Catastrophe

HIV/AIDS in Sub-Saharan Africa has been described as the "worst infectious disease catastrophe" since the bubonic plague killed a quarter of Europe in the 14th Century. Deaths due to AIDS in the region, the UN anticipates, might still surpass the 20 million people who perished in Europe during the plague of 1347, and the more than 20 million people worldwide who died in the influenza epidemic of 1917. Over the next decade, AIDS is expected to kill more people in Sub-Saharan Africa than total number lost in all wars during the 20th Century.

Antiretroviral

Declines in deaths from AIDS is largely ascribed to antiretroviral treatment services. More than 1.5 million people were receiving this therapy in low- and middle-income countries—up from a mere 400,000 people two years earlier. In sub-Saharan Africa recipients increased more than eight-fold (from 100 000 to 810 000) between 2003 and 2005 notably Botswana, Kenya, South Africa, Uganda and Zambia). Heterosexual intercourse remains the epidemic's driving force in sub-Saharan Africa.

Development crisis

Given the scale of the epidemic, it is no longer simply a public health problem. It is a development crisis that has been in the making for at least 10 years. HIV/AIDS has already reversed 30 years of hard-won social progress in some countries and has impacted on every level from the micro- to the macroeconomic. Companies have begun to realize that HIV/AIDS poses a genuine threat to the workforce and the marketplace. Alarming new costs are showing up on balance sheets. This is especially the case in Africa, where the private sector is feeling the cumulative impact of a severe, long-standing and still-emerging epidemic. Many businesses have started prevention programs at the workplace to try to protect their investment in human capital. They provide information and condoms to workers, often through peer education programs. Forward-thinking companies in high HIV/AIDS-prone countries, however, are looking beyond prevention to the inevitable dent that the disease will make in their workforce and their profits. The Global Business Coalition on HIV/AIDS was formed under UN auspices to mobilize the private sector. Employee turnover related to the disease increases training and recruitment costs. The effect of HIV/AIDS on the macro-level is hard to judge but expert studies point to a likely loss of real GDP growth in some African countries in the order of one to two percent. The Southern Africa AIDS Information Dissemination Service estimates that over the next 20 years HIV/AIDS might reduce some economies in sub-Saharan Africa by a fourth. The disease undermines agricultural systems and threatens the food security of rural families. The UN Food and Agriculture Administration (FAO) has estimated that in the 25 most-affected African countries, AIDS has killed seven million agricultural workers since 1985. Rural communities bear a higher burden of the cost of the disease as urban dwellers and migrant laborers return to their village of origin when they fall ill. Household expenditures rise as a result of medical bills and funeral expenses.

Increased cost

In Africa, the disease attacks educated urban professionals—the backbone of economic expansion—first. The loss of these people can rob the continent of much of its potential. Increased benefits and training costs, and the disruption of regular production due to sick and bereavement leave, are seriously affecting both the private and public sectors.

Projects

The UN Global Fund to Fight AIDS, Tuberculosis and Malaria was launched with $2.1 billion at its disposal—half the estimated amount needed. The US has pledged to spend $15 billion over five years to fight AIDS in Africa.

Water Wars

In many parts of Africa, water shortage is a part of everyday life. Many countries share one water resource and a large number depends almost totally on the weather to provide proper irrigation. Major sources such as the Nile, Volta, and Zambezi rivers, and the Niger Basin, are shared by a multitude of nations. Upstream water projects have led to the displacement of large populations and diminished flows downstream. With the growing demand for water resources, conflicts seem almost inevitable, especially with many African governments' history of poor management of resources and inadequate conflict resolution mechanisms.

Recent studies show water supplies diminishing in Africa and large parts elsewhere in the world—especially in underdeveloped arid regions. Population growth, depletion of groundwater, waste and pollution, and the effects of manmade climate change exacerbate the problem. It all leads to drought and famine, loss of livelihood, the spread of waterborne diseases, forced migrations, and in some instances open conflict.

Decline

The amount of water available per person in Africa is declining and only 26 of the continent's 53 countries are on track to reduce by half the number of people without sustainable access to clean drinking water by 2015, according to a survey by the United Nations Environment Programme (UNEP) released in November 2010. Furthermore, only five countries in Africa are expected to attain the target of reducing by half the proportion of the population without sustainable access to basic sanitation by 2015, the deadline of the Millennium Development Goals (MDGs)—a series of targets agreed to by all countries and leading development institutions to meet the needs of the world's poorest.

Arid areas

More than 40 percent of Africa's population lives in arid, semi-arid and dry humid areas. The amount of water available per person in Africa is far below the global average and is declining. Groundwater is falling and rainfall is also declining in some regions. Development of water resources is inadequate and prices to access water are generally distorted, with water provision highly inefficient.

After Australia, Africa is the world's second-driest continent. With 15 percent of the global population, it has only 9 percent of global renewable water resources. Water is unevenly distributed, with Central Africa holding 50.66 percent of the continent's total internal water and Northern Africa only 2.99 per cent.

The groundwater resources represent only 15 percent of total renewable water resources, but supply about 75 percent of Africa's population with most of its drinking water. In all regions except central Africa, water availability per person (4 008 m3 in 2008) is under global

A Sudanese student drinks and washes her face at a new water fountain built by volunteers at the Omer El-Mukhtar primary school for girls. (Photo:"Fred Noy—UN)

161

averages and lower than that of all of other world regions except Asia.

Most of the urban population growth has taken place in peri-urban squatter neighborhoods, overwhelming the capacity of water supply networks and resulting in an overall decline in piped water coverage. Between 2005 and 2010, Africa's urban population grew at a rate of 3.4 per cent, or 1.1 percent more than the rural population.

Mapping

The *Africa Water Atlas*, compiled by UNEP at the request of the African Ministers' Council on Water, reveals how irrigation projects in Kenya, Senegal and Sudan are helping to improve food security. It also draws attention to Africa's "water towers", which are sources for many of Africa's transboundary rivers that contribute largely to the total stream flow of African major rivers. These "towers" supply life-giving resources and services in downstream areas such as water for hydropower, wildlife and tourism, small and large scale agriculture, municipalities and ecosystem services. Most of these water towers, from the Middle Atlas Range in Morocco through to the Lesotho Highlands in Southern Africa, are under extreme pressure as a result of deforestation and encroachment.

Hopespots

Africa is known to be a global "hotspot" for water constrained, rain-fed agriculture and climate-driven food insecurity with about 100 million people in Africa living in these areas. But new research, captured in the Atlas, reveals that there are also "hopespots" in drought-prone environments where there is enormous potential for expanding simple water-harvesting techniques. Images from the *Water Atlas* show how the successful harvesting of rainwater in the Horn of Africa, particularly in Kenya, is already mitigating the risk for farmers and helping to reduce food insecurity in their communities. The Atlas also highlights positive examples of water management that are protecting against, and even reversing, degradation.

- The damming of the Logone River in the Lake Chad Basin in the 1970s coincided with a period of drought that reduced overbank flooding and disrupted local livelihoods on the Waza Logone Floodplain. Managed releases from the dam beginning in the 1990s restored some of the natural flooding, bringing improved grazing and the return of other valuable ecosystem functions.

- Sudan's massive Gezira Irrigation Project, built in the early 20th century, and other projects such as Rahad, New Halfa and the Kenana Sugar Plantation, which were built in the 1960s and 1970s, help to rank Sudan second in Africa after Egypt in terms of land under irrigation.

- Along the Senegal River, irrigation schemes beginning in the 1940s and other large investments in the

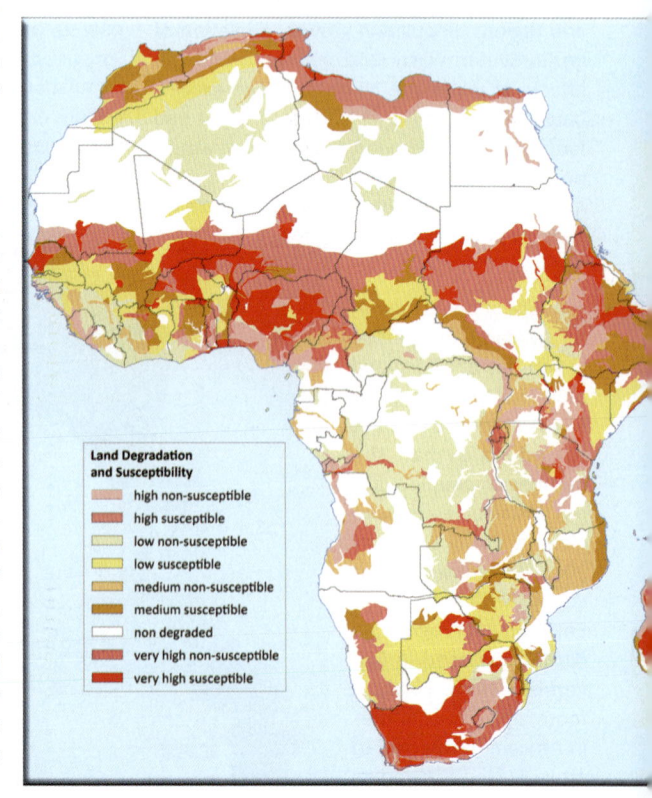

1980s, including the construction of the Manantali Dam in Mali and the Diama Dam in Senegal, have increased irrigation potential within the Senegal Basin.

- The Great Man-Made River Project in Libya, which began roughly 30 years ago, is among the largest civil engineering projects in the world. The project brings water from well fields in the Sahara to Libya's growing population. The majority of the system's water comes from Libya's two largest groundwater resources—the Murzuq and Kufra groundwater basins. As much as 80 per cent of Libya's groundwater is used for agriculture.

Opportunities to address the inadequate access to improved sanitation include a new drive to revolutionize toilets so they are as desirable as mobile phones. The vast improvements being made in access to communications technologies in Africa provides an example of how innovation and entrepreneurship in sanitation technologies could also reap economic benefits and improve health and well-being.

Preventing wars

Africa has 63 shared water basins with the potential of conflict over transboundary sharing. However, there are already at least 94 international water agreements in Africa to cooperatively manage shared waters. For example, the leaders of Uganda, Sudan and Egypt signed a pact to share the waters of the Nile River. Such solutions can potentially prevent water shortage and head off conflict.

Food security

Water scarcity challenges Africa's ability to ensure food security for its population. Agriculture uses the most water in Africa and the estimated rate of agricultural output increase needed to achieve food security is 3.3 percent per annum. Hydroelectricity supplies 32 percent of Africa's energy, but its electricity use is the lowest in the world. Africa's hydropower potential is under-developed. Africa is one of the most vulnerable continents as far as climate change and climate variability are concerned. Some regions are becoming drier and floods are occurring more regularly with severe impacts on people's livelihoods. Africa faces a situation of economic water scarcity, and current institutional, financial and human capacities for managing water are inadequate.

Solutions

"Practical solutions will include many components," Prof. Jeffrey Sachs of Columbia University noted, "including better water management, improved technologies to increase the efficiency of water use, and new investments undertaken jointly by governments, the business sector, and civic organizations." Organizations such as IRD and companies such as Coca-Cola have been actively engaged in improving water containment and distribution.

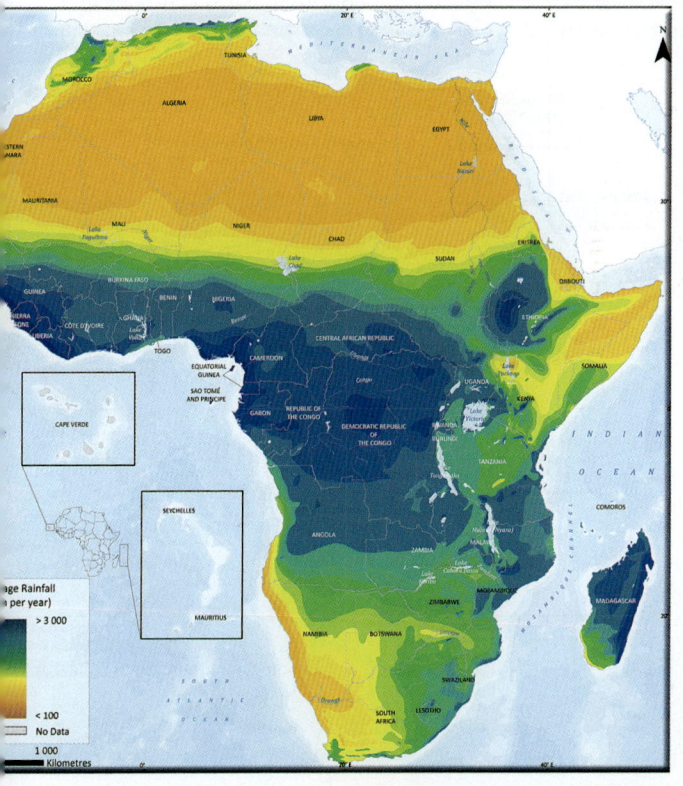

Maps: Africa Water Atlas—UNEP

THERE ARE 1,272 LARGE DAMS IN AFRICA
80.8% are single purpose dams
66% were built for irrigation
25% for water supply
South Africa has 539 major dams
Zimbabwe (213) and Algeria (107)

THE 6 LARGEST DAMS BY HEIGHT
Cahora Bassa Dam, Mozambique, 171 meters
Katse Dam, Lesotho, 155 meters
Hassan 1 Dam, Lakhdar River, Morocco, 145 meters
Akosombo Dam, Ghana, 134 meters
Bine El Ouidane Dam, Morocco, 133 meters
Kariba Dam, Zambia/Zimbabwe, 128 meters

THE 5 LARGEST DAMS BY CAPACITY
Kariba Dam, Zambia/Zimbabwe, 180 bn cu. meter
High Aswan Dam, Egypt, 162 bn cu. meter
Akosombo Dam, Ghana, 150 bn cu. meter
Cahora Bassa Dam, Mozambique, 52 bn cu. meter
Kossou Dam, Côte d'Ivoire, 28 bn cu. meter

Dams

Large scale water and hydro projects in Africa have in most cases met with a mixed reception from the local communities. More often than not it was a case of dam and be damned. In various parts of the Continent several large-scale projects have displaced communities, flooded sacred land and wildlife sanctuaries and adversely affected the livelihood of some while benefiting the population as a whole. In a continent where water is a scarce commodity and electricity needs are growing large hydro projects seem to be the obvious answer. But they come at a sacrifice over and above the billions of dollars spent on construction. The Lesotho Highlands Project followed the Aswan in Egypt, Volta in Ghana, Kariba in Zambia and Zimbabwe and Cahora Bassa in Mozambique as well as lesser known but equally impressive dams in Morocco and Côte d'Ivoire. On the drawing board is the Inga Rapids Project in the Democratic Republic of Congo that will generate enough electricity for Africa's needs and still have some left for export to Europe.

Aswan

Aswan is the name that conjures up when anyone mentions dams in Africa. Completed in 1902 the first Aswan Dam was merely the precursor of a much larger construction further up the river Nile. The High Aswan Dam, built with financial and technological assistance from the Soviet Union, was completed in 1971. At a height of 111 meters and a width of 3,800m it featured 180 watergates and 12 power-generating units supplying 2.1 million kw of electric power. Lake Nasser that swelled up behind this massive wall threatened to drown numerous priceless historic ruins, including the Abu Simbel shrine dedicated to Ramses II. With donations from across the world UNESCO assigned masterful Italian engineers to move these massive treasures in piecemeal fashion to higher ground. Less fortunate were the farmers downstream who are denied by the dam deposits of fertile sediment that used to flow seawards during the summer floods.

Kariba

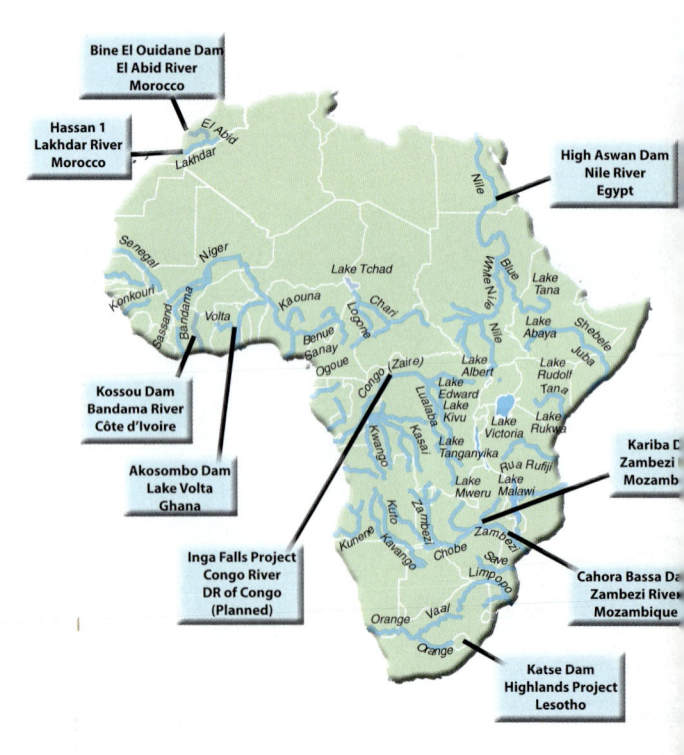

The story repeated itself at Kariba Dam on the Zambezi River between Zambia and Zimbabwe. Completed in 1977, it relegated High Aswan to second place and ranks as one of the largest dams in the world. At a height of 128m and 579m wide Kariba dam supplies electricity to both Zambia (the Copperbelt) and Zimbabwe. But it also changed the downstream ecology dramatically and forced the resettlement of 57,000 Tonga people living upstream along the Zambezi. Operation Noah involved the rescue of around 6,000 large animals and numerous small ones threatened by the lake's rising waters. While the animals thrive in their new sanctuaries the displaced Tonga never seemed to have adjusted after the lands where they had farmed, fished, worshipped, raised their children and buried their dead, were flooded. They were resettled to poor lands with no development assistance.

Cahora Bassa

Downstream in the Zambezi River construction started on the Cahora Bassa dam in 1969 in the Tete Province in Mozambique. This joint effort between Portugal, the then ruler of Mozambique, and South Africa, resulted in a flood area 250 km long and 38 km wide covering an area of 2,700 sq. km with an average depth of 20.9m. The Cahora Bassa lake is Africa's second-largest artificial lake. Only Egypt's Aswan dam is bigger in terms of surface water. The Cahora Bassa Dam system is the largest hydroelectric scheme in southern Africa with the powerhouse containing 5 x 415MW turbines.

Lesotho

Power hungry South Africa also inspired the Lesotho Highlands Water Project. Construction started ion the late nineties and it reached its final phase in 2006. Electricity has already started to flow into South Africa's Pretoria Witwatersrand Vereeniging (PWV) industrial complex. Current sales of electricity from this project account for 20 percent of Lesotho's national income. But once again, 30,000 of Lesotho's tribesmen had to be relocated as their traditional lands were drowned by the rising waters.

Inga

Grand Inga, the world's largest hydropower scheme, is proposed for the Congo River in the Democratic Republic of Congo (DRC). It will generate twice the power of the Three Gorges Dam in China and more than a third of the total electricity currently produced in Africa. It plans to harness the mighty Congo River and generate more than 40,000 megawatts that will be sufficient to power most of Africa's industrialized areas and still have a lot left to sell to southern Europe via a proposed Mediterranean connector. The project will incorporate and upgrade the existing two dams, Inga I and Inga II that fell into disrepair. The World Bank is said to have pledged as much as $500 million. The plan also calls for the construction of Inga III, a massive hydroelectric station, at a cost of $6 billion.

Lake Nasser (Photo: Michael Poliza)

Some of Africa's Challenges

	Water Coverage			Sanitation Coverage			Diseases		
	Total % 2006	Urban % 2006	Rural % 2006	Total % 2006	Urban % 2006	Rural % 2006	Malaria Total 2007/8	Tuberculosis 2007	Measles Total 2007
Algeria	85	87	81	94	98	87	196	8,439	0
Angola	51	62	39	50	79	16	1,377,992	21,422	1,014
Benin	65	78	57	30	59	11	861,847	...	341
Botswana	96	100	90	47	60	30	1,201	3,002	1
Burkina Faso	72	97	66	13	41	6	36,514	2,614	12
Burundi	71	84	70	41	44	41	876,741	3,595	43
Cameroon	70	88	47	51	58	42	313,083	13,220	100
Cape Verde	...	...	...	...	...	...	35	158	0
Central African Rep.	66	90	51	31	40	25	152,260	...	49
Chad	48	71	40	9	23	4	57,644	2,513	441
Comoros	85	91	81	35	49	26	20,559	...	0
Congo, Rep	71	95	35	20	19	21	157,757	3,552	84
Congo Dem. Rep.	46	82	29	31	42	25	1,462,300	66,099	55,577
Côte d'Ivoire	81	98	66	24	38	12	1,343,654	14,071	5
Djibouti	92	98	54	67	76	11	119	1,208	24
Egypt	98	99	98	66	85	52	76	4,887	1,684
Equatorial Guinea	43	45	42	51	60	46	50,758	...	5
Eritrea	60	74	57	5	14	3	4,702	694	55
Ethiopia	42	96	31	11	27	8	458,561	38,040	1,446
Gabon	87	95	47	36	37	30	40,701	1,462	0
Gambia	86	91	81	52	50	55	10,910	1,238	0
Ghana	80	90	71	10	15	6	827,438	7,429	6
Guinea	70	91	59	19	33	12	33,405	6,199	3
Guinea Bissau	57	82	47	33	48	26	11,299	...	1
Kenya	57	85	49	42	19	48	839,904	38,360	1,516
Lesotho	78	93	74	36	43	34	...	788	2
Liberia	64	72	52	32	49	7	606,952	...	1
Libya	...	...	...	97	97	96	...	772	59
Madagascar	47	76	36	12	18	10	89,138	15,344	0
Malawi	76	96	72	60	51	62	4,986,779	7,608	143
Mali	60	86	48	45	59	39	1291 853	3,894	2
Mauritania	60	70	54	24	44	10	302	1,714	11
Mauritius*	100	100	100	94	95	94	22	86	13
Morocco	83	100	58	72	85	54	118	11,937	2,248
Mozambique	42	71	26	31	53	19	4,831,491	18,214	267
Namibia	93	99	90	35	66	18	4,907	5,091	21
Niger	42	91	32	7	27	3	413,252	5 773	282
Nigeria	47	65	30	30	35	25	143,079	44,016	2,613
Rwanda	65	82	61	23	34	20	228,015	4,053	26
São Tomé & Príncipe	86	88	83	24	29	18	1 572	58	0
Senegal	77	93	65	28	54	9	202 466	7,108	9
Seychelles	...	100	...	...	...	100	...	...	1
Sierra Leone	53	83	32	11	20	5	154,459	5,347	0
Somalia	29	63	10	23	51	7	23,905	6,130	1 149
South Africa	93	100	82	59	66	49	12,098	135,604	31
Sudan	70	78	64	35	50	24	457,362	12,627	327
Swaziland	60	87	51	50	64	46	58	2,764	0
Tanzania	55	81	46	33	31	34	10,067	24,520	7 726
Togo	59	86	40	12	24	3	273,471	1,796	8
Tunisia	94	99	84	85	96	64	...	941	4
Uganda	64	90	60	33	29	34	894,505	21,303	3 776
Zambia	58	90	41	52	55	51	3,080,301	13,378	535
Zimbabwe	81	98	72	46	63	37	92,900	10,583	242
AFRICA	59	82	46	33	46	26	...	561,149	81,903

Source: AFDB

166

CORRUPTION

Major scandals in Germany, France, Britain, Italy, Japan and the United States have shown that corruption is hardly a problem confined to developing countries or emerging markets. But in underdeveloped parts of Africa the effect of corrupt practices is more devastating. Corruption not only siphons off funds that could have been utilized for infrastructure and other development. It inflates the cost of doing business and turns away foreign investors.

Billions of dollars diverted into secret foreign bank accounts represent a significant share of the continent's stock of flight capital, totaling, according to the UN Economic Commission for Africa, around $148 billion. Economists estimate that in some African countries bribes, "sales commissions" and the diversion of funds add between 10% and 20% to the cost of development projects. Serious efforts are underway in Africa to facilitate a business climate that is more conducive to foreign participation.

Transparency International

Berlin-based Transparency International (TI) leads a number of NGOs intent on quantifying global corruption and pressuring UN agencies and governments to take remedial action. A perfect score of 10 indicates a country with no corruption at all while 0 would signify total corruption. While both of these are obviously not practically possible, the scale inbetween provides useful measurement. In TI's 2010 Corruption Perceptions Index (CPI) survey seventy eight countries out of 178 scored less than a 3 out of a perfect 10 for a totally non-corrupt society. Corruption is perceived to be most acute in Somalia, Myanmar, Afghanistan, Iraq, Uzbekistan, Turkmenistan, Sudan, Chad, Burundi, Equatorial Guinea and Angola. Somalia with rating of 1.1 was placed last on the list. Countries with scores higher than 8.8 included New Zealand, Denmark and Singapore with 9.3, Sweden and Finland with 9.2, Canada with 8.9 and the Netherlands with 8.8. In 2010 TI ranked 15 African countries among the top 100 nations with the least corruption among those surveyed. Scoring above 3 were Botswana (5.8), Mauritius (5.4), Cape Verde (5.1), Seychelles (4.8), South Africa (4.5), Namibia (4.4), Tunisia (4.3), Ghana (4.1), Rwanda (4.0), Lesotho (3.5), Malawi (3.4), Morocco (3.4), Liberia (3.3), Djibouti (3.2), The Gambia (3.2), Swaziland (3.2), Burkina Faso (3.1), Egypt (3.1), and Zambia (3.0). According to TI, the poor nations that can least afford it as the monies are siphoned off important development projects, tend to be the greatest victims of corrupt practices and bribery. Levels of corruption in the public sector are recorded as perceived by business people, country analysts and ordinary citizens.

Convention

In 1999 the Organization for Economic Cooperation and Development (OECD) adopted its own *Convention on Combating Bribery*, based on the US Foreign Corrupt Practices Act. The *African Convention on Preventing and Combating Corruption* was initially approved by the African Union's Ministerial Conference in Addis Ababa in September 2002 and later adopted by its executive council. The new convention guarantees access to information and the participation of civil society and the media in the monitoring process. It also outlaws

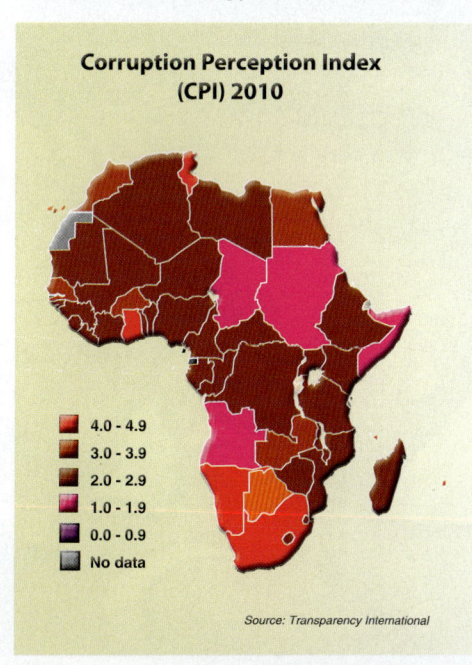

Corruption Perception Index (CPI) 2010

4.0 - 4.9
3.0 - 3.9
2.0 - 2.9
1.0 - 1.9
0.0 - 0.9
No data

Source: Transparency International

the use of funds acquired through illicit and corrupt practices to finance political parties. African leaders have laid part of the blame on foreign entrepreneurs who use bribes to beat their competition out of lucrative contracts. Corruption, they argue, can only be effectively contained if the leading industrial nations do their part in policing their own corporations doing business in Africa.

Bribe payers

While Transparency International's *Corrupt Perception Index* (CPI) focuses on officials in recipient countries, its *Bribe Payers Index* (BPI) focuses on bribe paying governments and corporations, seeking to win business and other favors abroad. TI found that many governments in developed countries preferred to turn a blind eye to bribes paid out to win business in the developing world. The Bribe Payers Index (BPI) showed high levels of bribery in the developing world, not only by corporations from Russia, China, Taiwan and South Korea, but also by those from leading industrial nations. The US, for example, with a score of 5.3 out of a possible clean 10, ranked 13th with Japan, below France, Spain, Germany, Singapore and the United Kingdom. Most likely areas where bribes might be demanded, according to the survey, are public works and construction, arms and defense, oil and gas, real estate, telecommunications, power generation, mining and transportation. Oil revenues have gone into the pockets of middlemen and local officials.

AFRICA'S TOP RATED 2010

Rank	Country	CPI
33	Botswana	5.8
39	Mauritius	5.4
45	Cape Verde	5.1
49	Seychelles	4.8
54	South Africa	4.5
56	Namibia	4.4
59	Tunisia	4.3
62	Ghana	4.1
66	Rwanda	4.0
78	Lesotho	3.5
85	Malawi	3.4
85	Morocco	3.4
87	Liberia	3.3
91	Djibouti	3.2
91	The Gambia	3.2
91	Swaziland	3.2
98	Egypt	3.1
101	Sao Tome & Principe	3.0

Children attending a primary school in Harar, Ethiopia.

Illiteracy

Although outstripped by South Asia (56.2%) in terms of illiteracy, Africa with an overall 33.3% rate poses a severe challenge to a continent trying to promote development and reduce poverty. Illiteracy in 7 of its 53 nations exceed 50%—going as high as 69.6% in Burkina Faso and 80% in Niger. Africa's most populous country, Nigeria, shows a 26.9% illiteracy rate. South Africa, Africa's most advanced nation, has an illiteracy rate of 12.2%—compared to rates in Europe and North America of about 1%. One disturbing facet of illiteracy and low school enrollment is the inability to educate youth and adults through the printed word about the dangers of HIV/AIDS infection.

Criteria

Statistics provided for adults aged 15 and older by UNESCO and the African Development Bank come with a disclaimer regarding their sources. "Different countries," UNESCO points out, "have different social and cultural contexts, different definitions and standards of literacy, different methodologies for collecting and compiling literacy data, as well as different quality of data collected." In some cases data may represent the whole country and in others only part. Some countries may identify literate persons by simply asking: "Are you literate or not" or "Can you read and write with understanding, while others may ask more comprehensive questions or administer literacy tests to identify different levels of literacy. The United Nations simply defines literacy as the inability to read and write a simple message in any language. Definitions and disclaimers aside, it is evident that large-scale illiteracy in Africa hinders poverty reduction, effective HIV/AIDS prevention education and general improvement of the human condition, and that massive input is required.

Illiteracy and Education

Country	Adult Illiteracy Rate (%) 2007	Illiteracy ratio M/F 2007	% Primary school enrollment 2007
Algeria	26.1	1.91	105
Angola	...	...	...
Benin	54.7	1.79	96
Botswana	17.2	0.73	112
Burkina Faso	69.6	1.35	67
Burundi	43.9	1.26	103
Cameroon	21.2	1.74	106
Cape Verde	20.6	2.19	106
Central Afr. Rep.	43.4	1.66	51
Chad	46.3	1.39	76
Comoros	42.9	1.39	85
Congo Rep.	12.6	2.21	108
Congo Dem. Rep	29.5	1.93	...
Côte d'Ivoire	44.5	1.56	71
Djibouti	27.8	1.93	42
Egypt	39.4	1.66	102
Equat.Guinea	11.4	3.38	122
Eritrea	37.8	1.79	66
Ethiopia	52.5	1.3	98
Gabon	...	...	...
Gambia	55.1	1.3	77
Ghana	21.1	1.91	92
Guinea	...	...	88
Guinea Bissau	...	52.5	0
Kenya	11.8	2.14	107
Lesotho	13.5	0.19	114
Liberia	39.3	2.37	...
Libya	14.6	4.11	104
Madagascar	27.8	1.52	139
Malawi	34.1	2.1	120
Mali	68.9	1.36	80
Mauritania	56.4	1.4	99
Mauritius	12.9	1.46	102
Morocco	44.9	1.7	107
Mozambique	47.0	1.91	102
Namibia	13.4	0.98	106
Niger	80.0	1.24	51
Nigeria	26.9	1.61	93
Rwanda	25.3	1.44	140
São T.& Principe	...	...	127
Senegal	56.0	1.4	80
Seychelles	...	...	116
SierraLeone	...	...	...
Somalia	...	...	...
South Africa	12.2	1.1	103
Sudan	34.9	1.74	57
Swaziland	16.0	1.09	102
Tanzania	18.2	2.06	110
Togo	34.2	2.26	102
Tunisia	22.1	2.4	97
Uganda	26.8	1.93	117
Zambia	16.5	1.87	115
Zimbabwe	7.2	2.39	...
AFRICA	33.3	1.59	96

Sources: ADB, UNESCO

DEBT BURDEN

The $326 billion that Africa owes its foreign creditors—amounting to more than $300 for every man, woman and child on the continent—represents a crippling burden to some of its nations. Africa carries 11% of the developing world's debt with only 5% of its income. In the past 17 years, Africa's total debt rose by 350%. In many African countries up to 40% of government revenue is allocated to servicing foreign debt, to the detriment of health, education and other essential social services. Sub-Saharan Africa spends over twice as much on debt service as it does on basic health care. In the past decade total debt service has risen by 39%, from $10.9 billion to $15.2 billion.

Even though its debt burden decreased from well over $300 billion to $285 billion from 2005 to 2006—in large part the result of a $40 billion write-off by its creditors—external debt still amounts an alarming 56% of its exports. Altogether 33 of the 41 countries identified by the World Bank as "Heavily Indebted Poor Countries" (HIPC) are in Africa and several countries are spending between 15% and 50% of their export earnings on interest and debt repayments. Development aid, which has been in steep decline in recent years, does not close the gap. For example, Sub-Saharan African countries have been paying $1.51 on debt service for every $1 received in grant aid from foreign donors.

Causes

In the 1960s and 1970s, international lenders readily pushed a high volume of loans on many African states. Neither the lenders nor the borrowers anticipated these to balloon due to exchange rate fluctuation and interest rate hikes. Other factors that

AFRICAN FOREIGN DEBT - 2008/9

Country	External debt US$ million 2008	External debt as % GDP 2008	External debt as % GDP 2009	Debt service % GDP 2008	Debt service % GDP 2009
Algeria	4,363	2.7	2.7	1.8	2.5
Angola	16,603	19.5	26.6	4.3	13.3
Benin	813	12.1	15.2	2.9	3.7
Botswana	1,248	9.3	22.5	7.2	12.0
Burkina Faso	1,592	19.6	24.1	6.1	6.0
Burundi	1,473	134.3	24.8	3.6	1.9
Cameroon	1,427	6.0	7.9	6.8	10.2
Cape Verde	966	55.4	61.3	16.5	20.8
Central Afr. Rep.	991	43.0	8.3	19.9	4.9
Chad	1,535	18.3	22.0	3.2	2.8
Comoros	265	49.7	48.4	12.3	10.2
Congo, Dem. R.	13,481	115.9	124.5	8.4	16.1
Congo, Rep.	5,654	52.5	24.6	2.6	15.9
Côte d'Ivoire	18,587	79.1	82.1	9.3	10.1
Djibouti	582	59.2	60.5	6.8	8.0
Egypt	33,893	20.8	16.8	8.4	12.2
Equat. Guinea	120	0.6	1.0	0.1	0.1
Eritrea	878	59.3	53.7	36.4	51.1
Ethiopia	2,907	11.0	12.9	2.4	2.8
Gabon	2,128	14.6	18.9	26.1	7.1
Gambia, The	301	37.1	43.6	31.0	32.
Ghana	6,227	37.4	49.4	4.7	7.7
Guinea	2,997	66.3	64.8	9.5	7.9
Guinea-Bissau	1,040	225.5	238.1	3.0	2.6
Kenya	6,312	21.4	24.2	4.7	5.5
Lesotho	627	38.8	39.5	2.8	5.
Liberia	3,675	432.6	290.1	0.0	0.
Libya	5,574	6.2	9.2	0.0	0.
Madagascar	2,368	25.0	28.0	1.6	4.
Malawi	683	16.0	17.7	1.3	2.
Mali	1,863	21.2	24.5	3.0	3.
Mauritania	1,892	59.9	59.6	8.8	3.
Mauritius	821	9.4	10.1	4.3	4.
Morocco	18,341	20.6	21.9	7.9	8.
Mozambique	5,127	51.8	53.9	20.0	30.
Namibia	1,999	22.6	23.9	27.3	21.
Niger	752	14.0	16.4	1.9	2.
Nigeria	4,460	2.2	3.0	0.7	1.
Rwanda	678	15.2	16.7	1.1	3.
São Tomé & Príncipe	123	70.0	40.3	182.2	275.
Senegal	5,546	41.5	50.9	5.1	7.
Seychelles	845	102.8	118.8	6.6	12.
Sierra Leone	647	33.1	36.0	2.3	3.
Somalia	2,949	...	...	...	...
South Africa	71,811	25.9	27.1	37.6	40.
Sudan	33,660	58.0	67.6	2.5	6.
Swaziland	451	15.9	17.3	25.1	32.
Tanzania	6,834	33.1	31.6	1.6	2.
Togo	1,501	51.9	53.2	2.8	6.
Tunisia	20,627	50.5	52.8	40.7	54.
Uganda	1,881	12.9	15.5	2.5	2.
Zambia	1,072	7.3	9.4	1.9	2.
Zimbabwe	6,046	192.2	186.9	22.7	19.
AFRICA	**326,287**	**21.3**	**23.6**	**10.6**	**14.**

Sources: AFDB, IMF

contributed to the debt crisis in Africa include poor government economic management, deteriorating terms of trade, shrinking market shares for major exports, and boom and bust cycles in recent years.

HIPC Initiative

In 1996, the International Monetary Fund, together with the World Bank and major creditor nations, adopted the Heavily Indebted Poor Countries (HIPC) initiative that entitled 41 developing countries to assistance beyond mere rescheduling of debt. To qualify, debtor nations had to have a GNP per capita of US$695 or less in 1993, and a present value of debt to exports higher than 220%, or a present value of debt to GNP higher than 80%. The program envisages the cancellation of as much 80% of external debt—one third owed to multilateral institutions. With the adoption of the Enhanced HIPC program in 1999, the international community agreed to make the Initiative broader and faster by increasing the number of eligible countries, raising the amount of debt relief, and speeding up the process.

Two stages

Eligible countries qualify for debt relief in two stages. During the first stage, before reaching the so-called decision point—usually after three years—the debtor country needs to establish a satisfactory track record in terms of IMF and (International Development Agency (IDA) supported programs. During the second stage, after reaching the decision point, the country is required to implement a full-fledged poverty reduction strategy. During this stage, the IMF and IDA, the Paris Club creditors and others, are expected to grant interim relief. At the end of the second stage, when the floating completion point is reached, the IMF and IDA provide the remainder of the committed debt relief while Paris Club creditors enter into a highly concessional stock-of-debt operation with the country. Other multilateral and bilateral creditors will be required to contribute to the debt relief on comparable terms. Twenty five countries (Benin, Bolivia, Burkina Faso, Cameroon, Chad, Ethiopia, The Gambia, Ghana, Guinea, Guinea-Bissau, Guyana, Honduras, Madagascar, Malawi, Mali, Mauritania, Mozambique, Nicaragua, Niger, Rwanda, São Tomé and Príncipe, Senegal, Tanzania, Uganda, Zambia) have reached their decision point under the enhanced HIPC Initiative and four countries (Bolivia, Mozambique, Tanzania and Uganda) reached completion point under the original HIPC Initiative.

Forgiven Debt

In 2005, the Group of Eight gathering in Gleneagles, Scotland, agreed to full cancellation of the more than $40 billion owed them by 18 African Heavily Indebted Poor Countries. This decision was taken after considerable pressure from various quarters including the Commission on Africa as public appeals by music stars Bob Geldof and Bono.

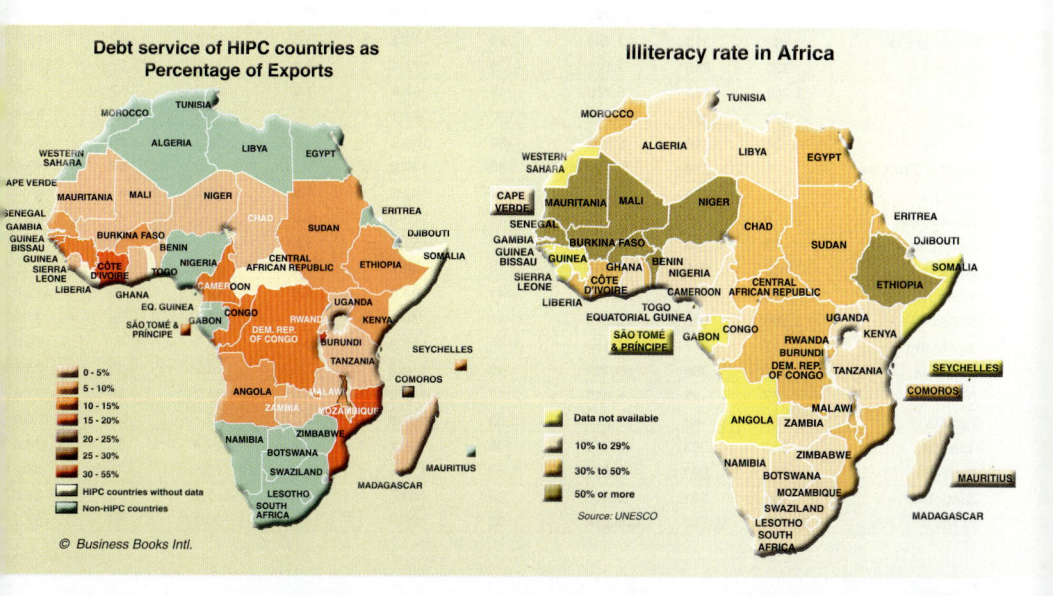

AFRICAN HUMAN INDICATORS

	Land Area sq km 000	Land Area sq. m 000	Total Pop. 000 2009	Pop. Density Pop/km² 2009	Prim. Sch Enroll Ratio 2008	Exp. on Education % of GDP 2008	Adult Illiteracy % 2008	Life Expect Years 2008	Health Exp. per cap.US$ 2009
Algeria	2,382	920	34,895	15	107.5	...	26.1	72	148.0
Angola	1,247	481	18,498	15	193.8	2.6	...	43	71.0
Benin	113	44	8,935	78	116.6	3.6	54.7	57	26.0
Botswana	582	225	1,950	3	109.7	8.1	17.2	51	379.0
Burkina Faso	274	106	15,757	58	73.4	3.7	69.6	52	27.0
Burundi	28	11	8,303	298	135.6	5.1	43.9	50	10.0
Cameroon	475	183	19,522	41	110.9	3.9	21.2	50	45.0
Cape Verde	4	2	506	125	101.3	5.7	20.6	72	112.0
Central Afr. Rep.	623	241	4,422	7	77.4	1.3	43.4	45	14.0
Chad	284	110	11,206	9	75.5	1.9	46.3	51	29.0
Comoros	2	1	676	302	122.0	3.8	42.9	65	16.0
Congo Rep.	342	132	3,683	11	114.0	1.8	12.6	55	44.0
Congo Dem. Rep	2,345	905	66,020	28	90.4	...	29.5	46	10.0
Côte d'Ivoire	322	124	21,075	65	74.5	4.6	44.5	48	35.0
Djibouti	23	9	864	37	55.5	8.7	27.8	55	63.0
Egypt	1,001	386	82,999	83	99.7	3.7	39.4	71	92.0
Equat.Guinea	28	11	676	24	98.7	0.6	11.4	52	440.0
Eritrea	118	46	5,073	43	56.9	2.0	37.8	58	8.0
Ethiopia	1,104	426	82,825	75	97.8	5.5	52.5	53	7.0
Gabon	268	103	1,475	6	139.8	3.8	...	57	351.0
Gambia	11	4	1,705	151	86.2	2.0	55.1	59	15.0
Ghana	239	92	23,837	100	101.8	5.4	21.1	60	33.0
Guinea	246	95	10,069	41	89.9	1.7	...	56	20.0
Guinea Bissau	36	14	1,611	45	69.7	5.2	...	46	12.0
Kenya	580	224	39,802	67	111.5	7.0	11.8	54	29.0
Lesotho	30	12	2,067	68	107.7	12.4	13.5	43	51.0
Liberia	111	43	3,955	36	90.6	...	39.3	46	7.0
Libya	1,760	680	6,420	4	110.3	2.7	14.6	74	219.0
Madagascar	587	227	19,625	33	151.7	2.9	27.8	59	9.0
Malawi	118	46	15,263	129	120.2	4.2	34.1	48	21.0
Mali	1,240	479	13,010	10	91.3	4.6	68.9	54	31.0
Mauritania	1,026	396	3,291	3	102.3	2.9	56.4	64	19.0
Mauritius	2	1	1,288	631	99.4	3.9	12.9	73	230.0
Morocco	711	275	31,993	45	106.9	5.5	44.9	71	113.0
Mozambique	802	310	22,894	29	114.2	5.0	47.0	42	16.0
Namibia	824	318	2,171	3	112.4	6.4	13.4	53	281.0
Niger	1,267	489	15,290	12	57.8	3.3	80.0	57	16.0
Nigeria	924	357	154,729	167	93.1	...	26.9	47	33.0
Rwanda	26	10	9,998	380	150.9	4.1	25.3	46	33.0
São T.& Principe	1	0	163	169	130.2	...	...	66	49.0
Senegal	197	76	12,534	64	83.5	4.8	56.0	63	44.0
Seychelles	0	0	84	185	125.3	5.0	...	72	565.0
SierraLeone	72	28	5,696	79	157.7	3.8	...	...	12.0
Somalia	638	246	9,133	14	20.7	...	...	48	...
South Africa	1,221	471	50,110	41	104.5	5.1	12.2	49	425.0
Sudan	2,506	968	42,272	17	74.0	...	34.9	59	37.0
Swaziland	17	7	1,185	68	107.9	8.3	16.0	40	155.0
Tanzania	945	365	43,739	46	110.2	...	18.2	53	23.0
Togo	57	22	6,619	117	105.0	3.8	34.2	58	21.0
Tunisia	164	63	10,272	63	107.6	7.1	22.1	74	156.0
Uganda	241	93	32,710	136	117.2	3.8	26.8	52	24.0
Zambia	753	291	12,935	17	119.1	1.4	16.5	42	58.0
Zimbabwe	391	151	12,523	32	103.6	4.6	7.2	43	38.0
AFRICA	30,307	11,702	1,008,354	33	100.9	4.5	33.3	54	57.7

Source: AFDB

Chapter 7
The Nations of Africa

Diversity should be expected on a continent of 1 billion people consisting of hundreds of ethnic groupings and thousands of tribal affiliations, speaking 2,000 languages in 53 countries. Business is conducted in English, French, Arabic, Portuguese, Spanish and Swahili, with English having an edge on the others.

AFRICA'S 53 NATIONS

Flag	Country
	ALGERIA
	ANGOLA
	BENIN
	BOTSWANA
	BURKINA FASO
	BURUNDI
	CAMEROON
	CAPE VERDE
	CENTR.AFR.REP.
	CHAD
	COMOROS
	CONGO (BR)
	CONGO D.R.
	CÔTE D'IVOIRE
	DJIBOUTI
	EGYPT
	EQ. GUINEA
	ERITREA
	ETHIOPIA
	GABON
	THE GAMBIA
	GHANA
	GUINEA
	GUINEA-BISSAU
	KENYA
	LESOTHO
	LIBERIA
	LIBYA
	MADAGASCAR
	MALAWI
	MALI
	MAURITANIA
	MAURITIUS
	MOROCCO
	MOZAMBIQUE
	NAMIBIA
	NIGER
	NIGERIA
	RWANDA
	SÃO TOMÉ & PRÍNC.
	SENEGAL
	SEYCHELLES
	SIERRA LEONE
	SOMALIA
	SOUTH AFRICA
	SUDAN
	SWAZILAND
	TANZANIA
	TOGO
	TUNISIA
	UGANDA
	ZAMBIA
	ZIMBABWE

Map of Africa showing all nations with their capitals and major cities, bordered by the Atlantic Ocean, Red Sea, and Indian Ocean.

COUNTRY PROFILES

Profiling political and economic conditions in 53 diverse countries spanning across the African continent and an array of adjoining islands would have been impossible without the kind cooperation of several institutions, including the United Nations and the IMF and a number of Africa-related organizations, including the African Development Bank and the UN Economic Commission for Africa. We have also received statistical data from several country sources.

In assessing business opportunities in specific countries, we are indebted to the US State Department (www.state.gov) and the US Department of Commerce (www.ita.doc.gov). We recommend that entrepreneurs who are seriously interested in conducting business in Africa consult with these departments.

Data

While every effort was made to cross-check statistics and to provide the most recent data available, there will no doubt be areas of dispute. Not all nations apply the same criteria and some are unfortunately lacking in up-to-date figures. Even in this book you will find conflicts and variations depending on which source we quote.

Maps

Our maps follow the official borders recognized by the United Nations. It is not within our power to adjudicate in border disputes and adjust maps to suit the preferences of either party in contested cases.

PPP

Apart from real GDP statistics based on current official dollar exchange rates, figures are also published based on purchasing power parity (PPP). The PPP method, considered by many economists as a more accurate measure of economic strength, weighs incomes against domestic costs and prices in specific countries. Exchange rates may suddenly go up or down by 10% or more as a result of market forces or official decisions while real output remains unchanged. On 12 January 1994, for example, the 14 countries of the Communauté Financière Africaine, or CFA, (whose currencies are tied to the French franc) devalued their currency by 50%. This did not, however, cut the real output of these countries by half as real GDP based on the new exchange rates would suggest. It should be noted that while PPP estimates for OECD countries are quite specific, the same estimates for developing countries are often mere approximations.

THE NATIONS

Country	Page
Algeria	177
Angola	181
Benin	185
Botswana	189
Burkina Faso	193
Burundi	197
Cameroon	200
Cape Verde	206
Central Afr. Rep.	210
Chad	213
Comoros	217
Congo, Dem Rep.	220
Congo, Rep. of	224
Côte d'Ivoire	227
Djibouti	231
Egypt	234
Equitorial Guinea	238
Eritrea	242
Ethiopia	246
Gabon	250
Gambia, The	254
Ghana	257
Guinea	261
Guinea-Bissau	265
Kenya	268
Lesotho	272
Liberia	276
Libya	280
Madagascar	284
Malawi	288
Mali	292
Mauritania	296
Mauritius	300
Morocco	304
Mozambique	308
Namibia	312
Niger	316
Nigeria	320
Rwanda	324
São T. & Príncipe	327
Senegal	330
Seychelles	334
Sierra Leone	337
Somalia	340
South Africa	343
Sudan	350
Swaziland	353
Tanzania	357
Togo	361
Tunisia	365
Uganda	369
Zambia	373
Zimbabwe	377
Western Sahara[1]	381

1. Territory under dispute

AFRICAN ECONOMIC INDICATORS

	Real GDP market prices US$million 2008	Real GDP Growth Rate % 2009	Real GDP Growth Average % 2001/9	Real GDP Per Capita US$ 2008	GDP PPP Value US$million 2009	GDP PPP Per Capita US$ 2009	Inflation CPI % 2009	External Debt US$million 2008	FDI Total US$million 2008
Algeria	158,974	2.2	3.7	6,054	256,542	7,352	5.7	4,363	2,646
Angola	119,370	-0.6	11.6	3,729	100,459	5,431	14.0	16,603	15,548
Benin	6,336	3.0	4.1	1,233	13,454	1,506	4.1	813	120
Botswana	11,522	-4.0	3.9	11,801	25,764	13,214	8.2	1,248	-4
Burkina Faso	8,188	3.0	5.4	1,026	19,395	1,231	2.8	1,592	137
Burundi	1,116	3.3	3.0	320	2,853	344	8.3	1,473	1
Cameroon	25,071	2.0	3.3	1,959	46,347	2,374	3.2	1,427	260
Cape Verde	1,952	3.9	6.1	2,690	2,002	3,959	2.2	966	209
Central Afr. Rep.	2,309	2.0	1.9	644	3,471	785	3.8	991	121
Chad	6,155	-0.8	8.4	1,464	17,067	1,523	10.5	1,535	834
Comoros	557	1.4	1.9	850	821	1,215	4.5	265	8
Congo Rep.	13,650	7.6	4.5	3,309	15,614	4,239	6.0	13,481	2,622
Congo Dem. Rep	12,541	2.6	4.7	272	21,304	323	44.2	5,654	1,000
Côte d'Ivoire	23,006	3.6	0.9	1,172	33,766	1,602	1.4	18,587	353
Djibouti	1,023	4.8	3.8	962	1,955	2,262	1.7	582	234
Egypt	166,019	4.7	4.9	4,576	471,509	5,681	16.2	33,893	9,495
Equat.Guinea	15,529	0.5	20.5	27,001	21,188	31,331	5.5	120	1,290
Eritrea	1,479	3.6	0.8	295	3,813	752	34.7	878	0
Ethiopia	25,163	9.9	8.0	597	72,196	872	36.4	2,907	93
Gabon	16,542	-1.0	1.9	13,821	21,951	14,886	2.5	2,128	20
Gambia	612	4.8	5.0	349	2,003	1,175	4.2	301	63
Ghana	14,657	4.7	5.5	612	36,558	1,534	18.8	6,227	2,120
Guinea	4,611	0.6	2.8	482	10,473	1,040	4.8	2,997	1,350
Guinea Bissau	442	2.9	1.1	253	817	508	-1.5	1,040	15
Kenya	41,896	2.5	4.1	1,349	62,423	1,568	9.3	6,312	96
Lesotho	1,323	1.1	3.1	655	2,482	1,201	4.8	627	199
Liberia	1,212	4.4	1.3	267	1,093	276	7.8	3,675	144
Libya	87,854	2.1	4.4	11,576	99,491	15,497	2.5	5,574	4,111
Madagascar	8,198	-4.5	3.0	406	18,230	929	8.9	2,368	1,477
Malawi	3,032	7.0	4.9	212	8,395	550	8.5	683	37
Mali	8,411	4.4	5.7	661	15,898	1,222	2.2	1,863	127
Mauritania	3,771	-1.1	3.9	1,684	8,157	2,479	2.2	1,892	103
Mauritius	9,180	2.8	3.7	10,175	17,489	13,576	2.5	821	383
Morocco	88,642	5.0	5.1	3,547	151,855	4,747	1.0	18,341	2,388
Mozambique	14,456	5.4	8.0	663	21,746	950	3.4	5,127	587
Namibia	8,159	-1.8	4.3	3,881	13,737	6,327	8.8	1,999	746
Niger	5,147	-0.9	5.0	349	10,392	680	4.3	752	147
Nigeria	216,755	3.0	8.2	1,431	327,822	2,119	12.0	4,460	20,279
Rwanda	3,816	4.5	6.5	381	9,526	953	10.3	678	103
São T.& Principe	160	4.1	6.1	1,547	339	2,083	17.3	123	33
Senegal	12 602	1.5	3.8	9,675	20,841	1,663	-1.1	5,546	706
Seychelles	842	-6.8	0.9	585	1,480	17,563	31.7	845	364
SierraLeone	2,391	3.5	10.1	401	4,509	792	10.7	647	30
Somalia	...	...	...	...	...	...	...	2,949	87
South Africa	259,452	-1.8	3.6	5,313	487,107	9,721	7.1	71,811	9,009
Sudan	54,270	4.9	7.1	1,376	95,466	2,258	10.5	33,660	2,601
Swaziland	2,584	0.2	2.2	1,049	5,806	4,900	4.1	451	10
Tanzania	18,346	5.5	6.9	442	53,167	1,216	12.1	6,834	744
Togo	2,526	2.2	1.8	373	6,071	917	1.9	1,501	68
Tunisia	42,457	3.1	4.6	4,067	89,010	8,666	3.5	20,627	2,761
Uganda	16,611	7.0	7.7	521	46,632	1,426	11.1	1,881	787
Zambia	14,320	6.1	5.4	1,178	19,606	1,516	13.4	1,072	939
Zimbabwe	4,723	3.7	-5.4	339	2,193	175	9	6,046	52
AFRICA	1,565,237	2.5	5.3	2,876	2,825,691	4,060	9.9	326,287	87,647

Sources: ADB, IMF, CIA Factbook

ALGERIA

With more than 30 million inhabitants, ample oil resources and an economy in transition, formerly socialist Algeria offers great potential for foreign investment. Responding to IMF and the World Bank programs, Algeria has made remarkable economic and financial progress, improving its trade and budget balances, reducing inflation and foreign debt and bolstering foreign currency reserves. Currently the main focus of foreign investors is on oil and gas, but as privatization progresses, this is likely to change.

Country profile

The Democratic and Popular Republic of Algeria (*Aljumhuriyah aljaza'Iriyah ad Dimuqra-tiyah ash Shabiyah*) is the largest of the countries in the northwestern corner of Africa, known as the Maghreb. It is, after Sudan, the second largest country on the continent. Regions vary from coastal plains along the Mediterranean, to high plateaus, mountains and the Sahara Desert—with large reserves of oil and natural gas that are so important to the economy. About 80% of the predominantly Muslim population speak Arabic. Berbers, including Kabyles, and the Tuaregs are major linguistic groups. A medium ranking on the United Nations Human Development Index reflects the comparatively high levels attained in education and health.

History

The Arab culture and Islam were introduced to the predominantly Berber peoples of Algeria in the 7th Century. It survived subsequent invasions by the Turks and the French, who came in 1830 and stayed until 1962 when the Algerians won their independence after a protracted war against France. President Ahmed Ben Bella and his successor, President Houari Boume-dienne, introduced various socialist reforms. In 1988 widespread strikes led to rioting and the killing of hundreds in Algiers and other cities. It also gave rise to the Islamic Salvation Front (FIS), an extremist fundamentalist movement bent on eradicating "European" influence in Algeria. As a result of violence backed by the FIS before the 1990 elections and pronouncements by its leaders that they intended to replace democracy with a theocracy, the rulers suspended the election. The FIS was dissolved by court order in 1992. In 1994 General Liamine Zeroual was appointed president to replace the High Council of State (HSC), which ruled in the interim. By mid-1994 some 4,000 Algerians and more than 30 foreigners had been killed by the FIS. Gen-

Pres. Abdelaziz Bouteflika
Born: March 2, 1937
Since April 1999

UN Photo Matt Campbell

POLITICAL	
Head of State	Pres. Abdelaziz Bouteflika
Majority Party	FLN
Other major paties	RND, MSP
Independence	5 July 1962
National capital	Algiers
Official language	Arabic

PHYSICAL	
Total area	920,000 sq. miles 2,382,000 sq. km (3½ x Texas)
Arable land	3% of land area
Coastline	746 m/1200 km

POPULATION	
Total	34 million
Av. yearly growth	1.2%
Life expectancy	74 years
Urban population	65%
Adult literacy	69.9%

ECONOMY	
Currency	Algerian dinar (DA)(US$1=74.70)
GDP (real)	$158.9 billion
GDP growth rate	2.2%
GDP per capita[1]	$6,054
GDP (ppp)[2]	$256 billion
GDP per cap. (ppp)	$7,352
Inflation rate	5.7%
Exports	$43.7 billion
Imports	$39.1 billion
External debt	$3.4 billion
Unemployment	10.25%

1. Atlas method.
2. See page 175 for an explanation of purchasing power parity (ppp).

eral Zeroual held elections in 1997, which the Rassemblement national démocratique (RND) won. Following President Zeroual's resignation in 1999, Abdelaziz Bouteflika was elected as Algeria's first civilian president. After an amnesty agreement in 1999 with some of the armed Islamic fundamentalist groups, violence diminished and in 1999 referendum Bouteflika's peace plan was adopted by a landslide 98% of the vote. Bouteflika was reelected in 2009 for a third term—a Constitutional amendment in 2008 abolished term limits.

Government

A bicameral parliament consists of a 389-seat National People's Assembly (*Al-Majlis Ech-Chaabi Al Watani*) elected by popular vote for five years and a Council of Nations which serves as an upper chamber. One third of the 144 members of the *Council* are appointed by the President and the rest elected by indirect vote. Council members serve six years. In the May 2007 National Assembly elections, with a voter turnout of 35%, the *Front de libération nationale* (FLN) captured 136 seats while 61 went to the Rassemblement national pour la démocratie (RND). The Islamist Movement of Society for Peace (MSP) (*Harakat Mujtama as-Silm/Mouvement de la Societé pour la Paix*) won 52 seats and independents and numerous smaller parties the rest.

Economic policy

In the first two decades after independence Algeria, heavily influenced by socialism, maintained a government-controlled economy. The petroleum industry was nationalized and collective ownership introduced in the agricultural sector. Legislation allowing foreign-owned companies to become involved in the "reconstruction" of the national economy was adopted since and several reforms introduced. In recent years government regulatory pricing was relaxed and more liberal tax policies introduced as part of an ongoing reform program. Structural reform within the economy, such as development of the banking sector and the construction of infrastructure, is moving ahead.

Sectors

Algeria has one of Africa's more advanced economies based on oil and natural gas. The oil production of 1.373 million bbl/day is of a high quality with a low sulphur content. The hydrocarbons sector accounts for roughly 60 percent of budget revenues, 30 percent of GDP, and over 95 percent of export earnings. Algeria has the world's seventh-largest reserves of natural gas and ranks second as a gas exporter. It is 14th in oil reserves. High oil prices along with macroeconomic policy reforms sanctioned by the IMF boosted the country's financial and macroeconomic indicators. Algeria's large trade surpluses helped it to build substantial foreign exchange reserves. A key player in this petroleum sector is the state oil company, SONATRACH, which has been courting overseas investors in recent years. There are four oil refineries and four natural gas liquefaction plants. Agriculture is confined to the Mediterranean coastal region where crops such as wheat, barley, vegetables, citrus fruits, dates, olives, peas, beans, lentils, tobacco a nd sugar beet are grown. Wine is the main agricultural export. Other mineral resources include iron ore, uranium, zinc, phosphates, gold, antimony, bituminous coal, tungsten, manganese, lead, mercury, gypsum and salt. Manufacturing largely consists of heavy industries such as iron and steel, and fertilizer and cement plants, but the emphasis is shifting towards textiles and the processing of food, tobacco and cigarettes.

Privatization

The government privatized or liquidated 1,000 state enterprises since 1996. Privatization of *Crédit Populaire d'Algérie* (CPA) was completed in 2007. The entry of HSBC (UK) and Deutsche Bank (Germany) into the country's financial services industry and the acquisition by Linde (Germany) of a controlling stake in a state-owned industrial gas company, contributed to a surge in foreign direct investment.

Trade

About 95 percent of Algeria's export revenues come from oil and natural gas exports. Major buyers are Spain, Portugal and Morocco. Algeria produces only about one-third of its own food requirements and relies heavily on imports from the United States and Europe for the rest.

Investment

Following the example of the state-owned petroleum corporation, SONATRACH, various sectors in Algeria have been courting foreign investors in recent years. American interest has mainly been in the petroleum sector. Other significant entrants were Coca-Cola and Pepsi Cola. It is expected that in the next few years others will follow suit in the service, food processing and mining sectors.

Financial sector

The Bank of Algeria controls monetary growth by setting bank lending limits. Interest rates are adjusted on a weekly basis by a government board. In 1998 the central bank opened a secondary market for government debt. Still, the lack of a modern financial services sector restricts growth of the private sector and has impeded foreign investment in Algeria. Reform efforts in the state-owned banking sector overall have progressed slowly. A few foreign banks have opened representational offices since the promulgation of the currency and credit law.

Taxes & tariffs

The government reformed its tax code to encourage business development by cutting rates in several categories. The corporate tax rate for non-residents is 24 percent and capital gains tax 20 percent. A value added tax (VAT) of 17 percent applies and exchange control is in effect. Taxes are levied on dividends (15%), interest (10 to 50%) and royalties (24%). (See page 138).

BUSINESS ACTIVITY

AGRICULTURE	Wheat, barley, oats, grapes, citrus, fruit, olives, livestock.
INDUSTRIES	Petroleum, natural gas, light industries, mining, electrical, petrochemical, food processing.
NATURAL RESOURCES	Petroleum, natural gas, iron ore, phosphates, uranium, lead, zinc.
EXPORTS	$43.7 billion (2009 est.): petroleum, natural gas and petroleum products.
IMPORTS	$39.1 billion (2009 est.): capital goods, food and beverages, consumer goods.
MAJOR TRADING PARTNERS	Italy, US, France, China, Spain, Germany

Doing Business with Algeria

▶ **Investment**

Algeria, with its large proven oil and gas reserves and potential for new discoveries, offers significant commercial opportunities to foreign investors. Investments in the hydrocarbon sector involve a minority partnership with the state-owned SONATRACH. The same rules apply in telecommunications and national transportation, but in all other sectors foreign investors have unlimited scope. Repatriation of profits, interest, dividends or any other form of revenue is permitted.

▶ **Trade**

Machinery for the exploration and exploitation of oil and gas offers the best potential for US exports. As the world's fifth largest and Africa's largest importer of wheat, this commodity, as well as other foodstuffs, present good opportunities. There is a strong demand for housing materials, consumer products, and equipment for water projects and telecommunications. Import licenses are no longer required for most of these items, but the government stipulates that imported products, particularly consumer goods, must be labeled in Arabic. Distribution is largely in private hands and can be done through legally authorized dealers.

▶ **Trade finance**

Eximbank programs apply to Algeria. The World Bank has assisted with loans for purchases relating to housing, water and sewage, and urban transport. The US-based Agricultural Mutual Bank, in partnership with a major insurance company and the private Union Bank, established a leasing corporation for agricultural equipment. Algerian state corporations have the reputation of honoring their purchase obligations, even though there may sometimes be bureaucratic delays.

▶ **Selling to the government**

Direct negotiation for contracts is only permitted in a few special cases. Tenders for primary raw materials, agricultural products, and construction are frequently limited to known suppliers. Public tenders are advertised in the dailies, the official weekly contract bulletin of the public agency (BOMOP) and sometimes in the international press. Algerian organizations rarely buy at the tendered price as further negotiation usually takes place with a short list of bidders. It is customary for companies to visit the state organizations beforehand and introduce their products and their company's capabilities. The use of agents or other intermediaries is strictly prohibited.

▶ **Exchange controls**

A government board manages a float for the dinar, which is convertible for all current account transactions. Private and public importers may buy foreign exchange from five commercial banks for transactions on proof that they can pay for hard currency in dinars.

▶ **Partnership**

The Algerian government is looking for outside resources to modernize its plants and encourages foreign investors to enter into joint ventures. In their search for partners Algerian companies usually look for technical expertise and financial assistance. Recent legislation gave foreign banks the freedom to establish in Algeria, paving the way for partnerships in the financial sector. Other state sectors are trying to emulate the success that the state-owned petroleum giant, SONATRACH, had in striking partnerships with major foreign investors both in the exploration and downstream processing of its oil and gas.

▶ **Establishing a presence**

To open a liaison office, foreign firms apply for an office leasing agreement at the Algerian Ministry of Commerce. They have to appoint a director and submit bank guarantee of $20,000.

▶ **Labor**

Trade unions are allowed. The law mandates a 40-hour work week and the government has set a guaranteed monthly minimum wage of 6,000 Algerian dinars ($100). A decree regulates occupational and health standards. Working conditions are largely left at the discretion of employers in consultation with employees.

▶ **Legal rights**

Even though Algeria is a member of the Paris Industrial Property Convention and the 1952 Convention on Copyrights, its protection of intellectual property is less than satisfactory. There is recourse to international arbitration to settle possible legal disputes with investors.

▶ **Business climate**

Algerian organizations usually deal only with foreign partners who have developed their trust by personal visits, follow-up, and who have shown ability to honor commitments. It is sometimes necessary to spend large amounts on market development, especially when the contracts are substantial.

ANGOLA

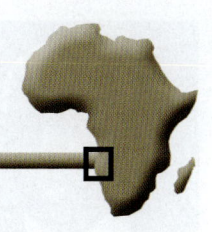

Rich in oil and diamonds and other natural resources, Angola is a sparsely populated country roughly the combined size of Texas and California. The country is rebuilding after the end of a civil war lasting twenty seven years. Its high growth rate is driven by its oil sector, benefiting from high oil prices coupled with rising production. Postwar reconstruction and the resettlement of displaced citizens have further boosted income from construction, agriculture, gold and diamond mining, and fishing. Reforms recommended by the IMF and greater transparency serve to encourage foreign investors.

Country profile

The Republic of Angola is slightly larger than South Africa and the combined size of Texas and California. The climate varies from tropical in the north to subtropical in the south. Major rivers are the Kunene, Zambezi and the Kwanza (after which the country's currency was named). The Bantu-speaking Ovimbundu, Kimbundu and Bakongo peoples are in the majority. Fifty-three percent are Christians (mostly Roman Catholic). The rest adhere to indigenous beliefs.

History

In the 16th Century, Portuguese interest in the region focused on the slave trade to supply the needs of its newfound colony, Brazil. Portuguese influence remained centered around Luanda (founded in 1575) and the kingdom of Ndongo ruled by chiefs referred to as ngola—which eventually served as an inspiration when naming independent Angola. It was not until the 1920s that Portugal managed to extend its influence to the borders of Angola, as defined by European treaties in the 1880s and 1890s. A protracted anti-colonial insurgent war ended in when Portugal granted independence to Angola in 1974 after army officers toppled the Salazar regime in Lisbon. Three movements were involved in the freedom struggle, largely divided on a regional and ethnic basis: The Popular Movement for the Liberation of Angola (MPLA) (receiving support from Cuba and the Soviet Union), the National Front for the Liberation of Angola (FNLA) and the National Union for the Total Independence of Angola (UNITA) (receiving assistance from the US and South Africa). On

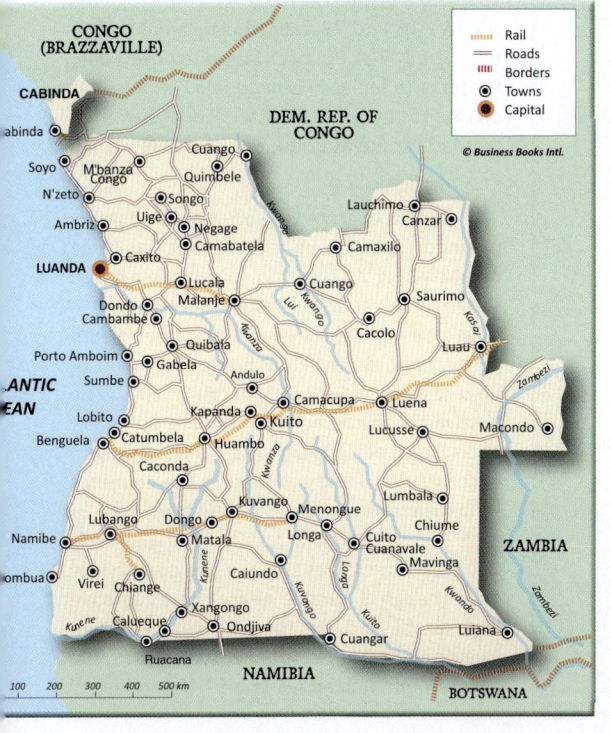

Pres. José Eduoardo dos Santos
Born: Aug.28, 1942
Since Sep 1979

UN Photo Marco Castro

POLITICAL	
Head of State	Pres. José Eduardo dos Santos (1979)
Ruling Party	MPLA
Main Opposition	UNITA
Independence	11 November 1975
National capital	Luanda
Official language	Portuguese

PHYSICAL	
Total area	481,000 sq. miles 1,247,000 sq. km. (3 x California)
Arable land	3% of land area
Coastline	994 miles/1,600 km

POPULATION	
Total	12.8 million
Av. yearly growth	2.1%
Urban population	57%
Life expectancy	38.2 years
Adult literacy	67.4%

ECONOMY	
Currency	New Kwanza (NKz) (US$1=92.2)
GDP (real)	$119.4 billion
GDP growth rate	-0.6%
GDP per capita[1]	$3,729
GDP (ppp)[2]	$100 billion
GDP per cap. (ppp)	$6,431
Inflation rate	14.0%
Exports	$40.7 billion
Imports	$15.7 billion
External debt	$12.8 billion
Unemployment	NA

1. Atlas method.
2. See page 175 for an explanation of purchasing power parity (ppp).

11 November 1975, MPLA leader Agostinho Neto was sworn in as the first president of an independent Angola under Marxist one-party rule. Both FNLA and UNITA turned their offensive against the new rulers. Even though US backing and South African support were eventually withdrawn, UNITA leader Jonas Savimbi continued the war. Dr. Neto died in 1979 and was succeeded as president by the new leader of the MPLA, José Eduardo dos Santos.

Government

In 1992 President dos Santos received a plurality of votes against 122 other legally recognized parties in Angola's first round of elections. The second round never took place as UNITA, the other major party, repudiated the first as fraudulent. In 1994 MPLA and UNITA signed the Lusaka Protocol in an effort to end 20 years of civil war and in April 1997, UNITA joined MPLA and 10 smaller opposition parties in a Government of Unity and National Reconciliation (GURN). In the second half of 1998, however, UNITA pulled out and resumed the war. After the death in battle of UNITA leader, Jonas Savimbi, in 2002 the civil war ceased. In the long-awaited first post-war elections in September 2008 dos Santos' MPLA captured 191 seats in the National Assembly against UNITA's 16 and 13 captured by smaller parties. The MPLA Political Bureau chose Paulo Kassoma to replace Fernando da Piedade Dias dos Santos as Prime Minister. Piedade was appointed President of the National Assembly.

Economic policy

Angola operated a Soviet-style centrally planned economy until 1991, but has since been making a transition to a market-based system. The country's robust growth rate is driven by high oil prices and rising petroleum production. Increased oil production contributed to a 34.7% GDP growth rate in 2007. The postwar reconstruction boom and resettlement of displaced persons led to high rates of growth in construction and agriculture. The country's infrastructure is, however, still damaged or undeveloped from as a result of a 27-year-long civil war. Land mines still mar the countryside even though a durable peace seems to have been established after the death of rebel leader Jonas SAVIMBI in February 2002. In 2005, the government started using a $2 billion line of credit, since increased to $7 billion, from China to rebuild Angola's public infrastructure, and several large-scale projects were completed in 2006. The central bank in 2003 implemented an exchange rate stabilization program using foreign exchange reserves to buy kwanzas out of circulation. It has significantly reduced inflation. Consumer inflation declined from 325% in 2000 to 11.8% in 2007. This stabilization policy has, however, placed pressure on international net liquidity. To take full advantage of its rich national resources—gold, diamonds, extensive forests, Atlantic fisheries, and large oil deposits—Angola needs to continue with reforms. Considerable progress are shown in terms of transparency in government spending. Postwar reconstruction and the resettlement of displaced citizens have boosted income.

Privatization

A privatization program has been developed but a weak private sector in Angola seems to lack the capacity to pick up on offers. A few smaller state-run enterprises have been sold but some have turned out to be nonviable. Most large enterprises such as telecommunications firms, insurance companies, and banks, remain government monopolies.

Sectors

Oil production and its supporting activities contribute about half of GDP and 90 percent of exports. Subsistence agriculture provides the main livelihood for half of the population. Half of the country's food must still be imported. The economy is largely driven by the petroleum sector which accounts for close to half of total GDP. Apart from significant diamond mining, the country also has deposits of iron ore, phosphates, copper, feldspar, gold, bauxite and uranium. Agricultural production continues to suffer from a degraded infrastructure, lack of funds for investment. Production is expected to increase once the infrastructure is repaired and upgraded with the assistance of foreign investors, notably China. The ports of Luanda, Lobito, and Namibe are all operational, but still require improvements.

Trading

With a production of approximately 1.6 million bbl/day of crude, oil accounts for 93 percent of Angola's export revenues. Refined petroleum, natural gas, and raw timber are also important export items. Diamonds are another major export with sales estimated at $400-$600 million per year. Angola imports most consumer items, capital goods, and transport equipment. The US buys 75% of Angola's oil exports.

Financial sector

Owned and operated by the Ministry of Finance, the *Caixa de Credito Agro-Pecuaria e Pescas* (CAP) took over all commercial operations from *Banco National de Angola* (BNA). CAP loans, often on concessionary and sometimes interest-free terms, have been used by the government to provide off-budget financing for parastatal entities. The *Banco de Comercio e Industria* (BCI) is a semiprivate bank, with a 40 percent government ownership.

Taxes

The corporate tax rate for non-residents is 35 percent and capital gains tax 35 percent. Exchange control is in effect. Taxes are levied on dividends (10%), interest (15%) and royalties (10%). (See page 138).

BUSINESS ACTIVITY

AGRICULTURE
Bananas, sugar cane, coffee, sisal, corn, cotton, manioc, tobacco, vegetables, plantains, livestock.
INDUSTRIES
Petroleum, diamonds, iron ore, phosphates, feldspar, bauxite, uranium, gold, cement, basic metal products, fish processing, food processing, brewing, tobacco products, sugar, textiles.
NATURAL RESOURCES
Petroleum, diamonds, iron ore, phosphates, copper, feldspar, gold, bauxite, uranium.
EXPORTS
$40.7 billion (2009 est.): crude oil, diamonds, refined petroleum products, gas, timber, cotton, fish products.
IMPORTS
$15.7 billion (2009 est.): machinery and electrical equipment, vehicles and spare parts, medicines, food, textiles, military supplies.
MAJOR TRADING PARTNERS
US, China, Portugal, France, South Africa, Brazil.

Doing Business with Angola

▶ **Investment**

The Foreign Investment Institute is the point of contact for investors and the Foreign Investment Code guarantees equal treatment for overseas entrepreneurs who are subject to the same tax regime as locals. Repatriation of profits is guaranteed, and prompt indemnification promised in cases of nationalization or expropriation. The country's rich resources—oil, diamonds and several other strategic minerals—have lured big foreign firms. Petroleum-related investments dominate but once the war ends, rebuilding and repair of roads and railways are expected to offer further opportunities, as will agribusiness and telecommunications.

▶ **Trade**

The best prospects for exports are in oil-field machinery and equipment, computers and parts, used clothing, cars and trucks, generators and parts, ships, and aircraft. Product distribution can be problematic as a result of poor infrastructure. Foreign companies may chose to sell through an established importer in Angola, by winning a tender, through investment, or by opening an office.

▶ **Trade finance**

In 1999 the US Eximbank resumed financing for US trade deals with Angola. Angola has in recent years been a recipient of US Department of Agriculture PL-480 Title I program foodstuffs.

▶ **Selling to the government**

The Angolan authorities solicit supplies and services in local and international publications. Bid documents are obtained from a specific government ministry, department or agency at a nonrefundable fee.

▶ **Exchange controls**

The government sets the official rate and has imposed limits on foreign exchange transactions. There are no restrictions on the total amount of foreign currency brought into Angola but it must be declared within 24 hours at an authorized agency. No national currency can be exported from Angola. It is legal to maintain accounts in dollars. All import payments must be made through the central bank, even if foreign exchange is held in another bank.

▶ **Partnerships**

Joint ventures are sanctioned under the foreign investment law, which also regulates the amount and form of capital invested. If an investment is valued at more than $50 million or involves activities that can only be carried out by concession (such as oil and diamond exploration and production), a contract must be established defining the project's objectives, the tax benefits and incentives to be granted, and providing for government monitoring. Such contracts are subject to the approval of the Ministry of Planning, the Prime Minister, and the Council of Ministers. Joint ventures must also be licensed by the Ministry of Commerce.

▶ **Establishing a presence**

A local attorney is needed to prepare the "Articles of Association" before registering a company and to conduct due diligence investigations prior to the conclusion of any purchase or other contractual agreement. The authorities assist foreign businesses interested in establishing agency, franchise, joint venture, or licensing relationships.

▶ **Project financing**

The country is experiencing difficulty in securing financing for projects other than those guaranteed by oil production. Under the Cabinda Trust arrangement, projects in the petroleum sector can receive financing secured by future oil production. Non-Cabinda Trust loans are often short term and at high interest rates.

▶ **Labor**

Labor is plentiful, but skills are scarce. The average level of education is sixth grade. There are two significant labor organizations in Angola.

▶ **Legal rights**

Under Angola's Foreign Investment Code all overseas investments are guaranteed protection and, in the event of expropriation, prompt compensation. Angola is a member of the World Intellectual Property Organization and makes use of its international classification of patents and products and services.

▶ **Business climate**

The buisness climate has improved drastically after the cessation of the war and several petroleum companies and other major foreign firms are involved in mining, banking and the service industry. Both domestic and international telecommunications can be problematic. Many large international corporations rely on high frequency radio transmissions for routine communication.

BENIN

In 1990 Benin, formerly known as Dahomey, turned away from a centrally planned economy under one-party Marxist-Leninist rule. The new democratically-elected government adopted reforms proposed by the World Bank and IMF aimed at developing a free market economy in this small West African country. After several structural adjustment programs (SAPs), Benin has managed a recovery that has caught the attention of US and European investors and traders. Political and economic relations with the capitalist world—once marred by Benin's hardline Marxism—are close and cordial.

Country profile

The Republic of Benin (formerly Dahomey) extends about 650 km north from the Bight of Benin (part of the Gulf of Guinea) to the Niger River. The southern equatorial region is covered with moist woodland savanna and oil palm trees along the coast. The poorer soil on the northern plateau is used for large-scale cotton cultivation and livestock. Along its borders with Niger and Burkina Faso, Benin maintains several national parks which constitute West Africa's premier wildlife conservation area. Most Beninese are related to peoples in neighboring countries. The Fon are closely related to the Ewe in Togo and the Yoruba are related to one of Nigeria's major ethnic groups. Also the Bariba (Borgu), Somba, Fulani, Dendi and Busa (Bussa) have relatives across the various borders. French is the official language and is spoken by groups of mixed descent and expatriates in the coastal towns and cities. Benin is one of only a few African countries where ethnic beliefs still hold sway over the Muslim and Christian faiths, with 70 percent adhering to indigenous beliefs and the rest evenly split between Christianity and Islam. The coastal regions of Benin and Togo practice voodoo (vodun or juju), a tribal ritual that spread to the Caribbean and the Americas during the slave trade era.

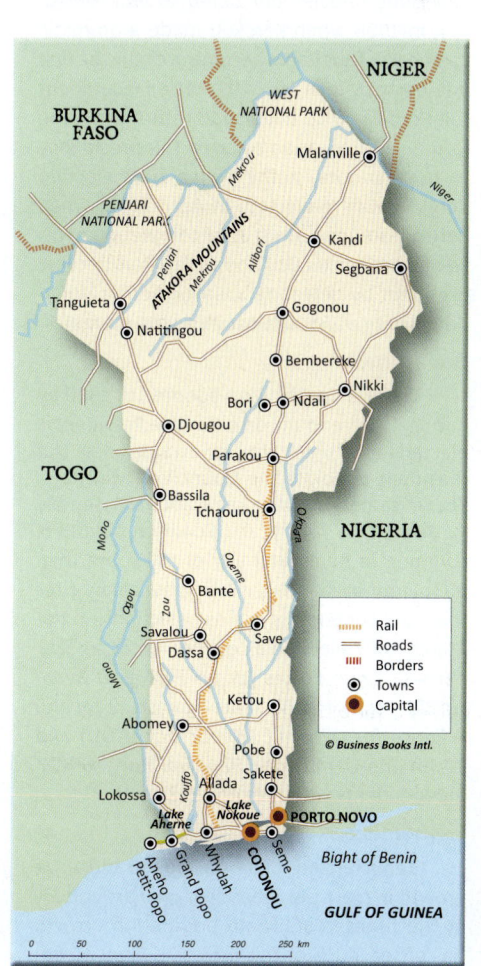

History

The Abomey kingdom of the Dahomey or Fon peoples was established in 1625. Its rich cultural life found expression in wooden masks, bronze statues, tapestries and pottery that have gained world renown in recent years. The Portuguese and the Dutch conducted slave trade from Porto Novo until the mid-19th Century before the French, with the approval

185

Pres. Thomas
Yayi Boni
Born: 1952
Since April 2006

UN Photo Eskinder Debebe

POLITICAL

Head of State	Pres. Yayi Boni
Ruling Party	FCBE
Main Opposition	ADD
Independence	1 August 1960
National capital	Porto Novo[3]
Official language	French

PHYSICAL

Total area	44,000 sq. miles 113,000 sq. km (± Tennessee)
Arable land	13% of land area
Coastline	75 miles/121 km

POPULATION

Total	8.8 million
Av. yearly growth	2.97%
Urban population	41%
Life expectancy	59
Adult literacy	34.7%

ECONOMY

Currency	CFA franc (CFAF) (US$1=495.40)
GDP (real)	$6.3 billion
GDP growth rate	3.0%
GDP per capita[1]	$1,233
GDP (ppp)[2]	$13.4 billion
GDP per cap. (ppp)[2]	$1,506
Inflation rate	4.1%
Exports	$1 billion
Imports	$1.6 billion
External debt	$1.2 billion
Unemployment	NA

1. Atlas method.
2. See page 175 for an explanation of purchasing power parity (ppp).
3. Official. Cotonou is the de facto capital.

of Britain and Germany, appropriated a colony extending from the Niger to the sea and named it Dahomey. Early in the 20th Century it became part of French West Africa and on 1 August 1960, was one of 14 former French African colonies granted independence. Several coups led to the assumption of power by Major Mathieu Kérékou in 1974. During his 17-year rule Kérékou turned Dahomey into the People's Republic of Benin under a Marxist dictatorship. In 1989, President Kérékou was forced by widespread opposition to his failed centralized economy to renounce Marxism-Leninism and implement a major privatization program. His cuts in the government payroll and reduction of social services promoted student and labor unrest. Fearing revolution Kérékou agreed to a new constitution and free elections in 1991. He lost to Nicéphore Soglo, who introduced economic reforms but failed to win reelection in 1996 when Kérékou made a dramatic comeback. Thus Benin became not only the first one-party state in Africa to vote an incumbent ruler out of office but also to return the same former authoritarian ruler to the presidency by popular vote. In the March 2001 election Kérékou was re-elected. In April 2006, when Kérékou stepped down after completion of his two terms, banker Dr. Thomas Yayi Boni became president by defeating Speaker Adrien Hounbendji with a 75% against 25% vote margin.

Government

Under a Constitution adopted in 1990 by national referendum, an executive President is elected for a 5 year term, renewable once. The President appoints the Council of Ministers. The unicameral 83-member National Assembly is elected for four years. Coalition politics is common in Benin and any of the more than 30 splinter parties might swing the balance for the main contenders in close elections. In the March 2007 election a coalition of 20 smaller parties—*Cauri Forces for an Emerging Benin* (FCBE)—captured 35 seats against 20 for the *Alliance for Dynamic Democracy* (ADD) and 10 for the *Democratic Renewal Party* (PRD). Independents won the other 18 seats.

Economic policy

Benin remains underdeveloped and while growth in real output has averaged around 5% in the reent years rapid population growth has offset much of this increase. Plans to improve the business climate by reforms to the land tenure system, the commercial justice system, and the financial sector were included in Benin's $307 million Millennium Challenge Account grant signed in February 2006. Benin has implemented changes in accordance with a structural adjustment program (SAP) sponsored by the World Bank and the IMF and qualified for $460 million in debt relief under the Heavily Indebted Poor Countries Initiative. (HIPC).

Privatization

Apart from selling state enterprises such as SONACOP (oil company), *Société Sucrière de Save* (a sugar refinery), *Société des Ciments d'Onigbolo* (cement company), SONICOG (vegetable oil refineries), and SONAR and IARD (national insurance companies), the government has liquidated several other failing enterprises. Privatization continues in telecommunications, water, electricity, and agriculture.

Sectors

Agriculture employs three-quarters of the population and accounts for 37% of GDP. Benin produces cotton, palm oil and kernels, coffee, and cocoa for export. It is generally self-sufficient in food production, though large quantities of foodstuffs, especially rice, are imported. Main food crops are millet, sorghum, maize, and root and tuber crops, such as cassava and yams. Livestock farming is important in the drier areas to the north. Fishing is popular in the rivers, lakes and lagoons. Timber production is negligible. Offshore oil is produced near Seme and further exploration is being undertaken. There are known deposits of phosphate, iron ore, chromium, gold and marble awaiting exploitation. Extensive limestone deposits are utilized for cement production. Manufacturing centers around the processing of agricultural products and consumer goods and construction materials. Tourism is a growing industry.

Trading

A substantial part of Benin's trade consists of goods smuggled across its border with Nigeria and therefore not accounted for in official trade statistics. Oil and cotton are major export items while food, fuel, energy and capital goods top the list of import items. Exports are mainly to Portugal, Morocco and the United States while France, Thailand and China supply in most of Benin's needs.

Investment

Benin has been emphasizing foreign investment opportunities in tourism, food processing, agriculture and ITC. Major foreign investors in Benin are France, Germany, and Canada. US firms have become increasingly involved in the petroleum sector. Other recent foreign investment came through acquisition of state-owned enterprises in textiles, tobacco, cement, beer brewing, petroleum and public transportation.

Financial sector

Five major commercial banks were established after the state-owned banking system failed. With foreign assistance and guidance from the World Bank and IMF, Benin took measures to attract foreign banks back. The present financial system includes the Credit Promotion Benin (CCB), the postal checking accounts (CCP), the Savings Bank (CNE) and the Sonar, a state-owned insurance company.

Taxes and tariffs

The corporate tax rate for non-residents is 30 percent and capital gains tax 30 percent. A value added tax (VAT) of 18 percent applies and exchange control is in effect. Taxes are levied on dividends (9%), interest (15%) and royalties (25 to 30%). (See page 138).

BUSINESS ACTIVITY

AGRICULTURE
Corn, sorghum, cassava (tapioca), yams, beans, rice, cotton, palm oil, peanuts, poultry, livestock.

INDUSTRIES
Textiles, cigarettes, beverages, food, construction materials, petroleum.

EXPORTS
$1 billion (2008 est.): cotton, crude oil, palm products, cocoa.

IMPORTS
$1.6 billion (2008 est.): petroleum products, intermediate goods, capital goods, light consumer goods.

MAJOR TRADING PARTNERS
China, India, US, France, Ghana, Indonesia, Niger, Nigeria, Thailand.

Doing Business with Benin

▶ Investment

Good investment opportunities stem from the privatization process, with the oil sector offering the best potential for foreign investors. The government is slowly, but not entirely, disengaging itself from the this sector. Further scope is offered by Benin's efforts to improve the infrastructure for telecommunications, electricity and roads. The country also holds potential for those who are able to offer modern techniques for cold storage, canning, and packing. Saltwater fishing is another area where foreign involvement is sought. Considerable cotton production and privatization of the textile industry open up further prospects.

▶ Trade

Agricultural products, food processing machinery, consumer goods and gas powered turbines for electricity generation are good prospects. Large foreign firms often enter into exclusive contracts with an agent/distributor. Overseas firms are cautioned to deal only with Beninese companies that are registered with the government. Among the long-established distributors of consumer goods are French firms and Lebanese and Indian traders. The main types of outlets are open-air markets, street displays and street vendors, and European-style supermarkets and convenience stores with a wide range of local and imported products.

▶ Trade finance

Eximbank operates programs in support of US capital goods and services. With properly documented trade transactions, authorization for overseas payments is easily obtained. There is, however, no protection against currency fluctuations. Several banks have reliable and efficient correspondent relationships with overseas banks.

▶ Selling to the government

There has been a concerted effort on the part of the authorities to promote transparency and eliminate favoritism when considering bids. Bureaucratic red tape remains a problem.

▶ Exchange controls

Any enterprise engaged in a commercial, industrial, agricultural, or artisan activity, or that provides services, is entitled to transfer capital, profits and dividends.

▶ Establishing a presence

A limited company (Inc.) is the most common form of entry. Its establishment is speedy and simple. Establishing of a company normally requires authorization by the relevant ministry after completion of specific forms. Some industrial firms may opt for preferential schemes under the Investment Code, offered by the Technical Investment Commission of the Ministry of Planning. In most cases overseas firms rely on the services of a local attorney.

▶ Project financing

Several infrastructure renovation contracts are funded by grants or loans from the World Bank or other International Development Banks. The Overseas Private Investment Corporation (OPIC) offers financial assistance to small US companies and provides political risk insurance, loans, and investment guarantees. Two World Bank-related institutions, FIAS (Foreign Investments Advisory Service) and MIGA (Multilateral Investment Guarantee Agency), are active in Benin. Potential development financing is also available through the African Development Bank, the West African Bank for Development (BOAD), the European Development Fund (FED), and the International Fund for Economic Development (FIDA).

▶ Labor

A largely unskilled workforce is organized in four trade union confederations. Due to high unemployment (no official statistics) there is a substantial surplus of workers. A considerable number of skilled workers also continue to reenter the job market as privatization eliminates jobs in former state enterprises. Foreign firms have also had considerable success with in-house training and the government has established several technical schools. Salaries have not kept pace with the cost of living after devaluation. Labor reforms aiming at greater flexibility are underway.

▶ Business climate

There are guarantees against nationalization and the post-Marxist Benin is going out of its way to make the country investor friendly. In disputes between the state and a foreign firm, Benin recognizes the Hague Permanent Arbitration Court as the final authority. It also subscribes to the International Center for Settlement of Investment Disputes, which is part of the World Bank Group. Laws protect against IPR infringements. Benin is a signatory of the OAPI Convention of Yaounde (African Organization for Intellectual Property) and the World Intellectual Property Organization.

BOTSWANA

Botswana has maintained a high growth rate since its independence in 1966 as well as four decades of exemplary democratic rule. It has transformed itself from one of the poorest countries in the world to a middle-income country with the best credit rating in Africa. Diamond mining accounts for more than one-third of GDP and for between seventy and eighty percent of the country's export earnings. Tourism, subsistence farming, and cattle are other key sectors. Botswana has one of the world's highest known rates of HIV/AIDS infection but also has in place one of Africa's most progressive and comprehensive programs for dealing with the disease.

Country profile

The Republic of Botswana is a large, sparsely populated, landlocked country sharing borders with five other countries. Its terrain varies from the arid Kalahari Desert to the lush forests of the Okavango Delta and the dry savannah of the Limpopo Valley. Botswana is constantly in need of rain, hence the national motto, Pula or rain. More than 80% of its 1.6 million citizens are Tswana (plural Batswana, singular Motswana). They speak various dialects of the Sotho language, Setswana. The rest are Herero, Mbukushu, Subia and Fwe, apart from a few whites. Half of the population are Christians and the rest still adhere to traditional tribal beliefs.

History

The earliest inhabitants of the area were the San, followed by the Tswana. Bechuanaland, as it was known before independence, had been the crossroads for missionaries, merchants and migrants before Britain annexed and declared it a protectorate in 1885 in a preemptive strike to prevent the Boers of the Transvaal from taking possession of the territory. Independence for Bechuanaland under its new name, Botswana, came in 1966. The first elected president, Sir Seretse Khama, remained in power until his death in 1980. Khama was succeeded by Vice President and later Sir Ketumile Masire who remained in power for seventeen years. When President Masire retired in 1998, his vice president—an Oxford-educated economist and former Finance Minister—Festus Mogae, was elected president. President Mogae stepped down in April 2008 in favor of his deputy, Vice President Seretse Ian Khama—the son of Botswana's first president. Khama was reconfirmed to the post in October 2009.

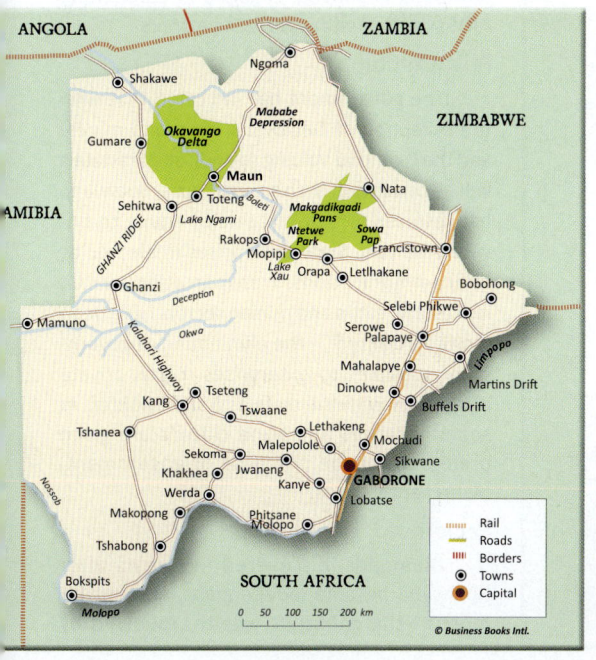

189

Pres. Seretse Khama Ian Khama
Born: Feb. 27, 1953
Since April 2008

UN Photo

POLITICAL	
Head of State	Pres. Ian Khama
Ruling Party	Botswana Democratic Party (BDP)
Main Opposition	Botswana National Front (BNF)
Independence	30 Sept. 1966
National capital	Gaborone
Official languages	English, Tswana

PHYSICAL	
Total area	225,000 sq. miles 582,000 sq. km. (± Texas)
Arable land	1% of land area
Coastline	Landlocked

POPULATION	
Total	2 million
Av. yearly growth	1.94%
Urban population	60%
Life expectancy	61.8 years
Adult literacy	81.2%

ECONOMY	
Currency	Pula (BWP) (US$1=6.64)
GDP (real)	$11.5 billion
GDP growth rate	-4.0%
GDP per capita[1]	$11,801
GDP (ppp)[2]	$25.8 billion
GDP per cap. (ppp)	$13,214
Inflation rate	8.2%
Exports	$3.4 billion
Imports	$4.2 billion
External debt	$1.2 billion
Unemployment	7.5%

1. Atlas method.
2. See page 175 for an explanation of purchasing power parity (ppp).

Government

Held out as a model of democracy in Africa, Botswana continues to adhere strictly to its 1966 constitution requiring the election of a president and National Assembly for a period of five years. The President, elected indirectly, is limited to two terms. In the October 2009 election Khama's Botswana Democratic Party (BDP) won 45 of the 57 parliamentary seats in the unicameral Assembly against 6 for the Botswana National Front (BNF), 5 for the Botswana Congress Party/Botswana Alliance Movement (BCP/BAM) and one independent.

Economic policy

At independence in 1966, Botswana was one of the 20 poorest nations. The discovery of diamonds in 1971 and sound economic policies enabled it to attain one of the world's highest economic growth rates. Under its Industrial Development Policy the government utilized mineral wealth to develop human resources and infrastructure, communications facilities and utilities. Two major investment services rank Botswana as the best credit risk in Africa. The stock exchange sought new listings to attract business on the foreign capital markets. HIV/AIDS, however, presents a major threat to the country, with some estimates putting the infection rate at 36%—the highest in the world. Botswana is actively engaged in combatting AIDS together with overseas partners.

Privatization

The government has indicated that with the exception of Debswana (diamond mines) and the Diamond Valuing Agency, all parastatals will be privatized. In some instances, Botswana has resorted to a partial sale of equity to private investors. State enterprises in electricity, telecommunications, transportation, water, real estate, cattle and mining sectors have been "commercialized"—the elimination of government subsidies to enterprises run as private businesses with the state as a shareholder. In some instances Botswana citizens are given preference in the purchase of government-owned enterprises.

Sectors

Diamonds, discovered five years after Botswana became independent, account for most of the country's wealth, followed by cattle farming. Diamonds constitute close to 80% of total export earnings. Botswana also has significant deposits of coal, copper-nickel, soda ash, potash and sodium sulphate. Livestock—especially cattle farming—constitutes 80% of the total agricultural income. Sorghum, maize, millet, beans and other crops are cultivated on a subsistence basis. A developing manufacturing sector entails motor vehicle assembly, and pharmaceuticals, leather and textiles, food processing and furniture. Due to the small size of the domestic market, most of these industries are export-oriented. Tourism is a major industry. Botswana's national parks and private game lodges lure safari enthusiasts from around the world.

Trading

Botswana's largest export market is the European Union with diamonds as the main commodity. South Africa is in second place, purchasing mostly vehicles and beef and supplying most of Botswana's imports. United States exports are mostly manufactured goods, including heavy machinery, electrical appliances, data processing machines, radar appliances, communication and electrical equipment. US imports consists largely of textiles, clothing and handicrafts.

Investment

Foreign direct investment (FDI) forms a major portion of overseas capital flows into Botswana, followed by portfolio investments. The latter have grown considerably since the establishment of the Botswana Stock Exchange in the 1990s. Not surprisingly, mining draws the largest percentage of FDI. Significant foreign capital has also gone into the development of infrastructure and, in recent years manufacturing and tourism. Most foreign equity and non-equity investments came from South Africa followed by the European Union with the U.K. and Luxembourg as major sources. Investments from the US went largely into the service, manufacturing and tourism sectors. The automobile industry remains a priority and vehicle assembly is now the country's second most important industry. By far the largest foreign investor in Botswana is South Africa's Anglo-American Corporation (De Beers), which has a multimillion dollar stake, along with the Government of Botswana, in the country's major diamond mining industry, Debswana.

Financial sector

The central bank—the Bank of Botswana—has an impressive track record managing the commercial banking sector and monetary policies. Foreigners have access to credit at local market rates and often receive preferential treatment over local borrowers. There are four commercial banks and one investment bank, all with correspondent arrangements in the US. Nonresidents are no longer restricted from issuing bonds on the stock market and are able to hold bonds with maturity periods of over one year. Dual listings are also permitted on the Botswana Stock Exchange. The establishment of an International Financial Services Center (IFSC) in the wake of progressive economic liberalization, the abolition of exchange controls, high foreign exchange reserves, and the maintenance of a favorable macroeconomic environment present a potentially lucrative business opportunity for foreigners interested in operating offshore banking, insurance and accounting.

Taxes and tariffs

The corporate tax rate for non-residents is 25 percent and capital gains tax 81.75 to 25 percent. A value added tax (VAT) of 10 percent applies and exchange control does not apply. Taxes are levied on dividends (15%), interest (10%) and royalties (15%). (See page 138).

BUSINESS ACTIVITY

AGRICULTURE
Sorghum, maize, millet, pulses, groundnuts (peanuts), beans, cowpeas, sunflower seed, livestock.
INDUSTRIES
Diamonds, copper, nickel, coal, salt, soda ash, potash, livestock processing.
NATURAL RESOURCES
Diamonds, copper, nickel, salt, soda ash, potash, coal, iron ore, silver.
EXPORTS
$3.4 billion (2009 est.): diamonds, nickel, copper, meat.
IMPORTS
$4.2 billion (2009 est.): foodstuffs, vehicles and transport equipment, textiles, petroleum products.
MAJOR TRADING PARTNERS
EU, Southern African Customs Union

Doing Business with Botswana

▶ **Investment**

There is scope for investment in motor vehicle assembly, photovoltaic manufacturing, financial services and tourism. Investment incentives are offered. The Botswana Export Development and Investment Agency assists investors through all the preliminary stages and provides support services, such as purchasing or leasing of property, obtaining work and residence permits, licenses, and grants. The Botswana Development Corporation seeks out suitable partners for specific projects and the National Development Bank offers long-term loans. Under the Financial Assistance Policy, grants are extended to labor-intensive projects outside the cattle farming and diamond sectors.

▶ **Trade**

State purchase of drugs (particularly to combat HIV/AIDS) and a growing need for computer hardware and software, mining, construction, telecommunications equipment, as well photovoltaic and water supply systems, offer trade opportunities. As a result of frequent droughts, there is often a need for corn, sorghum, wheat, and rice.

▶ **Trade finance**

Short-term finance, including pre-and-post-shipment credit, is available through the local commercial banking system and export credit insurance is offered by domestic insurance companies. Eximbank financing is available to US exporters.

▶ **Selling to the government**

The Central Tender Board (CTB) awards government tenders in an open process. Lobbying of the CTB is strictly prohibited. Occasionally preferential treatment is given to local participants. Firms are encouraged to make contact with the relevant government ministries or parastatals to ensure proper presentation of tenders for major projects.

▶ **Exchange controls**

Botswana has abolished exchange controls but the authorities monitor capital flows for early warning signals of potentially destabilizing activity. Commercial banks require investors to fill out basic forms for outward and inward transactions.

▶ **Partnerships**

Partnership with a local investor has occasionally been an unwritten requirement for winning government tenders. The government, however, does not impose any performance requirements or local participation on foreign enterprises.

▶ **Establishing a presence**

Foreign private entities may freely establish, acquire, and dispose of interests in local business enterprises. The government does not set any conditions regarding location, local content, local equity, import substitution, export targets, or financing. There is no restriction on the repatriation of profits and dividends, debt service, capital gains, returns on intellectual property, royalties, franchise fees and service fees. Upon disinvestment, foreigners are allowed to reclaim all proceeds.

▶ **Project financing**

OPIC finance and insurance programs apply to US operations in Botswana. Botswana is a member of the Multilateral Investment Guarantee Agency and all four major local commercial banks as well as an investment bank offer financing for new businesses. Six separate development financial institutions also offer specialized services. The borrowing provisions for US and other foreign firms are liberal.

▶ **Labor**

With high unemployment, there is no shortage of workers. Due to the low skill base employers may have to undertake significant training, depending on the industry. Only a small portion of the formal sector—mostly mining and banking— is unionized and strikes are rare. An industrial court ensures impartial adjudication in labor disputes.

▶ **Legal rights**

Civil law is based on Roman-Dutch law and the English criminal legal system applies. Botswana is a member of the International Center for the Settlement of Investment Disputes (ICSID) and the Multilateral Investment Guarantee Agency. The Industrial Property Act and recently revamped Copyright Act brought the country in conformity with the WTO's Trade Related Aspects of International property Rights. The Constitution prohibits nationalization of private property.

▶ **Business climate**

Botswana's business and government community tend to be reserved and formal. English is the official language and used extensively in business, but Setswana is widely spoken. It is wise to reconfirm appointments 24 hours ahead. Meetings may start late and are sometimes interrupted by telephone conversations. Neither is an indication of disrespect or lack of interest.

BURKINA FASO

Formerly known as Upper Volta, Burkina Faso is the smallest of West Africa's landlocked states. Despite its relatively small population of ten million and limited natural resources, Burkina has managed to attract foreign interests by streamlining its public sector, privatizing, lifting trade barriers and liberalizing prices. Since the early nineties it has worked closely with the World Bank and the IMF in a structural adjustment program. Burkina Faso depends on Ghana and Côte d'Ivoire for outlets to the sea and job opportunities for some of its citizens. foreign entrepreneurs, especially those involved in mining and minerals, are increasingly focusing on Burkina Faso—"the land of the honorable."

Country profile

The Democratic Republic of Burkina Faso, formerly known as Upper Volta, is the smallest of Western Africa's landlocked states. It spans the headwaters of the Great Volta River. Burkina is rich in historical relics but relatively poor in natural resources. The climate is tropical. The Gur (or Voltaic) peoples, who also inhabit northern parts of Togo, Ghana and Côte d'Ivoire, dominate Burkina. The largest group of Gur-speaking peoples is the Mossi (or Moore) around Ouagadougou, the nucleus of their ancient kingdom. The Mande-speaking Bobo and Dyula, found in the southwest around the town of Bobo-Dioulasso and the with the Bisa, who live further east, are related to the people of Mali. In the dry north are the pastoral Fulani. Half the population adheres to traditional ethnic faiths and the rest are largely Muslim.

History

Burkina Faso's original inhabitants were the Bobo, Lobi and Gurunsi peoples. The Mosi and Gurma peoples migrated to the region in the 14th Century. From the 15th to the 18th Century the Mossi successfully resisted incorporation into the Mali and Songhai empires as well as Fulani invasions. France conquered the territory between 1895 and 1904. Responding to insurrection in Upper Volta, the French introduced military rule until 1919, when it became a separate colony in the union of French West Africa. Upper Volta received self-government following a referendum in 1958 and full independence in 1960. Shortly after he won the first election, President Maurice Yameogo banned all opposition parties. He was overthrown in 1966 and succeeded by Gen. Sangoule Lamiza-

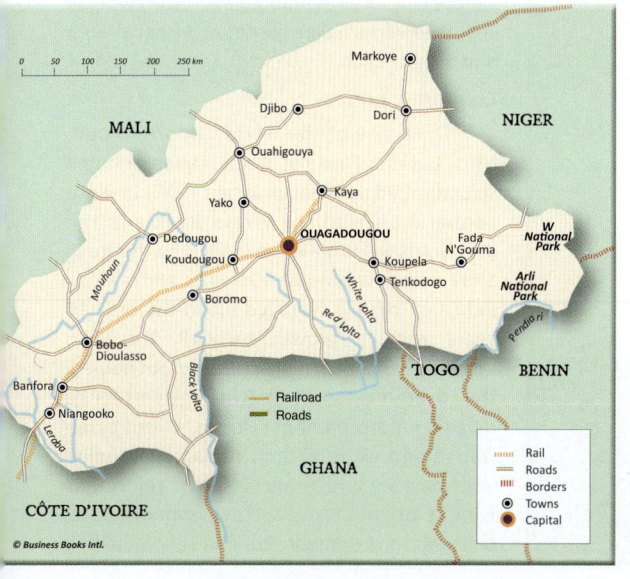

193

Pres. Blaise Compaoré
Born: February 3, 1951
Since October 1987

UN Photo Ryan Brown

POLITICAL	
Head of State	Pres. Blaise Compaoré
Ruling Party	CDP
Main Opposition	ADF-RDA
Independence	4 August 1960
National capital	Ouagadougou
Official languages	French

PHYSICAL	
Total area	106,000 sq. miles
	274,000 sq. km.
	(± Colorado)
Arable land	13% of land area
Coastline	Landlocked

POPULATION	
Total	15.7 million
Av. yearly growth	3.1%
Urban population	20%
Life expectancy	52.9
Adult literacy	21.8%

ECONOMY	
Currency	CFA franc (CFAF) (US$1=495.40)
GDP (real)	$8.2 billion
GDP growth rate	3.0%
GDP per capita[1]	$1,026
GDP (ppp)[2]	$19.4 billion
GDP per cap. (ppp)	$1,231
Inflation rate	2.8%
Exports	$855 million
Imports	$1.5 billion
External debt	$1.6 billion
Unemployment	77%

1. Atlas method.
2. See page 175 for an explanation of purchasing power parity (ppp).

na, who, as promised, returned the country to civilian rule in 1970 but reverted to authoritarian rule four years later. Until the early 1980s, several further attempts to establish multiparty politics failed. In August 1983 Capt. Thomas Sankara, a 34-year admirer of Libya's Colonel Qaddafi, came to power. He changed the name of Upper Volta to Burkina Faso, a blend of local words meaning "the land of the honorable," and introduced a Libyan-style "Jamahiriya." After several failed attempts, Sankara was assassinated in 1987 and succeeded by Capt. Blaise Compaoré who reversed hardline socialist policies and introduced economic reforms in cooperation with international banks. Attempts by the opposition to have Compaoré excluded from the November 2005 presidential election on the grounds that it violated the two-term stipulation in the Constitution, failed. He won easily against a fractured opposition and was reelected in November 2010 for another term.

Government

The unicameral National Assembly or *Assemblee Nationale* is elected by popular vote for a 5-year term. In the May 2007 election for the National Assembly Pres. Blaise Compaoré's *Congrès pour la Démocratie et le Progrès* or Congress for Democracy and Progress (CDP) captured 73 out of 111 seats. The main opposition party, the *Alliance pour la démocratie et la féderation-Rassemblement démocratique africain* or African Democratic Rally-Alliance for Democracy and Federation (ADF-RDA) won 14 seats. Eleven smaller parties won between 1 and 5 seats each.

Economic policy

Once one of the world's poorest countries, Burkina Faso has been implementing a structural adjustment program (SAP) in close cooperation with the World Bank and the IMF. Starting from a mere 0.4% growth rate in 1989 with few natural resources and a weak industrial base it averaged 6% in the next 10 years, reaching a growth rate of 18.6% in 2007. While an increase in agricultural output helped, the government is credited in large part for its diligent enforcement of reforms. Price liberalization and external tariff reduction coupled with banking and financial sector reform, as well as privatization, further enhanced the business environment. Burkina Faso qualified for $700 million in debt relief under the Heavily Indebted Poor Countries Initiative (HIPC) and a Millennium Challenge Account threshold education grant.

Privatization

In the nineties Burkina Faso's parliament approved the restructuring of 42 state-owned enterprises. These included 19 major corporations in banking, brewing, mining, medicine, manufacturing and advertising that have already been restructured. Since then several others have been liquidated or turned over to private control. Further privatization of the state-owned electricity, water and telecommunications utilities is underway.

Sectors

Burkina has few natural resources and depends in part on foreign aid remittances by its citizens employed in neighboring countries such as Côte d'Ivoire and Ghana. The rural population is largely dependent on subsistence farming and nomadic stock raising. Main food crops are sorghum, millet, yams, maize, rice and beans. Cotton is grown for export. Mining activity is confined to gold, manganese, phosphates, marble and antimony. There are also viable deposits of zinc, silver, limestone, bauxite, nickel and lead. Small scale manufacturing entails flour milling, sugar refining, manufacture of cotton yarn and textiles and the production of consumer goods.

Trading

Importation of most consumer and other manufactured goods and equipment causes a chronic unfavorable trade balance. The largest exporter to Burkina is still France but imports from other countries and are growing. China has become a major buyer of goods from Burkina. Cotton, livestock and gold are principal exports. Abidjan's harbor in Côte d'Ivoire is used for bulk imports and exports.

Investment

Mining is the area of greatest interest for foreigners. The authorities have lured foreign mining companies by easing of regulatory laws, reducing taxes, adopting standard investment contracts, and improving the dissemination of geological data. American, Australian and South African corporations have obtained exploration and mining permits in recent times. French and Lebanese investors dominate in other sectors.

Financial sector

The financial and banking sectors have been restructured during the past seven years. Non-performing banks have been liquidated or privatized with the help of foreign partners. Three large commercial banks (with correspondent relationships with New York banks) and four credit institutions provide credit for investment and commercial transactions.

Taxes and tariffs

The mining investment code provides special customs and fiscal privileges for mining companies during both the exploration and production stages. Only after the existence of extractable mineral deposits is proven may the holder of the exploration license obtain a mining license or concession allowing total exemption from customs fees on raw materials, components, and equipment necessary for production. The license holder also enjoys a seven year exemption from other taxes. The corporate tax rate for non-residents is 10 to 30 percent and capital gains tax 10 percent. A value added tax (VAT) of 18 percent applies and exchange control is in effect. Taxes are levied on dividends (12.5%), interest (6 to 25%) and royalties (20%). (See page 138).

BUSINESS ACTIVITY

AGRICULTURE
Peanuts, shea nuts, sesame, cotton, sorghum, millet, corn, rice, livestock.
INDUSTRIES
Cotton lint, beverages, agricultural processing, soap, cigarettes, textiles, gold.
NATURAL RESOURCES
Manganese, limestone, marble, gold, antimony, copper, nickel, bauxite, lead, phosphates, zinc, silver.
EXPORTS
$855 million (2009 est.): cotton, animal products, gold.
IMPORTS
$1.5 billion (2009 est.): machinery, food products, petroleum.
MAJOR TRADING PARTNERS
China, Côte d'Ivoire, France, Singapore, Togo, Thailand, Ghana.

Doing Business with Burkina Faso

▶ **Investment**

Tax exemptions apply to investments in mining and other sectors and an investment code guarantees foreign investors the right to transfer any funds associated with an investment, including dividends, receipts from liquidation, assets, and salaries. Transfers are authorized in the original currency of the investment. Gold mining and diamond exploration are priority areas. Foreign and domestic investors are treated equally. The Ministry of Industry, Commerce, and Mines approves all new investments on the recommendation of the national investment commission.

▶ **Trade**

Telecommunications and computer equipment, pharmaceuticals, and used clothing are areas where US exporters have managed to capture a share of the market. A local agent/distributor is not required by law but can be helpful. There is a market for wheat, yellow corn, semolina, and rice. Most trade restrictions have been removed and tariffs have been steadily reduced.

▶ **Trade finance**

Burkina is eligible for foreign credit insurance assistance through Eximbank programs and is a member of the Multilateral Investment Guarantee Agency.

▶ **Selling to the government**

Road, dam and other construction projects are at times awarded to local companies in partnership with foreign firms. Purchases by state-owned utilities are done on tender.

▶ **Exchange controls**

Transfer of all funds associated with an investment, including dividends, receipts from liquidation, assets, and salaries is allowed without delay.

▶ **Partnerships**

There is a limited number of business people available with the practical experience and financial capacity needed to form a successful partnership There are several Burkinabé joint ventures in the mining sector involving foreign companies.

▶ **Establishing a presence**

Wholly owned foreign ownership in companies is allowed. Proposed foreign businesses operations are, however, subject to a screening process to ensure full compliance with local laws.

▶ **Project financing**

Burkina Faso is eligible for OPIC programs and the potential exists for direct loans and loan guarantees from the World Bank, the European Union and the African Development Bank.

▶ **Labor**

There is a scarcity of skilled workers, mainly in management, and in the engineering and the electrical trades. Burkinabé workers have a reputation for industriousness and loyalty. A code guaranteeing worker's rights is administered by a labor court. There is a well organized trade union movement. Employers must advise workers at least 30 days prior to termination and except in cases of theft or flagrant neglect of duty they have the right to termination benefits.

▶ **Legal rights**

Basic property rights are protected. In a few cases where the government deems expropriation necessary, compensation must be paid in advance. Since 1960, there have only been three cases: In 1968, the electric company (Safelec) was nationalized; in 1970 Comacico-Benin and SECM, film making and distribution companies, were taken over by the state; and in 1980, a manufacturer of ammunition, Carvolt, was expropriated. If an attempt at settlement of a dispute between the government and an investor fails, arbitration is prescribed. Burkina belongs to the African Intellectual Property Organization as well as the World Intellectual Property Organization. A local attorney and/or notary public may be required when securing or closing a contract.

▶ **Business climate**

Business is almost exclusively conducted in French but adequate translation services are available. There is a small but dynamic Chamber of Commerce, which conducts feasibility studies and training, develops business links, and organizes trade shows. It also serves as a bridge between government authorities and business associations. All matters regarding investments and import-export regulations and procedures are handled by the Ministry of Commerce, Industry and Crafts. Most sales and distribution are conducted from the major cities of Ouagadougou and Bobo-Dioulasso. The main commercial banks and insurance companies have, however, branches in secondary urban areas.

BURUNDI

Like neighboring Rwanda, Burundi took center stage in the mid-1990s for the wrong reasons. Situated in the scenic Great Lakes region of Africa, this land-locked, resource-poor former Belgian colony has been the scene of some of the modern world's worst carnage. The assassination in 1993 of Burundi's first democratically elected president triggered widespread ethnic violence between Hutu and Tutsi factions, causing more than 200,000 to perish. The mounting cost in human lives was accompanied by worsening economic conditions. An internationally brokered power-sharing agreement between the Tutsi-dominated government and the Hutu rebels in 2003 paved the way for a freely elected Hutu majority government and the opportunity to rebuild.

Country profile

The Republic of Burundi is situated in the high rainfall region bordering Lake Tanganyika. Most of the people are Rundi or Barundi, comprising the Bantu Hutu (Bahutu) peoples (85%) and Nilotic Tutsi (Batutsi) (15%). The Twa (Batwa), descendants of the early Pygmy population, number only in the thousands. The majority of both Tutsi and Hutu are Christians—overwhelmingly Roman Catholic. Kirundi and French are official languages and Swahili is widely spoken.

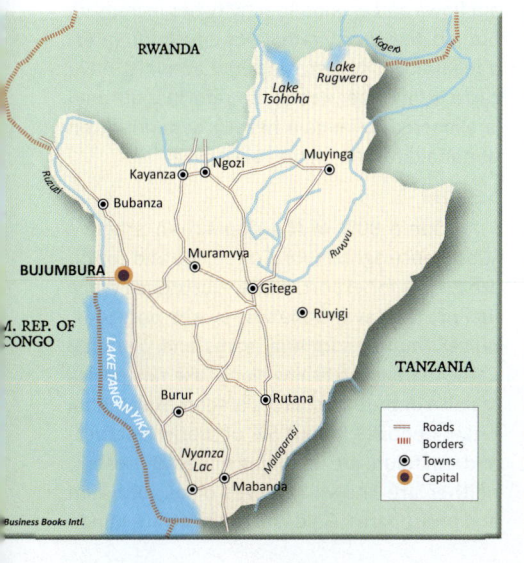

History

The simple version of history has the Tutsi (Nilotic) cattle breeders arriving in the area from the 15th Century and subjugating the Hutu inhabitants. In reality, the situation is much more complex as boundaries of race and class became less distinct over the years as a result of intermingling. Some put part of the blame for the racial animosity that led to the recent mass-scale killings on the shoulders of German and Belgian colonial rulers who pitched the Hutu against Tutsi for their own gain. When Burundi and neighboring Rwanda were incorporated into German East Africa in 1899, they had been kingdoms for several centuries headed by mwamis (kings). After Germany's defeat in World War I these nations were transferred to Belgium under the joint name of Ruanda-Urundi. They were, however, "separated at birth" when they gained their independence in 1962. In 1972, after an abortive coup attempt, between 200,000 and 400,000 Hutus were killed in Burundi and about 200,000 fled the country. Following elections in 1993, a Hutu assumed the presidency for the first time. He was assassinated by the Tutsi-dominated army after only 100 days in office, triggering widespread ethnic violence between the Tutsi and Hutu. Over 200,000 Burundians perished during the ensuing conflict lasting more than a decade. In 1995, the Hutu-led *Front pour la démocratie au Burundi* (Front for

Pres. Pierre Nkurunziza
Born: 18 Dec.1963
Since August 2005

UN Photo Eskinder Debebe

POLITICAL	
Head of State	Pres. Pierre Nkurunziza
Ruling party	CNDD-FDD
Main opposition	FRODEBU & UPRONA
Independence	1 July 1962
National capital	Bujumbura
Official languages	French & Kirundi

PHYSICAL	
Total area	11,000 sq. miles 28,000 sq. km. (± Maryland)
Arable land	45% of land area
Coastline	Landlocked

POPULATION	
Total	9.5 million
Av. yearly growth	3.7%
Urban population	10%
Life expectancy	57.8 years
Adult literacy	59.3%

ECONOMY	
Currency	Burundi franc (FBu)(US$1:1,217)
GDP (real)	$1.1 billion
GDP growth rate	3.3%
GDP per capita[1]	$320
GDP (ppp)[2]	$2.9 billion
GDP per cap. (ppp)	$344
Inflation rate	8.3%
Exports	$68 million
Imports	$275 million
External debt	$1.5 billion
Unemployment	NA

1. Atlas method.
2. See page 175 for an explanation of purchasing power parity (ppp).

the Democracy in Burundi) (FRODEBU) and the Tutsi-dominated opposition *Union pour le progrès national (Union of National Progress* (UPRONA), formed a coalition government under Hutu president Sylvestre Ntibantunganya, but unrest continued. In September 1996, Major Pierre Buyoya, a former Tutsi president, staged a coup, toppled the Hutu-run government and assumed the leadership. In accordance with a transition agreement Buyoya stepped down as president after 18 months in favor of his Hutu deputy, Domitien Ndayizeye. An internationally brokered power-sharing agreement between the government and the Hutu rebels paved the way for elections in July 2005 that swept Pierre Nkurunziza, as leader of the Hutu-dominated *Conseil national pour la defense de la democratie-Forces pour la defense de la democratie* (CNDD-FDD) into power as president. He was re-elected in July 2010.

Government

A bicameral parliament consists of the National Assembly with 100 seats (60% Hutu, 40% Tutsi and at least 30% reserved for women) and a Senate with 54 seats. In the July 2010 Assembly election the CNDD-FDD won 81 of the 100 contested seats against 17 for UPRONA and 5 for FRODEBU with 3 going to other parties. The president is elected indirectly by the Assembly.

Economic policy

Before the massacres and instability, the country had already been among the poorest in the world. Political stability since has improved aid flows and economic activity has increased, but a high poverty rate, poor education rates, a weak legal system, and low administrative capacity hamper economic reforms. Burundi is expected to remain heavily dependent on donor aid for the forseeable future.

Sectors

Some 90% of the population practice subsistence agriculture. Coffee, tea and cotton are grown for export, while subsistence crops include cassava, bananas, sweet potatoes, pulses, maize, sorghum, yams and peanuts. Cattle rearing and fishing along Lake Tanganyika are also important sources of food. Substantial nickel deposits (about 5% of world reserves) and vanadium are not being mined at present; neither are known reserves of oil, uranium and phosphates. Gold and tungsten are mined on a small scale. Manufacturing involves beer brewing, soft drinks, cigarettes, coffee and tea.

Privatization

There were efforts to privatize the deeply indebted water and electricity state enterprises.

Trade

Coffee and tea exports account for 90% of foreign exchange earnings and the ability to pay for imports depends primarily on weather conditions and coffee and tea prices.

Investment

Nickel exploration and gold and vanadium mining present opportunities.

Financial Sector

International banking transactions can be carried out through the *Banque de la République du Burundi*, the *Banque Commerciale du Burundi* and the Banque Burundaise pour le Commerce et l'Investissement. The banking sector suffered mass withdrawals in 1994.

BUSINESS ACTIVITY

AGRICULTURE
Coffee, cotton, tea, corn, sorghum. potatoes, bananas, manioc, beef, milk, hides.
INDUSTRIES
Light consumer goods such as blankets, shoes, soap, components assembly, public works construction, food processing.
NATURAL RESOURCES
Nickel, uranium, rare earth oxides, peat, cobalt, copper, unexploited platinum, vanadium, and gold.
EXPORTS
$68 million (2009 est.): coffee, tea, cotton, hides.
IMPORTS
$275 million (2009 est.): capital goods, petroleum products, foodstuffs, consumer goods.
MAJOR TRADING PARTNERS
Germany, Belgium, Switzerland, Saudi Arabia, France, Uganda, Kenya.

Doing Business with Burundi

▶ **Investment**

Even though minerals such as nickel, vanadium and phosphate have attracted foreign interest, no one is making a serious move until Burundi manages to establish stability and provide security for foreign entrepreneurs.

▶ **Trade**

Foreigners who offer goods are advised to appoint an experienced agent, even though it is not legally required. A sizeable portion of the country's basic needs are handled through purchases by donor countries.

▶ **Selling to the government**

The purchase of petroleum, a major import item, is supervised by the Ministry of Industry.

▶ **Investment**

Burundi maintains strict control over its supplies of hard currency, all of which are held by the Central Bank. Repatriating profits requires permission from the Central Bank. The conversion of Burundi Francs to dollars often a lengthy and cumbersome undertaking.

▶ **Project finance**

International development assistance is at a virtual halt, apart from humanitarian relief efforts. Financing is not available from OPIC or other known international bodies.

▶ **Project finance**

The majority of the workforce consists of illiterate and semi-literate displaced farmers. Unionized employees, especially in the urban areas, earn somewhat more than the minimum wage which stood at $0.40 per day in the cities of Bujumbura and Gitega and $0.35 in the rest of the country. Many schools have been destroyed in the civil war, leading to lower rates of student enrollment and a limited pool of educated potential employees.

▶ **Business climate**

French and Kirundi are official languages and are widely used in business. Relatively few people speak English.

CAMEROON

Cameroon's economy is the most diversified in Central Africa and makes up more than half of the total GNP of the Central African Economic and Monetary Community (CEMAC). Its abundant natural resources, a favorable climate, and well-educated work force make it one of Africa's potentially most competitive economies. Apart from its own oil resources Cameroon also largely benefits from the recently completed pipeline transporting oil for export from the Doba field in Chad to Kribi. Apart from additional revenues the pipeline serves to stimulate foreign investment in Cameroon in related industries. The country has successfully completed several economic reform programs to spur business development and attract invetsment from abroad.

Country profile

The Republic of Cameroon is situated on a plateau rising to 1,500 m in the Adamawa Mountains. Mount Cameroon is one of a series of volcanoes running southward, into the ocean, and northward, to Bamenda. In the rain forests of the south an equatorial climate prevails while the fertile soil of the western volcanic zone allows cultivation of a variety of tropical crops. There are more than 200 language groups. The largest single group is the Bamileke. Other major peoples include the Fulani, the Chadic, and the Bantu-speaking Fang. The northern Fulani and Chadic are mainly Muslim, while those in the west and south are predominantly Christian, though many still adhere to traditional ethnic beliefs.

History

Cameroon is part of the original home of the Bantu cultural grouping who migrated east and south into the countries now known as the Central African Republic, Gabon and Congo. Little was known about the territory until the arrival of the Portuguese in 1472. Explorer Fernando Po named the Wuri River Rio dos Camarôes (shrimp or prawn) after large crustaceans found at its mouth. This evolved into the country's present name, Cameroon. During the following three centuries several other European nations and American traders operated along the Cameroon coast. In 1884, it became the German protectorate of Kamerun, but after the First World War the League of Nations allocated 80% of the territory to France (French Cameroun) and the remaining 20%, consisting of two separate areas along the Nigerian border, to the British as Northern and Southern Cameroons. After a protracted insurgency led by the Bamileke, French Cameroun gained its independence in 1960 under President Ahmadou Ahidjo who adopted single-party rule. In 1982 Ahidjo resigned on grounds of ill health and handed power over to Prime Minister Paul Biya. A war of words between the two former allies led to a trial and a death sentence *in absentia* for Ahidjo—found guilty of subversion. Biya won re-election in 1992, 1997 and again in 2004—the latter for a seven year term.

Bakassi Peninsula

Parts of the British Cameroons opted to join newly-independent Cameroon in 1960 while others voted to merge with Nigeria. In August 2006, Nigeria, under pressure from then UN Secretary General Kofi Annan, agreed to honor a ruling by the International Court of Justice to cede the oil-rich Bakassi Peninsula to Cameroon. This ended a long row over ownership of the oil-rich territory. The handover was completed in August 2008. Around 90 percent of the population in the Bakassi Peninsula, estimated at between 200,000 to 300,000, are Nigerian fishermen and their families.

Government

Cameroon has a central government led by a President, elected for a 7 year term. The president appoints the prime minister and cabinet. The 180-member unicameral National Assembly serves a 5 year term. In the 2007 elections Biya's *Rassemblement démocratique du Peuple Camerounais* or Cameroon People's Democratic Movement (CPDM) captured 140 seats. The *Front Social Démocratique* (SDF) forms the main opposition with 14 seats followed by the National Union for Democracy and Progress (UNDP) and the Cameroonian Democratic Union (UDC) each with 4.

Economic policy

The IMF, World Bank and Paris Club have instituted programs to help reinvigorate Cameroon's economy. However, economic growth continues to be inhibited by a large inefficient parastatal sector, excessive public sector employment, growing defense and internal security expenditures, and by the Government's inability to collect internal revenues effectively, especially in economically important pro-opposition regions. Cameroon has, however, conformed to a triennial economic program and undertook a number of reforms

Pres. Paul Biya
Born: Feb. 13, 1933
Since November 1982

UN Photo Eskinder Debebe

POLITICAL

Head of State	Pres. Paul Biya
Ruling Party	CPDM
Main Opposition	SDF
Independence	20 May 1960
National capital	Yaoundé
Official languages	English & French

PHYSICAL

Total area	475,000 sq. km.
	183,000 sq. miles
	(± California)
Arable land	15% of land area
Coastline	248 miles/400 km

POPULATION

Total	18.9 million
Av. yearly growth	2.19%
Urban population	57%
Life expectancy	53.7 years
Adult literacy	67.9%

ECONOMY

Currency	CFA franc (CFAF) (US$1=495.40)
GDP (real)	$25 billion
GDP growth rate	2.0%
GDP per capita[1]	$1,959
GDP (ppp)[2]	$46.3 billion
GDP per cap. (ppp)	$2,374
Inflation rate	3.2%
Exports	$3.6 billion
Imports	$4.4 billion
External debt	$1.4 billion
Unemployment	30%

1. Atlas method.
2. See page 175 for an explanation of purchasing power parity (ppp).

to reduce its own stake in the economy and promote private sector development.

Sectors

Although agriculture is the dominant sector and employs about three-quarters of the labor force, Cameroon has one of the few diversified economies in sub-Saharan Africa. Cocoa is the main cash crop—Cameroon is the world's fifth largest producer—followed by coffee, cotton, tobacco, rubber, palm oil, sugar and bananas. It is the fifth largest producer of petroleum in sub-Sahara Africa. The acquisition of the oil-rich Bakassi Peninsula will boost Cameroon's declining oil production. A consortium including Chevron and ExxonMobil constructed a pipeline to carry petroleum from Chad to Kribi in Cameroon. Unexploited mineral wealth includes bauxite, cobalt, chromium, gold, iron, nickel, sapphires, tin, titanium, uranium, and limestone. Cameroon has the largest tropical rain forest after the Democratic Republic of Congo and produces tropical wood (ebony, mahogany, and iroko) both for export and the local industry. During good rainfall years Cameroon is largely self-sufficient in foodstuffs. Understandably, International oil and cocoa prices have a significant impact on the economy

Privatization

Cameroon is in the midst of a privatization process that will eliminate all public sector monopolies, except for aluminum. Privatized to date are, among others, CAMSUCO (national sugar company), SOCAPALM (the palm oil complex), the CDC (agricultural plantation complex), BICEC (a state-owned bank) and SOCAR (insurance company). Parastatals that are scheduled for privatization include the national airline (CAMAIR), the telecommunication companies (CAMTEL and CAMTEL-MOBILE) and the national insurance retirement fund (CNPS).

Trade

Petroleum and gas account for 33% of Cameroon's exports, tropical wood (24%), and aluminum 5.5%. Other exports are coffee, cocoa, cotton, rubber, timber, bananas and pineapples. US sales to Cameroon include bauxite for an aluminum smelting plant as large local bauxite deposits (the 5th largest worldwide) are too expensive to mine. Other major imports from the US are wheat and flour, petroleum coke and pitch additives for aluminum smelting, used clothing and gross lot discounted and discontinued consumer products.

Investment

France is the leading investor. Construction of the multinational $1.5 billion Chad/Cameroon pipeline has, however, lead to larger US participation. Apart from oil production, US firms are involved in security services, hygiene products, and fresh fruit production.

Financial sector

There are nine commercial banks under control of the Banque des Etats de l'Afrique Centrale (BEAC), a common central bank also serving the five other member countries of the Central African sub-region and regulated by the French government. Cameroon has no securities market or bond market but the Banque Nationale de Paris has been mandated to draw up a model for a small, screen-based securities market for the Central African franc zone.

Taxes & tariffs

The corporate tax rate for non-residents is 38.5 percent and capital gains tax 38.5 percent. A value added tax (VAT) of 19.25 percent applies and exchange control is in effect. Taxes are levied on dividends (16.5%) and royalties (15%). (See page 138.)

BUSINESS ACTIVITY

AGRICULTURE
Coffee, cocoa, cotton, rubber, bananas, oilseed, grains, root starches, livestock, timber.
INDUSTRIES
Petroleum production and refining, food processing, consumer goods, textiles, timber.
NATURAL RESOURCES
Petroleum, bauxite, iron ore, timber, hydropower.
EXPORTS
$3.6 billion (2009 est.): crude oil and petroleum products, lumber, cocoa beans, aluminum, coffee, cotton.
IMPORTS
$4.4 billion (2009 est.): machines and electrical equipment, fuel, food.
MAJOR TRADING PARTNERS
Spain, France, Italy, South Korea, Netherlands, Nigeria, Belgium, China, US.

AES-SONEL

One Community, One Vision, One common Goal for the Future

Since its acquisition by the AES Corporation in 2001, AES-SONEL has been **relentlessly committed to operational excellence and is dedicated to improving the quality of life of the local communities and the people we serve in Cameroon, guided by the company's core values: Put Safety First, Act with Integrity, Strive for Excellence, Honor Commitments and Have Fun Through Work.**

Breadth of Our Operations

AES-SONEL is the sole power company *energizing Cameroon* with a diversified portfolio of power generation, distribution and transmission businesses across the national territory. Between 2001 and 2010 AES helped the Republic of Cameroon to increase its generation capacity by 25%, representing F.CFA 377 billion of private investments (approximately USD 754 million).

AES currently operates in Cameroon with a total installed capacity of 1,017 MW (720 MW Hydro, 297 MW Thermal) and serves over 570,000 customers in the country. Additionally, AES plans to double the number of families with access to reliable electricity to 1 million by 2021.

AES-SONEL is currently the 5th largest company in Cameroon and has a workforce of 3,600 people with 98% of the employees being from Cameroon.

Community Outreach and Our Commitment to Sustainability

In our efforts to promote the social and economic development of the local communities, AES-SONEL provides access to electricity to around 60,000 new families in Cameroon every year. Over the past two years, around 100 villages and remote areas of large cities have been electrified.

In addition to providing safe and reliable electricity to its customers, AES-SONEL supports the local population through a variety of corporate social responsibility programs which focus on health, education, culture as well as agriculture. Giving back to the community is an important part of our work and corporate responsibility is simply how we do business.

A strong energy sector is essential to a country's continued economic development. At AES-SONEL, we are pleased with the progress we have made so far and we will keep on honoring our commitment by striving to continuously improve our performance as we provide safe, affordable and sustainable power to the people of Cameroon.

AES
the power of being global

Doing Business with Cameroon

▶ **Investment**

A new code simplified foreign investment and introduced financial incentives coupled with minimal eligibility/performance requirements. Equity ownership is subject to limitation only in small and medium size enterprises (SMEs) where a 35% local ownership is required. Privatization in agriculture, reinsurance, banking, telecommunications, water and electrical utilities, rubber production, and transportation has opened up new opportunities. The Industrial Free Zone creates conditions for investors to operate virtually outside the country's established legal and regulatory systems but requires that 80% of the product be sold outside Cameroon.

▶ **Trade**

Cameroon is a favored base for foreign trade with Central Africa. Products with potential include fertilizer, used clothing, heavy machinery and material for forestry, transport and road construction, pipeline construction and related services such as security and communications, computer, electronic equipment, and aircraft parts. Local agents with established links to wholesalers and market knowledge are often the best way into this competitive market. Apart from retail outlets operated by large international oil companies and international car rental companies, franchising is limited.

▶ **Trade finance**

Eximbank finances US goods and services sold to Cameroon. Exporters usually rely on irrevocable, confirmed letters of credit.

▶ **Selling to the government**

Government procurement is handled by the *Direction Générale des Grands Travaux* (DGTC) or Public Works Directorate. Local companies are allowed preferential price margins on all state procurement and development projects. Direct purchases are often made through domestic middlemen who require cash up front on behalf of their foreign clients. Foreign participation in government-subsidized R&D is restricted to programs beyond the technical capability of local firms.

▶ **Exchange controls**

The currency continues to be pegged to the French franc, ensured by the French Treasury, and remains readily convertible. Dividends, return of capital, interest and principal on foreign debt, lease payments, royalties and management fees, and returns on liquidation may all be remitted abroad.

▶ **Partnership**

Foreign firms are free to join with any local entity of their choosing in any form desired. Most foreigners obtain expert local counsel when entering into joint ventures and licensing arrangements.

▶ **Establishing a presence**

The Investment Code Management Unit was established in 1991 to assist foreign and domestic business start-ups. It provides investment authorization and a variety of other services through a network of official correspondents in all the relevant ministries. The law requires at least a 35% local ownership for enterprises under the Small and Medium-Size Enterprise (SME) regime.

▶ **Project finance**

OPIC underwrites viable projects and Cameroon is a member of the Multilateral Investment Guarantee Agency. The World Bank and African Development Bank are further sources of financing.

▶ **Labor**

Even though Cameroon has a high literacy rate and a relatively well-educated labor force most of the unemployed are unskilled and non-technical laborers. The labor code removed government control over layoffs and firings, and reduced official involvement in labor unions.

▶ **Legal rights**

The IMF and the World Bank, through their structural adjustment oversight, are assisting Cameroon in the reform of its judicial system. Cameroon accepts binding international arbitration of investment disputes and is a member of the International Center for the Settlement of Investment Disputes. It is also the headquarters for the 14-nation West African intellectual Property Organization or *Organisation Africaine de la Propriété Intellectuelle (OAPI)* and is a signatory of the Paris Convention on Industrial Property and the Universal Copyright Convention.

▶ **Business climate**

Cameroon has the largest private sector in French-speaking Central Africa. English is also widely spoken in a business community that does not necessarily conform to western practices. Local business people will first try to "get to know" a potential partner before venturing into concrete discussions. Punctuality is not the norm and patience and persistence are vital.

Connected.
Trained.
Prepared.

In Africa, IRD is developing sustainable food and agriculture systems. We provide training and equipment to individual farmers and small- to medium-sized agribusinesses throughout the continent. By strengthening entrepreneurial capacity and farm-to-market linkages, we help increase farmers' incomes, improve nutrition, and alleviate hunger.

The case of Niger. In Niger, families who lost their livestock to drought and flood have reason to be hopeful. With funds generated by the sale of US government-donated vegetable oil, IRD is distributing goats to more than 2,000 pastoralist families. Because these families depend on their livestock for both nutrition and wealth, IRD is also repairing or creating water points for the herds, promoting pasture reserves, and training local organizations to provide veterinary care. In Niger and elsewhere, IRD is improving livelihoods, one goat at a time.

In Niger, Cameroon, Zimbabwe, and a dozen other African countries, IRD is giving the most vulnerable people a strong voice in their development and the tools they need for self-sufficiency.

Learn more at www.ird.org/food

INTERNATIONAL RELIEF & DEVELOPMENT
1621 N. KENT ST., 4TH FLOOR | ARLINGTON, VA 22209 | 703.248.0161

IRD

CAPE VERDE

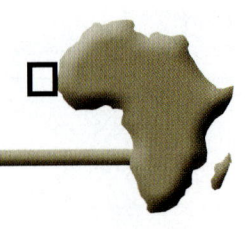

Cape Verde consists of a group of islands strategically located off Africa's West Coast. It depends largely on income from services to foreign shipping and airlines, remittances from some 700,000 Cape Verdean émigrés and foreign aid. Since opening its economy to the outside world, however, the island group nation has attracted foreign investment in light manufacturing, tourism, fishing, transportation and communications. Foreign firms are beginning to take advantage of Cape Verde's under-utilized quotas in the US and European markets by establishing manufacturing and assembly plants in its export free zones.

Country profile

The Republic of Cape Verde consists of ten windswept Atlantic islands about 500 km west of Dakar. The largest is São Tiago (992 sq. km) and the smallest, Santa Lucia (34 sq. km). Mt. Fogo (2,829 m) is an active volcano island that last erupted in 1995. The islands lie in the North Atlantic high pressure belt, are poor in natural resources and prone to droughts and high temperatures. Afro-Europeans make up 71% of the population and the rest are African. Whites account for about 1% of the total. An estimated 700,000 Cape Verdeans are living and working abroad, most of them sending regular remittances to the 420,000 remaining on the islands. Portuguese is the official language, but the vernacular is Crioulo (Creole), derived from Portuguese and West African languages.

History

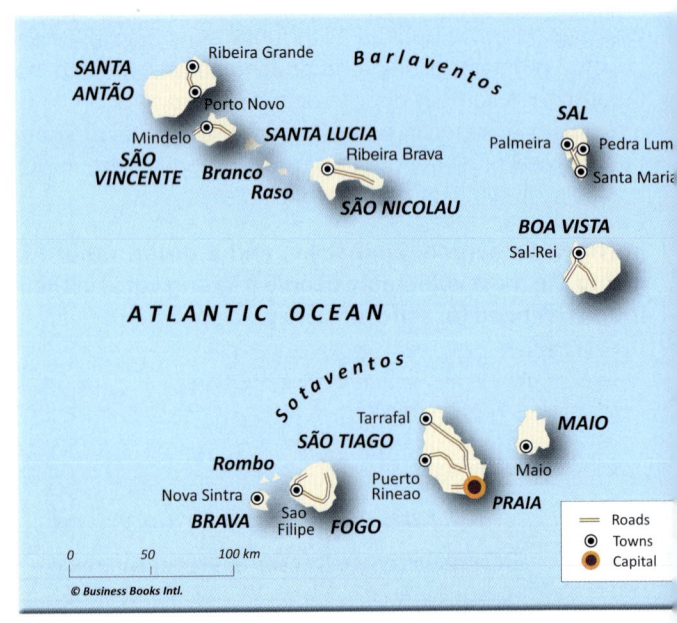

The islands were uninhabited when Portuguese mariners discovered them during their voyages in search of a sea route around Africa. The first Portuguese governor, appointed in 1462, was based at Ribeira Grande on Sao Antiago, the largest of the islands. A Creole population resulted from intermingling between the Portuguese and the imported slaves from Western Africa. The Cape Verde islands remained obscure until 1975 when they achieved independence from Portugal under President Aristides Pereira of the African Party for the Independence of Guinea and Cape Verde (PAICV). Pereira turned the islands into a one-party state with a centrally controlled economy. Under pressure from the Movement for the Democracy (MPD) led by Carlos Veiga, Cape Verde was eventually transformed into a multi-party democracy in 1990. The following year, the MPD won and Veiga took over as prime minister. A former supreme court judge, Antonio Mascarenhas Monteiro, won the presidential election. The MPD was returned to power with a larger majority in the general elections held in December 1995, but in March 2001 Pedro Pires was inaugurated as president after beating his rival, Carlos Veiga. He was re-elected in February 2006, once again defeating Veiga.

Government

The President, elected for 5 years, has limited powers as real authority rests with the Prime Minister, elected by the unicameral 72-member National Assembly. In February 2006, José Maria Pereira Neves was reappointed Prime Minister as leader of the *Partido Africano da Independência de Cabo Verde* (PAICV) which defeated the *Movimento para Democratia* (MPD)(29 seats) and several smaller parties by capturing 41 seats.

Economic policy

After years of state control, the new government adopted a development strategy in the early nineties based on market-oriented policies, including an ambitious privatization program. It showed a strong commitment to the implementation of sound macroeconomic and structural reforms and the development of institutions and an infrastructure. Despite slow progress in some sectors, Cape Verde's economic reform policies appear to be paying off, as new businesses are being created, private investment projects are implemented, especially in the tourism sector, construction is booming, and the business community is eager to explore new import markets. Financial and economic legislation has been revised and the government's role in the economy has shifted from a participant in the economy to being a promoter and regulator.

Sectors

The islands suffers from a lack of natural resources coupled with serious water shortages resulting from recurrent droughts. Fishing (mainly tuna and shellfish) is an important activity in the Atlantic ocean economic zone with 28,350 sq. miles (734,265 sq. km.) assigned exclusively to Cape Verde. With only one third of a potential 50,000 tons of fish products per year exploited due to the lack of adequate technology for deep sea fishing,

Prime Minister José Maria Pereira Neves
Born: Aug. 20, 1943
Since February 2001

UN Photo Marco Castro

POLITICAL
Head of State	Pres. Pedro Rodrigues Pires
Prime Minister	José Maria Pereira Neves
Ruling Party	PAICV
Main Opposition	MPD
Independence	5 July 1975
National capital	Praia
Official language	Portuguese

PHYSICAL
Total area	2,000 sq. miles 4,000 sq. km. (± Rhode Island)
Arable land	10% of land area
Coastline	600 miles/965 km

POPULATION
Total	430,000
Av. yearly growth	0.56%
Urban population	60%
Life expectancy	71.6
Adult literacy	76.6%

ECONOMY
Currency	Cape Verde escudo (US$1=83.25)
GDP (real)	$1.95 billion
GDP growth rate	3.9%
GDP per capita[1]	$2,690
GDP (ppp)[2]	$2 billion
GDP per cap. (ppp)	$3,959
Inflation rate	2.2%
Exports	$106 million
Imports	$858 million
External debt	$966 million
Unemployment	21%

1. Atlas method.
2. See page 175 for an explanation of purchasing power parity (ppp).

this sector holds great potential. Agriculture can be practiced on only about one-fifth of the total area and meets about 10% of local consumption needs. Cape Verde emigrant communities in the United States and Europe provide a continuous inflow of foreign exchange and other informal assistance to relatives back home. The economy is largely service-oriented with commerce, transport, tourism, and public services accounting for two-thirds of GDP. The dry, tropical climate, diverse terrain, warm, clear waters and beautiful, deserted beaches provide ample resources for growing tourism. An international airport on the island of Sal is used as a refueling stop by international air carriers. About 30% of traffic through the airport is cargo moving between Europe and South America. Traffic between the islands is by air and ferry. Mining is confined to pozzolana (a volcanic substance used in the manufacturing of cement) and the production of salt, on Sal, through evaporation.

Privatization

Several state-owned enterprises have been privatized, including three hotels, the national telecommunications company, *Cabo Verde Telecom*, and the oil distribution company, Enacol. Two commercial banks, an insurance company, the state-run power supply company and the Cape Verdean port authority are on the block.

Trade

Cape Verde depends almost completely on imports to meet its basic consumer needs and for industrial inputs. Portugal is Cape Verde's most important trading partner and accounts for almost half of the total trade. Non-factor services to international maritime and air transport top the list of foreign currency earners, followed by bananas, lobster and fresh and frozen fish.

Investment

Economic reforms are aimed at developing the private sector and attracting foreign investment to diversify the economy. Projects for foreign participation center around fishing and tourism. Most foreign direct investment came from Portugal, Italy, Spain and other European countries. Recently US and Asian investors have also been targeted by the Cape Verdean foreign investment promotion agency, PROMEX.

Financial sector

The World Bank has been assisting the government of Cape Verde to restructure its financial sector. The first step was to split the Bank of Cape Verde into a central and a commercial bank. The Stock Market of Cape Verde (BVC) was launched in March 1999 with six listed companies. The financial sector includes four commercial banks (two foreign-owned), two insurance companies and a venture capital company created to promote development of the private sector.

Taxes & tariffs

The corporate tax rate for non-residents is 25 percent. There is no capital gains tax. A value added tax (VAT) of 6 to 15 percent applies and exchange control is in effect. Taxes are levied on interest (20%) and royalties (20%). (See page 138).

Expatriates

US-Cape Verdean contacts date from the early 19th Century when the New England whaling industry was at its peak. Today, substantial Cape Verde-American communities live in Massachusetts and Rhode Island. Cape Verde's large trade deficit is in part financed by remittances from expatriates and foreign aid.

BUSINESS ACTIVITY

AGRICULTURE
Bananas, corn, beans, sweet potatoes, sugar cane, coffee, peanuts, fish.
INDUSTRIES
Food and beverages, fish processing, shoes and garments, salt mining, ship repair.
NATURAL RESOURCES
Salt, basalt rock, pozzuolana (volcanic ash used to produce hydraulic cement), limestone, kaolin, fish.
EXPORTS
$106 million (2009 est.): shoes, garments, fish, bananas, hides.
IMPORTS
$858 million (2009 est.): foodstuffs, consumer goods, industrial products, transport equipment.
MAJOR TRADING PARTNERS
Japan, Spain, Portugal, France, UK, Brazil, Netherlands, Côte d'Ivoire.

Doing Business with Cape Verde

▶ Investment
A competitive incentive package is offered through the Center for Tourism, Investment and Exports Promotion (PROMEX) which acts as a one-stop shop for foreign investors. While favoring free zone enterprises geared to exports, these incentives also apply in large part to other investments based on infusion of foreign capital. Investors establishing export-driven operations are in many instances assured of generous preferential access to the markets of Europe, West Africa and the United States. Apart from light manufacturing, fishing and tourism offer opportunities.

▶ Trade
There is great receptivity for foreign goods, especially items from Portugal which enjoys strong cultural and linguistic links. The smallness of the market and lack of credit have inhibited trade development but the growing need for high-cost items required in the expansion of the country's airports, fishing fleets, telecommunications systems and other infrastructural projects are of special interest to foreign suppliers.

▶ Trade finance
The US Department of Agriculture's Commodity Credit Corporation (CCC) administers the Export Credit Guarantee program (GSM-102) providing financing for sales of US agricultural products. Other agencies that provide financing and insurance programs are the International Finance Corporation, the Overseas Private Investment Corporation, Eximbank and the US Small Business Administration.

▶ Selling to the government
Government procurement is by tender and typically financed by a multilateral lending institutions such as the World Bank or the African Development Bank. Recent projects include a longer runway at the international airport of Sal, a runway at Praia and the modernization of Sao Vicente's airport. Other plans involve harbor improvements and modernization of telecommunications.

▶ Exchange controls
Under current law, revenues and profits, capital gains, and loan repayments may be transferred overseas within 60, 90, and 30 days, respectively, after submission of an application to the Bank of Cape Verde (BCV). The BCV pays interest on all transfers where waiting periods exceed 30 days. Transfers are at times delayed when requests involve large sums which might affect Cape Verde's balance of payments. In some instances, the government might opt to make the transfer in installments.

▶ Establishing a presence
Joint ventures are allowed and encouraged in fisheries, airlines and telecommunications. Apart from these partnerships, foreigners have the option of establishing a branch, a limited liability company or a full corporation. Franchising is limited.

▶ Financing projects
Multilateral Investment Guarantee Agency and Overseas Private Investment Corporation programs apply. The US Trade and Development Agency, the World Bank and the African Development Bank provide funding for feasibility studies and other investment planning services. Bank credit is available to foreign investors under the same conditions as those for national investors. The private sector has access to credit instruments such as loans, letters of credit and lines of credit. There are clear legal guidelines for accounting but they are not totally consistent with international norms.

▶ Labor
With an unemployment rate of about 28% labor is readily available, much of it unskilled. Technical, managerial and professional talent is difficult to find. The recently revised labor code makes work contracts more flexible. There is no set minimum wage and prevailing levels are around $0.70 per hour.

▶ Legal rights
Disputes between foreign investors and the government are settled either through a single referee or an arbitration commission. Referees may be foreigners of a different nationality than the parties involved in the dispute. Final appeals can be made to the International Center of Settlement of Investment Disputes (ICSID). There have not been any such disputes in recent years. Since 1990 Cape Verde has had copyright laws and it is a signatory to several treaties providing protection.

▶ Business climate
Business practices and customs follow the Portuguese model. While Portuguese is spoken in most business circles, English is gaining wider acceptance and some French is spoken as well.

CENTRAL AFRICAN REPUBLIC

The Central African Republic (CAR) is, as its name indicates, at the center of the African continent. It is a sparsely populated country, well endowed with natural resources. Its remoteness from the nearest seaports is a drawback. Plagued in the past by slavery, colonial neglect and brutal tyrants, the CAR has somehow managed to nurture and strengthen the fragile democracy introduced in 1993 when it held its first free elections. Temporarily under transitional rule when President Ange-Félix Patassé was ousted in a coup by François Bozizé in 2003, CAR returned to civilian rule after elections in 2005. CAR is actively courting foreign investors, especially in diversified mining to augment its income from diamonds and gold.

Country profile

The Central African Republic is a landlocked and sparsely populated undulating plateau. During the rainy season much of the southeast is impassable as several rivers overflow into the Ubangi, the great tributary of the Congo River. Vast parts of the northern and eastern regions have been set aside for nature conservation. There are two major ethnic groups: the river peoples (Yakoma and Mabaka) and the savannah peoples (such as the Sara). Sango is widely spoken and used in broadcasting. More than two-thirds of the total population are Christians, though many still profess traditional ethnic beliefs.

History

The slave trade, especially during the 17th and 18th centuries, had a massive impact on the old kingdoms in this region, decimating their populations. By the turn of the 19th Century the French established themselves at Bangui and founded the colony of Ubangi-Chari (named after two major rivers). Local resistance to excesses by French companies who administered the territory culminated in the Kongo Wara wars from 1928 until 1931. In 1960 CAR achieved independence under the one party rule of President David Dacko. Five years later his cousin, sergeant Jean-Bédel Bokassa, seized power, declared himself president in 1972 and ultimately crowned himself emperor five years later. In 1979, Bokassa's brutal rule came to an end when French troops reinstated Dacko. Two years later Dacko was once again ousted in a military coup, this time by Gen. André Kolingba. In 1993 internal and international pressures forced Kolingba to hold a multi-party presidential election. He lost to Ange-Félix Patassé, who once served in

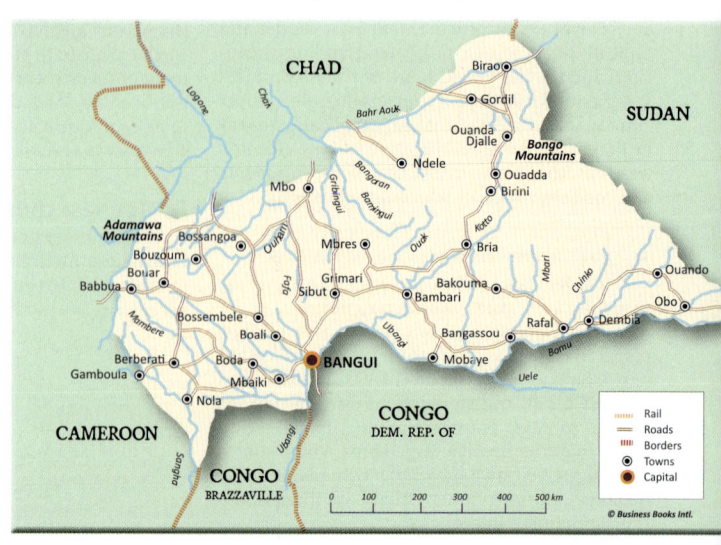

210

Bokassa's cabinet. Patassé was reelected in September 1999, defeating Kolingba and several other candidates. Patassé's rule was plagued by unrest and rebel incursions and the UN Mission in the Central African Republic (MINURCA) were called in to help maintain stability until March 2003, when he was ousted in a coup by François Bozizé. In the May 2005 presidential election Bozizé easily defeated Martin Ziguélé, a former prime minister.

Government

The President is elected for a maximum of two 6-year terms. It provides for a bicameral legislature consisting of a 109 member National Assembly, elected for 5 years, and a nominated Economic and Regional Council. In 2005 the *Convergence Kwa na Kwa* (KNK) coalition, supported by Bozizé, won 42 seats against 11 by the *Mouvement pour la Libération du Peuple Centrafricain* (MLPC). Independents and smaller parties make up the rest.

Economic policy

The government has agreed to a framework for economic reform, including the privatization of key parastatals under an IMF-approved Extended Structure Adjustment Facility (ESAF). The country's landlocked position, poor infrastructure and largely unskilled work force have, however, place constraints on development and economic growth.

Sectors

The agricultural sector contributes more than half of the GDP and employs an estimated 80% of the labor force. Key primary food crops include bananas, cocoa beans, coffee and sugar cane. Meat products range from beef, chicken, goat meat and mutton to pork. The CAR is almost self-sufficient in food and has the potential of becoming a net exporter. Export crops are cotton, coffee, cattle, organic material and tobacco leaves. Mining largely involves alluvial diamonds and gold, together contributing about 4% of the nation's gross domestic product. Key industries are diamond mining, sawmills, breweries, textiles, footwear, and assembly of bicycles and motorcycles.

Privatization

Privatization of had just begun when the civil unrest broke out in 1996 and delayed the process. The national telecommunications operator, Socatel has been partly privatized.

Pres. François Bozizé
Born: 1946
Since March 2003

UN Photo Eskinder Debebe

POLITICAL	
Head of State	Pres. François Bozizé
Ruling Party	KNK
Major Opposition	MPLC
Independence	13 August 1960
National capital	Bangui
Official language	French

PHYSICAL	
Total area	241,000 sq. miles 623.000 sq. km. (2 x New Mexico)
Arable land	3% of land area

POPULATION	
Total	4.5 million
Av. yearly growth	1.49%
Urban population	39%
Life expectancy	45 years
Adult literacy	48.6%

ECONOMY	
Currency	CFA franc (CFAF) (US$1=495.40)
GDP (real)	$2.3 billion
GDP growth rate	2.0%
GDP per capita[1]	$644
GDP (ppp)[2]	$3.5 billion
GDP per cap. (ppp)	$765
Inflation rate	3.8%
Exports	$147 million
Imports	$237 million
External debt	$991 million
Unemployment	8%

1. Atlas method.
2. See page 175 for an explanation of purchasing power parity (ppp).

Investment

Foreign direct investment is primarily concentrated in the diamond mining, gold and timber sectors.

Trade

France continues to be the major trade partner while the US, Japan, and Iran are significant suppliers of products such processed foods, pharmaceuticals, consumer goods, industrial products, vehicles, and petroleum products.

Financial sector

Banking in the CAR is under control of the French-controlled Banque des Etats de l'Afrique Centrale (BEAC).

Taxes and tariffs

Corporate tax rate for non-residents is 20 to 30 percent. A value added tax (VAT) of up to 19 percent applies and exchange control is in effect. A tax of 15% is levied on dividends, interest and royalties. (See page 138).

BUSINESS ACTIVITY

AGRICULTURE
Cotton, coffee, tobacco, manioc, yams, millet, corn, bananas, timber.

INDUSTRIES
Diamond mining, sawmills, breweries, textiles, footwear, bicycles and motorcycles.

NATURAL RESOURCES
Diamonds, uranium, timber, gold, oil.

EXPORTS
$147 million (est. 2007): diamonds, timber, tobacco, coffee, cotton, yams, bananas.

IMPORTS
$237 million (est. 2007): food, textiles, petroleum products, machinery, electrical equipment, motor vehicles, chemicals, consumer goods, industrial products.

MAJOR TRADING PARTNERS
Canada, Belgium, France, Italy, Spain, China, France, Indonesia, Netherlands, Japan, US, Cameroon.

DOING BUSINESS WITH CENTRAL AFRICAN REPUBLIC

▶ **Investment**

Several American firms have expressed interest in mechanizing the largely manual diamond sector and getting involved in the mining and exploration of gold, copper, iron ore, tin, uranium and zinc. The mining industry is regulated by the Ministry of Energy, Mines, Geology and Water Resources. The government has invited foreign participation in the underdeveloped telecommunications sector by freeing up value added network services and partially lifting restrictions on cellular services development. The CAR shows good potential for foreign involvement in ecotourism in its rain forest and savanna regions. Tentative steps have been taken by foreign entrepreneurs to develop facilities in areas such as the primeval rain forest, Dzanga-Sangha National Park, in the southwestern region of the country.

▶ **Trade**

Even though there is a strong interest in American goods, US exporters should expect tough competition from France with which the CAR has maintained strong commercial ties. Importers of consumer items and personal vehicles have expressed an interest in US goods, but logistic problems tend to impede sales and distribution.

▶ **Selling to the government**

In selling to the government foreign firms usually concentrate on projects financed by donors.

▶ **Exchange controls**

Capital, profits and dividends can be freely transferred. The transfer of more than CFA 500,000 requires permission from the Ministry of Finance.

▶ **Partnerships**

As tax and customs laws may be more strictly enforced against foreigners, it is useful to have a local partner to negotiate the complex web of regulations required to establish a business.

▶ **Labor**

The workforce is largely unskilled.

▶ **Legal rights**

Foreign investors are assured of equal treatment under law which guarantees freedom from expropriation and nationalization, barring special circumstances, and freedom from political or economic interference.

CHAD

Landlocked Chad is Africa's fifth largest country and one of its poorest. This, however, is likely to change as it continues to demonstrate macroeconomic stability, capacity building, democratic reform and social progress. A 665 mile/1,070 km pipeline completed in 2004 that carries oil from Chad's Doba basin to the port of Kribi in Cameroon has begun to stimulate growth and boost income. In the next decade oil is expected to transform Chad from a country largely dependent on agricultural exports, subsistence crops and livestock to a manufacturing and mining base. The pipeline has opened up new opportunities for foreign investors, not only in petroleum-related industries but in a range of other manufacturing and service areas. Chad also has substantial deposits of gold, marble and natron.

Country profile

The landlocked Republic of Chad is the fifth largest country in Africa. Its capital, N'Djamena, is situated near the confluence of the country's only two rivers, the Chari and the Logone, which flow from the south into Lake Chad. There are sharply contrasting climatic zones varying from wet savannah in the south to arid Sahara Desert conditions in the north. Except for scattered Arab-speaking and Chadic groups, most of the peoples are of Nilo-Saharan origin, comprising the Bagirmi and the Sara of the south, the Maba in the Waddai region, and the Kanuri in the Sahara region. The desert peoples also include the Zaghawa along the eastern border, and the Tubu of the Tibesti Mountains. French and Arabic are official languages but some English is spoken, apart from 100 local languages. More than half the country is Muslim and the rest is divided evenly between Christianity and traditional African religions.

History

Artifacts dating back to 5000 BC have been discovered at burial sites in the Sahel and Southern Sahara regions, inhabited by nomadic Negroid people, many of whom turned to the Muslim faith as early as the 10th Century. Towards the end of the 19th Century, converted Christians from the south sided with French troops against the north. In 1910 Chad was incorporated into French Equatorial Africa. In 1957 the Chadians formed their first elected government and a year later voted to become a self-governing member of the French Com-

Pres. Idriss Déby Itno
Born: 1952
Since Dec. 1990

UN Photo Devra Berkowitz

POLITICAL	
Head of State	Pres. Idriss Déby
Ruling Party	MPS
Major Opposition	RDP
Independence	11 August 1960
National capital	N'Djamena
Official languages	French & Arabic

PHYSICAL	
Total area	110,000 sq. miles
	284,000 sq. km.
	(3 x California)
Arable land	3% of land area

POPULATION	
Total	10.3 million
Av. yearly growth	2.0%
Urban population	27%
Life expectancy	47.7 years
Adult literacy	25.7%

ECONOMY	
Currency	CFA franc (CFAF) (US$1=495.40)
GDP (real)	$6.2 billion
GDP growth rate	-0.8%
GDP per capita[1]	$1,464
GDP (ppp)[2]	$17 billion
GDP per cap. (ppp)	$1,523
Inflation rate	10.5%
Exports	$3.5 billion
Imports	$2.2 billion
External debt	$1.5 billion
Unemployment	NA

1. Atlas method.
2. See page 175 for an explanation of purchasing power parity (ppp).

munity. The territory became independent on 11 August 1960 with southerner Francois Tombalbaye as its first president. Two years later, in response to growing internal unrest, he banned the opposition. Muslim opponents formed the Chad Liberation Front (Frolinat) and took control of the north. French assistance to Tombalbaye was countered by Libyan financial and military aid to Frolinat. After the withdrawal of the French military in 1972, Libya laid claim to and annexed the Aozou Strip in northern Chad. Tombalbaye perished during a military coup in April 1975, setting off a series of destabilizing events that prompted incursions by Libyan, Nigerian and French troops. In 1990, former army chief Idriss Déby finally deposed the French-favored ruler, Hissene Habre, declared himself president and announced his commitment to a multiparty system. In 1994 the International Court of Justice ruled in Chad's favor in the Aozou dispute, forcing Libya to withdraw. Déby emerged as the winner in the presidential election of 1996 and was re-elected in 2001 and again in May 2006. Déby added Itno to his name on 26 January 2006. In 2005 new rebel groups emerged in western Sudan and made incursions into eastern Chad.

Government

The 155-seat unicameral National Assembly is elected for four years. In the April 2002 elections Pres. Déby's *Mouvement patriotique du Salut* (MPS), won 110 seats, followed in distant second and third place by the *Rassemblement pour la Démocratie et le Progrès* (RDP) (12 seats) and the *Front des Forces d'Action pour la République* (FAR) (9). A June 2005 referendum replaced the Senate with an Economic, Social, and Cultural Council and scrapped term limits on the presidency. Both the presidential and parliamentary elections were postponed to 2011.

Economic policy

The government has begun to disengage itself from key sectors of the economy, liberalized pricing, and is promoting competition. Chad's return of internal security prompted a number of international business representatives to make exploratory visits to Chad. By far the most important venture to date is the oil extraction project in southern Chad that came on stream in 2003. Beginning in late 2000, the Doba Basin oil project has brought in billions in foreign direct investment from a consortium led by two US oil companies. In 2006 President Deby landed in a dispute with Chevron and ExxonMobil over alleged failure on the part of the corporations to pay taxes on oil revenues.

Sectors

Growth in some sectors has been constrained by Chad's lack of outlets to the sea. There are no railways and the roads are inadequate. Despite rapid growth in the oil sector, agriculture still accounts for 80% of the work force. Cotton is cultivated in the south and livestock in the north. Food crops include sorghum, millet, dry beans, sesame, potatoes, rice and maize. The only minerals extracted in quantity are soda and rock salt but there are known reserves of chromium, tungsten, titanium, iron ore, wolfram, gold, uranium and tin. The exploitation of oil deposits at Doba in the south after the construction of a 665 mile/1,070-km pipeline across Cameroon to an offshore tanker terminal at the Atlantic port of Kribi has stimulated industrial activity way beyond the current cotton processing and small scale food, textiles, brewing, tobacco, and leather plants. The nation's total oil reserves have been estimated to be in excess of 1.5 billion barrels.

Privatization

There has been steady progress towards privatization. The *Banque Meridien BIAO Tchad* (BMBT-BIAT) and *l'Office National Hydraulique Pastoral et Villageois* (ONHPV) have already been reconstructed. Slated for privatization were SONASUT (sugar monopoly), STEE (water and electricity), TIT (telecommunications), ONPT (post office/telecommunications), Air Chad, and Cotontchad (cotton monopoly).

Investment

Foreign direct investment represents more than half of the total capital invested in Chadian enterprises. As a result of historical ties, France leads the way with an estimated 50 to 60 percent of the total. Other significant investors are the Benelux countries, Italy, Taiwan, US, Japan, Saudi-Arabia, and Libya. In 2004, a consortium including Chevron, ExxonMobil and Malaysia's Petronas completed a pipeline from the Doba basin to the coast of Cameroon. At a construction cost of $3.7 billion production is currently at about 225,000 bbl/day—an expected total of 2 billion barrels over its 30-year life.

Trade

Cotton is the most important cash crop, accounting for about 90% of export revenues. Gum Arabic, groundnuts, sesame, sugar cane and tobacco are additional cash crops. Livestock is a source of traditional wealth and exported either on the hoof or as frozen meat, hides and skins. Mineral exports include soda and rock salt (mainly to Nigeria) and natron, used in the preservation of meat and in tanning. Oil has become the major export item. Major imports include machinery and transportation equipment, industrial and consumer goods.

Financial sector

As a member of *Communautè Financiére Africaine* (CFA) zone, Chad belongs to the regional central bank, *Banque des Etats de l'Afrique Centrale* (BEAC), which controls distribution of its money and the transfer of funds.

Taxes and tariffs

The corporate tax rate for non-residents is 25 percent and capital gains tax 25 to 40 percent. A value added tax (VAT) of 18 percent applies and exchange control is in effect. A tax of 20% is levied on dividends, interest and royalties. (See page 138).

BUSINESS ACTIVITY

AGRICULTURE
Cotton, sorghum, millet, peanuts, rice, potatoes, manioc, cattle, sheep, goats, camels.
INDUSTRIES
Cotton textiles, meat packing, beer brewing, natron, kaolin (sodium carbonate), soap, cigarettes, construction materials.
NATURAL RESOURCES
Petroleum, uranium, natron, kaolin, fish.
EXPORTS
$3.5 billion (est. 2009): oil, cotton, cattle, textiles, gum arabic.
IMPORTS
$2.2 billion (est. 2009): machinery and transportation equipment, industrial goods, petroleum products, foodstuffs, textiles.
MAJOR TRADING PARTNERS
US, China, Taiwan, France, Cameroon, Netherlands, Germany, Saudi Arabia.

Doing Business with Chad

▶ **Investment**

ExxonMobil affiliate, Esso Chad—leading a consortium including Chevron and Petronas—constructed a 665 miles (1,070 km) oil pipeline from the Doba basin in Chad to Kribi in Cameroon at a cost of $3.5 billion. This massive development opened up significant opportunities for foreign firms in finance, construction, oil-related industries and telecommunications. Chad's mineral reserves, including gold, marble and natron, have also attracted interest from investors. Livestock, still largely unexploited, present opportunities in meat and dairy production, leather, glue, fertilizer and other products. Spirulina (blue-green algae) in Lake Chad, shea trees, sesame seed oil, and a need for solar and wind power are other potential areas of investment. Privatization opens up further areas for foreign private participation. While currently uneconomic as a result of poor infrastructure, deposits of copper, silver, zinc and other metals hold future promise. Tax incentives apply to most investment.

▶ **Trade**

Imports include pharmaceutical products, flour milling products, malt, starchy food gluten, industrial chemicals, organic and non-organic, cellulose acetates, tire tubes, new and used tires for buses and trucks, paper products, greaseproof paper, rags, used and new textiles and shoes, steel, cable and tubes, tools and hardware, compressor parts, pumps, and air conditioners. There is a growing need for electric power systems; construction, mining, and agriculture machinery; telecommunications equipment and services; and food processing and packaging equipment.

▶ **Trade finance**

Eximbank has financed projects for ventures in the past. Short- to medium-term trade financing can also be obtained from the commercial banks and longer term arrangements through multilateral lending institutions such as the World Bank, African Development Bank, the *Fonds Europeen de Development* (FED), and the Islamic Development Bank.

▶ **Selling to the government**

Government tenders are published in the local press. The Minister of Finance and Economy together with his staff act as the National Authorization Office (NAO), selecting tenders on behalf of the relevant ministries. Large procurements are usually financed by the multilateral lending institutions.

▶ **Exchange controls**

There are no restrictions on the transfer of funds. As a member of the Central African Regional Customs Union (UDEAC) and the regional monetary union (CEMAC), Chad uses the CFA franc, supported by France at a fixed value.

▶ **Partnerships**

Foreign firms have entered into joint venture opportunities in the textile, agricultural and transportation sectors.

▶ **Establishing a presence**

Structuring can be in terms of a limited liability company (*Société à Responsabilité Limitée*—SARL) or a *Corporation Societe Anonyme* (SA) with at least seven shareholders. Both have to be registered with a number of state agencies before authorization is granted by the Ministry of Commerce.

▶ **Financing projects**

Major development projects are funded by multilateral donors such as the World Bank and African Development Bank. Foreign investors might be able to obtain financing on the local market but credit allotments are limited in range and lending criteria are rigid.

▶ **Labor**

Over 80 percent of the workforce is engaged in unpaid subsistence farming, herding and fishing. Unionized labor has no ties to the government and a new labor code has been drawn up in conjunction with the World Bank. Mandatory allowances to workers include transportation, health indemnity, bonuses, and vacation pay.

▶ **Legal rights**

Law is based on the French Napoleonic Code and Chadian customary law. Chad is a member of the Cameroon-based West African Intellectual Property Rights Organization but due to administrative limitations protection against copyright infringements is not guaranteed.

▶ **Business climate**

There is local tendency to take time developing a broad base of understanding and mutual trust during personal contact before proceeding with serious business discussions. When visiting Chad, it is advisable to have corporate and business materials available in French.

COMOROS

Consisting of four major and a number of minor islands in the Indian Ocean east of Mozambique, the Comoros archipelago has been struggling to attain political stability and economic growth since its independence in 1975. Comoros has limited natural resources and a population torn by ancient divisions. Since 1997 the Comorian federal state has been threatened with secession by the islands of Anjouan and Mohéli and endured some 20 coups or attempted coups. Efforts continue to stabilize the political situation with the help of the African Union and other international organizations, and to make the islands more attractive for much-needed foreign economic involvement.

Country profile

The four main islands and islets of the Comoros Islamic Federal Republic are scattered like stepping stones across the northern end of the Mozambique Channel, a stretch of Indian Ocean between the African coast and Madagascar. Three of the islands, Grande Comore (Ngazidja), Anjouan (Ndzuani) and Moheli (Mwali), constitute the federal republic, while the fourth, Mayotte (Maore) is a disputed French territory. These islands are the summits of a submerged volcanic ridge. Mount Karthala (2,040 m) on Grande Comore has the largest live crater in the world. The climate on all the islands is tropical, hot and humid, with abundant rainfall in most places. More than 100,000 Comorians live in France. The island population is mainly of Arab, African (Swahili) and Malagasy origin. Arabic and French are the official languages but Kiswahili is the common tongue. Most Comorians are Sunni Muslims.

History

Originally part of an extensive trade network in the northern Indian Ocean, these islands became known as Comoros—a corruption of the name Jazair al-Komr (Islands of the Moon) given by Arab mariners. A thousand years ago Ndzuani (Anjouan) was settled by Arabs and Shirazi (Persian) Muslims, replete with slaves. Since 1912 the Comoros had been administered as a colony by the French from Madagascar. In 1946 it was separated and in 1961 granted limited self-government. In 1974, when Comoros voted for independence, Mayotte, with its Christian majority, voted against joining the other largely Islamic islands and opted for continued French rule. The first post independence president, Ahmed Abdallah, was ousted after less than a month in office and replaced by a young populist, Ali Solihi. Since then coups, attempted coups and mercenary incursions have been part and parcel of the nation's political life. Elected in 1996, President Mohammed Taki died in November 1998 under sus-

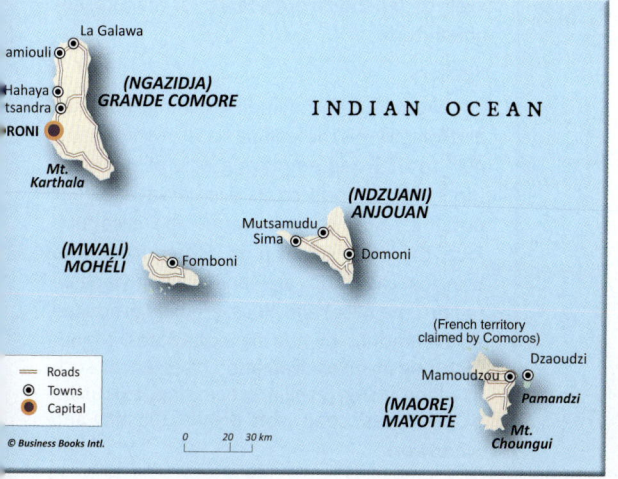

217

Pres. Ahmed Sambi
Born: 5 June 1958
Since May 2006

UN Photo Marco Castro

POLITICAL	
Head of State	Pres. Ahmed Sambi
Independence	6 July 1975
National capital	Moroni
Official languages	Arabic & French

PHYSICAL	
Total area	1,000 sq. miles 2,000 sq. km. (12 x Washington, DC)
Arable land	35%
Territorial sea	12 nautical miles

POPULATION	
Total	752.500
Av. yearly growth	2.76%
Urban population	28%
Life expectancy	63.5 years
Adult literacy	56.5%

ECONOMY	
Currency	Comoron franc (CF) (US$1=371.41)
GDP (real)	$557 million
GDP growth rate	1.4%
GDP per capita[1]	$850
GDP (ppp)[2]	$821 million
GDP per cap. (ppp)	$1,215
Inflation rate	4.5%
Exports	$32 million
Imports	$143 million
External debt	$266 million
Unemployment	20%

1. Atlas method.
2. See page 175 for an explanation of purchasing power parity (ppp).

picious circumstances and was succeeded by the president of the High Court, Tadjidine Ben Said Massoude. He was in turn replaced in 1999 in the latest of 20 coups since independence in 1975, engineered by Col. Azali Assoumani, who headed a military government until 2002. Under severe outside pressure Assoumani and other combatants signed a new constitution in March 2002, providing for elections. In June 2002 Assoumani became federal president by virtue of his election to the post of president of the Grand Comoros island. He was succeeded in May 2006 by Ahmed Abdallah Sambi, a resident of Anjouan.

Government

In terms of the March 2002 constitution, the three islands—Grand Comoros (Ngazidja), Anjouan and Mohéli—each elects its own president. The federal presidency rotates every four years between the three islands. Late December 2010 the next president will be elected for the first time from three finalists on the island of Moheli—Ikililou Dhoinine, Mohamed Said Fazul, and Djabir Abdou. Both Grand Comoros and Anjouan have had their turn. Fifteen of the 33 deputies in the unicameral Assembly of the Comoros Union are selected by the assemblies in the three islands and the remainder by universal suffrage. They serve for five years.

Economic policy

In the early nineties Comoros embarked on free market reforms under a structural adjustment program supported by the World Bank and the IMF. However, the islands seem likely to depend on outside aid for the foreseeable future.

Sectors

Agriculture,—including fishing, hunting, and forestry—is the leading sector, contributing 40% to GDP and employing 80% of the work force. Major food crops are cassava, sweet potatoes, rice, bananas, yams and coconuts. Rice, the main staple food, is imported. The principal cash crops are vanilla, ylang-ylang oil (a perfume base) and cloves, mostly produced on plantations owned by expatriates. Manufacturing involves distillation of essences such as ylang ylang, vanilla processing, extrusion of plant oils, soap, soft drinks, plastics and woodwork.

Privatization

A French company in mid-1997 took over management of the country's ailing electrical utility and other French companies are likely to follow suit as privatization continues. A South African firm has purchased government hotels.

Investment

Efforts by the government to attract foreign investment have been marred by political instability. South Africa is considered to be the prime candidate for investment capital.

Trade

Vanilla, cloves and ylang-ylang are major exports. France, Germany, and the United States are major buyers and France, Pakistan, South Africa, the United Arab Emirates and Kenya are the major suppliers of goods. Rice accounts for the bulk of the imports. Remittances from more than 150,000 Comorians living overseas are another important source of foreign currency.

Financial sector

Comoros is a member of the Communauté financière africaine The Banque Nationale de Paris Intercontinentale is the country's only international financial institution. Increased foreign support is needed to help Comoros meet its goal of an annual 4% growth in GDP.

Taxes and tariffs

The corporate income tax rate is 40%. There is a 15% tax on distributed dividends.

BUSINESS ACTIVITY

AGRICULTURE
Vanilla, cloves, perfume essences, copra, coconuts, bananas, cassava (tapioca).

INDUSTRIES
Tourism, perfume distillation, textiles, furniture, jewelry, construction materials, soft drinks.

EXPORTS
$32 million (est. 2006): ylang-ylang, cloves, perfume oil, copra.

IMPORTS
$143 million (est. 2006): rice and other foodstuffs, consumer goods, petroleum products, cement, transport equipment.

MAJOR TRADING PARTNERS
France, Singapore, Japan, Germany, South Africa, US, Netherlands, Kenya, Singapore, Pakistan, Belgium, UAE.

DOING BUSINESS WITH COMOROS

▶ **Investment**

The government has encouraged foreign investment by offering a number of special tax and other incentives. Opportunities for profitable trade and investment will, however, remain underutilized until Comoros resolves its deep-seated political problems and follows through with much needed economic reforms. Telecommunications, road construction, fishing and tourism are promising potential future areas for investment once longer term stability is restored.

▶ **Trade**

The US can be competitive in supplying items such as medical equipment and supplies, cellular telephone systems and solar energy units, once the political and economic climate improves. The Japanese have helped fund a satellite facility for Comoros which should stimulate growth in the communications sector and create a demand for equipment. Current commerce between the United States and Comoros is limited.

▶ **Exchange controls**

The government allows transfer of capital, profits and dividends.

▶ **Labor**

Unemployment and underemployment are widespread. The low educational level of the labor force contributes to a subsistence level of economic activity, high unemployment, and a heavy dependence on foreign grants and technical assistance.

▶ **Business Climate**

French is the language of business and daily life in Comoros, although some Arabic and Swahili are spoken. Comoros is a Muslim country, and visitors should observe conservative norms of dress and behavior.

CONGO, DEM. REP.

As Africa's third largest country, in size the equivalent of Western Europe, richly endowed with mineral and other natural resources, the Democratic Republic of Congo (DRC) or Congo (Kinshasa) has the potential to become one of the Continent's most prosperous nations. However, until peace and stability are restored and effective economic reforms introduced it seems destined to be little more than the renamed ravaged continuation of Mobutu's Zaire. In July and October 2006, the DRC held its first elections in 45 years—declared by the United Nations, who supervised this landmark event, as its largest and most complex task to date. Although violence marred the proceedings there is hope that it might lead to greater stability in the long run.

Country profile

The Democratic Republic of Congo—commonly referred to as Congo Kinshasa to prevent confusion with the neighboring Republic of Congo or Congo Brazzaville—is Africa's third largest country after Sudan and Algeria. The entire Congo Basin is well watered and dense rainforests extend along the Congo River and its tributaries. The eastern border is fringed with mountains overlooking a series of lakes including Albert, Edward, Kivu and Tanganyika. Roughly 80% of the country's inhabitants speak Bantu languages, ranging from the predominant Kongo to the Mongo, the Tumba and Lulua. The remainder, concentrated along the northern border, belong to the Adamawan Ubangian and Sudanic linguistic families. Kiswahili is widely spoken in the eastern parts of the country and in Shaba. More than 75% of the population adhere to Christianity.

History

Some 3,000 years ago the original hunter-gatherer Pygmies in the Congo Basin were joined by land-tilling Bantu speaking peoples from the north and northeast. Building on the explorations of American journalist Henry Morton Stanley in the 1870s, Belgian King Leopold I assembled an international consortium of bankers to exploit the Congo's natural resources. At the Berlin Conference of 1884-1885 the European powers recognized Leopold's claim to this vast region. Following widespread public concern over inhumane labor practices in the

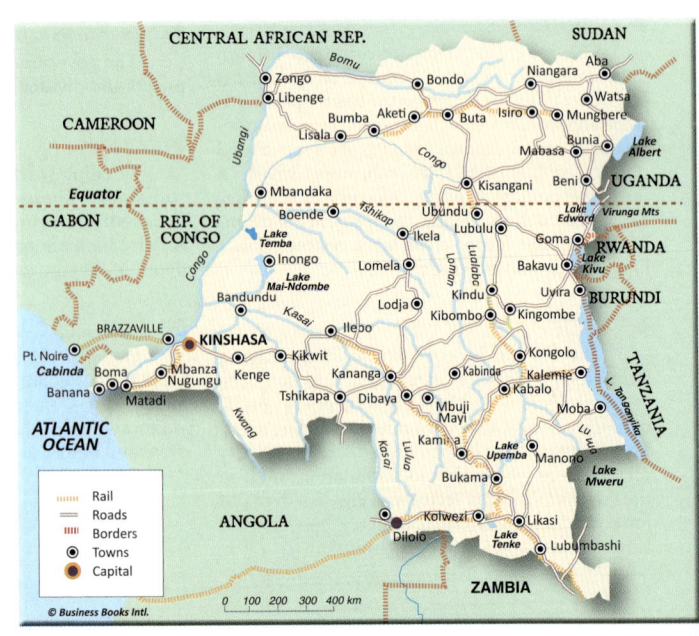

Congo, the Belgian government took over the administration of the territory in 1908. In 1960, when Belgium granted independence to an ill-prepared colony, a power struggle ensued, fueled in part by the big powers. Brief appearances by Joseph Kasavubu, Moise Tshombe and Patrice Lumumba was followed by Col. Joseph-Desiré Mobutu who exercised autocratic rule over Zaire for more than three decades. In 1997 an ailing Mobutu was ousted by Laurent Desiré Kabila and his Alliance of Democratic Forces for the Liberation of Congo-Zaire (ADFL) with the support of the Rwandan and Ugandan governments. Kabila renamed Zaire the Democratic Republic of Congo (DRC). A new insurrection by disillusioned former compatriots in the northeast, backed by Rwanda and Uganda, prompted Angolan, Namibian and Zimbabwean troops to come to Kabila's aid. In January 2001, Joseph Kabila became president after his father's assassination. In July 2003, under outside pressure, Kabila swore in as vice presidents in his cabinet Jean-Pierre Bemba of the Uganda-backed Congolese Liberation Movement and Azarias Ruberwa of the Rwanda-allied Congolese Rally for Democracy as well as Abdoulaye Yeroda Nbombasi, allied to Kabila, and Arthur Z'Ahidi Ngoma, a member of the country's unarmed political opposition. In the 2006 election—lasting from July until November—held under UN auspices with tight security, Kabila emerged the victor over Bemba. Despite apparent flaws this election represented a step toward ending a conflict that cost 4 million lives through fighting and the attendant hunger and disease. Fighting continues in the Northeastern region.

Government

Neither Kabila's *Parti du peuple pour la reconstruction et la democratie* (PPRD) with its 111 seats nor former Vice-President Jean-Pierre Bemba's *Mouvement pour la libération du Congo* (MLC) party with its 64 seats managed to win an outright majority in the 500 seat legislature in the July 2006 election. The rest of the seats were won by 63 smaller parties and independents. The PPRD (22 seats) and MLC (14) also failed to gain outright control of the 108 seat Senate.

Economic policy

The government has Implemented reforms and a degree of transparency and economic stability were accomplished. Cited as

Pres. Joseph Kabila
Born: 1972
Since Jan. 2001

UN Photo Eskinder Debebe

POLITICAL
Head of State	Pres. Joseph Kabila
Major parties	PPRD & MLC
Independence	30 June 1960
National capital	Kinshasa
Official language	French

PHYSICAL
Total area	905,000 sq. miles
	2,345,000 sq. km.
	(¼ of US)
Arable land	3%
Coastline	23 miles/37 km

POPULATION
Total	68.7 million
Av. yearly growth	3.2%
Urban population	34%
Life expectancy	54.3 years
Adult literacy	67.2%

ECONOMY
Currency	Congolese franc (US$1=890.00)
GDP (real)	$12.5 billion
GDP growth rate	2.6%
GDP per capita[1]	$272
GDP (ppp)[2]	$21.3 billion
GDP per cap. (ppp)	$323
Inflation rate	44.2%
Exports	$6.1 billion
Imports	$5.2 billion
External debt	$5.7 billion
Unemployment	NA

1. Atlas method.
2. See page 175 for an explanation of purchasing power parity (ppp).

priorities are the revitalization of the mining, agricultural and transport sectors.

Sectors

Arable land is plentiful and inland waters contain abundant supplies of fish. DRC was the world's largest producer of cobalt, the second largest of industrial diamonds and the fourth largest of copper. Diamonds are largely retrieved from alluvial and kimberlite deposits. Crude oil production is small compared to other Sub-Saharan African oil producers, but output from its small offshore fields remained steady during the 1990s and continues to serve as a reliable source of revenues. Due to extensive smuggling gold production is estimated to be much higher than quantities reflected in official statistics. The country has a hydroelectric potential of 100,000 megawatts (MW) or 13% of the world's total. Manufacturing is concentrated in Kinshasa and the mining centers of Shaba and ranges from brewing, food processing and textiles to vehicle assembly.

Privatization

At the peak of the Mobutu-driven nationalization more than 140 enterprises belonged to the state. Since then, several were liquidated, privatized, or replaced by new ones. Today there are 116 of which 56 are fully publicly owned and 60 with mixed ownership.

Investment

In recent years, foreign investments were mostly concentrated in transportation, chemical products and pharmaceuticals, wood, food processing, mining, and services. The largest US investment is in oil with ChevronTexaco in the lead. Belgian-owned firms are prominent as minority owners in several major parastatal firms. Lebanese, Chinese, South Asian and South African business enterprises have a growing economic influence and French interest is reviving. The diamond industry is controlled by the state-owned *Societe Miniere de Bakwanga* (Miba), which markets its diamonds through Sediza, a subsidiary of the international De Beers Central Selling Organization.

Trade

Copper, cobalt, coffee, petroleum, and diamonds account for most of the country's foreign exchange earnings. In the mid-1990s diamonds contributed nearly half of export earnings while copper and cobalt contributed 20%. The US is, after the Benelux countries the biggest buyer of Congolese products.

Financial sector

The banking system comprises the central bank, twelve commercial banks and a development bank—the Société Financière de developpement (SOFIDE). Most commercial banks maintain correspondent arrangements with banks operating in the US.

Taxes and tariffs

Corporate tax is 40% of income, capital gains and branch profits. Foreign investments valued between $200,000 and $10 million (local currency equivalent) receive extensive tax concessions on profits and dividends.

Foreign presence

Over the years the country's size, population, economic potential, resources and location have made it attractive to Western business, apart from official strategic considerations during the Cold War. Many foreign firms that withdrew amidst civil disorder and an economic downturn are returning.

BUSINESS ACTIVITY

AGRICULTURE
Coffee, sugar, palm oil, rubber, tea, quinine, cassava, bananas, root crops, corn, fruit, wood products.

INDUSTRIES
Mining, mineral processing, consumer products, cement, diamonds.

NATURAL RESOURCES
Copper, cobalt, cadmium, petroleum, industrial and gem diamonds, gold, silver, zinc, manganese, tin, germanium, uranium, radium, bauxite, iron ore, coal, hydropower potential, timber.

EXPORTS
$6.1 billion (est. 2007): diamonds, copper, coffee, cobalt, crude oil.

IMPORTS
$5.2 billion (est. 2007): foodstuffs, mining and other machinery, transport equipment, fuel.

MAJOR TRADING PARTNERS
China, Belgium, US, South Africa, France, Finland, Zambia, Zimbabwe, Kenya.

Doing Business with the DRC

▶ **Investment**

With the exception of the minerals extraction sector, the government neither requires nor seeks participation in foreign investments. There is minimal screening of foreign investment. A bilateral investment treaty (BIT) has been in place with the US since 1989, guaranteeing reciprocal rights and privileges to each country's investors. A *Zone Franche d'Inga* (ZOFI) was established to attract potential investors, especially heavy industry users of energy.

▶ **Trade**

Export opportunities exist in used clothing, telecommunications and computer equipment, refrigeration and air conditioning equipment, electrical generators and distribution equipment, pharmaceuticals, aircraft and related equipment, cosmetics, four-wheel drive passenger vehicles, commercial trucks, mining, construction, agricultural, and forestry equipment, and food products such as rice, wheat, dried milk products, processed tomato products, canned meat and fish, and poultry. Trained professionals without regular employment offer a range of services from the complex to the mundane, including translating and interpreting, setting up appointments with key officials, following-up with local businesses, arranging accommodation and transportation, and facilitating passage through DROC's notoriously slow airports.

▶ **Trade finance**

Although hard-currency accounts are available at commercial banks, most businesses avoid them because of high maintenance costs. International transfers and transfers between various regions of the country are frequently done by direct agreement between businesses. Local banks sometimes serve as matchmakers.

▶ **Selling to the government**

Due to political unrest and a drop in revenues, government procurement is currently in a state of flux.

▶ **Exchange control**

The transfer of dividends and other funds associated with investments is allowed but licenses are required for all transactions in foreign exchange, including import payments.

▶ **Establishing a presence**

A branch office or sales subsidiary may be a useful method of representation where a large ongoing market exists or frequent contacts are required. Sometimes exporters rely on a group of firms selling complementary items by establishing a jointly owned sales subsidiary. There are five possibilities: *Société Privée à Responsibilité Limitée* (SPRL)— a limited liability company that combines the character of a partnership and a corporation; *Société Privée à Responsabilité Limitée* (SARL) — a joint stock company; *Société Cooperative* (SC)— where each member has a single vote; *Société en Nom Collectif* (SNC)—a simple partnership; and the *Société en Commandité Simple* (SCS)—a limited partnership.

▶ **Financing projects**

DROC is a member of the World Bank's Multilateral Investment Guarantee Agency, which offers insurance to new foreign investments against foreign exchange risk, expropriation and civil unrest.

▶ **Labor**

Even though a large urban population provides a ready pool of available labor—some with high school and university education—skilled industrial labor is in short supply. Minimum wages are set on a regional basis by the government for all workers in private enterprise. Strict labor laws can make termination of employees difficult. Outside the major cities, large companies often become involved in providing infrastructure including roads, schools, and hospitals. As foreign undertakings mature, the government expects the number of expatriates employed to diminish.

▶ **Legal rights**

Although arbitrary seizure of property was a problem during the early months of the Kabila regime, the government has brought the practice under control in recent months. DROC is a member of the World Intellectual Property Organization and the Paris Convention for the Protection of Industrial Property. However, enforcement of IPR regulations has been lax due to bureaucratic disarray. The complexities of DROC law make the hiring of local legal professionals necessary.

▶ **Business Climate**

French is the business language and little English is spoken. European traditions of social etiquette apply. A suit or coat and tie (for men) and a business suit (for women) are appropriate for business appointments or meetings with officials.

CONGO, REP. OF

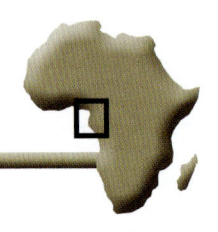

The Republic of Congo or Congo (Brazzaville) is sub-Saharan Africa's fourth largest oil producer (after Nigeria, Angola, and Gabon). Most of its remaining estimated proven reserves of 1.5 billion barrels is offshore, making it heavily dependent on foreign expertise and technology. Foreign companies are heavily engaged in the exploration and production of oil and gas and as suppliers of equipment and machinery. ethnic rivalry and political unrest has not disrupted this vital sector but prompted potential investors in other sectors to put their plans on hold.

Country profile

The Republic of Congo (commonly referred to as Congo Brazzaville to distinguish it from the Democratic Republic of Congo or Congo Kinshasa) lies within the catchment areas of the Congo and Ubangi rivers. The climate is tropical. The population is Bantu-speaking with the Kongo, Teke and Mboshi forming 85% of the total. About 45% are Christians.

History

Some 600 years ago when the Bantu-speaking people moved into the region it was inhabited by Pygmies. Towards the end of the 15th Century Portuguese merchant mariners established relations with the Kongo kingdom at the mouth of the Congo river and conducted slave trade until it was abolished in the 19th Century. French colonization began in the late 19th Century when Count Savorgnan de Brazza signed a treaty with the chief of the Batekes, Makoko. In 1910 Congo became part of French Equatorial Africa and in 1960 gained its independence under Pres. Fulbert Youlou. After several coups Col. Denis Sassou-Nguesso took control in 1979 and established a one-party regime. In 1993, Pascal Lissouba won the presidency but his party failed to obtain an absolute majority. A four month civil war erupted which led to the large-scale destruction of Brazzaville. In 1997 Lissouba's fragile coalition government came to an end when Sassou-Nguesso took control with the help of Angolan forces. At the end of 1999 a peace agreement was signed between Sassou-Nguesso, from the north, and the rebels representing the populous south. Continuing conflict led to a peace accord in March 2003. In 2002 and again in 2009 Nguesso was reelected president.

Government

The present constitution, adopted after a referendum held in March 1992, provides for bicameral parliament—a 137-member *Assemblée Nationale* (National Assembly) and a 72-member *Sénat* (Senate), both elected for five year terms—the latter by indirect vote. In the two-stage June and August 2007 elections the Congolese Party of Labor (PCT) won 46 seats against 11 each for the Congolese Movement for Democracy and Integral Development (MCDDI) and the Pan-African Union for Social Democracy (UPADS). Independents captured 37 seats and smaller parties the rest.

Economic policy

Economic reforms have been undertaken with the support of the World Bank, IMF and other international organizations. Progress was, however, slowed by the resumption of armed conflict in December 1998. The most recent peace agreement has kindled new hope.

Sectors

Oil is a major revenue source. The economy also presents a mixture of village agriculture and handicrafts, an industrial sector based largely on oil, support services. The main food crops are maize, cassava, rice and yams; the main cash crops are cocoa, coffee, sugar and palm oil. With its more than 90 bridges and 12 tunnels, the over 500 km stretch of Congo-Ocean Railway, built in the colonial era, is not only an engineering feat but provides a vital link in the transport system of equatorial Africa. The railway starts at Pointe Noire with its modern deep-water harbor, opened in 1939 and still regarded as one of the best equipped in Africa. After Nigeria and Cameroon, Congo is the third largest gas resource base in Sub-Saharan Africa. Pointe Noire, Congo's economic and petroleum capital, has not been directly affected by the insecurity elsewhere in the country.

Privatization

In April 1998, the Congolese government established a new national petroleum company, the *Société Nationale des Pétroles du Congo* (SNPC), to market Congo's crude oil and to assume all upstream functions of the former state-owned company, Hydro-Congo. Privatization of Hydro-Congo's downstream operations has been underway since 1997 with Elf and Shell as major participants. Prior

Pres. Denis Sassou-Nguesso
Born: 1943
Since October 1997
UN Photo Devra Berkowitz

POLITICAL

Head State	Pres. Denis Sassou-Nguesso
Ruling party	PCT
Independence	15 August 1960
National capital	Brazzaville
Official language	French

PHYSICAL

Total area	132,000 sq. miles
	342,000 sq. km.
	(± Montana)
Arable land	0.5%
Coastline	105 miles/169 km

POPULATION

Total	4 million
Av. yearly growth	2.75%
Urban population	61%
Life expectancy	54 years
Adult literacy	83.8%

ECONOMY

Currency	CFA franc (CFAF) (US$1: 495.40)
GDP (real)	$13.7 billion
GDP growth rate	7.6%
GDP per capita[1]	$3,309
GDP (ppp)[2]	$15.6 billion
GDP per cap. (ppp)	$4,239
Inflation rate	6.0%
Exports	$8.2 billion
Imports	$3.3 billion
External debt	$13.5 billion
Unemployment	NA

1. Atlas method.
2. See page 175 for an explanation of purchasing power parity (ppp).

to the 1997 civil war, Congo's national utility, *Société Nationale d'Electricité* (SNE), was one of the several government entities considered for privatization.

Investment

Elf Aquitaine (Elf) holds a dominant position in exploration, production, and refining with Italy's ENI-Agip playing an important secondary role. US firms are engaged in offshore exploration and production include Chevron and ExxonMobil.

Trade

Oil accounts for 70% of the Congolese government's revenue and 85% of Congo's exports. It is the 15th largest supplier of crude to the United States.

Taxes and tariffs

The corporate tax rate for non-residents is 20 to 35 percent. There is no capital gains tax. A value added tax (VAT) of 18 percent applies and exchange control is in effect. Taxes are levied on dividends (20%), interest (20%) and royalties (20%). (See page 138.)

BUSINESS ACTIVITY

AGRICULTURE
Cassava, sugar, rice, corn, peanuts, vegetables, coffee, cocoa, forest products.

INDUSTRIES
Petroleum extraction, cement, lumbering, brewing, sugar milling, palm oil, soap, cigarettes.

NATURAL RESOURCES
Petroleum, timber, potash, lead, zinc, uranium, copper, phosphates, natural gas.

EXPORTS
$8.2 billion (est. 2009): petroleum products, lumber, plywood, sugar, cocoa, coffee, diamonds.

IMPORTS
$3.3 billion (est. 2009): capital equipment, construction materials, foodstuffs.

MAJOR TRADING PARTNERS
US, China, Taiwan, India, Belgium, Italy, France, Germany, South Korea.

DOING BUSINESS WITH THE CONGO

▶ **Investment**

The success of deepwater exploration off the coast of the Congo and neighboring Cabinda (Angola) has sparked renewed interest in these areas. Hydrocarbon legislation enacted in 1994 offers production-sharing agreements (PSAs) to foreign oil companies in partnership with the national oil company, SNPC. Contractors finance all investment and recover their expenditure when the production begins. In 1995, foreign companies were given the option of converting existing exploration and production joint venture contracts to PSAs and since then all major operators in Congo have signed up. Other sectors of interest to foreign investors are forestry, mining, agriculture, pharmaceuticals, and construction.

▶ **Trade**

Major imports by Congo include heavy machinery, vehicles, business equipment, clothing, pharmaceuticals, consumer goods, and foodstuffs. US exports are inhibited in part by high transport costs, a cumbersome local bureaucracy, and lack of established networks between US and Congolese traders. The French, with extensive local knowledge and an on-the-ground presence have the edge.

▶ **Exchange controls**

As a member of the franc zone, the Congo shares the BEAC as a central bank with neighboring central African states.

▶ **Establishing a presence**

A center for business enterprises (known by its French acronym, CFE) assists foreigners who wish to establish themselves in the Congo.

▶ **Financing projects**

The International Finance Corporation was a major lender to the N'Kossa offshore project. Most of the financing for projects in the growing oil and gas sector is, however, arranged by the major oil companies themselves.

▶ **Labor**

A new labor code aims at making the country more investor-friendly.

▶ **Business climate**

Conducting business in the Congo requires a knowledge of French. Business customs conform to the European model as a result of years of French influence in the region.

CÔTE D'IVOIRE

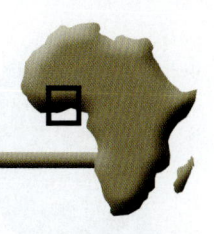

Cocoa exports coupled with ample foreign investment and close ties to France helped Côte d'Ivoire become one of the most prosperous nations in the West African region. Côte d'Ivoire is not only the world's largest producer of cocoa. It is also a significant exporter of coffee, forest products, cotton, rubber, bananas, pineapples, and palm oil. A relatively well-developed infrastructure and a sophisticated financial sector have prompted several foreign firms to establish their regional West-African headquarters in Côte d'Ivoire. Recent political turmoil has, however, impacted negatively on the country.

Country profile

The Republic of Côte d'Ivoire forms a low plateau less than 500 m. above sea level, bordered in the west by the Nimba mountains stretching northwards to the confluence of the Sassandra, the Red and the White Bandama, and the Komoe rivers. Rainfall along the coast averages 2,000 mm. per year and gradually decreases northward, to around 1,000 mm. The Baoule dominates with 23% of the total population, followed by the Bete (18%), the Senoufou (15%), and Malinke (11%). The country has an immigrant and expatriate population of over 2 million. More than 120,000 Lebanese are mostly engaged in business and French expatriates number around 50,000. French is the official language. About 38% of the population are Muslim, especially in the north, and 28% Christian, mainly in the southeast.

History

First settled by the Kru and subsequently the Mande-speaking people (including the Muslim Malinke) and the Kwa, Côte d'Ivoire came into French orbit in the 1840s. Forts were built along the coast to facilitate ivory and slave trade. The colony of Côte d'Ivoire was established in 1893 and French colonists, encouraged by the colonial government, began with cocoa and coffee cultivation on large estates with the help of forced labor. In the 1930s a Baoulé medical officer, Félix Houphouet-Boigny, took up the cause of black farmers. The name Boigny, which was added to signify "irresistible force," proved prophetic. In 1960 Houphouet Boigny became the executive President of newly independent Côte d'Ivoire and for the next 30 years exercised one party rule. In the country's first free elections in 1990 he was reelected by a margin of 82%. Houphouet Boigny died on 7 December 1993, at the age of 88 and was succeeded by the speaker of the National Assembly, Henri Konan Bédié. On 24 December 1999, Bédié and his elected government

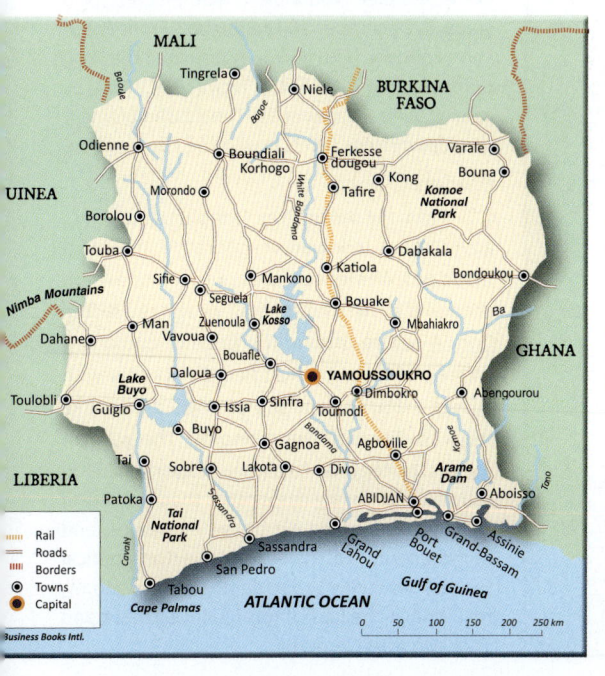

Pres. Laurent Gbagbo
Born: May 31, 1945
Since October 2000

UN Photo Ky Chung

POLITICAL
Head of State	Pres. Laurent Gbagbo
Prime Minister	Guillaume Soro
Ruling Party	FPI
Main Opposition	PDCI-RDA
Independence	7 August 1960
National capital	Yamoussoukro
Official language	French

PHYSICAL
Total area	124,000 sq. miles
	322,000 sq. km.
	(± New Mexico)
Arable land	9%
Coastline	320 miles/515 km

POPULATION
Total	20.6 million
Av. yearly growth	2.13%
Urban population	49%
Life expectancy	55.5 years
Adult literacy	48.7%

ECONOMY
Currency	CFA franc (CFAF) (US$1=495.40)
GDP (real)	$23 billion
GDP growth rate	3.6%
GDP per capita[1]	$1,1724
GDP (ppp)[2]	$33.8 billion
GDP per cap. (ppp)	$1,602
Inflation rate	1.4%
Exports	$8.8 billion
Imports	$6.5 billion
External debt	$18.5 billion
Unemployment	NA

1. Atlas method.
2. See page 175 for an explanation of purchasing power parity (ppp).

were deposed in a military coup led by former army chief of staff General Robert Guei who promised to stay in power only "to sweep the house clean." Instead he decided to run for president in the October 2000 elections. After declaring himself the winner in what was considered to be a rigged race, Guei was forced by public outcry to step down in favor of his main rival, Laurent Gbagbo. A failed coup in September 2002 split Côte d'Ivoire between a rebel-held north and government-controlled south, resulting in civil strife. An 8,000-strong UN peacekeeping mission (UNOCI) and 2,000 French troops intervened. A new presidential elections, originally scheduled for 2005, was held in October 2010 after several postponements. Even though Alassane Ouattara, representing the north, won the second round of an election which initially also included Henri Bédié, Laurent Gbagbo refused to vacate the office, claiming fraud. At the end of the year efforts by the UN and the African Union to have Gbagbo step down, were unsuccessful.

Government

The constitution provides for an executive president elected by popular vote for a 5-year term. He appoints a Prime Minister, who in turn selects the Council of Ministers. The 225-member *Assemblée Nationale* is also elected for 5 years. In December 2002 Gbagbo's *Front Populaire Ivoirienne* (FPI) narrowly defeated the *Parti Démocratique de la Côte d'Ivoire* (PDCI-RDA) by gaining 96 seats against 94. The *Rassemblement des républicains* (RDR) boycotted the election.

Economic policy

From the outset Pres. Houphouet-Boigny's government followed conservative and pragmatic pro-Western policies, with emphasis on economic growth rather than wealth redistribution. A severe drop in the price of cocoa and coffee in the eighties saddled the country with a large external debt and prompted it to take steps to diversify the economy. The government's strategy has four goals: export diversification; encouraging crops other than coffee and cocoa; encouraging extractive industries; and reinforcement of the services sector. Political turmoil has continued to damage the economy, resulting in the loss of foreign investment and slow economic growth.

Sectors

Côte d'Ivoire is the world's leading exporter of cocoa and a significant producer of cotton, coffee, sugar and rubber. In recent years there has been considerable expansion into the cultivation and export of mangoes, cashews, flowers and silk. New mining and petroleum codes were enacted in the mid-nineties to encourage foreign exploration of gold and nickel and offshore oil production. Mining plays a small role in the economy but oil has been extracted from offshore fields since the late 1970s. The country has considerable largely unexploited iron ore, bauxite and manganese deposits. Manufacturing revolves mostly around the processing of agricultural, forestry and petroleum products, and textiles, chemicals and import substitution. Tropical weather and a well-developed infrastructure make tourism a promising sector.

Privatization

Most of the 60 state-owned enterprises earmarked in a privatization program in the early nineties have been privatized—including restructuring of the telecommunications company, a vegetable-oil producer, the country's leading hotel, an electricity company, the state oil refinery and the national airline.

Investment

Foreign firms have focused largely on mining and oil exploration. Gold and nickel exploration contracts have been concluded with Canadian, Australian and South African mining houses. Offshore oil and gas exploration and production involve US, Canadian and European firms. France, however, continues to be the most important foreign investor. Following the liberalization of cocoa and coffee exports, US-based Cargill and other commodity trading multinationals have invested in both local processing and the export of raw cocoa beans.

Trade

Côte d'Ivoire is the world's leading exporter of cocoa beans, contributing over 30% of the world's output. It ranks third in Africa in the export of coffee beans, after Ethiopia and Uganda, and is the leading sugar cane producer in West Africa. It competes with Mali and Nigeria for first place in West Africa as producer of cotton lint and with Nigeria as a supplier of tobacco leaves. Rice and meat are imported despite significant local production. Imports—primarily from France, Nigeria, the US, Ghana, and Germany—range from industrial inputs to transportation equipment, food and beverages, fuel and lubricants to consumer goods.

Financial sector

Côte d'Ivoire is a member of the Communauté Financière Africaine (CFA), a financial grouping of Francophone African countries and belongs to the Union Economique et Monétaire de l'Afrique de l'Ouest (UEMOA). The BCEAO, located in Dakar, is the central bank for UEMOA members and the French Treasury guarantees convertibility of its currency. There are 15 commercial banks, regional stock exchange, and over 30 insurance companies. The African Development Bank is headquartered in Abidjan.

Taxes and tariffs

The corporate tax rate for non-residents is 25 percent and capital gains tax 25 percent. A value added tax (VAT) of 15 percent applies and exchange control is in effect. Taxes are levied on dividends (12%), interest (18%) and royalties (20%). (See page 138).

BUSINESS ACTIVITY

AGRICULTURE
Coffee, cocoa beans, bananas, palm kernels, corn, rice, manioc, sweet potatoes, sugar, cotton, rubber, timber.

INDUSTRIES
Foodstuffs, beverages, wood products, oil refining, automobile assembly, textiles, fertilizer, construction materials, electricity.

NATURAL RESOURCES
Petroleum, diamonds, manganese, iron ore, cobalt, bauxite, copper.

EXPORTS
$8.8 billion (est. 2009): cocoa, coffee, tropical woods, petroleum, cotton, bananas, pineapples, palm oil, fish.

IMPORTS
$6.5 billion (est. 2009): food, consumer and capital goods, fuel, transport equipment.

MAJOR TRADING PARTNERS
France, Netherlands, US, Italy, Nigeria, Singapore, Germany, China.

Doing Business with Côte d'Ivoire

▶ **Investment**

Investors who establish themselves in regions outside Abidjan are entitled to an 8-year tax exemption instead of 5 years. Companies seeking priority enterprise status, eligible for these tax holidays and other benefits, might be required to purchase Ivorian products. The *Centre de Promotion des Investissements en Côte d'Ivoire* (CEPICI) serves as a "one-stop-shop" for foreign investors, helping them to find suitable opportunities and serving as a link with the public sector. Investments from outside the Franc Zone must be approved by the external finance and credit office of the Ministry of Economy and Finance. Apart from privatization and the relaxation of state monopolies, a variety of opportunities exists in projects such as waste water and solid waste collection networks in regional cities, the connection of the Mali-Côte d'Ivoire and the Guinea-Côte d'Ivoire electrical grids, and the Abidjan-Ghana expressway, many on a BOT (Build-Own-Transfer) basis.

▶ **Trade**

Opportunities exist in high value food products, paper products, telecommunications, computers and software, consumer electronics and agricultural, irrigation, mining, construction, air-conditioning, refrigeration, medical, security, and power generation equipment, as well as textile, forestry and woodworking machinery, and cosmetics, toiletries, pharmaceutical and health care products. In the past 5 years, several oil and gas projects have come into production creating a need for field equipment.

▶ **Trade finance**

Eximbank financing is available. Competitive credit terms are important considerations in purchasing decisions.

▶ **Selling to the government**

The Ivorian Government periodically issues procurement tenders in local newspapers and sometimes in international media. The *Bureau National d'Etudes Techniques et de Developpement* (BNETD) usually acts on behalf of other ministries in projects financed by the World Bank and the African Development Bank.

▶ **Exchange controls**

By law all exchange transactions relating to foreign countries must be handled by authorized banks. Foreign exchange for import payments must be purchased either on the date of settlement specified in the commercial contract or at the time the required down payment is made. French Franc-based transactions are the easiest and more common.

▶ **Partnerships**

Many foreign firms rely on local partners or agents. An increasing number of Ivorians who trained abroad are available as partners.

▶ **Establishing a presence**

The CEPICI assists foreign firms with formalities such as registration, incorporation, and the modification or dissolution of a local entity. The four most common forms of business are *Association et Participation* (Joint Venture); *Succursale* (Foreign Branch), a *Société à Responsabilité Limitée* (Limited Liability Company); and *Société Anonyme* (Stock Corporation).

▶ **Financing projects**

The Overseas Private Investment Corporation offers loans, loan guarantees and insurance products to US investors. The US Trade and Development Agency finances feasibility studies and the World Bank and the African Development Bank support government procurement. Côte d'Ivoire is a member of the Multilateral Investment Guarantee Agency.

▶ **Labor**

Unskilled labor is readily available but clerical, technical, managerial, and professional talent is more difficult to find. Wage rates are relatively high by regional standards.

▶ **Legal rights**

A new arbitration tribunal has been established under the auspices of the Chamber of Commerce. Côte d'Ivoire is a member of the international center for the settlement of investment disputes (ICSID) and a party to the Paris Convention and the African Intellectual Property Organization (OAPI), which recently adopted revisions to conform to the WTO agreement on trade-related intellectual property issues (TRIPS).

▶ **Business climate**

Business customs in Côte d'Ivoire are decidedly European. French is the official language and prevalent in business. Academic titles and degrees are frequently used by members of the expatriate community or those who received their schooling abroad.

DJIBOUTI

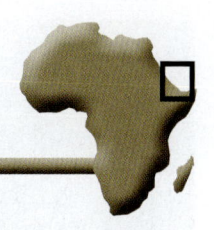

As one of the smallest countries on the African continent and with limited natural resources, Djibouti is largely dependent on its service sector. Its strategic location at the mouth of the Red Sea makes it a convenient transshipment point for goods entering or leaving the East African Highlands. It provides a rail link from Djibouti harbor to Ethiopia's Addis Ababa as well as telecommunication cable connections between Northern Europe and Asia. The government is actively seeking to redress the problem of recurrent deficits by encouraging foreign involvement in mining, shipping and services. Djibouti is host to several thousand French military personnel and allows the US naval and air defense access.

Country profile

The Republic of Djibouti is a small country at the juncture of the Red Sea and the Gulf of Aden, slightly larger than Swaziland and The Gambia. It consists mainly of a volcanic rock-strewn desert interrupted by patches of arable land, salt lakes and pans, and has high temperatures, high humidity and a low annual rainfall. Its population consists largely of the Issa Somali clan. There is also a strong Afar minority. Both groups are Muslim Cushitic-speaking peoples with a traditionally nomadic lifestyle. The small but influential Arab element comes mainly from Yemen and the expatriate community is mostly French, some of them refugees from Somalia. More than two thirds of the population live in the port city of Djibouti.

History

Around the 3rd Century B.C. Arabs migrated to what is today Djibouti. Their descendants, the Afars or Danakil people, were joined a century later by the Issas who migrated from southern Ethiopia. Both the Afar and the Issa were nomadic livestock herders who spoke related Cushitic languages and adopted the Muslim faith. Portuguese and Turkish slave traders in the region were eventually followed by the French, British and Italians who competed for control of the sea route through the Red Sea and the Suez Canal. The French prevailed. From 1888, they developed the port of Djibouti on the southern side of the Gulf of Aden and in 1917 connected it by means of a 480 mile (780 km) railway to Addis Ababa in Ethiopia. In 1958 the Afar voted to remain a self-governing part of France in a referendum boycotted by most of the Issas. The same happened in 1967 when the French Territory of the Afars and Issas was granted responsible self-government and renamed French Somaliland. The quest

Pres. Ismail Omar Guelleh
Born: 1947
Since May 1999

UN Photo Mark Garten

POLITICAL	
Head of State	Pres. Ismail Omar Guelleh
Ruling Party	UMP Coalition
Independence	27 June 1977
National capital	Djibouti
Official language	French & Arabic

PHYSICAL	
Total area	9,000 sq. miles 23,000 sq. km. (±Massachussetts)
Arable land	0.04%
Coastline	314 km

POPULATION	
Total	724,000
Av. yearly growth	2.1%
Urban population	87%
Life expectancy	60.3 years
Adult literacy	67.9%

ECONOMY	
Currency	Djiboutian franc (DF) (US$1=175.75)
GDP (real)	$1.0 billion
GDP growth rate	4.8%
GDP per capita[1]	$962
GDP (ppp)[2]	$1.95 billion
GDP per cap. (ppp)	$2,262
Inflation rate	1.7%
Exports	$100 million
Imports	$644 million
External debt	$582 million
Unemployment	59%

1. Atlas method.
2. See page 175 for an explanation of purchasing power parity (ppp).

for national unity was, however, stimulated by the territorial claims made on the territory by the independent Somali Republic to the south. In a third referendum in March 1977, the electorate voted overwhelmingly in favor of independence. A senior Issa politician, Hassan Gouled Aptidon, became executive president of the Republic of Djibouti, a single party state. In September 1992 the voters adopted a multiparty constitution and in April 1999 Aptidon finally stepped aside opening the door for Ismail Omar Guelleh to be elected president. He was re-elected in April 2005, unopposed.

Government

The 1992 Constitution provides for a president elected for a maximum of two 6-year terms. It is customary for the prime minister to be appointed from the Afar minority. The National Assembly, elected for a 5-year term, has 33 seats assigned for the Issa and 32 for the Afar. In the February 2008 election the ruling coalition, the Union for the Presidential Majority (UMP), captured all 65 seats. The opposition boycotted the election, declared fair by the African Union and Arab League.

Economic policy

Djibouti's economy has been weakened by battles against Afar rebels during the 1990s. In March 2000 they signed a peace accord with the new government. In October 1995 the entire country was declared a free export zone to encourage foreign involvement.

Sectors

Djibouti is largely dependent on foreign assistance to finance development and buttress its balance of payments. The agricultural sector in Djibouti contributes only 3.5% of the GDP but employs an estimated 75% of the people. The service sector constitutes 76.0% of GDP. Djibouti serves as both a transit port for the region and an international transshipment and refueling center. Its port facility and railroad linking To Addis Ababa account for most of the economic activity. container facilities have been greatly expanded but are challenged by improved facilities at Saudi Arabia's Jeddah harbor and Ethiopia's Assab port. The country hosts a state-of-the-art submarine cable running from Northern Europe to East Asia. At least ten international airlines use the airport at Djibouti as a stopover. An oil refinery was built in 1990. A small fishing industry is being developed. Surveys have indicated the presence of a few minerals such as copper, gypsum and sulfur. The main source of energy is thermal plants. An expatriate community contributes significantly to its economy.

Privatization

Recent attempts at privatization of state enterprises have met with some response from potential investors.

Investment

Although efforts were made to reduce restrictions on foreign investors, recent warfare and harsh environmental conditions in the region have deterred investors.

Trade

Exports consisting of cattle, refined sugar, crude organic material, fish, hides and skins, and coffee are mostly transshipments from Ethiopia. A large portion of Djibouti's imports are destined for Ethiopia, Somalia and other neighboring regions.

Financial sector

A sophisticated private banking service in place. With its almost unrestricted commercial and financial sectors, Djibouti is actively courting offshore banking and insurance firms.

Taxes and tariffs

The corporate income, capital gains, and branch tax rates are 20%. There is a 10% withholding tax on dividends for nonresidents. Residents are exempt from the withholding tax on dividends and interest.

BUSINESS ACTIVITY

AGRICULTURE
Fruit, vegetables, goats, sheep, camels.
INDUSTRIES
Limited to a few small-scale enterprises such as dairy products and mineral-water bottling.
NATURAL RESOURCES
Geothermal areas.
EXPORTS
$100 million (2006): hides and skins, coffee (in transit).
IMPORTS
$644 million (2006): food, beverages, transport equipment, chemicals, petroleum products.
MAJOR TRADING PARTNERS
Saudi Arabia, Ethiopia, Somalia, India, Yemen, France, Italy, China, Japan.

DOING BUSINESS WITH DJIBOUTI

▶ **Investment**

Shipping and other port-related activities are seen as prime candidates for investment. The country also shows potential for geothermal and solar energy production. There are small known gold deposits as well as diatomite, geothermal fluids, mineral salts, gypsum, perlite, pumice, and possibly petroleum. Oil interest focuses on the southern region and the offshore area along the Gulf of Aden. Djibouti is trying to lure offshore banking with its liberal economic regime.

▶ **Trade**

Merchandise exports of local origin are insignificant and almost all food requirements and consumer goods have to be imported. Djibouti's well- equipped harbor is a transshipment point for products to and form Ethiopia by rail. It is also used by both French and US naval ships.

▶ **Exchange controls**

The currency, the Djibouti franc, is pegged to the dollar and is freely convertible. There are no foreign exchange restrictions.

▶ **Labor**

An unemployment rate of 40% to 50% continues to be a major problem. Skilled labor is, however, relatively expensive.

▶ **Business climate**

The business practices are Middle Eastern and the language French.

233

EGYPT

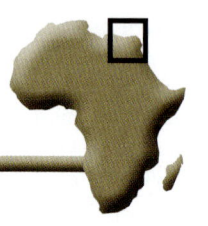

As the most populous Arab country, Egypt is both African and Middle Eastern. Egypt's total population of more than 70 million is steadily developing western consumption patterns and even among the poor consumer taste is rapidly changing and expanding the potential for imported goods. Because of its strategic position in the region, Egypt continues to receive strong donor support, including substantial US economic and military assistance, of which a good portion returns in orders for American products. Despite infrequent fundamentalist acts of terror, Egypt enjoys political stability and its economy has made great strides towards integration into the global market.

Country profile

The Arab Republic of Egypt is today as dependent on the river Nile as it was in the days of the Pharaohs. Agriculture centers around the valley of the Nile. Even though they speak Arabic, Egyptians are not Arabs but a mixture of peoples tracing their ancestry back to the Nubians, Berbers, Arab-Berber groups and Europeans. About 90% are Muslim and 6% Christian Copts, apart from Roman Catholic, Protestant and Jewish minorities.

History

Today Egypt has virtually the same borders as in the era of the Pharaohs. First conquered in 332 BC by Alexander the Great it passed on to Roman control in 31 BC. In 639 Muslims from Arabia conquered Egypt and transformed it into an Arabic-speaking Muslim country. Turkish rule, a brief French presence under Napoleon, and British caretaker rule led to a sovereign, independent state under King Fuad on 28 February, 1922. Violent protests against the continued British military presence at the Suez Canal in the 1950s led to a bloodless coup. Farouk was replaced by Col. Gamal Abdel Nasser who ruled until his death in 1970. He was succeeded by his deputy, Anwar Sadat, who signed the Camp David Peace Accords in 1979 and was assassinated two years later by members of the Islamic Jihad organization. Sadat was succeeded by his deputy, General Hosni Mubarak.

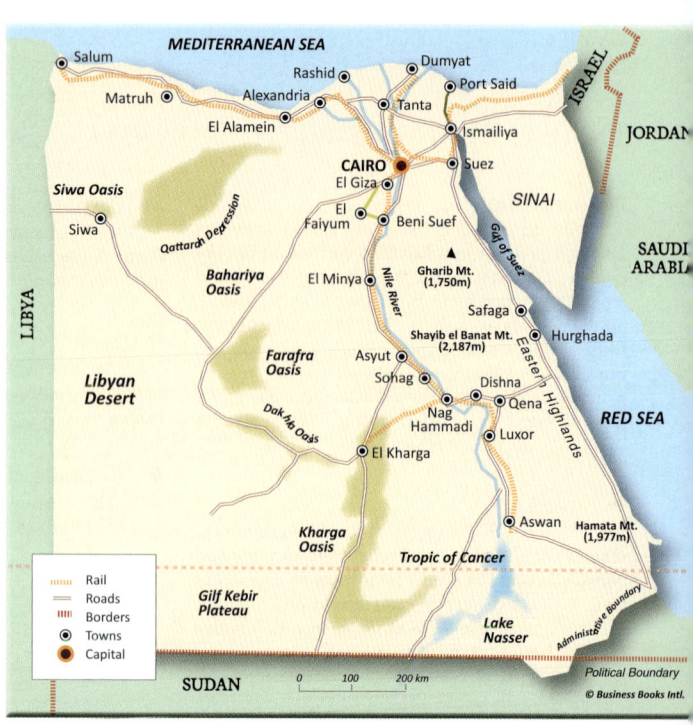

Government

Until 2005 the president was appointed by a two-thirds majority of the People's Assembly (*Majlis al-Sha'ab*) and confirmed by referendum. Under a new rule adopted by referendum President Hosni Mubarak was elected for the first time by popular vote to a fifth six year term in September 2005. In the bicameral parliament all but ten nominated members of the 454-seat People's Assembly are directly elected for a five-year term while the *Mailis al-Shura* or Advisory Council consists of 176 elected members and 88 apointed by the president. The *Hizb al Dimuqratiyah al Wataniyah* (HDW) (National Democratic Party—NDP) has dominated the Assembly since its establishment in 1978. It won 420 seats in the November 2010 election against a splintered opposition including the *New Wafd Party* (NWP), the Progessive National Union Party and a few others.

Economic policy

Egypt maintains a market economy with the state sector accounting for 30 percent of GDP and the private sector 70 percent. Continued decentralization has stimulated growth. Legislation has been passed to increase private sector activity and allow greater foreign participation. Privatization in key areas such as insurance, banking, and telecommunications is underway. A reduction in 2005 of personal and corporate tax rates, reduction of energy subsidies and further privatization measures by the government has led to a boom on the stock market and impressive GDP growth.

Privatization

Since January 1996 serious steps have been taken toward selling off state-owned enterprises. The basis has been laid for expanded participation by the private sector and foreign investors in the banking and insurance sectors. Private investment in key infrastructure areas has increased significantly. All future power generation projects will be constructed on a build-own-operate-transfer (BOOT) basis. The government has sold cellular phone concessions and has opened airports, ports, and port services to private investors.

Sectors

Tourism and the Suez Canal account for one third of GDP and total earnings from goods and services. The oil and gas sector accounts for

Pres. Hosni Mubarak
Born: May 4, 1929
Since October 1981

UN Photo

POLITICAL	
Head of State	Pres. Hosni Mubarak
Prime Minister	Ahmed Nazif
Ruling Party	HDW or NDP
Main Opposition	NWP
Independence	1922
National capital	Cairo
Official language	Arabic

PHYSICAL	
Total area	386,000 sq. miles 1,001,000 sq. km. (3 x New Mexico)
Arable land	3%
Coastline	1,522 miles/2,450 km

POPULATION	
Total	78.8 million
Av. yearly growth	2.0%
Urban population	43%
Life expectancy	72 years
Adult literacy	71.4%

ECONOMY	
Currency	Pound (£E) (US$1=5.79)
GDP (real)	$166 billion
GDP growth rate	4.7%
GDP per capita[1]	$4,576
GDP (ppp)[2]	$471 billion
GDP per cap. (ppp)	$5,681
Inflation rate	16.2%
Exports	$24.3 billion
Imports	$47.6 billion
External debt	$33.8 billion
Unemployment	9.4%

1. Atlas method.
2. See page 175 for an explanation of purchasing power parity (ppp).

about 7% of Egypt's GDP and 34% of its exports. Agriculture's share of GDP has declined but it still accounts for one third of the work force.

Trading

Egypt is one of the world's largest food importers. It is also a significant importer of oil and gas field machinery, military equipment, automotive parts, construction and medical equipment, telecommunications equipment, packaging and paper material and, more recently, environmental equipment and materials. Egypt is the single largest overseas market for American wheat and a significant importer of other agricultural commodities, machinery, and equipment. Crude oil and petroleum products, cotton, textiles, metal products, and chemicals are important merchandise exports and tourism is a major foreign exchange earner.

Investment

The US is the second largest investor in Egypt, after the United Kingdom. Roughly two-thirds of total US investment is in the oil and gas sector, but it also includes iareas such as consumer goods, automobile production, and financial services. Other major investord include France, Italy, and several Arab countries. Given its strategic position in the region, Egypt continues to benefit from strong donor support. The US Government has worked closely with Egypt on its economic reform program, and is its largest bilateral aid donor. Privatization and new customs reforms should further encourage investment.

Financial sector

Banks are supervised by the central bank of Egypt. There are 61 banks in Egypt, 22 of them joint ventures with foreign participation. Egypt does not limit foreign equity participation in local banks and several foreign banks have majority shares in Egyptian banks, while other foreign banks are registered as branches of the parent bank (rather than subsidiaries). The Cairo and Alexandria Stock Exchange (CASE) is one of Africa's major stock markets. European and U.S. mutual funds now include Egyptian stocks, and 52 local issues are included in the International Finance Corporation's general index. Companies listed on the CASE are required to apply international accounting and disclosure standards.

Taxes and tariffs

Since the early nineties, under an economic reform program developed in conjunction with the IMF and the World Bank, Egypt has reduced its tariff rates. The 2003 establishment of the Model Customs and Tax Center (MCTC) helped modernize customs and tax administration in Egypt. The Cairo-based MCTC is a "one-stop shop" where taxpayers registered in Greater Cairo can settle income taxes, sales taxes and customs for goods passing through any of Egypt's ports. The corporate tax rate for non-residents is 20 percent and capital gains tax 20 percent. There are no value added taxes (VAT) or exchange controls in effect. Taxes are levied on royalties (20%). (See page 138).

US relations

An annual aid program administered by USAID since 1975 promotes infrastructure development and privatization. The US finances most of Egypt's big-ticket defense procurements at an average yearly rate of $1.3 billion. Egypt and the US signed a Trade and Investment Framework Agreement (TIFA).

BUSINESS ACTIVITY

AGRICULTURE
Cotton, rice, corn, wheat, beans, fruit, vegetables, cattle, water buffalo, sheep, goats, fish.

INDUSTRIES
Textiles, food processing, tourism, chemicals, petroleum, construction, cement, metals.

NATURAL RESOURCES
Petroleum, natural gas, iron ore, phosphates, manganese, limestone, gypsum, talc, asbestos, lead, zinc.

EXPORTS
$24.3 billion (est. 2009): crude oil and petroleum products, cotton yarn, raw cotton, textiles, metal products, chemicals.

IMPORTS
$47.6 billion (est. 2009): machinery and equipment, food, fertilizers, wood products, durable consumer goods, capital goods,

MAJOR TRADING PARTNERS
US, Italy, UK, China, France, Germany, Spain, Saudi Arabia, Syria, UK.

Doing Business with Egypt

▶ **Investment**

As a result of the government's privatization program, the private sector's role has steadily expanded in key sectors such as metals (aluminum, iron, and steel), petrochemicals, cement, automobiles, textiles, consumer electronics, and pharmaceuticals. The government has made development of high technology a priority and seeks to attract export-oriented manufacturing firms. Generous tax and other incentives are offered. Franchising of fast-food restaurants and clothing stores is a growing business in Egypt.

▶ **Trade**

The huge US favorable trade balance with Egypt is ample proof of the possibilities existing beyond the supply of military equipment funded largely by US government grants. Wheat and other agricultural products, medical equipment, computers, construction equipment and a whole range of consumer goods are imported. Foreign firms can sell directly within Egypt as long as they register, but most rely on domestic companies for wholesale and retail distribution.

▶ **Trade finance**

Apart from Eximbank facilities, USDA/FAS operates an Export Credit Guarantee Program for Egyptian private sector importers of US food and agricultural commodities. USAID/Egypt sponsors a Private Sector Commodity Import Program (CIP) that makes dollars available to Egyptian private sector importers through some 22 Egyptian banks.

▶ **Selling to the government**

Egyptian procurement is either done with national budgetary funds or by using aid funds from USAID or other donors. In the case of USAID-funded procurement, project announcements are made in the US "Commerce Business Daily," published in Chicago. US military aid finances most of Egypt's big-ticket defense procurements. Only registered commercial agents can work on tenders. Government employees are judged on their ability to squeeze the final penny from the lowest bidder— a practice commonly referred to in Arabic as "momarsa."

▶ **Exchange controls**

The Foreign Exchange Law of May 1994 allows individuals and legal entities to retain and transfer foreign exchange abroad and entitles banks to conduct foreign exchange transactions.

▶ **Partnerships**

In most sectors foreigners are allowed any measure of shareholding in a partnership, ranging from a few percentage points to close to 100 percent.

▶ **Establishing a presence**

There are several choices, depending on the nature and size of the intended business. Some companies, which intend to conduct market research in scientific, technical or consulting fields, might resort to representative offices funded entirely by remittances from abroad and not subject to Egyptian tax. Oil, construction, and consulting firms often rely on branch offices.

▶ **Project financing**

OPIC and US TDA support US investment. Egypt is currently included in the International Finance Corporation index for emerging markets and there has been an increase in corporate bonds issued by private sector companies.

▶ **Labor**

The abundance of labor has led to low prevailing wages and the use of labor-intensive technologies. Workers may join trade unions but are not required to do so.

▶ **Legal rights**

The government guarantees against nationalization. The US-Egypt Bilateral Investment Treaty also protects against expropriation and provides for nonbinding, third party arbitration in investment disputes. Even though Egypt is a signatory of several international IPR treaties, the US Trade Representative felt obliged to place Egypt on a priority watch list in April 1998—a designation retained through 1999. In the meantime, the US assisted Egyptian authorities in their efforts to increase intellectual property rights (IPR) protection, primarily through USAID programs.

▶ **Business climate**

Egyptians with whom foreigners do business are typically trilingual (English-French-Arabic), well-traveled individuals who pride themselves on seeking out good deals at decent prices. The Egyptian market is a complex and highly competitive one and an Egyptian agent is frequently essential. Be prepared to bargain. Negotiations are bound by an unspoken culture that assumes that there is not any final, best price that cannot be reduced.

EQUATORIAL GUINEA

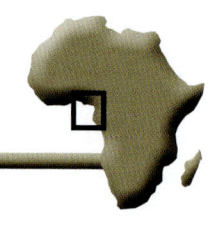

Once largely dependent on cocoa and coffee, Equatorial Guinea has had the world's fastest growing economy in recent years, largely as a result of offshore oil discoveries. Referred to by some as the "Kuwait of Africa" tropical Equatorial Guinea has become the third largest oil producing country in Sub-Saharan Africa. Forestry, farming, and fishing continue to be important components of GDP. The government has declared its intention to reinvest some oil revenue into agriculture to help subsistence farmers. Despite the windfall from oil improvement of living standards among the general population has been modest.

Country profile

The Republic of Equatorial Guinea covers an area roughly the size of Hawaii, consisting of widely scattered regions—Rio Muni or Mbini on the mainland (which constitutes 92% of the total land area), Bioko island (with 22% of the population and the capital of Malabo), tiny Annobon Island, some 650 km to the south, and the islets of Corsico and Elobey off the mainland estuary. Some 80% of nearly a half million Equato-Guineans live in Mbini—about 150 km wide and extending 200 km inland. Its equatorial climate supports extensive rainforests where mahogany and okoume are grown. Some 125 miles (200 km) from Mbini is Bioko (formerly known as Fernando Po Island), which forms part of a submerged volcanic mountain range with exposed points as far as Annobon Island to the south and Mt. Cameroon to the north. The Bantu-speaking Fang is the largest group in Mbini while the original inhabitants of Bioko Island are the Bubi and the Fernandino—the latter descendants of former slaves whose Krio language has become the lingua franca. Annobon is inhabited by a fishing community of mixed origin. Both French and Spanish are official languages. Most people in the mainland region profess ethnic faiths, but Bioko Island is overwhelmingly Roman Catholic.

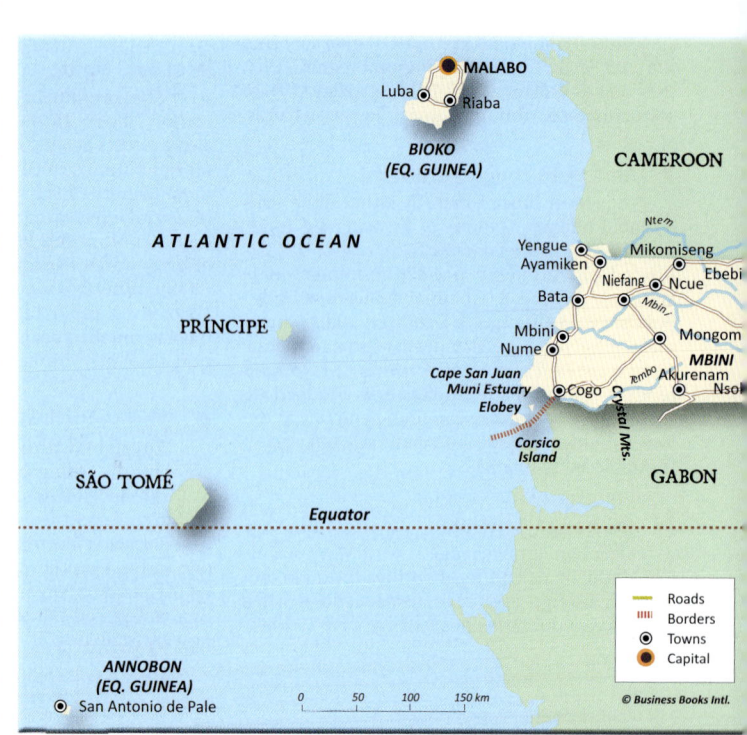

238

History

In the 1470s the Portuguese reached Fernando Po (later renamed Bioko) and three other tropical islands in the Gulf of Guinea. Bubi hostility and Bioko's hot, humid climate prompted the Portuguese to concentrate on the deserted islands of Sao Tome, Principe and tiny Annobon further south. In 1778 Portugal bartered Bioko and Annobon to Spain for territory in South America. Until 1858, when the Spanish finally took possession, the British leased Bioko as a naval base for anti-slavery operations. The British developed the port of Clarence, renamed Santa Isabel by the Spanish. Today its known as Malabo, the capital of Equatorial Guinea. Rescued slaves who chose to remain are today known as the Fernandinos. They spoke pidgin English that evolved into Krio. In the 1880s, Spain added a slither of territory on the mainland to its island possessions, named it Rio Muni (today's Mbini) and formed Spanish Guinea. In response to pressures from so-called emancipados, the colony was granted independence on 12 October 1968 under Pres. Macias Nguema who led a decade-long campaign of terror resulting in the death of 20,000 people. One-third of the total population of 300,000 sought asylum in neighboring countries. Cubans and North Koreans helped to keep Macias in power and the Soviet Union was allowed to exploit fish resources from a base on Bioko Island. In the process Macias drove one of Africa's most prosperous colonies into bankruptcy. On 3 August 1979, the chief of the army, Lt.-Col. Teodoro Obiang Nguema Mbasogo, replaced his uncle by force, took immediate steps to stabilize the country and cultivated relations with Western donor countries and organizations. He was elected president for a 7-year term in June 1989 and reelected in 1996, 2002 and 2009.

Government

The present Constitution, endorsed by referendum on 16 November 1991, provides for a multiparty system. The President, vested with executive powers, is elected by the voters for 7-year terms and appoints the Prime Minister who heads the government and appoints the Council of Ministers. The 100-member House of People's Representatives serves a 5 year term. In the May 2008 election Obiang's *Partido Democratieo de Guinea Ecuatorial* (PDGE)

Pres. Teodoro Obiang Nguema Mbasogo
Born: 1942
Since August 1979

UN Photo Paulo Filgueiras

POLITICAL

Head of State	Pres. Teodoro Obiang Nguema Mbasogo
Ruling Party	PDGE
Main Opposition	EC
Independence	12 October 1968
National capital	Malabo
Official languages	Spanish & French

PHYSICAL

Total area	11,000 sq. miles
	28,000 sq. km.
	(± Maryland)
Arable land	5%
Coastline	184 miles/296 km

POPULATION

Total	633,440
Av. yearly growth	2.7%
Urban population	39%
Life expectancy	61.6 years
Adult literacy	87%

ECONOMY

Currency	CFA franc (CFAF) (US$1=495.40)
GDP (real)	$15.5 billion
GDP growth rate	0.5%
GDP per capita[1]	$27,001
GDP (ppp)[2]	$21.1 billion
GDP per cap. (ppp)	$31,331
Inflation rate	5.5%
Exports	$8.8 billion
Imports	$3.3 billion
External debt	$120 million
Unemployment	30%

1. Atlas method.
2. See page 175 for an explanation of purchasing power parity (ppp).

won 89 seats. The Electoral Coalition (EC) won 10 and the *Convergencia para la Democracia Social* (Convergence for a Social Democracy) (CPDS) holds 1 seat. The constitution vests all authority in the presidency.

Economic policy

At independence in 1968, Equatorial Guinea's per capita income was one of the highest in Africa. It dropped to one of the lowest after a decade of mismanagement under the Macias regime. The new government liberalized the economy to some extent. Since the late nineties Equatorial Guinea has had the world's fastest growing economy, largely as a result of new oil discoveries. There are long-term incentives for job creation, training, promotion of non-traditional exports, support of development projects and indigenous capital participation, freedom to repatriate profits, exemption from certain taxes and capital and other benefits. Investors, especially in the fast growing oil sector, are given ample scope by a government keen to lure foreigners. Not much of this newfound wealth has trickled down to the general population. Government officials and their family members own most businesses.

Sectors

Limited oil production began in 1991 and since the discovery of major additional oil reserves off Bioko Island in 1995 Equatorial Guinea has been referred to by some as the "Kuwait of Africa." Other sectors with good potential include fishing, timber, tourism, and mining. There are modest deposits of iron ore, lead, zinc, manganese, uranium, tantalum and molybdenum. Prospects also exist in agriculture with cocoa, coffee, palm oil, bananas and coconuts as major crops. Deep water port facilities serve as outlets for neighboring countries. The small, isolated island of Annobon lies in a 314,000-square kilometer exclusive maritime economic zone amid some of the Atlantic's richest fishing grounds.

Privatization

A decision was taken to privatize the distribution of petroleum products in the country. Private investors have been co-opted to increase electrical capacity and parastatals and public enterprises have been earmarked for privatization in the agro-industry (cocoa), transport (airline, shipping and maritime transport), public utilities (electricity, water and telecommunications) and several other sectors.

Investment

The US is a major investor in oil and gas operations in Equatorial Guinea but Spain as the former colonial power maintains a sizeable portion of the holdings in the country. China has become a serious player in recent times.

Trade

Spain, France, Italy, Cameroon, Nigeria and the US are important suppliers of food, petroleum products, automobiles, machinery, and iron and steel. The US, China, Cameroon and Côte d'Ivoire are major buyers of oil and fuels and the Netherlands, Spain, Germany, France and Italy top the list of purchasers of cocoa, timber and coffee.

Financial sector

Interest rates are set by the regional central bank (BEAC), monitored and regulated by the French Government. There are two commercial banks regulated by the Banking Commission for Central African States (COBAC).

Taxes and tariffs

A flat tax of 6.25 % applies to all petroleum revenues. Generalized preferential tariffs apply to goods being shipped to other CEMAC countries.

BUSINESS ACTIVITY

AGRICULTURE
Coffee, cocoa, rice, yams, cassava (tapioca), bananas, palm oil nuts, manioc, livestock, timber.

INDUSTRIES
Petroleum, fishing, sawmilling, natural gas.

NATURAL RESOURCES
Timber, petroleum, small unexploited deposits of gold, manganese, uranium.

EXPORTS
$8.8 billion (est. 2009): petroleum, timber cocoa, methanol.

IMPORTS
$3.3 billion (est. 2009): petroleum, food, beverages, clothing, machinery.

MAJOR TRADING PARTNERS
China, US, Taiwan, Japan, Italy, Spain, UK, France, Portugal.

Doing Business with Equatorial Guinea

▶ **Investment**

The investment code allows repatriation of profits and offers tax and other incentives for job creation, training, the promotion of non-traditional exports, and the support of development projects. Investments in non-traditional products in rural areas are favored. Foreign investment is not subject to screening and foreign equity ownership is not restricted. The government is offering attractive terms to foreign entrepreneurs willing to explore and exploit the country's mineral wealth. Fisheries, salting, livestock feeds, cocoa paste, palm oil, transportation and communications, water purification and sanitation, and power and energy have been identified as priority areas for investment.

▶ **Trade**

Apart from oil production equipment, airplanes, watercraft, heavy road and logging equipment, construction materials, agricultural inputs such as fertilizers and equipment, foodstuffs, used clothing and shoes offer sales opportunities. Foreign firms are advised to obtain the services of agents with local knowledge. There are few franchise operations in Equatorial Guinea but international oil companies might soon be able to retail petroleum products, currently limited to Total, the government's partner.

▶ **Trade finance**

Importers and exporters use internationally accepted methods of settlement. Foreign firms sometimes grant credits of 180 days for consumer goods and 24 months for small machinery and equipment but an irrevocable, confirmed letter of credit is standard practice.

▶ **Selling to the government**

Programs financed jointly by international financial institutions and the Government are open to unrestricted competition. Privatization of specific industries might in future present opportunities in the transport sector (both the national airline and the national shipping corporation), and in public utilities (water, electricity and telecommunications).

▶ **Exchange controls**

Foreign exchange controls are enforced primarily for statistical purposes and to enable the Ministry of Finance to certify that remittances conform with established regulations. Authorizations for foreign transfers are routinely granted.

▶ **Partnerships**

Partnerships in certain areas are mandatory as local entrepreneurs have exclusive rights in the manufacture of arms, explosives and other weapons, the gathering, treatment and storing of toxic, dangerous and radioactive materials or waste products and the production of alcoholic beverages excluding beer.

▶ **Financing projects**

The World Bank's resident representative in Yaoundé, Cameroon, and its affiliate, the International Finance Corporation's regional offices in Douala also handles applications from Equatorial Guinea. The African Development Bank Group has been involved in the country and OPIC operates in the country. The International Development Association has on occasion provided loans for projects involving foreigners.

▶ **Labor**

Unemployment is difficult to quantify in a developing economy where so many of the citizens are toiling the land or underemployed in rural areas but the UN Development Program has estimated it to be as high as 88 %. A Spanish company (FTF-First Training and Finance) was contracted by the government to regulate labor supplies, initially for the petroleum industry, but subsequently for other sectors.

▶ **Legal rights**

Foreign and domestic investors are provided with guarantees that comply with international norms. Trademark enforcement is weak as Equatorial Guinea is not a member of the 14nation West African intellectual property organization, *Organisation Africaine de la Propriété Intellectuelle*. Equatorial Guinea does, however, accept binding international arbitration of investment disputes with foreign investors and is a member of the International Center for the Settlement of Investment Disputes. It is also a signatory to the Convention on the Recognition and Enforcement of Foreign Arbitral Awards.

▶ **Business Climate**

The business community closely follows Spanish customs and the language most often used is Spanish, with some French. Equato-Guineans insist on getting to know a potential partner before starting concrete discussions.

ERITREA

Eritrea, Africa's youngest country, gained its freedom from Ethiopia in 1991 after a 30-year war of liberation and achieved statehood after a referendum in 1993. It triumphed over tremendous odds in a struggle that reduced substantial parts of a once fairly prosperous country to ashes. Recovery was impeded by a border war with Ethiopia that erupted in 1998 and ended with a UN-sponsored peace agreement in December 2000. Eritrea has liberalized its economy and with the help of foreign investment made remarkable progress while a UN Peacekeeping force continues to monitor the temporary security zone on its border with Ethiopia.

Country profile

As an extension of Ethiopia's mountains, the Eritrean highlands form a steep escarpment, overlooking a narrow coastal plain. With an annual rainfall of 500-1,000 mm the escarpment is the most productive agricultural region. The Tekeze river forms part of the border with Ethiopia and drains into the Nile. The Danakil Depression (130 m below sea level) is one of the hottest places on earth. Nomadic livestock herders occupy the coastal plain. Eritrea's economic zone in the Red Sea includes more than 350 islands of various shapes and sizes, fringed by coral reefs, with a total land area of 515 sq. miles (1,335 sq km). Eritrea's people are of Ethio-Semitic, Cushitic and Nilotic origin. The main language is Tigrinya, spoken by the Tigray—the principal Ethio-Semitic group. Cushitic groups live on both sides of the border with Sudan in the northwest. The Afar (a.k.a. the Adal or Danakil) roam the southern coastal strip. English is the most widely spoken European language. The Tigray are predominantly Christian, belonging to the Eritrean Orthodox Church. There are sizeable minorities of other Christian denominations and Muslims.

History

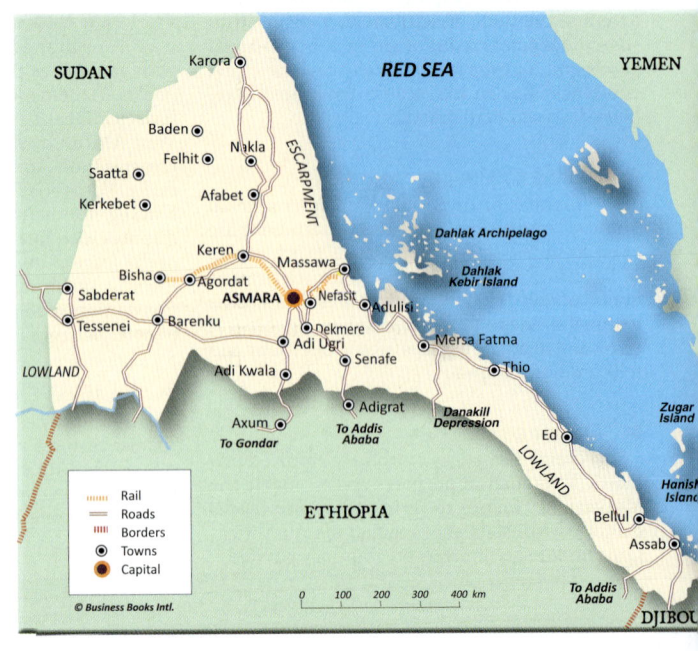

Eritrea used to be part of the ancient Ethiopian empire built around Axum (Aksum). During the 4th Century AD Ethiopia's emperors converted to Christianity and established the Ethiopian Orthodox Church throughout the realm. From about the 8th Century Axum went into decline. When Emperor Menelik II came to power at the turn of the 19th Century and founded a new capital, Addis Ababa (the new flower) to replace Asmara (the flower), the Tigray in the north revolted. In 1889, Menelik ceded to Italy the northern and northeastern fringes of his empire in the hope of satisfying Rome's territorial ambitions. The Italian colony of Eritrea—a name derived from Mare Erythraeum, the old Roman designation for the Red Sea—was adopted in 1890. After a humiliating defeat when they tried to expand their influence south into Ethiopia, the Italians concentrated on colonizing Eritrea. In 1936 Italy finally conquered Ethiopia and ruled over both colonies until 1941 when the Allied forces defeated Mussolini's troops and returned Ethiopian emperor Haile Selassie to the thrown. Selassie pressed for the re-incorporation of Eritrea into its "motherland." In 1952 the UN General Assembly decided Eritrea should become an autonomous state federated with Ethiopia. Barely ten years later, however, Emperor Haile Selassie abrogated the federation, dissolved Eritrea's national assembly and absorbed the country as Ethiopia's 14th province. Various liberation movements became active and eventually the Eritrean People's Liberation Front (EPLF) won Eritrea's independence in May 1993. The EPLF leader, Isaias Afwerki was appointed interim president. He is still in power. Since its independence, Eritrea and Ethiopia have disagreed about the exact demarcation of their borders and in May 1998 border clashes began. It erupted into a war that lasted until the beginning of 2000, resulting in the loss of tens of thousands of lives on both sides and depleted state coffers. A cease-fire was signed in June 2000 and a peace agreement concluded later in the year. The UN agreed to provide peace-keeping troops to patrol the buffer zone.

Government

The Constitution adopted in May 1997 provided for an executive President elected for a maximum of two 5-year terms by the National Assembly. The 104-member Assembly (*Hagerawi Baito*)consists of 60 appointed and 44 representing the members of the Central Committee of the People's Front for Democracy and Justice (PFDJ). The PFDJ, formerly known as the Eritrean People's Liberation Front (EPLF) has ruled the country since independence. Elections scheduled for December 2001 were postponed indefinitely.

Pres. Isaias Afwerki
Born: 1946
Since June 1993

UN Photo Eskinder Debebe

POLITICAL

Head of State	Pres. Isaias Afwerki
Ruling party	PFDJ
Independence	24 May 1993
National capital	Asmara
Working languages[4]	Tigriñya, Arabic and English

PHYSICAL

Total area	46,000 sq. miles 118,000 sq. km. (± Pennsyvania)
Arable land	4.95% of land area
Coastline	1388 miles/2,234 km (incl. islands)

POPULATION

Total	5.6 million[3]
Av. yearly growth	2.5%
Urban population	21%
Life expectancy	61.78 years
Adult literacy	58.6%

ECONOMY

Currency	Nafka (US$1=15.00)
GDP (real)	$1.5 billion
GDP growth rate	3.6%
GDP per capita[1]	$295
GDP (ppp)[2]	$3.8 billion
GDP per cap. (ppp)	$752
Inflation rate	34.7%
Exports	$17 million
Imports	$627 million
External debt	$876 million
Unemployment	NA

1. Atlas method.
2. See page 175 for an explanation of purchasing power parity (ppp).
3. Not including 0.5 million refugees awaiting repatriation.
4. No official language.

Economic policy

In coordination with the World Bank and the IMF Eritrea developed a liberal macroeconomic policy with an investment code that offers significant incentives to foreign investors. The border dispute with Ethiopia has substantially impacted the Eritrean economy.

Sectors

Like the economies of many other African nations Eritrea's is largely dependent on subsistence agriculture. Around 60% of the population is engaged in or relies on crop cultivation and livestock raising. Agriculture and fishing account for about half the national product (GDP) and two-thirds of exports. Main crops are teff, millet, wheat, sesame, sorghum, barley, vegetables, pulses, cotton, fruit and coffee. Fishing waters offer sardine, anchovy, shrimp and lobster in abundance. Eritrea has deposits of salt and other minerals such as basalt, limestone, marble, granite, sands, silicates, gold, silver, copper, nickel, zinc, chrome, sulphur and potash. Prospecting is underway for oil and gas. Eritrea's substantial mineral deposits are largely unexplored as a consequence of the war with Ethiopia. Eritrea is estimated to have some 14,000 kilograms of gold reserves. Western observers also have noted Eritrea's excellent potential for quarrying ornamental marble and granite. Some 10 mining companies (including Canadian and South African firms) had obtained licenses to prospect for different minerals. The presence of hundreds of thousands of land mines in Eritrea, particularly along the border with Ethiopia, presents a serious impediment to future development of the mining sector. Major products include processed food and dairy products, alcoholic beverages, glass, leather goods, marble, textiles, and salt.

Privatization

A dozen public enterprises have been privatized so far—including a dairy factory, a brewery, and a corrugated iron sheet factory—some in the form of public-private partnerships and others through outright sale to foreign or local investors.

Investment

No precise country breakdown of foreign direct investment statistics is available. Apart from the United States other major investors include South Korea, Italy, and China.

Trade

Multilateral lenders who have been impressed with the government's fiscal discipline, despite the recently concluded border war, readily provided financing for imports needed for reconstruction and development. Principal sources for imports consisting largely of machinery, petroleum products, food and manufactured goods are Malaysia, Italy, Egypt India, Japan and Germany. Principal buyers, mostly of unfinished raw materials, textiles and livestock include Ireland, US, Italy and Turkey.

Financial sector

A housing and commerce bank, an agriculture and industry development bank and the commercial bank of Eritrea operate alongside the central bank of Eritrea. The central bank of Eritrea, though a government entity, operates independently from the ministry of finance. Foreign banks are allowed in the country.

Taxes and tariffs

The corporate tax rate for non-residents is 10 percent and capital gains tax 10 percent. A sales tax of 5 to 12 percent applies and exchange control is in effect. Taxes are levied on interest (10%) and royalties (10%). (See page 138).

BUSINESS ACTIVITY

AGRICULTURE
Sorghums, lentils, vegetables, maize, cotton, tobacco, coffee, sisal, livestock, fish.

INDUSTRIES
Food processing, beverages, clothing and textiles.

NATURAL RESOURCES
Gold, potash, zinc, copper, salt, potential of oil and natural gas, fish.

EXPORTS
$17 million (est. 2009): livestock, sorghum, textiles, food, small manufactures.

IMPORTS
$627 million (est. 2009): processed goods, machinery, petroleum products.,

MAJOR TRADING PARTNERS
China, Italy, US, France, Netherlands, Ethiopia, Turkey, Taiwan, Germany, Taiwan.

Doing Business with Eritrea

▶ **Investment**

Investment policy gives domestic and foreign investors equal access to land, utilities, and other production units in all sectors of the economy except domestic retail and wholesale trade and import agencies. A variety of tax and export incentives are extended to investors, especially those involved in relatively depressed areas. Foreign firms are encouraged to participate in the privatization process where, in some cases, the government has favored partnership agreements over outright sales. Among the target areas for foreign investment are fishing, offshore oil and gas exploration, mining, tourism, the development of alternative energy sources such as thermal, wind, and solar, as well as construction enterprises to repair roads, bridges, airports, and railways, rehabilitate port facilities, improve water and sewage networks, and build houses and office and industrial sites.

▶ **Trade**

Energy, mining, agribusiness, construction, telecommunications, transportation, tourism, heavy equipment, light industry, and marine resources offer significant opportunities for trade. There is a constant shortage of heavy construction equipment and a demand for agricultural and mining equipment. Suppliers of used equipment may find a ready market in a country with the reputation of being able to keep anything running. (During their war for independence the Eritreans thrived on Soviet style vehicles captured from their Ethiopian opponents]. There is an expanding English speaking middle class with an appetite for Western consumer products.

▶ **Trade finance**

Nearly all import financing is done on a letter of credit basis. There are two banks in Eritrea authorized to issue LCs—the commercial bank of Eritrea and the housing and commerce bank.

▶ **Selling to the government**

Many government purchases are associated with donor financed projects and are subject to bidding and procurement rules of the donors. There is no central procurement office and each ministry handles its own needs. The tenders are open to public bidding and advertised in the local papers. Major governmental infrastructure projects, including road, airport, harbor and hospital construction, create an ongoing need for foreign equipment, expertise and materials.

▶ **Exchange controls**

The national bank of Eritrea has adopted a free-floating exchange rate. Foreign investors are allowed to remit profits and dividends, principal and interest on foreign loans, and fees related to technology transfer as well as the proceeds from the sale of liquidation of assets.

▶ **Partnerships**

The government encourages joint ventures with foreign firms, especially in mining and the privatization of state-owned businesses. Franchising is a relatively new concept but former expatriate Eritreans tend to be good candidates as licensing partners.

▶ **Establishing a presence**

A business licensing office has been established as a one-stop shop to short-circuit procedures. Private entities, both domestic and foreign, have the right to establish, acquire, own, and dispose of most forms of business enterprise but companies affiliated with the ruling party, the People's Front for Democracy and Justice (PFDJ) enjoy certain advantages over other firms.

▶ **Financing projects**

The Overseas Private Investment Corporation offers risk insurance and loans to US investors. Eritrea is a member of the Multilateral Investment Guarantee Agency.

▶ **Labor**

Eritrea has an inexpensive but industrious and disciplined workforce but skilled manpower in certain fields is hard to obtain. All workers in public and private enterprise are members of the national confederation of Eritrean workers.

▶ **Legal rights**

Foreign investors may choose to submit disputes to local settlement under the laws of Eritrea, in terms of The Hague convention or by presenting its case to the Eritrea investment center. Eritrea also abides by the International Convention on the Settlement of Investment Disputes. There are currently no formal mechanism to protect intellectual property rights, patents, and copyrights.

▶ **Business climate**

Business customs are Western and English. Italian and Arabic are widely spoken. Everyone in the business community seems to know each other and considerable value is placed on character.

ETHIOPIA

The land of kings and legends, Ethiopia is the oldest independent country in Africa and the original home of coffee. It has been under colonial rule only for a brief period during Italian occupation from 1936 until 1941. Political and economic reforms and the conclusion of a costly war against Eritrea should enable it to make economic progress. Ethiopia not only holds the promise of becoming a significant exporter once it has fully utilized its resources but as Africa's third most populous country—after Nigeria and Egypt—could develop into a major market for foreign products as per capita incomes rise. The new government has introduced economic reforms to lure foreign investors.

Country profile

More than half of the Federal Democratic Republic of Ethiopia is at high altitudes. Its highest point, Ras Dashen (4,620 m) is Africa's fourth highest mountain. The national capital, Addis Ababa, is 2,450 m above sea level. The mountainous region is bisected by the Great Rift Valley. South of Addis Ababa a chain of freshwater and salt lakes extends along the valley floor to Lake Turkana at the country's southwestern corner. Numerous large rivers, including the Blue Nile, flow from east to west towards the Nile Basin. The highest rainfall (over 1,000 mm) occurs in the west and southwest. Ethiopian society is a mixture of Caucasoid and Negroid peoples. The three principal groups are the Ethiopian Semites, the Cushites and the Omotic cluster of peoples and tongues, with two subgroups, the Amhara and the Oromo, accounting for 70% of the total population. A much smaller group, the Tigray, speaking Tigrinya, inhabits the far northern highlands and extends across the border into Eritrea. Half the population are Orthodox Christians, 35% are Muslims and the remainder adhere to ethnic beliefs.

History

Early mixing between the Cushitic, Omotic and Nilotic Negroid peoples produced a racially mixed population in ancient Ethiopia. From about 800 BC there was an influx of Semitic peoples from Saba (now Yemen) across the Red Sea into the highlands of present-day Eritrea and northern Ethiopia. The name Ethiopia (a Greek name meaning "land of dark people") began to apply to the empire centered around the city of Axum. In 333 AD Ethiopian Emperor Ezana was converted to Christianity and, by the

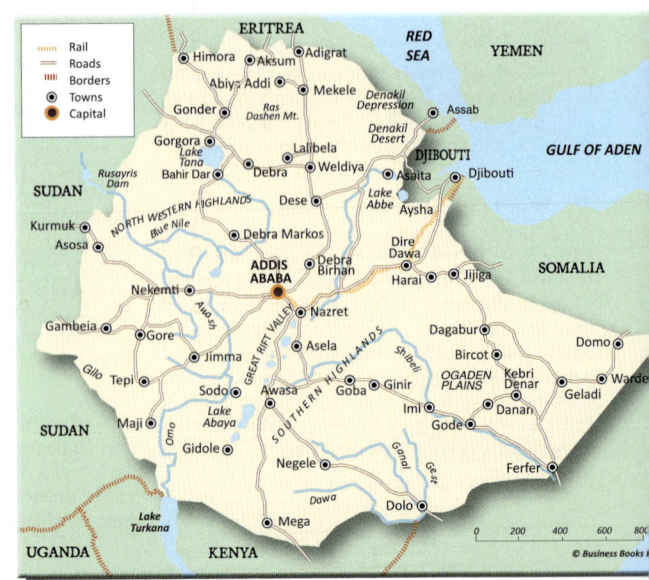

14th and 15th centuries when this territory was surrounded by Muslim regions, tales were told in Europe about the mysterious Christian kingdom of Prester John. Emperor Menelik II came to power at the turn of the nineteenth century and founded a new capital, Addis Ababa, to replace Asmara. Shortly after his ascension to the throne in 1889, Emperor Menelik ceded to Italy the northern and northeastern fringes of his empire to placate Rome but the Italians still tried to incorporate Ethiopia, suffering a humiliating defeat. In 1936 Italy extended its rule over Ethiopia as well and in 1941, with Mussolini's defeat by the Allied forces. Emperor Haile Selassie was restored to the throne. At his insistence that Eritrea be rejoined to the "motherland" the UN General Assembly made it an autonomous state within an Ethiopian federation. In 1962 Selassie abrogated the federation and absorbed the country as Ethiopia's 14th province. Setbacks in the ensuing war with Eritrea and internal dissension led to the imprisonment and alleged strangling in jail of Haile Selassie in 1974. His successor, Major Mengistu Haile Mariam, introduced a Soviet-style regime—known as the Dergue—killing some 100,000 opponents. In 1991 the brutal 14-year dictatorship ended when the Tigray-led Ethiopian *People's Revolutionary Democratic Front* (EPRDF) marched into Addis Ababa. Mengistu fled, making way for Meles Zenawi who became executive prime minister in the first multiparty elections in 1995 and relected in 2000, 2005 and 2010. Girma Wolde-Giyorgis was re-elected president in 2007.

Government

The 1994 constitution provides for a bicameral parliament consisting of a 117-member upper chamber (Council of the Federation) and 527-member lower chamber (Council of People's Representatives). A President is elected by both houses for a 6-year term but power rests with the Prime Minister, chosen by the majority party in the Council of People's Representatives. In the May 2010 election Zenawi's ruling Ethiopian People's Revolutionary Democratic Front (EPRDF) won 499 seats against 24 for its main contestant, the Somali Peoples Democratic Party (SPDP). The rest of the seats were split between six parties and one independent member.

*Prime Minister
Meles Zenawi
Born: May 9, 1955
Since August 1995*

UN Photo Evan Schneider

POLITICAL

Head of State	Pres. Girma Wolde-Giyorgis
Prime Minister	Meles Zenawi
Ruling Party	EPRDF
Main opposition	CUD, UEDF
Independence	2,000 years
National capital	Addis Ababa
Official language	Amharic

PHYSICAL

Total area	426,000 sq. miles
	1,104,000 sq. km.
	(2 x Texas)
Arable land	11% of land area
Coastline	Landlocked

POPULATION

Total	85.2 million
Av. yearly growth	3.2%
Urban population	17%
Life expectancy	55.4 years
Adult literacy	42.7%

ECONOMY

Currency	Birr (BR)
	(US$1=16.50)
GDP (real)	$25.2 billion
GDP growth rate	9.9%
GDP per capita[1]	$597
GDP (ppp)[2]	$72.2 billion
GDP per cap. (ppp)	$872
Inflation rate	36.4%
Exports	$1.7 billion
Imports	$7.0 billion
External debt	$2.9 billion
Unemployment	NA

1. Atlas method.
2. See page 175 for an explanation of purchasing power parity (ppp).

Economic policy

Since its return to civilian rule in 1991, Ethiopia has established new relationships with international financial institutions and secured funding from the World Bank to implement structural adjustment programs with the International Monetary Fund (IMF). It received $3.6 billion in support from the international donor institutions for the period from mid-2002 to mid-2005. Under these programs, Ethiopia has made substantial progress in shifting expenditures from defense to social and economic sectors and in reforming its banking system.

Sectors

Agriculture accounts for more than half of GDP, more than 60% of foreign earnings and over 80% of total employment. Coffee exports, averaging more than $150 million a year, are crucial to the economy. Cotton and sugar are other major cash crops and food crops include cereals, particularly teff, maize, and sorghum. Ethiopia's cattle population of around 30 million head is by far the largest in Africa, yet commercial slaughtering (2.3 million head annually) is lower than that of South Africa. Mineral resources include appreciable reserves of natural gas (in the eastern region), gold, copper, zinc, potash and iron ore. Manufacturing is largely in processed foods, consumer goods and textiles for the home market, and hides for export, handicrafts and leather. Tourism is a growth industry in this country with its cultural diversity, mountains, lakes, rivers, ancient cities.

Privatization

Since the nineties when the government started selling state-owned enterprises, 180 entities have been privatized, including the Pepsi Cola and Coca-Cola bottling plants. In the agricultural sector most marketing boards have been abolished, enabling farmers to sell their crops to the highest bidder. Coffee marketing has been opened to competition.

Investment

The Ethiopian Investment Authority encourages foreign investment projects. Major foreign investors include Saudi Arabia, South Korea, Kuwait, the US, Italy and China. In 2003 the Ethiopian government promulgated new regulations to stimulate foreign investment, including lowering of the required investment minimum by foreign firms from $500,000 to $100,000. Some sectors, such as banking, remain wholly or partially off-limits to foreigners.

Trade

Primary exports are coffee, hides and skins, sesame seeds, pulses, chat, live animals, honey and beeswax, and fruits and vegetables. Coffee (arabica) is by far the most important export commodity, constituting about two-thirds of exports by value. Main imports are semi-finished goods, crude petroleum and petroleum products, transport and industrial capital goods, medical and pharmaceutical products, motor vehicles, civil and military aircraft, raw materials, and agricultural machinery.

Financial sector

There are six private banks and seven private insurance companies. The National Bank of Ethiopia (NBE) regulates credit and exchange. Foreign banking is not permitted but most commercial banks have correspondent relations.

Taxes and tariffs

The corporate tax rate for non-residents is 30 percent and capital gains tax 15 to 30 percent. A value added tax (VAT) of 15 percent applies and exchange control is in effect. Taxes are levied on dividends (10%), interest (5%) and royalties (5%). (See page 138).

BUSINESS ACTIVITY

AGRICULTURE
Cereals, pulses, coffee, oilseed, sugar cane, potatoes, hides, cattle, sheep, goats.

INDUSTRIES
Food processing, beverages, textiles, chemicals, metals processing, cement.

NATURAL RESOURCES
Small reserves of gold, platinum, copper, potash, natural gas.

EXPORTS
$1.7 billion (est. 2009): coffee, leather products, gold, oilseed, live animals.

IMPORTS
$7.0 billion (est. 2009): food and live animals, petroleum and petroleum products, chemicals, machinery, motor vehicles and aircraft.

MAJOR TRADING PARTNERS
China, Italy, Djibouti, Saudi Arabia, US, Germany, Netherlands, India.

Doing Business with Ethiopia

▶ Investment
Investors in relatively underdeveloped regions of Ethiopia are eligible for exemption from income tax for up to five years. With the lowest telephone line density in Africa and plans to award a series of contracts to expand services, telecommunications offers good potential. Foreign firms are excluded from the domestic banking, insurance services, high volume air transport or freight services, forwarding and shipping agency services, rail transport services, and non-courier postal services. Foreigners are welcomed to participate in privatization but in some instances the government promotes joint ventures with Ethiopian private concerns rather than outright sales.

▶ Trade
The country's main imports include motor vehicles, petroleum products, civil and military aircraft, spare parts, construction equipment, medical and pharmaceutical products, agricultural and industrial chemicals, agricultural machinery, fertilizers, irrigation equipment, and food grains. The government requires that all imports be channeled through Ethiopian nationals registered with the government as official import or distribution agents. Ethiopia maintains restrictions and taxes on the export of coffee and chat and regulates the sale of petroleum products.

▶ Trade finance
The Ethiopian government relies on grants and external borrowing on highly concessionary terms to finance the external current account deficit.

▶ Selling to the government
Road building, telecommunications development and other infrastructural projects are open for international competitive bidding and are funded by either the Ethiopian government or major international financial institutions such as the International Development Association of the World Bank and the African Development Fund.

▶ Exchange controls
All foreign exchange transactions must be carried out through authorized dealers under the control of the National Bank. Foreign investors may freely remit profits and dividends, principal and interest on foreign loans, fees related to technology transfer, proceeds from liquidation of assets or transfer of shares, and funds required for debt service or other international payments.

▶ Partnerships
Foreign investors are encouraged to go into joint ventures especially where there is the prospect of technology transfer, improvement of the country's foreign exchange position, utilization and development of natural and human resources and added value in various economic sectors.

▶ Establishing a presence
Both foreign and domestic private entities have the right to establish, acquire, own, and dispose of most forms of business enterprises. State-owned enterprises have, however, considerable *de facto* advantages over private firms when it comes to cutting red tape, access to credit and swift customs clearance.

▶ Financing projects
The Overseas Private Investment Corporation offers risk insurance and loans to US investors. Ethiopia is also a member of the Multilateral Investment Guarantee Agency. Capital is sometimes available from the International Development Association of the World Bank or the African Development Bank for roads, energy, health and education projects. The International Finance Corporation also offers some equity financing.

▶ Labor
Labor is readily available and inexpensive, but skilled manpower is scarce. About 300,000 workers are members of unions and approximately 40% of the urban workforce is unemployed.

▶ Legal rights
There has been no expropriation since the transitional government replaced the Mengistu rule. Disputes arising out of foreign investment may be submitted to a competent Ethiopian court or to international arbitration. There are no regulations for the registration of patents and copyrights. Some protection can be secured through registration of trademarks at the Ministry of Trade and Industry and the publication of cautionary notices in local newspapers.

▶ Business climate
While Amharic is spoken throughout the country and Oromiffa and Tigrinya also widely used, English is the second official language and understood in most business circles. Ethiopians are universally addressed by first name even in formal situations.

GABON

Gabon is one of Sub-Saharan Africa's wealthiest countries and a major supplier of oil to the United States. It is also a significant exporter of manganese and timber. Gabon is seen as having the potential of becoming a regional hub for services to other countries in the region. There is an active recruitment of foreign investors and privatization has opened up opportunities in transport, telecommunications and manufacturing. The discovery of a range of strategic minerals has stimulated interest in this sector, as well.

Country profile

The Republic of Gabon is a small equatorial country of rivers, estuaries and lagoons. Most of Gabon lies in the basin of the Ogoue river and its main tributary, the N'Gounie. The Ogoue is navigable from its delta to Booue, some 300 km upstream. The interior plateau rises to 1,300 m at the southern Chaillu Mountains on the Congo border and the northern Crystal Mountains reaching into Equatorial Guinea. Equatorial forest covers three quarters of the land surface. The climate is hot and humid. The majority of the Bantu-speaking peoples are Fang and there are sizeable minorities of Mbeti, Tsogo, Njabi, Shira, Teke, Omyene, Mpongwe Punu. One-tenth of the population are expatriates from neighboring countries and France. The majority is Christian, due in part to the efforts of the famous Dr. Albert Schweitzer who spent most of his adult life in his missionary leper hospital at Lambarene on the Ogoue River. French is the official language.

History

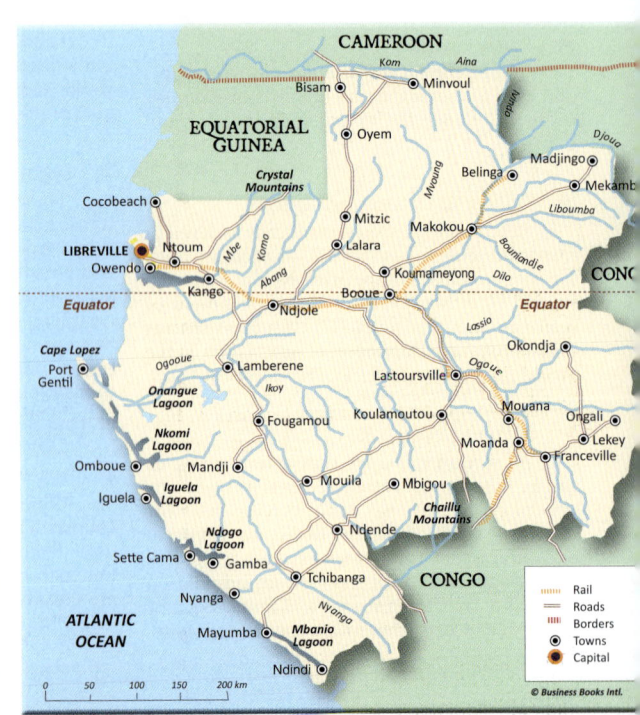

The earliest inhabitants of the Gabonese jungles were small bands of Pygmies or Babinga. Some 600 years ago Bantu-speaking peoples from the north started settling the coastal areas. They moved to the interior during the 16th Century. The Portuguese established contact in 1472 and were followed by Dutch, British and French who traded in slaves, ivory and precious tropical woods with the coastal kingdoms. The French established a fortified settlement on the Gabon estuary which evolved into Libreville, a community for liberated slaves. At the urging of explorer Count Pierre Savorgnan de Brazza, the areas known as Gabon and the Middle Congo were occupied by France in 1886. In 1910 part of Gabon was incorporated into French Equatorial Africa but a year later the northern parts of Gabon and Congo Brazzaville were ceded by treaty to German Cameroon. They were returned to the French after World War I and in 1960 a unified Gabon became an independent republic. When its first president, Leon M'Ba, died in 1967 Vice-President Albert Bernard Bongo took over and continued his pre-decessor's one-man rule until 1992 when he was obliged to call general elections in response to strong internal student and worker pressures. (After his conversion to Islam in 1973, Bongo changed his given names, Albert Bernard to El Hadji Omar). Pres. Bongo died in June 2009 after serving 32 years and was succeeded by his son Ali Bongo Ondimba after winning in an election held in August.

Government

An executive President is directly elected by the voters for 7-year terms without term limits. He appoints the Prime Minister and the Council of Ministers. The bicameral legislature consists of a 102-member Senate (*Sénat*), elected for six years, and a 120-member National Assembly or *Assemblée Nationale*, elected for a 5-year term. In 2009 President Omar Bongo's *Parti démocratique gabonais* (PDG) won 75 seats in the Senate with several minor parties splitting the rest. In the December 2006 National Assembly election the PDG also gained an unassailable majority of 82 seats with seven other parties and several independents splitting the rest.

Economic policy

Recent reforms in coordination with the World Bank aim to build a stronger and more diversified economy and reduce debt through privatization and diversification. The government has stepped up its efforts to attract foreign skills and technology to assist in the effort. Gabon enjoys a per capita income four times that of most of Sub-Saharan African nations. but due to high income inequality, a large portion of the population remains poor.

Sectors

The economy is dominated by the oil sector, which accounts for about half of GDP and government revenue, sixty percent of gross

Pres. Ali Ben
Bongo Ondimba
Born: Feb. 9, 1959
Since August 2009

POLITICAL

Head of State	Pres. Ali Bongo Ondimba
Ruling Party	PDG
Independence	17 August 1960
National capital	Libreville
Official language	French

PHYSICAL

Total area	103,000 sq. miles
	268,000 sq. km.
	(± Colorado)
Arable land	1.26% of land area
Coastline	550 miles/885 km

POPULATION

Total	1.5 million
Av. yearly growth	1.9%
Urban population	85%
Life expectancy	53 years
Adult literacy	63.2%

ECONOMY

Currency	CFA franc (CFAF) (US$1: 495.40)
GDP (real)	$16.5 billion
GDP growth rate	-1.0%
GDP per capita[1]	$13,821
GDP (ppp)[2]	$21.9 billion
GDP per cap. (ppp)	$14,886
Inflation rate	2.5%
Exports	$5.9 billion
Imports	$2.3 billion
External debt	$2.1 billion
Unemployment	21%

1. Atlas method.
2. See page 175 for an explanation of purchasing power parity (ppp).

investment, and over three quarters of merchandise exports. Offshore and onshore wells make Gabon Africa's third largest oil producer. After oil, timber and manganese are major foreign currency earners. The government is encouraging investors to develop value added operations in the timber industry. Okoume, a soft mahogany, represents 75% of wood production. The remainder consists of a large variety of exotic hardwoods. Gabon is Africa's second largest producer of manganese after South Africa and the fourth largest uranium source (after Niger, South Africa and Namibia). High-grade iron ore is still largely unexploited and there is scope for small-scale gold mining. Agriculture, livestock and fishing make up a little less than 8% of GDP. The principal food crops are cassava, maize, manioc, fruit and vegetables. Palm oil, cocoa, coffee, sugar cane, cotton and rubber are cultivated for export. Industry, including energy and construction, accounts for only 10% of GDP and consists of the SOGARA oil refinery in Port Gentil, a cement plant, paint factory and the processing of sugar, flour, beer, cigarettes and bread. The telecommunications system is one of the most advanced in Africa.

Privatization

Privatization is underway in various sectors. Targets include the Trans-Gabonese railway (OCTRA), the state electricity and water monopoly (SEEG), and the telecommunications monopoly, Office des Postes et Télécommunications du Gabon (OPT). Experienced international consultants have been engaged to help evaluate needs and to manage tenders.

Investment

French firms maintain an edge over competitors from other countries. US firms are most active in the petroleum sector but in recent years some have started focusing on fisheries, port development, transport, and light industry. Spain, Germany, Italy, and Britain are also significant players.

Trade

Until oil was discovered, tropical timber was the main export item. Today timer products account for only 10% of exports compared with petroleum's 80% share and around 10% for uranium and manganese. The US buys about two-thirds of Gabon's oil (averaging $1.5 billion per year), as well as minerals and timber. US sales to Gabon consist largely of petroleum-related machinery and other heavy equipment.

Financial sector

French banks dominate in a relatively sophisticated system offering full corporate banking services. Gabon is a member of the French franc zone. The BEAC, headquartered in Yaoundé, issues currency and controls liquidity within the zone. There is no stock exchange.

Taxes and tariffs

Although there have been tariff disputes over the importation of exploration equipment in the past, there are few barriers in the crude oil sector where most of US firms are involved. Normally equipment used in the crude oil sector—such as seismic boats and drilling equipment—enters on a duty free basis. The corporate tax rate for non-residents is 35 percent. There is no capital gains tax. A value added tax (VAT) of 10 to 18 percent applies and exchange control is in effect. Taxes are levied on dividends (15%), interest (10 to 20%) and royalties (10%). (See page 138).

Foreign presence

Since its independence Gabon has been pro-West and has maintained a strong relationship with the United States and Europe.

BUSINESS ACTIVITY

AGRICULTURE
Cocoa, coffee, sugar, palm oil, rubber, cattle, okoume (tropical softwood), fish.
INDUSTRIES
Food and beverage, textiles, lumbering, plywood, cement, petroleum, extraction and refining, manganese, uranium, gold, chemicals, ship repair.
NATURAL RESOURCES
Petroleum, manganese, uranium.
EXPORTS
$5.9 billion (est. 2009): crude oil, timber, manganese, uranium.
IMPORTS
$2.3 billion (est. 2009): machinery and equipment, foodstuffs, chemicals, construction materials.
MAJOR TRADING PARTNERS
US, China, Japan, France, Netherlands, Cameroon, Begium, Cameroon, Malaysia.

Doing Business with Gabon

▶ **Investment**

Apart from ongoing opportunities in the petroleum sector, Gabon offers considerable scope in mining of alkaline, niobium, titanium, gold, diamonds and phosphates. Privatization opens up new investment opportunities to foreigners in transport, telecommunications and manufacturing, involving parastatals such as Air Gabon, the Trans-Gabonese railway (OCTRA), the national post and telecommunications authority (OPT), the sugar monopoly (SOSUHO) and the oil refinery (SOGARA). There is also an active recruitment of investment in wood processing, light industries, fisheries and port development.

▶ **Trade**

The largest portion of foreign sales to Gabon relates to petroleum exploration and mining equipment, as well as other heavy machinery. Major local mining operations—manganese (COMILOG), uranium (COMUF) and phosphate (SOMIMO)—maintain large inventories of US cranes, drag lines, trucks and tractors. Foreign manufacturers have also developed a share in the growing market for state-of-the-art equipment in the telecommunications sector. Gabon is a net food importer.

▶ **Trade finance**

Credit is provided through six commercial banks and payment is usually by irrevocable letters of credit. A parastatal funded by the African Development Bank helps finance purchases by small and medium-sized firms owned by Gabonese nationals.

▶ **Selling to the government**

In the past a poor payment record discouraged the Eximbank and other overseas agencies from extending credit to the government. As Gabon gets its house in order and better utilizes its substantial petroleum revenues this is bound to change. For the present, however, firms are advised to ensure that funds have been set aside in the official budget for specific items when they make the deal.

▶ **Exchange controls**

There are no restrictions on foreign capital and funds may be transferred freely for commercial transactions through regular banking channels. Funds can be transferred with minimal formality within the franc zone (including to France) and repatriation of capital is not subject to onerous restrictions.

▶ **Partnerships**

Joint ventures and licensing are limited but will increase as Gabon's proceeds with privatization. Both US and European soft drinks and beers are produced in Gabon under license.

▶ **Establishing a presence**

To open a branch, applications must be filed with the Ministry of Commerce, the Tax Office of the Ministry of Finance, and the Social Security Office (*Caisse Nationale de Sécurité Sociale*— CNSS). The process can take up to three months and local legal assistance is advisable. Gabonese law allows foreign and local firms to operate as branches constituted locally as limited corporations, *Sociétés à Responsabilité Limitée* (SARL), or corporations, *Sociétés Anonymes* (SA).

▶ **Financing projects**

Gabon is a member of the Multilateral Investment Guarantee Agency. OPIC involvement has been minimal.

▶ **Labor**

Some 20% of Gabon's population are alien Africans active in the informal sector as well as in low and high skill jobs in the formal sector. A serious shortage of Gabonese managers compels firms to recruit non-Gabonese Africans and the Department of Labor reluctantly authorizes such employment, mindful of the objective of the National Employment Commission to replace these expatriates with qualified Gabonese citizens. Labor unions and confederations are active.

▶ **Legal rights**

There have been no instances of expropriation or nationalization of foreign firms. In some cases the government has mediated settlements of commercial or labor disputes on terms more favorable to foreign firms than those offered by the courts. Gabon is a member of the African Intellectual Property Office (OAPI) based in Yaoundé, Cameroon, and its courts enforce property rights. Registration is handled by the Ministry of Commerce.

▶ **Business climate**

Experience has shown that to be successful an overseas firm needs tenacious, Frenchspeaking representatives who make repeated visits to potential customers. Personal contact and a knowledge of the territory are important. French is the only language of commerce.

GAMBIA, THE

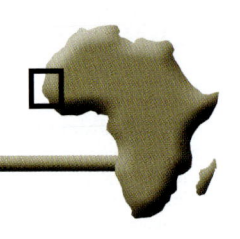

In 1996, The Gambia exchanged military for civilian rule and liberalized its economy. Most of the population continue to depend on crops and livestock for their livelihood. Small scale manufacturing involves processing peanuts, fish and hides. As the smallest country on the African continent, this slither of land along the Gambia river jutting into the heart of Senegal has found a niche in tourism and as a trading post between West Africa and the world. Reexporting is a major economic activity. Construction projects and tourism have drawn foreign participants to this former British colony. The Gambia, however, continues to rely heavily on bilateral and multilateral aid as well as IMF technical advice and assistance.

Country profile

The Republic of The Gambia meanders for 470 km along the banks of one of Africa's most navigable rivers, the Gambia, into Senegal. The capital and main psrt of Banjul is built on a small peninsula on the south bank of a large, lake-like estuary. Beautiful beaches and warm coastal waters are the main tourist attractions. The climate is hot and humid. Ethnic groups comprise the Mande, including the rural Mandinka, and the Atlantic peoples, including the Wolof. English is the official language but Wolof is spoken in the towns and Mandinka in rural areas. About 85% of the population are Muslim. There is also a sizeable Christian minority.

History

From the 13th Century the Wolof, Malinke and Fulani peoples settled in the region. Portuguese mariners explored the waters of the Gambia river in the 1450s reaching far into the interior. In 1651, the Duchy of Courland (today's Latvia) took possession of islands in the river and small tracts of land alongside, notably Banjul and St. Andrew (now James Island), starting the first organized European settlement on the African mainland south of the Sahara. (The Cape of Good Hope was settled by the Dutch in the following year). In 1681 the French founded an enclave at Albredabut and during the 17th Century Gambia was occupied by various English merchant companies. From the 17th to the 18th Centuries Gambia was at the center of the slave trade and in 1888 it was declared a British colony. Dawda Jawara, the leader of the People's Progressive Party, led Gambia to independence in 1965. For a few years in the 1980s, Sir Dawda acted as vice-president of Senegambia, an experimental union with surrounding Senegal. After its dissolution he and his party again won elections in 1987 and 1992 but in July 1994 Dawda Jawara was ousted in a bloodless military coup by Lieut. Yaya Jammeh. In September 1996 Jammeh was elected president over three other candidates and He was reelected in October 2001 and again in September 2006 in a landslide victory alleged by the opposition to have been unfair.

Government

The unicameral National Assembly has 48 members elected for a five year term and 5 appointed members. In January 2007 Jammeh's Alliance for Patriotic Reorientation and Construction (APRC) scored a landslide victory with 47 seats against 4 for its nearest rival, the United Democratic Party (UDP).

Economic policy

The government launched an economic development program under the banner "Vision 2020—The Gambia Incorporated" to capitalize further on a macroeconomic framework put in place with the help of successive IMF and World Bank structural adjustment programs.

Sectors

The Gambia has no significant mineral or natural resources. A limited agricultual base accounts for one-quarter of GDP and employs more than three-quarters of the labor force. Peanuts is a major corp, while livestock and fishing are important sectors. Other food crops include rice, maize, millet, sorghum, cassava and pulses. Manufacturing involves groundnut and fish processing, brewing, footwear, perfume, cement and brick production. Known mineral deposits include kaolin, tin, ilmenite, zircon and rutile. The Gambia's natural beauty and proximity to Europe has made it one of the larger markets for tourism in West Africa.

Trade

Reexport trade normally constitutes a major segment of economic activity. India is The Gambia's major export market, accounting for more than 37%. China is its major supplier, followed by Senegal, Côte d'Ivoire and Brazil. The Gambia is an important entrepot for goods distributed to neighboring countries. However, a government-imposed preshipment inspection plan and currency instability has had a negative impact on The Gambia as a reexport base.

Investment

Growth sectors include construction, tourism, transportation, and to a limited degree, agriculture crop production and fisheries. Schools, roads, hospitals, a new airport terminal building, a new national television station (the first in The Gambia), and Arch 22, a tourist attraction, have been built in recent years. The tourism sector continues to attract private sec-

Pres. Yaya A.J.J Jammeh
Born: May 25, 1965
Since October 1994

UN Photo Michelle Poiré

POLITICAL
Head of State	Pres. Yaya Jammeh
Ruling Party	APRC
Main Opposition	UDP
Independence	18 February 1965
National capital	Banjul
Official language	English

PHYSICAL
Total area	4,000 sq. miles
	11,000 sq. km.
	(2 x Delaware)
Arable land	25% of land area
Coastline	50 miles/80 km

POPULATION
Total	1.8 million
Av. yearly growth	2.6%
Urban population	57%
Life expectancy	53.8 years
Adult literacy	40.1%

ECONOMY
Currency	Dalasi (D) (US$1=26.90)
GDP (real)	$612 million
GDP growth rate	4.8%
GDP per capita[1]	$349
GDP (ppp)[2]	$2.0 billion
GDP per cap. (ppp)	$1,175
Inflation rate	4.2%
Exports	$86 million
Imports	$285 million
External debt	$301 million
Unemployment	NA

1. Atlas method.
2. See page 175 for an explanation of purchasing power parity (ppp).

BUSINESS ACTIVITY

AGRICULTURE
Peanuts, millet, sorghum, rice, cassava (tapioca), palm kernels, livestock, forestry and fishing (not fully exploited).
INDUSTRIES
Processing peanuts, fish and hides, tourism, beverages, agricultural machinery assembly, wood working, metal working, clothing.
NATURAL RESOURCES
Fish.
EXPORTS
$86 million (est. 2009): peanut products, fish, cotton, palm kernels.
IMPORTS
$285 million (est. 2009): food, manufactures, fuel, machinery, transport equipment.
MAJOR TRADING PARTNERS
India, China , Netherlands, Senegal, UK, Indonesia, France, Japan, Brazil, Belgium.

tor investment. Despite announced plans to this effect, privatization of key parastatals has been slow in materializing. The seizure of a private peanut firm, Alimenta, has eliminated the largest buyer of Gambian groundnuts.

Financial Sector

Foreign exchange earnings are too small to pay for the country's imports, leaving it heavily dependent on bilateral and multilateral aid to cover the deficit. Foreign aid contributes 80% of the government's revenue.

Taxes & tariffs

The corporate tax rate for non-residents is 35 percent and capital gains tax 10 to 25 percent. A sales tax of 15 to 18 percent applies and exchange control is in effect. Taxes are levied on dividends (15%), interest (15%) and royalties (15%). (See page 138).

Doing Business with The Gambia

▶ **Investment**

Designated as priority sectors for investment are manufacturing, agriculture, livestock, fisheries, forestry, mining and quarrying, tourism, and support services such as air cargo, transportation, banking and finance. Investments in these sectors qualify for exemption from customs duty and sales tax on imported capital goods and construction materials as well as special land lease arrangements. Investment incentives need to be negotiated up front. A one-stop office simplifies the establishment of foreign enterprises.

▶ **Trade**

Most trade restrictions in the form of quotas, licensing, or other restrictive instruments of commerce have been removed.

▶ **Exchange controls**

There are no exchange controls in effect. Profits and dividends from nonresident investments can be transferred without any restriction.

▶ **Establishing a presence**

Under the Companies Act, foreigners may establish public or private companies either unlimited or limited in terms of shares or guarantees. Incorporation simply requires a memorandum and articles of association and registration is swift.

▶ **Project finance**

The Gambia is a member of the Multilateral Investment Guarantee Agency.

▶ **Labor**

With a relatively high unemployment rate and less than 40% of the population literate, semi-skilled and unskilled workers are readily available.

▶ **Legal rights**

There are constitutional safeguards for the payment of adequate compensation in case of property acquisition or nationalization and the right to appeal to the Supreme Court. This generally positive record was marred by a January 1999 state takeover of the Gambia Groundnut Corporation, a subsidiary of the Swiss-based Alimenta group.

▶ **Business Climate**

The business language is English but French is also spoken as a result of The Gambia's close relationship with Senegal and Côte d'Ivoire.

GHANA

Ghana is well endowed with natural resources such as gold, timber and cocoa and is one of the wealthier nations in the region. It has emerged as one of the most attractive bsuienss destinations in West Africa. It has been ranked near the top by the the U.S.-based Millennium Challenge Corporation (MCC) particularly in the areas of good governance, economic freedom, anti-corruption, the rule of law and human rights. Recent oil discoveries gave a further boost to the economy.

Country profile

The Republic of Ghana lies on a low plateau ranging between 500 and 1,000 ft. (150 to 300 m) above sea level. The Volta River feeds off its White and Black tributaries and has been dammed at Akosombo to form the vast Lake Volta stretching 250 miles (400 km) inland and covers 3.5% of the land area. English is the official language, but 75 native languages and dialects are also spoken. The Akan cultural group (consisting of the Asante, Fante, and Brong) forms 40% of the population. About 38% adhere to ethnic beliefs while Christianity (43%) dominates in the south and the Muslim faith (12%) remains strong in the far north.

History

Gold first attracted European exploration along what became known as the Gold Coast. In 1482 the Portuguese built the first fort at Elmina (The Mine). The Dutch, French, British and Germans followed. From the 16th until the 19th Century trade in gold was overshadowed by the slave trade. During this period the Asante people gained dominance and prompted weaker tribes such as the Fante to seek British protection. Britain took control and abolished slavery from the mid-19th Century. The British colony, Gold Coast, together with the former UN trust territory, British Togoland, was granted independence as Ghana in 1957, under the leadership of Kwame Nkrumah. After he was ousted in 1966, Nkrumah's military successors—Generals Joseph Ankrah, Kofi Busia, Ignatius Acheompong and Frederick Akkuffo—perpetuated one party rule. Inflation soared and corruption went unchecked. In 1979 a young Flight Lieutenant, Jerry Rawlings, seized power and installed Hilla Limann as president. In 1981 Rawlings seized power again. As head of the Provisional National Defense Council (PNDC) he abolished the constitution and jailed Limann. In 1992 a multiparty system was adopted and a presidential election held, which Rawlings won easily. He won reelection in 1996 but in

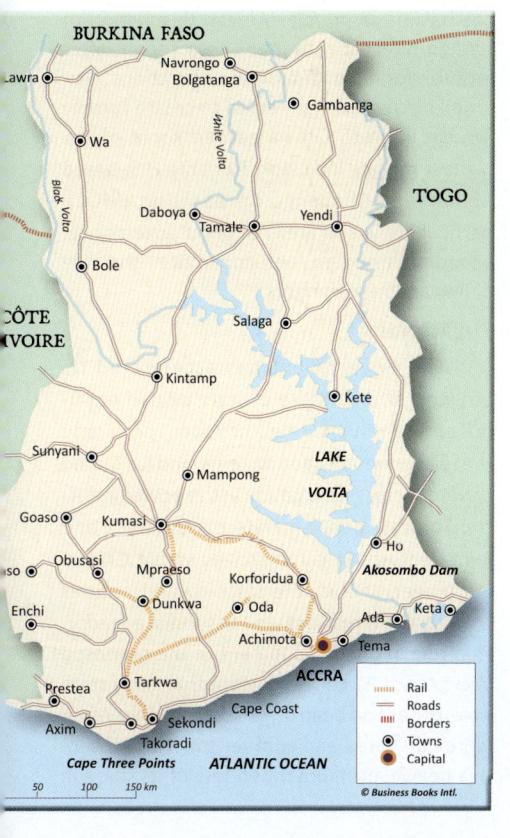

Pres. John Evans Atta Mills
Born: July 21, 1944
Since January 2009

UN Photo Eskinder Debebe

POLITICAL	
Head of State	Pres. John Evans Atta Mills
Ruling Party	NDC
Main Opposition	NPP
Independence	6 March 1957
National capital	Accra
Official language	English

PHYSICAL	
Total area	92,000 sq. miles 239,000 sq. km. (± Oregon)
Arable land	16% of land area
Coastline	335 miles/539 km

POPULATION	
Total	23.8 million
Av. yearly growth	1.9%
Urban population	50%
Life expectancy	59.8 years
Adult literacy	57.9%

ECONOMY	
Currency	Cedi (US$1=1.4550)
GDP (real)	$14.6 billion
GDP growth rate	4.7%
GDP per capita[1]	$612
GDP (ppp)[2]	$36.5 billion
GDP per cap. (ppp)	$1,532
Inflation rate	18.8%
Exports	$5.7 billion
Imports	$8.4 billion
External debt	$6.2 billion
Unemployment	11%

1. Atlas method.
2. See page 175 for an explanation of purchasing power parity (ppp).

December 2000 his deputy in the National Democratic Congress (NDC), John Evans Atta Mills, was defeated in his bid for the presidency by John Agyekum Kufuor of the New Patriotic Party (NPP). Kufuor was re-elected in December 2004 but in 2008 Mills and his party triumphed at the polls, winning both a majority in parliament and the presidency. Fullbright scholar and law professor Mills captured the top post after a keenly contested three round election.

Government

The President holds executive power and legislative power is vested in the unicameral 200-member National Assembly, both elected for four year terms. In the December 2008 elections John Atta Mills' National Democratic Congress (NDC) narrowly defeated the ruling New Patriotic Party (NPP), winning 114 seats against 107. Minor opposition parties share the remaining 7 seats.

Economic policy

Ghana has emerged as one of the most attractive places in West Africa to do business, according to World Bank indicators. It has become a premier African destination of foreign direct investment and a sought-after location for regional business operations. Major oil discoveries has served to create further foreign interest. Ghana earned some of the highest-ranking indicators from the U.S.-based Millennium Challenge Corporation (MCC), particularly in the areas of good governance, economic freedom, anti-corruption, the rule of law and human rights..

Privatization

The Government has accelerated its program of divestiture of state owned enterprises and rehabilitation of roads, ports and the telecommunication systems, and facilitated private sector participation in the power industry. Through public-private partnerships and joint ventures in commercially viable Ghanaian power utilities the state-owned entities transform themselves and assumed a leadership role in the development of the proposed West Africa Power Pool. More than sixty state enterprises had been divested, while thirty-four were liquidated and another thirty privatized. In a heavily oversubscribed sale of its share in

Ashanti Goldfields, the government earned $320 million. The Ghanaian government also sold most of its shares in Standard Chartered Bank (Ghana), Accra Breweries, Equity Insurance, Guinness Ghana, Kumasi Breweries, Pioneer Tobacco and Unilever (Ghana).

Sectors

Ghana has large deposits of gold, diamonds, bauxite and manganese, as well as sizeable forests and arable land. It has a good potential in hydroelectric power. Recent oil discoveries gave a major boost to Ghana's economy as it attracted billions of foreign investment. Agriculture remains important. Ghana is among the world's largest exporters of cocoa. Timber is another major foreign currency earner. Crops grown for sale to local agro-industries include sugar, cotton, oil palms and rubber. Subsistence crops are rice, maize, sorghum, millet, groundnuts, yams and fruit. Mining is the second largest earner of foreign exchange. Gold tops the list with diamonds and manganese gaining in importance. Manufacturing remains relatively modest. Apart from a large aluminum smelter, most other industrial activity revolves around agro-business such as the processing of cocoa and beer brewing.

Trading

Ghana's largest overall trading partner is the United Kingdom, followed by the United States, Netherlands, Nigeria and China. Nigeria is, however, the largest importer of Ghanaian goods, followed by China.

Investment

Foreign direct investment is aggressively pursued by the Ghanaian government in an effort to stimulate growth as donor assistance is expected to diminish. Foreign investment in Ghana is mostly in mining and manufacturing. The United Kingdom is the largest investor with direct investments exceeding $750 million, much of it attributable to Lonrho's 41% stake in Ashanti Goldfields Corporation. US investments are largely in mining and foods and are expected to rise as there have been expressions of interest by American companies in the acquisition of state-owned communications and manufacturing firms earmarked for divestiture. There are significant investments by other foreign nationals through the government's privatization program. Norwegian investors are part owners of the state's Ghana Cement Works (GHACEM). Ghana Telecom is operated by the state in partnership with Telecom Malaysia. South African companies have become active in the mining sector. The private sector can now source equity and loans through venture capital companies and equity through the Ghana Stock Exchange.

Financial sector

The Central Bank oversees 11 commercial banks, 5 merchant banks and over 100 rural banks. In recent years, however, several state-owned banks have been privatized. Nonbank financial institutions (NBFIs) include a Stock Exchange, 21 insurance companies, the Social Security and National Insurance Trust (SSNIT), two discount houses, the Home Finance Company, numerous building societies, a venture capital company, a unit trust and 5 leasing companies.

Taxes and tariffs

The corporate tax rate for non-residents is 25 percent and capital gains tax 5 percent. A value added tax (VAT) of 15 percent applies and exchange control is in effect. Taxes are levied on dividends (8%), interest (8%) and royalties (10%). (See page 138).

BUSINESS ACTIVITY

AGRICULTURE
Cocoa, coffee, rice, cassava (tapioca), peanuts, corn, shear nuts, bananas, timber.
INDUSTRIES
Mining, lumbering, light manufacturing, aluminum smelting, food processing.
NATURAL RESOURCES
Gold, timber, industrial diamonds, bauxite, manganese, fish, rubber.
EXPORTS
$5.7 billion (est. 2009): gold, cocoa, timber, tuna, bauxite, aluminum, manganese ore, diamonds.
IMPORTS
$8.4 billion (est. 2009): capital equipment, petroleum, consumer goods, food, intermediate goods.
MAJOR TRADING PARTNERS
UK, US, Netherlands, Nigeria, China, France.

Doing Business with Ghana

▶ **Investment**

Ghana's telecommunications sector and roads need repair and expansion and deregulation opened up this field for foreign investment. Gold mining remains the focus of growth and exploration by foreign mining companies continues. The Ghana Investment Promotion Center Act of 1994 extends incentives to foreign investors, including tax holidays, accelerated depreciation, locational privileges and other inducements.

▶ **Trade**

Food processing and packaging equipment, telecommunications equipment, secondhand clothing and motor vehicles, mining machinery, construction and earth-moving equipment, computers and peripherals as well as hotel and restaurant equipment offer opportunities for exporters. The channels of distribution available to foreign suppliers of goods and services in Ghana are wholesalers, retail outlets, and agents or distributors.

▶ **Trade finance**

Traditional trade finance instruments such as letters of credit, collections, and funds transfers are available to the exporter. USDA credit guarantee programs provide access to financing for imports of wheat, rice, feed grains, vegetable oil, protein meal, dairy products, as well as agricultural equipment.

▶ **Selling to the government**

The Ghana Supply Commission (GSC) handles procurement on behalf of the government and its agencies. Procurement is typically financed by a multilateral lending institution such as the World Bank, the African Development Bank or the International Finance Corporation.

▶ **Exchange Control**

The government of Ghana has moved away from exchange controls and has permitted the establishment of Foreign Exchange Bureaus. The cedi can now be readily exchanged for foreign currency.

▶ **Partnerships**

The Ghanaian Investment Code provides legislative encouragement for joint venture activities. The government guarantees transfers of capital, profits and dividends.

▶ **Establishing a presence**

Foreigners intending to invest in Ghana should first contact the Ghana Investment Promotion Center (GIPC), a one-stop shop for economic, commercial and investment information. The minimum required equity for foreign investors is $10,000 in joint ventures or $50,000 for enterprises wholly owned by foreign nationals. Trading companies either wholly or partly owned by non-Ghanaians require a minimum foreign equity of $300,000 and employment of at least 10 locals.

▶ **Project financing**

Private sector projects in Ghana might qualify for International Finance Corporation assistance and, in the case of US firms, Overseas Private Investment Corporation loans, loan guarantees and insurance. All the programs of the Eximbank apply. The US Trade and Development Agency finances feasibility studies.

▶ **Labor**

Ghana has a large pool of inexpensive, unskilled labor. Even though there is no legal requirement to involve labor in management deliberations, joint consultative committees involving management and labor are common.

▶ **Legal rights**

Ghana follows British common law and recognizes the right of foreign and domestic private entities to own and operate business enterprises. Ghana is a member of the World Intellectual Property Organization and the English-speaking African Regional Industrial Property Organization (ESARIPO). In 1996, the Ghana Arbitration Center was established to strengthen the legal framework for the protection of commercial and economic interests.

▶ **Business climate**

English is the official language and is used in most business transactions. Normally Ghanaian businessmen wear business suits during working hours and resort to traditional attire for social functions. Often, however, they may also be found in traditional attire during business hours. Businesswomen wear African attire during business hours as well as for social functions.

GUINEA

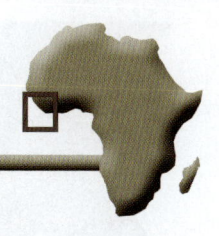

Guinea's economy has been reconstructed since 1984 when the socialist dictatorship of Sékou Touré came to an end. While the informal sector response to the more liberal economic policies introduced after Touré has been impressive, international trade, agricultural production, and manufacturing have showed slower progress. Poor physical and institutional infrastructure, an erratic and unpredictable judicial system, and corrupt practices contributed to the weak formal sector response. The country is rich in minerals and fertile land and has by all accounts the potential to be relatively prosperous. President Conté has instituted economic reforms, including financial and judicial reform. After his death in December 2008 the country has been in turmoil. The election of Alpha Condé as president is seen as a positive development.

Country profile

The Republic of Guinea is a kidney-shaped country with a coastline marked by shallow estuaries and mangrove swamps. Apart from French, the official language, several native languages are spoken. The Ful (or Fulani), inhabiting the Futa Jallon Highlands, is the largest single group but collectively the Mande people (comprising the Baga, Nalu, Kisi and Landuma) form the majority. Guinea is largely Muslim with less than 2% Christians, mostly Roman Catholic.

History

Portuguese explorers arrived in the second half of the 15th Century. Though not a major slave trading region, the Los Islands near Conakry were used as slave depots. After the Portuguese came the British and eventually the French, who gained possession of the territory in 1884. Under the leadership of a trade union leader, Sékou Touré, Guinea voted in a 1958 referendum to reject an offer by France of autonomy within the French Community. The French granted Guinea independence and withdrew all assistance and personnel. Touré's socialist dictatorship led to economic decay and large-scale emigration. After Touré's death in 1984, Gen. Lansana Conté seized power. In 1992 a multi-party system was introduced and Conté elected president. He was re-elected in 1998 and 2003 but following his death in December 2008, Captain Moussa Dadis Camara seized power in a military coup. Guinea was further destabilized at the end of 2009 when an assassination attempt on Camara by an aide forced his transfer to a hospital in Rabat,

Pres. Alpha Condé
Born: March 4, 1938
Since Dec. 2010

Condé flckr

POLITICAL

Head of State	Pres. Alpha Condé
Independence	2 October 1958
National capital	Conakry
Official language	French

PHYSICAL

Total area	95,000 sq. miles
	246,000 sq. km.
	(± Oregon)
Arable land	3.6% of land area
Coastline	199 miles/320 km

POPULATION

Total	10 million
Av. yearly growth	2.6%
Urban population	34%
Life expectancy	57 years
Adult literacy	29.5%

ECONOMY

Currency	Guinea franc (GNF) (US$1=6,950)
GDP (real)	$4.6 billion
GDP growth rate	0.6%
GDP per capita[1]	$482
GDP (ppp)[2]	$10.5 billion
GDP per cap. (ppp)	$1,040
Inflation rate	4.8%
Exports	$981 million
Imports	$1.1 billion
External debt	$2.9 billion
Unemployment	NA

1. Atlas method.
2. See page 175 for an explanation of purchasing power parity (ppp).

Morocco, where he died. His vice-president, General Sekouba Konate, acted as head of state, until elections were held in November 2010. Alpha Condé, returning from exile in Paris to head the Rally of the Guinean People (RPG), emerged the surprise winner in a runoff election against Cellou Dalein Diallo of the Union of Democratic Forces of Guinea (UFDG). After placing second with a mere 18.2% to Cellou Dalein Diallo's 43.7% in the first round, Condé turned the tables in the final round by winning 52.5% of the popular vote against Diallo's 47.5%—thus becoming Guinea's first freely elected president since its independence from France in 1958. Condé, a former professor, faces the tough challenge of restoring peace and democracy.

Government

In terms of the constitution the president is elected for a seven year term and a 114-seat unicameral National Assembly for five years. In last election in June 2002 Conté's Party for Unity and Progress (PUP) won 85 seats against 20 for the main opposition, the Union for Progress and Renewal (UPR). The Assembly has been in limbo since the coup in December 2008.

Economic policy

In 1984 President Conté inherited a country impoverished by his predecessor's socialist-driven policies. He launched an ambitious program of reform, aimed at dismantling the 24-year-old centralized, state-run economy. Significant progress has been made in downsizing and improving the performance of the public sector, the regulatory environment, liberalizing the price controls, exchange and trade system, and increasing the efficiency of the tax collection. Recently, political upheavals have had an adverse impact on the country's economy.

Privatization

Although there were several publicized investment failures in 1996 and 1997 (mainly due to corruption and poor management), reforms and privatization efforts in the energy sector are bound to create opportunities for foreign investment. Water and electricity production grew significantly. A significant increase in energy production followed the completion of the hydroelectric site at Garafiri. The French and Canadians are primary investors in the energy sector.

Sectors

Guinea has major mineral, hydropower and agricultural resources. Even though only 3% of the land is under cultivation, agriculture accounts for about one-third of the GDP and provides work for three-quarters of the labor force. Coffee is the most important export crop. Bananas, cotton, pineapples, palm oil, groundnuts and citrus fruits are also grown. Forestry shows considerable potential. Mining remains the most dynamic sector and accounts for most of Guinea's export earnings. The country's bauxite reserves, estimated at 20 billion tons, constitute the world's largest. Guinea is the world's second largest supplier of bauxite and ranks third in aluminum production. Apart from aluminum smelting, the manufacturing sector is small and mostly geared to the local market.

Trading

Guinea remains largely dependent on mineral exports. Mining receipts account for about three-quarters of the country's foreign exchange earnings. It is a large importer of agricultural products, tobacco, and alcoholic and non-alcoholic beverages. Flour imports originate largely in France with some Belgian contribution. Principal sugar suppliers include France, Belgium, and Italy. Guinea has no free trade or export processing zones or warehouses, but a temporary license to conduct free trade transactions can be obtained.

Investment

Full foreign ownership is permitted in commercial, industrial, mining, agricultural and service sectors. Industries that are restricted from having a majority of foreign ownership are radio, television, and newspapers. The government currently controls, owns, and operates the electronic media, although a presidnetial decree has established a process for private ownership of broadcast media. France is Guinea's strongest traditional economic partner and provides extensive development assistance. Canadians and Belgians also have a strong local presence. Malaysians began investing in Guinea in telecommunications and banking and showed an interest in construction, tourism and agriculture. Lebanese are involved in real estate, small manufacturing enterprises, and telecommunications, supermarkets, wholesale food, and electronics. Outside of the mining sector, foreign-aid projects continue to provide the largest source of business opportunities for expatriate firms and are critical driving forces in developing Guinea's infrastructure. Priority areas are education, health, agricultural marketing, rural road construction, and rural enterprise development. During the past few years, USAID has supported the construction of over 1,000 km of rural roads in Guinea. Fighting along Guinea's borders with Liberia and Sierra Leone and large-scale refugee movements, has had a negative impact on investor confidence.

Financial sector

The banking system has been reconstructed with the assistance of the IMF and the World Bank. Guinea is, however, not receiving multialteral aid as both the IMF and World Bank has ceased such assistance in 2003.

Taxes and tariffs

The corporate tax rate for non-residents is 35 percent. A value added tax (VAT) of 18 percent applies and exchange control is in effect. Taxes are levied on dividends (10%), and royalties (10%). (See page 138).

BUSINESS ACTIVITY

AGRICULTURE
Rice, coffee, pineapples, palm kernels, cassava (tapioca), bananas, sweet potatoes, cattle, sheep, goats, timber.

INDUSTRIES
Bauxite, gold, diamonds, alumina refining, light manufacturing, agricultural processing.

NATURAL RESOURCES
Bauxite, iron ore, diamonds, gold.

EXPORTS
$981 million (est. 2009): Bauxite, alumina, diamonds, gold, coffee, fish, agricultural products.

IMPORTS
$1.1 billion (est. 2009): petroleum products, metals, machinery, transport equipment, textiles, grain and other foodstuffs.

MAJOR TRADING PARTNERS
Russia, South Korea, US, China, Belgium, Netherlands, Ireland, Spain, France, Ukraine, Germany.

Doing Business with Guinea

▶ **Investment**

Privatization in the telecommunications, banking and energy sectors has opened up new areas for foreign investment. Under the auspices of The United Nations Development Program and the United Nations Industrial Development Organization Guinea listed over 100 private and public investment projects, totaling more than $150 million in the agriculture, fishing, industry, and public works sectors. Other targeted sectors include mining, manufacturing, transportation, and energy. Investing is simplified by the Office of Private Investment Promotion (OPIP), a one-stop business registration office, centralizing the administrative, legal, fiscal, and other formalities.

▶ **Trade**

Apart from agricultural products, good prospects for exports to Guinea are machinery and equipment, petroleum products, construction/semi-finished material, industry/manufacturing, telecommunications and hi-tech equipment (computers, soft/hardware), and consumer goods (canned/dry supermarket goods, textiles, cosmetics, used clothing, alcoholic and other beverages, and tobacco products). Expansion of telecommunication and Internet services should increase the demand for cellular phones, relay towers, and switches.

▶ **Trade finance**

Guinea qualifies for three US Department of Agriculture export promotion programs: the dairy export incentive program, a GSM-102 credit program, and a wheat export enhancement program.

▶ **Selling to the government**

Donor countries and institutions usually stipulate the bidding rules for foreign-financed public investment projects. The AGCP (Guinean Central Procurement Agency) handles projects/contracts over one million dollars. The Public Market (*Marché Publique*) handles projects/contracts under one million dollars.

▶ **Exchange control**

All initial capital investments and earnings generated can be converted and repatriated, but only 50% of Guinean capital can be converted or transferred.

▶ **Partnership and presence**

The US Embassy commercial officer, local Chamber of Commerce, the Employers' Association, and Guinean Offices of Investment Promotion are all useful points of contact for business people contemplating establishing a presence. No franchises currently exist in Guinea.

▶ **Project financing**

The African Development Bank's private sector window in Abidjan has funding available for development-oriented business projects. The Overseas Private Investment Corporation will also accept applications for investment projects in Guinea. The US Trade and Development Agency assists in the financing of feasibility studies.

▶ **Labor**

Labor is ample but there is a critical shortage of skilled managers and administrators with private sector experience. Employers no longer need to go through the labor office to hire or fire an employee, and there is no obligation to employ only Guineans. The labor code legalizes labor unions and the right to collective bargaining.

▶ **Legal rights**

The legal, regulatory, and accounting systems are based upon French civil law but are not always applied uniformly or transparently. While Guinea's laws are designed to promote free enterprise and competition, senior government officials have publicly acknowledged shortcomings due to corruption and lack of training. The government has committed itself to strengthening the judicial and legal institutions to attract more foreign investment and improve economic conditions. The establishment of an independent Arbitration Court is specifically aimed at protecting foreign business people from corruption within the judicial system. Guinea is a member of the African Intellectual Property Organization comprised of 15 African countries and the World Intellectual Property Organization. The country is in the process of modifying its intellectual property right laws to bring them up to international standards.

▶ **Business climate**

Most Guineans are Muslim, and Islam plays a major role in shaping the customs and habits of the local business culture. Foreigners should be familiar with the basic tenets of Islam to facilitate business dealings. Friendship and trust are very important and it takes time to build a successful working relationship. Patience and face-to-face contact are requirements for successful business.

GUINEA-BISSAU

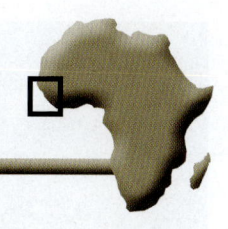

Guinea-Bissau counts among the world's five poorest countries. As the world's sixth largest producer of cashew nuts Guinea-Bissau relies heavily on this export, as well as sales of peanuts, palm kernels and timber. These products could be eclipsed by the mining of phosphate and other minerals and the exploitation of petroleum. So far high cost and lack of infrastructure have, however, discouraged potential foreign investors in mining but offshore oil prospecting has started. The domestic economy relies heavily on fishing and farming, with rice as a major crop.

Country profile

The Republic of Guinea-Bissau consists mostly of low-lying marshland. The name of its capital, Bissau, is included in its name to distinguish it from its larger neighbor, Guinea. Its coastline is interrupted by meandering rivers, wide estuaries and adjoined by 18 islands known as the Bijagos (Bissagos) Archipelago. The climate is tropical, hot and wet. Rainfall in the north ranges between 1,000 and 2,000 mm. Within a relatively small area, Guinea-Bissau contains an ethnically diverse population consisting of seven significant cultural groups alongside the dominant Balanta. There is a sizable expatriate community of Portuguese, Syrian and Lebanese traders, most of them involved in commerce. The majority of Guinea-Bissau's inhabitants adheres to traditional ethnic beliefs while one-third is Muslim and about ten percent Christian. Portuguese is the official language but several native tongues are spoken as well as French, mostly in business circles.

History

In the 13th Century Guinea-Bissau was part of the Kingdom of Gabu in ancient Mali. During the 15th Century Portugal built forts along the coast and engaged in slave trade with the rulers of the region. Rios de Guine, (as it was called then) was administered by the Portuguese from Cape Verde until 1879 when it became a separate colony. After the abolition of slavery, groundnut cultivation became the mainstay of the economy. At the Berlin Conference in 1885, Portuguese Guinea was formally recognized by the European powers. By the 1950s the Balanta and other coastal peoples joined with Cape Verdean dissidents to form the *Partido Africano da Independêndia da Guiné é Cabo Verde* (PAIGC)

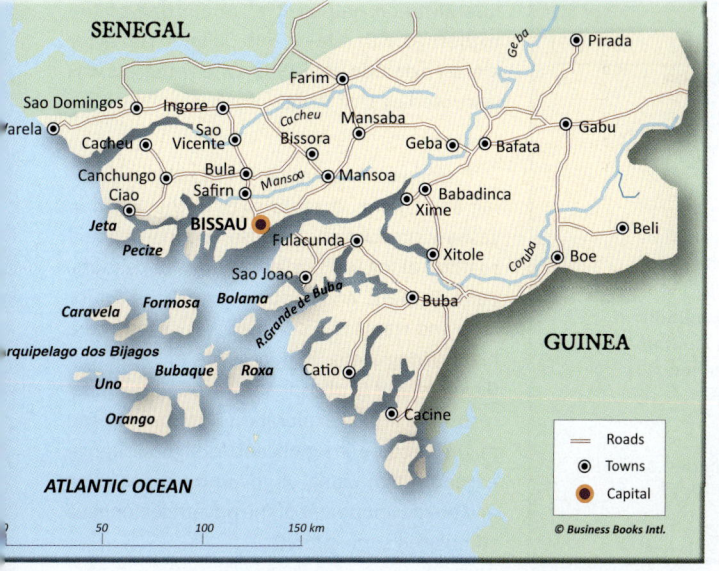

Pres. Malam Bacai Sanhá
Born: May 5, 1947
Since Sept. 2009

Official photo

POLITICAL

Head of State	Pres. Malam Bacai Sanhá
Ruling Party	PAIGC
Main Opposition	PRS
Independence	24 September 1973
National capital	Bissau
Official language	Portuguese

PHYSICAL

Total area	14,000 sq. miles
	36,000 sq. km.
	(3 x Connecticut)
Arable land	11% of land area
Coastline	217 miles/350 km

POPULATION

Total	1.5 million
Av. yearly growth	2.0%
Urban population	30%
Life expectancy	47.9 years
Adult literacy	42.4%

ECONOMY

Currency	CFA franc (CFAF) (US$1=495.40)
GDP (real)	$442 million
GDP growth rate	2.9%
GDP per capita[1]	$253
GDP (ppp)[2]	$817 million
GDP per cap. (ppp)	$508
Inflation rate	-1.5%
Exports	$133 million
Imports	$200 million
External debt	$1 billion
Unemployment	NA

1. Atlas method.
2. See page 175 for an explanation of purchasing power parity (ppp).

and engaged in an armed struggle against the Portuguese rulers. In September 1974 when the Portuguese army overthrew the Caetano dictatorship in Lisbon, Guinea-Bissau was the first of the five Portuguese African territories to achieve independence. Its first ruler, Pres. Luiz Cabral, was deposed by the military veteran prime minister João Bernardo "Nino" Vieira in 1980 who remained in power until 2000 when he was defeated at the polls by Kumba Ialá. Ialá was toppled in a bloodless coup in September 2003. After a caretaker period a presidential election was held in July 2005. Vieira won and returned to power. He was assassinated in March 2009. Malam Bacai Sanhá became president in September 2009 after defeating Kumba Ialá at the polls.

Government

In terms of the constitution the president is elected by popular vote for a 5-year term, has executive power and appoints the Prime Minister and the Council of Ministers. Members of the 102-member unicameral People's National Assembly are elected for 4-years. In the November 2008 elections the PAIGC won 67 seats against 28 for the *Partido para a Renovaçao Social* (PRS) and 5 for smaller parties. Carlos Gomes, as leader of the majority party, assumed the premiership.

Economic policy

The country's structural adjustment program involving trade reform and price liberalization helped it to attain one of the highest growth rates in Sub-Saharan Africa for almost a decade until 1998, when progress was disrupted by civil strife.

Sectors

Guinea-Bissau depends mostly on farming and fishing. It ranks sixth in the world in cashew production and also exports fish and seafood along with small amounts of peanuts, palm kernels, and timber. Rice is the major crop and staple food. Livestock is raised in the higher-lying areas. High cost has impeded the development of phosphate and other minderal resrouces but oil exploration is continuing and might become a significant foreign exchange earner. A tightening of government spending and the development of the private sector have stimulated some growth.

Privatization

A new investment law was adopted to facilitate private participation in all key sectors. A privatization council appointed to oversee the restructuring of state-owned businesses resumed its activity after the restoration of peace.

Investment

Offshore oil was discovered in 1958 near Guinea-Bissau's border with Senegal but it took until the 1980s to obtain funding for seismic survey. Exploration agreements signed with foreign oil companies were held up by a border dispute with Senegal. An agreement was reached entitling Senegal to 85% of the mineral resources in the disputed area.

Trade

At about three quarters of export revenue, cashew nuts are the major foreign exchange earner. The downstream petroleum industry is largely dependent on refined petroleum products imported from neighboring countries.

Financial sector

Guinea-Bissau joined the West African Monetary Union (WAEMU) in 1997 and incorporated its central bank into the Central Bank of West Africa (BCEAO).

Taxes and tariffs

Comprehensive tax reform was adopted with the introduction of a generalized sales tax, review of customs tariffs.

BUSINESS ACTIVITY

AGRICULTURE
Rice, corn, beans, cassava (tapioca), cashew nuts, peanuts, palm kernels, cotton, timber, fish.
INDUSTRIES
Agricultural products processing, beer, soft drinks.
NATURAL RESOURCES
Fish, timber, phosphates, bauxite, unexploited deposists of petroleum.
EXPORTS
$133 million (est. 2006): cashews, peanuts, palm kernels, sawn lumber, shrimp.
IMPORTS
$200 million (est. 2006): foodstuffs, transport equipment, petroleum products, machinery and equipment.
MAJOR TRADING PARTNERS
India, Senegal, France, Nigeria, Portugal, Ecuador.

DOING BUSINESS WITH GUINEA-BISSAU

▶ Investment

Since 1993 when it reached a settlement in an offshore territorial dispute with Senegal, Guinea Bissau has placed 4 offshore blocks on offer. The government is also actively seeking foreign participation in the development of its underutilized fish and timber sectors. In mining there is also good potential for exploration and exploitation. Guinea-Bissau's considerable hydropower potential is another area that attracts the attention of foreign investors. Railroad repair and other infrastructure projects are in the offing.

▶ Trade

Substantial quantities of rice are being imported. Once further developed, the country's fish and timber resources could be of special interest to foreign importers. Gasoline and kerosene form a significant portion of the country's import needs.

▶ Selling to the government

Future business with the government will most likely be in petroleum equipment, timber and mining machinery, road and rail construction equipment and rolling stock. Procurement, distribution and marketing of fuel products are carried out by the state owned oil company, *Distribudora de Combustiveis e Lubrificantes* (DICOL) together with the Portuguese oil company, Petrogal.

▶ Exchange controls

As a member of the West African Monetary Union (WAMU), Guinea Bissau offers currency convertibility and applies few controls.

▶ Business climate

Although Portuguese is the official language, French is widely used. Customs in the business community are French-European.

KENYA

Kenya serves as a regional hub for trade and finance in East Africa. For some time growth has been impeded by to much reliance on primary goods and corruption. After considerable progress under the new government installed in 2003 in the combat of corruption, there were serious setbacks as evidenced by high-level scandals in 2005 and 2006. Still, recent reforms and market deregulation are expected to stimulate interest among foreign investors. There has been increased foreign participation in Kenya's capital markets after the liberalization of foreign exchange flows.

Country profile

The Republic of Kenya is bisected by the Great Rift Valley extending from Lake Turkana in the north to Lake Natron on the Tanzanian border. There are some 20 national parks, including Masai Mara (adjoining Tanzania's Serengeti park), Amboseli and Tsavo. The equator runs across the foothills of snow-capped Mount Kenya (17,057 ft/5,199 m), Africa's second highest mountain. Three quarters of the population consist of Bantu-speaking peoples (Kikuyu, Luhya and Kamba) while the remainder are Nilotic (Luo, Maasai or Masai, Samburu, Turkana and Kalenjin). Other minority groups include the Indian, Arab and European expatriates. English and Swahili are official languages. About three-quarters of the population is Christian while the rest adhere to ethnic beliefs.

History

The discovery of fossilized remains of humanlike beings and Stone Age relics from archaeological sites in Kenya gave rise to the belief that this region might well be the cradle of humanity. Paleontologists estimate that people may first have inhabited Kenya 2 million years ago. The Nilotic people expanded southward during the beginning of Christian era into western Kenya where they absorbed the Cushitic and Omotic communities. They were joined by the Bantu-speaking peoples and in the 10th Century Muslim merchants began to develop ports and trading stations along the coast. Portuguese explorer Vasco da Gama was the first European to drop anchor at Mombasa in 1498. The region became a British protectorate in 1890 and a crown colony in 1920. In 1905 Nairobi, strategically located halfway along the newly completed railway to Lake Victoria, became the capital of the British East Africa. To the chagrin of the locals, white settlers had occupied almost all the prime agricultural land by the 1950s. Discontented with the slow progress towards meaningful land reform and political change, the Kikuyu-dominated Mau Mau movement under the leadership of

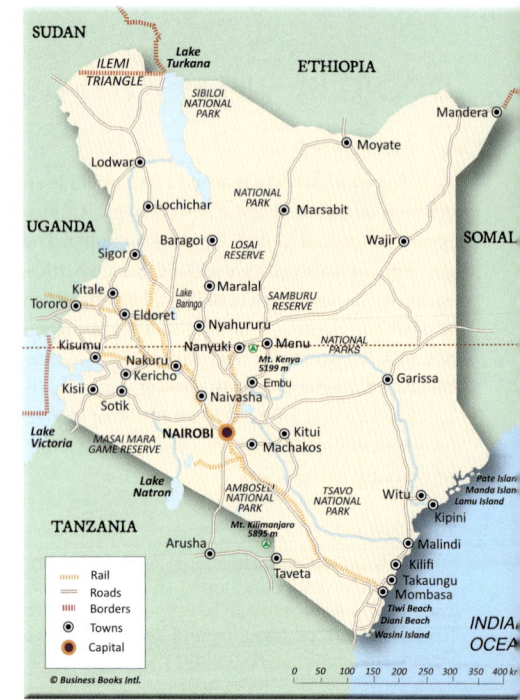

Jomo Kenyatta engaged in a drawn-out, costly struggle. Independence was granted by Britain in 1963 and Kenyatta was elected president as leader of the Kenya African national Union (KANU). In 1978 when Kenyatta died, he was succeeded by Vice-President Daniel arap Moi, a member of the minority Kalenjin group, chosen as a compromise candidate by the Kikuyu-dominated KANU to promote unity. From 1964 until 1992, when President Moi, under severe pressure, called elections, KANU exercised single party control over Kenya. Moi was reelected in 1992 and 1998 and stepped down in 2003 when Emilio Mwai Kibaki became president. In December 2007 Pres. Kibaki claimed victory by narrow margin over Raila Amolo Odinga, leader of the Orange Democratic Movement (ODM). Charging widespread fraud, the ODM took to the streets and in the ensuing struggle more than a thousand perished on both sides. Peace was restored in February 2008 after Pres. Kibaki agreed to share power with Odinga as his prime minister.

Government

An executive President is elected for a maximum of two 5-year terms. In the unicameral National Assembly 210 members are elected by popular vote, 12 are appointed and 2 are *ex officio* members. In the December 2008 election Raila Odinga's ODM won 99 seats against 43 for Kibaki's Party of National Unity (PNU). ODM-Kenya won 16 and Kenya African National Union (KANU) led by Uhuru Kenyatta, 14. According to an agreement signed by Kibaki and Odinga in February 2008, the Prime Minister will coordinate and supervise the execution of the functions and affairs of the Government including those of ministries and perform other duties assigned to him by the President.

Economic policy

In the wake of an economic downturn after 30 years of sustained growth, the government embarked on a substantive reform program, dismantling foreign exchange controls, allowing a free-floating exchange rate, removing import licensing, and liberalizing marketing and decontrolling prices. Privatization and tax reform are vital ingredients. In July 2000 the World Bank resumed loans to Kenya, ending a three year suspension; then halted lending a year later when the Moi government

Pres. Emilio Mwai Kibaki
Born: 15 Nov. 1931
Since December 2002

UN Photo Evan Schneider

POLITICAL
Head of State	Pres. Emilio Mwai Kibaki
Prime Minister	Raila Odinga
Ruling Party	ODM
Main Opposition	PNU
Independence	12 December 1963
National capital	Nairobi
Official languages	English & Swahili

PHYSICAL
Total area	224,000 sq. miles
	580,000 sq. km.
	(2 x Nevada)
Arable land	8% of land area
Coastline	333 miles/536 km

POPULATION
Total	39 million
Av. yearly growth	2.7%
Urban population	22%
Life expectancy	57.8 years
Adult literacy	85.1%

ECONOMY
Currency	Kenyan shillings (KSh) (US$1=80.50)
GDP (real)	$41.9 billion
GDP growth rate	2.5%
GDP per capita[1]	$1,349
GDP (ppp)[2]	$62.4 billion
GDP per cap. (ppp)	$1,568
Inflation rate	9.3%
Exports	$4.5 billion
Imports	$9.2 billion
External debt	$6.3 billion
Unemployment	40%

1. Atlas method.
2. See page 175 for an explanation of purchasing power parity (ppp).

failed to introduce anti-corruption measures. Kenya's tourist industry suffered and investor confidence were shaken in the aftermath of the 2008 post-election trauma.

Sectors

Agriculture provides employment to 75% of the workforce and accounts for about 30% of GDP and 50% of merchandise export value. Kenya is among the world's leading exporters of tea and coffee (mostly high-grade arabica). It is the world's largest supplier of pyrethrum, a natural insecticide. It also exports cut flowers, vegetables and fruit, cotton, sugar, pineapples, sisal, hides and skins. The country is self-sufficient in maize, the major staple food. Soda ash is mined and large deposits of titanium and zircon have been discovered along the coast. Other minerals include fluorspar, salt, limestone and precious stones. Manufacturing includes beverages, tobacco, textiles, electric and electronic appliances, metal products, food products, petroleum products, machinery, glass, cement, pulp and paper products, sugar and confectionery. Relying on wildlife and game reserves, tourism has become one of Kenya's major sources of foreign exchange.

Privatization

A privatization program that started in the nineties Kenya divested from more than 160 public enterprises. The container terminal operations at Mombasa harbor and the airport operations are privatized.

Investment

More than 200 foreign companies are registered in Kenya—most of them from the United Kingdom, Germany, and the US—and engaged in the manufacturing of products ranging from shoes to pharmaceuticals, petroleum products to beverages, foodstuffs, vehicles and automobiles. Established in 1954, the Nairobi Stock Exchange (NSE) is the oldest and largest Exchange in East and Central Africa.

Trade

A substantial portion of Kenya's exports (especially manufactured products and re-exported petroleum) go to COMESA countries. The European Union (including the UK) is Kenya's main supplier and second largest export market. However, in recent years South Africa has become a major source, while Kenya's exports to South Africa have also shown substantial growth. Tea exports, Kenya's largest single foreign exchange earner. Tourism, catering is second and coffee third.

Financial sector

Kenya has a well-developed financial sector comprising 48 licensed national and internationally-affiliated banks, 11 non-bank financial institutions, 4 building societies, 2 mortgage finance companies and 48 foreign exchange bureaus. Several major foreign banks offer a full range of services. The Capital Markets Authority regulates the stock market and the brokerage firms. More than sixty firms are listed on the Nairobi Stock Exchange (NSE)—a compliant member of the African Stock Exchanges Assocation (ASEA).

Taxes and tariffs

The corporate tax rate for non-residents is 37.5 percent. There is no capital gains tax. A value added tax (VAT) of 16 percent applies. There is no exchange control in effect. Taxes are levied on dividends (10%), interest (15 to 25%) and royalties (20%). (See page 138).

BUSINESS ACTIVITY

AGRICULTURE
Coffee, tea, corn, wheat, sugar cane, fruit, vegetables, dairy products, beef, pork, poultry, eggs.

INDUSTRIES
Small-scale consumer goods (plastic, furniture, batteries, textiles, soap, cigarettes, flour), agricultural products processing, oil refining, cement, tourism.

NATURAL RESOURCES
Gold, limestone, soda ash, salt barytes, rubies, fluorspar, garnets, wildlife.

EXPORTS
$4.5 billion (est. 2008): tea, coffee, petroleum products, fish, horticultural products.

IMPORTS
$9.2 billion (est. 2008): machinery and transportation equipment, consumer goods, petroleum products.

MAJOR TRADING PARTNERS
Uganda, South Africa, Tanzania, UK, US, UAE, Netherlands, Japan, China, India, Saudi Arabia, Pakistan.

Doing Business with Kenya

▶ Investment

Investment opportunities exist in tourism, agriculture (including ostrich and crocodile farming), and the manufacturing of electronics, plastics, chemicals, pharmaceuticals and engine parts. Foreign manufacturers are encouraged to use Kenya as a base to access and penetrate the larger East and Central African market. Special incentives are extended to factories in Export Processing Zones. Incentives offered to investors in the manufacturing and hotel sectors include tax breaks on the cost of buildings and capital machinery. The Investment Promotion Center provides a one-stop entry. As privatization proceeds new opportunities are offered in infrastructure development.

▶ Trade

There is a growing need for equipment relating to power generation, telecommunications, road building and food processing. A US firm has been successful in selling solar panels. Since the reduction of duties and VAT on computers, US and other foreign suppliers have been enjoying a healthy growth. US exporters who do not manufacture or assemble locally usually rely on local distributors with a thorough knowledge not only of the Kenyan but the regional market. Other than Coca-Cola, franchising has not been particularly successful.

▶ Trade finance

The US Eximbank is open to short- and medium-term financing for government and private sector entities in Kenya. Several banks and specialized financial institutions finance Kenyan exporters and importers.

▶ Selling to the government

Extensive road and rail repair with funding from the World Bank, African Development Bank, and other multilateral and bilateral sources should provide ample opportunity for foreign construction and engineering firms.

▶ Exchange controls

The Exchange Control Act has been repealed and there are no restrictions on converting or transferring funds associated with an investment or trade.

▶ Partnerships

Unlike franchising, joint ventures and licensing are common as they combine local marketing expertise with foreign manufacturing competence.

▶ Establishing a presence

To establish a presence, foreign firms merely need to register with the Kenyan Registrar of Companies. Incorporation of a company in Kenya as a subsidiary of a foreign entity is more complicated and usually requires the services of a local attorney.

▶ Financing projects

The Overseas Private Investment Corporation provides services to US investors. Kenya is also a member of the Multilateral Investment Guarantee Agency. Apart from the World Bank, IFC and African Development Bank, the Industrial Development Bank (IDB)—a Kenyan government-funded financial institution—provides medium and long term loan finance.

▶ Labor

Women constitute more than 25% of the work force in finance, insurance, and other business services and over 29% in public administration and agriculture. Some textile factories are almost exclusively staffed by women. The informal sector, known as *jua kali*, employs about 64% of all workers and accounts for about 90% of all new jobs outside the agricultural small holdings. Kenyan law provides safeguards and benefits for workers and spells out mechanisms and procedures to address complaints relating to worker rights. Wage scales for 12 different categories of employees are stipulated. Often benefits include housing and transportation.

▶ Legal rights

The Foreign Investment Protection Act protects investors against expropriation. There is also legislation to control monopolies and restrictive trade practices. Patents, trademarks and trade secrets are the responsibility of the Kenya Industrial Property Office in the Ministry of Research, Technical Training and Technology. Copyrights are handled by the Attorney General's office. Kenya is a member of several international and regional intellectual property conventions.

▶ Business Climate

Business executives are relatively informal and open to new ideas. The use of first names at an early stage of a business relationship is acceptable. Friendship and mutual trust are highly valued. English is spoken across the country.

LESOTHO

The small mountainous Kingdom of Lesotho is entirely surrounded by South Africa on which many of its citizens have traditionally depended for labor, especially in the gold mines. The sale of water to its large neighbor from the massive Lesotho Highlands Project is compensating in part for an erosion of job opportunities in the mines. the domestic economy is still largely dependent on subsistence farming but a small manufacturing base has developed in the milling, canning, leather, and jute industries. a rapidly expanding apparel-assembly sector exports to South Africa and other countries where Lesotho enjoys duty-free privileges.

Country profile

The terrain of the small, mountainous Kingdom of Lesotho has been likened to Switzerland and Andorra. Altitudes in the eastern half exceed 2,440 m and peaks in the northeast and along the Drakensberg mountains go beyond 3,350 m. Thabana Ntlenyana (3,482 m) in this range is the highest point in Southern Africa. Lesotho receives heavy rainfall (averaging 1,900 mm) and winter snow. Water is the country's most valuable natural asset. Lesotho has one of Africa's most homogeneous populations, consisting almost exclusively of Basotho. More than 90% are Christians, of whom about 45% belong to the Roman Catholic Church and the rest to various Protestant denominations. English is the official language but Sesotho is widely spoken.

History

In the 19th Century King Moshoeshoe I brought together a number of splinter groups in this mountainous stronghold, giving birth to the Basotho nation. It was in reality a kingdom made up of refugees from the fierce tribal wars in neighboring regions. Through smart military and diplomatic strategies Moshoeshoe managed to keep his enemies at bay until he was challenged by the Dutch-descended Boers who established their own Orange Free State Republic alongside his kingdom and then started making territorial claims. War ensued that led to the defeat of the Basotho at Thaba Bosiu. Moshoeshoe was forced to cede some of his best land to the Boers. Fearing further intrusion from the Boer republic the king asked for British protection. It was annexed to the British Cape Colony in 1871 but in 1884 it was restored to direct control by the British Crown. Lesotho functioned as the so-called Basutoland Protectorate until 1966, when it regained its independence. It functioned as a multiparty democracy until 1986—most of these years under Chief Lebowa Jonathan, a descendant of Moshoeshoe—when a military regime took power. The country returned to an elective political system in 1993 as a constitutional monarchy. Recent years have seen considerable political intrigue, an abortive coup attempt and unrest that necessitated the intervention of South African and Botswana forces to maintain the status quo. These troops left in March 1999 after peace was restored. King Letsie III has ruled since the death of his father, King Moshoeshoe II, in 1996. Prime Minister Pakalitha Mosisili heads the government as leader of the dominant Lesotho Congress for Democracy (LCD).

Government

Lesotho is a constitutional monarchy with real authority vested in the Prime Minister as the leader of the strongest party. A 120-member National Assembly is elected for a 5 year term. The 33 member Senate is made up of 22 principal chiefs (descendants of chiefs originally appointed by King Moshoeshoe I) and 11 appointed by the ruling party. In February 2007, Prime Minister Mosisili's LCD won 61 Assembly seats. The National Independent Party (NIP) took 21 seats and several smaller parties the rest.

Economic policy

Despite impressive gains in recent years, the government still faces severe and growing unemployment and underemployment in some areas as cutbacks in the South African mining sector continue to eliminate job opportunities for expatriate workers. Since 1988 reform policies have been aimed at flexibility and efficiency in tax collection, deregulation of the agricultural markets, and privatization.

Sectors

Agriculture employs a quarter of the workforce. Subsistence farming—mainly animal husbandry and maize cultivation—is the predominant activity, with wool and mohair as major exports. Other crops include wheat, sorghum, beans and sunflower oil. Since 1990, the contribution of the industrial sector to GDP has increased from 34 per cent to more than 45 percent. It provides employment for a quarter of the workforce. Most of the activity is in labor-intensive small to medium-sized cloth-

King Letsie III
Born: July 17, 1963
Since February 1996

POLITICAL

Head of State	King Letsie III
Prime Minister	Pakalitha Mosisili (May 1998)
Ruling Party	LCD
Main Opposition	NIP
Independence	4 October 1966
National capital	Maseru
Official languages	English & Sesotho

PHYSICAL

Total area	12,000 sq. miles 30,000 sq. km. (± Maryland)
Arable land	11% of land area
Coastline	Landlocked

POPULATION

Total	2.1 million
Av. yearly growth	0.12%
Urban population	25%
Life expectancy	40.38 years
Adult literacy	84.8%

ECONOMY

Currency	Loti (US$1=6.88)
GDP (real)	$1.3 billion
GDP growth rate	1.1%
GDP per capita[1]	$655
GDP (ppp)[2]	$2.5 billion
GDP per cap. (ppp)	$1,201
Inflation rate	4.8%
Exports	$821 million
Imports	$1.6 billion
External debt	$627 million
Unemployment	45%

1. Atlas method.
2. See page 175 for an explanation of purchasing power parity (ppp).

ing, footwear and textile enterprises. Limited mining operations consist largely of artesian digging for diamonds. There are, however, reserves of uranium, iron ore, lead and peat. Tourism is a growing sector. Lesotho's single most important asset is the Lesotho Highlands Water Project (LHWP). Delivering water from the highlands of Lesotho to South Africa's Vaal River system and generating hydropower for Lesotho, the project is Africa's largest. Water from the highlands is diverted to South Africa's thirsty Pretoria Witwatersrand Vereeniging (PWV) industrial complex and at full capacity the LHWP will contribute an estimated 5% of Lesotho's GDP. The project is expected to be completed in 2020 at a final cost of $8 billion. Lesotho has signed an Interim Poverty Reduction and Growth Facility with the IMF and a Millennium Challenge Account Compact with the US worth $362.5 million.

Privatization

Some of the 31 parastatals slated for privatization have been sold. One of the first to be spun off was Lesotho Airways and the most recent involved Lesotho Bank, when a private South African bank purchased a 70% share. There is speculation that the Lesotho Telecommunications Corporation (LTC) and the Lesotho Electric Company (LEC) may soon be on the block.

Investment

Lesotho has had considerable success in diversifying its traditional export base by moving into the production of textiles and electrical goods, footwear, radios and television sets with the help of foreign entrepreneurs, mostly from Europe, South Africa, Hong Kong, Singapore and Taiwan. The Lesotho Highlands Water Project (LHWP) represents major involvement by foreign firms from Europe, South Africa, Hong Kong, Singapore and Taiwan, as well as the US. Two Canadian mining companies, Messina Diamond Corp. and Diamond Works, have taken options on diamond exploration.

Trade

Most of Lesotho's exports go to other SADC countries and half of its imports originate from the region, primarily South Africa. Export growth has been strong in livestock, leather products, furniture, and garments—the latter produced for the most part by Taiwanese-owned factories. Its textile industry has largely benefited from the trade benefits extended by the United States under the Africa Growth and Opportunity Act (AGOA).

Financial sector

Lesotho is a member of the South African Common Monetary Area (CMA) and its currency, the Loti (plural Moloti) is at parity with the South African rand. It is therefore easily convertible for business transactions. Three local banking groups have branches throughout the country and two international banks have entered the market. The Lesotho Agricultural Development Bank (LADB) serves the agricultural sector.

Taxes and tariffs

As a member of the South African Customs Union (SACU), Lesotho's import tariffs and trading regime are determined collectively with other member states. Customs regulations allow temporary importation of raw materials on a duty-free basis. The corporate tax rate for non-residents is 25 percent. There is no capital gains tax. A value added tax (VAT) of 0 to 15 percent applies and exchange control is in effect. Taxes ranging from 0 to 25 percent are levied on income from dividends, interest and royalties. (See page 138).

BUSINESS ACTIVITY

AGRICULTURE
Corn, wheat, pulses, sorghum, barley, livestock.
INDUSTRIES
Food, beverages, textiles, handicrafts, construction, tourism.
NATURAL RESOURCES
Water, agricultural and grazing land, some diamonds and other minerals.
EXPORTS
$821 million (est. 2009): manufactures (clothing, footwear, road vehicles), wool and mohair, food and live animals.
IMPORTS
$1.6 billion (est. 2009): food, building materials, vehicles, machinery, medicines, petroleum products.
MAJOR TRADING PARTNERS
SADC, Hong Kong, China, US, Taiwan, Belgium, Germany, India, Canada.

Doing Business with Lesotho

▶ **Investment**

As the principal government investment agency, the Lesotho National Development Corporation (LNDC) assists with loans, serviced sites, training grants and work permits. New factories are allowed duty-free importation of raw materials and components and effective export processing zone status anywhere in the country. A non-repayable skills training grant covers 75% of the wage bill during the initial training period at newly-established manufacturers. Loan finance is provided by the LNDC for projects which can demonstrate long-term economic viability and sometimes it will take equity in new developments considered to be in the national interest. Continuing privatization provides new opportunities.

▶ **Trade**

Imports include agricultural products, pharmaceuticals, iron tubes and pipes, metalwork and office machinery. As the Lesotho Highlands Water Project (LHWP) enters its second phase there is a continuing need for construction equipment and engineering services. The consumer market is relatively small but several foreign companies have taken advantage of Lesotho's extensive preferential trade privileges in southern Africa, Europe and elsewhere by establishing export-oriented factories and assembly points.

▶ **Trade finance**

The customary irrevocable letter of credit is supported by a sophisticated private banking system.

▶ **Selling to the government**

Purchases of heavy equipment and engineering services by the LHWP are handled independently in accordance with internationally-accepted tendering procedures. There are several other government projects where outside donors control tenders. To date, for example, the World Bank assists with projects in agriculture, infrastructure, health, population, education, water, and land management and conservation.

▶ **Exchange controls**

As a member of the Common Monetary Area (CMA) Lesotho applies the same controls as South Africa, Swaziland and Namibia. Although closely monitored, the transfer of funds for trade and investment purposes and the repatriation of profits and dividends present no serious problem.

▶ **Partnerships**

The Lesotho-South Africa treaty governing the LHWP stipulates that all foreign companies working on this multi-billion dollar project must enter into joint ventures with local firms. In all other operations foreign investors, have the option of either involving local partners or setting up on their own.

▶ **Establishing a presence**

The LNDC serves as a one-stop shop for any foreign firm that wishes to establish an office, a branch or a manufacturing plant in the country. The process is relatively uncomplicated and does not take long.

▶ **Financing projects**

The World Bank, the International Development Association and the International Finance Corporation have been financing projects seen as vital to the national interest. Lesotho is a founding member of the Multilateral Investment Guarantee Agency. The LNDC provides loan finance for up to 15 years.

▶ **Labor**

The formal sector work force has a high literacy rate and an aptitude for new skills. Training grants are extended to new factories for up to 50% of the payroll. Wages are considerably lower than in neighboring South Africa. While this can be an advantage it also poses the danger of turnover as workers are lured to higher incomes across the border.

▶ **Legal rights**

Lesotho has no history of expropriation or nationalization of private property. It is a member of the International Center for the Settlement of Disputes. Like South Africa, Lesotho's legal system is based on Roman Dutch law. Intellectual Property rights are protected under laws drafted in cooperation with the World Intellectual property Organization . Lesotho is a signatory to the convention on the settlement of investment disputes between states.

▶ **Business climate**

The business environment shows a strong British influence and can be likened to that of neighboring South Africa. It is, however, customary to approach serious business at a slow and deliberate pace. English is widely spoken in both business and social circles.

LIBERIA

Africa's oldest republic, established more than two centuries ago by freed American slaves, Liberia suffered from years of turmoil caused by tribal strife and exacerbated by the intrusion of kinsmen from neighboring states. Hopes of recovery when Charles Taylor became president in July 1997 in an election declared free and fair by foreign observers, were dashed as he abused his powers and civil war resumed. In August 2003 Taylor was forced to step down and go into exile and 2005 Dr. Ellen Johnson-Sirleaf became Africa's first female head of state when she won a hotly contested election against world soccer star George Weah. The new government has aggressively pursued foreign investors to reinvigorate the economy.

Country profile

The Republic of Liberia has a hot and humid monsoon climate lasting from April to November. The coastline is straight, with shallow, mangrove-fringed lagoons and no natural harbors. The land rises from the broad coastal plain to a plateau and high mountain ranges on the northern borders. Diamonds are extracted from the river valleys and timber and rubber from the forests. Some 30 indigenous groups belong to three cultural or linguistic groupings—the Mandé and Atlantic Mel in the northern half of the country and the Kru (or Kruan) in the southern half of the country. The Liberians of African-American lineage, who dominated the country's politics from the 1820s to 1980, account for only 5% of the total population and are concentrated around Monrovia and other coastal centers. There are also small groups of Lebanese and Ful (Fulani) in these cities and towns. English is the official language but a Creole version referred to as Merico or Liberian English is the mother tongue of the Americo-Liberians. More than 70% of the population profess ethnic religious beliefs, 20% practice the Muslim faith and 10% are Christians.

History

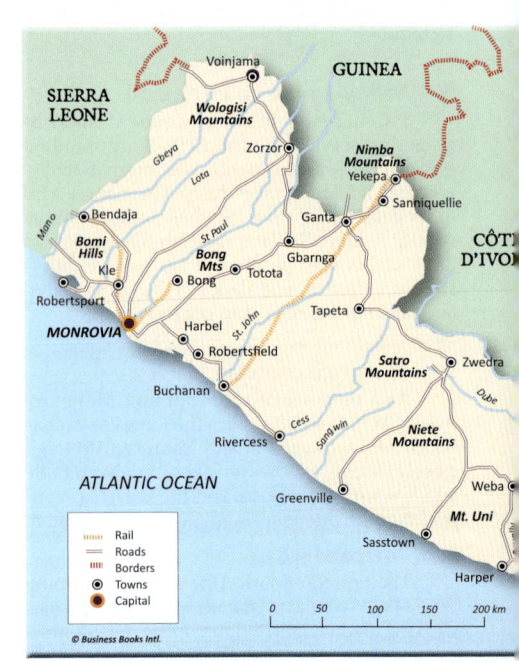

A thousand years ago the territory now known as Liberia was occupied by the Mandé, Kru and Atlantic Mel-speaking peoples from the north and east and in the mid-15th Century the coastal towns were conducting a flourishing slave trade with European merchants. Modern Liberia (derived from the Latin liber or freedom) was the creation of the American Colonization Society (ACS) founded in 1816 to encourage the return of freed slaves to Africa, similar to a program organized by the British in Sierra Leone. Over a period of 40 years some 12,000 slaves were voluntarily resettled. The original constitution denied indigenous Liberians equal rights with these American emigrants and their descendants. With modest assistance from the US government, Monrovia, named after President James Monroe, and other settlements such as Robertsport, Buchanan, Greenville and Harper, were established. On 26 July 1847 Liberia declared itself a sovereign and independent republic. Effective administration from Monrovia was limited to the coast where the settlers and their descendants lived. It was only since 1920 that real progress was made towards opening up the interior with the help of a 43 mile (69 km) railroad from Monrovia to the Bomi Hills. American influence remained strong. The US dollar was then, and still is, the preferred currency. Firestone rubber company was the first major investor. President William Tubman, a descendant of the African American settlers, served seven consecutive terms and his successor, William Tolbert, ruled from 1971 to 1980, when he was killed by Master Sergeant Samuel Doe, self-styled leader of the National Democratic Party of Liberia (NDPL). A devastating civil war raged from 1989 until 1996. In accordance with the Abuja Accord the warring Liberian factions agreed to participate in elections during July 1997. Charles Taylor's National Patriotic Front of Liberia won. Faced with renewed insurgency, Taylor involved himself in destabilizing neighboring Sierra Leone and Guinea. In August 2003, Taylor was forced to go into exile and was replaced by Deputy President Moses Blah who in turn stepped down in favor of entrepreneur Gyude Bryant who promised free elections. In the November 2005 presidential election, Harvard graduate and former World Bank official, Dr. Ellen Johnson-Sirleaf, defeated world soccer star George Weah to become Africa's first female head of state.

Government

The president is elected for a six year term. The bicameral National Assembly consists of a 30-seat Senate elected for a nine year term and a 64-seat House of Representatives elected for 6 years. In the October 2005 election Weah's Congress for Democratic Change (CDC) captured 15 seats in the House against 9 for the main opposition Liberal Party (LP). The United Party (UP) associated with Johnson-Sirleaf won 8 seats.

Pres. Ellen Johnson-Sirleaf
Born: 1939
Since Jan 2006

UN Photo Erin Siegal

POLITICAL
Head of State	Pres. Ellen Johnson-Sirleaf
Independence	26 July 1847
Ruling party	CDC
Main opposition	LP
National capital	Monrovia
Official languages	English

PHYSICAL
Total area	43,000 sq. miles
	111,000 sq. km.
	(± Tennessee)
Arable land	4% of land area
Coastline	360 miles/579 km

POPULATION
Total	3.4 million
Av. yearly growth	2.7%
Urban population	60%
Life expectancy	41.8 years
Adult literacy	57.5%

ECONOMY
Currency	Liberian dollar (L$) (US$1=68.50)
GDP (real)	$1.2 billion
GDP growth rate	4.4%
GDP per capita[1]	$267
GDP (ppp)[2]	$1.1 billion
GDP per cap. (ppp)	$276
Inflation rate	7.8%
Exports	$1.2 billion
Imports	$7.1 billion
External debt	$3.7 billion
Unemployment	85%

1. Atlas method.
2. See page 175 for an explanation of purchasing power parity (ppp).

Economic policy

Civil war and official mismanagement have seriously impaired Liberia's economy. Much of the infrastructure around Monrovia has been destroyed in the war while international trade sanctions imposed against the Taylor government prevented the country from marketing diamonds and timber on the open world markets. Numerous businessmen left the country, siphoning off capital and causing a serious brain drain. Only the registration of foreign merchant vessels under the Liberian flag continued operating smoothly from a small Washington office. President Johnson-Sirleaf, a Harvard-trained banker and administrator, has taken steps to reduce corruption, build support from international donors, and encourage private investment.

Sectors

More than two-thirds of Liberia's workforce is dependent on agriculture. Rubber is the principal cash crop and provided 28% of export revenue before the war. Starting with Firestone many years ago, significant rubber plantations are still foreign-owned even though smallholders are today responsible for over half the total production. Coffee and cocoa are grown for export while palm oil is mainly produced for the domestic market. Food crops include rice, cassava and vegetables. Commercial ocean fishing concentrates on shrimp. Iron ore is the premier mining activity and normally accounts for more than half of all exports. In some years, however, the value of diamond sales exceeds that of iron ore. There are known deposits of bauxite, manganese, columbite, uranium, tantalite, copper, tin, lead, and zinc. Manufacturing is confined mainly to textiles, food processing, wood products, cement and chemicals.

Investment

Civil war and government mismanagement destroyed much of Liberia's economy and the infrastructure in and around the capital, Monrovia. Many entrepreneurs fled, causing a drain in capital and expertise. After the expulsion of Taylor, restoration of peace and the establishment of a democratically-elected government in 2006, many have returned. Richly endowed with water, mineral resources, forests, and a climate favorable to agriculture, Liberia has the potential of once again becoming a significant producer and exporter of basic products such as raw timber and rubber. Local manufacturing, mainly foreign owned, has always been small in scope. The reconstruction of infrastructure and the raising of incomes in this ravaged economy will largely depend on generous financial and technical assistance from donor countries and foreign investment in key sectors, such as infrastructure and power generation.

Trade

Major exports from Liberia include diamonds, iron ore, rubber, timber and coffee, while exports consists of mostly of fuels and lubricants, chemicals, machinery and transport equipment, manufactured goods, and rice and other foodstuffs. In 2001 the United Nations imposed sanctions on Liberian diamonds and timber exports, along with an arms embargo and a travel ban on government officials in an effort to dissuade the Taylor government from supporting rebel insurgents in Sierra Leone. Embargoes on timber and diamond exports have been lifted opening new sources of revenue for the government. Rubber exports also resumed.

Investment

In 1925 the US Firestone Rubber Company became a major foreign player in Liberia

BUSINESS ACTIVITY

AGRICULTURE
Rubber, coffee, cocoa, rice, cassava (tapioca), palm oil, sugar cane, bananas, sheep goats, timber.
INDUSTRIES
Rubber and palm oil processing, diamonds.
NATURAL RESOURCES
Iron ore, timber, diamonds, gold.
EXPORTS
$1.2 billion (est. 2006): diamonds, iron ore, rubber, timber, coffee, cocoa.
IMPORTS
$7.1 billion (est. 2006): fuel, chemicals, machinery, transportation equipment, manufactured goods, foodstuffs.
MAJOR TRADING PARTNERS
Malaysia, US, South Africa, South Korea, Poland, Spain, Japan, China, Singapore.

when it obtained a 99-year lease on 1 million acres of forest near Monrovia. For decades Firestone was the country's largest employer. It branched into a number of other financial and commercial areas, but rubber remained its major export until the 1950s when iron ore production gained dominance.

Financial Sector

Currently, banks in Liberia operate only as a repository for funds. A fee is charged to receive a wire transfer, to make a deposit or withdrawal, or to cash checks. Banks do not pay interest or make loans.

Taxes and tariffs

The corporate tax rate for non-residents is 35 percent and capital gains tax 15 percent. Exchange control is in effect. A taxes of 15% is levied on dividends, interest and royalties. (See page 138).

Special ties

Special ties between the US and Liberia date back to its creation in the 1820s. Over the years this close relationship was severely tested by human rights abuses, corruption and lawlessness. Since the ousting of Taylor and restoration of democracy the close relationship has been restored.

Doing Business with Liberia

▶ **Investment**

A National Investment Commission was established to grant incentives to foreign investment, some in the form of monopolies in areas such as rice and gasoline importation. This practice has served to stifle further foreign interest. Also still in force is the 1975 "Liberianization" law that prohibits foreign ownership of businesses such as travel agencies, retail gasoline stations, and beer and soft drink distributorships. Investors also have to cope with a myriad of ministries and agencies, conflicting rules and regulations, and bureaucratic red tape. To build investor confidenece the Governance and Economic Management Action Plan (GEMAP) was created, aimed at ensuring transparent revenue collection and allocation.

▶ **Trade**

Relatively cheap products such as used clothing, used cars, and used equipment offer trade prospects. There is also a demand for US consumer goods such as toiletries, hair products, and other personal care items. It is expected that the market for pesticides and chemical fertilizers should improve as post-conflict Liberia returns to full production in the agricultural sector.

▶ **Selling to the government**

As economic conditions improve, the Liberian government is likely to become a significant market. New infrastructural projects will create a need for foreign supplies and services.

▶ **Exchange controls**

There is no difficulty obtaining Liberian currency at the unofficial rate and there are no restrictions on converting or transferring investment funds.

▶ **Establishing a presence**

Foreign firms considering establishing an office are strongly advised to retain the services of a local attorney. They should also take cognizance of a law that mandates that Liberian nationals should be employed at all levels, including upper management.

▶ **Project financing**

Liberia does not participate in OPIC or other investment insurance programs. Foreign investors will also find it difficult obtain credit on the local market.

▶ **Labor**

A considerable number of skilled professionals emigrated during the civil war. There is, however, no shortage of unskilled and semiskilled labor in Liberia. Unofficial unemployment figures are as high as 85%. Current law requires that Liberian nationals should be employed at all levels and the Ministry of Labor has on occasion held up work permits for expatriates and intervened in disputes between investors and their Liberian employees.

▶ **Legal rights**

Liberia's judiciary has at times been subjected to political, social, familial, and financial pressures. Currently several US firms are in litigation over the expropriation of property during the seven-year civil conflict. In past cases the government has been accused of settling such claims at well below market value.

LIBYA

Top quality oil reserves—the largest on the African continent—coupled with a relatively small population, enable Libya to be among the top on the African continent in per capita income. UN sanctions introduced in 1992 against Libya in the wake of the terrorist bombing of US and a French commercial airliners were lifted in September 2003 after Muammar Qaddafi accepted responsibility and paid compensation to the families of victims. However, US sanctions prohibiting US-Libyan business remained in place until April 2004 when the Bush Administration lifted most restrictions and opened the way for investment and commercial activities. Certain controls on US exports to Libya are, however, still maintained.

Country profile

The *Great Socialist People's Libyan Arab Jamahiriya* sits on a vast plateau. The Tripolitania region, centered around Tripoli has a Mediterranean climate. To the south is the dryer Jefara Plateau and in the east the high escarpment of Cyrenaica, with Benghazi at its hub. Sabha, Kufra and Jofra are clusters of oases, with extensive croplands under irrigation. The predominantly Arab and Muslim population speak Western Arabic dialects. There are various Berber and Tuareg minorities around Tripoli and at oases in the desert.

History

The first inhabitants of Libya were Berber tribes. Ancient Libya was invaded by Phoenicians, Numidians, Greeks, Romans, Vandals and Byzan-tines, followed in 648 by Arabs and the Turks in 1551. Both Tripolitania and Cyrenaica became part of the Ottoman Empire. Tripolitania became one of the outposts for the Barbary pirates who exacted "tribute" payments from merchant ships in the Mediterranean. This practice led to a four year war between the Pasha of Tripoli and the US ending in a peace treaty in June 1805, exempting US ships from this "tribute." Before World War II Italy took control of the coastal towns while the Turks ruled the interior. After the war, the Italians began to pacify the country. Its dominance ended in 1942 when the German-Italian Axis was defeated in the Western Desert. The British took Tripolitania and Cyrenaica and the French occupied the Fezzan. In 1951 Libya became independent under King Idris. Wealth followed the discovery of oil in 1960 and led to corruption and discontent. On 1 September 1969, a 28-year-old army captain, Muammar

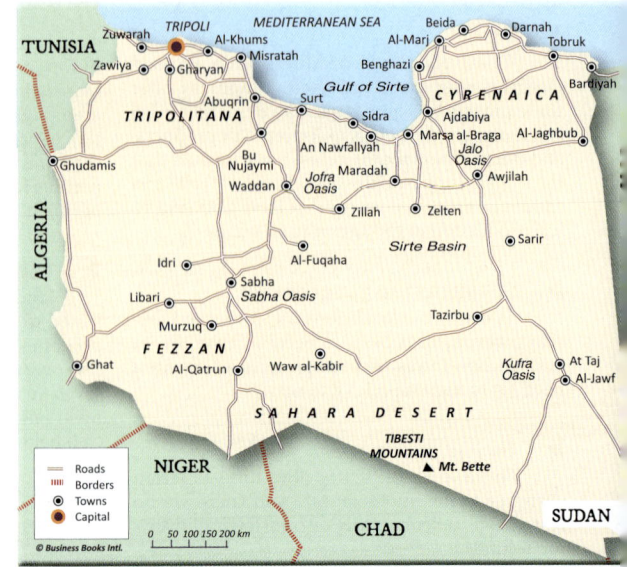

Qaddafi, seized power. Eight years later he formed a monolithic General People's Congress and renamed the country, the *Great Socialist People's Libyan Arab Jamahiriya*.

Government

Since March 1977 Libya has been ruled according to the tenets of Qaddafi's Third Universal Theory enunciated in his Green Book. The electorate is divided into some 1,500 People's Congresses, each electing 13-member People's Committees (local governments) which in turn send two members each to a General People's Congress (national legislature) that meets briefly once a year. The General People's Congress elects the General Secretariat (the highest executive body) and the General People's Committee (cabinet). In 1977 Muammar Qaddafi was elected Revolutionary Leader and head of state.

Economic policy

Oil revenues and a small population should give Libya one of the highest per capita incomes in Africa, but there is considerable inequality in actual incomes. Non-oil manufacturing and construction sectors have expanded from largely processing agricultural products to include the production of petrochemicals, iron, steel, and aluminum and currently account for about 20% of GDP. Dry conditions and poor soils severely limit agricultural output. Libya imports most of its food. The country relies heavily on the Great Manmade River Project for agricultural irrigation but significant additional investment is devoted to desalinization research to meet the growing water demand. Another major project involves rail links with Egypt and Tunisia. Libya has reduced state subsidies and implemented privatization but it still has some way to go in transforming and modernizing its state-driven socialist economy. It has implemented significant economic reforms as part of a broader campaign to reintegrate the country into the international fold.

Privatization

The centrally planned economy began to be opened up for free enterprise in the 1980s. In 2007 the state-owned Oilinvest Group sold a 65% stake in Tamoil to Colony Capital (United States) for $5.4 billion. A few economic and social services formerly performed by the state are now handled by private enterprise.

Col. Muammar Qaddafi
Born: 1945
Since Sept 1969

UN Photo Evan Schneider

POLITICAL	
Head of State	Col. Muammar Qaddafi
Ruling Party	Arab Socialist Union
Independence	24 December 1951
National capital	Tripoli
Official language	Arabic

PHYSICAL	
Total area	680,000 sq. miles 1,760,000 sq. km. (± Alaska)
Arable land	1% of land area
Coastline	1,100 miles/1,770 km

POPULATION	
Total	6.3 million
Av. yearly growth	2.2%
Urban population	78%
Life expectancy	77.26 years
Adult literacy	82.6%

ECONOMY	
Currency	Libyan Dinar (LD) (US$1=1.24)
GDP (real)	$87.8 billion
GDP growth rate	2.1%
GDP per capita[1]	$11,576
GDP (ppp)[2]	$99.5 billion
GDP per cap. (ppp)	$15,497
Inflation rate	2.5%
Exports	$34.2 billion
Imports	$22.1 billion
External debt	$5.6 billion
Unemployment	30%

1. Atlas method.
2. See page 175 for an explanation of purchasing power parity (ppp).

Sectors

The economy depends largely on revenues derived from the oil sector that contributes 95% of export earnings, one-quarter of GDP, and 60% of public sector wages. There are deposits of iron, potassium, magnesium, sulphur, gypsum and phosphate.

Trade

Petroleum exports account for most of Libya's foreign hard currency earnings. The government claims that UN sanctions during the nineties have cost the country more than $24 billion in revenues. The state-owned National Oil Corporation maintains a virtual monopoly over the marketing of all Libyan oil and gas. State enterprises also control most manufacturing, agriculture and trade outside the petroleum sector. Poor soils and an unfavorable climate limit agricultural output and Libya currently imports about 75% of its food requirements.

Investment

Since 1968, Libya's oil industry has been run by the state-owned National Oil Corporation (NOC) along with a number of smaller subsidiary companies. The leading foreign oil producer in Libya is Italy's Agip-ENI, operating in the country since 1959. Two US oil companies—Exxon and Mobil—withdrew from Libya in 1982, following a US trade embargo in 1981. Five other US companies—Amarada Hess, Conoco, Grace Petroleum, Marathon, and Occidental—remained active in Libya until 1986, when the Reagan administration ordered all US firms to cease activities against a state charged with sponsoring terrorism. US oil companies have been returning to Libya since the US government lifted of sanctions in 2004.

Lockerbie

Relations between Libya and the US and its western partners reached an all-time low following the "Lockerbie Affair" in December 1988 when all 259 passengers aboard Pan Am flight 103 died in an explosion over Lockerbie in Scotland—an event blamed by London and Washington on two Libyan nationals. Qaddafi's initial refusal to extradite the two suspects led to the imposition of mandatory economic sanctions against Libya by the UN Security Council on 31 March 1992. The US formulated its own sanctions under the Iran and Libya Sanctions Act. In 2000 Qaddafi sought a way out of the impasse by extraditing the suspects for trial in The Hague. This led to the suspension of UN sanctions and the re-establishment of economic and diplomatic relations by most nations, excluding the US. Early in 2001, one of the two accused, Abdel Baset Ali Mohmed Al-Megrahi, was convicted and sentenced to twenty years in a Scottish jail. After Libya accepted responsibility for Pan Am 103 and undertook to make payments to the families of the victims of both Pan Am 103 and a UTA flight downed over Niger in 1989, UN sanctions were finally lifted by the UN Security Council in 2003. The US kept its embargo in place until April 2004 when the Bush administration lifted it in response to Libya's commitment to open its weapons programs to international inspectors and to dismantle its weapons of mass destruction. On June 30, 2006, the U.S. rescinded Libya's designation as a state sponsor of terrorism and today most US commercial business, investment and trade with Libya is possible.

Taxes

The corporate tax rate for non-residents is 15 to 40 percent and a capital gains tax of 15 to 40 percent as well. Exchange control is in effect. There is 10 percent tax on income from interest but no taxes on dividends and royalties. (See page 138).

BUSINESS ACTIVITY

AGRICULTURE
Wheat, barley, olives, dates, citrus, vegetables, peanuts, beef, eggs.
INDUSTRIES
Petroleum, food processing, textiles, handicrafts, cement.
NATURAL RESOURCES
Petroleum, natural gas, gypsum.
EXPORTS
$34.2 billion (est. 2009): Crude oil, refined petroleum products, natural gas.
IMPORTS
$22.1 billion (est. 2008): machinery, transport equipment, manufactured goods, food.
MAJOR TRADING PARTNERS
Italy, Germany, US, Spain, France, Turkey, China, Greece, UK, Tunisia.

Doing Business with Libya

▶ **Investment**

Since the lifting of UN sanctions the overseas focus has been on the development of several dormant oil exploration and production projects. Continued expansion of gas production remains a high priority in Libya. The National Oil Corporation is offering concessions to foreign partners. Libya has had no railroad in operation since 1965, as all previous systems were dismantled. Current plans are to construct a 890 mile (1,435 km) standard gauge line from the Tunisian frontier to Tripoli and Misratah, continuing inland to Sabha, the center of a mineral-rich area, as well as another that will link Tobruk with As Sallum in Egypt.

▶ **Trade**

Since the lifting of UN sanctions Libya has resumed purchases of oil industry equipment. Latest trade figures show a growing market in food and live animals, manufactured goods, machinery and equipment and chemicals. Most purchasing is done by the government and foreign currency payments, even in the case of private sector purchases, are state-monitored and controlled. The National Oil Corporation prefers to sell crude to refiners under long-term contracts and very little Libyan oil finds its way onto the spot market.

▶ **Trade finance**

Since April 1999 Libya has been eligible for international export credit guarantees and risk assurance. In the past commodity imports have been purchased by confirmed letters of credit at standard terms. Despite occasional administrative delays, Libya has maintained a good payment record in the past.

▶ **Selling to the government**

Most sales to Libya are in fact to the government. State agencies hold monopolies on a broad range of products. For example, pharmaceuticals—one of the areas where US firms are once again allowed to trade—are purchased at public tender by the Medical Supply Organization. In several other areas the Export-Import Board allocates foreign exchange for the importation of specific products by state or even to private enterprises. Libya is a major purchaser of agricultural products and US producers of wheat, barley and other products are expected to gain largely after sanctions were lifted. There are constant modifications and a local expert is needed to keep potential exporters current. Equipment for the National Oil Corporation and its subsidiaries is largely sourced through a central purchasing agency in London.

▶ **Exchange controls**

Controls apply. Even though the government has declared the intention to unify the official and parallel market exchange rates, a large differential persists.

▶ **Partnership**

To ensure that overseas interests were not subject to the asset freeze imposed by UN sanctions in the early nineties, Libyan holdings, both outright and in partnership with foreign firms, went out of their way to obfuscate and disguise their partnerships. Since the lifting of sanctions, the Libyan authorities have actively sought new partnerships.

▶ **Establishing a presence**

Since the final departure of its oil companies in 1986, the US has not had any formal links with Libya. The return of US business has been actively sought after the lifting of sanctions.

▶ **Project financing**

Despite occasional instances of administrative delays, Libya has maintained a good payment record on foreign service contracts. Although international financing has become available after the lifting of UN sanctions, Libya is not likely to be a candidate for major loans. The government is expected to continue shying away from long-term debt in its endeavors to maintain a balanced financial position in foreign transactions.

▶ **Labor**

A constraint is imposed on the economy by the shortage of skilled and unskilled labor. The country relies on a large contingent of foreign technicians and about a million migrant manual workers from Egypt and other neighboring countries. Most Libyan workers are absorbed by an extensive state bureaucracy. In 1990, some 70% of all Libyan salaried workers were on the state's payroll.

▶ **Business climate**

Even though Arabic is the official language and often the only one spoken by officials, both English and Italian are widely used in the business community. Local representatives are essential to establish a long-term presence and make inroads.

MADAGASCAR

The world's fourth largest island, Madagascar, is emerging from several years of neglect and beginning to attract the attention of investors with its ample supply of natural resources, labor, and an ecosystem with great potential for tourism. The government, in cooperation with the IMF and World Bank, reduced budget deficits, corrected the overvaluation of the currency and removed trade barriers. In recent years, foreign investors have been taking a closer look at this Indian Ocean island, said by experts to have formed part of the main African continent in prehistoric times. Agriculture, fishing and forestry, are the main components of the economy.

Country profile

The Republic of Madagascar (known as the Malagasy Republic from 1959 to 1975 and as the Democratic Republic of Madagascar from 1975 until 1992) is situated 400 miles off the east coast of Africa. It is the world's fourth largest island after Greenland, New Guinea and Borneo, and nearly twice the size of the British Isles, measuring 1,570 km from north to south and 570 km at its widest. The highest point is the volcanic Mt. Tsaratanana (2,876 m) in the far north. The east coast is hot and humid, the central highlands around Antananarivo temperate, and the savanna regions in the southwest, arid. There are 18 ethnic groups of Malay-Polynesian, African and Arab origin. The Merina highlanders are the largest group, followed by the coastal Betsimisisaraka. Later arrivals include French, Comorians, Indians and Chinese. More than half the population follow traditional tribal beliefs brought from Borneo. The remainder are mostly Christians apart from a few Muslims.

History

The Malagasy are of mixed Malayo-Indonesian and African-Arab ancestry. Settled originally around the 10th Century by Borneo mariners who arrived in outrigger canoes, the island was first claimed by the Portuguese early in the 16th Century. They named it Madagascar after a reference to such an island in the writings of Marco Polo. After destroying existing Arab settlements on the island, the Portuguese were displaced by the French. Towards the end of the 19th Century the island was formally handed over to France by the British in return for a free hand in Egypt and Zanzibar. After several uprisings, a referendum called by France in

1958 showed Madagascans overwhelmingly in favor of independence within the French community. In 1959, pro-French Philibert Tsiranana became the first president. Admiral Didier Ratsiraka, who was named president in June 1975 after coup in 1973, nationalized banks, insurance companies, shipping companies, the oil refinery and a leading foreign trading company. In response to riots following his reelection in 1989, Pres. Ratsiraka agreed to share power with Albert Zafy. Elected in 1993 President Zafy was impeached by parliament for abusing his constitutional powers during an economic crisis. In 1996, Ratsiraka won again only to be defeated in the 2001 election by Marc Ravalomanana. Re-elected in 2006, Ravalomanana was ousted in a coup by Andry Rajoelina early in 2009. At the age of thirty-five Rajoelina became Africa's youngest head of state when a deal was negotiated in Addis Ababa in November 2009 whereby he accepted two co-presidents in a transitional government—one closely associated with Ravalomanana (living in exile in South Africa) and the other with former President Zafy. Andry Rajoelina is a radio and TV station owner and former mayor of Antananarivo.

Government

The executive President serves four-year terms and appoints the Council of Ministers. The bicameral parliament comprises a 90-member Senate (60 members elected for a six year term, 10 for each province by provincial electors, and 30 members appointed); and the National Assembly whose 127 members are elected for 4 years. A Council of Ministers is appointed by the Prime Minister. In November 2010 Rajoelina had a new constitution validated by referendum to reduce the minimum age for the presidency from 40 to 35, enabling him to be a candidate in the election scheduled for May 2011.

Economic policy

The Malagasy government began to implement market-oriented reforms in the mid-nineties. Under a program directed by the World Bank and IMF it liberalized exchange, trade, and price systems; eliminated restrictions in key economic sectors, such as petroleum, food, and transportation; and began to tighten fiscal and monetary policies. The country has

Pres. Andry Nirina Rajoelina
Born: 30 May 1974
Since March 2009

POLITICAL

Head of State	Pres. Andry Rajoelina
Transitional	2 Co-presidents
Independence	26 June 1960
National capital	Antananarivo
Official languages	Malagasy & French

PHYSICAL

Total area	227,000 sq. miles 587,000 sq. km (2 x Arizona)
Arable land	5% of land area
Coastline	3000 miles/4,828 km

POPULATION

Total	20.6 million
Av. yearly growth	3.0%
Urban population	29%
Life expectancy	62.9 years
Adult literacy	68.9%

ECONOMY

Currency	Malagasy Ariary MGA (US$1=2,090)
GDP (real)	$8.2 billion
GDP growth rate	-4.5%
GDP per capita[1]	$406
GDP (ppp)[2]	$18.2 billion
GDP per cap. (ppp)	$929
Inflation rate	8.9%
Exports	$1.0 billion
Imports	$1.8 billion
External debt	$2.4 billion
Unemployment	23%

1. Atlas method.
2. See page 175 for an explanation of purchasing power parity (ppp).

been on a steady albeit slow growth pattern since—recording an impressive 32.6% growth in GDP in 2007. Broadening of the tax base and strengthening of tax administration achieved a major increase in revenues and a reduction in deficits. Returning confidence boosted domestic financial savings and investment. Poverty reduction and combating corruption have been priorities in recent years.

Sectors

Agriculture, including fishing and forestry, is the mainstay of the economy, accounting for a third of GDP. Major capital-intensive industries are oil refining, fertilizer and cement production, textile manufacturing and the processing of agricultural products. Madagascar is the world's 10th largest chrome producer. Prospecting by US and European companies since the 1970s has led to the discovery of small deposits of oil and gas. Madagascar also has substantial reserves of high quality chrome ore, graphite, mica, bauxite and iron ore as well as small deposits of uranium, quartz, monazite, garnet, amethyst, ilmenite, zircon and titanium. Tourism is a growing sector and expected to become a major foreign exchange earner.

Privatization

In the course of the privatization of the public bank, BFV, its nonperforming loans were transferred to a debt workout unit (SOFIRE), which is responsible for continuing the recovery effort. The second public bank (BTM) was offered for sale in 1998. The petroleum company (SOLIMA) was also put up for sale. Forty other state enterprises are earmarked for sale.

Trade

Agriculture, including fishing and forestry, contributes 70% of export earnings. Minerals, with chromium in the lead, form about 5% of exports. Other export items include iron ore, graphite, mica, and bauxite.. Exports of apparel have boomed in recent years primarily due to duty-free access to the US. The Multilateral Investment Guarantee Agency (MIGA) supported reforms in the country's customs clearance process.

Investment

France is the leading foreign investor, followed by Hong Kong, Singapore, Germany and Italy. Some 125 foreign companies are involved in the island's Export Processing Zones (EPZ). Offshore fishing and shrimp farming have also developed into significant foreign exchange earners in recent years, attracting both Japanese and European investors. The discovery of important deposits of sapphires in the north and the south of the country has attracted investors from the United States, Thailand, Indonesia, Israel and Europe. The local Internet service has grown considerably since 1998.

Financial Sector

The banking system comprises six commercial banks, of which several are under foreign control. Union Commercial Bank (UCB) and State Bank of Mauritius (SBM) are branches of Mauritian parent companies of the same name. The former state bank BFV was purchased by the French bank Société Générale, and BTM bank is in the process of privatization. Financial statements are required from banks in compliance with international standards.

Taxes and tariffs

The corporate tax rate for non-residents is 10 to 23 percent. A value added tax (VAT) of 20 percent applies and exchange control is in effect. Taxes are levied on interest (23%) and royalties (10%). (See page 138).

BUSINESS ACTIVITY

AGRICULTURE
Coffee, vanilla, sugar cane, cloves, cocoa, rice, cassava (tapioca), beans, bananas, peanuts, livestock.

INDUSTRIES
Meat processing, soap, breweries, tanneries, sugar, textiles, glassware, cement, automobile assembly, paper, petroleum, tourism.

NATURAL RESOURCES
Graphite, chromite, coal, bauxite, salt, quartz, tar sands, semiprecious stones, mica, fish.

EXPORTS
$1.0 billion (est.2009): coffee, vanilla, cloves, shellfish, sugar, petroleum products, cotton.

IMPORTS
$1.8 billion (est. 2009): capital goods, petroleum, consumer goods, food.

MAJOR TRADING PARTNERS
France, US, Germany, Italy, South Africa, Mauritius, China, Iran.

Doing Business with Madagascar

▶ **Investment**

A *"guichet unique"* or one-stop office co-ordinates new investment proposals. In recent years the government has dismantled some of the regulatory and tax constraints impeding foreign investment, especially in the energy, mining, hydrocarbon, telecommunication, and air transportation sectors. Other areas with good investment potential include hotels and other tourist facilities, aqua-culture, and apparel manufacturing. An Export Processing Zone (EPZ) is a major area for foreign direct investment.

▶ **Trade**

Manufacturers of telecommunications, mining and petroleum extraction equipment, road-building and repair machinery, automotive spare parts, lubricants, hardware and civil aviation equipment will be able to sell in Madagascar as the country's development and reconstruction programs unfold. A need for wheat, flour and edible oils in a liberalized market offers further potential for exporters. Import licenses are not needed except for a few strategic items. Telecommunications items, however, do require prescreening to ensure compatibility.

▶ **Trade finance**

Eximbank has introduced a new program to assist US trade with Madagascar. Local credit is available to exporters of traditional agricultural products such as vanilla, coffee, cocoa and cloves at relatively high interest rates.

▶ **Selling to the government**

Tenders for government-funded projects are usually announced in official and local journals or on radio and television. Normally these bids are handled in a transparent fashion although on occasion international bids have been awarded to favored local suppliers without explanation. Lack of transparency does not, however, appear to have affected the privatization process where public bidding has generally been open and foreign investors have been welcomed.

▶ **Exchange controls**

Exchange controls were eliminated in 1996 and there are no restrictions on converting or transferring funds associated with a foreign investment, including remittances of investment capital, earnings, loan repayments, and lease payments into foreign currency at a legal market clearing rate.

▶ **Partnership**

Local partners are helpful in finding a way through a bureaucratic maze requiring from investors a series of permits from several government ministries. The Malagasy partner is likely be a minority shareholder.

▶ **Establishing a presence**

In 1996, in a drastic departure from its socialist past, Madagascar adopted laws allowing for the first time not only local private interests but foreigners the freedom to establish, acquire, and dispose of business interests.

▶ **Project finance**

On March 31, 1998, OPIC and Madagascar signed a bilateral Investment Incentive Agreement. Madagascar is a member of the Multilateral Investment Guarantee Agency. The World Bank and the African Development Bank have also financed a variety of infrastructure projects.

▶ **Labor**

There is widespread unemployment and wage rates in the country are among the lowest in the world. Malagasy workers are easily trained and skills are readily available in areas such as textiles, knitting, and clothing assembly.

▶ **Legal rights**

Madagascar is busy restoring foreign trust after the seizure by its socialist government in the 1970s of property owned by foreign oil companies to create SOLIMA, the state oil company. The expropriation claims of some of the affected companies have been settled. Today the government is committed to a system of arbitration for commercial conflicts under a new arbitration law. Madagascar is a member of the World Intellectual Property Organization and has two offices for IPR protection: OMAPI, *Office Malgache de la Propriété industrielle* (Malagasy Office for Industrial Property) and OMDA, *Office Malgache des Droits d'Auteurs* (Malagasy Office for Copyrights).

▶ **Business climate**

Malagasy people are culturally reserved. The concept of sales service and customer support is relatively new to the island and is primarily practiced by distributors of computers and automobiles. Retailers of most consumer goods rarely accept returns. French is the language of business but a substantial number of people also speak English.

MALAWI

Landlocked Malawi is one of the most densely populated countries on the African continent. With some of the continent's most fertile soil and ample rainfall, it relies heavily on agricultural products such as tobacco, tea and sugar. Recent reforms aimed at liberalizing and diversifying the economy have led to higher growth rates, reduction of deficits, and lower inflation. Removal of government controls and privatization are expected to attract a higher degree of foreign direct investment and expertise not only in agriculture but also its largely undeveloped mining sector. Privatization has involved several foreign purchases in recent years. Export processing zones offer tariff-free access to neighboring countries and quota privileges to overseas markets.

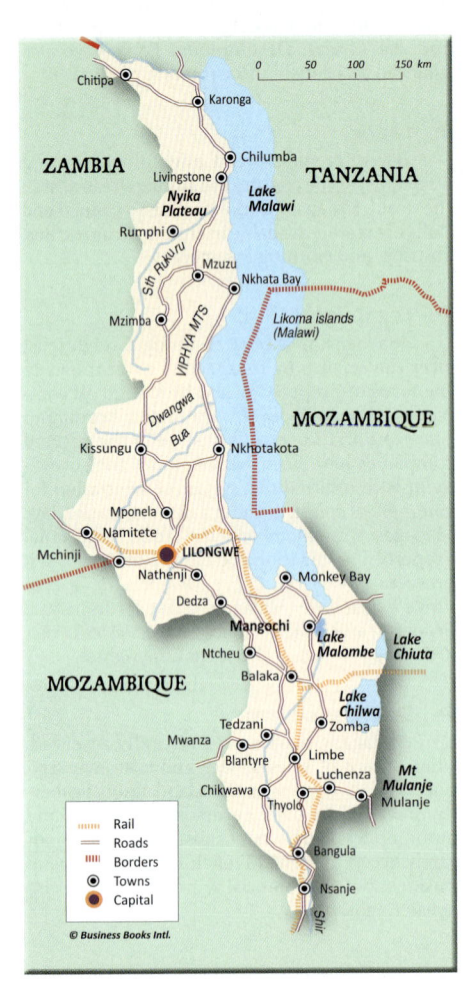

Country profile

The landlocked Republic of Malawi stretches for 840 km along the fertile western and southern sides of Africa's third largest lake—Lake Malawi. The country's width varies between 80 and 160 km. Lake Malawi and the much smaller Malombe, Chiuta and Chilwa lakes take up 20% of the total area. The Shire River, a tributary of the Zambezi, feeds into the Malawi and Malombe lakes while the Shire Highlands, which peak at Mount Mulanje (3,050 m), overlook the country's principal tea-growing region. Further to the north are the Viphya Mountains and the Nyika Plateau. The climate is temperate, with high rainfall and moist savanna woodland vegetation in the high-lying areas and dry savanna along the lakes. The closely related Chewa and Nyanja ethnic groups account for about half of the total population. Other significant groups in the south are the Lomwe, Yao, and Ngoni and in the north the Tumbuka, Tonga and Nkhonde. English and Chichewa are official languages. More than half of the population is Christian with the remainder split evenly between the Muslim faith and their own ethnic beliefs.

History

Lake Malawi was named after the 16th Century Maravi empire that extended to the Indian Ocean and comprised peoples such as the Chewa, Nyanja, Nyasa, Nsenga, Phiri and

Zimba, who broke away from the Lunda-Luba kingdom in the southern Congo Basin. There was early contact with Portuguese along the Mozambican coast and Arab traders who settled along the coast of modern-day Tanzania. David Livingstone first visited Lake Malawi in 1859 and was followed by other missionaries and a group of Glasgow businessmen, who set up the African Lakes Company and established Blantyre—named after David Livingstone's Scottish birthplace—that became the territory's largest urban center. In 1891 Malawi (then known as Nyasaland) became a British colony and in 1953 it was incorporated into the Federation of Rhodesia and Nyasaland together with Northern Rhodesia (Zambia) and Southern Rhodesia (Zimbabwe). Dr. Hastings Banda led the opposition against this federation and ultimately forced the British in 1962 to grant independence to the new state of Malawi. In the 1970s, over objections from the OAU, President Banda established diplomatic relations with apartheid South Africa and accepted considerable financial and technical assistance, including funding for the new capital at Lilongwe to replace Blantyre. In 1994 an ailing Banda was pressured into holding the first free elections since independence. He and his ruling Malawi Congress Party were swept from office by the United Democratic Front (UDF). Muslim businessman Bakili Muluzi became president and was re-elected in 1999. In 2004 Dr. Bingu wa Mutharika, Economic Minister in Muluzi's cabinet, won a hotly contested presidential race. He was re-elected in 2009.

Government

The executive President and Vice President are elected on one ballot by popular vote for 5-year terms. The unicameral 193-member National Assembly is also elected for a 5-year term. In the May 2009 election the Democratic Progressive Party (DPP) led by Wa Mutharikawon 114 seats against 26 for the Malawi Congress Party or MCP and 17 for the United Democratic Front (UDF). The other seats were split between smaller parties and independents.

Economic policy

Economic structural adjustment programs have been applied with the help of the World Bank, International Monetary Fund. As a for-

Pres. Bingu wa Mutharika
Born: Feb. 27, 1934
Since May 2004
UN Photo

POLITICAL
Head of State	Pres. Bingu wa Mutharika
Ruling Party	DPP
Main Opposition	MCP
Independence	6 July 1964
National capital	Lilongwe
Official languages	English & Chichewa

PHYSICAL
Total area	46,000 sq. miles 118,000 sq. km. (± Pennsylvania)
Arable land	23% of land area
Coastline	Landlocked

POPULATION
Total	15.0 million
Av. yearly growth	2.7%
Urban population	19%
Life expectancy	50 years
Adult illiteracy	62.7%

ECONOMY
Currency	Malawian Kwacha (MK) (US$1=150)
GDP (real)	$3.0 billion
GDP growth rate	7.0%
GDP per capita[1]	$212
GDP (ppp)[2]	$8.4 billion
GDP per cap. (ppp)	$550
Inflation rate	8.5%
Exports	$912 million
Imports	$1.5 billion
External debt	$683 million
Unemployment	NA

1. Atlas method.
2. See page 175 for an explanation of purchasing power parity (ppp).

mer UN Director for Trade and Development Finance for Africa and Secretary-General of the Common Market for Eastern and Southern Africa (COMESA), Dr. Wa Mutharika exhibited financial discipline. In 2000 Malawi was approved for relief under the Heavily Indebted Poor Countries (HIPC) program. Poverty, improvements in agriculture, unemployment, and the HIV/AIDS epidemic are ongoing issues. Severe droughts in 2005 and 2006 have hampered growth.

Sectors

Fertile soil and ample rainfall form the basis of a thriving agricultural sector that employs nearly half of the workforce and supports mots of the population. Smallholders grow food crops such as maize, potatoes, groundnuts, cassava and plantains, and keep livestock. Estate farmers account largely for the major export crops such as tobacco, tea and sugar. Both fishing and forestry are being developed and coal is mined on a scale sufficient to supply the country's domestic needs. Limestone is extracted for cement production. Major bauxite deposits at Mount Mulanje are not mined due to prohibitive transportation costs. Manufacturing largely involves agricultural processing and includes tea factories, sugar refineries, cotton gins, tobacco plants, sawmills and plywood manufacturers, oil and grain mills, abattoirs and cold storage plants. Other manufacturing includes textiles, footwear, cement, fertilizer, soap, and matches. Lake Malawi and the national parks are tourist attractions.

Privatization

Foreigners are allowed to participate in all phases of the privatization program but in some cases nationals are given preferential treatment ranging from discounted share prices to subsidized credits. These concessions are extended to locals on condition that the shares or assets be retained for at least two years.

Investment

The Malawi Investment Promotion Agency puts private foreign direct investment at an amount of about $10 million per year. Understandably, this level is considered insufficient to complement local private and public sector investment and new investment is aggressively pursued through promotional programs abroad.

Trade

Major overall trading partners are South Africa, Zimbabwe, UK, Japan and Germany. The US, UK, South Africa, Japan, and Germany are the largest purchasers. With a 60% share of the total, tobacco tops the list of exports.

Financial sector

Malawi has a sound banking sector, monitored and regulated by the Reserve Bank of Malawi (RBM). There are five full-service commercial banks of which the largest two—the NBM and CBM—are state-owned. As of June 25, 1999, 1,159.01 million shares with a market capitalization of some $170 million were traded on the Malawi Stock Exchange.

Taxes and tariffs

There are efforts to reduce or eliminate various tariff and non-tariff barriers. In 1998, the Government removed export taxes on tobacco, sugar, tea and coffee. The corporate tax rate for non-residents is 15 to 35 percent and capital gains tax 15 percent. A value added tax (VAT) of 16.5 percent applies and exchange control is in effect. Taxes are levied on dividends (10%), interest (15%) and royalties (15 to 20%). (See page 138).

BUSINESS ACTIVITY

AGRICULTURE
Tobacco, sugar cane, cotton, tea, corn, potatoes, cassava (tapioca), sorghum, pulses, cattle, goats.

INDUSTRIES
Tea, tobacco, sugar, sawmill products, cement, consumer goods.

NATURAL RESOURCES
Limestone, uranium, coal, bauxite.

EXPORTS
$912 million (est. 2009): tobacco, tea, sugar, coffee, peanuts, wood products.

IMPORTS
$1.5 billion (est. 2009): food, petroleum products, semimanufactures, consumer goods, transportation equipment.

MAJOR TRADING PARTNERS
US, South Africa, Germany, Egypt, Japan, UK, Netherlands, China, India, Russia, Zimbabwe, Tanzania.

Doing Business with Malawi

▶ **Investment**

Investment incentives include duty-free importation of raw materials for manufacturing industry, and tax holidays. There are several export processing zones (EPZs) that offer tariff free access into South Africa as well as quota privileges for textiles and sugar in the European Union and the US. Manufacturers also enjoy export advantages to neighboring countries such as Zambia, Tanzania, Congo (Kinshasa). Agriculture is the sector where Malawi competes most successfully internationally and there is a concerted effort to find alternatives to tobacco growing with its uncertain future.

▶ **Trade**

There is a growing Malawi market for computers, peripherals and software. Used clothing, equipment and vehicles are major imports. Product distribution in Malawi can be problematic as some rural areas become inaccessible during the rainy season from November to April. Infrastructural and community programs sponsored by USAID, the World Bank, and the African Development Bank present opportunities for the sale of materials, equipment, and expertise.

▶ **Trade Finance**

Overseas purchases are financed primarily through secured letters of credit. Short-term export finance Eximbank insurance is available to US exporters.

▶ **Selling to the government**

The government issues tender notices for supplies and services in local and international publications 15 to 90 days in advance. Completed bids accompanied by the required deposit are submitted to Malawi Government Central Tender Board (MGCTB) and opened in the presence of bidders or their representatives. As Malawi upgrades its transport and telecommunications systems, major purchases and service contracts are imminent.

▶ **Exchange controls**

There are no restrictions on remittance of foreign investment funds (including capital, profits, loan repayment and lease repayment) as long as it was originally sourced from abroad and registered with the Reserve Bank of Malawi (RBM).

▶ **Partnerships**

Joint ventures are allowed under the Partnership Act. The amount and shareholding are not regulated but joint ventures must be licensed by the Registrar General in the Ministry of Justice.

▶ **Establishing a presence**

Foreign businesses are allowed to establish themselves either through a subsidiary, branch, franchise, joint venture, or licensing relationship. Currently, US subsidiary or affiliate US companies operate in the agro-industry (mostly tobacco), computers and office equipment, and petroleum products. MIPA, as well as organizations such as the Malawi Chamber of Commerce and Industry, the Malawi Development Corporation (MDC), and the Malawi Export Promotion Council (MEPC) all assist foreign firms with registration.

▶ **Financing projects**

Malawi has had an OPIC investment guarantee agreement since 1967 and is a signatory to the Multilateral Investment Guarantee Agency. The World Bank's International Development Agency, the African Development Bank, and USAID are principal donors.

▶ **Labor**

Unskilled labor is readily available but skilled staff is scarce. Union membership is still low and there is a general lack of awareness of worker rights and benefits. Only 13% of the formal sector workforce belongs to unions.

▶ **Legal rights**

The legal system is based on British common law. The courts accept and enforce foreign court judgments that are registered in accordance with established legal procedures. Malawi is a member of the International Center for Settlement of Investment Disputes and accepts international arbitration of investment disputes. Malawi is a member of the World Intellectual Property Organization, the Berne Convention, and the Universal Copyright Convention. The Copyright Society of Malawi (COSOMA) administers the Copyright Act and the Registrar General administers the Patent and Trademarks Act and oversees the protection of industrial intellectual property rights.

▶ **Business climate**

Malawians are courteous and easygoing in business. Their approach shows the strong influence of the British. It is a small country where most prominent business people know each other well.

MALI

Economic activity in landlocked Mali depends largely on farming and fishing along the Niger river that meanders through the desert. In the nineteenth century explorers braved the difficult route to Timbuktu in search of legendary gold-paved streets that turned out to be a figment of the imagination. Today, however, Mali is Africa's fourth largest gold producer and both South African and Canadian mining companies are exploring for more. In 1992 a long period of post-independence autocracy bent on socialism made way for a democratically elected government and economic reform policies supported by international agencies. The country is actively seeking foreign participation to help boost agricultural production and develop mining prospects.

Country profile

Most of landlocked Republic of Mali consists of monotonous plains, less than 500 m above sea level. The more than 4,000 km long Niger river flows northeast from Guinea through the heart of Mali into the Sahara desert. Between the towns of Ségu and Timbuktu it branches into lakes and swamps forming the Masina Delta. Both the Niger and its tributary, the Bani, are vital for transport and irrigation. In the summer moist maritime winds move in from the Gulf of Guinea and in winter the dry harmattan blows from the Sahara Desert in the north. The Sahel Belt, bordering the desert, extends from Senegal and Mauritania through Mali. Mandé-speaking peoples, consisting of the Bambara, Malinké (Manding or Mandinka) and Soninké, account for half the population. Other significant groups include the Ful (or Fulani), the Senufo, the Dogon, and the Songhai. The nomadic Tuareg are concentrated around the scattered oases of the Sahara to the north of Timbuktu and Gao and speak Berber. About 80% of the population are Muslim and the rest is split between Christianity and ethnic beliefs. French has official status and Bambara is the lingua franca.

History

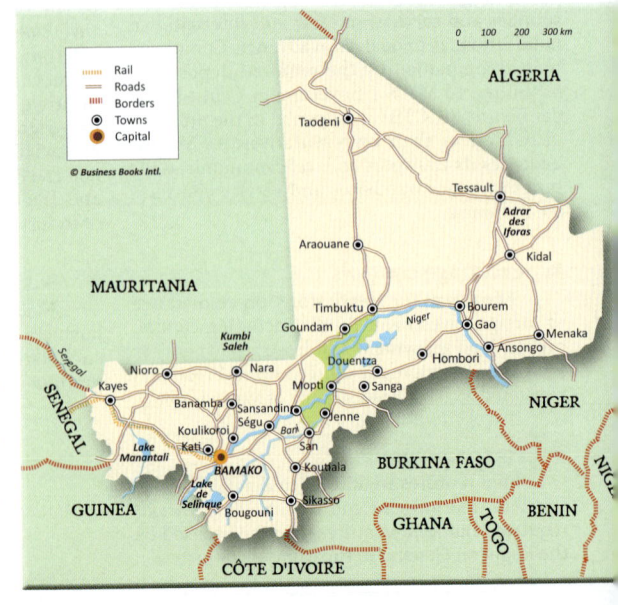

The advent of the camel as a means of transport across the desert some 1,800 years ago stimulated trade between Mediterranean Africa and ancient Mali, a creation of a Mandé group, the Malinké. The Malinké empire ruled regions of Mali from the 12th to the 16th Century while the Songhai empire reigned over the Timbuktu-Gao region in the 15th Century. Originally explorers braved the arduous route inland in search of the legendary golden riches of Timbuktu, only to discover that the tales were heavily inflated. Morocco conquered Timbuktu in 1591 and controlled it for two centuries. In the late 19th Century the French set out from their colony in Senegal to establish a colonial empire that would stretch to the Red Sea. With their claims validated at the 1885 Berlin Conference, the French applied a combination of diplomacy and military force to overpower several Sahelian states, including Mali. As French Soudan it was first incorporated into French West Africa and afterwards given joint independence with Senegal in the Federation of Mali. Shortly after independence in 1960, the federation split up and French Soudan became Mali. The first Malian president, Modibo Keita, opted for a one-party state, severed ties with France, introduced socialist policies and sought assistance from the Soviet Union. In 1968 the Keita dictatorship was overthrown by Lieutenant Moussa Traoré who retained one-man rule while adopting some free-market policies. Violent repression of pro-democracy forces prompted Lt.-Col. Amadou Toumani Touré to depose Traoré and facilitate the country's first free elections in 1992. Alpha Konaré won the presidential election and was re-elected in 1997 for a second term. In May 2002 Amadou Touré returned to power by gaining 64.4% of the popular vote and in 2007 he was re-elected with an increased margin.

Government

The 1992 constitution provides for an executive President, elected for a five year term. The President appoints the Council of Ministers and the Prime Minister. The 147-member unicameral *Assemblée Nationale (*National Assembly) also serves for a 5-year term. In the July 2007 election a multi-party coalition under the umbrella of the Alliance for Democracy and Progress (ADP) gained 113 seats against 15 for its rival, the Front for Democracy (FDR) coalition.

Economic policy

With 65% of its land area desert or semi-desert and an unequal distribution of income, Mali counts among the world's poorest countries. Since 1992 the emphasis has been on free trade and private enterprise, promoted in cooperation with the IMF, World Bank, and bilateral donors, including the United States. Strict adherence to IMF guidelines has stimu-

Pres. Amadou Tomani Tourê Born: Nov. 4, 1948 Since June 2002

UN Photo Mak Garten

POLITICAL
Head of State	Pres. Amadou Tomani Touré
Ruling Party	ADP
Main Opposition	FDR
Independence	22 September 1960
National capital	Bamako
Official languages	French

PHYSICAL
Total area	479,000 sq. miles 1,240,000 sq. km. (2 x Texas)
Arable land	3.8% of land area
Coastline	Landlocked

POPULATION
Total	13.4 million
Av. yearly growth	2.6%
Urban population	32%
Life expectancy	51.78 years
Adult literacy	46.4%

ECONOMY
Currency	CFA franc (CFAF) (US$1=495.40)
GDP (real)	$8.4 billion
GDP growth rate	4.4%
GDP per capita[1]	$661
GDP (ppp)[2]	$15.9 billion
GDP per cap. (ppp)	$1,222
Inflation rate	2.2%
Exports	$294 million
Imports	$2.4 billion
External debt	$1.9 billion
Unemployment	30%

1. Atlas method.
2. See page 175 for an explanation of purchasing power parity (ppp).

lated foreign investment and enabled Mali to become the second largest cotton producer in Africa. Export taxes, import duties, and price controls have been reduced or eliminated and a new investment code adopted. Landlocked Mali remains vulnerable to unrest in neighboring countries both as far as trade routes and worker remittances are concerned.

Sectors

Even though only 3% of the total land area is arable more than 80% of the people make a living in agriculture, accounting for half of Mali's GDP. Some 10% still live a nomadic life. Mali is Africa's fourth largest and Sub-Saharan Africa's largest producer of cotton. Other cash crops are groundnuts, sugar cane and rice. Food crops include millet, sorghum and maize. Livestock is responsible for half of the agricultural sector's activity. The country is self-sufficient in freshwater fish and a significant exporter. Gold mining has become an important contributor to GDP and has attracted considerable foreign interest, including the leading mining producers in South Africa. Mali also has deposits of bauxite, iron ore and tin. Prospecting is underway for petroleum, copper, lithium and diamonds. Manufacturing is mainly confined to small-scale agricultural processing for domestic consumption and export. Other industries include soft drinks, textiles, soaps, plastics, cigarettes, cement, bricks, and agricultural tools.

Privatization

Around 90% of all production is still in the hands of state enterprises, but privatization is continuing.

Investment

Foreign direct investment in Mali's manufacturing sector is modest but growing. Canadian and South African mining houses have become prominent players in the gold mining sector while the French are dominant in cotton production, food processing, and petroleum retailing—a sector where ExxonMobil has also been a significant player for some time.

Trade

Mali is heavily dependent on foreign aid and vulnerable to fluctuations in world prices for cotton, its main export, along with gold. Mali is the largest producer and exporter of cotton in Sub-Saharan Africa. Gold accounts for one third of its foreign exchange earnings. Although the French dominate the automobile and consumer goods market, North American, Asian, and other African nations are steadily gaining. Côte d'Ivoire and Senegal supply a whole range of essential consumer goods.

Financial sector

As a member of UEMOA, Mali's banking system is regulated from the regional central bank in Dakar, Senegal. Commercial banks enjoy considerable liquidity but tend to invest in Western capital markets instead of local enterprises. The ongoing privatization program is expected to make the local market more attractive. In 1994, the government started issuing treasury bonds that carry tax advantages for investors. Companies in Mali are expected to list on the UEMOA stock exchange.

Taxes and tariffs

Except for a 3% levy on cotton and gold, taxes on exports were eliminated in 1990. Import duties on some goods were reduced or eliminated in 1994. The tax system remains complicated and in the view of some outsiders needs further overhaul to make it more attractive for foreign investors.

BUSINESS ACTIVITY

AGRICULTURE
Cotton, millet, rice, corn, vegetables, peanuts, cattle, sheep, goats.

INDUSTRIES
Minor local consumer goods production, food processing, construction, phosphate and gold mining.

NATURAL RESOURCES
Gold, phosphates, kaolin, salt, limestone, uranium, bauxite, iron ore, manganese, tin, unexploited copper deposits.

EXPORTS
$294 million (2006): cotton, gold, livestock.

IMPORTS
$2.4 billion (2006): machinery and equipment, construction materials, petroleum, foodstuffs, textiles.

MAJOR TRADING PARTNERS
China, Thailand, Taiwan, Bangladesh, Taiwan, France, Côte d'Ivoire, France, Senegal, Australia.

Doing Business with Mali

▶ **Investment**

The investment code favors investment in export-oriented and labor-intensive businesses. The mining code encourages investments in medium and small mining enterprises and allows two year exploration permits free of charge. The investment, mining, and commercial codes all offer duty-free importation of capital equipment, tax advantages for new ventures in priority industries and repatriation of profits and capital. Foreign investors go through the same one-stop screening process as domestic investors. Criteria for approval include the size of capital investment, the potential for added value, and the level of job creation. Any company that exports at least 80% of its production is entitled to tax-free status.

▶ **Trade**

Mali imports petroleum products, chemicals, vehicles, machinery, processed foods, pharmaceutical products, used clothing, cosmetics, electronics, telecommunications equipment, mining equipment, and most manufactured items. Most exporters to Mali make use of local agents or distributors.

▶ **Trade finance**

Payment is usually by irrevocable letters of credit. US investors in Mali enjoy short and medium term Eximbank coverage.

▶ **Selling to the government**

Significant government purchases usually involve programs sponsored by international agencies and donors such as USAID. These procurement contracts offer opportunities for foreign suppliers of agricultural, construction, irrigation, computer, and telecommunications equipment and services. Bidding rules are normally set by the donors.

▶ **Exchange controls**

Although there are no restrictions or limits on the repatriation of capital or profits, the regional central bank requires that all remittances be channeled through it, together with supporting commercial documents.

▶ **Partnerships**

Several overseas investors in the manufacturing and service sector have opted for partnerships or joint ventures. Such arrangements are encouraged but not required by the government. In the case of joint ventures involving the government, its share is limited to 20%.

▶ **Establishing a presence**

Establishing a presence requires a one-stop procedure (*guichet unique*). Manufacturers apply at the National Directorate of Industries and Trading Companies and at the National Directorate of Economic Affairs. The Chamber of Commerce and Industry assists in the process and registration takes on an average between 30-45 days. Foreign investors are allowed full ownership. They are also permitted to purchase shares in privatized parastatal and other domestic companies.

▶ **Financing projects**

Mali is eligible for Overseas Private Investment Corporation financing and insurance programs. It is a member of the World Bank's Multilateral Investment Guarantee Agency.

▶ **Labor**

Skilled workers laid off by the state and college and high school graduates without employment prospects are available in the job market. Workers have the right to belong to unions and although a warning notice is not required, mediation is generally sought before workers resort to striking. Although not mandatory, firms often find it useful to liaise with official labor inspectors—especially when hiring and firing.

▶ **Legal rights**

In rare instances of expropriation of property the Malian government has done so in accordance with international law. The investment code allows a foreign company which signs an agreement with the government to refer to international arbitration in cases where the local courts are unable to resolve disputes in a satisfactory manner. Mali is a member of the International Center for the Settlement of Investment Disputes and New York Convention of 1958 on the recognition and enforcement of foreign arbitrage awards. The *Direction Nationale des Industries* implements copyright and patent protection. Mali is a signatory to the WTO TRIPS agreement. Intellectual property right infringement has not been a serious problem.

▶ **Business climate**

Very little English is spoken in the French-oriented business community. Malians place great emphasis on protocol and courtesy and discussions normally start with an extensive exchange of pleasantries. Although most Malians are Muslim and do not drink, smoke, or eat pork, they usually do not object to foreigners doing so.

MAURITANIA

Making the most of its resources despite large stretches of desert and the world's third lowest population density after Namibia and Mongolia, Mauritania has made notable progress in recent years. Extensive iron ore deposits account for almost half of its total exports. A new investment code widened the scope for foreign participation in key sectors such as mining, fishing and agriculture. There is prospecting for mineral resources, including oil and gold. Mauritania's coastal waters are among the richest fishing areas in the world.

Country profile

More than 70% of the Islamic Republic of Mauritania consists of the Sahara Desert. Both the desert and the Sahel regions rise from monotonous coastal plains in the west to a low plateau eastward and northward, exceeding heights of 500 m above sea level at the iron-bearing hills around Fderik and Zouerate. Only the southernmost strip, along the northern bank of the Senegal River receives sufficient rainfall (up to 800 mm) for intensive crop cultivation. Most Mauritanians are descendants of Berbers and Arab immigrants, but black groups such as the Wolof, Tukulor, and Soninke and the nomadic Tajakant and Regeihat are present in significant numbers. Hassaniya Arabic, which had enjoyed equal status with French since 1967, became the only official language in 1991. The Mandé languages of the Soninké, Fula and Wolof are also recognized as national languages and used in schools. French is still widely spoken in commerce. The Muslim faith prevails.

History

Mauritania was first inhabited by black peoples and Berbers. From the 7th Century, following the advent of the Arabs in Northern Africa, the Berbers in the region were converted to the Islamic faith and they in turn proselytized the Tukulor and other black communities in the Sahel region. As was the case in Morocco, Arab and Berber intermixing led to the emergence of Moors (derived from the Latin *Mauri* or French *Maures*) who viewed themselves as al-Bidan (white) as opposed to their al-Sudan (black) neighbors. Portuguese slave traders established a base on Arguin Island (Tidra) from 1443. The French took over the region in the 1930s. In 1960, over strenuous opposition from Morocco, which laid claim to the territory, Mauritania became independent under President Moktar Ould Daddah (son-in-law of French president Charles de Gaulle). Ould

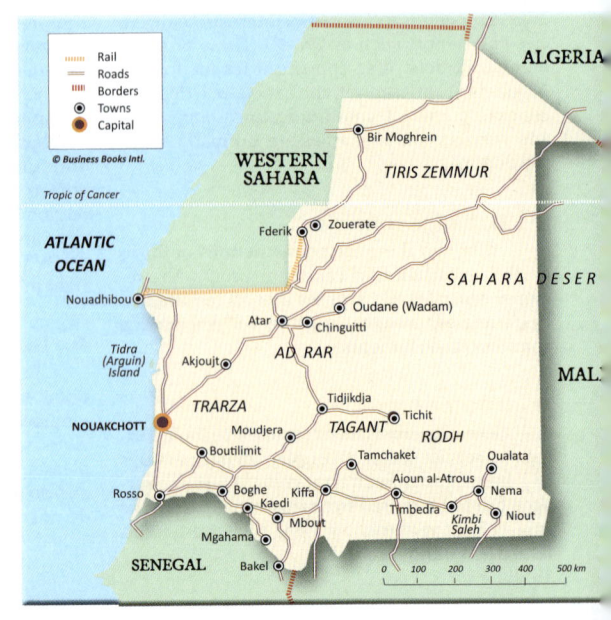

Daddah's party had won all the seats in a 1959 general election. In 1976 Spain ceded Spanish (Western) Sahara on a 50/50 basis to Morocco and Mauritania. The Polisario guerrillas, who sought independence for Western Sahara, attacked targets in Mauritania, drawing it into a protracted and costly war. In 1997, in the midst of growing opposition to this unpopular war, Ould Daddah was ousted by Lt-Col. Khouna Ould Haidalla, who assumed the presidency and appointed Col. Maaouiya Ould Sid'Ahmed Taya as his prime minister. Mauritania dropped its territorial claims, leaving the way clear for Morocco to expand its influence over all of Western Sahara. In 1984 Taya assumed the presidency. He exercised autocratic rule until 1992 when his *Parti Républicain Démocratique et Social* (PRDS) won at the polls. Pres. Taya was re-elected in 1997 and again in November 2003 but deposed two years later in bloodless military coup led by Gen. Mohamed Ould Abdel Aziz. Sidi Ould Cheikh Abdellahi was elected president in March 2007 and served briefly before being ousted in August 2008 by Gen. Aziz, who initially supported him. Apparently Abdallahi angered General Aziz and his supporters by reaching out to Islamic hardliners, freeing several suspected terrorists, and using state funds to build a mosque on the grounds of the presidential palace. General Ould Abdel Aziz was sworn into office in August 2009 after winning 52.47 per cent of the votes cast in the July presidential election. He appointed a government of 27 ministers, mostly composed of supporters and for the first time a woman as foreign minister—Naha Mint Hamdi Ould Mouknass, who heads up a small pro-Aziz party.

Government

In terms of the constitution the president is elected by popular vote for a six year term. A bicameral parliament consists of a 56-member Senate or *Majlis al-Shuyukh* elected for a 6-year term, 53 by municipal leaders and the other three by Mauritanians living abroad; and a 95-member National Assembly *(Majlis al-Watani)* elected by popular vote for five years. After the December 2006 Assembly election the five party Coalition of Majority Parties (CPM) held 63 seats against the four party Coordination of Democratic Opposition (COD) with 27 seats. The rest is held by smaller parties outside these two coalitions.

Pres. Mohamed Ould Abdel Aziz
Born: 1956
Since Aug 2009

Photo: VOA

POLITICAL	
Head of State	Pres. Mohamed Ould Abdel Aziz
Ruling Party	Al Mithaq
Main Opposition	CFCD
Independence	28 November 1960
National capital	Nouakchott
Official languages	Hasaniya Arabic

PHYSICAL	
Total area	396,000 sq. miles
	1,026,000 sq. km.
	(3 x Arizona)
Arable land	0.48%
Coastline	469 miles/754 km

POPULATION	
Total	3.1 million
Av. yearly growth	2.4%
Urban population	41%
Life expectancy	60.37 years
Adult literacy	51.2%

ECONOMY	
Currency	Ouguiya (UM)
	(US$1=284.50)
GDP (real)	$3.8 billion
GDP growth rate	-1.1%
GDP per capita[1]	$1,684
GDP (ppp)[2]	$8.2 billion
GDP per cap. (ppp)	$2,479
Inflation rate	2.2%
Exports	$1.4 billion
Imports	$1.5 billion
External debt	$1.9 billion
Unemployment	30%

1. Atlas method.
2. See page 175 for an explanation of purchasing power parity (ppp).

Economic policy

The government has implemented an IMF and World Bank-sponsored structural adjustment program. Reforms include privatization and restructuring of the banking sector, liberalization of the exchange rate system, and reduction of trade and investment barriers. These reforms resulted in an increase in real GDP. But they did not come without a certain measure of political risk. An investment code approved in 2001 widened the scope for direct foreign investment in key sectors. Mauritania qualified for debt relief under the Heavily Indebted Poor Countries (HIPC) initiative.

Sectors

The economy depends largely on the mining of iron and copper ore and fishing in the Atlantic. Less than 3% of Mauritania is cultivable and only one-fifth of its food crop requirements is produced locally. Imported cereals supplement the locally-grown food crops consisting mainly of millet, sorghum, maize, rice and vegetables. Livestock (cattle, sheep, goats and camels) account for about 15% of GDP or three-quarters of the total agriculture production. Only 10% of the working-age population is employed in the formal sector of the economy. Mauritania's coastal waters are among the richest fishing areas in the world but indiscriminate fishing by foreigners threatens to deplete this source of income. Marine fishing around Nouadhibou contributes 5% of GDP. Joint-venture companies are responsible for about 95% of output, most of it processed locally. At an estimated 6 billion tons, Mauritania's iron ore reserves are among the largest in the world. Other mineral resources include gold, copper, phosphates, sulphur, gypsum and uranium. Development is hampered by large-scale deforestation, over-exploitation of fishing grounds and a chronic water shortage. In 2001 exploratory drilling 80 km offshore indicated potential profitable oil extraction and production.

Investment

Foreign investment dried up during ethnic clashes between 1989 and 1991 but resumed modestly towards the mid-1990s after the government introduced new incentives. Foreign investors include firms from the US, France, Saudi Arabia, China, Belgium, Australia and Ireland in areas such as petroleum, mining, food processing, banking, fishing and manufacturing.

Trade

With 58% of the total, iron ore is the country's leading export earner, followed by fishing, which accounts for 38% of the total. Mauritania imports almost all its food, machinery and consumer needs, including foodstuffs, vehicles and spare parts, petroleum products, building materials, mining equipment, telecommunications equipment, electronics, cosmetics and most other manufactured items. French, Spanish and Asian goods dominate the market.

Financial sector

Banking supervision has been strengthened to encourage development of an interbank market and to ensure solvency. There are five commercial banks and about 30 exchange offices in Mauritania. The Central Bank fixes the exchange rate for the ouguiya.

Taxes and tariffs

Recent laws focus on a more efficient and simplified revenue collection system coupled with lower rates. The corporate tax rate for non-residents is 25 to 30 percent and capital gains tax 25 percent. A value added tax (VAT) of 14 to 18 percent applies and exchange control is in effect. Taxes are levied on dividends (10%), and interest (10%). (See page 138).

BUSINESS ACTIVITY

AGRICULTURE
Dates, millet, sorghum, root crops, cattle, sheep, fish products.

INDUSTRIES
Fish processing, mining of iron ore and gypsum.

NATURAL RESOURCES
Copper, iron ore, gypsum, fish, phosphate.

EXPORTS
$1.4 billion (est. 2006): fish and fish products, iron ore, gold.

IMPORTS
$1.5 billion (2006): foodstuffs, consumer goods, petroleum products, capital goods.

MAJOR TRADING PARTNERS
Japan, Italy, France, UK, US, Germany, Belgium, Spain, Russia, China.

Doing Business with Mauritania

▶ Investment
Incentives are offered to investors in small- and medium-sized enterprises and export-oriented manufacturing utilizing local manpower and raw materials in areas outside of Nouakchott and Nouadhibou. Government priorities range from reorganization of the fishing sector to gold and other mineral prospecting, increased water supply and improved irrigation systems to rural road construction and rehabilitation, and telecommunications expansion to increased electricity generation.

▶ Trade
Three market segments are considered to be prime prospects for US exporters: foodstuffs (especially wheat, flour, rice, powdered milk, and canned food), mining equipment (machinery and trucks), and telecommunications. Foreign firms have also been successful in supplying fishing gear, wind and solar energy equipment, pharmaceutical and medical products, computers and software, cosmetics, toiletries, and oil and clothing.

▶ Trade finance
Most imports are by irrevocable and confirmed letters of credit issued by local banks. Some Mauritanian importers hold bank accounts abroad and pay for imports without involving their local bank. The Foreign Credit Insurance Association (FCIA) insures purchases by the state mining company, SNIM.

▶ Selling to the government
Purchases are usually by tenders (*avis d'appel d'offres*) but direct negotiations are common in small transactions involving local suppliers. Major projects are often guaranteed and controlled by international donors. The Central Procurement Board (*Commission Centrale des Marchés*) monitors all government procurement.

▶ Exchange controls
The foreign exchange system has been liberalized, and repatriation of dividends and capital as well as payments for overseas goods and services are possible through commercial banks without prior approval from the Central Bank.

▶ Partnerships
The government offers a wide range of incentives to encourage partnership arrangements. Current joint ventures are primarily with other Arab countries in the mineral, fishing, and banking sectors.

▶ Establishing a presence
An official investment agency (*Guichet Unique de l'Investissement*) and the Mauritanian Chamber of Commerce and Industry offer assistance and advice to foreigners who wish to establish an office. Even though procedures can be handled without a local lawyer, foreign investors with long-term plans usually retain one to ensure strict compliance from the outset.

▶ Financing projects
Mauritania relies for about 85% of its project funding on loans from The African Development Bank, IMF, and European Investment Bank, and the Islamic Bank.

▶ Labor
Even though unemployment is high among high school and college graduates, there is a shortage of factory-skilled workers and managerial staff in all sectors, with the possible exception of mining. Workers are free to associate with and establish unions at local and national levels. Work stoppages are rare. Foreign firms are normally at liberty to hire any number of expatriates, except in areas such as industrial fishing where crews are required to have five Mauritanians per vessel.

▶ Legal rights
Since Mauritania's independence, there has only been one case of nationalization when in 1974 the government took over a mining company from a majority French partner. It paid a mutually agreed sum in compensation. Disagreements over investment issues are settled in the courts or in terms of arbitration procedures in conformance with the rules of the World Bank. Mauritania is a member of the African Intellectual Property Organization, the Paris, Berne and Hague conventions and the World Intellectual Property Organization.

▶ Business Climate
A working knowledge of French or Arabic is an advantage but interpreters are readily available. As a Muslim country, consumption of alcohol and pork is taboo. A handshake is customary when initiating and closing a business meeting but it should be remembered that some conservative Muslim men will not shake a woman's hand.

MAURITIUS

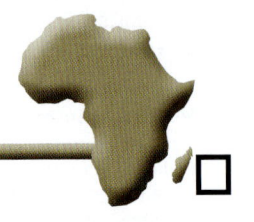

When Mauritius became independent in 1968, this small island country in the Indian Ocean was an underdeveloped single crop community. Since then it branched out from sugar into several other sectors and raised its per capita income to the second highest in Africa. While sugar cane still covers more than ninety percent of the cultivated land area and accounts for 25% of export earnings, the emphasis today is on banking and the information industry. Mauritius has attracted more than nine thousand offshore entities. Textiles and tourism have become significant sectors.

Country profile

The Republic of Mauritius comprises the main island and a much smaller Rodrigues Island, about 500 km northeast, as well as two dependencies, the virtually uninhabited Cargados Carajos (600 km north), and Agalega, with a few hundred inhabitants (1,200 km north). It also lays claim to the uninhabited French island of Tromelin (500 km north) and the British Chagos Islands about halfway to Sri Lanka. The Chagos group includes Diego Garcia, used as an American military communications base. Mauritius itself measures about 58 km by 47 km and has a subtropical climate, beaches, coral reefs and scenery that attract thousands of upscale tourists. Its inhabitants trace their ancestry to three continents—Africa, Asia and Europe. The Indian group (Hindu and Muslim) accounts for 69% while citizens of mixed Afro-European origin (Creoles) constitute 27%. Education levels and health standards are high. About 52 percent of the population is Hindu and 16 percent Muslim.

History

The Dutch first came to this island in 1638 and named it Mauritius (after the Dutch leader, Mauritz of Nassau). They made way for the French in 1715, who renamed it Isle de France, stayed until 1810 and lost it to the British, who reinstated the name Mauritius. Indentured Hindu workers were brought from India to work on sugar estates. Their descendants are in the majority, followed by Creoles (of mixed, predominantly African slave origin), Muslim Indians, Chinese and a few Europeans. The Creole population gave birth to a language based on the French, Malagasy and African languages, which became the lingua franca of the island. Mauritius received its independence under the British crown in 1968 and became a Republic in 1992. Continuous political squabbles, splits and shifting alliances do not seem to have derailed a climate of continuity and stability. Prime Minister Navin Ramgoolam headed an unstable coalition government for 5 years before being ousted at the polls by an opposition alliance in September 2000. Sir Aneerood Jugnauth, leader of the *Movement Socialiste Miltant* or

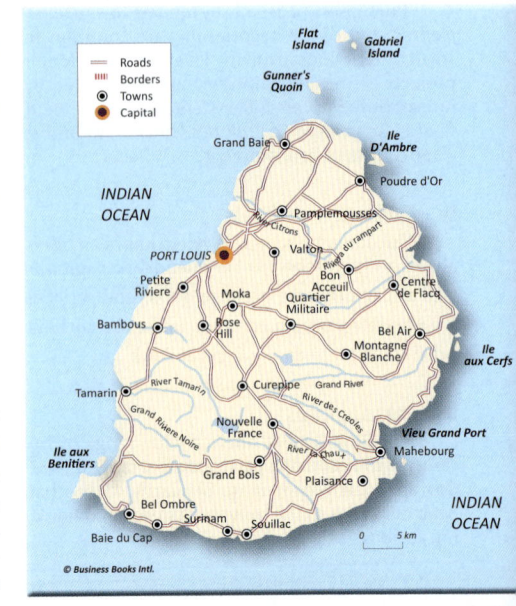

Militant Socialist Movement (MSM), served as prime minister for 3 years before handing over to his coalition partner, Paul Bérenger, of the *Mouvement Militant Mauricien* (MMM). In 2005 Navinchandra Ramgoolam regained the Prime Minister's post by defeating Berenger at the polls. In the May 2010 National Assembly elections, the Alliance for the Future Coalition (AF) spearheaded by Ramgoolam once again defeated Berenger's Mauritian Militant Movement (MMM).

Government

Both the ceremonial president and the prime minister, who heads the government, are elected for 5 years. The unicameral National Assembly, elected by the voters for 5-year terms, has 62 members plus an additional maximum of eight seats allocated to the "best losers"— the unsuccessful minority candidates with the largest number of votes. After the May 2010 election the Alliance for the Future (AF) led by incumbent Prime Minister Navinchandra Ramgoolam won 41 seats against 18 for its closest rival, Berenger's the Mauritian Militant Movement (MMM). President Sir Anerood Jugnauth, was reaffirmed in his post in September 2008.

Economic policy

Starting with a monocrop, impoverished island nation some 30 years ago, Mauritius has earned the top spot among African countries on the UN Human Development Index. Today it is a diversified economy, relying not only on exports of sugar, but textiles and services such as tourism and financial and offshore business. Mauritius has attracted more than 9,000 offshore entities, mostly aimed at commerce in India and South Africa. Investment in the banking sector alone generates more than $1 billion per year. The country, however, faces new challenges as both sugar and textiles are losing their preferential access to major overseas markets. It has compensated by taking full advantage of the Africa Growth and Opportunity Act (AGOA) for textile exports to the US. The emphasis is on productivity and turning some of its most successful companies into multinationals. The aim is to make Mauritius a regional trade and financial center. Impressive annual economic growth has resulted in more equitable income distribution, increased life expectancy, lowered infant mortality and improved infrastructure.

Navinchandra Ramgoolam
Born: July 13, 1947
Since July 2005

UN Photo Mark Garten

POLITICAL

Head of State	Pres. Anerood Jugnauth
Prime Minister	Navinchandra Ramgoolam
Ruling Coalition	AF
Main Opposition	MMM/MSM
Independence	12 March 1968
National capital	Port Louis
Official languages	English & French

PHYSICAL

Total area	1,000 sq. miles
	2,000 sq. km.
	(11xWashington DC
Arable land	50% of land area
Coastline	110 miles/177 km

POPULATION

Total	1.3 million
Av. yearly growth	0.78%
Urban population	42%
Life expectancy	74 years
Adult literacy	84.4%

ECONOMY

Currency	Rupee (MauR) (US$1=30.20)
GDP (real)	$9.2 billion
GDP growth rate	2.8%
GDP per capita[1]	$10,175
GDP (ppp)[2]	$17.5 billion
GDP per cap. (ppp)	$13,575
Inflation rate	2.5%
Exports	$1.9 billion
Imports	$3.5 billion
External debt	$821 million
Unemployment	7.2%

1. Atlas method.
2. See page 175 for an explanation of purchasing power parity (ppp).

Privatization

The government's share of GDP is modest but it still controls key sectors. The State Trading Corporation regulates imports of rice, flour, petroleum products, and cement, and the Agricultural Marketing Board the importation of potatoes, onions and spices.

Sectors

Initially heavily dependent on sugar, Mauritius has developed a strong manufacturing and tourism sector in the past few decades. Agriculture's share of GDP shrank to 9%, while manufacturing's contribution rose to 23%. Sugar, however, remains the basis of the economy. It is grown on about half the total land area and employs 14% of the labor force. Apart from high-value textiles, local manufactures include pharmaceuticals, publishing, software, light engineering, and jewelry. Tourism is the third pillar on which the Mauritian economy rests, accounting for 5% of GDP and providing direct and indirect employment for some 50,000 people. Offshore banking has become a major source of income.

Trade

Sugar and textiles together with a variety of light manufactures account for most of the country's exports. Other significant exports are tea and cut flowers. Mauritius imports three-quarters of its food, especially rice, a staple food. Main imported raw materials are textile yarn and fabrics (55%), cotton, wool and synthetic fibers (6%), and chemicals (4%). Caterpillar and John Deere are major suppliers of derocking machinery for sugar farms, followed by a few European manufacturers. The US also leads in supplying pivot irrigation systems for these estates.

Investment

Foreign direct investment fell sharply since the early 1980s when many Hong Kong firms, the leading investors in textile manufacturing, relocated. There are a few US investors in the Export Processing Zone (mostly diamond cutting/polishing and garment manufacturing). Most recent foreign direct investment has gone into information technology, printing and publishing, pharmaceuticals, light engineering, high-quality garments, and jewelry. India, UK, France, Germany and South Africa are leading investors.

Financial sector

A sophisticated banking system comprises 10 commercial banks (seven foreign-owned) and 10 financial intermediaries, including the Development Bank of Mauritius, the State Investment Corporation, the Mauritius Leasing Company (a joint private-public venture), as well as two private leasing companies. There are seven offshore banks and 4,600 non-banking off-shore companies providing insurance, funds management, aircraft leasing, consultancy, and data processing. The Stock Exchange of Mauritius has 45 listed companies (including two foreign) and an over-the-counter market with 60 companies. The Bank of Mauritius oversees domestic and offshore banks and implements monetary policies. Much of the country's offshore business involves US investment in India, channeled through Mauritius for tax reasons.

Taxes & Tariffs

The corporate tax rate for non-residents is 15 percent. There is no capital gains tax. A value added tax (VAT) of 15 percent applies and tehre is no exchange control in effect. Non-residents are not subject to any taxes on dividends, interest or royalties (24%). (See page 138).

BUSINESS ACTIVITY

AGRICULTURE
Sugar cane, tea, corn, potatoes, bananas, pulses, cattle, goats, fish.

INDUSTRIES
Food processing (largely sugar milling), textiles, clothing, chemicals, metal products, transport equipment, nonelectrical machinery, tourism.

NATURAL RESOURCES
Arable land, fish.

EXPORTS
$1.9 billion (est. 2009): clothing, textiles, sugar, cut flowers, molasses.

IMPORTS
$3.5 billion (est. 2009): manufactured goods, capital equipment, foodstuffs, petroleum products, chemicals.

MAJOR TRADING PARTNERS
UK, France, US, China, Italy, South Africa, India, Germany, UAE, Madagascar, Belgium.

Doing Business with Mauritius

▶ **Investment**

Tax concessions and other incentives are offered in Export Processing Zones scattered around the island. Textiles and apparel account for 80% of EPZ exports, but there has been diversification into the manufacture of watches, electronic measuring instruments, jewelry, leather goods, toys, and optical goods. The Mauritius Export Development and Investment Authority assists investors and promotes exports. Generous incentives are also available to foreign companies operating from the Mauritius Freeport in transshipment and re-exportation, offshore banking and other financial services, light manufacturing, and information technology. The authorities encourage both local and foreign private investment in major infrastructure projects ranging from energy to roads and airport construction.

▶ **Trade**

There is growing interest in foreign technology, especially in telecommunications, computers, software, and farm machinery. Opportunities also exist in restaurant and food-processing equipment and design consulting. The government controls prices and markups on items such as rice, flour, cement, cooking gas, infant milk powder, cheese, fertilizer, frozen fish, iron and steel bars, and petroleum products. Major expansion of both traditional and nontraditional sources of energy such as electricity from bagasse and wind power-created demand for turbo-alternators, boilers, machinery to handle bagasse, coal and ash, and associated electrical equipment. There is an ongoing need for machinery and irrigation systems.

▶ **Trade finance**

Mauritius qualifies for the full range of Eximbank loans extended to US exporters. The government-controlled Development Bank of Mauritius provides loans to large and medium-sized industrial enterprises and manages various concessionary lending schemes for small-scale enterprises.

▶ **Selling to the government**

Infrastructure projects such as airport and port development, energy, telecommunications, health, sewage, road and dam construction, and computerization offer opportunities.

▶ **Exchange controls**

There are no exchange control regulations and dividends and royalties are freely repatriated.

▶ **Partnership**

Joint ventures are rare except in architecture, construction and civil engineering projects. Several Mauritian firms, however, manufacture foreign products under license.

▶ **Establishing a presence**

Foreigners usually opt for a limited company or a branch. It is common procedure to nominate two residents to form the company and transfer the shares to the foreign investor after approval. A foreign investor in export-oriented manufacturing is permitted 100% equity, but the government encourages local participation. Foreign participation may be limited to 49% in investments serving the domestic market, and is generally not encouraged in areas where Mauritius has already mastered the technology.

▶ **Project financing**

Mauritius is eligible for OPIC programs and major infrastructure projects are financed by the World Bank, the African Development Bank, the European Investment Bank/European Development Fund, the Kuwait Fund, and the Arab Bank for Economic Development in Africa.

▶ **Labor**

It is not difficult to recruit workers with basic secondary education and some technical training. There is, however, a shortage of skills in financial services and management, especially human resource management. Labor-management relations are generally good and unions account for less than 25 percent of the workforce.

▶ **Legal rights**

The legal system, based on both the Napoleonic code and British common law, protects property, patents and trademarks. Mauritius is a member of the World Intellectual Property Organization and party to the Paris and Bern Conventions for the Protection of Industrial Property and the Universal Copyright Convention. Its copyright law is in conformity with WTO's Trade Related Aspects of Intellectual Property Rights (TRIPS).

▶ **Business climate**

Business customs are Western. For men, normal business wear is a suit. Lunches and cocktail receptions are common business events. International mail, telephone, fax and e-mail services are reliable. The official language is English but French and Creole are used in everyday life.

MOROCCO

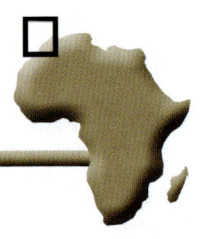

As the African country closest to Europe, Morocco's economic fate is closely tied to markets across the Mediterranean sea. Separated from Spain by the 13 kilometer Strait of Gibraltar, most of Morocco's trade is directed towards the European Union but there is a concerted effort to expand business relations with the United States. Despite diversity and the lingering Western Sahara dispute, Morocco is one of the most stable countries in the Arab world—due largely to the efforts of the late King Hassan, a consummate politician, and his successor, King Mohammed VI. Morocco has the largest phosphate reserves in the world, a thriving agricultural sector, rich fisheries, a sizeable tourist industry, and a growing manufacturing sector. Since the early 1980s Morocco has pursued an economic reform program that has led to rising per capita incomes, lower inflation, and smaller deficits.

Country profile

The Kingdom of Morocco is part of a region dominated by the Atlas Mountains that extends into Algeria and Tunisia. The port city of Ceuta at Morocco's northernmost point is Spanish territory, as is Mellila further east. Mount Toubkal in the High Atlas is 13,670 ft (4,165 m) above sea level and snow-capped during much of the year. The much lower Anti-Atlas mountains stretch into in the desert borderlands with large clusters of oases. Between the Atlantic coast and the mountain ranges is fertile agricultural land. Earthquakes sometimes occur and in 1960 one razed Agadir, causing the death of some 15,000 people. About 60% of the population is of Arab and mixed Arabo-Berber origin and speak Arabic, while the remainder still speak various Berber dialects. Arabic is the official language but French is widely used in business, government and education. Many people in the far north speak Spanish. Islam is the state religion and but there are about 100,000 Christians, mainly Roman Catholic, and several thousand Jews.

History

When the Phoenicians started trading with the region it was already occupied by people of caucasoid origin. These Africans were called barbarians by the ancient Greeks and Romans and the name Berber is probably derived from barberoi (Greek) or barbari (Latin). Arab-Muslim conquerors in the course of the 7th Century succeeded in converting many Berbers to Islam. Marriages between Arab warriors and Berber women started a process of assimilation. In 1492 the Christians

304

in Spain and Portugal finally overpowered the Moors and caused a considerable migration to Morocco of Muslims and Jews. Following their victory, the Spaniards and Portuguese seized most of the ports along the Maghreb coast. Ceuta and Tanger were already under Portuguese control and Melilla became a Spanish stronghold. In 1684 the city of Tanger, which had been donated to the English by the Portuguese, was reoccupied by the Moroccans. However, Spain held on to Melilla and to Ceuta, which it had acquired from the Portuguese as well. In 1912 France took possession of the larger (central) part of Morocco, with all its important cities, and later that year ceded to Spain two territories to the north and south including Ceuta and Melilla and Rio de Oro (later to become known as the Spanish or Western Sahara). The nationalist opposition in Morocco defeated a combined Franco-Spanish force of over 250,000 in 1926 and forced France to grant it self-government in 1956. Spain had to cede all its possessions except Ceuta, Melilla, Ifni and Spanish Sahara. As the neighboring states (Algeria, Mauritania and Mali) became independent, Morocco claimed, on historic grounds, parts of their territory, as well as the entire Spanish Sahara. King Mohammed V ruled from 1957 until his death in 1961. He was succeeded by his son Mulay Hassan II who ruled until his death in 1999. King Hassan was followed to the throne by his heir, King Mohammed VI.

Government

The current constitution, dating back to 1972, combines limited democracy with strong, virtually unlimited royal authority. As head of state, the king may introduce and veto legislation, dissolve the legislature and rule by decree. He appoints the Prime Minister and the cabinet. After the 2007 election Abbas El Fassi was appointed Prime Minister. The bicameral parliament consists of the 270-seat *Majlis al-Mustasharin* or Chamber of Counselors elected for a nine year term by local councils, professional organizations, and labor syndicates, and the *Majlis al-Nuwab*—a 325 seat lower house or Chamber of Representatives elected by for five years by popular vote. In the September 2007 election the Independence Party *(Hizb al-Istiqlal/Parti d'Independence)* (PI) won 52 seats against 46 for Justice and Development Party *(Parti de la Justice et du Développement)*

King Mohammed VI
Born: Aug. 12,1963
Since July 1999

POLITICAL

Head of State	King Mohammed VI
Prime Minister	Abbas El Fassi
Ruling Party	Independence Party
Main Opposition	Peoples Movement
Independence	2 March 1956
National capital	Rabat
Official language	Arabic

PHYSICAL

Total area	172,000 sq. miles 446,000 sq. km. (± California)
Arable land	20% of land area
Coastline	1,140 m/1,835 km

POPULATION

Total	31.2 million
Av. yearly growth	1.0%
Urban population	56%
Life expectancy	75.5 years
Adult literacy	52.3%

ECONOMY

Currency	Moroccan dirham (DH) (US$1=8.41)
GDP (real)	$88.6 billion
GDP growth rate	5.0%
GDP per capita[1]	$3,547
GDP (ppp)[2]	$151.9 billion
GDP per cap. (ppp)[2]	$4,747
Inflation rate	1.0%
Exports	$14.8 billion
Imports	$31.2 billion
External debt	$18.3 billion
Unemployment	9.1%

1. Atlas method.
2. See page 175 for an explanation of purchasing power parity (ppp).

(PJD). Other major parties include the People's Movement *(Mouvement Populaire)* with 41 seats, the National Rally of Independents *(Rassemblement National des Indépendants)* with 39 and the Socialist Union of People's Forces *(Union Socialiste des Forces Populaires)* with 38. Twenty different parties are represented in Moroccan Assembly.

Economic policy

Although its economic policies brought stability, unemployment remains a concern in Morocco. Plans have been announced to reduce poverty and provide jobs. It launched a $2 billion National Initiative for Human Development (INDH) plan to address poverty. The introduction by 2010 of a free trade area with the EU will force Moroccan producers to become more amenable to foreign partnerships. A free trade agreement with the United States and large scale privatization projects—including the sale of government shares in the state-owned bank telecommunications company—boosted foreign direct investment.

Sectors

Agriculture, fishing and forestry employ two-thirds of the working population, account for 15% of GDP and contribute about 25% of the country's export revenues. At 21% a comparatively high proportion of the total area is arable and utilized by large-scale commercial farmers, producing citrus and wine, as well as peasant smallholders. The principal food crops are wheat, barley, maize and vegetables. Sugar cane, sugar beet, olives and cotton are major industrial crops but the principal agricultural exports are citrus, tomatoes, canned fruit, vegetables and wine. The country is self-sufficient in livestock production, mainly sheep. Canned fish and fresh fish, including shellfish, account for around 14% of total exports. Together with Western Sahara, Morocco accounts for 75% of the world's known phosphate reserves and is, after Russia and the US, the world's third largest producer. Other mineral resources are silver, zinc, copper, fluorine, lead, barite, and iron.

Privatization

Morocco has sold more than half of its 114 state enterprises. A 35% interest in the state telecommunications monopoly, Maroc Telecom, was sold to France's Vivendi Universal for $2.7 billion.

Investment

Foreign investment has grown considerably since privatization started and the government opened infrastructural projects to private participation.

Trade

The export of phosphates and derivatives accounts for over a quarter of the total. Morocco is a net exporter of fruits and vegetables, but a net importer of cereals. Textile and clothing comprise 70% of all manufactured exports.

Financial sector

There are 12 major banks, five government-owned specialized financial institutions, some 15 credit agencies and 10 leasing companies. Insurance companies, pension funds, and a stock market are the other components of a modern, well developed financial sector. The Casablanca stock exchange enjoyed a recent revival after new laws made it more efficient.

Taxes and tariffs

The corporate tax rate for non-residents is 10 percent and capital gains tax 30 percent. A value added tax (VAT) of 20 percent applies and exchange control is in effect. A tax rate of 10% applies to dividends, income from interest and royalties. (See page 138).

BUSINESS ACTIVITY

AGRICULTURE
Barley, wheat, citrus, wine, vegetables, olives, livestock.
INDUSTRIES
Phosphate rock mining and processing, food processing, leather goods, textiles, construction, tourism.
NATURAL RESOURCES
Phosphates, iron ore, zinc, fish, salt, lead, manganese.
EXPORTS
$14.8 billion (est. 2009): food and beverages, semiprocessed goods, consumer goods, phosphates, clothing, petroleum products.
IMPORTS
$31.2 billion (est. 2009): crude petroleum, textile fabric, transistors, plastics.
MAJOR TRADING PARTNERS
France, Spain, UK, China, US, Belgium, Germany, Italy, Saudi Arabia

Doing Business with Morocco

▶ **Investment**

Apart from agricultural land and a few sectors still reserved for the state such as phosphate mining, air and rail transport, and public utilities, foreign participation is strongly encouraged. Under Morocco's privatization program most of these restricted areas are expected to be opened up. A Moroccanization decree limiting foreign ownership in the petroleum refining and distribution sector was repealed and allowed, among others, Mobil Oil to buy back the government's 50 percent share of its local subsidiary. There are no foreign investor performance requirements and incentives apply. In the building of power plants, telephone network expansion and other infrastructural developments the government relies largely on foreign entrepreneurs.

▶ **Trade**

The favored port of entry is Casablanca and foreign manufacturers and exporters are represented in the market either through their own affiliate branch office or by authorized agent/distributors who import, install and service the equipment. There seems to be ample scope in the fast food sector. Additional franchising opportunities include hotels and motels, automotive parts and services, dry cleaning business equipment and services. Among the top prospects for sales are water distribution equipment, electrical power systems, pollution control, mining, medical and telecommunications equipment, computers and software, and architectural, engineering, tourism and other services. Agricultural needs range from large quantities of wheat to vegetable oil, sugar, and cotton.

▶ **Trade finance**

Local financing is available for Moroccan investors and importers, but real interest rates are high by overseas standards. Most Moroccan imports are by irrevocable confirmed letters but intense competition at times requires attractive payment terms. The Eximbank provides assistance to US exporters and the US Department of Agriculture extends credit guarantee programs.

▶ **Selling to the government**

While government purchases are at times directly negotiated, tenders are common. So-called medium and major projects are open to international firms while minor ones are reserved for locals. Major projects are often guaranteed by an international financial entity.

▶ **Exchange controls**

Foreign exchange is available through the commercial banks upon presentation of documents for the repatriation of dividends and capital by foreign investors, for remittances by foreign residents, and for payments for foreign technical assistance, royalties and licenses.

▶ **Partnerships**

There is growing local interest joint ventures and at latest count 1,500 have been operating in the manufacturing sector, mostly with French, Spanish and German partners.

▶ **Establishing a presence**

To form a local company foreigners merely need to file documents with the Secretariat of the Court of First Instance.

▶ **Financing projects**

In most instances project financing comes from the World Bank, the African Development Bank, the European Investment Bank, the Kuwaiti Fund, the Saudi Fund and the Abu Dhabi Fund.

▶ **Labor**

Workers are free to form and join unions but only about 6% of Morocco's nine million workers are unionized, mostly in the public sector. Collective bargaining has, however, been a long-standing tradition in some parts of the economy, notably heavy industry.

▶ **Legal rights**

The law protects and facilitates acquisition and disposition of property rights, including intellectual property rights. Morocco is a member of the World Intellectual Property Organization and party to the Berne copyright, Paris industrial property, and universal copyright conventions. Still dating from the era of French and Spanish protectorates is the requirement that patent and trademark applications to be filed in both Casablanca and Tangier. Morocco is a member of the International Center for the Settlement of Investment Disputes and a party to the 1958 convention on the recognition and enforcement of foreign arbitrary awards.

▶ **Business climate**

Morocco is a Muslim country and business meetings are best avoided on Friday. Although Arabic is the official language, French is widely used.

MOZAMBIQUE

Once plagued by internal strife and failed socialist policies Mozambique changed its fortunes in recent years through political stability and sound economic policies that lured foreign investment. Important fiscal reforms and the introduction of value-added tax boosted state revenues. A major aluminum smelter, titanium extraction and textile manufacturing are among the foreign-driven projects that stimulated growth. Mozambique, however, continues to depend on foreign assistance for much of its annual budget.

Country profile

Much of the Republic of Mozambique consists of a coastal plain and lowland less than 500 m above sea level. The Zambezi River is the largest of 25 rivers in the region. The climate is hot and humid, with temperatures and rainfall rising to the north. Most of the people are Bantu-speaking. The Makua and Lomwe account for 40% of the total. Other inhabitants range from the Yao, Makonde, Sena, Chewa, Shona, to the Tsonga, and Shangaan. Minority groups such as the mestizos (people of mixed descent), Indians and whites—Portuguese and a growing number of South Africans—are prominent in the economy. Portuguese is the official language, but English is widely spoken in business and professional circles.

History

In ancient times northern Mozambique formed part of the trade network in slaves, gold and ivory between Arabs and Persians and the Bantu kingdom of Mwene Mutapa. Intermarriage between these merchants and their African slaves gave rise to a distinct Swahili culture. Portuguese involvement started in 1498 when Vasco da Gama reached Mozambique Island. By 1510 the Portuguese had control of all the former Arab sultanates on the east African coast. Portugal participated in the partitioning of Africa among the European powers in the last two decades of the 19th Century and Mozambique took its present shape on the map in 1890. Mozambique was ruled as an overseas Portuguese province. In 1964 the Frente da Libertação de Moçambique or Liberation Front of Mozambique (Frelimo), led by Dr. Eduardo Mondlane, began an armed revolt against the Portuguese rulers. The

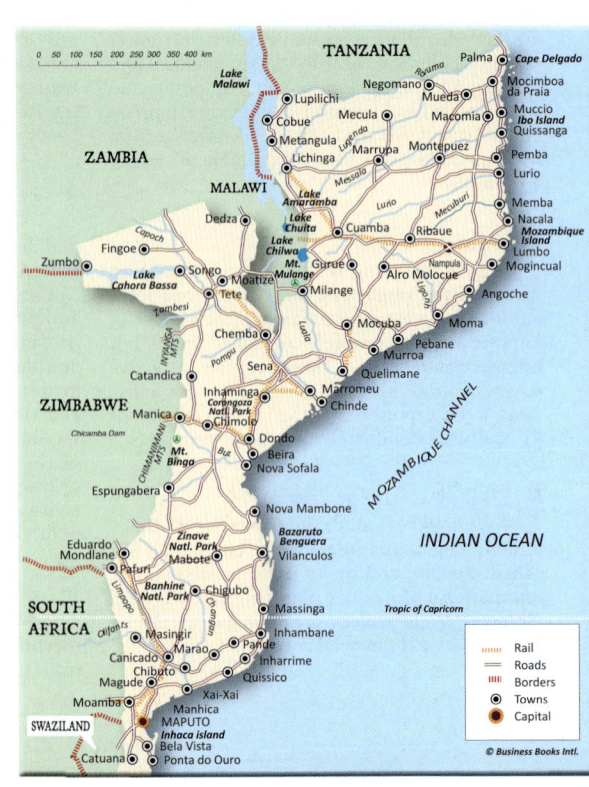

308

struggle was continued after his death in 1969 by Samora Moises Machel. After a military coup in Portugal in 1974, a peace agreement was concluded and on 25 June 1975, 470 years of Portuguese rule ended. Machel became president of an independent Mozambique. Asset-stripping by the fleeing Portuguese, Marxist-Leninist centralization and nationalization, and a paralyzing and five year civil war against the Resistencia Nacional Moçambicana or Mozambican National Resistance (Renamo) contributed to the country's rapid economic decay. In October 1986 President Machel was killed when his aircraft crashed. Following the collapse of the Soviet Union, Machel's successor, President Joaquim Alberto Chissano, turned to the West and post-apartheid South Africa to jumpstart the economy. A peace agreement between Frelimo and Renamo led to the adoption of a new democratic constitution in 1994. In November 1995, Mozambique was the first non-former-British colony to become a member of the Commonwealth. In 2005 Chissano was succeeded as head of state by Armando Guebuza who was re-elected in a land-slide victory in October 2009.

Government

Under the new constitution, both the president and the 250-member unicameral Assembly, or the *Assembleia da República*, are elected for 5-year terms. In the October 2009 elections Frelimo presidential candidate Armando Guebuza gained 75 percent of the popular vote. With 191 seats Frelimo maintained a comfortable majority in the Assembly over Renamo and its and its coalition partners with their 59 seats.

Economic policy

At independence Mozambique was one of the world's poorest countries. In the nineties the failed Marxist policies were abandoned in favor of free market practices. Mozambique's creditors decided to write off most of its debt. Foreign debt was further reduced by rescheduling and forgiveness under the IMF's Heavily Indebted Poor Countries (HIPC) and Enhanced HIPC initiatives. Privatization is proceeding well. Outside investors reacted positively to the improved investment climate in Mozambique. Despite impressive growth in recent years Mozambique remains dependent on foreign assistance for part of its budget.

Pres. Armando Guebuza
Born: Jan 20, 1943
Since February 2005

UN Photo Evan Schneider

POLITICAL
Head of State	Pres. Armando Guebuza
Ruling Party	Frelimo
Main Opposition	Renamo
Independence	25 June 1975
National capital	Maputo
Official language	Portuguese

PHYSICAL
Total area	310,000 sq. miles
	802,000 sq. km.
	(±2 x California)
Arable land	5.1% of land area
Coastline	1,535 m/2,470 km

POPULATION
Total	22 million
Av. yearly growth	1.8%
Urban population	37%
Life expectancy	41.37 years
Adult literacy	47.8%

ECONOMY
Currency	Metical (Mt) (US$1=34.15)
GDP (real)	$14.5 billion
GDP growth rate	5.4%
GDP per capita[1]	$663
GDP (ppp)[2]	$21.8 billion
GDP per cap. (ppp)	$950
Inflation rate	3.4%
Exports	$1.96 billion
Imports	$3.0 billion
External debt	$5.1 billion
Unemployment	21%

1. Atlas method.
2. See page 175 for an explanation of purchasing power parity (ppp).

Sectors

Agriculture is the mainstay of the economy, employing up to 60% of the workforce, mainly in subsistence farming. Principal cash crops are cashew nuts, tea, sugar, sisal, cotton, copra and oil seeds. Maize is the main subsistence crop, but cassava, millet, sorghum, groundnuts, beans and rice are also grown. The country has a rich variety of minerals including large deposits of iron and bauxite ore and coal, tantalite (used in the electronics industry and for special steels) and pegmatite (a source of tantalite), beryl, mica, bismuth and semiprecious stones. Along the coast are also titanium-bearing beach sands. Plans are underway to develop the large natural gas fields at Pande, west of Inhambane, and in the Buzi swamps, near Beira. Manufacturing includes food processing and industrial crops, fertilizer, agricultural implements, cement, textiles, beverages, ceramics, wood processing, tires, and radios. Pristine beaches and national wildlife parks are important assets and tourism is a growing sector. Cahora Bassa Dam on the Zambezi—Africa's largest hydropower station after the Aswan High in Egypt—has the potentialk of supplying not only in the needs of Mozambique but those of its neighbors.

Privatization

Over 900 state-owned enterprises have been sold including a cement plant, flour mills, breweries, commercial agriculture operations, cashew processing plants, and fishing and trading companies. The management of coal, sugar, citrus, and container terminals at ports has been entrusted to private consortia. In most of these transactions, there was substantial foreign participation. As a final step to privatizing the financial sector, two of the country's largest state-owned banks have been sold.

Investment

Just under $4 billion in foreign direct investment has been registered during the past five years. South Africa surpassed Britain and Portugal as the most important source of investment after its Industrial Development Corporation (IDC) became an active participant in large projects such as the Mozal aluminum smelter. Several major US firms have also become involved. These projects, along with the toll road under construction from South Africa and the upgrading of the port of Maputo should provide the impetus for further investment along the Maputo Development Corridor.

Trade

Exports are largely cashews, sugar, cotton, and other agricultural commodities, textiles, seafood, and minerals. the Mozal aluminum smelter, the country's largest foreign investment project to date, has greatly increased export earnings. Electric power, natural gas and related products, as well as tourism, are other potential important foreign currency earners.

Financial sector

Nowhere is the dramatic effect of recent reforms more apparent than in the banking system. The Banco de Mozambique, which acted as both the central bank and the major commercial bank in the past has been replaced by a separate central bank and a number of private banks.

Taxes and tariffs

The corporate tax rate for non-residents is 32 percent. There is no and capital gains tax. A value added tax (VAT) of 17 percent applies and exchange control is in effect. Taxes are levied on dividends (20%), interest (20%) and royalties (20%). (See page 138).

BUSINESS ACTIVITY

AGRICULTURE
Cotton, cashew nuts, sugar cane, tea, cassava (tapioca), corn, rice, tropical fruit, beef, poultry.

INDUSTRIES
Food, beverages, chemicals (fertilizer, soap, paints), petroleum products, textiles, cement, glass, asbestos, tobacco.

NATURAL RESOURCES
Coal, titanium, natural gas.

EXPORTS
$1.96 billion (est. 2009): aluminum, bulk electricity, prawns, cashews, cotton, sugar, copra, citrus.

IMPORTS
$3.0 billion (est. 2009): food, clothing, machinery, metal products, chemicals, fuel.

MAJOR TRADING PARTNERS
South Africa, US, UK, Belgium, China, Spain, Italy, Australia, Zimbabwe.

Doing Business with Mozambique

▶ **Investment**

The Investment Promotion Center (CPI) offers a variety of tax incentives according to regions and the type of investment. Specific performance requirements are built into mining concessions and management contracts and sometimes into the sale of state-owned entities. Approval for investment follows automatically in 10 days if no objections are voiced by the relevant ministries, provincial governor (for investments under $100,000), or the Minister of Planning and Finance (in the case of investments under $100 million). The Council of Ministers must review investments over $100 million as well as those involving large tracts of land. Legislation supports the creation of "Industrial Free Zones." There are good opportunities in energy, mining, fishing, timber, tourism, agriculture and manufacturing of inexpensive goods.

▶ **Trade**

Trade opportunities exist in the energy, mining, fishing, timber, tourism, and agriculture (cashews, cotton, and sugar) sectors. There is a growing demand for construction, telecommunications, agricultural, plastic, food processing and packaging and fishing equipment. Planned new projects such as an aluminum smelter, natural gas pipelines, a direct reduced iron and steel plant, and new mineral sands processing are bound to increase the demand for engineering and construction equipment and expertise. Wheat, rice, and edible oils are imported in reasonably large quantities.

▶ **Trade finance**

Eximbank provides short-, medium-, and long-term financing to US exporters. The US Trade and Development Agency assists with feasibility studies and reverse trade missions.

▶ **Selling to the government**

Major government purchases might be subject to the procurement rules set by international donors as Mozambique often relies on outside financial support. It is, however, necessary for bidders to establish personal contacts within the government and to keep abreast of frequent changes in the procurement process.

▶ **Exchange controls**

Repatriation of profits and repayment of offshore loans are allowed. Investment laws guarantee foreign investors the right to remit loan repayments, dividends, profits and invested capital.

▶ **Partnerships**

Joint ventures are encouraged by the government and can help ease potential problems with regulatory issues and red tape. The government itself favors partnerships with foreign firms in privatization deals.

▶ **Establishing a presence**

The official Investment Promotion Center (CPI) has developed a package of services to assist foreign investors with this process.

▶ **Financing projects**

OPIC has an Investment Incentive Agreement in place. Mozambique is also a member of the Multilateral Investment Guarantee Agency. Some major projects are financed by the World Bank, the African Development Bank, and donor agencies such as USAID. The International Finance Corporation and the Commonwealth Development Corporation provide medium-term loans and equity finance in Mozambique. The US government-sponsored $100 million Southern African Enterprise Development Fund (SAEDF) assists Mozambican entrepreneurs out of its Johannesburg offices.

▶ **Labor**

Most working Mozambicans derive income from more than one activity, and grow corn and vegetables on small parcels of land for personal consumption. Labor unions, created during the socialist years, are gradually asserting their independence from the ruling Frelimo Party.

▶ **Legal rights**

The government grants land-use concessions for periods of up to 50 years with options to renew. Foreign investors have recourse to arbitration through the UNCITRAL (United Nations Commission on International Trade Law) model. The government has also acceded to the New York Convention on the Recognition and Enforcement of Foreign Arbitral Awards. Mozambique has signed the Bern Convention on International Copyrights, as well as the New York and Paris Conventions. Intellectual property right infringement is not considered a significant problem.

▶ **Business climate**

Portuguese is widely spoken but the use of English is growing in business circles. The business community in Maputo is small enough for most to know each other.

NAMIBIA

Despite its sparse population and lack of rainfall, Namibia seems poised to become a convenient gateway to the growing Southern African regional market. Good infrastructure and an efficient, deep-water port at Walvis Bay, coupled with a strong mining and agricultural base, make Namibia a good candidate for investment and future trade. In its effort to bring previously-disadvantaged Namibians into the economic mainstream via private sector commercial development, the Namibian government is actively courting foreign investors. Since independence, personal and corporate tax rates have been cut to improve the business climate.

Country profile

The Republic of Namibia consists of three regions running from north to south: the Namib Desert along the coast, the great escarpment which reaches its highest elevation at the Auas mountains near Windhoek, and the semi-arid Kalahari Basin continuing into Botswana and South Africa. Average annual rainfall for the country is only 270 mm—about 70% of the land is classified as arid and 22% as desert. Underground water sources sustain large herds of cattle on the northern savanna pastures and sheep, including karakul, on the desert scrub in the south. Wildlife abounds and is protected in a number of nature reserves and wilderness areas. The three Bantu-speaking groups—the Ovambo, Kavango and Herero—account for about two-thirds of the population. Whites comprise about 5 percent of the total. Even though English is the official language, Afrikaans is widely spoken, as well as some German. More than 90% of the population is Christian.

In the 19th Century German merchants settled in the territory around the British possession of Walvis Bay. German forces moved inland to claim what became known as German West Africa, almost annihilating the Herero and the Nama in the process. During the First World War South Africa defeated the Germans in the territory and in 1919 the League of Nations confirmed its control over the mandate of South West Africa (SWA). South African attempts after the Second World War to incorporate the ter-

History

The San and Nama or Khoikhoi peoples were already in the region 500 years ago when Ovambo and Kavango groups migrated south from present-day Angola.

ritory instead of submitting it to the control of the newly-formed UN Trusteeship Council led to a lengthy political struggle in the UN. The South West African Peoples Organization (SWAPO), under leadership of Sam Daniel Shafiishuna Nujoma, resorted to arms in 1966 after the International Court of Justice gave a ruling favorable to the South African government. In 1988, a US-inspired peace agreement ended hostilities on the northern border where South Africa was engaged in a protracted battle with Cuban and Angolan MPLA troops, assisted by SWAPO commandos. SWAPO emerged as the victor in an election held in 1989 under supervision of a UN Transitional Assistance Group (UNTAG) and on 21 March 1990, Nujoma was sworn in as president of independent Namibia and reelected several times until he stepped down in 2005. He was succeeded by Hifikepunye Pohamba as leader of SWAPO and as president after winning the November 2004 presidential election. Pohamba was re-elected by a landslide vote in November 2009.

Government

The executive President is elected for a 5-year term. He appoints the Prime Minister and other cabinet ministers. The 72-member National Assembly is also elected for 5 years on a party-list proportional basis, while the 26-member National Council—elected every six years by the Regional Councils—serves as an upper house. In November 2009 Swapo captured 54 seats in the National Assembly against 8 for the Rally for Democracy and Progress (RDP) with the rest of the seats split between seven parties.

Economic policy

There is considerable state involvement in sectors such as postal services, telecommunications, development banking, electricity and water supply, transport, and agricultural commodity marketing. The government has advocated an interventionist role in major infrastructure projects or "high risk ventures." At the same time, it has adopted a free market-based investment code with wide-ranging incentives to encourage private sector involvement. The goal is to diversify the economy away from heavy dependence on diamonds, uranium, and base metals. The economy is closely linked to South Africa with the Namibian dollar pegged one-to-one to the South African rand.

Pres. Hifikepunye Pohamba
Born: August 8, 1935
Since March 2005

UN Photo Evan Schneider

POLITICAL

Head of State	Pres. Hifikepunye Pohamba
Ruling Party	Swapo
Main Opposition	RDP
Independence	21 March 1990
National capital	Windhoek
Official language	English

PHYSICAL

Total area	318,000 sq. miles 824,000 sq. km. (½ x Alaska)
Arable land	1%
Coastline	977 m/1,572 km

POPULATION

Total	2.1 million
Av. yearly growth	0.95%
Urban population	37%
Life expectancy	51.24 years
Adult literacy	85%

ECONOMY

Currency	Namibian dollar (N$) (US$1=6.88)
GDP (real)	$8.2 billion
GDP growth rate	-1.8%
GDP per capita[1]	$3,881
GDP (ppp)[2]	$13.7 billion
GDP per cap. (ppp)	$6,327
Inflation rate	8.8%
Exports	$3.5 billion
Imports	$4.5 billion
External debt	$2 billion
Unemployment	51.2%

1. Atlas method.
2. See page 175 for an explanation of purchasing power parity (ppp).

Sectors

Heavily dependent on this sector, Namibia ranks among the top 20 mining countries in the world. It is the fourth largest exporter in Africa of nonfuel minerals. Currently mining accounts for 20% of its GDP. Namibia is a major producer of uranium, pyrites, cadmium, arsenic, gold, silver, fluorspar, and semi-precious stones, but gem quality diamonds are the country's largest generator of foreign exchange. The mining sector, however, employs only about 3% of the population. Most of the population is still dependent on subsistence agriculture. The agricultural sector forms only 11.7% of Namibia's GDP but 70% of the population depend on it. Cattle farming is predominant in the central and northern regions, while karakul sheep, goat, and ostrich are raised in the south. Pilchard, hake, horse mackerel, anchovy and rock lobster are the main catches off the coast, rated among the world's richest fishing grounds. The primary industrial activity (excluding mining) is meat and fish processing. The tourism industry shows great growth potential. Large offshore natural gas reserves have been discovered.

Privatization

Even though the state continues to control key economic sectors such as electricity, telephones, water, the national airline and the railway, it is moving towards private sector-led growth, Despite strong union opposition, it is proceeding with privatization of select state-owned companies, with minority shares reserved for black empowerment groups.

Investment

The five major foreign investor countries in Namibia are South Africa, Germany, Britain, the US and Malaysia. Namibia obtained a stake in the diamond industry previously monopolized by De Beers in 1994 when it struck an agreement with the company that gave the state a 50 percent share of the new entity, NAMDEB. Diamond output was boosted further through offshore mining by the UK-based Namibian Minerals Corporation. Other mining opportunities such as the Australian owned Haib copper prospect in the far south are among recent areas of focus. Shell has identified a promising gas field offshore that could make the country a significant energy exporter in the next century.

Trade

Exports consist largely of gem-quality diamonds, uranium, base metals, cattle, karakul hides and fish. Imports are similarly high. Around 85% of Namibia's imports originate in or transit through South Africa. Normally Namibia imports about half of its cereal requirements and during drought periods food shortages become a major problem in the rural regions.

Financial sector

The Bank of Namibia has formal authority over the country's foreign exchange dealings. Namibia enjoys good creditworthiness in international financial circles, and is eligible to draw on the resources of the IMF, the World Bank, and the African Development Bank. Commercial banks provide comprehensive domestic and international services. The Namibian Stock Exchange (NSE) is the second largest African stock market in terms of value of shares listed.

Taxes and tariffs

The corporate tax rate for non-residents is 34 percent. There is no capital gains tax. A value added tax (VAT) of 15 percent applies and exchange control is in effect. Taxes are levied on dividends (10%), interest (10%) and royalties (30%). (See page 138).

BUSINESS ACTIVITY

AGRICULTURE	
Millet, sorghum, peanuts, livestock, fish.	
INDUSTRIES	
Meat packing, fish processing, dairy products, mining (diamond, lead, zinc, tin, silver, tungesten, uranium, copper).	
NATURAL RESOURCES	
Diamonds, copper, uranium, gold, lead, tin, lithium, cadmium, zinc, salt, vanadium, natural gas, fish, suspected deposits of oil, coal, iron ore.	
EXPORTS	
$3.5 billion (est. 2009): diamonds, copper, gold, zinc, lead, uranium, cattle, processed fish, karakul skins.	
IMPORTS	
$4.5 billion (est. 2009): foodstuffs, petroleum products and fuel, machinery and equipment, chemicals.	
MAJOR TRADING PARTNERS	
South Africa, US, China.	

Doing Business with Namibia

▶ **Investment**

An Investment Center within the Ministry of Trade and Industry assists foreign investors. Investment and tax incentives are available for new and existing manufacturing firms, and an Export Processing Zone (EPZ) has been set up at the port of Walvis Bay. A well-developed infrastructure in Namibia is a good asset for prospective foreign investors looking at Namibia as a gateway to the Southern Africa region. The fishing, tourism, manufacturing, mining, water and energy sectors offer prospects for development and expansion by foreign entrepreneurs.

▶ **Trade**

Namibia, with its solid managerial and physical infrastructure, provides a useful springboard to the central and southern African markets. Useful areas for exporters are agricultural equipment and chemicals, consumer food products, and telecommunications equipment. South African and German-linked concerns dominate the marketing and distribution networks and many of the product line markets.

▶ **Trade finance**

The Eximbank provides insurance and guarantees for US exporters to Namibia. The US Department of Agriculture provides credit guarantees for up to three years for qualifying exports.

▶ **Selling to the government**

Government purchases are usually by tender. Often Namibian government needs are too modest to interest the larger US supplier, but there are notable exceptions. In an effort to diversify sources of supply, the government contracted in late 1996 with Detroit-based Barden International to supply more than 800 General Motors vehicles to its motor pool. Barden invested about $15 million in right-hand drive conversion at a plant in Windhoek.

▶ **Exchange controls**

Under the CMA Agreement, the South African rand is also legal tender and exchange controls are similar to those applied in South Africa.

▶ **Partnerships**

The government sometimes allocates business rights to Namibian companies on more favorable terms. For example, in the fishing sector joint ventures with Namibian concession holders are obviously the best route for foreigners.

▶ **Establishing a presence**

A presence may be in the form of a public or private company, branch of a foreign company, partnership, joint venture, or as a sole trader. A branch of a foreign company must register within 21 days of establishing itself in Namibia. Namibian accountants and auditors should be engaged to ensure strict adherence to local tax and labor laws.

▶ **Financing projects**

The Overseas Private Investment Corporation provides funding and political risk insurance to qualified US investors. Namibia is also a member of the Multilateral Investment Guarantee Agency. Local commercial banks provide project financing in agriculture, commercial fishing, tourism, housing, minerals and mining.

▶ **Labor**

There is a large pool of qualified workers in varying professions but a shortage of highly skilled personnel. A special tax deduction of up to 25% is extended to manufacturing companies that provide technical training. The government will also reimburse companies for costs directly related to employee training under approved conditions. Most workers belong to trade unions. The NUNW, an affiliate of the ruling SWAPO party, represents the workers of seven affiliated trade unions. Wage rates of $200 per month and a 45 hour work week are common. Overtime pay plus annual and maternity leave are standard.

▶ **Legal rights**

Namibia's legal system is based on Roman-Dutch law. The Foreign Investment Act protects investors against expropriation and stipulates steps for the settlement of disputes by international arbitration. The local court system provides an effective means to enforce property and contractual rights. An independent, transparent legal system protects and facilitates acquisition and disposition of property rights. The issue of intellectual property is understood and generally respected by most companies operating in Namibia and, unlike some other developing countries, IPR infringement is not a major problem.

▶ **Business climate**

Business customs are similar to those practiced in neighboring South Africa. Most business with foreigners is conducted in English but among the locals Afrikaans and German are also spoken.

NIGER

The Niger river flowing through Sahel terrain is as much of a lifeline for Niger as the Nile is for Sudan and Egypt—both as a source of water and a means of transport. With some of the world's largest reserves A slowdown in world market for uranium has severely damaged this landlocked country's economy. The current emphasis is on exploration and development of alternative mineral resources and the expansion of its agricultural base with the help of foreign investors. Foreign firms have been focusing on gold, coal and oil. economic reforms have been introduced to make the country more investor-friendly.

Country profile

The Republic of Niger covers a plateau less than 500 m (1,640 ft) high reaching northwards into the Sahara Desert. In the central region the partly volcanic Air Mountains rise to 1,800 m (6,000 ft) above sea level. The perennial Niger River meanders for about 500 km (310 miles) through the southwestern tip of the country. During the flood season from July to September it is navigable by smaller boat and provides irrigation along its banks. The Hausa people extending across the Nigerian border form the largest cultural group, accounting for more than half of Niger's population. The closely related Songhai and Zarma (or Djerma), concentrated along the Niger River, account for about a quarter of the population. These groups and the smaller Kanuri, Daza and Teda factions speak Nilo-Saharan languages. About 10% of the population are Fulani (or Ful) and 3% Tuareg. Over 85% of the population are Muslims, but among some ethnic faiths still prevail.

History

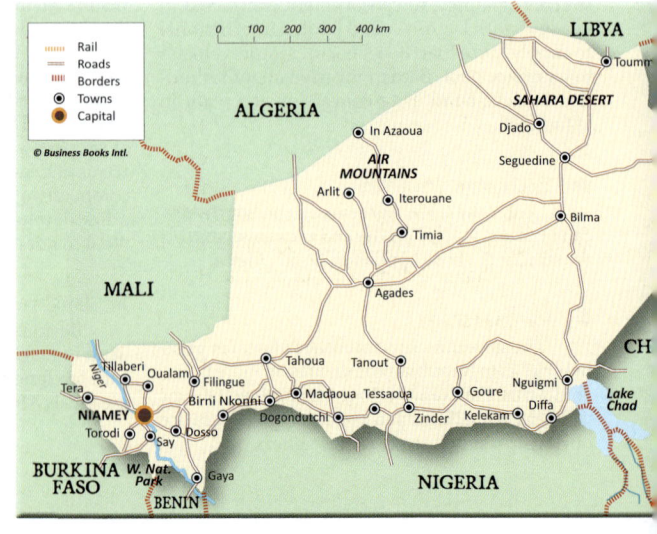

The nomadic Tuaregs were the first inhabitants of this Sahara region. They were followed by the Hausa (14th Century), the Zerma (17th Century), the Goboir (18th Century) and the Fulani. About 1,000 years ago, Arab traders first made contact with the Hausa in the Sahel region and introduced them to the Muslim faith. The Hausa were subjugated by Songhai around 1500 but regained their independence in 1591. In 1806 Mungo Park, the first European to reach this remote region, encountered Hausa, Songhai, Fulani and Tuareg. In 1903 the French created colonies in the Sahel and southern Sahara, extending from Senegal through French Sudan (Mali) and Upper Volta (Burkina Faso) to Niger. Due to stiff resistance from the Tuareg and Kanuri peoples, France's conquest of Niger was not finalized until 1922. Niger was granted independence in 1960 under Hamani Diori who drove out Marxist rivals headed by his cousin Djibo Bakary. In 1974, Diori was overthrown by Col. Seyni Kountché who invited back Bakary and others and included them in a new government of national unity. When Kountché died in 1987 he was succeeded by Colonel Ali Saibou who solidified one-party rule under the Mouvement National de la Société de Devéloppement or National Movement for the Development Society (MNSD). He in turn lost to Mahamane Ousmane and the Alliance des Forces du Changement (AFC) in free elections in 1993. Ousmane was ousted in a coup by Ibrahim Baré Mainassara in 1996. Baré, considered corrupt and ineffective as a leader, was assassinated in April 1999 and succeeded by Pres. Mamadou Tandja, who was subsequently reaffirmed in his post in elections in 1999 and 2004. On 18 February 2010 Lt. Gen. Salou Djibo deposed Tandja in a military coup. As head of the Supreme Council for the Restoration of Democracy, Djibou is the *de facto* head of state. The military junta has declared its intention to reshape the country into a "model democracy."

Government

The unicameral National Assembly consists of 113 seat chamber elected by popular vote for five years. In the 2009 election the National Movement for a Developing Society (MNSD) won 76 seats against 15 for the Social and Democratic Rally (RSD) and 7 for the Rally for Democracy and Progress (RDP). The rest of the seats were split between smaller parties and independents.

Economic policy

The government is committed to reform of the economy by implementing of a structural adjustment program (SAP) together with the World Bank and IMF. The uranium-led boom of the seventies is something of the past. Foreign investors are encouraged to explore alternative mineral sources. In December 2000 Niger qualified for enhanced debt relief under the Highly Indebted Poor Countries (HIPC) program. This led to a significant reduction of annual debt service obligations. Nearly half of the national budget depends on foreign donor resources.

Sectors

The economy is largely based on subsistence farming and uranium mining. Less than

Pres. Salou Djibo
Born: 15 April 1965
Since Feb. 2010

UN Photo: Rick Bajornas

POLITICAL	
Head of State	Pres. Salou Djibo
Ruling Parties	MNSD
Main Opposition	RSD
Independence	3 August 1960
National capital	Niamey
Official language	French

PHYSICAL	
Total area	489,000 sq. miles
	1,267,000 sq. km.
	(2 x Texas)
Arable land	3.5% of land area
Coastline	Landlocked

POPULATION	
Total	15.8 million
Av. yearly growth	3.66%
Urban population	16%
Life expectancy	52.99 years
Adult literacy	28.7%

ECONOMY	
Currency	CFA Franc (CFAF) (US$1=495.40)
GDP (real)	$5.1 billion
GDP growth rate	-0.9%
GDP per capita[1]	$349
GDP (ppp)[2]	$10.4 billion
GDP per cap. (ppp)	$680
Inflation rate	4.3%
Exports	$428 million
Imports	$800 million
External debt	$752 million
Unemployment	NA

1. Atlas method.
2. See page 175 for an explanation of purchasing power parity (ppp).

3% of the land is arable—including the irrigated areas along the Niger River, where food and cash crops such as millet, sorghum, cassava, rice and cowpeas are grown. Livestock (mainly cattle) are sold to neighboring countries, and hides and skins overseas. Niger has, after South Africa, the largest uranium reserves in Africa. Foreign exchange earnings from this mineral has shrunk as the world market declined considerably from its peak. Other minerals in reasonable quantity include tin-bearing casserite ore, phosphates, molybdenum, coal and salt. Foreign firms are involved in exploration for gold along the border with Burkina Faso and oil in the Lake Chad region. Future growth may be sustained by exploitation of oil, gold, coal, and other mineral resources such as uranium. Manufacturing comprises sugar refining, brewing, cotton ginning, tanning, rice milling, and small-scale production of cement, metals, textiles, plastics, soft drinks and construction materials.

Privatization

Although the government has shown a receptiveness to foreign acquisition of privatized parastatals, the process has been slow.

Investment

The uranium bust of the early 1980s has led to the withdrawal of French and other European firms. ExxonMobil (in partnership with Elf-Aquitaine) discovered oil in southeastern Niger near Lake Chad while Hunt Oil Company concentrated on the northeastern Djado plateau. Coal mining is another area of interest.

Trade

Uranium which contributed around 40% of the export revenue in the boom years, today accounts for merely 8%. There is also an effort to fill the void with any of a range of proven and still to be explored gold, oil, phosphates, molybdenum, coal and salt reserves. Even though Niger currently shows deficits on its trade balance, the long-term outlook is for a modest surplus.

Financial sector

There is one large international bank, the Meridien-BIAO, which serves as a regional institution and has close connections with the French banking system. Smaller banks include the Banque Commerciale du Niger (BCN), jointly owned by the governments of Niger and Libya. All these banks offer an array of financial instruments including letters of credit and short- and long-term loans.

Taxes and tariffs

Despite continuing efforts to make the tax laws more transparent, investors find it prudent to spell out details beforehand in contractual arrangements with the government. Import duties are as high as 66%. The corporate tax rate for non-residents is 30 percent. There is no capital gains tax. A value added tax (VAT) of 19 percent applies and exchange control is in effect. Taxes are levied on dividends (7.5%), interest (13 to 25%) and royalties (16%). (See page 138).

Assistance

While France remains a major donor, aid has also been coming from the US and various multilateral sources. In the eighties when an estimated 2 million people were in danger of starvation in Niger, 200,000 tons of imported food (largely from the US) helped avert the famine. The USAID has been involved in a number of programs aimed at promoting political and democratic reform while the US Department of Defense has extended assistance

BUSINESS ACTIVITY

AGRICULTURE
Cowpeas, cotton, peanuts, millet, sorghum, cassava (tapioca), rice, cattle, sheeps, goats, camels, donkeys, horses, poultry.

INDUSTRIES
Cement, brick, textiles, food processing, chemicals, slaughterhouses, light industries, uranium mining.

NATURAL RESOURCES
Uranium, coal, iron ore, tin, phosphates, gold, petroleum.

EXPORTS
$428 million (2006): uranium ore, livestock products, cowpeas, onions.

IMPORTS
$800 million (2006): consumer goods, machinery, vehicles and parts, petroleum, cereals, foodstuffs.

MAJOR TRADING PARTNERS
US, France, Nigeria, Russia, Côte d'Ivoire, China, Italy, French Polynesia.

Doing Business with Niger

▶ **Investment**

Incentives offered to investors include tax holidays, duty-free importing, subsidized energy and assistance in setting up industrial sites. There are no screening or local ownership requirements but a clear preference for labor-intensive operations exists. The government is actively seeking investment in energy production, mineral exploration and mining, agriculture, food processing, forestry, fishing, low-cost housing, construction, handicrafts, hotels, schools, health centers and transportation. Gold, coal and oil are three mining sectors where US companies have been noticeable in recent years. The planned modernization of the telecommunications system is expected to become an area of keen competition between US and other firms with know-how and equipment.

▶ **Trade**

Overseas suppliers usually approach Niger as part of a larger West African market and supply goods and services via neighboring states. Among the proven markets for US goods are computers and related products, telecommunications equipment, vehicles (especially four-wheel drive), machinery, office equipment, pharmaceuticals (particularly generic drugs), heavy construction and earth-moving equipment, and coal-fired electrical generating equipment.

▶ **Trade finance**

The cost of local credit is high and the most common form of payment remains irrevocable letters of credit. Eximbank extends financing to US exporters.

▶ **Selling to the government**

Aside from donor-financed development projects requiring engineering consulting services, technical assistance, agricultural planning, and specialized equipment, recent government purchases ranged from generic drugs to four-wheel drive vehicles. A local agent may be helpful in the process.

▶ **Exchange controls**

Niger is a member of the Franc zone and its currency is fully convertible into French francs. Investment capital and earnings on invested capital—dividends, interest, loan and lease payments, royalties, and fees—are usually transferred to and from Niger through French banks. There are no restrictions on payments and transfers.

▶ **Establishing a presence**

Private entities can freely establish, acquire, and dispose of interests in business enterprises. Attempts have been made to cut red tape and authorization for investment is guaranteed within three months of the date of application. For those unfamiliar with French law, on which Niger bases its own system, the advice of a local attorney is recommended.

▶ **Financing projects**

The OPIC investment guarantee program has applied since 1962 but there has been little activity on this front.

▶ **Labor**

There is a shortage of professionals as more than half of the 65,000 salaried, formal sector workers are employed in the public sector. Even though wages are low the government considers organized labor a key "social" partner in running and developing the country. Labor-management relations are generally good but there have been instances where the National Federation of Labor Unions (USTN) has practically shut down the country with general strikes as part of politically-inspired protests.

▶ **Legal rights**

Niger has an independent court system which respects and protects property and commercial rights. The investment code guarantees against acts of nationalization or expropriation except when deemed to be in the public interest. There is provision for the settlement of disputes and indemnification either by local arbitration or through the International Center for Settlement of Disputes on Investments. Niger is a member of the West African Intellectual Property Organization (OAPI) and a signatory to the Paris Convention for the Protection of Industrial Property. It is also a member of World Intellectual Property Organization and a signatory to the Universal Copyright Convention.

▶ **Business climate**

The culture is largely Muslim and business is conducted in a calm and deliberate fashion. Rushing the deal is not only considered unseemly but is often self-defeating The official language is French and the services of an interpreter might be necessary to prevent misunderstandings.

NIGERIA

With 148 million people, Nigeria is Africa's most populous nation. Its economy is second in size only to South Africa's. It is the continent's major oil producer and the fifth largest supplier of crude to the United States. Since 1999 elected governments have been implementing market-oriented reforms and made an effort to have Nigeria's riches trickle down to the broader population and rectify the inequities of past dictatorships. Nigeria offers investors a low-cost labor pool, abundant natural resources, and by far the largest domestic market on the continent. Its return to democracy reopened one of Africa's major markets for overseas business. American, European and Asian investors have not been slow in taking advantage as evidenced by impressive foreign direct investment not only in the oil sector but in manufacturing and telecommunications.

Country profile

Nigeria is the largest of several West African countries on the Gulf of Guinea. The Niger and Benue rivers flow through a Y-shaped delta into the Gulf of Guinea. The Hausa-Fulani, mostly Muslim, dominate in the north while the Ibo are in the majority in the southwestern part of the country. Major cities, apart from Lagos with a population of 9 million, are Abuja (the capital), Kano, Port Harcourt, and Kaduna.

About 50% of Nigeria's population is Muslim, 40% Christian and the rest adhere to ethnic religions.

History

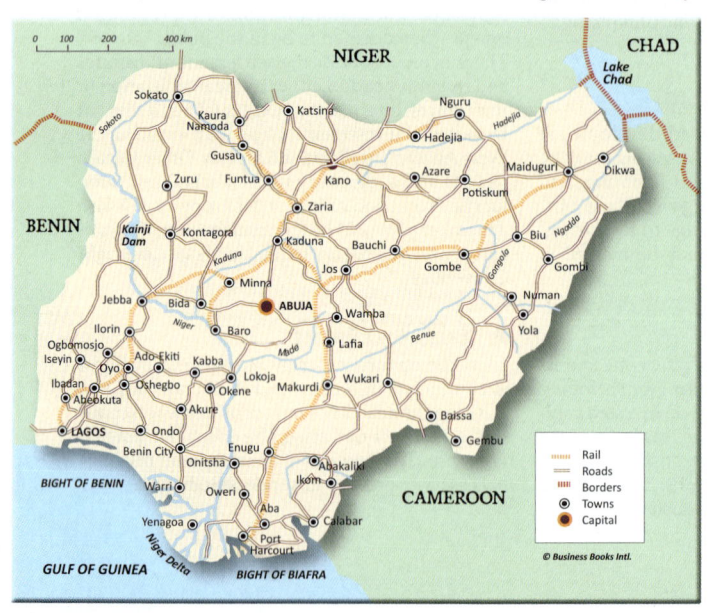

Old kingdoms were flourishing when Portuguese mariners first visited the shores of Nigeria in 1472. In 1914 they were united in one British colony and on 1 October 1960 Nigeria gained its independence. The 40 years since were marred by a series of coups and a major civil war. The Biafra War broke out in May 1967 when the Ibo-controlled Eastern Regional legislature proclaimed an "independent" republic and took up arms to defend itself. Hundreds of thousands of people were killed in a struggle which, despite support from some African and Western countries, ended in defeat for Biafra in January 1970. Following another abortive attempt at installing a democratically-elected government in 1993, General Sani Abacha took charge. In 1995 the execution by the Abacha regime of nine political prisoners, including the renowned writer Ken Saro-Wiwa, led to Nigeria's temporary suspension from the Commonwealth and the imposition of sanctions. Following Abacha's death in 1998, four separate elections culminated in the establishment of local, state and federal governments and the swearing in of Olusegun Obasanjo as president in May 1999. After two terms he was succeeded by Umaru Musa Yar'Adua after the April 2007 election. YarAdua died in May 2010 after several months of illness. His Vice President, Goodluck Jonathan, who acted in his place since January, was confirmed as president.

Pres. Goodluck Jonathan
Born: 20 Nov. 1957
Since May 2010
UN Photo Evan Schneider

Government

The 1999 constitution provides for a President elected by popular vote for a maximum of two 4-year terms. A 109-member Senate and a 360-seat House of Representatives are elected to 4 year terms. In the April 2007 election the People's Democratic Party (PDP) associated with Goodluck Jonathan, won 263 House seats against its closest rivals: the All Nigeria Peoples Party (ANPP) with 63 and Action Congress (AC) with 30. In the Senate the split was PDP (85), ANPP (16) and AC (6).

Economic policy

With oil prices likely to remain high in the foreseeable future, the Nigeria has the potential of greater wealth distribution. Nigeria has started implementing IMF reforms. Market-oriented reforms include modernization of the banking system, curbing inflation by resisting excessive wage demands and elimination of regional disputes over oil income share. In November 2005, Nigeria won Paris Club approval for a debt-relief deal that eliminated $18 billion of debt in exchange for $12 billion in payments—a total package worth $30 billion $37 billion external debt. The National Economic Empowerment Development Strategy—styled after the IMF's Poverty Reduction and Growth Facility—was formed to tighten fiscal and monetary management.

Privatization

There are plans to privatize most of Nigeria's state-owned companies. Banks, state-run cement companies and oil marketing companies, already listed on the Nigerian Stock

POLITICAL	
Head of State	Goodluck Jonathan
Ruling Party	PDP
Main Opposition	ANPP
Independence	1 October 1960
National capital	Abuja
Official language	English

PHYSICAL	
Total area	357,000 sq. miles 924,000 sq. km. (2 x California)
Arable land	31% of land area
Coastline	530 miles/853 km

POPULATION	
Total	152.2 million
Av. yearly growth	2.0%
Urban population	48%
Life expectancy	47 years
Adult literacy	68%

ECONOMY	
Currency	Naira (N) (US$1=151.76)
GDP (real)	$216.8 billion
GDP growth rate	3.0%
GDP per capita[1]	$1,431
GDP (ppp)[2]	$327.8 billion
GDP per cap. (ppp)	$2,119
Inflation rate	12.0%
Exports	$47.8 billion
Imports	$33 billion
External debt	$4.5 billion
Unemployment	4.9%

1. Atlas method.
2. See page 175 for an explanation of purchasing power parity (ppp).

Exchange, were to be sold. In the second phase, all the state's interest in hotels, automotive plants and similar industries will be sold. In the third stage the Nigeria Electric Production Authority (NEPA), Nigeria Telecommunications Limited (NITEL), oil refineries, and the state-owned National Fertilizer Company of Nigeria (NAFCON) were to be privatized. In 2003 the government started deregulating fuel prices and announced the privatization of Nigeria's four state-owned oil refineries.

Sectors

Some 70 percent of the population is engaged in agriculture. In the south, rubber trees, oil palm and cocoa are cultivated for export and in the north groundnuts, cotton and cattle. Currently the agricultural sector accounts for 40 percent of the GDP. Nigeria has, however, slipped in recent years from being a net exporter to becoming a major importer of agricultural products. Petroleum continues to power the Nigerian economy, accounting for almost all of the country's foreign exchange earnings. The current government is attempting to move away from this over-independence on the lucrative and capital-intensive oil sector. Despite some diversification in recent years manufacturing still consists largely of import substituting products. Other manufacturing activities include iron and steel and fertilizer production, and automobile assembly.

Trading

Nigeria is currently the fifth largest importer of US wheat. Its oil export revenues accounted for 95 percent of total exports with the US purchasing anout half of the total. Other substantial American exports to Nigeria include computers and software, medical equipment, automotive parts, cosmetics, textiles and fabrics. Nigeria is the fifth largest supplier of crude oil to the US after Saudi Arabia, Canada, Venezuela and Mexico.

Investment

Since 1999, foreign companies, particularly in the oil and gas sector, have been looking at new or expanded investments in Nigeria. Abundant oil reserves have kept the economy afloat and once again hold the key to the future. Total US foreign direct investment in Nigeria is estimated at around $4 billion, largely in the petroleum sector. A newly planned Export Processing Zone (EPZ) at Port Harcourt aims at attracting foreign investments in the manufacturing sector. Incentives have also been approved to encourage investment in downstream oil and gas processing and marketing. The privatization of state-owned properties is diversifying and intensifying foreign investment.

Financial sector

The Central Bank of Nigeria (CBN) monitors the banking system to ensure compliance with monetary, credit, and foreign exchange guidelines. There are 89 commercial and merchant banks, 67 of them classified as healthy. There are also a number of finance houses and mortgage and community banks throughout the country. Some 200 companies are listed on the Lagos (formerly Nigerian) Stock Exchange, in operation since 1961.

Taxes and tariffs

The corporate tax rate for non-residents is 6 percent and capital gains tax 10 percent. A value added tax (VAT) of 5 percent applies and exchange control is in effect. Taxes are levied on dividends (10%), interest (10%) and royalties (5 to 10%). (See page 138).

BUSINESS ACTIVITY

AGRICULTURE
Cocoa, peanuts, palm oil, corn, rice, sorghum, millet, cassava (tapioca), yams, rubber, cattle, sheep, goats, pigs, timber, fish.
INDUSTRIES
Crude oil, coal, tin, columbite, palm oil, peanuts, cotton, rubber, wood, hides and skins, textiles, cement and other construction materials, food products, footwear, chemicals, fertilizer, printing, ceramics, steel.
NATURAL RESOURCES
Petroleum, tin, columbite, iron ore, coal, limestone, lead, zinc, gas.
EXPORTS
$47.8 billion (est. 2009): petroleum, cocoa, rubber.
IMPORTS
$33 billion (est. 2009): machinery, chemicals, transportation equipment, manufactured goods, food, live animals.
MAJOR TRADING PARTNERS
US, China, UK, Spain, France, Netherlands, Brazil, Germany.

Doing Business with Nigeria

▶ **Investment**

The new government in 1999 signaled its intention to make Nigeria investor-friendly and to encourage foreign participation. Its privatization program should present foreign investors with new opportunities in oil exploration, banking, hotels, and automotive parts manufacturing. Plans to install 3 million telephone lines per year will require foreign private sector participation will be required.

▶ **Trade**

Oil and gasfield machinery will continue to be prime import items. There is a growing market for computers, cellular phone sets, transmission and switching and other telecommunications equipment. Other prime items include medical supplies, pharmaceuticals, textiles, and wheat and used cars and buses. The demand for earthmoving and roadbuilding machinery will increase as road reconstruction begins.

▶ **Trade finance**

In July 1999 Eximbank returned to Nigeria with a $100 million pilot program, once again making medium-term financing available to US exporters. The Nigerian Export-Import Bank (NEXIM) was established in 1991 to assist banks to provide pre- and post-shipment financing in local currency to support non-oil exports.

▶ **Selling to the government**

Nigeria buys products and services through a "tender board" composed of senior government officials, sometimes together with local consultants or foreign firms represented in Nigeria. *The Central Bank of Nigeria (CBN) does not buy products and services for the government or its agencies and purported inquiries and business proposals emanating from the CBN on behalf of the Nigerian government or any of its agencies should be disregarded as scams.*

▶ **Exchange controls**

Foreign exchange control applies. All applications must be channeled through selected banks to the Central Bank of Nigeria (CBN).

▶ **Partnerships**

Establishment of a joint venture is in itself not sufficient to constitute a legal entity. A foreign firm may, however, participate as a shareholder in a local company incorporated as a joint venture.

▶ **Establishing a presence**

Foreign firms are not allowed to operate through a branch office but obliged to establish a place of business and incorporate to conduct business in Nigeria. A local presence can also be established on the basis of equity participation, joint ventures, an arrangement for the provision of technical services to a Nigerian company, or the purchase of securities in existing Nigerian companies. All foreign companies must register with the NIPC to obtain a business permit.

▶ **Project financing**

Overseas Private Investment Corporation programs are available to US ventures in Nigeria. The US Trade and Development Agency extends funding for feasibility studies. Financing can also be obtained through any of the local commercial, merchant or industrial banks and, to a limited extent, from insurance companies, building and property development companies, pension funds and institutional investors.

▶ **Labor**

Nigeria has a large, English-speaking workforce, generally better educated and skilled than elsewhere on the continent. Any nonagricultural firm with more than 50 workers must recognize trade unions and deduct dues for union members. Collective bargaining is common.

▶ **Legal rights**

The legal system is fashioned after English Common law. Nigeria is a signatory to the major world agreements on Intellectual Property Protection and a member of the World Intellectual Property Organization. The government's Patents and Design Decree of 1970 and Trademark Act of 1965 regulate the registration of patents and trademarks.

▶ **Business climate**

English is widely spoken. Visitors should make their contacts well before departure for Nigeria. *A fraudulent practice that has received wide publicity is known as "419." It involves an offer to transfer large sums of money with promises of commissions after up-front payments are made by the potential victim. While remaining on their guard against such practices, foreign citizens should also be aware that these scams do not represent the Nigerian business community at large. Scam attempts should be reported to the nearest Nigerian embassy.*

RWANDA

The 1994 genocide decimated Rwanda, damaged its fragile economic base, severely impoverished the remaining population, and eroded the country's ability to attract private and external investment. This tragic setback came on the heels of an economic downturn in the 1980s as the world price of coffee plunged. Since peace was restored Rwanda has, however, made significant progress in stabilizing and rehabilitating its economy—GDP has rebounded, and inflation has been curbed. Currently the emphasis is on diversification away from coffee and tea towards mining and tourism.

Country profile

In the west the Republic of Rwanda borders on Lake Kivu. On its eastern border with Tanzania it shares marshy lakes along the Kagera River. The climate is tropical with rainfall ranging between 800 and 1,400 mm (32 and 55 inches). Much of the terrain is covered with lush vegetation. Conservation regions include well-known game parks such as Akagera National Park and *Parc National des Volcans* where the mountain gorilla and other endangered species are found. Most inhabitants are Banyarwanda, of whom 80% are Hutu and the rest Tutsi. They speak Kinyarwanda which, together with French and English, is an official language. Most Rwandans are Christians.

History

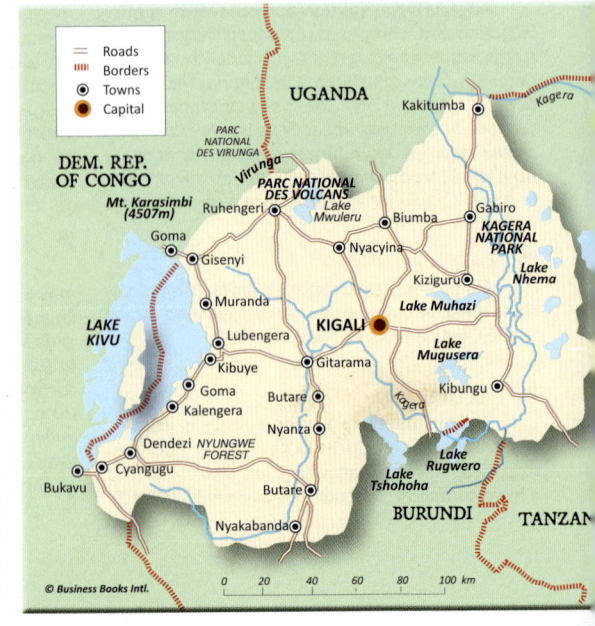

The original inhabitants of Rwanda were the Pygmies or Twa, today numbering barely 1% of the total population. The simple version of history has the Tutsi (Nilotic) cattle breeders arriving in the area from the 15th Century and subjugating the Hutu inhabitants. In reality, the situation is much more complex as boundaries of race and class became less distinct over the years as a result of intermingling. Some put part of the blame for the racial animosity that led to the recent mass-scale killings on the shoulders of German and Belgian colonial rulers who pitched the Hutu against Tutsi for their own gain. When Burundi and neighboring Rwanda were incorporated into German East Africa in 1899, they had been kingdoms for several centuries headed by *mwamis* (kings). After Germany's defeat in World War I these nations were transferred to Belgium under the joint name of Ruanda-Urundi. They were, however, "separated at birth" when they gained their independence in 1962. After periodic outbursts of violence, conciliation between Hutu and Tutsi leaders finally seemed to be in the making when Pres. Juvenal Habyarimana, under international and domestic pressure, began reforms in 1994. The reform process was, however, short-lived as Habyarimana perished in an aircraft downed by a rocket near Kigali on 6 April 1994, along with the president of neighboring Burundi. The next day, the Rwandan government mobilized the country's ethnic Hutu majority in a genocide against the Tutsi and moderate Hutus, a campaign that claimed over 800,000 lives. Maj. Gen. Paul Kagame and his Tutsi-dominated multi-ethnic *Front Patriotique Rwandais* or Rwanda Patriotic Front (FPR) invaded from Uganda and defeated the Rwanda regime in July 1994. Shortly afterwards, Kagame was appointed Vice President and Defense Minister, and in March 2000 he was sworn in as President. The FPR formed a coalition government with Paul Kagame as a Tutsi serving as president and Bernard Makuza, leader of the Hutu-dominated *Mouvement Démocratique Républicain* or Republican Democratic Movement (MDR), appointed prime minister. Although much of the country is now at peace, members of the former regime continue their efforts to destabilize the northwest area of the country from a base in the neighboring Democratic Republic of Congo. Pres. Kgama was reaffirmed in his post in the August 2003 election and reelected in August 2010.

Government

The president is elected by popular vote for a seven year term. The bicameral parliament consists of a 26-seat Senate with an 8-year term (12 members elected by local councils, 8 appointed by the president, 4 by the Political Organizations Forum and 2 by institutrions of higher learning) and an 80-seat Chamber of Deputies with a 5-year term (53 elected by popular vote, 24 women elected by local bodies, and 3 selected by youth and disability organzations). In the September 2008 election Kagame's Tutsi-dominated FPR won 42 of the 53 popular seats against 7 for the Hutu-dominated *Parti Social-Démocrate* (PSD) and 4 for the *Parti Libéral* (PL).

Economic policy

Rwanda is the most densely populated and one of the poorest countries in Africa. Despite the ravages of civil war and the 1994 genocide it has made great strides towards recovery. The government has implemented with

Pres. Paul Kagame
Born: October 1957
Since April 2000

UN Photo Ryan Brown

POLITICAL	
Head of State	Pres. Paul Kagame
Prime Minister	Bernard Makuza
Majority party	FPR
Main Opposition	PSD
Independence	1 July 1962
National capital	Kigali
Off. languages	Kinyarwanda, French & English

PHYSICAL	
Total area	10,000 sq. miles
	26,000 sq. km.
	(± Maryland)
Arable land	40% of land area
Coastline	Landlocked

POPULATION	
Total	11 million
Av. yearly growth	2.8%
Urban population	18%
Life expectancy	50.5 years
Adult literacy	70.4%

ECONOMY	
Currency	Rwandan franc (RF)(US$1=588.00)
GDP (real)	$3.8 billion
GDP growth rate	4.5%
GDP per capita[1]	$381
GDP (ppp)[2]	$9.5 billion
GDP per cap. (ppp)	$953
Inflation rate	10.3%
Exports	$191 million
Imports	$867 million
External debt	$678 million
Unemployment	NA

1. Atlas method.
2. See page 175 for an explanation of purchasing power parity (ppp).

the help of the IMF structural reforms, focusing on improving the civil service, privatization, reducing tariffs, and the restructuring of banks.

Sectors

Agriculture is the mainstay of the economy and the largest employer, with coffee and tea as major cash crops. Other export crops are pyrethrum and quinquina. Privatization started in the late nineties. About half of the 46 enterprises earmarked have been restructured and another 18 were ceded to the private sector.

Trade

Coffee and tea account for about 85% of total export revenues. Consumer products are imported from neighbors and Europe.

Taxes

The corporate tax rate for non-residents is 30 percent and capital gains tax 30 percent. A value added tax (VAT) of 18 percent applies. Taxes of 15 % are levied on dividends, interest and royalties. (See page 138).

BUSINESS ACTIVITY

AGRICULTURE
Coffee, tea, pyrethrum , bananas, beans, sorghum, potatoes, livestock.
INDUSTRIES
Cement, agricultural processing, beverages, soap, furniture, shoes, plastic goods, textiles, cigarettes.
NATURAL RESOURCES
Gold, casseterite (tin ore), wolframite (tungsten ore), natural gas, hydropower.
EXPORTS
$191 million (est. 2009): coffee, tea, hides, tin ore.
IMPORTS
$867 million (est. 2009): foodstuffs, machinery and equipment, steel, petroleum products, construction material.
MAJOR TRADING PARTNERS
China, Germany, Kenya, US, Uganda, Belgium, Thailand.

Doing Business with Rwanda

▶ **Investment**

With the passage of an investment code and creation of a one-stop investment promotion agency, Rwanda hopes to attract foreign direct investment. Tax breaks are offered to new firms as well as expatriate employees. While the tea and coffee sectors remain prime targets for investment, privatization will also open up the telecommunications, energy and water supply sectors for foreign participation.

▶ **Trade**

There is also a growing demand for used clothing, 4-wheel drive vehicles, trucks, communications and computer equipment, cosmetics, and consultant services.

▶ **Trade finance**

Unless orders are placed by international agencies, irrevocable letters of credit are the standard mode of payment.

▶ **Selling to the government**

A tender board handles procurement and sets guidelines and policies. It is involved in purchases by all government departments and international donors.

▶ **Exchange controls**

Controls have been relaxed and commercial banks are able to assist in the transfer of overseas payments of profits and dividends.

▶ **Financing projects**

In 1996, humanitarian relief began to shift to reconstruction and development assistance. Rehabilitation and expansion of road, water, health and educational facilities and agricultural projects involve overseas funding. The World Bank, the UN Development Program, the European Development Fund and various countries provide aid.

▶ **Labor**

Four prewar independent trade unions are back in operation. The largest union, CESTRAR, was created in the early nineties as a government institution but has since become fully independent. Minimum wage and social security regulations are in force.

▶ **Business Climate**

Business in Rwanda is conducted in both English and French. There is a strong desire to expand relations with US firms and in sophisticated circles a taste for American goods.

SÃO TOMÉ & PRÍNCIPE

Comprising two small former Portuguese islands off the West African coast, the state of São Tomé and Principé is located in the oil-rich Gulf of Guinea, off the coast of Nigeria, Africa's largest oil producer. The two countries are closely linked by a joint oil exploitation pact. The islands, heavily dependent on foreign aid since their independence in 1975, sit on top of a potential oil bonanza estimated at over a billion barrels of crude. In the meantime economic reforms aim at making the islands less dependent on a single cash crop, cocoa.

Country profile

The island country of São Tomé and Príncipe comprises two extinct volcanic islands and four rocky islets about 300 km off the coast of Gabon. The larger island, São Tomé, located on the equator, rises at its peak to over 2,000 m (6,500 ft). The eastern slopes are covered with cocoa plantations and smallholdings cut out of dense rainforest. To the north, Principé rises to 948 m (3,100 ft) above the sea. The climate of both islands is equatorial Annual rainfall decreases from 5,000 mm (197 inches) on the southwestern slopes of the islands to 1,000 mm (39 inches) on their northeastern sides. Society on both islands is fairly homogeneous, consisting largely of native-born descendants of the early Portuguese settlers and African slaves. There are also a number of Chinese, Cape Verdeans, Mozambicans and Angolans. Portuguese is the official language, but the more common lingua franca is Portuguese Crioulo (Creole). Most are Roman Catholic.

History

The island of São Tomé was discovered by Portuguese mariners in 1478 and granted to Portugal's crown prince, together with its sister island, Principé (Prince). After the prince's accession to the throne as Joao II, he encouraged settlement of the uninhabited islands to expand the Portuguese presence in this region and promote trade with Africa. The settlers imported slaves from the mainland and a mixed Afro-European population emerged who spoke a creole language based on Portuguese and various African languages. In the face of fierce competition from Brazil, sugar was replaced by cocoa as the main crop. In 1975 the *Movimiento de Libertaçao de São Tomé e Príncipe* or Movement for the Liberation of São Tomé and Príncipe (MLSTP) under the leadership of Manuel Pinto da Costa, led the islands to independence. Under pressure from foreign donors in the late 1980s, the MLSTP government began to liberalize the economy and

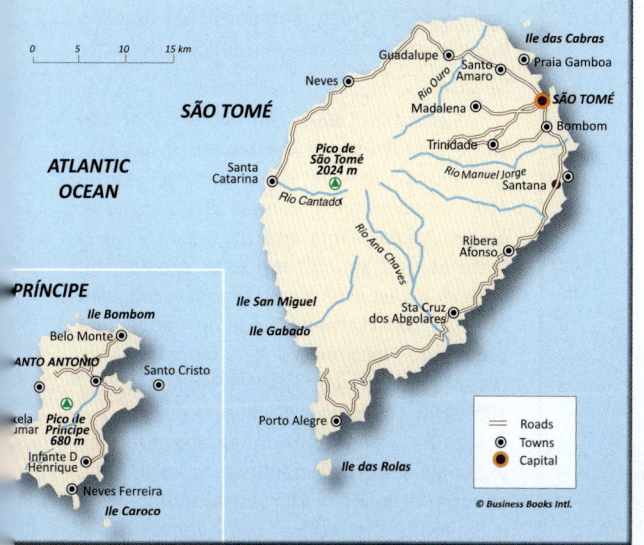

Pres. Fradique
de Menezes
Born: Mar. 21, 1942
Since Sept. 2001

UN Photo Marco Castro

POLITICAL
Head of State	Pres. Fradique de Menezes
Prime Minister	Joachim Rafael Branco (2008)
Ruling Party	ADI
Main Opposition	MLSTP
Independence	12 July 1975
National capital	São Tomé
Official language	Portuguese

PHYSICAL
Total area	386 sq. miles 1,000 sq. km. (5 x Wash. DC)
Arable land	6.25% of land area
Coastline	130 miles/209 km

POPULATION
Total	175,800
Av. yearly growth	2.1%
Urban population	61%
Life expectancy	62.7 years
Adult literacy	84.9%

ECONOMY
Currency	Dobra (US$1=18,615)
GDP (real)	$160 million
GDP growth rate	4.1%
GDP per capita[1]	$1,547
GDP (ppp)[2]	$339 million
GDP per cap. (ppp)	$2,083
Inflation rate	17.3%
Exports	$8 million
Imports	$88 million
External debt	$123 million
Unemployment	NA

1. Atlas method.
2. See page 175 for an explanation of purchasing power parity (ppp).

removed the ban on opposition parties. It was voted out of office in 1990 but returned victorious in 1994 when the interim government failed to cope with economic problems. Miguel Trovoada, who returned from exile to win the presidency in 1991, was reelected in 1996. In July 2001 Fradique de Menezes of the *Acçao Democrática Independente* or Independent Democratic Action (ADI) won the presidency. In July 2003 his government survived a military coup when Major Fernando "Cobo" Pereira and his rebel soldiers caved in under pressure from the African Union, released their captives and returned to their barracks. Pres. de Menezes was reelected in July 2006.

Government

An executive President is elected for a maximum of two 5-year terms and appoints the Prime Minister. The 55-member unicameral National Assembly is elected for a 4-year term. In the August 2010 election Pres. Fradiquede Menezes' ADI won 26 seats against 21 for the Movement for the Liberation of São Tomé and Príncipe (MLSTP) and 7 for the Party for Democratic Convergence (PCD).

Economic policy

After a period of economic decline and chronic deficits, São Tomé and Príncipe, together with the IMF, implemented vigorous adjustment measures. It still depends on concessional aid and benefited from $200 million in debt relief under the Highly Indebted Poor Countries (HIPC) program. Its successful implementation of structural reforms has drawn a positive response from international donors.

Sectors

Since the 1800s, the economy of São Tomé and Principé was based on plantation agriculture—first sugar and later cocoa. After independence, control of Portuguese-owned cocoa plantations passed to various state-owned agricultural enterprises. The second-largest export crop is coffee, followed by copra, palm kernels, cinnamon, pepper and breadfruit. The principal food crops are taro, cassava, breadfruit and maize. Fishing employs 10% of the economically active population and is seen as a valuable future earner of foreign exchange. Efforts are underway to exploit the country's timber resources. Manufacturing is limited to the production of items such as soap, soft drinks, palm oil, bricks and textiles as well as timber processing. The island's beaches and tropical environment offer good tourism potential. Considerable additional income is expected from the exploitation of São Tomé and Príncipe's offshore oil resources in the Gulf of Guinea in a 60/40 split arrangement with Nigeria.

Privatization

The government has been turning over management of the parastatals, as well as the agricultural, commercial, banking, and tourism sectors, to the private sector. The focus has been on restructuring of the state-run agricultural and industrial sectors. Agricultural privatization involving several cocoa estates has met with mixed success due to a lack of domestic capital.

Investment

Private investment is expected to grow from 18.4% of GDP in 1998 to 45% of GDP in 2002. Two American oil companies, ExxonMobil and Environmental Remediation Holding Corporation, have begun oil exploration activities in São Tomé's recently delineated exclusive economic deep water zone.

Trade

The dominant crop on São Tomé is cocoa, representing about 98% of exports. Other export crops include copra, palm kernels, and coffee. Netherlands and Belgium are major trading partners.

Financial Sector

The authorities have set a relatively high reserve requirement ratio of 22% and the government's counterpart funds were transferred to the Central Bank, enhancing liquidity in the banking system. The collection of proceeds from privatization and the sale of oil exploration concessions contributed to government liquidity.

BUSINESS ACTIVITY

AGRICULTURE
Cocoa, coconuts, palm kernels, copra, cinnamon, pepper, coffee, bananas, papayas, beans, poultry, fish.
INDUSTRIES
Light construction, textiles, soap, beer, fish processing, timber.
EXPORTS
$8 million (est. 2009): cocoa, coffee, copra, palm oil.
IMPORTS
$88 million (est. 2009): machinery and electrical equipment, food products, petroleum products.
MAJOR TRADING PARTNERS
Netherlands, Belgium, Portugal, Japan.

Doing Business with São Tomé & Príncipe

▶ **Investment**

An aggressive pursuit of potential foreign investors has met with limited success. The task is complicated by the small size and relative isolation of the islands, remaining foreign exchange controls, and low productivity and human resource development. There are attempts to stimulate interest abroad not only in tropical agriculture, but in areas such as tourism, industrial fishing, and manufacturing in a regional free trade zone. Expectations are that São Tomé and Príncipé, situated in the oil-rich Gulf of Guinea near Nigeria, will strike petroleum in large quantity and join other nations in the region who built new economies on such bonanzas. In 1993, the government announced plans to designate a free trade zone to attract offshore investors and stimulate development of the country's shipping and manufacturing sectors.

▶ **Trade**

Even though priority is given to the development of food crops in an effort to reduce the large food import bill, the islands are still heavily reliant on foreign sources. In the 1990s foodstuffs accounted on average for about 35% of total imports.

▶ **Financing projects**

The government relies on foreign assistance from various donors. The UN Development Program, the World Bank, the European Union, and the African Development Bank have all at different stages financed projects.

▶ **Labor**

The local workforce is largely involved in agricultural activity. Lack of employment has led to an exodus of workseekers abroad.

SENEGAL

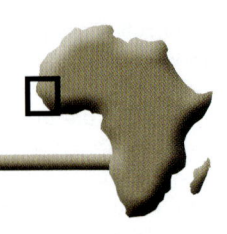

Historically Senegal and its capital, Dakar, served as the gateway to West Africa. Although its industrial and commercial base is smaller than that of rival Côte d'Ivoire, it is equipped with one of Africa's most efficient and modern infrastructures and populated by a sophisticated people with an international, distinctly French, outlook. Senegal has met all IMF benchmarks in its macroeconomic program. A decent supply of minerals coupled with a cosmopolitan environment have attracted many European and—more recently— an increasing number of American entrepreneurs. However, Senegal still relies on outside donor assistance.

Country profile

The Republic of Senegal consists largely of a low plateau between 100-200 m above sea level. Three perennial rivers flow through the region—the Senegal, Gambia and Casamance. All three open up in large deltas or estuaries, replete with expansive beaches, national parks and tourist resorts. The Senegalese Peninsula with its ample rainfall was appropriately named Cape Verde or Green Cape. The Wolof in the northwest are the largest ethnic group and account for about 40% of the total population. Their language is a lingua franca in Senegal along with French, the official tongue. Other significant groups include the Serer, Tukulor, Ful (or Fulani), Mandé and a large Mauritanian (Moorish) community. More than 90% adhere to the Muslim faith but there is a small Christian minority in Dakar. Ethnic beliefs survive.

History

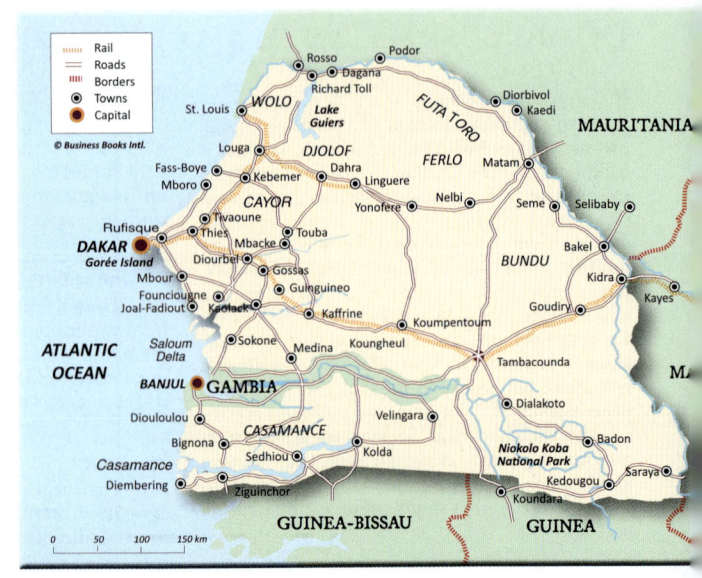

The earliest evidence of civilization in this region are mysterious circles of huge stone columns (megaliths) in the vicinity of the Gambia and Saloum rivers. The inhabitants of modern Senegal and The Gambia are descendants of Negroid peoples who settled some 1,400 years ago. From 1445 Portuguese mariners traded with the Wolof and Serer kingdoms but in 1588 they were driven out by the Dutch. Ultimately the French gained dominance from their settlement on St. Louis Island in the estuary of the Senegal, capturing Rufisque and Gorée Island, which served as slave trading posts until the abolition of this trade in the first half of the 19th Century. Millions of Africans were shipped from Gorée to the New World during the 1700s. Eventually these coastal centers and Dakar became integral parts of France, electing their own deputies to the National Assembly. France not only annexed Senegal, but used the colony as a base for further expansion eastward. A Catholic poet-politician, Léopold Sedar Senghor, led Senegal to independence in 1960 and exercised virtual one-man rule until his voluntary retirement in 1981 when he stepped down in favor of his prime minister, Abdou Diouf. During his term as president, Diouf witnessed the creation in 1982 together with The Gambia, of the Confederation of Senegambia as well as its breakup in 1989. In the presidential election of March 2000, Diouf, as leader of the *Parti Socialiste du Sénégal* or Socialist Party of Senegal (PS), was defeated at the polls and succeeded as president by Abdoulaye Wade, representing the *Parti Démocratique Sénégalais* or Senegalese Democratic Party (PDS). Wade was re-elected in February 2007. He inherited an ongoing problem posed by the secessionist *Mouvement des forces democratiques de Casamance* (MFDC), led by the Rev. Augustin Diamacoune in southern Senegal.

Government

The executive President is directly elected by the voters for a term of five years, renewable once. (When Pres. Wade was first elected in 2000, the term was seven years). The president appoints the Prime Minister who forms the cabinet. The legislature consists of a 100-member Senate and a 150-member National Assembly serves for five years (90 members elected by direct popular vote with the remaining members elected by proportional representation from party lists). In the August 2007 election the SOPI Coalition—comprising President Wade's PDS and a half dozen smaller parties—captured 131 seats in the Assembly. The election was boycotted by 12 opposition parties causing a record low turnout of 35 percent of the voters.

Economic policy

With an ambitious economic reform program started in the nineties Senegal has met all IMF benchmarks and macroeconomic indicators show a respectable performance with a real growth in GDP averaging 5% and reaching 19.2% in 2007. Inflation has also been pushed down significantly. There has been an increasing emphasis on measures to attract

Pres. Abdoulaye Wade
Born: May 29, 1926
Since April 2000

UN Photo Evan Schneider

POLITICAL	
Head of State	Pres. Abdoulaye Wade
Ruling Party	SOPI (Coalition)
Independence	4 April 1960
National capital	Dakar
Official language	French

PHYSICAL	
Total area	76,000 sq. miles
	197,000 sq. km.
	(± South Dakota)
Arable land	12% of land area
Coastline	330 miles/531 km

POPULATION	
Total	12.3 million
Av. yearly growth	2.6%
Urban population	42%
Life expectancy	59.3 years
Adult literacy	39.3%

ECONOMY	
Currency	CFA franc (CFAF) (US$1=495.40)
GDP (real)	$12.6 billion
GDP growth rate	1.5%
GDP per capita[1]	$993
GDP (ppp)[2]	$20.8 billion
GDP per cap. (ppp)	$1,663
Inflation rate	-1.1%
Exports	$1.9 billion
Imports	$4.5 billion
External debt	$5.5 billion
Unemployment	48%

1. Atlas method.
2. See page 175 for an explanation of purchasing power parity (ppp).

private sector investment after completion of the first phase of economic liberalization. Private activity currently accounts for more than 80% of the country's GDP. However, Senegal still relies on on outside donor assistance and under the IMF's Highly Indebted Poor Countries (HIPC) debt relief program had two-thirds of its bilateral multilateral, bilateral and private sector debt eliminated..

Sectors

The economy remains heavily dependent on agriculture which employs about 75% of the working population and accounts for more than a fifth of GDP. Groundnuts, cotton and sugar are major cash crops. Staple foods are millet, sorghum, maize and rice. Livestock is raised across the country. Fresh and canned marine fish is the principal export and involves about 10% of the labor force. Even though the mining sector accounts for less than 2% of GDP, exports of phosphate rock, phosphate acid and fertilizers contribute more than a quarter of foreign earnings. There are large unexploited iron ore and limited gold reserves. Titanium, zirconium and rutile are mined south of the Cape Verde Peninsula. Natural gas from offshore wells fuel a power station near Dakar and modest oil deposits off the Casamance coast are still to be exploited. Manufcaturing involves food processing, textiles, chemicals and petroleum products, plastics, paint, soap and pharmaceuticals.

Privatization

Privatization is considered key to attracting foreign investment. Enterprises were earmarked for restructuring include the state-owned telecommunications company, a peanut oil processor, the national power utility, the railroad company and several hotels. A subsidiary of France Telecom purchased a one-third share in SONATEL and the government retained 51% control over the power utility SENELEC.

Investment

As privatization offers new opportunities, firms are expected to challenge the historic dominance of the French in the industrial sector. Irish and Canadian companies are involved in gas exploration while South African and Australian firms have become involved in gold and other mining operations.

Trade

Fresh and canned marine fish is the principal export, contributing over 30% of export revenue. Senegal is the largest exporter of groundnuts on the continent and the fifth largest exporter of phosphates. Major imports include crude and refined petroleum products, machinery, electrical appliances, rice, grain, lubricants, and dairy products. Tourism is also a major foreign exchange earner .

Financial sector

Senegal shares the Banque Central Des Etats de L'Afrique de L'Ouest (BCEAO), or Central Bank of West African States, with other members of the CFA franc zone. In the wake of a serious banking crisis in the 1980s, significant reforms were introduced. Five stronger banks emerged with greater liquidity, tighter controls and a full range of services.

Taxes and tariffs

Corporate tax rate for non-residents is 25 percent. A value added tax (VAT) of 18 percent applies and exchange control is in effect. Taxes are levied on dividends (10%), interest (6 to 16%) and royalties (20%). (See page 138).

BUSINESS ACTIVITY

AGRICULTURE
Peanuts, millet, corn, sorghum, rice, cotton, tomatoes, green vegetables, cattle, poultry, pigs, fish.

INDUSTRIES
Agricultural and fish processing, phosphate mining, fertilizer production, petroleum refining, construction materials.

NATURAL RESOURCES
Fish, phosphate, iron ore.

EXPORTS
$1.9 billion (est. 2009): fish, groundnuts (peanuts), petroleum products, phosphates, cotton.

IMPORTS
$4.5 billion (est. 2009): food and beverages, consumer goods, capital goods, petroleum products.

MAJOR TRADING PARTNERS
France, India, China, Nigeria, UK, Mali, Brazil, The Gambia, Italy, Netherlands, Belgium, Thailand.

Doing Business with Senegal

▶ **Investment**

The Dakar Industrial Free Zone (DIFZ) is an industrial park dedicated primarily to export-oriented and labor-intensive manufacturing. Investors in the DIFZ and other designated areas enjoy tax-free status and duty-free entry of raw materials and components. Foreign investors need to register at a central one-stop facility to qualify for these and other incentives. The emphasis is on investment outside the Dakar region, small- and medium-sized enterprises and sectors such as agriculture, fishing, manufacturing, mineral extraction, and tourism. US investors are engaged in hotel renovation programs on the historic slave site, Gorée Island, off the coast of Dakar. Majority Senegalese ownership is a requirement in food production and fishing projects and most enterprises are obliged to employ a certain number of local workers.

▶ **Trade**

Although Senegal has until now offered a relatively limited market for US products, the liberalization of the economy, freer access for imports, and new developments in power generation and in telecommunications are expected to broaden the scope. Best deals in the past were in agricultural commodities, mining, tourism, information technology, and used clothing. There is a strong growth in the computer market and products ranging from air conditioners to cosmetics. US and other importers have concentrated on groundnuts and phosphates from Senegal. Distribution is mostly through large French-owned or Lebanese firms.

▶ **Trade finance**

Irrevocable letters of credit are the preferred form of payment. Local financing is tight.

▶ **Selling to the government**

Both in privatization deals and major government purchases foreign firms are invited to present bids. Procurement of goods and services with the help of multilateral funds is in accordance with international rules for competitive bidding. In recent years, major government contracts involved telecommunications, energy and water projects.

▶ **Exchange controls**

Senegal's currency, the CFA Franc, is freely convertible into French francs at a fixed rate. Foreign investors are guaranteed repatriation of profits and capital. Transactions are channeled through authorized banks, the postal administration, or the regional central bank, the BCEAO.

▶ **Partnerships**

In major privatization deals involving telecommunications, energy projects and the like, the government insists on being a partner with foreign private investors. It is also actively promoting joint ventures between foreign and domestic entrepreneurs in certain sectors of the economy.

▶ **Establishing a presence**

There is provision for several types of companies, including general partnerships, limited liability companies (LLC), public limited companies (PLC), and joint venture enterprises. Incorporation costs are moderate. Copies of all agency agreements between foreign principals and local distributors or agents must be submitted to the Department of Internal Trade and Prices for final approval.

▶ **Financing projects**

The Overseas Private Investment Corporation provides insurance and assistance to US investors. Several international agencies are involved in major projects.

▶ **Labor**

There is a reasonable availability of unskilled and semi-skilled labor but investors with a need for specialized skills need to factor in expenditure for training purposes.

▶ **Legal rights**

Property rights are protected and there are no known cases of expropriation involving US or other overseas firms. Senegal is a member of the Cameroon-based African Intellectual Property Organization or *Office African et Malagache de la Propiété Industrielle* (OAMPI), which safeguards trademarks, patents, and industrial designs among its members. It is also a member of the Paris Convention for the Protection of Industrial Property and the Berne Convention for the Protection of Literary and Artistic Works.. Trademarks are filed through the Central Office and granted protection by OAMPI for 20 years, renewable indefinitely.

▶ **Business climate**

The business culture has a decidedly French flavor. Still, usage of English is growing as efforts intensify to lure larger investment from the United States, Britain and countries such as South Africa and Australia.

SEYCHELLES

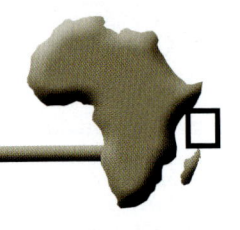

Income from tourism has helped Africa's smallest state, Seychelles, to rank near the top in Africa in terms of GNP per capita. Since its independence in seventies the per capita output of this Indian Ocean archipelago has increased sevenfold. Already a crossroad for sea and air travelers and freight shipping, the multi-island nation has become a major offshore banking and insurance center by offering facilities comparable to places like the Bahamas. Investor-friendly reforms and privatization have lured investment in fishing and manufacturing from the US and Europe. A tuna processing plant partly owned and operated by a US firm is the biggest single employer on the islands.

Country profile

The Republic of Seychelles comprises 115 small islands scattered over an area of about 1.3 million sq. km (0.5 million sq. miles) in the Indian Ocean, just south of the equator some 1,600 km (1,000 miles) east of Mombasa. The main island, Mahe, about 27 km (17 miles) long and 8 km (5 miles) at its widest, is the largest of 40 non-volcanic Inner Islands formed by granite rock, renowned for their unique flora and fauna. The outlying islands consist of nine archipelagos, including coralline atolls and groups of volcanic islands. The Aldabra, Farquhar and Desroches island groups are all included in the Republic of Seychelles.

Most Seychellians are of mixed descent, primarily African and European. French-Kreol is the lingua franca and an official language, together with English. The population is predominantly Christian.

History

The Seychelles were uninhabited when the British East India Company discovered the archipelago in 1609. It soon became a haven for pirates. The islands were claimed by the French in 1756 and administered as part of the colony of Mauritius. In the Peace Treaty of Paris in 1814 the French signed over *Séchelles* to the British who anglisized the name to its current spelling. The Seychelles islands gained independence in 1976 under a coalition government headed by Sir James Mancham, leader of the *Mouvement Seychellois pour la Democratie* or Seychelles Democratic Party (DP), as president, and Marxist nationalist, France Albert René of the *Front Progressiste du Peuple Seychellois* or the Seychelles Peoples Progressive Front (SPPF) as prime minister. In 1977 while Mancham was abroad, René overthrew him and set up a one-party pro-Soviet state. (The American space agency's radar

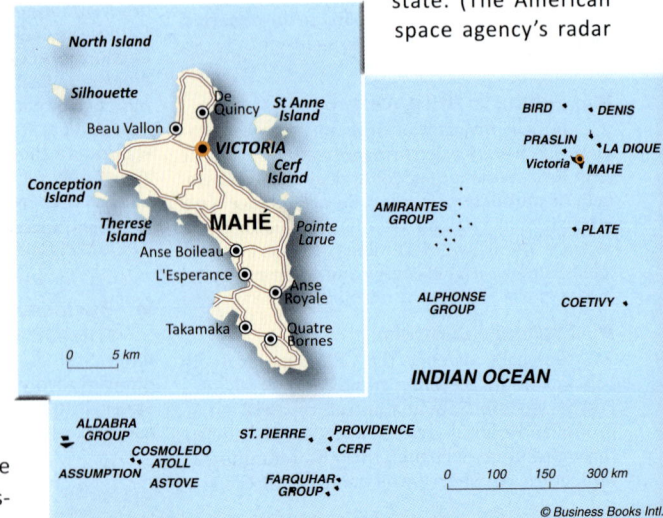

334

station which paid a substantial rent, was allowed to stay). In 1992, in the wake of Soviet Union's demise, René lifted restrictions on opposition parties and won handsomely. He was reelected president in 1998 and 2001. In April 2004 René stepped down and Vice President James Michel took over. Michel was reaffirmed in the post in the July 2006 election by defeating Wavel Ramkalawan.

Government

An executive President is elected by popular vote for a 5-year term and appoints a Council of Ministers. A unicameral 34-seat National Assembly, or *Assemblée Nationale* consists of 25 elected seats and 9 appointed on a proportional basis to parties that won 9% or more of the popular vote. In May 2007 the SPPF captured 23 seats against 11 for the centrist Seychelles National Party (SNP).

Economic policy

The government encourages foreign investment in the hotels and other services. At the same time, it tries to reduce dependence on tourism by promoting farming, fishing, and manufacturing.

Sectors

Tourism, tuna fishing, agriculture and small-scale manufacturing are key sectors. Tourism employs a third of the workforce and accounts for 70% of foreign currency earnings. A sharp decline in tourist revenues during the Gulf War and after the 11 September 2001 terrorist attacks on the US, prompted the government to diversify. A fully equipped international airport on Mahe island not only handles an inward tourist flow but serves as a stopover on international routes. Victoria has the deepest port in the Indian Ocean and serves as a major fish and freight transshipment point.

Privatization

Privatization has created new investment opportunities. A celebrated case is the partial purchase several years ago by a subsidiary of US-based Heinz of a state-owned tuna plant.

Investment

Foreign investment is largely in telecommunications, tourism and manufacturing. A tuna processing plant owned and operated by Heinz in partnership with the government into the largest employer on the islands.

Pres. James Alix Michel
Born: Aug. 18, 1944
Since April 2004
UN Photo Marco Castro

POLITICAL
Head of State	Pres. James Alix Michel
Ruling Party	SPPF
Main Opposition	SNP
Independence	29 June 1976
National capital	Victoria
Official languages	English & French-Kreol

PHYSICAL
Total area	175 sq. miles
	455 sq. km.
	(2½ x Wash. DC)
Arable land	2% of land area
Coastline	305 miles/492 km

POPULATION
Total	88,300
Av. yearly growth	0.96%
Urban population	54%
Life expectancy	73.2 years
Adult literacy	91.8%

ECONOMY
Currency	Seychelles Rupee (SRe (US$1=12.08)
GDP (real)	$842 million
GDP growth rate	-6.8%
GDP per capita[1]	$9,675
GDP (ppp)[2]	$1.4 billion
GDP per cap. (ppp)	$17,563
Inflation rate	31.7%
Exports	$428 million
Imports	$703 million
External debt	$845 million
Unemployment	2%

1. Atlas method.
2. See page 175 for an explanation of purchasing power parity (ppp).

Trade

Leading foreign exchange earners are tourism and fishing, largely geared to exporting of canned tuna, fish, and frozen shrimp and prawns. Recently tea has been added to its exports.

Financial sector

Corporate tax, withholding tax on dividends and interests, wealth tax, capital gains tax, customs duties, stamp duty, and exchange controls have been waived for offshore investors. The Insurance Act, modeled on similar legislation in Singapore, makes provision for the licensing of offshore insurance companies. Like Mauritius, Seychelles is aggressively courting offshore banking business.

Taxes and tariffs

Investors are exempted from withholding tax on dividends, personal income tax, and wealth tax. Imports usually require government approval in one form or another and price controls apply to imports.

BUSINESS ACTIVITY

AGRICULTURE
Coconuts, cinnamon, vanilla, sweet potatoes, cassava (tapioca), bananas, broiler chickens, tuna fish.

INDUSTRIES
Fishing, tourism, processing of coconuts and vanilla, coir (coconut fiber), rope, boat building, printing, furniture, beverages.

EXPORTS
$428 million (est. 2008): fish, cinnamon, bark, copra, petroleum products (reexports).

IMPORTS
$703 million (est. 2008): manufactured goods, food, petroleum products, machinery and equipment, chemicals.

MAJOR TRADING PARTNERS
France, UK, Saudi Arabia, Japan, Netherlands, South Africa, Singapore, Spain, Italy, Mauritius.

Doing Business with Seychelles

▶ **Investment**
Several government organizations have been established to assist potential foreign investors. A one-stop shop, the Seychelles International Business Authority (SIBA), is largely preoccupied with the registration of offshore companies and promoting the Seychelles as a hub in the Indian Ocean region while the Seychelles International Trade Zone concentrates on tax-exempt, export-oriented operations in the zone. The greatest potential for US investors is in tourism, fisheries, light manufacturing and infrastructure. There is growing foreign interest in newly created opportunities for secure and confidential offshore banking and insurance facilities.

▶ **Trade**
Marketing of products is inhibited by a lack of adequate foreign exchange and the government policy of restricting non-essential imports.

▶ **Trade finance**
The foreign exchange shortage is one of the main obstacles to doing business in the Seychelles.

▶ **Selling to the government**
The state-owned Seychelles Marketing Board has a monopoly on the importation of essential products such as rice, sugar and dairy products.

▶ **Financing projects**
Major infrastructure investments are typically financed by bilateral donors such as France, Kuwait and China and multilateral agencies such as the World Bank, the European Development Bank and the African Development Bank.

▶ **Legal rights**
By its own admission, the Seychelles is not sufficiently equipped by law to provide intellectual property protection. Steps are underway to tighten the laws and improve monitoring.

▶ **Labor**
The local workforce is easily adaptable to manufacturing and service sector tasks. In the fishing sector, there is a wealth of talent.

▶ **Business Climate**
Business is conducted at a an easy pace in either English, French or Creole. Seychellians are quite informal and casual dress is the norm even at the senior government and company levels.

SIERRA LEONE

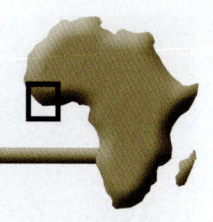

In recent years, this promising former British protectorate suffered heavily as rival forces engaged in fierce fighting. Substantial mineral, agricultural and fishing resources in Sierra Leone remain underutilized as potential foreign investors steer clear. Interruption in the mining of diamonds, bauxite and rutile has practically dried up the flow of foreign currency and the mass exodus of professionals from Sierra Leone is continuing. the new democratically elected government is reestablishing order after a costly decade-long civil war.

Country profile

The Republic of Sierra Leone is a country of many rivers perched on a mountainous peninsula. From the coast the land rises gradually to the Loma and Tingi mountains near the northern border. As the capital of a country with an average rainfall of between 79 and 197 inches (2,000 and 5,000 mm) per year, Freetown is one of the world's wettest cities. Rainforest covers much of the terrain. The Temne and Mende are major groups, There are substantial Creole (or Krio) and Lebanese minorities. English is the official language, but Krio, an English-based Creole language, is the lingua franca.

History

The Bulom people were the first to settle in the region, followed by the Mende and the Temme in the 15th Century and the Fulani. In the middle of the 15th Century, Portuguese mariners began to sail up the broad mouth of the Sierra Leone River in search of fresh water. They named the mountainous peninsula, Serra Lyoa and traded in gold, ivory and slaves. During the last half of the 16th Century a Mende warrior people invaded the region and subjugated the local communities. Towards the end of the 18th Century liberated slaves from North America sponsored by private British patrons found a province in Sierra Leone. In 1808 Britain turned the capital, Freetown, into a naval base to enforce the abolition of slavery and in 1896 declared a protectorate over the interior to prevent it from falling into French hands. After the discovery of gold, diamonds, iron ore, bauxite and rutile, the colony experienced considerable economic growth. Since Dr. Milton Margai and his Sierra Leone People's Party (SLPP) led Sierra Leone to independence in 1961, the colony has experienced more than its fair share of coups and counter-coups. On 25 May 1997, the democratically-elected government of President Ahmad Tejan Kabbah was overthrown by a disgruntled coalition of personnel of the Armed Forces Revolutionary Council (AFRC)

Pres. Ernest
Bai Koroma
Born: Oct. 2, 1953
Since Sept. 2007

UN Photo Eskinder Debebe

POLITICAL	
Head of State	Pres. Ernest Bai Koroma
Ruling Party	APC
Main Opposition	SLPP
Independence	27 April 1961
Capital	Freetown
Official languages	English

PHYSICAL	
Total area	28,000 sq. miles 72,000 sq. km. (± South Carolina)
Arable land	7% of land area
Coastline	250 miles/402 km

POPULATION	
Total	5.2 million
Av. yearly growth	2.2%
Urban population	38%
Life expectancy	55.69 years
Adult literacy	35.1%

ECONOMY	
Currency	Leone (Le) (US$1=4,175)
GDP (real)	$2.4 billion
GDP growth rate	3.5%
GDP per capita[1]	$401
GDP (ppp)[2]	$4.5 billion
GDP per cap. (ppp)	$792
Inflation rate	10.7%
Exports	$216 million
Imports	$560 million
External debt	$647 million
Unemployment	NA

1. Atlas method.
2. See page 175 for an explanation of purchasing power parity (ppp).

and the Revolutionary United Front (RUF) under the command of Major Johnny Paul Koroma. In 1998 Kabbah was reinstated by the Economic Community of West African States Cease-Fire Monitoring Group (ECOMOG). In January 1999, renewed fighting broke out between the AFRC/RUF and ECOMOG troops, bringing commerce to a standstill. Until May 2002 sufficient stability was restored to enable Sierra Leone to have its first free postwar presidential election. Tejan Kabbah won more than 70% of the popular vote. Ernest Bai Koroma became president in August 2007 when he defeated Kabbah's designated successor, Solomon Berewa, at the polls. The new government still faces the challenge of rebuilding infrastructure after a drawn-out war that cost the lives of tens of thousands and left 2 million (one-third of the population) homeless.

Government

The current constitution provides for an executive President, directly elected for a maximum of two 4-year terms. The 124 members of the House of Representatives serve for a 5-year term—112 are elected on a proportional basis and 12 seats are for representatives of the traditional chiefs. In August 2007 Koroma's All People's Congress (APC) won 59 seats agaist Sierra Leone People's Party's (SLPP) 43. The People's Movement for Democratic Change (PMDC) came third with 10 seats.

Economic policy

A Poverty Reduction and Growth Facility program by the IMF helped to stabilize economic growth and reduce inflation. The International Finance Corporation, assisted with financing. Recovery depends to a large extent on the ability of the government to maintain peace and assistance from overseas donors.

Sectors

Agriculture, mostly on smallholdings, provides a livelihood for about 70% of the population. Rice is grown by most farmers, but despite government efforts to promote self-sufficiency, increasing quantities have to be imported. Other food crops include maize, cassava, sweet potatoes and sorghum. The major export crops are coffee, cocoa, palm kernels and ginger. Fishing is a growing industry with oysters and shrimp as major products. Diamonds are mined in alluvial fields around the eastern towns of

Koidu-Sefadu and Kenema by numerous individual diggers and a government-controlled corporation. Rutile (titanium dioxide) mined in the sands on Sherbro Island has overtaken diamonds as the principal export. Sierra Leone is currently the world's second largest producer of this mineral, an essential ingredient in paints. Bauxite ore, which has overtaken diamond mining in importance, has resumed after the new government took control. Manufacturing is largely concentrated around the porcessing of raw materials and light industry aimed at the domestic consumer market.

Investment

Foreign investment, mostly British, is largely concentrated in the mining sector. Output in diamond mining is expected to increase once stability returns.

Trade

Diamonds have for many years been the principal export, but in recent years rutile accounted for over 40% of export earnings, followed by bauxite ore and diamonds.

Taxes

A corporate and capital gains tax rate of 30 percent applies to non-resident holdings. There is no value added tax but exchange control is in effect. Taxes are levied on dividends (10%), interest (15%) and royalties (25%). (See page 138).

BUSINESS ACTIVITY
AGRICULTURE
Rice, coffee, cocoa, palm kernels, palm oil, peanuts, poultry, cattle, sheep, pigs, fish.
INDUSTRIES
Mining (diamonds), small-scale manufacturing (beverages, textiles, cigarettes, footwear), petroleum refining.
NATURAL RESOURCES
Diamonds, bauxite, iron ore.
EXPORTS
$216 million (est. 2006): diamonds, rutile, cocoa, coffee, fish.
IMPORTS
$560 million (est. 2006): foodstuffs, machinery and equipment, fuel and lubricants.
MAJOR TRADING PARTNERS
Belgium, Côte d'Ivoire, US, UK, South Africa, China, Netherlands, India.

DOING BUSINESS WITH SIERRA LEONE

▶ **Investment**

Foreigners who passed on the considerable potential in Sierra Leone when rebels operated in the mineral-rich northern and eastern portions of the country, are now showing interest. With the fighting that has caused suspension of most mineral operations apparently something of the past, foreign entrepreneurs are returning. In the past the mineral industry accounted for 20% of the nation's gross domestic product, 80% to 90% of export earnings, and employed almost 15% of the total workforce, primarily in rural areas. There are opportunities in the mining of bauxite, cassiterite, clays, columbite, diamonds, gold, iron ore, kaolin, lignite, platinum, dimension stone, and tantalite.

▶ **Trade**

Reconstruction and repair of roads, schools, hospitals, airports and telecommunications connections, largely with the help of donor funding, are areas where foreigners are bound to play a meaningful role in the future. Some projects have already been initiated with the help of funding from international donor agencies. Sales of food, clothing and other supplies at this time are mostly to humanitarian and specialized agencies that will insist on giveaway pricing to augment donations. Once Sierra Leone has regained its equilibrium it should again become a small but vibrant market for a wide range of consumer goods.

▶ **Exchange controls**

The foreign exchange rate is market-determined. Private foreign exchange bureaus operate freely and bank accounts in foreign currencies are allowed.

▶ **Financing projects**

Sierra Leone has been a MIGA member since 1996 and has pending applications with the institution for projects in agribusiness, mining and telecommunications. World Bank activities have focused on sectoral programs and projects in the agriculture, education, infrastructure, and health sectors. The IFC's portfolio as of July 31, 1998 totalled $5.2 million (in Sierra Rutile).

SOMALIA

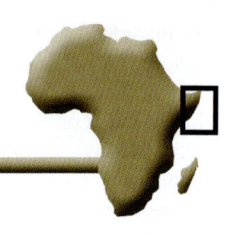

Foreign business with Somalia remains on hold as the struggle between the fighting factions continues. Economic progress has stalled in most parts of the country in the wake of the unrest and instability that followed the fall of the military regime in 1991. After failed attempts by US and UN military forces to impose a settlement while overseeing the distribution of international food and other humanitarian aid in the nineties, Somalia has been left largely to its own devices. A transitional government still faces strong opposition from rival factions in their efforts to reunite the breakaway Republic of Somaliland in the central region and Puntland State with a central authority in Mogadishu.

Country profile

The largely inoperative Somali Democratic Republic has a rhino-horn shaped coastline of more than 3,000 km (1,684 miles)—the longest in Africa—which earned it the designation, Horn of Africa. The Ras Hafun peninsula, to the south of Cape Guardafui at the Horn's tip, is the African continent's most easterly point. Ethiopia cuts into Somalia, virtually dividing it into northern Somalia (the former British Somaliland) and southern Somalia (formerly Italian Somaliland). In the north a steep escarpment rises inland from a narrow coastline towards Ethiopia. The south consists largely of monotonous plains below 500 m (1,650 ft) and the region adjoining the Juba and Shibeli rivers provides grazing for livestock. About half of the largely homogenous population is nomadic and the other half evenly divided between settled farming regions of Juba-Shebeh and the towns. Islam is the prevailing faith and most Somalians speak Somali, which, together with Arabic, is an official language. English and Italian are the main European languages.

History

While early civilizations were flourishing in the lower Nile Valley several thousand years ago, there was a migration southward into this region. Most of these early settlers were Cushites of caucasoid origin such as the Berbers and the ancient Egyptians and Nubians. About 1,500 years ago Negroid peoples arrived from the west and in the course of time extensive intermixing occurred. Arab and Persian merchant mariners founded the port of Mogadishu in the

10th Century and subsequently Merca, Brava, Kismayu, Lamu, Kilwa and other settlements further to the south. First the Hawiya Cushite clan near Mogadishu and in the ensuing years most others adopted the Muslim faith. In the 16th Century the area bordering the Gulf of Aden was part of the Turkish Ottoman empire. The Portuguese controlled the coastal centers in the south but were driven out early in the 18th Century by the Omani Arabs who gained control of the coast from Zanzibar and Mombasa to Mogadishu. Through all this activity the Somali peoples remained divided. At the height of the colonial era at turn of the 19th Century the Somalis were ruled by three European powers—France, Britain and Italy—and Ethiopia, in five separate regions. By mutual agreement, Italian and British Somaliland were united and given their independence as the united Republic of Somalia in 1960, while French Somaliland became the independent Republic of Djibouti in 1977. Somalis continue to live in Kenya's North-West Frontier province and in Ethiopia's Ogaden desert. After a brief period of democracy, the Republic of Somalia fell under the power of General Mohammed Siad Barre, who nationalized the economy as part of his economically disastrous policy of "scientific socialism."

Recent developments

In 1977 Barre attempted to distract attention from his domestic failures by sending army units to help Somali rebels trying to take over Ethiopia's Ogaden with the help of Cuban troops An estimated one million ethnic Somalis sought refuge in Somalia. In 1991 the Majerteen and Hawiye clans formed the United Somali Congress (USC) and forced Barre to flee. Once in control of Mogadishu, the USC found itself split between two warlords, triggering another internal battle. Intervention by US and UN troops to enforce a peace and oversee the delivery of international food and medical supplies to refugees saved numerous lives but ended in political failure. The fighting resumed in 1995 after the foreign forces evacuated. In the early nineties Somaliland (primarily former British Somaliland) seceded from Somalia. So did Puntland in the northeast along the Horn of Africa. While both lay claim to greater stability than the rest of the country neither has been recognized internationally.

Pres. Sharif Sheikh Ahmed
Born: Jul. 25, 1964
Since January 2009

UN Photo Marco Castro

POLITICAL	
Head of State	Sharif Sheikh Ahmed
Prime Minister	Mohamed Abdullahi Mohamed
Independence	1 July 1960
Capital	Mogadishu
Official language	Somali

PHYSICAL	
Total area	246,000 sq. miles 638,000 sq. km. (± Texas)
Arable land	2% of land area
Coastline	1,880 miles/3,025 km

POPULATION	
Total	10.1 million
Av. yearly growth	2.8%
Urban population	37%
Life expectancy	50 years
Adult literacy	37.8%

ECONOMY	
Currency	Somali shilling (US$1=1,600)
GDP (real)	$2.7 billion
GDP growth rate	2.6%
GDP per capita[1]	NA
GDP (ppp)[2]	$5.7 billion
GDP per cap. (ppp)	$600
Inflation rate	NA
Exports	$300 million
Imports	$798 million
External debt	$3 billion
Unemployment	NA

1. Atlas method.
2. See page 175 for an explanation of purchasing power parity (ppp).

Government

In August 2000 a Somalia parliament was convened in neighboring Djibouti. Despite recognition of this Transitional Federal Assembly (TFA) by several neighboring countries, Somali warlords in Mogadishu and the breakaway regions of Somaliland and and Puntland did not. It was also challenged by the Union of Islamic Courts (IUC) from its stronghold in Magadishu. In January 2009, the former chairman of the Islamic Courts Union movement, Sheikh Sharif Ahmed, was elected president of Somalia in the second round of balloting held in Djibouti. The 550-seat transitional governing entity with a five-year mandate, known as the Transitional Federal Institutions (TFIs), relocated to Somalia in 2004 and in 2009 was given a two-year extension until October 2011. In October 2010 Mohamed Abdullahi Mohamed was appointed Prime Minister by President Ahmed.

Economic policy

The continuing power struggle in and around the former capital, Mogadishu, and along the routes of communication has severely impeded serious economic planning.

Sectors

A large section of the population consists of nomads who depend on livestock for their livelihood. The major cash crop is bananas. Also grown are cotton, sugar cane, sorghum and maize. Northern Somalia is the world's largest source of incense and myrrh. With the longest coastline in Africa, Somalia's fishing industry is relatively undeveloped. Mining is confined to the commercial extraction of salt and gypsum but there are reserves of iron ore, uranium, beryl and columbite. Somalia has the world's largest reserves of gypsum hydrite. Despite the continuing anarchy the country's service sector continues to grow. Modagishu offers a variety of goods ranging from exotic imported foods to the newest electronic gadgets— as well as Africa's lowest international wireless call rates.

BUSINESS ACTIVITY

AGRICULTURE
Bananas, sorghum, corn, sugar cane, mangoes, sesame seeds, beans, cattle, sheep, goats, fish.
INDUSTRIES
Small industries, including sugar refining, textiles , petroleum refining (shut down).
NATURAL RESOURCES
Uranium.
EXPORTS
$300 million (2006): livestock, bananas, hides, fish, charcoal, scrap metal.
IMPORTS
$798 million (2006): manufactures, petroleum products, foodstuffs, construction materials.
MAJOR TRADING PARTNERS
UAE, Djibouti, Kenya, Yemen, Brazil, Oman, Bahrain, India.

Doing Business with Somalia

▶ Investment

Once peace is restored, foreign activity in oil exploration and mining is bound to follow. A large number of minerals have been discovered, including gold, gypsum, iron ore, kynite, lead barite, limestone piezo-quartz, tin, sepiolite titaniferous sand, and uranium. To date, only limestone and gypsum deposits have been exploited commercially. The recovery of gas reserves in the Ogaden region of Ethiopia and oil across the Red Sea in North and South Yemen spurred interest in Somalia on the part of Chevron, Conoco, Exxon Mobil and others. Since the disintegration of Somalia most of this activity ceased but the self-proclaimed Somaliland Republic has recently indicated that oil prospecting contracts signed by the former government of united Somalia in its region would be honored. Telecommunications and fishing are future prospects.

▶ Trade

The only potential sales to most of Somalia at this stage are in food and other supplies to UN and other agencies involved in relief programs.

▶ Financing

Most of Somalia's international financing consist of humanitarian assistance and disaster relief with UN agencies and some NGO programs involved.

SOUTH AFRICA

Rated by the UN as one of the world's 26 industrialized nations and by the US Commerce Department as one of a few select Big Emerging Markets (BEMs), South Africa offers great potential for exporters and investors with the right products, resources and commitment. South Africa has a substantial and sophisticated market with significant growth potential, well-developed financial institutions and capital markets, first-rate communication and transport links and ample raw materials. It offers easy access not only to neighboring markets but elsewhere in Africa. In areas such as mining, information technology, paper production and beverages South African companies have become major international players.

Country profile

The Republic of South Africa at the southern tip of the African continent comprises 1,219,090 sq. km. or 470,893 sq. miles (including two island possessions more than 1,920 km/1,193 miles southeast of Cape Town—Prince Edward and Marion. The country is within the subtropical high pressure belt and wide expanses of ocean have a moderating influence on the climate. More than 76% of the population is of black African heritage; some 12.7% whites; 8.5% Colored; and 2.5% East Indian. Two-thirds of black South Africa belongs to the Nguni group and speak Xhosa, Zulu, Swazi and Ndebele. The rest belongs to the South, North and West Sotho (Tswana), the Tsonga, and the Venda. The Coloreds are a mixed race and Indians are the descendants of indentured laborers brought to Natal by Britain in the 1860s to work on sugar plantations. Forebears of the Afrikaners and English-speaking whites came from the Netherlands, France and Britain in the 17th and early 19th centuries, and, more recently, Germany, Portugal, Italy, Greece and other European countries. There is also a sizeable Chinese community. Next to English and Afrikaans, nine major Bantu languages enjoy official status. South African society is predominantly Christian but there are also sizeable minorities of Muslims, Jews and Hindu.

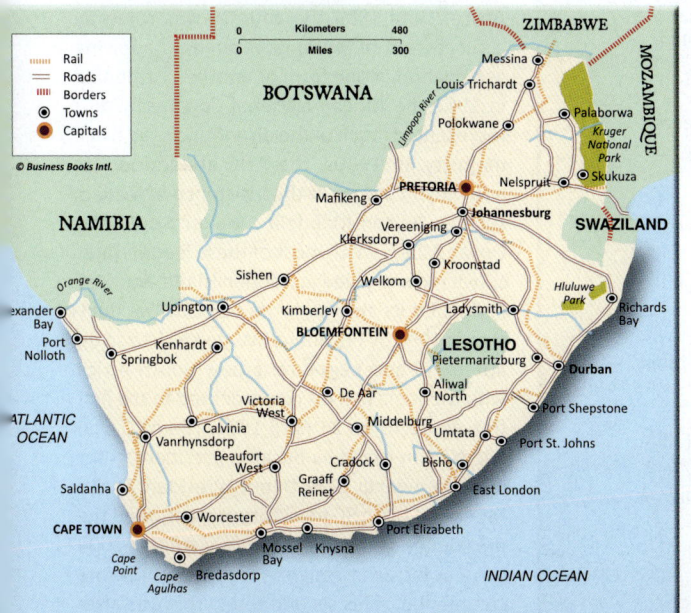

History

The region is said to have been occupied by small nomadic groups of San or

Pres. Jacob Zuma
Born: April 12, 1942
Since: May 2009

POLITICAL

Head of State	Pres. Jacob Gedleyihlekisa Zuma
Ruling Party	ANC
Main Opposition	DA
Independence	31 May 1910
Freedom Day	27 April 1994
Capitals	Pretoria Cape Town, Bloemfontein
Official languages	English & 10 other

PHYSICAL

Total area	471,000 sq. miles 1,221,090 sq. km. (2 x Texas)
Arable land	12% of land area
Coastline	1,738 ml/2,798 km

POPULATION

Total	49 million
Av. yearly growth	0.05%
Urban population	61%
Life expectancy	49.2 years
Adult literacy	86.4%

ECONOMY

Currency	Rand (R) (US$1=6.88)
GDP (real)	$259.5 billion
GDP growth rate	-1.8%
GDP per capita[1]	$5,313
GDP (ppp)[2]	$487 billion
GDP per cap. (ppp)	$9,721
Inflation rate	7.1%
Exports	$66.6 billion
Imports	$66 billion
External debt	$71.8 billion
Unemployment	24%

1. Atlas method.
2. See page 175 for an explanation of purchasing power parity (ppp).

Bushmen hunter-gatherers 100,000 years ago. Some 2,000 years ago they were gradually displaced by the pastoral Khoi or Hottentot and 1,500 years ago migrant Bantu entered the region from the north-central part of the continent. Portuguese explorer Bartholomeu Dias was the first European to set foot on South African soil in August 1487. It was, however, only on 6 April 1652 that a small group of Dutch under command of Jan van Riebeeck of the Dutch East India Company settled at the Cape. In 1689 they were joined by French Huguenots who developed the settlement into a notable wine producer. Britain took control of the Cape in 1806. The new British settlers aligned themselves with the Dutch frontiersmen. However, relations between the British authorities and the Boers (farmers)—as these descendants of the original Dutch and French settlers called themselves—were strained. The Boers trekked north and established their own independent Republics of the Transvaal and the Orange Free State. In the process the Boers had numerous battle encounters with the various black or Bantu peoples who settled in the northern part of the country. After their defeat by Britain in the Anglo-Boer War of 1899-1902 both Boer Republics were ruled from Westminster for eight years until 31 May 1910 when, together with the Cape and Natal colonies, they received independence as part of the Union of South Africa. Until 1994 the country was ruled by a succession of white governments applying segregation in one form or another. Beginning in 1912 the African National Congress (ANC) represented much of the disenfranchised black majority. In 1960s, the ANC abandoned its non-violent stance at the insistence of leaders such as Nelson Mandela, Walter Sisulu and Govan Mbeki. With most of these leaders later convicted and jailed at Robben Island, the ANC continued its struggle from abroad. The decision in 1990 by President F.W. de Klerk to scrap apartheid and negotiate a new South Africa with Mandela and his comrades led to the first free elections on 24 April 1994. The ANC won and Nelson Mandela became president. After his retirement in 1999, Deputy President Thabo Mbeki led the ANC to victory and assumed the presidency. He scored another victory in 2004 but was forced to resign by is own party before completion of his second term. This was after a court ruling in favor of his former Deputy President Jacob Zuma, whom he dismissed in 2005 on charges of fraud and corruption. In December 2007 Zuma defeated Mbeki in his bid for reelection as president of the ANC and in September 2008, the Supreme Court of KwazuluNatal dismissed charges against him —finding that they might have been motivated by political considerations. Zuma's deputy in the party, Kgalema Motlanthe, served as Acting President until the April 2009 election when Zuma led the ANC to victory to become president.

Government

Parliament consists of a National Assembly with 400 members elected on a proportional basis, and a National Council of Provinces (NCOP), consisting of 54 permanent members and 36 special delegates representing provincial interests. The President, formally elected by the National Assembly, is both the Head of State and leads the Cabinet. He serves for a maximum of two five year terms. Each of the nine provinces has its own legislature of between 30 and 80 members and is headed by a premier representing the majority party. In the April 2009 election the ANC captured almost 66% in the national parliament with 264 seats against 67 for the largely white Democratic Alliance led by Helen Zille and 30 for the newly formed Congress of the People (COPE) under leadership of the former Defense Minister, Mosiuoa Lekota. The Inkatha Freedom Party (IFP) headed by Zulu Chief Mangosuthu Buthelezi won 18 seats. Smaller parties include the United Democratic Movement (UDM) (4), Independent Democrats (4), the *Vryheidsfront Plus* (Freedom Front Plus) (4), the African Christian Democratic Party (3), and the United Christian-Democratic Party (UCDP) (2). The Minority Front (MF), the Pan African Congress (PAC), the Azanian Peoples Organization (AZAPO) and the African Peoples Convention (APC) each won a single seat.

Economic policy

The South African government sees its broad goals as the creation of a strong, dynamic and balanced economy; the elimination of poverty; meeting the basic needs of every South African; development of human resources; protection against racial or gender discrimination in hiring, promotion or training; the development of a prosperous and balanced regional economy in southern Africa; and integration into the world economy. Its Growth, Employment and Redistribution (GEAR) macroeconomic strategy set specific goals in all spheres of economic activity, ranging from gross domestic product growth to budget deficits, interest rates, inflation and job creation. Even though the country has fallen short in terms of GDP growth and job creation, it held its own on inflation and deficit targets. The government continues to receive good ratings from Moody's, Standard & Poors, Fitch and other rating agencies.

Sectors

South Africa has a modern, well-diversified economy. Agriculture contributes about 4.5% of the gross domestic product (GDP) and accounts for 13% of the total employment. Mining and mineral processing—even though they have been outstripped by manufacturing in recent years—remain vital to the economy. They still make an 8% direct contribution to GDP and employ more than half a million workers. South Africa's mineral wealth is found in diverse geological formations. The Witwatersrand Basin around Johannesburg yields 98% of South Africa's gold output while the Bushveld Complex, spanning the North-West and Mpumalanga provinces, contains the world's largest reserves of platinum group minerals (PGMs), chromium, vanadium, nickel, fluorspar and andalusite, apart from substantial supplies of antimony, asbestos, diamonds, coal, fluorspar, phosphates, iron ore, lead, zinc, uranium, vermiculite and zirconium. Both South Africa's fishing and forestry industries have developed into key economic players on the domestic scene and important currency earners. The sophistication of its manufacturing industry places South Africa in the company of the world's thirty top industrial nations. Nearly 32% of GDP is derived from secondary industry and policy-makers are devoting particular attention to sound, accelerated development of this sector. South Africa manufactures a wide range of consumer goods, including food products, textiles, footwear and clothing, metal and chemical products, and paper and paper products. The production of capital goods such as machinery, transport and electrical equipment is also expanding. In 1997, manufacturing, electricity, gas, water and construction contributed almost a third of the nation's total GDP, compared to agriculture's 4.5% and mining's 7.8%. South Africa's modern and extensive transport system places it in the company of top industrialized nations. A number of countries in southern Africa use this network to move their imports and exports. At the end of 2007, South Africa began to experience an electricity crisis because state power supplier Eskom suffered supply problems with aged plants, necessitating "load-shedding" cuts to residents and businesses in the urban centers.

Privatization

Under a "National Framework Agreement" (NFA), government, business, and labor agreed to a substantial program of restructuring and privatization of state assets. Partially or fully privatized so far are the Airports Company, six radio stations of the state-owned SA Broadcasting Corporation, Telkom (the national telecommunications company), and South African Airways (SAA). The two biggest deals to date are the sale of 30% percent of Telkom SA to a consortium of SBC Communications of the US and Telekom Malaysia for $1,261 million and the sale of 20% of SAA to Swissair for $230 million. Deals in the offing involve an additional stake in Telkom and the restructuring of Denel (a defense contractor), Eskom (a power utility), and Transnet (the country's major transport group). So far the government has managed to overcome opposition from the strong trade unions movement, COSATU, and the South African Communist Party.

Investment

The US tops the list of major foreign investors including Britain, Malaysia, Germany and Japan with. In the megadeal section, the US telecommunications giant SBC Communications ranks a close second on the FDI list to Malaysia's Petronas. Dow Chemicals, Coca-Cola, IBM, Salem, Goodyear, Duracell, Ford and McDonalds are other big US investors. Main sectors for investment are telecommunications, energy and oil, automobile manufacturing, food and beverages, chemicals and plastics and mining. Dow Chemical's takeover of Sentrachem for $850 million in the late nineties is the largest single outright purchase of a South African private company in recent years. During the past six years, however, direct investment abroad by South African multinational firms has outpaced FDI inflows. South Africa has also become the largest source of investment not only in neighboring SADC nations but much of the rest of Africa.

Trade

Significant trading partners are the US, United Kingdom, Germany, Japan, Italy and France. The U.S. and South Africa signed a Trade and Investment Framework Agreement (TIFA)—the first in Sub-Saharan Africa. The US is a major supplier of wheat and rice to South Africa and accounts for more than 10% of the country's total agricultural imports. The US also has a significant share of the growing market for high technology equipment, computers and software, and machinery. As a result of the liberalization of its economy, South Africa's ratio of trade in goods and services to gross domestic product increased from to 65%.

Economic Empowerment

Increasingly both foreign and local companies are seeking Black Economic Empowerment (BEE) partners to secure good working relationship with other entrepreneurs in the private sector and to secure approval in lucrative government tenders. In terms of the Broad-Based Black Economic Empowerment Act of 2003 companies doing business with the government are obliged to promote black advancement in business. Broad Based Black Economic Empowerment (BBBEE) is an extension of Black Economic Empowerment initiated in response to criticism against the more narrow-based empowerment that measured only equity ownership and management representation and led to the enrichment of a few black (Black African, Coloured or Indian) individuals but failed to distribute wealth across a broad a spectrum of the disadvantaged population. The success of BEE in the upper echelons of business is evident from a growth from almost zero black ownership in public companies before 1994 to an estimated at 9.4% in 2002.

BEE Targets

The goal is to attain a black share in the economy of between 25 and 30% in 2014. Black economic empowerment has had a profound effect on the South African economy, with BEE transactions representing R200-billion over the past decade, according to ratings agency Moody's in its May 2008 report. BEE is a key driver of corporate activity, such as mergers and acquisitions, and Moody's forecasts that this trend will continue, with 52% of South African privately held businesses experiencing a change in ownership in the next 10 years. The various sectors of industry in South Africa are setting their own targets in accordance with their own specific needs. In the mining, petroleum, maritime, tourism and financial sector charters declared so far set an average target of 25% black ownership in the next decade. The government has been at great pains to try and reassure multinationals that they are not required to give away shares to BEE partners to do business in South Africa. All BEE deals, the government insists, should take place at market value or at most a 10 percent discount. Any company that does not conform to BEE practices drastically reduces its chances of doing business in South Africa.

Financial sector

The South African Reserve Bank (SARB) oversees a world-class banking system comprising 56 fully licensed institutions and 60 representative offices of foreign banks. The JSE Securities Exchange is Africa's largest and ranked 18th worldwide in terms of market capitalization in 2007 with 422 companies valued at more than to $836 billion. Trading volume of $1.2 trillion placed it 23 worldwide. The JSE offers screen trading through its Johannesburg Equities Trading (JET) system. Its Share TRAnsactions Totally Electronic (STRATE) system eliminates paper transactions by making settlement and the transfer of ownership of scrip possible through electronic book entry. Foreign trade accounts for a sizeable portion of the daily volume.

Sophistication

The level of sophistication of South Africa can best be judged by looking at the size of the top one hundred companies and tracing the success that its private sector has had in capturing world market share not only in mining and minerals but manufacturing and information technology. Notable among these are Sappi, which leads the world in the production of fine coated paper and dissolving pulp. Other South African giants include South African Breweries which ranks second worldwide and operates breweries in the US, Africa and Europe, and Anglo American and Billiton that dominate mining around the globe and IT companies Datatec and Didata.

Key partners

The Development Bank of Southern Africa (DBSA) works with donors and partners at international, national and regional levels on targeted infrastructural and strategic developments. It is playing an increasingly important role in the Southern African Development Community (SADC). The state-run Industrial Development Corporation is another potential partner for investors.

Taxes & tariffs

With the exception of mining companies that are subject to special rates, the corporate tax rate is 33%. Non-residents pay a capital gains tax of 10 to 14 percent. A value added tax (VAT) of 14 percent applies and exchange control is in effect. Taxes are levied royalties at rate of 12 percent. (See page 138).

BUSINESS ACTIVITY

AGRICULTURE
Corn, wheat, sugar cane, fruit, vegetables, beef, poultry, mutton, wool, diary products.
INDUSTRIES
Mining (world's largest producer of platinum, gold, chromium), automobile assembly, metalworking, machinery, textiles, iron and steel, chemicals, fertilizer, foodstuffs.
NATURAL RESOURCES
Gold, diamonds, platinum, uranium, coal, iron ore, phosphates, manganese.
EXPORTS
$66.6 billion (est. 2009): gold, diamonds, other minerals and metals, food, chemicals, manufactured goods.
IMPORTS
$66 billion (est. 2009): machinery, transport equipment, chemicals, petroleum products, textiles, scientific instruments.
MAJOR TRADING PARTNERS
US, UK, Germany, Netherlands, Japan, China, Saudi Arabia, Angola, Iran.

Doing Business with South Africa

▶ **Investment**

Since 1994 steps have been taken to make South Africa more attractive to foreign investment by reducing import tariffs and subsidies to local firms; eliminating discriminatory non-resident shareholders tax; removing remaining limits on hard currency repatriation; reducing by half secondary tax on corporate dividends; lowering the corporate tax rate on earnings to 30 percent; and allowing foreign investors 100 percent ownership. Foreign investors are not screened or subjected to performance or other special requirements. The government, however, encourages investments that will strengthen, expand, or enhance technology in various industries.

Foreign firms are entitled to the same export incentive programs, tax allowances and other trade regulations applicable to domestic enterprises. As the Government pushes ahead with plans to attract strategic equity partners for its large parastatal organizations, there is an increased sensitivity to the concerns of foreign investors. In terms of Black Economic Empowerment goals investors are well advised to partner with local previous disadvantaged individuals (PDIs)—black, Colored and Indian—as it will enhance their chances of qualifying for lucrative government contracts. In fact, most local private companies tend to require a good measure of black economic empowerment in dealing with other enterprises. This is simply good business. Incentives and assistance are available to both locals and foreigners under the Small/Medium Manufacturing Development Program (SMMDP). Major areas for investment have been in telecommunications, energy and oil, motor and components, food and beverages, chemicals and plastics, mining, manufacturing and hotels. A Government program of Spatial Development Initiatives (SDIs) has enhanced investment opportunities outside the major industrial centers. An official agency, Investment South Africa (ISA), provides information and assistance to prospective investors, helps identify opportunities, and assists them in finding joint venture partners and obtaining technology and capital. Franchising is an established practice. The Department of Trade and Industry must approve manufacturing royalties.

▶ **Trade**

Rapid development and expansion of telecommunications, large new pollution and waste management systems, increased use of computers and high technology devices, modernization of airports, the introduction of managed health care and a growing market for security systems are only a few areas where American products have found ready acceptance in recent years. The US remains a major exporter of agricultural products and current estimates indicate that for the medium term South Africa will continue to rely in part on imports to meet its food needs. Principal imports for include wheat, corn, rice, vegetable oils and a variety of consumer-oriented food products. Prospective exporters to South Africa from industrial nations find that this country replicates on a smaller scale their own domestic market, both in product preference and marketing methods.

At the same time, US importers have been able to purchase sophisticated local manufactures and sold them back into the US market at handsome profits. Lately the rapidly growing tourism sector has provided a market for US suppliers of information systems, marketing, design, architecture, finance and management planning. E-commerce is expected to play a significant role in future business. South Africa is an extremely competitive marketplace and it is essential that exporters provide adequate servicing, spare parts, and components, as well as qualified personnel capable of handling inquiries. It is common to appoint a single agent or distributor capable of providing national coverage either through a single office or a network of branch offices and outlets. South Africa is an ideal springboard for trading with the 13 other countries of the Southern African Development Community (SADC) and the neighboring members of the South African Customs Union (SACU).

▶ **Trade finance**

All Eximbank programs are available to US exporters of goods and services to South Africa. South Africa's sophisticated financial sector provides overdraft facilities and short- to long-term credit. Key areas of business for foreign banks include trade finance, letters of credit, foreign exchange activities and services to offshore investors.

▶ **Selling to the government**

Not only the central government but nine provincial governments and hundreds of local authorities present a market for overseas suppliers of sophisticated goods and services. Government purchasing is done through competitive bidding on tenders published in the State Tender Bulletin and some of the leading newspapers. A local agent is needed to act on behalf of foreign bidders. When selling to the government, consideration should be given to the government's goal to expand black participation in the economy. Even though there are no set rules pressure is growing to include "set-asides" for black businesses. In doing business with South Africa a foreign enterprise should seriously consider black partners. In some large-scale infrastructural projects a Black Economic Empowerment (BEE) partner is mandatory. The government's Industrial Participation Program

(IPP) mandates a countertrade/offset package for all state and parastatal purchases of goods, services, and lease contracts above $10 million. Under this program, bidders on governmental and parastatal contracts must submit an industrial participation package worth 30 percent of the imported content value. The bidder has seven years to fulfill this obligation.

▶ **Exchange controls**

Exchange controls are administered by the South African Reserve Bank's (SARB) Exchange Control Department through commercial banks that are authorized to deal in foreign currency. In March 1997, the Finance Ministry started to relax foreign exchange controls. Royalties, software license fees, and certain other remittances to non-residents still require the approval of the SARB.

▶ **Legal rights**

An independent judiciary allows full recourse without political interference in disputes over property or any other facet of business. Patents may be registered for 20 years and trademarks for 10 years, renewable for an additional 10 years. While South African IPR laws and regulations are largely TRIPS-compliant, there is still concern over copyright piracy and trademark counterfeiting and the US is working with the government to find ways of reducing infractions.

▶ **Partnerships**

In looking for partners, foreign firms have a range of choices between sophisticated large, medium-sized and smaller entities. Often the choice is determined by prevailing politics which favor black enterprise participation in government contracts. The government has leaned towards Private Public Partnerships (PPPs) in some projects, inviting foreign firms to enter in a joint venture with the authorities. It also makes good sense for foreigners with designs on the regional SADC market and other areas of Africa to join forces with South African firms with extensive local knowledge.

▶ **Establishing a presence**

South Africa's Companies Act provides for clear, transparent regulations concerning the establishment and operation of businesses. Foreign investments are organized under the same rules and regulations as domestic firms with one exception: overseas companies may opt to operate as "external companies" which do not pay tax on undistributed profits. Share capital duty is based instead on the shares of the parent firm. Foreigners may normally buy into local firms without limitation, either by acquiring shares or assets. There is no record of any expropriation or nationalization of American or any other foreign investment in South Africa.

▶ **Financing projects**

The Development Bank of Southern Africa and the Industrial Development Corporation assist in the financing of projects involving local partners. The Overseas Private Investment Corporation backs and insures US projects in South Africa. The US Trade and Development Agency funds feasibility studies, consultancies, training programs, and other project planning services in the area. Under current exchange controls foreigners need special permission to borrow locally as part of an effort to prevent excessive "gearing" through local financing. The World Bank's International Finance Corporation has established the Africa Enterprise Fund (AEF) to finance projects ranging from $100,000 to $1.5 million at market interest rates.

▶ **Labor**

The government has promised to review labor legislation in response to complaints that the South African labor market is over-regulated. Unemployment rates are highest among black South Africans (29%), followed by Coloreds (16%), Indian (10%), and Whites (4%). Nearly 35% of the workers belong to unions. The strongest among them, the 1.8 million member Congress of South African Trade Unions (COSATU), is a full partner in the ANC governing alliance. Even though strike activity has declined sharply under the ANC-led government, COSATU and others have not been slow at using mass stayaways for political purposes.

▶ **Business climate**

Business customs in South Africa are similar to those in the US and Western Europe. South African business people tend to dress conservatively and those of the old school make every effort to be on time for appointments. Even though English dominates, business ignores Afrikaans at its own peril, especially if it is consumer-oriented. There is a level of language sensitivity among Afrikaners that prompts most local firms and many foreign entities to advertise and print their literature in both languages.

SUDAN

The mineral and agricultural potential in Africa's largest country, Sudan, remains largely untapped as foreign investors await a resolution to the on-going internal strife. Since 2004 Sudan found itself under pressure from the major powers and the UN to stop "genocide" in the Darfur region. As long as it remains at war with itself, Sudan will have to defer its dreams of becoming the breadbasket of Africa through large scale irrigation of fertile land along the Nile and its tributaries. There has, however, been considerable foreign activity in oil and minerals, especially from China.

Country profile

The Republic of Sudan spans more than 2,000 km (1,243 miles) from north to south along the Sahel Belt on the fringe of the Sahara Desert. The Arabs named the territory the territory *bilad al-sudan*—land of the blacks. Except for a few peaks such as Mount Kinyeti (3,187 m/10,456 ft) on the Ugandan border and Mount Marra (3,070 m/10,072 ft)) on its border with Chad, Sudan consists largely of plains below 1,000 m/3,280 ft). The White and Blue Nile tributaries join in Sudan to form the world's longest waterway as it flows north into Egypt. All three of the continent's major linguistic supergroupings —Afroasiatic, Nilo-Saharan and Niger-Congo—are present. More than 70% of the population is Muslim, mostly in the north. There are substantial numbers of Christians in the south. Arabic is the official language.

History

In ancient times the stretch of desert along the Nile drew Negroid people from the south and Caucasoids from the north. Based at Meroe, Nubian civilization reached its zenith in the third and second centuries BC. Sudan became an Anglo-Egyptian condominium in 1899 and gained its independence in 1956. It has been plagued since by ethnic and religious strife between the Arab Muslim rulers and largely black Christian population in Darfur region. In 2004 the United Nations focused on what the US termed genocide in Darfur. International pressure led to peace talks between the Khartoum government and the southern Sudan People's Liberation Army (SPLMA). In July 2005 the joint appearance in Khartoum of rebel leader John Garang as Vice President of Sudan's new Government of National Unity, and Omer Hassan Al-Bashir, the President of

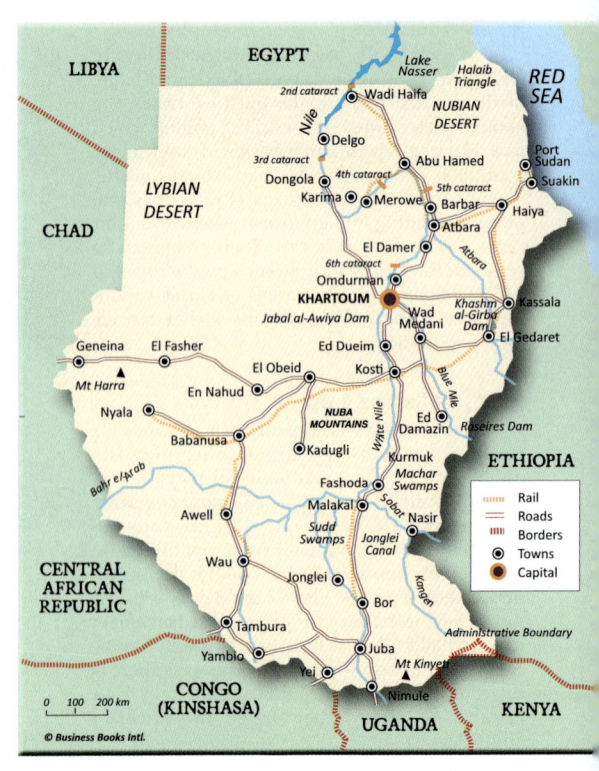

Sudan, seemed to herald an end to the war. Umar Hassan Ahmad al-BASHIR had assumed the presidency in 1989 as chairman of Sudan's Revolutionary Command Council for National Salvation (RCC)before serving concurrently as chief of state, chairman of the RCC, prime minister, and minister of defense. Garang died a few weeks after signing the peace agreement in a helicopter crash on his way back from a visit to Uganda. Riots broke out and hostilities between the SPLA and the government forces resumed, continuing a battle that took nearly two million lives and left millions displaced.

Government

Under the 2005 Comprehensive Peace Agreement (CPA) a power-sharing Government of National Unity (GNU) was formed between the National Congress Party (NCP) and Sudan People's Liberation Movement (SPLM). National elections were scheduled for 2009 and subsequently rescheduled and held in April 2010. Despite a warrant for his arrest by the International Criminal Court to stand trial on charges of war crimes, President Omar al-Bashir captured 68 percent of 10 million valid ballots and to win another five year term. International observers claimed the election was marred by intimidation, gerrymandering and fraud. In southern Sudan, which is preparing to vote in January 2011 on whether to split off from the north, incumbent Salva Kiir of the SLPM prevailed as well, winning 93 percent of the vote to remain president of that semi-autonomous region.

Economic policy

Sudan embarked on an IMF reform program to streamline investment procedures, promote privatization, eliminate most of the non-targeted consumer subsidies, and liberalize foreign trade and exchange regimes. It has managed to make impressive strides in turning around an ailing economy.

Sectors

Two-thirds the population depend on crop farming or grazing. With the help of several major water projects, Sudan accounts for 16% of Africa's total irrigated land. Food crops include sorghum, wheat, peanuts, dates, yams, sugar cane, and a variety of fruits and vegetables. Cotton for export is grown in the region between the Blue and White Niles. Sudan accounts for about four-fifths of the world's supply of gum

Pres. Omar Hassan al-Bashir
Born: Jan. 1, 1944
Since October 1989

UN Photo Eskinder Debebe

POLITICAL
Head of State	Pres. Omar Hassan al-Bashir
Ruling Party	NCP
Independence	1 January 1956
National capital	Khartoum
Official languages	Arabic

PHYSICAL
Total area	968,000 sq. miles 2,506,000 sq. km. (¼ USA)
Arable land	6.8% of land area
Coastline	530 miles/853 km

POPULATION
Total	43.9 million
Av. yearly growth	2.5%
Urban population	43%
Life expectancy	54.2 years
Adult literacy	61.1%

ECONOMY
Currency	Sudanese pound (US$1=2.49)
GDP (real)	$54.3 billion
GDP growth rate	4.2%
GDP per capita[1]	$1,376
GDP (ppp)[2]	$92.7 billion
GDP per cap. (ppp)	$2,258
Inflation rate	10.5%
Exports	$7.6 billion
Imports	$8.3 billion
External debt	$33.6 billion
Unemployment	18.7%

1. Atlas method.
2. See page 175 for an explanation of purchasing power parity (ppp).

Arabic and is the largest producer of sesame seeds. There is fishing along the rivers and the coast. A recently completed pipeline carries oil for export to Port Sudan. Increased oil production has given the economy a boost, enabling Sudan to show a trade surplus for the first time in recent history. Small amounts of chromium, manganese, and mica are produced. Other minerals with potential include gold, magnesite, and salt. Manufacturing involves processing of agricultural products, textile, paper mills, sugar and consumer goods. Foreign investment focuses largely on oil exploration and exploitation in the southern region.

Taxes

The corporate tax rate for non-residents is 35 percent and capital gains tax 2 to 5 percent. A value added tax (VAT) of 15 to 20 percent applies and exchange control is in effect. Taxes are levied on royalties (10%). (See page 138).

BUSINESS ACTIVITY

AGRICULTURE
Cotton, groundnuts, sorghum, millet, wheat, gum arabic, sesame, sheep.
INDUSTRIES
Cotton, textiles, cement, edible oils, sugar, soap, shoes, petroleum.
NATURAL RESOURCES
Crude oil, some iron ore, copper, chrome, industrial metals, gold, uranium.
EXPORTS
$7.6 billion (est. 2009): petroleum, cotton, sesame, livestock, meat, gum arabic, sugar.
IMPORTS
$8.3 billion (est. 2009): foodstuffs, manufactured goods, refinery and transport equipment, chemicals, textiles, medicines.
MAJOR TRADING PARTNERS
China, Saudi Arabia, Japan, UAE, India, Indonesia, Egypt.

DOING BUSINESS WITH SUDAN

▶ **Investment**

In February 2000, acting on reports of government atrocities against the local population around the newly built pipeline to Port Sudan, the US Treasury imposed sanctions on the Greater Nile Oil Project, the consortium set up to exploit the oil. China, aggressively seeking oil and other raw materials in Africa, has more than picked up the slack. China first established a presence in the unexploited Muglad oilfields of southern Sudan 10 years ago. Now it imports 50% of the region's crude oil, and 13 of the 15 most important foreign companies operating in Sudan are Chinese, from the China National Petroleum Corporation to the Zhongyuan Petroleum Corporation. More than 80% of all available concessions in oil exploration has been allotted to international companies. There is an ongoing effort to involve foreign firms in iron ore, manganese, magnesite, silver, gold, chromium ore, gypsum, mica, zinc, tungsten, copper and uranium mining. High grade deposits of gold have, however, been discovered in the Red Sea Hills, with reserves estimated at 100 tons. Expansion of Sudan's hydroelectric station at Roseires on the Blue Nile and a new station the 4th cataract are built in conjunction with foreign partners.

▶ **Trade**

Sudan offers opportunities to exporters of machinery, transportation equipment, metal goods, and textiles.

▶ **Selling to the government**

The $400 million Roseires dam extension project and a hydroelectric project, the Al Hamdab hydroelectric dam, provided construction contracts with foreign loan funding.

▶ **Financing projects**

There has been some progress toward normalizing Sudan's relations with international and regional financial institutions.

▶ **Labor**

Most of the work force is engaged in agricultural or pastoral occupations. Some 1.75 million workers belonged to the principal trade union federation, the Sudan Workers Trade Unions Federation, until it was banned after the 1989 coup.

▶ **Legal rights**

Sudan's judicial system comprises a civil branch that handles most cases and an Islamic branch dealing exclusively with personal and family matters.

▶ **Business Climate**

The government enforces strict adherence to the Muslim faith and the business environment conforms.

SWAZILAND

The Kingdom of Swaziland—the second smallest country on the mainland of Africa after The Gambia—has enjoyed steady economic growth through free market policies that attracted sizeable foreign investment from neighboring South Africa and abroad. The monarchy has been under considerable pressure from within and outside to unban political parties and allow true democracy. While progress on the political front is slow, Swaziland continues to rank among the leaders on the continent as far as economic reforms are concerned. This, together with a good measure of stability, present an environment conducive to investment and free trade.

Country profile

The Kingdom of Swaziland is a stamp-sized country squeezed between the Drakensberg and Lebombo mountains and bordered by South Africa and Mozambique. Rainfall is highest in the elevated region (more than 1,000 mm/39 inches) and lowest in its so-called lowveld (less than 750 mm/30 inches). Four large rivers flowing from South Africa—the Komati, Mbuluzi, Great Usutu and Ngwavuma—provide irrigation. Several nature reserves and game sanctuaries combined with a temperate climate, spectacular scenery and Swazi cultural life, attract visitors. More than 80% of the population are Swazi belonging to the Nguni-speaking peoples. Most are Christians and English and siSwati are official languages.

History

Late in the 16th Century the Embo-Nguni people moved into southern Africa and settled in what is today southern Mozambique. Towards the middle of the 18th Century, King Ngwane III led the Dlamini and related clans across the Lebombo Mountains into Swaziland. Culminating with the rule of King Mswati the Dlamini clan extended their power over an area much larger than modern Swaziland and became known as the amaSwati or Swazi. In 1846 white migrants from the Cape Colony laid claim to a large portion, insisting that Mswati II had ceded it to them by treaty. Swazi denials were fruitless and the kingdom continued to shrink. In 1895 Swaziland came under the administrative control of President Paul Kruger's Transvaal Republic. The Anglo-Boer War of 1899-1902 brought this arrangement to an end and in 1903 Britain took over. In 1968 Swaziland's independence was restored under King Sobhuza who ruled as an absolute monarch until his death in 1982. Several of Sobhuza's 67 sons from marriages to 100 wives

King Mswati III
Born: Apr. 19, 1968
Since April 1986

UN Photo Evan Schneider

POLITICAL	
Head of State	King Mswati III
Prime Minister	Barnabas Sibusiso Dlamini (2008)
Ruling Party	Elections on a non-party basis
Independence	6 September 1968
National capital	Mbabane
Official languages	English & siSwati

PHYSICAL	
Total area	7,000 sq. miles 17,000 sq. km. (± New Jersey)
Arable land	11% of land area
Coastline	Landlocked

POPULATION	
Total	1.35 million
Av. yearly growth	1.2%
Urban population	25%
Life expectancy	47.9 years
Adult literacy	81.6%

ECONOMY	
Currency	Lilangeni (E) (US$1=6.88)
GDP (real)	$2.58 billion
GDP growth rate	0.2%
GDP per capita[1]	$1,049
GDP (ppp)[2]	$5.8 billion
GDP per cap. (ppp)	$4,900
Inflation rate	4.1%
Exports	$1.4 billion
Imports	$1.5 billion
External debt	$451 million
Unemployment	40%

1. Atlas method.
2. See page 175 for an explanation of purchasing power parity (ppp).

engaged in a power struggle which was eventually resolved when King Mswati III took to the throne in 1986. King Mswati has reintroduced Swaziland's old, non-party political system of *Tinkhundlas*—a collection of chiefdoms serving as constituencies.

Government

Swaziland is a modified traditional monarchy ruled by King Mswati III together with an prime minister appointed by him. An advisory 5-year term Parliament or *Libandla* consists of 30-seat Senate (10 members elected by the House of Assembly and 20 appointed) and the 65-seat House of Assembly (10 appointed by the monarch and 55 elected by popular vote). Political parties are banned and balloting is done on a nonparty basis and candidates are nominated by the local council of each constituency. The last election was held in 2008. The king can veto any law passed by the legislature and at times rules by decree.

Economic policy

With a modern infrastructure, Swaziland has attained one of the largest per capita manufacturing sectors in Africa. The government aims at further development of a modern export-oriented sector producing side-by-side with a traditional subsistence sector producing for local consumption. Swaziland's economy compares favorably with most of Africa but even though the government has taken the right steps to encourage further investment it has been, in the view of some critics, slow in responding to international pressures to introduce labor reforms. Privatization of some sectors previously dominated by the state is underway. King Mswati has taken the lead in facing up to the dangers of HIV/AIDS, which has become a major threat to the nation. It recently surpassed Botswana as the couyntry woith the world's highest known rates of infection. Apart from active campaigns to promote awareness, the king has ordered his subjects to follow his own example and that of his seven wives by undergoing routine AIDS tests.

Sectors

More than 10% of the population is directly dependent on the sugar industry— the country's single largest employer and leading exporter. Other important crops are cotton, maize, tobacco, rice, vegetables, citrus fruits and pineapples. Swaziland has Africa's largest manmade forest covering 7% of the country's total land area and earning valuable foreign currency through the sale of wood and pulp. Iron ore, asbestos, industrial-quality diamonds and coal are being exploited. Until the late 1980s when diversification spawned textiles, footwear, beverages, sweets and beer processing, four-fifths of the industrial sector depended largely on the processing of agricultural and forestry products, sugar, cotton and meat. Tourism plays an important role in the economy.

Privatization

The Swazi Post and Telecommunications Corporation (SPTC) is among the key state enterprises earmarked for privatization. Joint venture partners are sought for Royal Swazi National Airways and the building of a new terminal at Matsapa International Airport.

Investment

Foreign direct investment has long been a vital element in an economy favorably disposed towards outsiders. During years of sanctions against the apartheid regime in South Africa, foreign firms found a convenient escape across the border in Swaziland. With sanctions something of the past, Swaziland has continued to lure foreign entrepreneurs, among them South African beer, and paper and pulp conglomerates. The Central Bank does not track foreign direct investment (FDI) by country but statistics indicate a preponderance of South African firms. British firms are second followed by the Taiwanese. There have also been modest inflows from the US, Denmark, the Netherlands, and Germany.

Trade

South Africa—a fellow member of the South African Customs Union—accounts for 80% of Swaziland's imports and 50% of its exports. Sugar is a major export item but there has in recent years been a strong growth in the export of electronic appliances, textiles, and processed food. It is likely that trade liberalization measures within the SACU and the Southern African Development Community (SADC) will lessen Swaziland's heavy dependence on South Africa. Customs duties from the Southern African Customs Union and remittances from Swazi workers in South Africa contribute largely to the economy.

Financial sector

There are four commercial banks monitored by the Central Bank of Swaziland. The government-owned Swaziland Development and Savings Bank was liquidated in June 1995 and is being restructured. An exchange was established in July 1990 by Sibusiso Dlamini, a former World Bank executive who became Swaziland's prime minister, to enable ordinary Swazis to become stakeholders in their economy. It remains closely tied to the South African market and operates under similar conditions.

Taxes and tariffs

Companies are taxed at a 30 percent rate on profits derived from a Swaziland source. Three provisional tax payments are made and the balance is payable or refundable at the close of the tax year. Dividends are exempt from company tax but subject to a non-resident shareholders tax of 15 percent. Sales tax at 12 to 20 percent is charged on certain transactions, imported goods, and the sale of locally-manufactured goods and services. There is a 15 percent tax levied on income from interest, royalties and management fees. (See page 138).

BUSINESS ACTIVITY

AGRICULTURE
Sugar cane, cotton, maize, tobacco, rice, citrus, pineapples, corn, sorghum, peanuts cattle, goats, sheep.
INDUSTRIES
Mining (coal and asbestos), wood pulp, sugar, soft drink concentrates.
NATURAL RESOURCES
Diamonds, asbestos.
EXPORTS
$1.4 billion (est. 2009): soft drink concentrates, sugar, wood pulp, cotton yarn, citrus and canned fruit, refrigerators.
IMPORTS
$1.5 billion (est. 2009): motor vehicles, machinery, transport equipment, foodstuffs, petroleum products, chemicals.
MAJOR TRADING PARTNERS
South Africa, EU, Mozambique, Japan, UK, Singapore, US.

Doing Business with Swaziland

▶ **Investment**

Four industrial areas have been set aside for special development. The principal estate is at Matsapha between Mbabane and Manzini, offering easy rail and road access to the ports of Durban and Port Richards in South Africa and Maputo in Mozambique. Incentives include tax allowances for new and existing businesses and, in the case of pioneering enterprises that bring unique operations and skills, a tax holiday of five years. Far from discriminating against foreigners, the government has been accused at times of favoring expatriate business over local entrepreneurs. In some instances overseas entrepreneurs have been able to avail themselves of government-financed research programs. Opportunities exist in sugar, wood pulp, timber, citrus, canned fruit and the manufacturing of textiles, electrical and electronic goods.

▶ **Trade**

Many foreign firms opt for assembly and distribution points in South Africa to sell computers and software, telecommunications equipment, and a range of consumer goods in Swaziland and other smaller markets in the SACU. The sugar, wood pulp, and fruit industries have in the past offered good markets for US sales of harvesting, loading, weeding, fertilizing, and irrigation equipment. The upgrading of the infrastructure continues to create demands for air traffic control and other airport equipment, road building machinery, and rolling stock for the railroads and trucks.

▶ **Trade finance**

Export financing is available through Eximbank. Irrevocable letters of credit are common practice.

▶ **Selling to the government**

Sometimes the government gives preferential treatment to local tenders. A large proportion of government contracts are filled by South African and other southern African companies. Privatization of the fixed line system, hydroelectric projects, low- and middle-income housing and railroad construction are projects where foreign participation is actively sought.

▶ **Exchange controls**

As a member of the Common Monetary Area, Swaziland permits repatriation of profits and dividends (after a withholding tax of 15%) upon application to the Central Bank. There are no exchange regulations affecting transactions within the CMA.

▶ **Partnerships**

US firms are noticeable in the franchising of fast food restaurants and retail stores, usually established as an extension of their South African network. In recent years, however, Swazi entrepreneurs have been insisting on cutting their own deals directly with US firms instead of going through South Africa.

▶ **Establishing a presence**

Registration of either a wholly-owned foreign enterprise or a joint venture takes approximately two weeks and is usually carried out by local attorneys and accounting firms. Business sites for industrial operations are available from the Ministry of Enterprise and Employment and the Swaziland Industrial Development Corporation (SIDC).

▶ **Financing projects**

The Overseas Private Investment Corporation, the US Trade and Development Guarantee Agency, and the Multilateral International Guarantee Agency are active in Swaziland. Project financing for infrastructure development is available through the World Bank and African Development Bank.

▶ **Labor**

An estimated 10% of the work force is employed in South Africa. Relations between organized labor and government have been strained over political issues in the past few years. After the banning of political parties, labor unions have taken on the role of activists.

▶ **Legal rights**

Although a dual legal system comprising Roman-Dutch and customary law is a source of confusion to some foreigners, it is generally administered in a fair and reasonably swift manner. There are also traditional royal courts where the king as supreme authority adjudicates in disputes. Swaziland is in the process of tightening its patent and copyright legislation. Under new legislation, the government relies on technical assistance from the African Regional Industrial Property Organization in Harare and coverage has been extended to pharmaceutical and agricultural chemical products. An updated Copyright Act is styled after that of the World Intellectual Property Rights Organization .

▶ **Business climate**

The business culture shows a strong British and South African influence.

TANZANIA

Although renowned for its political stability, Tanzania suffered severely from three decades of decay under a centralized socialist economy. It proceeded on the road to recovery with the election of a capitalist-minded democratic government in the mid-nineties. Considering the degree to which this potentially prosperous nation was allowed to slip during the socialist one-party regime of the late President Jules Nyerere, the challenge is quite formidable. Encouraging progress in infrastructure rebuilding and privatization with the help of foreign capital and expertise has, however, placed Tanzania among the bright prospects on the continent. It is Africa's fourth largest gold producer.

Country profile

The United Republic of Tanzania is a land of lakes and offshore islands. It includes the southern half of Lake Victoria, most of the eastern half of Lake Tanganyika [at depths of 1,433 m (4,700 ft) the world's deepest after Russia's Lake Baikal] and borders on Lake Malawi in the south. Its offshore areas include the densely populated spice islands of Zanzibar and Pemba and the fishing resort, Mafia Island. In the north is Africa's highest mountain, snow-capped Mount Kilimanjaro (5,896 m/19,344 ft). Rainfall inland averages 750 mm (29.5 inches). The coastal region and the islands of Zanzibar and Pemba share a humid tropical climate. The savanna plains of mainland Tanzania support a rich and diverse wildlife in at least 12 national parks, 10 game reserves and various other conservation areas. There are 120 Bantu-speaking groups, none of them large enough to dominate the rest. There are also a number of non-Bantu groups speaking Maasai, Cushitic and Khoisan languages. Influential Arab and Indian minorities reside in the coastal centers and on Zanzibar and Pemba. The 60% who do not adhere to ethnic beliefs are evenly split between Christianity and Islam. Swahili and English are official languages.

History

The discovery of the remains of the Australopithecus hominid family in Tanzania's Olduvai Gorge supports claims that this region gave birth to humanity. About 3,000 years ago Khoisan peoples entered the region, followed by caucasoid Cushites and Negroid Nilotes from the north. As long

Pres. Jakaya Kikwete
Born: Oct. 7, 1950
Since Dec. 2005

UN Photo Ryan Brown

POLITICAL
Head of State	Pres. Jakaya Kikwete
Ruling Party	CCM
Main Opposition	CHADEMA
Independence	26 April 1964
National capital	Dar es Salaam/ Dodoma[3]
Official languages	English & Swahili

PHYSICAL
Total area	365,000 sq. miles 945,000 sq. km. (2 x California)
Arable land	4.5% of land area
Coastline	885 m./1,424 km

POPULATION
Total	41.9 million
Av. yearly growth	2.0%
Urban population	25%
Life expectancy	52.5 years
Adult literacy	69.4%

ECONOMY
Currency	Shilling (TSh) (U$1=1,475.50)
GDP (real)	$18.3 billion
GDP growth rate	5.5%
GDP per capita[1]	$442
GDP (ppp)[2]	$53.1 billion
GDP per cap. (ppp)	$1,216
Inflation rate	12.1%
Exports	$2.97 billion
Imports	$5.7 billion
External debt	$6.8 billion
Unemployment	NA

1. Atlas method.
2. See page 175 for an explanation of purchasing power parity (ppp)
3. The National Assembly is in Dodoma but many government offices remain in Dar-es-Salaam.

as 2000 years ago traders from Egypt (Greeks and Romans), Axum (Ethiopians), Arabia, the Persian Gulf, India and Indonesia visited the shores and around 500 AD the Bantu-speaking peoples moved in from the great lakes. Portuguese explorers reached the coastal regions in 1500 and held some control until the 17th Century. Most strongholds established by the Portuguese fell into Arab hands by the early 19th Century. In 1840 Sayyid Said, the Imam of Muscat (Oman), took up residence on Zanzibar Island and established a sultanate that spanned over the entire coastal belt and associated islands of present-day Tanzania and Kenya. Homegrown spices, slaves, and ivory from the mainland were traded in Zanzibar, which eventually became a base from where the likes of Livingstone and Stanley explored. In 1871 American journalist Henry Stanley went from Zanzibar to look for Livingstone and found him at the slave depot of Ujiji (close to Kigoma) on Lake Tanganyika, using the memorable phrase, "Dr. Livingstone, I presume?" A German East African Protectorate formed in 1891 included Tanganyika and its coastal belt (formerly part of the Zanzibar Sultanate), as well as the kingdoms of Ruanda and Rundi. After Germany's defeat in World War I, Tanganyika was handed over to Britain and Ruanda-Urundi to Belgium. The Zanzibar Protectorate remained a separate sultanate under British rule. Julius Nyerere and his Tanganyika African National Union (TANU) gained independence for Tanganyika in 1961. Three years later it joined with Zanzibar in the United Republic of Tanzania and Zanzibar. Over the next 30 years Nyerere's socialist communes (ujaama) led to economic disaster. In 1984 he was succeeded by his vice president, Ali Hassan Mwinyi, who introduced some changes and in 1995 newly-elected President Benjamin Mkapa set Tanzania firmly on the road to reform. In December 2005 Jakaya Kikwete was elected president. He was relected in October 2010.

Government

The executive President and the Vice President of the Republic of Tanzania are directly elected by the voters for a 5-year term. Zanzibar elects its own president to handle internal affairs on the island. The unicameral 274-seat National Assembly or *Bunge* also serves for 5 years—232 members are elected by popular vote, 37 seats allocated to women nominated by the president, and five seats reserved for representatives of the Zanzibar House of Representatives.

National Assembly

In the October 2010 election Pres. Kikwete's *Chama Cha Mapinduzi* (CCM) or Revolutionary State Party captured 251 seats against 45 won by The *Chama Cha Demokrasia na Maendeleo* (Party of Democracy and Development) (CHADEMA) and 31 for the *Chama Cha Wananchi* or Civic United Front (CUF).

Economic policy

With the assistance of the IMF, economic reforms were implemented, including cuts in state expenditure, reduction of the civil service, devaluation of the currency, privatization of state corporations and removal of price controls. Growth rates rose to a healthy 6% and inflation was drastically curbed. Bilateral donors have contributed funds to assist in the refurbishing of Tanzania's dilapidated infrastructure.

Sectors

Even though topography limits cultivation of crops to 4% of the total land area, agriculture employs about 75% of the working population. The principal cash crops on the mainland are coffee and cotton, followed by cashew nuts, tobacco, tea and sisal. On the islands of Zanzibar and Pemba, cloves, copra, tobacco, vanilla, peppermint, rubber and seaweed are produced. Maize, millet, sorghum, cassava, rice and bananas are the main food crops. Fishing involves marine activity around the islands and freshwater catches in Lake Victoria and Lake Tanganyika. The cattle population of over 13 million is the fourth largest in Africa. Added recently to well-established supplies of gemstones such as diamonds, rubies, sapphires and a variety of semiprecious stones are discoveries of gold, nickel, copper and cobalt. There are also confirmed reserves of phosphates, graphite, uranium, niobium, titanium, vanadium and natural gas. With ample wildlife and spectacular beaches tourism is a major industry.

Privatization

Most of the state properties privatized are medium-sized manufacturing enterprises and trading companies. The government is, however, committed to restructuring major public utilities in telecommunications, power, water and sewerage and transport.

Investment

Since Tanzania established its Investment Promotion Center in 1990, it has approved more than a thousand projects worth some $3 billion involving investors from Britain, Germany, Italy, Thailand, India, Canada, South Africa and the US. Sectors that have attracted most of the foreign capital are manufacturing, tourism, agriculture, fisheries and mining.

Financial sector

After nearly 25 years of government monopoly, legislation was passed in August 1991 to allow private banks back into Tanzania. Banking reforms since have encouraged private sector growth and investment.

Taxes and tariffs

The corporate tax rate for non-residents is 30 percent and capital gains tax 20 to 30 percent. A value added tax (VAT) of 18 percent applies and exchange control is in effect. Taxes are levied on dividends (10%), interest (10%) and royalties (15%). (See page 138).

BUSINESS ACTIVITY

AGRICULTURE
Coffee, sisal, tea, cotton, pyrethrum (insecticide made from chrysanthemums), cashew nuts, tobacco, cloves (Zanzibar), corn, wheat, cassava (tapioca), bananas, fruit, vegetables, cattle, sheep, goats.
INDUSTRIES
Primarily agricultural processing (sugar, beer, cigarettes, sisal twine), diamond and gold mining, oil refining, shoes, cement, textiles, wood products, fertilizer, salt, tourism.
NATURAL RESOURCES
Hydroelectric potential, phosphates, iron and coal.
EXPORTS
$2.97 billion (est. 2009): gold, coffee, manufactured goods, cotton, cashew nuts, minerals, tobacco, sisal.
IMPORTS
$5.7 billion (est.2008): consumer goods, machinery and transportation equipment, industrial raw materials, crude oil.
MAJOR TRADING PARTNERS
China, India, Japan, South Africa, UAE, US, Germany, Netherlands, Kenya.

Doing Business with Tanzania

▶ Investment

The Tanzania Investment Center (TIC) seeks out, directs and assists foreign investment. In designated priority areas investors are entitled to generous incentives. Opportunities range from large infrastructural projects to smaller industrial developments. Through foreign participation, internal air charter services have increased from five to more than twenty. Road reconstruction and tourism are other areas targeted by foreign investors. Foreign firms have teamed up with locals in the mining of gemstones, gold, ferrous metals and petroleum and gas exploration.

▶ Trade

Trade opportunities exist in industrial equipment, textiles and used clothing, telecommunication equipment, aircraft and parts, computers and software, corn, and soy bean and wheat, much of the latter destined for refugees from the troubled Great Lakes area who spilled across the border into Tanzania. There are a number of bonded warehouses in Dar es Salaam which serve as transit points for shipments to Uganda, Rwanda, Burundi, the Democratic Republic of Congo, Zambia, and Malawi.

▶ Trade finance

An irrevocable letter of credit confirmed by an outside bank is normal practice. Local financing is available, usually at high interest rates, while a parastatal insurance company provides cover against loss, damage and destruction.

▶ Selling to the government

Procurement is by tender boards although in certain unspecified instances the government purchases on a direct basis. Tenders are usually issued at the beginning of each calendar year. Sometimes international donor agencies help set the requirements and the rules.

▶ Exchange controls

Although Tanzania continues to be plagued by intermittent shortages of foreign exchange, the advent of exchange bureaus has made it easier to transfer profits, dividends and other investment returns.

▶ Partnerships

Several local firms rely on franchising arrangements with US firms, an arrangement that is expected to grow in popularity as Tanzania progresses into a free enterprise environment. Privatization also presents increased opportunities for joint ventures and licensing arrangements. The use of local legal advice might be necessary to ensure that both parties in such arrangements are on the same page as misunderstandings sometimes arise due to cultural differences.

▶ Establishing a presence

In establishing a presence, foreign firms have the choice of entering into a joint venture with a local firm or creating a wholly-owned subsidiary. Both are reasonably easy to set up, especially with local legal advice and the assistance of the TIC.

▶ Financing projects

The Overseas Private Investment Corporation supports US investors. Project financing is also available from institutions such as the World Bank, Tanzania Development Finance Co. Ltd, Tanzania Investment Bank, Tanzania Venture Capital Fund, East African Development Bank, African Development Bank and the International Finance Corporation.

▶ Labor

Although labor is plentiful in Tanzania, it is largely unskilled. The few jobless but highly educated Tanzanians often lack managerial experience and need further training.

▶ Legal rights

While property rights, including intellectual property, are protected by law, enforcement might be lacking in some instances. The establishment of commercial courts is expected to expedite cases involving commercial disputes. Still, many of the antiquated provisions dating from the colonial and post-independence socialist era still need to be revised. After a long history of expropriation which culminated in 1973 with the nationalization of several European firms, Tanzania has in recent times maintained a clean record on this score. Tanzania is a member of both the International Center for Settlement of Investment Disputes and Multilateral Investment Guarantee Agency.

▶ Business Climate

Strong traces of European influences in the business community and a fluency in English might be deceptive. Americans are advised to ensure complete understanding on important issues when entering into agreements. In most cases it does help to engage a local legal adviser with past experience in international business negotiations.

TOGO

Togo's capital, Lomé, was once the hub of a regional economy but in recent years it has been seriously challenged by political and economic difficulties and developments in neighboring states. In efforts to regain its prominence, Togo is relying on a superior port and airport, high quality telecommunications, one of the most liberal trade regimes in the region, and an experienced, vibrant business community. known for its coffee, cotton and cocoa, as well as large supplies of phosphate, Togo also offers ample opportunity for entrepreneurs interested in manufacturing for export.

Country profile

The Republic of Togo extends about 540 km (335 miles) inland from a narrow, 56 km (35 mile) coastline along the Bight of Benin in the Gulf of Guinea. Sandy barrier beaches separate a chain of lagoons and lakes, including Lake Togo, from the sea. Most of the land lies below 500 m (1640 ft). The southern two-thirds of the country is drained by the Mono River, flowing from the Atakora Mountains. Vegetation varies from moist savanna, oil palm plantations and patches of dense forest in the south, to dry savanna in the northern lower rainfall areas. The Ewe, including the Mina and other related groups, account for about 45% of the total population. The Kabre (Kabye), Fulani, Mande and the Gurma make up the rest. Both Ewe and Kabre have the status of national languages and are taught in the schools. The voodoo (vodun) religion is prevalent in the coastal regions of Togo and Benin from where it spread during the slave trade era to the Caribbean and the Americas. Christians and Muslims number less than half of the population.

History

The Voltaic peoples and the Kwa were the earliest known inhabitants. Unlike its neighbors, ancient Togo was not an area of kingdoms but settled by refugees from the strong neighboring military states. When European traders visited these shores towards the end of the 15th Century the Ewe and the Mina were already entrenched on the coastlands and the Kabre established in the north. In the late 1880s, while the British and the French were focusing on other parts of the so-called Slave Coast, the Germans took the land of the Ewe and the Kabre by treaty. Togoland's borders were finally fixed in 1897. Although their rule was as authoritarian

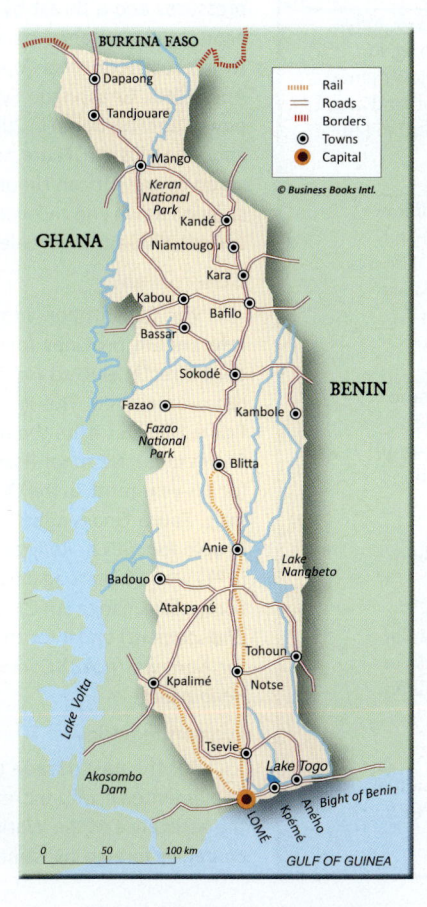

Pres. Faure Gnassingbé
Born: June 6, 1966
Since May 2005

UN Photo Rick Bajomas

POLITICAL

Head/State	Pres. Faure Gnassingbé
Ruling Party	RPT
Main Opposition	UFC
Independence	27 April 1960
National capital	Lomé
Official languages	French

PHYSICAL

Total area	22,000 sq. miles 57,000 sq. km. (± West Virginia)
Arable land	46% of land area
Coastline	35 miles/56 km

POPULATION

Total	6.6 million
Av. yearly growth	2.8%
Urban population	42%
Life expectancy	62.25 years
Adult literacy	60.9%

ECONOMY

Currency	CFA franc (CFAF) (US$1:495.40)
GDP (real)	$2.5 billion
GDP growth rate	2.2%
GDP per capita[1]	$373
GDP (ppp)[2]	$6 billion
GDP per cap. (ppp)	$917
Inflation rate	1.9%
Exports	$709 million
Imports	$1.2 billion
External debt	$1.5 billion
Unemployment	NA

1. Atlas method.
2. See page 175 for an explanation of purchasing power parity (ppp).

as that of other colonial governments, Germany turned Togoland into a model colony with good roads and railways and a well-equipped harbor at Lomé. After Germany's defeat in World War I, Togo was split into two parts. The western section was placed under British administration and the larger eastern part given to the French. A UN referendum in the mid-forties in both territories—largely boycotted by the Ewe—decided against reunification and when the Gold Coast became the independent state of Ghana in March 1957 it included British Togoland. French Togoland became the independent Republic of Togo in 1960. In 1967 the government led by the Polish-descended Nicolas Grunitzky was overthrown in a bloodless coup by Kabre army colonel Etienne Eyadema. After interim rule by a newly constituted National Reconciliation Committee, Eyadema took over as President. Gnassingbé Eyadema's autocratic rule was initially marked by rapid economic growth but turned sour in the eighties. Internal pressures and a threat by France to withhold economic assistance persuaded Gnassingbé to lift restrictions on opposition parties in April 1991. Gnassingbé Eyadema remained in power until his death in 2005 when Parliament appointed his son, Faure, to succeed him. Pressured by the African Union, Faure Gnassingbé stepped down and called and election. He won in April 2005 and was reelected in March 2010.

Government

The Constitution adopted after the 1992 referendum provides for an executive President directly elected for a term of five years, renewable once. The President appoints the Prime Minister from the majority party in the 81-member National Assembly, also elected for a 5-year term. In the October 2007 election Pres. Faure Gnassingbé's *Rassemblement du Peuple Togolais or Rally of the Togolese People* (RPT) won 50 seats against 27 for the Union of Forces for Change (UFC) *(Union des Forces du Changement)* and 4 for the Action Committee for Renewal *(CAR)(Comité d'Action pour la Renouveau)*.

Economic policy

For the past decade the government has implemented economic reform measures with the assistance of the World Bank and IMF, encouraging foreign investment and trying to balance its budget. Current structural adjustment programs stress privatization and liquidation of state-owned enterprises, withdrawal of the government from commodity marketing and agricultural inputs, the streamlining of government operations, and promotion of both administrative and judicial transparency.

Sectors

Agriculture employs about 80% of the working population and contributes 35% of the GDP. The main export crop is cotton, followed by coffee, cocoa, palm kernels and shea nuts. The three Cs—cocoa, coffee and cotton—currently accounts for 40% of the country's export earnings. Sugar cane and groundnuts are also grown. The country is largely self-sufficient with food crops such as rice, sorghum, millet, yams, cassava, vegetables and tropical fruit but basic foodstuffs are still imported. Livestock is important in the northern savanna regions. There is small-scale marine fishing and limited forestry. Mining activity concentrates on phosphates which account for more than a third of export earnings. Limestone, marble and salt are extracted and there are known reserves of iron ore, bauxite, dolomite and chromite. Manufacturing involves beverages, footwear, textiles and plastics.

Privatization

The government has been working with the World Bank, setting as future benchmarks the privatization of phosphate mining and telecommunications. The ginning of cotton has already been opened to private firms competing with SOTOCO, a restructured parastatal, and the agricultural commodity marketing monopoly was liquidated. Some 20 private firms have been granted marketing licenses for coffee and cocoa.

Investment

In recent years foreign firms have purchased from the government an oil refinery, dairy, cement plant, brewery, spaghetti factory, flour mill, and an edible oil refinery. Toward the end of 1999 there were more than 30 firms from the US, Denmark, Germany, Norway, and Hong Kong active in Togo's EPZs, manufacturing, assembling and distributing cement, textiles, leather goods, automobiles, and petroleum products.

Trade

Togo's major agricultural export crops are coffee, cocoa, and cotton but phosphates tops the list in terms of total foreign exchange earnings. The well-established modern harbor of Lomé serves as a convenient entry point for trade with the surrounding region.

Financial sector

Over the years Togo developed an efficient, modern banking system to support its role as regional trading center. After the economic and political crisis years a review of the financial sector—undertaken together with the World Bank—has led to restructuring and recapitalization. However, Togo still has some way to go before it regains its reputation or position as a regional banking center. All major banks maintain correspondent relationships with US banks.

Taxes and tariffs

Good progress was made towards simplifying and streamlining the tax system. The corporate tax rate for non-residents is 15 to 30 percent. There is no capital gains tax. A value added tax (VAT) of 18 percent applies and exchange control is in effect. Taxes are levied on dividends (20%), interest (15%) and royalties (15%). (See page 138).

BUSINESS ACTIVITY

AGRICULTURE
Coffee, cocoa, cotton, yams, cassava (tapioca), corn, beans, rice, millet, sorghum, livestock, fish.

INDUSTRIES
Phosphate mining, agricultural processing, cement, handicrafts, textiles, beverages.

NATURAL RESOURCES
Marble, phosphate, limestone.

EXPORTS
$709 million (est. 2009): cotton, phosphates, coffee, cocoa, re-exports.

IMPORTS
$1.2 billion (est. 2009): machinery and equipment, consumer goods, petroleum products.

MAJOR TRADING PARTNERS
Burkina Faso, Benin, Ghana, China, Mali, India, Netherlands, France, Thailand, Belgium, Brazil.

Doing Business with Togo

▶ Investment

The recently resumed privatization process is expected to attract foreign direct investment in energy, telecommunications, banking, and hotels. Togo has distinguished itself throughout the 1980s as an investor-friendly, western-oriented country but foreign interest waned during the period of political unrest. The government is trying to restore the investment levels of the past in areas such as agriculture, manufacturing, mining, and tourism. Applications are evaluated by the Planning Ministry in consultation with the National Investment Commission, which sets conditions once approved. The process takes about a month. Investors can obtain EPZ status in two designated zones entitling them to a less restrictive labor code, foreign currency-denominated accounts and tax advantages.

▶ Trade

Togo offers a limited domestic market but a good potential in its traditional role as a transshipment point to neighboring countries. Imports include used clothing and shoes, computer equipment, cosmetic products, and wheat and meat, but as privatization proceeds the need for telecommunications and power generation equipment is expected to grow. Togo operates a free port.

▶ Trade finance

Normally irrevocable letters of credit are used. Eximbank facilitates trade. Some of the larger trade prospects involve development projects funded by the World Bank, the West African Development Bank, and the African Development Bank.

▶ Selling to the government

Plans to develop self-reliance in power generation and improve telecommunication will require large-scale purchases of services and equipment. Tenders will most likely be handled by the international and individual country donor agencies.

▶ Exchange controls

There are no restrictions on the transfer of funds to other West African franc zone countries or to France but the transfer of funds elsewhere requires Finance Ministry approval.

▶ Partnerships

Even though Togolese business people eagerly pursue partnerships with American and other foreign firms, most of them offer local expertise and management instead of funding. The government encourages joint ventures. Although a few US firms, including Coca-Cola, rely on licensing agreements, franchising is limited.

▶ Establishing a presence

Establishing an office in Togo is in theory relatively simple, but administrative obstacles and delays are common. If there are expatriate managers they must obtain residence permits. The authorization to open an office comes from the Ministry of Commerce. Companies also need to register with the Commercial Court and the Togolese Chamber of Commerce at a minimal fee. The final step is the purchasing of an importer's card from the Ministry of Commerce, at about $150 per year.

▶ Financing projects

Multilateral institutions involved in funding projects in Togo include the African Development Bank, the ECOWAS fund, the West African Development Bank, and the World Bank.

▶ Labor

There is a large pool of qualified university graduates and unskilled workers but a shortage of workers with technical skills and practical experience. Separate wage scales are negotiated by employers, workers, and the government for industry, construction, public works, commerce, and banking. Although several labor confederations have combined forces to negotiate more effectively with the government and business, they have had limited impact.

▶ Legal rights

The investment code provides for the resolution of investment disputes involving foreigners under bilateral agreements with various governments or prearranged conciliation and arbitration procedures between the interested parties. Togo is a member of the International Center for the Settlement of Investment Disputes. Lack of transparency and predictability of the judiciary in the enforcement of property rights is being addressed in conjunction with the World Bank.

▶ Business Climate

French is the language of business and so is the culture itself. While foreigners without a working knowledge of French might have problems conversing, deal-making should not be a problem for those who have operated in the European market. There is no shortage of professional interpreters.

TUNISIA

Tunisia—Africa's northernmost country—has enjoyed modernization, stability and relative prosperity over a long period and is arguably the most cohesive and progressive society in the Maghreb region. Women have been liberated in what is the oldest Muslim stronghold on the continent. Metro railways run across the sites of ancient cities. Its former socialist government spawned a market-oriented economy. This middle-income country offers a good potential for foreign entrepreneurs, not only as a market in itself but to serve as a convenient springboard to the EU with which Tunisia has a free trade agreement.

Country profile

The Republic of Tunisia, on the western side of the great Gulf of Sirte, is the smallest country in North Africa with the largest proportion of arable land. Its northern portion enjoys a Mediterranean climate with winter rainfall varying from at least 400 to over 1,000 mm (16 to 39 inches). The country's only perennial river is the Medjerda, opening into wide coastal plains around the city of Tunis. Apart from a small Berber presence, Tunisians are largely descendants of migrants who in Carthaginian times made this crossroads region their home. Their culture is predominantly Arab and the Muslim faith prevails. French is widely spoken and taught in schools.

History

More than 3,000 years ago the Phoenicians established trading posts in the region and, according to legend, in 814 BC a group of exiles under the leadership of Princess Dido fled from Tyre (in present-day Lebanon) and founded Carthage (the New City). Carthaginian colonizers in Sicily and Spain encountered Roman opposition and became embroiled in a protracted struggle known as the Punic Wars which lasted from 264 until 146 BC when Carthage was finally defeated and razed. The Romans called their conquered territory Africa, a name probably derived from Afrig (Arab: Ifriqiya), the name also given to the Berber group living to south of Carthage. Carthage was rebuilt by Julius Caesar and became an important center for Christianity in the Roman empire. Except for an interval of Vandal rule from 439-533, Carthage remained part of the Roman Empire until 669 when the Arabs invaded. After the Arabs took control of the region which they

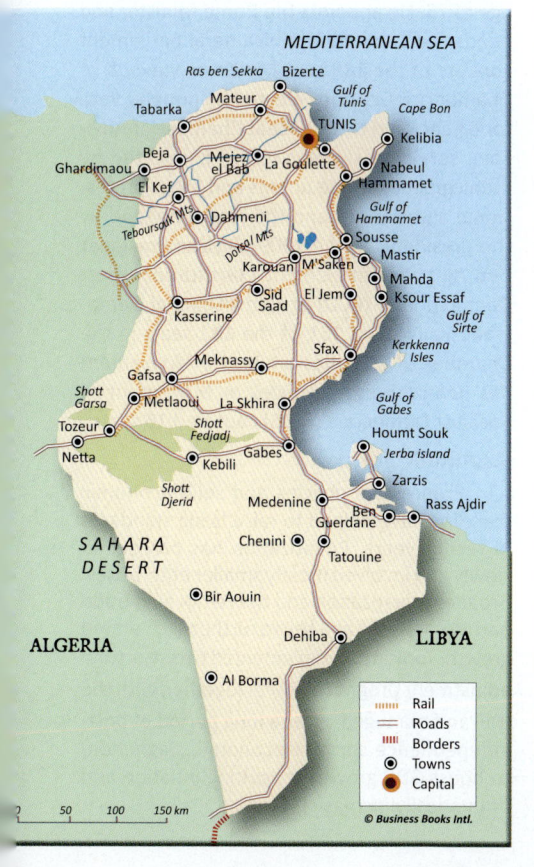

365

Pres. Zine El Abidine Ben Ali
Born: Sept. 3, 1936
Since Nov. 1989

UN Photo Mark Garten

POLITICAL	
Head of State	Pres. Zine El Abidine Ben Ali
Prime Minister	Mohamed Ghannouchi (1999)
Ruling Party	RCD
Main Opposition	MDS
Independence	20 March 1956
National capital	Tunis
Official languages	Arabic

PHYSICAL	
Total area	63,000 sq. miles
	164,000 sq. km.
	(± Georgia)
Arable land	18% of land area
Coastline	713 miles/1,148 km

POPULATION	
Total	10.6 million
Av. yearly growth	0.9%
Urban population	67%
Life expectancy	75.99 years
Adult literacy	74.3%

ECONOMY	
Currency	Tunisian dinar (TD) (U$1=1.44)
GDP (real)	$42.5 billion
GDP growth rate	3.1%
GDP per capita[1]	$4,067
GDP (ppp)[2]	$89 billion
GDP per cap.(ppp)	$8,666
Inflation rate	3.5%
Exports	$14.4 billion
Imports	$19.0 billion
External debt	$20.6 billion
Unemployment	14.7%

1. Atlas method.
2. See page 175 for an explanation of purchasing power parity (ppp).

called the Maghreb, they virtually annihilated Carthage and founded the new city of Tunis. In Tunisia, as elsewhere in the Mahgreb region, Berbers assimilated with the Arab rulers and adopted their faith. Tunisia became part of the Ottoman Empire in 1570. France invaded Tunisia in 1881 and ruled it as a protectorate until 1956 when a freedom movement under Habib Bourguiba finally forced it to grant independence. Bourguiba stayed in office until the age of 84 in 1989 when he was declared physically and mentally unfit by a panel of medical doctors. The life-presidency was abolished and an age limit of 70 years introduced. He was succeeded as president by Zine El Abidine Ben Ali in 1989. Ben Ali was reelected in 2004 and again in Octoiber 2009. After a referendum held in 2002 the presidential three term limit was scrapped and the age limit raised to 75 to enable Ben Ali to stay in power.

Government

The executive president is elected for 5-year terms and remains in power up to the age of 75. He appoints the Prime Minister and heads the Cabinet. The bicameral parliament consists of the 189-seat *Maijlis al-Nuwaab* or Chamber of Deputies elected by popular vote for 5 years and the 126-seat Chamber of Advisors, serving a six year term—85 elected by municipalities, trade unions and other professional associations and the rest appointed by the president. In the 2009 election President Ben Ali's *Rassemblement Constitutionelle et Démocratique* (RCD) or Constitutional Democratic Rally won 161 of the 182 seats in the Chamber of Deputies while the *Mouvement des démocrates socialistes o*r Movement of Socialist Democrats (MDS) captured 16 seats.

Economic policy

Progressive policies and solid economic planning have helped to raise living standards in recent years. Privatization has proceeded slowly and involved mostly smaller enterprises. Broader privatization and the removal of trade barriers are seen as a key to further accelerated growth. Tunisia has implemented two structural adjustment programs (SAPs) together, with the IMF and managed, after a long period of post-independence socialist economic stagnation, to boost GDP growth to, cutting inflation and dramatically increase exports.

Sectors

Tunisia has a diverse economy. Despite its modest natural resources, it has made impressive economic strides. Agriculture, fishing and forestry provide employment to a third of the workforce. One-third of the cultivated land is under olive trees, making Tunisia one of the largest producers and exporters of olive oil in the world. Tunisia is, after Morocco, the largest producer of phosphates in North Africa but the quality of the rock is poor and extraction is largely geared towards the production of fertilizer. Tunisia is one Africa's smaller oil producers, managing a modest export after supplying its domestic needs. The recent discovery of the Miskar gasfield in the Gulf of Gabes will make the country self-sufficient in natural gas and a significant exporter. Iron ore, zinc, lead, aluminium fluoride and salt are mined. Textiles and leather goods account for about 85% of manufactured exports, with mechanical and electrical goods and chemicals growing industries. Some four million tourists (mainly from Germany and other European countries) visit Tunisia each year.

Privatization

Mindful of labor opposition, the government has been moving slowly on privatization. A 20% share was sold in Tunis Air and two cement plants and several semi-public firms were privatized through offerings on the stock exchange and direct sales. The tender for Tunisia's first private build-own-operate (BOO) power generation was awarded to an American-led consortium.

Investment

As much as 75% of foreign direct investment (FDI) has been in the energy sector, largely in petroleum exploration and development. There is, however, a growing interest in manufacturing and official statistics list some 1,600 companies fully or partially owned by foreigners. France is the largest single source of foreign investment, followed by Italy, Germany, Belgium, Switzerland and the United Kingdom. The US has been the third-largest source of FDI.

Trade

Textiles and tourism are major foreign currency earners, followed by hydrocarbons, agricultural products, phosphates and chemicals. The European Union represents 80% of total trade. In recent years Tunisia hads become one of Africa's prime tourist countries.

Financial sector

The banking system is a mixture of private and state-owned institutions comprising 13 commercial banks, 8 development banks, one savings bank, 5 portfolio management institutions, 8 leasing companies, 8 offshore banks, and 2 merchant banks. The government is still a controlling shareholder in most of these banks which are regulated by the Central Bank of Tunisia. The financial markets, consisting of a semi-privatized stock exchange and a number of bond and stock funds, showed impressive growth. To encourage firms to list on the exchange, the government introduced tax incentives, reducing the corporate tax rate from 35 to 20 percent for companies with at least 30% of their shares traded on the exchange.

Taxes and tariffs

Tunisia forms a free trade area with the EU with few protective barriers. The first phase of tariff reduction and elimination of quantitative import restrictions envisaged in the EU agreement was completed.

BUSINESS ACTIVITY

AGRICULTURE
Olives, dates, oranges, almonds, grain, sugar beets, grapes, poultry, beef, dairy products.
INDUSTRIES
Petroleum, mining (particularly phosphate and iron ore), tourism, textiles, footwear, food, beverages.
NATURAL RESOURCES
Petroleum, phosphate, iron ore.
EXPORTS
$14.4 billion (est. 2009): hydrocarbons, textiles, agricultural products, phosphates, chemicals, mechanical goods.
IMPORTS
$29 billion (est. 2009): machinery, hydrocarbons, food, consumer goods, textiles.
MAJOR TRADING PARTNERS
France, Italy, Germany, Spain, Libya.

Doing Business with Tunisia

▶ Investment
A broad range of incentives for foreign investors includes tax relief, reduced tariffs on imported capital goods, and depreciation schedules for production equipment. Companies exporting at least 80% of their production enjoy a ten-year tax holiday. Additional incentives are available to attract investment in designated depressed areas and in sectors such as health, education, training, transportation, environmental protection, waste treatment, and research and development in technological fields. The best investment opportunities are in the infrastructure improvement (hydrocarbons, power generation, transportation, telecommunications) or in offshore, export-oriented, labor-intensive industries such as textiles and light manufacturing. Tunisia has two free trade zones—one at Bizerte and the other at Zarzis—offering tax and customs duty exemptions to manufacturers.

▶ Trade
The best prospects for exporters are in agricultural products such as wheat, barley, livestock and meat, agricultural equipment, and luxury and durable goods. It is customary to rely on local agents and distributors. Exclusive distribution contracts are, however, forbidden by law.

▶ Trade finance
Most transactions are by irrevocable letters of credit. Reputable importers usually have no problem in obtaining the necessary financing from local bank. For US exporters Eximbank financing and insurance are available.

▶ Selling to the government
Government purchases are usually by tender published in the local media and sometimes in selected foreign journals. Factors that might influence the selection of bids are their contribution to the local economy and employment, the level of transfer of skills or technology, and impact on the balance of trade. US bidders have typically been stronger on price and technology while European firms have offered better financing packages and links to the local economy. Depending on the size and complexity of the project, the decision-making procedure can take several months. Decisions on major projects might even require the approval of the Chamber of Deputies, which goes into session for only about half of the year. Performance bonds of between one and ten percent are common on government contracts.

▶ Exchange controls
Central bank authorization is needed for some foreign exchange transactions.

▶ Partnerships
Even though there are examples of successful US joint ventures, many businesses are family-owned and often resist outside management. The government has blocked several proposed partnerships in department stores and restaurants.

▶ Establishing a presence
Registering an office of a foreign company in Tunisia is relatively simple. The Foreign Investment Promotion Agency (FIPA) offers a one-stop shop to investors and it generally takes about two weeks to complete the process. When it involves fisheries, tourism, transportation, communications, and other specified sectors it might take longer as government approval is needed. Foreign investors are permitted to purchase up to 49% of the shares in resident firms.

▶ Financing projects
OPIC provides political risk insurance and other services while the World Bank and African Development Bank support projects relating to the environment, privatization, road construction, dams and irrigation.

▶ Labor
About 15% of the workforce belongs to the national labor confederation, the General Union of Tunisian Workers (UGTT). Working conditions are established through triennial collective bargaining agreements between the UGTT and the National Employers Association (UTICA). Tunisian law limits the number of expatriate employees per company.

▶ Legal rights
To ensure enforcement, foreign firms must register their trademarks and industrial designs with the Tunisian Institute for Standardization and Intellectual Property (INNORPI). Tunisia is a member of the World Intellectual Property Organization, and has signed the agreement on the protection of patents and trademarks.

▶ Business climate
Tunisia is a relatively open society that sees itself as a bridge between the European and Arab worlds. Although the official language is Arabic, French is widely spoken.

UGANDA

The Ugandan government has shown a singular commitment to economic reform and a determination to attract foreign investors and traders through privatization and other incentives. It has substantial natural resources including copper and cobalt. It's Soil is fertile and rainfall regular. Agriculture is the most important sector and employs over 80% of the workforce. Coffee accounts for the bulk of Uganda's export revenues. Early in 2009 an oil exploration company announced oil discoveries in the Lake Albert region that, it claims, could be the largest on shore discovery in Sub-Saharan Africa.

Country profile

The Republic of Uganda is situated north of Lake Victoria and consists largely of prime agricultural land. The equator cuts across the northern shores of this lake. The Victoria Nile links Lake Victoria with Lake Kyoga and Lake Albert. Much of the country is covered by moist woodland savanna, with large tracts of equatorial forest. There are 10 national parks and a number of other game and forest reserves. The largest population groups are of Nilotic origin. The Bantu-speaking people account for 20%. English is the official language, but, as elsewhere in Eastern Africa, Swahili is the lingua franca. Some 75% of the population are Christians, with Roman Catholics in the majority. Many people, mostly in the north, have ethnic beliefs.

History

About 500 BC Bantu-speaking peoples migrated to the area now known as Uganda. By the 14th Century there were three dominant kingdoms in the region—the Buganda, Bunyoro and Ankole. In the 19th Century explorers such as Richard Burton and Robert Livingstone found Uganda settled by the Nilotic peoples in the north and Bantu in the south, including the Baganda, from whom the country derived its name. In the 1890s Britain in a deal with Germany took possession of Uganda and Kenya while Germany apportioned Tanganyika (Tanzania) for itself. Independence from Britain in 1962 was followed by several decades of turmoil. Milton Obote seized power with the help of the second-in-command of the army, Colonel Idi Amin, and took Uganda down the road of nationalization before he was ousted in

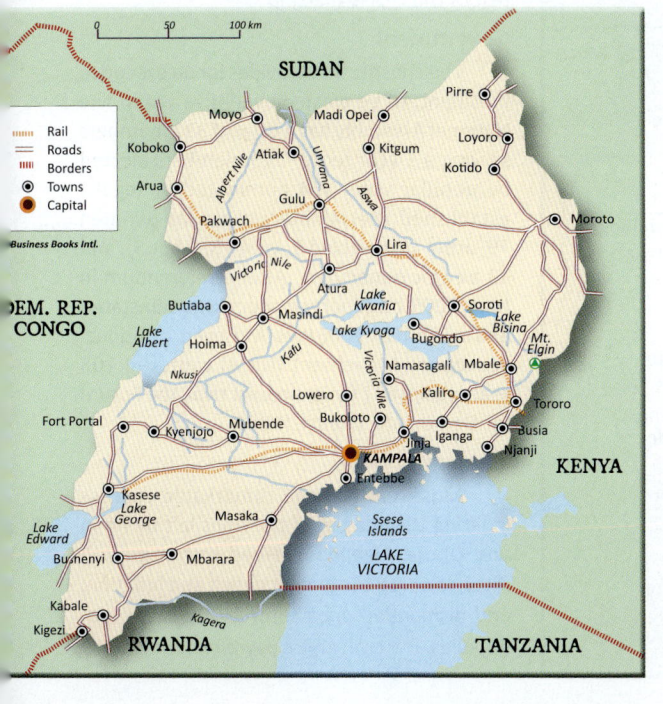

369

Pres. Yoweri
Kaguta Museveni
Born: 1944
Since Jan. 1986

UN Photo Eskinder Debebe

POLITICAL
Head of State	Pres. Yoweri Kaguta Museveni
Ruling Party	NRM
Main Opposition	FDC
Independence	9 October 1962
National capital	Kampala
Official language	English

PHYSICAL
Total area	93,000 sq. miles
	241,000 sq. km.
	(± Oregon)
Arable land	26% of land area
Coastline	Landlocked

POPULATION
Total	33.4 million
Av. yearly growth	3.6%
Urban population	13%
Life expectancy	52.98 years
Adult literacy	66.8%

ECONOMY
Currency	Ugandan shilling (Ush)(US$=2,308)
GDP (real)	$16.6 billion
GDP growth rate	7.0%
GDP per capita[1]	$521
GDP (ppp)[2]	$46.6 billion
GDP per cap. (ppp)	$1,426
Inflation rate	11.1%
Exports	$3.7 billion
Imports	$4.2 billion
External debt	$1.8 billion
Unemployment	NA

1. Atlas method.
2. See page 175 for an explanation of purchasing power parity (ppp).

1971 by Amin. Considered by many as one of Africa's most brutal leaders ever, Amin expelled the large Asian (mainly Indian) community and carried out massive purges resulting in the death of thousands. After exiled Ugandans with the help of neighboring Tanzania toppled Amin, Obote bounced back by winning a presidential election in 1980. This time he pursued liberal IMF-style economic policies to obtain aid from western donors and the economy perked up slightly until another coup in 1985 led to further instability. In 1986 a rebel army led by Yoweri Museveni, leader of the National Resistance Movement (NRM), took control. President. Museveni banned rallies by other political groups and invited his opponents to join the NRM. He was reelected for the third time in 2006. The Lord's Resistance Army has been engaged in an armed rebellion against the Ugandan government in one of Africa's longest-running conflicts. Led by Joseph Kony, who proclaims himself a spirit medium who wishes to establish a state based on his unique interpretation of the Acholi religious syncretism and Biblical millenarianism, the LRA has been accused of widespread human rights violations. While efforts are ongoing to broker a ceasefire agreement with the rebels the International Criminal Court has issued warrants for the arrest of the LRA leadership.

Government

The constitution provides for an executive President, to be elected every five years. The National Assembly has a total of 332 members serving a 5-year term—215 members elected by popular vote, 104 nominated by legally established special interest groups [women 79, army 10, disabled 5, youth 5, labor 5], and 13 *ex officio* members. After a referendum in June 2005 multiparty politics was reinstated and in February 2006 Pres. Museveni's National Resistance Movement (NRM) captured 205 seats against 37 for its nearest rival, the Forum for Democratic Change (FDC).

Economic policy

Museveni has had remarkable success in lifting Uganda out of the ruins left by Amin and Obote. Uganda attained higher growth rates, lowered the budget deficit and inflation, and dismantled price controls and state monopolies. The civil service payroll was drastically reduced. Growth in manufacturing, mining, transport, communications, and construction led to a doubling of the size of the economy since the late eighties. Improved economic conditions and government assurances led to the return of a number of Indian-Ugandan entrepreneurs who were exiled during the Amin and Obote regimes. In 2000 Uganda qualified for enhanced Highly Indebted Poor Countries (HIPC) and Paris Club debt relief worth $1.5 billion. Uganda been a leader among African nations in the fight against HIV/AIDS, reducing the rate of new infections.

Sectors

Agriculture and fishing are the mainstay of the economy, employing more than 80% of the working population. The country has long been famous for its robusta coffee, grown around Mount Elgon and in the foothills of the Ruwenzori Mountains. Other cash crops are cotton, tea, tobacco and sugar cane. Commercial cattle and dairy farming is undertaken in the southwest. Freshwater fish from the country's many lakes meets a high proportion of the population's protein needs and is also exported. Mining has been neglected for some time, but a revival is underway. There are extensive copper and iron ore reserves and hitherto less viable deposits of tungsten, tin, phosphates, columbo-tantalite, beryl, bismuth and limestone. Manufacturing revolves largely around food processing and import-substituting items such as textiles, cement, soap, plastics and metal products. Tourism is a growth industry. In January 2009 Heritage Oil announced a large oil discoveryin the Lake Albert region, which, it claimed could be the largest onshore discovery in sub-Saharan Africa. It was unclear how much of this would be recoverable.

Privatization

The government has committed itself to privatization but the program has been marred by several failed deals, a lack of transparency, and rampant asset stripping. Latest to be privatized is the Uganda Electricity Board (UEB).

Trade

Agricultural production, with coffee as a major component, represents the major portion of Uganda's export earnings. Other agricultural exports include flowers, vanilla, silk, cotton, tobacco and tea.

Investment

Most investors are companies and individuals with experience in Africa. They include British and Indian firms, as well as growing numbers of Kenyan and South African entities. There has been significant foreign investment in the past two years in the beverage industry by Coca-Cola, SA Breweries and Guinness.

Financial sector

The Bank of Uganda (BOU) monitors 18 commercial banks and two development banks. A stock exchange was established on 6 June 1997 by the Uganda Securities Exchange (USE) Ltd.—a company formed by licensed broker/dealers and investment advisers.

Taxes & Tariffs

Businesses with annual revenues of more than $35,000 are subject to a 18% value added tax (VAT). All 30% import duties have been reduced to 15%. Excise surcharges are set at 10%. The corporate tax rate for non-residents is 30 percent and capital gains tax at the same rate. There is no exchange control in effect. Taxes at a rate of 15 percent are levied on dividends, interest income and royalties. (See page 138).

BUSINESS ACTIVITY

AGRICULTURE
Coffee, tea, cotton, tobacco, cassava (tapioca), potatoes, corn, millet, pulses, beef, goat meat, milk, poultry.

INDUSTRIES
Sugar, brewing, tobacco, cotton, textiles, cement.

NATURAL RESOURCES
Copper, gold, cobalt, limestone, salt.

EXPORTS
$3.7 billion (est. 2009): coffee, gold, fish and fish products, cotton, tea, corn.

IMPORTS
$4.2 billion (est.2009): transportation equipment, petroleum, medical supplies, iron and steel.

MAJOR TRADING PARTNERS
Kenya, Belgium, South Africa, India, China, Germany, US, France, Rwanda, Netherlands, Italy, UAE, Japan.

Doing Business with Uganda

▶ Investment
Food processing, livestock, tourism, infrastructure, and transportation, import substitution, light manufacturing, mining, and telecommunications offer prospects for foreign investment. In an effort to revive mining, the government is encouraging foreigners to exploit deposits of copper, cobalt, gold, tin, tungsten, and oil. Accelerated depreciation incentives are offered. Acquisition, takeovers and greenfield investments are permitted.

▶ Trade
A small but growing middle class offers a ready market for quality consumer goods but new products often have to compete with used goods, especially in automobiles and clothing. The Uganda Manufacturers Association (UMA) and the Ugandan National Chamber of Commerce and Industry offer assistance to local agents and distributors.

▶ Trade finance
Eximbank provides short- to medium-term loans for US exporters. The Bank of Uganda supports export credit guarantees by commercial banks. Letters of credit and other standard instruments are also used. Sellers are advised to collect as much as possible of the price in cash and to collateralize all loans in cases where buyers are unknown.

▶ Selling to the government
The Central Tender Board controls tenders and advertises in the newspapers or sends invitations to organizations in Kampala. SWIPCO, a US-based company, is responsible for auditing all procurement of $50,000 and above by Ugandan ministries and parastatals.

▶ Foreign exchange
Foreign exchange, based on a market-determined exchange rate, can be freely purchased. The Investment Code of 1991 allows foreign exchange remittances with respect to transfer of foreign technologies. There are no foreign exchange controls affecting legitimate trade.

▶ Partnership
There are no restrictions on foreign ventures with local investors.

▶ Establishing a presence
The Uganda Investment Authority (UIA) offers advice on registry, licensing, immigration, tax, and customs matters, and sublicenses and permits. Foreign investors may form wholly-owned companies or joint ventures with local investors. There is no minimum equity capital requirement for companies. A branch of a foreign company may operate in Uganda if it registers with the Registrar of Companies and delivers to the Registrar a certified copy of the Memorandum and Articles of Association.

▶ Project financing
Most development projects are funded by outside donors who often give preference to purchases from companies based in their own country. In March 1998, Uganda signed an agreement allowing OPIC to broaden the scope of its activities. Local banks are generally weak and hesitant lenders.

▶ Labor
The private sector resorts to on-the-job training of unskilled and semiskilled workers to compensate for a shortage of skilled workers. Unions are relatively weak and labor unrest is rare. Employers must contribute an amount equal to 10% of the employee's gross salary to the National Social Security Fund (NSSF). Monthly salaries range from $60 to $140 for unskilled labor, $160 to $270 for skilled labor, and $350 to $670 for a junior manager.

▶ Legal rights
The law allows expropriation for public purposes through a transparent process and investors are guaranteed fair market value compensation within 12 months. The leadership has repeatedly reaffirmed Uganda's resolve that private property will never again be arbitrarily expropriated as it was in the dreaded Amin era. Instead, Uganda is in the process of returning land expropriated at the time, mostly from the Indian population. Commercial laws are based on the British mode. The Registrar of Patents awards patents for an initial period of 15 years, with a possible five-year extension. Uganda is a member of the International Center for the Settlement of Investment Disputes and opened a commercial court in August 1996.

▶ Business climate
Business decisions are often made by consensus. Initial business meetings are focused more on people's backgrounds and families than the business on hand. It is not uncommon for Ugandans to arrive late and for meetings to run over their scheduled time. Most business is conducted in English.

ZAMBIA

Transition to multiparty democracy in the early nineties enabled landlocked Zambia to change its fortunes through drastic economic reforms and a privatization program. Despite depressed mineral prices inhibiting growth, liberalization and diversification of its economy helped set Zambia on a firm road to recovery. It remains largely dependent on copper, cobalt, zinc and lead. Privatization of state-owned mines has increased foreign holdings and productivity and stimulated overseas interest in a variety of other sectors. Zambia continues to implement internationally endorsed poverty reduction programs.

Country profile

The landlocked Republic of Zambia shares boundaries with eight other countries. It is part of the high African plateau averaging more than 1,000 m (3,280 ft) and rising towards the northeastern Muchinga Mountains. Most of the country consists of savanna terrain. The Bantu-speaking population comprises more than 70 ethnic groups with the Bemba dominant in the northeastern Copperbelt region, the Nyanja in the east and around Lusaka, the Tonga in the south and the Lozi in the west. English is the official language. About two-thirds of the people are Christians and the rest profess traditional ethnic beliefs.

History

Paleontologists claim that humans inhabited the region between one and two million years ago. During the 15th Century the Luba, Lunda (Kazembe), Bemba (Chitimukulu) and Lozi (Barotse) kingdoms flourished in the region stretching from Shaba (in Congo Kinshasa) to Zambia. They were joined in 1840 by fugitives from upheavals in the Zulu kingdom in South Africa. By the 1880s, driven by his dream of a British Empire from the Cape to Cairo, Cecil John Rhodes and his British South Africa Company (BSA) claimed the region. In 1924 Northern Rhodesia, as it was known, was transferred to the British government and in the late 1920s the discovery of vast copper reserves lured mining moguls from Britain, South Africa and America and thousands of white settlers. In 1953 Northern Rhodesia (over strong objections from its inhabitants) was linked together with Nyasaland (later Malawi) and Southern Rhodesia in a white-ruled Federation of Rhodesia and Nyasaland. Agitation by Northern Rhodesia's Kenneth Kaunda and his United

Pres. Rupiah Bwezani Banda
Born: 3 Sept. 1948
Since August 2008

UN Photo: Erin Siegal

POLITICAL
Head/State	Pres. Rupiah Banda
Ruling Party	MMD
Main Opposition	PF
Independence	24 October 1964
National capital	Lusaka
Official languages	English

PHYSICAL
Total area	291,000 sq. miles 753,000 sq. km. (± Texas)
Arable land	7% of land area
Coastline	Landlocked

POPULATION
Total	13.5 million
Av. yearly growth	3.12%
Urban population	35%
Life expectancy	52.0 years
Adult literacy	80.6%

ECONOMY
Currency	Kwacha (ZK) (US$1=4,765.00)
GDP (real)	$14.3 billion
GDP growth rate	6.1%
GDP per capita[1]	$1,178
GDP (ppp)[2]	$19.6 billion
GDP per cap. (ppp)	$1,516
Inflation rate	13.4%
Exports	$4.4 billion
Imports	$1 billion
External debt	$3.3 billion
Unemployment	50%

1. Atlas method.
2. See page 175 for an explanation of purchasing power parity (ppp).

National Independence Party (UNIP) and Dr Hastings Banda of Nyasaland led to the dissolution of the Federation in 1963. In October 1964 President Kaunda led Zambia to independence. He consolidated his rule by banning the opposition and nationalizing the copper mines and other assets. In 1991, the relaxation of the ban propelled trade union leader and head of the Movement for Multiparty Democracy (MMD), Frederick Chiluba, to victory against Kaunda at the polls. He restored democracy and instituted drastic economic reforms. Chiluba was reelected in November 1996 and after completion of his second five year term stepped down. He was succeeded after the 2001 presidential election by Levy Mwanawasa of the MMD. In the September 2006 election Mwanawasa was reelected but died of a stroke in August 2008. His deputy, Rupiah Banda, served as Acting President until his election to the post in November 2008—claiming 40% of the popular vote over 38% for Michael Sata, leader of the Patriotc Front.

Government

Under the constitution an executive President is elected by popular vote for a maximum of two 5-year terms. He presides over a cabinet appointed by the majority party in the 158-seat National Assembly—150 members elected by popular vote and 8 appointed by the president to serve five-year terms. In the September 2006 election the MMD won 72 seats against 44 for the Patriotic Front (PF). The rest is held by several minority parties.

Economic policy

Since 1991 Zambia has moved towards a freer investor-friendly economy by removing price controls, reducing tariffs and privatizing. Tight fiscal and monetary policies coupled with democratic governance have resulted in renewed balance of payments support from donors and helped restore foreign investor confidence. The World Bank and other donor and lending institutions who agreed to cancel nearly all of Zambia's $7.2 billion foreign debt.

Sectors

Zambia has six times as much agricultural land as Zimbabwe but only 20% is cultivated. Currently agriculture employs about 40% of the workforce, largely on a subsistence basis. Cash crops include tobacco, seed cotton, coffee, fresh flowers and groundnuts. The main food crops are maize, rice, sorghum, millet, soy beans and wheat. Livestock farming is largely under control of small-scale farmers in the southern and western provinces. There is a reasonably large fresh fishing sector and half of the land area is forest, providing fuel wood and timber for mining and industrial use. The economy depends primarily on the copper industry. Zambia is the second largest producer after Congo (Kinshasa) of cobalt and also exports lead and zinc. Its gemstones, especially emeralds, remain largely unexploited. Over one-third of its manufacturing output consists of processed food and beverages. Other major products include textiles, chemicals and metal products. Zambia has good tourist potential and shares with Zimbabwe popular attractions such as Victoria Falls and Lake Kariba. Zambia is becoming increasingly popular as a destination for safari enthusiasists. Recently, oil was discovered in the Northern provinces of Zambezi and Chavuma, near the border with Angola.

Privatization

Most of Zambia's 330 parastatal companies have been privatized since the early nineties, including a major brewery, bakery, farms, several hotels, a mill and the copper mining conglomerate Zambia Consolidated Copper Mines (ZCCM). Among the other state enterprises slated for privatization are the telecommunications parastatal (ZAMTEL), Nitrogen Chemical of Zambia (NCZ), Zambia State Insurance Corporation (ZSIC), Zambia Postal Services Corporation (ZAMPOST), Zambia Electricity Supply Corporation (ZESCO) and Zambia Railways (ZR). Heavily indebted Zambia Airways could not find a buyer and was closed down.

Investment

Large-scale privatization and the freeing up of sectors previously reserved for government monopoly has boosted foreign direct investment over the past ten years. Among the megadeals were the selling of the large state copper mining giant ZCCM to South Africa's Anglo American. Manufacturing operations have sprung up, involving several American investors.

Trade

Zambia derives about 80% of its export earnings and about half of its government tax revenue from copper. The mining and marketing of copper, cobalt, lead and zinc are handled by the recently privatized Zambia Consolidated Copper Mines (ZCCM). Diversification efforts are underway to help expand the export share of tourism, agricultural products and manufactured goods.

Financial sector

The financial sector experienced rapid growth after liberalization of banking, and insurance, and the easing (and eventual elimination) of capital controls. Today there are 15 banks—6 of them foreign-owned subsidiaries, 7 belonging to local investors, 1 to the government and 1 under joint ownership of the Zambian and Indian governments. The banking sector is supervised by the central bank, the Bank of Zambia. The Lusaka Stock Exchange (LSE) trades the shares of a few major companies.

Taxes and tariffs

Duty-free goods include mining and agricultural machinery, medicines and medical equipment, chemicals, fertilizers, and seeds. The corporate tax rate for non-residents is 35 percent. A value added tax (VAT) of 16 percent applies.There is exchange control in effect. A 15 percent tax is levied on dividends, interest income and royalties. (See page 138).

BUSINESS ACTIVITY

AGRICULTURE
Corn, sorghum, rice, peanuts, sunflower seed, tobacco, cotton, sugarcane, cassva (tapioca), cattle, goats, pigs, poultry, beef, pork.
INDUSTRIES
Copper mining and processing, construction, foodstuffs, beverages, chemicals, textiles, fertilizer.
NATURAL RESOURCES
Copper, zinc, lead, cobalt, coal.
EXPORTS
$3.7 billion (est. 2009): copper, cobalt, zinc, lead, tobacco, cut flowers.
IMPORTS
$3.3 billion (est. 2009): machinery, transportation equipment, foodstuffs, fuel,petroleum products, electricity, fertilizer, clothing.
MAJOR TRADING PARTNERS
South Africa, Italy, China, India, Switzerland, Tanzania, Saudi Arabia.

Doing Business with Zambia

▶ **Investment**

The Zambian Investment Center (ZIC) seeks and an investment board screens foreign direct investments. The privatization process is open to foreign bidders and there are no requirements relating to local content, equity, financing, employment or technology transfer. Incentives are offered in regard to investments in rural enterprises, farming, and the manufacturing of non-mineral exports. Companies listed on the Lusaka Stock Exchange qualify for reduced corporate income tax. Mining, tourism, insurance, telecommunications and energy are prime areas of investment.

▶ **Trade**

Horticultural inputs, veterinary medicines, wheat and corn are significant import items. There is also a growing demand for heavy machinery and construction equipment as Zambia introduces major new infrastructure rehabilitation projects. Franchising is expanding in printing, fast food, postal services, computer/office supplies, telecommunications, education, and business services.

▶ **Trade finance**

Short-term local borrowing is expensive. Many buyers either undertake their own financing or seek funding outside the country. An irrevocable letter of credit is the most common method of payment. Eximbank programs are available.

▶ **Selling to the government**

The government has an ongoing need for products and services relating to rehabilitation of the country's railway and road networks, hydroelectric power, mining, and telecommunications. Many of these projects are funded by multilateral lending institutions and bilateral donors and subject in part to their tender requirements. All government purchases are channeled through the National Tender Board.

▶ **Exchange controls**

There are no controls on the movement of capital in or out of Zambia. Bank accounts may be held in local or foreign currency, and funds are easily transferred or allowed to be held offshore.

▶ **Partnerships**

In the few instances where franchising arrangements have been made they were done on the basis of British law. Joint ventures and licensing are inhibited by a shortage of local capital.

▶ **Establishing a presence**

To establish itself in Zambia a foreign firm must register with the Registrar of Companies at the Ministry of Commerce, Trade and Industry. Payment of a fee and submission of the company's charter are required. The minimum nominal capital required is approximately $200 and a registration fee of 2.5% of this startup capital is charged. Certificates of Incorporation are usually issued within 24 hours.

▶ **Financing projects**

Apart from bilateral and multilateral government agencies, commercial banks and venture capital funds are playing an increasing role in the financing of projects. The Overseas Private Investment Corporation, the International Finance Corporation and the Commonwealth Development Corporation also offer project financing, political risk insurance, and investor services.

▶ **Labor**

Labor is readily available although companies often have to invest in training to make up for a lack of skills. While the government stipulates preference for locals in positions where qualified, foreign firms are allowed automatic allowed work and residence permits for five expatriate workers when they invest, and more when justified later.

▶ **Legal rights**

The investment code allows for international arbitration should internal attempts at settlement of a commercial dispute fail. US companies have been successful in getting court rulings enforcing their contracts, even against parastatal companies. Trademark protection is considered adequate and there are fines for revealing business proprietary information. Copyright protection is limited and does not yet cover computer software. Zambia is a signatory to a number of international agreements on patents and intellectual property, including the Paris and Bern Convention and the African Regional Industrial Property Organization (ARIPO), and is a member of the World Intellectual Property Organization.

▶ **Business climate**

Business customs were shaped and influenced by the British (and Americans) since the end of the 19th century. Visitors who have conducted business in any of Southern Africa's English-speaking countries will find the environment in Zambia quite familiar.

ZIMBABWE

Once one of Africa's most prosperous countries, Zimbabwe has gone into a free fall in recent years due to mismanagement on the part of the Mugabe government. With inflation going through the roof, the economy in ruins, a massive brain drain and property rights subject to political whim, investors are seeking other greener pastures on the Continent. But Zimbabwe is also home to the world's second biggest platinum reserves and numerous other strategic minerals. A neglected infrastructure will need to be rebuilt with international financing once Zimbabwe is reintegrated into the global community. Thousands of highly skilled workers who have fled may be tempted back once responsible government is restored.

Country profile

The Republic of Zimbabwe is situated on an extension of the South African Highveld Plateau. The Zambezi and Limpopo rivers run along the country's northern and southern borders. At Victoria Falls the Zambezi plunges for 100 m (328 ft) over a width of 1.5 km (1 mile) into a narrow ravine, sending up a spray that earned it the indigenous name of Mosi-oa-Tunya—the "smoke that thunders." Downstream is Kariba Dam, the second largest human-made lake in Africa after Lake Volta in Ghana. Hwange National Park is one of several national parks. Rainfall in the highveld region averages 800 mm (31.5 inches) and along the lower regions less than 400 mm (15.7 inches). More than three-quarters of the population are Shona or Mashona. The second largest group is the Ndebele or Matabele, accounting for about 15% of the total. The white population number some 80,000 and Asians around 15,000. English is the official language. Well over half of the population is Christian and the rest adhere to traditional beliefs.

History

The remains of humans dating back 500,000 years have been discovered in the region. The country traces its history back to about 500 when the city of Great Zimbabwe (house of stone) was developed by the ancestors of the Shona. Around the middle of the 19th Century, the territory was invaded by Ndebele or Matabele migrants from

Pres. Robert
Gabriel Mugabe
Born: Feb.21, 1924
Since 1980

UN Photo Devra Berkowitz

POLITICAL

Head of State	Pres. Robert Gabriel Mugabe
Prime Minister	Morgan Tsvangirai
Ruling Party	MDC
Main Opposition	ZANU-PF
Independence	18 April 1980
National capital	Harare
Official language	English

PHYSICAL

Total area	151,000 sq. miles 391,000 sq. km. (± Montana)
Arable land	8.3% of land area
Coastline	Landlocked

POPULATION

Total	11.6 million
Av. yearly growth	2.9%
Urban population	37%
Life expectancy	47.55 years
Adult literacy	90.7%

ECONOMY

Currency	Zim.dollar (Z$) (U$1=361.90)[3]
GDP (real)	$4.7 billion
GDP growth rate	3.7%
GDP per capita[1]	$339
GDP (ppp)[2]	$2.1 billion
GDP per cap. (ppp)	$175
Inflation rate	9.0%
Exports	$1.2 billion
Imports	$2.4 billion
External debt	$6 billion
Unemployment	95%

1. Atlas method.
2. See page 175 for an explanation of purchasing power parity (ppp).
3. In 2009 new Zim dollars were issued at 1 for 1 trillion of the old currency. Trading has been suspended.

the south. In 1890 Cecil John Rhodes' British South Africa Company (BSA) started a white settlement at Salisbury (today's Harare, the capital of Zimbabwe). The territory was named Rhodesia, after Rhodes, and in 1923 white settlers were given the choice of joining South Africa or becoming a self-governing colony within the British Empire. They opted for the latter. By law the best cropland was reserved for a rapidly-growing white settlement. Joshua Mqabuko Nkomo's Zimbabwe African Peoples Union (ZAPU) and Robert Gabriel Mugabe's Zimbabwe African National Union (ZANU) led the black protest against this inequity. They resorted to arms in 1965 when Prime Minister Ian Smith and his ruling Rhodesian Front issued a unilateral declaration of independence (UDI). UN-imposed sanctions and a protracted guerilla war on two fronts involving ZAPU and ZANU forced Smith to the negotiating table and in April 1980 Zimbabwe gained independence under Prime Minister (later President) Robert Mugabe. Land resettlement remained a hot political issue with one-third of the country's arable land occupied by 4,000 white farmers. Mugabe's open support for forceful occupation of white farmland by "displaced war veterans" placed him at the center of a storm that led to the rise of the Movement for Democratic Change (MDC). In 2008 Mugabe was re-elected president unopposed in a runoff election after Morgan Tsvangirai of the MDC, who won the first round, pulled out, alleging large-scale intimidation and violence.

Government

The 1980 independence constitution was changed in 1987 to eliminate the 20 seats reserved for representatives of white voters and create the post of president—elected for 6 years without term limits. A bicameral parliament consists of a 93-seat Senate (60 of whom are elected by popular vote) and a 210-seat House of Assembly elected by popular vote. Both houses serve 5 year terms. In the March 2008 election marred by intimidation and violence the Movement for Democratic Change (MDC) managed to win 109 seats against the ruling Zimbabwe African National Union-Patriotic Front (ZANU-PF) who finished up with 97 seats. The other 4 seats were won by independents. One independent was elected. In the Senate ZANU-PF won 30 of the elected seats which, together with the appointees gave them a clear edge over the 30 captured by the MDC. In a three-way presidential race in March 2008 Tsvangirai won 47.9% of the popular vote against Mugabe's 43.2%. As Tsvangirai failed to get a clear majority in the first round a second round was called from which the MDC leader withdrew in fear of "further intimidation and violence." Mugabe, running unopposed, emerged in June 2008 with 85.5% victory against 9.3% for the absentee opponent. The EU and the United States, prevented from sending observers, accused the Mugabe regime of large-scale fraud and vote-rigging and took punitive economic measures to coerce Mugabe into power-sharing. In September 2008 Mugabe signed a so-called Global Political Agreement (GPA) under which he remained president and Tsvangirai became prime minister in February 2009. Intimidation of the MDC and Mugabe's autocratic rule continue despite pressures from abroad.

Economic policy

In December 2008 the inflation rate stood at 11.2 million million percent. In 2009 the old Zimbabwe dollars were exchanged for a new one at the rate opf 1 for 1 trillion. An estimated 80 percent of the population are living below the poverty threshold and thousands crossing into South Africa, Zambia and Botswana every week in search of work and food. There has been some economic improvement since the new government took over.

Sectors

Until Zimabawe's economy went into a free fall the agricultural sector contributed 20% of GNP and employed about 70% of the total labor force. Some 4,400 large commercial farms, covering 29% of the total land area, used to account for 80% of the country's commercial agricultural output. Maize, wheat, barley, cassava, soy beans, bananas and oranges were popular food crops. There was also a substantial production of cotton, sugar, coffee and beef but tobacco was by far the most important cash crop. Serious disruption of established farms have, however, resulted in drastic cutbacks. Mining of gold, chrome, nickel and asbestos used to provide employment to some 60,000 workers. Other important minerals are coal, copper, iron ore, tin, silver, platinum, phosphate, limestone, cobalt and lithium.

Investment

A survey conducted by the Confederation of Zimbabwe Industries (CZI) in the late 1980s indicated that 25% of all industrial concerns had some foreign ownership. Foreign investment accounted for 40% to 50% of the country's industrial output. Latest estimates put the total foreign investment at $5 billion, mostly British and South African. In recent years, however, many Zimbabwean companies have relocated to neighbouring Botswana and Zambia.

Trade

Tobacco used to be by far the most important cash crop, contributing more than 25% of Zimbabwe's total export revenues. Mining of gold, chrome, nickel and asbestos accounted on average for about 40%.

Taxes

The corporate tax rate for non-residents is 25.75 percent and capital gains tax 20 percent. A value added tax (VAT) of 15 percent applies and exchange control is in effect. A tax rate of 15 percent applies to dividends, income from interest, royalties and management fees. (See page 138).

BUSINESS ACTIVITY

AGRICULTURE
Corn, cotton, tobacco, wheat, coffee, sugar cane, peanuts, cattle, sheep, goats, pigs.
INDUSTRIES
Mining (coal, clay, numerous metallic and non-metallic ores), copper, steel, nickel, tin, wood products, cement, chemicals, fertilizer, clothing and footwear, foodstuffs, beverages.
NATURAL RESOURCES
Gold, copper, chrome, nickel, tin, asbestos.
EXPORTS
$1.2 billion (est. 2009): tobacco, chromium, gold, ferro alloys, cotton, clothing.
IMPORTS
$2.4 billion (est. 2009): machinery and transport equipment, other manufactures, chemicals, fuels.
MAJOR TRADING PARTNERS
South Africa, China, Botswana, Japan, DRC, Zambia, Italy.

Doing Business with Zimbabwe

▶ **Investment**

The Zimbabwe Investment Center (ZIC) was created as one-stop shop for potential investors. Incentives for investors include allowances on the purchase of industrial and commercial buildings, implements and machinery, and for training, as well as special mining leases. The government, however, still prefers majority Zimbabwean participation in new investment projects and the degree of local ownership remains an important criterion in the evaluation of investment proposals. Its privatization program announced in late 1998 limits foreign ownership to between 15 and 20%, down from previous levels of 30 to 35%. There are a number of sectors reserved for domestic investors such as horticulture, game, wildlife ranching, forestry, fishing, freight and passenger transport (excluding airlines), and tobacco products. Investing in export processing zones entitles foreigners to a five-year tax holiday and duty-free importation of raw materials and capital equipment.

▶ **Trade**

There is a market for transportation equipment, construction and farm machinery, computers and peripherals, chemicals and plastics, textile machinery, telecommunications equipment and food products. Exports include ferrochrome, nickel, tobacco, gold, sugar, and clothing.

▶ **Trade finance**

Eximbank offers facilities to US exporters and financing is also available from local banks at relatively high interest rates.

▶ **Selling to the government**

There is an increasing demand for equipment related to telecommunications, power generation and road building and repair. Purchases are through tender and sometimes involve multilateral and bilateral financing.

▶ **Exchange controls**

Foreign investors are allowed to remit all their after-tax profits. The government monitors all capital outflows relating to prospective outward investment and dividend remittances.

▶ **Partnerships**

Partnership is the preferred form of foreign investment, especially if it advances black economic empowerment. Several US firms have entered the market through franchising agreements relating to consumer goods and services.

▶ **Establishing a presence**

Approval from the Zimbabwean Investment Center is required in all cases where a new business is established, an existing one expanded, or part or all of a business acquired.

▶ **Financing projects**

There are investment agreements in place with the Overseas Private Investment Corporation and the World Bank's Multilateral Investment Guarantee Agency. Project financing is also available from two Zimbabwean development banks and a venture capital company.

▶ **Labor**

Unskilled and semi-skilled labor is readily available but there is a growing shortage of technical skills. The 1985 Labor Relations Act sets strict standards for occupational health and safety, working hours and minimum wage. The Zimbabwe Congress of Trade Unions (ZCTU), the country's umbrella labor organization, consisting of 35 member unions and about 300,000 members, is a powerful advocate for workers.

▶ **Legal rights**

Zimbabwe's judiciary had a reputation for fairness and independence. The country is a member of the World Intellectual Property Organization but efforts to honor intellectual property ownership and rights are sometimes hampered by ineffective means of enforcement. Recently, remittances for royalties, technical services and management fees have been suspended in some instances due to the severe hard currency shortage. Government buyouts of both foreign investors and commercial farmers since independence have generally been on a mutually agreed basis. Recently, however, the government sanctioned white commercial farmland invasions by "war veterans" without proper compensation, causing a serious dent in foreign investor confidence. Once investors have exhausted local remedies, appeal to private arbitration is allowed in accordance with the rules and procedures of the UN Commission on International Trade Law.

▶ **Business climate**

Business customs generally follow the British model and are fairly formal. Despite bureaucratic red tape and a lack of transparency in some instances, patient and persistent companies with experienced local representation manage to develop profitable businesses.

WESTERN SAHARA

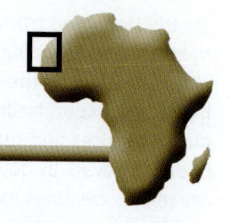

Editor's Note: The situation in Western Sahara is complex. In previous years, our description has displeased either Morocco or Algeria, depending on how it was described. The following represents what we believe to be a factual representation of the situation as it now stands.

At present Western Sahara is administered by Morocco as part of its greater Southern Region. However, the territory has also been proclaimed the Saharan Arab Democratic Republic (SADR) by a government-in-exile, based in Algeria, led by Mohammed Abdal-Aziz. The population of this disputed territory, currently under UN observation, is awaiting a referendum to decide whether they wish to become part of Morocco or establish an independent state. The United States government does not recognize either Moroccan rule over Western Sahara or the government-in-exile in Algeria.

As Algeria, Mauritania and Mali became independent, Morocco had laid claims on historic grounds to parts of their territory, as well as the entire Spanish Sahara. The latter claim was pursued forcefully by King Hassan. After a proposed UN referendum on the future of the territory failed to materialize, Western Saharan voters were allowed to participate in Moroccan elections in 1993.

Profile

Western Sahara's covers an area of 252,000 km consisting of a low plateau and desert, scattered oases and dry river beds. It shares contested borders with Morocco, Algeria and Mauritania. The climate along the 1,500 km coastline is moderated by the Northern Atlantic Ocean's cold Canaries current. Most of its 220,000 inhabitants (not including thousands of refugees in adjoining lands) are Muslim. They call themselves Saharans or Sadirawi and are of mixed Arabo-Berber origin. The largest group is the northern Tekna, who are preponderantly Berber and related to the inhabitants of southern Morocco. The Regeihat and the Imragen along the coast are nomadic fishermen. Arabic and Berber dialects are widely spoken, apart from a smattering of French and Spanish. More than 80% of the population is concentrated in Al-Aaiun (Laayoune) and settlements along the Saguia al-Hamra Valley in the far north.

Economy

Crop growing, mainly for subsistence, takes place at the numerous oases, and goats, sheep and camels are raised along the coast where the moisture sustains some pasturage. Both the rich offshore fishing waters and vast phosphate deposits at Boukra (Bou Craa) are important economic resources for Morocco. The phosphate rock is transported on a 62 mile (100 km) conveyor belt to the port of Al-Aaiun. The northern region of Western Sahara has greatly benefited from the Moroccan government's large spending on military operations in recent years. In the process, social services, housing and sport facilities, roads, air transport, postal services and telecommunications have been improved. By developing the economy of the region, creating employment opportunities, and improving social services the Moroccan government aims not only at fostering goodwill among the locals but also to encourage its own citizens to settle here.

History

At different stages and even as late as the mid-18th Century a vast region that included present-day Western Sahara, was controlled by different tribal and regional interests. The nomadic desert peoples, however, continued to resist the so-called makhzan or world of government control. In 1884, during the "scramble" for Africa, Spain grabbed a piece of this desert and declared a protectorate over it. When the territory's international borders were finally established, Spain controlled only the coastlands. The discovery of rich phosphate deposits at Boukra in 1963 intensified the resistance to Spanish domination and stimulated a desire for independence among the indigenous inhabitants. Responding to their appeals, the UN General Assembly adopted several resolutions from 1967 to 1973, condemning the Spanish presence in Western Sahara and affirming the right of the Saharans to self-determination. The Frente Popular para la Liberacion de Saguia al-Hamray Rio de Oro (Polisario) was founded in 1973.

Takeover

Under pressure from the Polisario, the UN and Morocco, Spain decided to hold a referendum in Western Sahara on the independence issue. With the referendum still pending, a UN mission reported that the majority of Saharans whom it consulted in the territory were in favor of independence and rejected Morocco's territorial claims. This was interpreted by an infuriated King Hassan as an attempt to influence the outcome of the referendum. Hassan had in the meantime struck a deal with Mauritania to partition Western Sahara between them to counter Algeria in its support of the Polisario. In November 1975 King Hassan responded to the untimely UN interference by mobilizing Moroccans of all political parties and persuasions to stage a massive peaceful march into Western Sahara. In what was known as the Green March, some 350,000 Koran-bearing civilians obliged Spain to capitulate and evacuate, allowing Moroccan troops to move in. A subsequent tripartite agreement between Spain, Morocco and Mauritania paved the way for a formal partitioning of the area between Morocco and Mauritania in 1976. Morocco claimed the phosphate-rich northern two-thirds of the territory and Mauritania the remainder, including the port of Dakhla. In 1997, Mauritania dropped its territorial claims, leaving the way clear for Morocco to expand its influence over all of Western Sahara.

SADR

In defiance the Polisario proclaimed the Saharan Arab Democratic Republic (SADR) and set up a government-in-exile in Algeria, a move that resulted in severance of diplomatic relations between Morocco and Algeria. Thousands of Polisario supporters followed their leaders into exile, settling around the oasis of Tindouf, not far from Algeria's border with Western Sahara. The Polisario subsequently embarked on a guerrilla war against Morocco and Mauritania. In the 1980s it also managed to obtain recognition for its "independent republic" when a majority of OAU member states conferred membership on the SADR over objections and the eventual resignation from the organization by Morocco. Some 70 UN member states recognize the SADR but lately support among African states has begun to erode.

Recent developments

In recent years relations between Morocco and its neighbors have been improving. Algeria joined with Morocco and several others in the Arab Maghreb Union. A cease-fire agreement between Morocco and the Polisario was concluded on 6 September 1991 and a UN Mission for the Organization of the Referendum in the Sahara (Minurso) was established to oversee Western Sahara until the quarrelling parties agree on the details of a long-awaited referendum.

Chapter 8
Travel Tips and Trivia

Travel to Africa can be complicated, cumbersome and sometimes downright difficult or it can be smooth, simple and soothing. In part it depends on where you are going and what you want to do. But mostly it is a matter of proper preparation and prudent pre-planning. In these pages we offer the traveler a few tips and suggestions that might make for smoother travel and greater enjoyment of their journey into Africa.

Travel Tips

These travel tips are mere general guidelines and travelers are advised to check with authoritative sources at embassies, their own respective government departments, travel agencies and airlines before they start on their journey.

ACCOMMODATION

Major international hotel chains such as Marriott, Intercontinental, Hilton and Le Meridien have established themselves in cities across Africa. There are also a number of homegrown hotel groups that offer economy to luxury services. Some countries grade hotels according to the quality and extent of their services on a scale of one to five stars. In the past five years hotels in South Africa have on several occasions been voted best in the world by readers of Condé Nast, Travel & Leisure, Tattler and other travel magazines.

AIR TRAVEL

International links to Africa are provided by a host of major international airlines and a number of African carriers. Although most other African nations have their own national airlines, only few serve intercontinental routes. Major international entry points such as Johannesburg, Cairo, Dakar, Nairobi, Dar es Salaam, Addis Ababa, Windhoek, Lagos and Abidjan provide multiple links to neighboring countries and remote destinations on the continent,

BUSINESS HOURS

Across the continent the variation in business hours is minimal. North African countries usually go for longer lunch breaks and later closings. Foreigners should not interpret lack of punctuality in some cultures as a sign of disrespect or disinterest. Keep in mind that there are Africans who find the Western obsession with speed and immediacy in conducting business not only strange but downright rude. Not much can be gained by insisting on fast decisions in a societies where ample group discussion and consensus are prerequisites.

CREDIT CARDS

While major credit cards are widely used and accepted in the larger cities across the continent and even in remote parts in some countries, it is prudent to enquire beforehand whether this form of payment is accepted in any specific part of Africa. In a few countries, travelers are cautioned against widespread credit card fraud and might be advised to rely on travelers checks or cash payments instead.

CAR RENTAL

Multinational car rental firms all have a presence in some but not all African countries—mostly on a franchise basis. There are also domestic services but for those who are just passing through and do not know the country well enough to judge their reliability, the familiar names might be a better option. Be prepared to pay heavy insurance rates and do not assumed that your American Express or other international insurance coverage will be accepted. Also shop around as rates differ drastically between different operators but be prepared to pay considerably more than the going rate in the United States and some other countries. Keep in mind that outside urban areas roads and driving conditions can present quite a challenge and chauffeur-driven vehicles or public transport should be considered. For obvious reasons, foreigners—unless they are adventurous and amply equipped with water and other supplies—are dissuaded from taking long trips into the desert or African hinterland. Driving in most of the former British colonies is on the left-hand side of the road and in the former French, Spanish, Italian and Portuguese possessions on the right-hand side. There are exceptions, such as former British-ruled Ghana, where driving is on the right.

CLIMATE

Hollywood's Africa conjures up images of people in khaki and pith helmets braving steamy jungles and forbidding deserts. Most visitors will do neither. Safarigoers usually find themselves in savanna terrain where most of the animals live. While the weather in some West African countries might be summed up in terms of hot and humid, most areas present a much more complex weather profile. During summer in South Africa, for instance, travelers find themselves moving between Mediterranean-type weather at the southern coast to subtropical and humid weather on the east coast and dry heat inland. Countries such as Egypt, Algeria, Libya and Tunisia offer pleasant Mediterranean climates on their coast in contrast to searing hot days in the inland desert, followed by cold nights. For a description of climate and weather patterns in African countries visit *www.worldtravelguide.net/navigate/region/afr.asp.* and for a daily updated weather forecast in major African cities visit *www.usatoday.com/weather.* Also see the climate chart on **page 388** for average temperatures and rainfall in major African centers.

CLOTHES

While locals in North African and West African countries wear sensible traditional dress to cope with hot weather, foreigners are often obliged to wear suit and tie to business meetings. Even though the trend is towards greater informality in some countries, this formal dress code largely prevails. Travelers who plan to go on safari outings are should take along a smaller bag for travel to game reserves. The feeder aircraft that serve these routes maintain strict baggage limits, requiring travelers to leave the bulk of their baggage in safekeeping at their hotel or the airport.

EMAIL

Business travelers who rely on email to communicate will find an increasing number of major hotels in the larger African cities offering not only cable and other data transmission connections for laptop carriers but also business centers, replete with computers. Some major hotels have introduced wireless broadband connection for guests with suitably equipped laptops, enabling them to connect anywhere within the hotel. Another growth industry in Africa is Internet cafés. The continent still has some way to go but the pace is picking up towards full connection to the information highway. As elsewhere, email is bound to replace snail mail and faxes as the preferred communication mode.

ELECTRICITY

Consider Africa 220/240 volts AC 50Hz territory—and at a few places power might surge up to 380 volts. There is a whole array of power connections in use, ranging from two and three-prong round to bayonet type plugs. Most hotels provide the necessary converters on loan to patrons. Remote areas and some game parks rely on their own power generation. Some have no electricity at all.

FOOD

Expect on a continent with hundreds of cultures and customs to find a wide choice of local dishes. Middle Eastern fare dominates in North Africa and down south traditional tribal dishes are mixed in with colonial and other imported culinary delights from India, Malaysia and Indonesia. For centuries Zanzibar has been an important source for spices. When served uncooked or unprocessed food, such as salads and fruit, call for the same caution as applies in the case of drinking water.

HEALTH

In most African countries a valid yellow fever vaccination certificate is required for travellers over one year of age. Cholera remains a serious risk in some regions. Although largely contained and eradicated in the urban and developed areas of the continent, malaria remains a risk, especially for those touring game park regions. Mefloquine or other medication should be taken on a prophylactic basis and in sometimes mosquito nets and repellents are used at night. Experts caution against swimming in fresh water in some outlying areas as Bilharzia (schistosomiasis) might be present. Hepatitis A, B and E are present and meningococcal meningitis may occur. Leishmaniasis and human trypanosomiasis (sleeping sickness) occur in a few isolated areas. Avoid ticks which spread African tick typhus. Wear shoes to avoid soil-borne parasites. Even though most of these cautionary statements do not apply to city centers but it is better to err on the safe side. When in doubt, call your physician or health department for advice.

MEDIA

In this modern day and age where CNN and other 24-hour news channels are piped into hotel rooms all over the continent, travelers are able to stay on top of the news without understanding the local language. Being conversant in both French and English will, however, enable a visitor to read local papers from Cape to Cairo and understand most of the local TV and radio news broadcasts. Those who have access to the Internet or international telephone connections can obviously stay abreast of news developments on their laptops or cellphones and other handheld devices.

MEDICAL SERVICES

Medical facilities across the continent run the gamut from poor to fair and excellent. At the one end of the spectrum is war-torn Sierra Leone where medical facilities are extremely limited and continuing to decline and at the other South Africa where hospitals are modern and medical staff well trained. (It is in Cape Town where the world's first heart transplant was performed.) Health insurance is recommended and travelers are advised to take an ample supply of their own personal medication along. Insurance is available that provides accident protection and emergency assistance in Africa. Programs for remote areas also include Flying Doctors insurance which facilitates emergency medical evacuation.

MONEY MATTERS

In most African countries the US dollar is the preferred currency but in former French and British colonies franc and pounds are widely used. Sometimes additional exchange rate charges can be avoided by using travelers checks. However enticing, black market exchange of foreign into local currency is always a risk and official bureaus at airports, banks or hotels should be used instead. Normally banks offer the best legal rates. In the Democratic Republic of Congo, locals in possession of US dollars are liable to be charged with treason. In most cases the uswe of credit cards is advisable. Take along just enough cash for tipping, cabs and incidental expenses. *[For past and current exchange rates see our chart on page 398 and for real-time exchange rates visit www.gocurrency.com or ask your bank].*

PHOTOGRAPHY

Safarigoers who intend to take pictures of animals will need telephoto lenses even in private game reserves where visitors are afforded the opportunity to see lions, leopards, elephants and others closer up. Africa also presents a treasure house of scenery, cultures and creations where ordinary photographic equipment can produce outstanding results. Photographic stores in major cities stock the products of leading manufacturers. It is prudent, however, to bring along spare custom batteries and other maintenance items.

PUBLIC HOLIDAYS

In North Africa Muslim holidays are observed and in the southern region mostly Christian holidays. In several West African countries where both faiths are practised extensively, both Muslim and Christian holidays are observed. Add in national days, workers' days and a number of other specials and some African countries may have 14 public holidays per year. Others have as few as four. As Muslim festivals are timed according to local sightings of various phases of the moon, there are no fixed dates. Ethiopia and Eritrea still use the Julian calendar, divided into 12 months of 30 days each, and a 13th month of five or six days at the end of the year, resulting on Christmas Day 2001 falling on January 7. The Julian calendar is seven years and eight months behind that of the rest of the world. (For an up-to-date listing of national public holidays in specific African countries visit *www.worldtravelguide. net/navigate/region/afr.asp*).

PUBLIC TRANSPORT

Most major cities are served by reasonably well-run and reliable taxis. While public transport offers a cheaper way of getting around, buses and trains—with few exceptions—tend to be overcrowded.

SECURITY

Seasoned travelers know the potential pitfalls when leaving valuables unattended or strolling down dark and lonely alleys in cities anywhere in the world. While some might marvel at the great sense of decency that prevails in Africa at large, it is advisable to apply the same caution and alertness that one would in large cities anywhere. Hotels have mini-safes in bedrooms for personal valuables or alternatively provide safekeeping at the front desk. It should be noted that even though South Africa, for example, ranks alarmingly high on the world's crime charts, comparatively few visitors have been personally affected. In a few isolated regions of Africa, the problem of crime pales in comparison to the brutality and dangers of fierce civil upheaval and war. The US State Department *(www.state.gov)* provides online travel advisory updates.

SHOPPING

Africa markets itself as the continent of curios. Wood carvings of people, animals and masks come in all sizes, some in dimensions that necessitate shipping. In the latter case it is obviously advisable to purchase from reputable dealers instead of street vendors. Other items include ivory, gold and silver objects and jewelry, bead work and weaving. Vendors of animal skins will provide treatment certificates and other documentation required by customs in the United States and other countries. There is a ban on the importation of ivory in the United States and several other countries. Do not expect to get diamonds or gold items at bargain prices in Africa. Outside the risky black market, prices are controlled and commensurate to what you might pay at home. African artists, however, add a special local flavor and charm to their jewelry designs that attract foreign buyers. Another popular purchase in South Africa are wines from estates visited during a wine tasting wine tour. These wines can be shipped or transported as checked baggage.

SPORT

Travelers with a penchant for sport will find plenty to do or to watch, depending on their preference. Soccer is big throughout the continent and cricket is widespread. Rugby—traditionally played in South Africa, Zimbabwe and Namibia—is gaining ground as far as Morocco. Angling and fishing along the continents coastline or in its major rivers are popular pastimes for visitors and golf course abound, especially in South Africa where courses designed by the likes of Gary Player, Jack Nicklaus, and Greg Norman supplement century old country clubs. Most clubs offer rental clubs so there is no need to cart along your own equipment. Most hotels have fitness centers.

TELECOMMUNICATIONS

Visitors whose cell phones are on GSM integrate seamlessly with their own equipment into cellphone networks in most major African countries. Those visitors who operate on a different mobile system will find convenient stalls and stores at some airports and in major cities where they can rent phones. Cellphone communication has grown at a faster pace in the African continent than anywhere else in the world. Visitors with GSM capable telephones or rental instruments simply purchase and insert a simcard and purchase time as they go along. Calls from hotels are usually subject to a heavy surcharge. Most hotels offer facsimile services. In South Africa and a few other countries services are provided for data transfer to laptops and a variety of handheld devices.

TRAINS

Train buffs looking for the unusual will find it in several parts of the continent. Kenya's Nairobi to Mombasa train and South Africa's renowned state-of-the-art luxury Blue Train are favorites. Sadly, however, in many parts of the continent railroads have fallen in disrepair.

TRAVEL INSURANCE

It is prudent to buy travel insurance, especially when going on big ticket safaris. This should cover both trip cancellation and evacuation and other medical costs. There are some tour operators that will not accept clients unless they obtain medical coverage as evacuation from remote areas are by helicopter and aircraft and costly.

VISAS

Citizens of the United States, United Kingdom and other European countries, as well as Japan need visas (obtainable at fees ranging from $20 to $100) for travel to most African countries. Exceptions are Botswana, Lesotho, Mauritius, Morocco, Namibia, Senegal, Seychelles, and South Africa, where no visas are required. In Zambia, US and Japanese citizens are not exempted and in Zimbabwe only the British and Canadians are exempted. In some cases a fee is charged for visas and arrival and departure taxes levied. *[Regulations change and travelers are advised to contact the respective embassies or consulates before embarking on their trip]*.

WATER

Even though drinking water in some African countries poses no danger, it is better to err on the safe side. While South Africans, for example, might find it peculiar to see anyone resort to bottled water unless they prefer the taste and don't mind paying extra, drinking water out of the faucet in many other countries borders on being reckless. There may be the risk of diarrhoea diseases, the dysenteries and various parasitic worm infections in both water and uncooked vegetables or fruit washed in contaminated water. Where there are no signs posted in bathrooms, the rule of thumb is not to drink water from any faucet anywhere before asking the question: "Is the water safe?" While this question might offend some of the locals, most will understand. Most establishments provide guests with bottled water in their rooms.

WHEN TO GO

Business travelers usually do not have the luxury of picking the best time to visit based on weather but the chart on the opposite page should provide a useful guideline to those who do. These are averages based on conditions over several years but no guarantees. Like anywhere else the weather in Africa at times shows total disregard for neat tables and median numbers. Those who visit Africa for pure pleasure should keep in mind that the best time of the year is not necessarily purely a matter of sunshine and warmth. In Southern Africa, for example, the best time to go on safari is during the winter months when the foliage is sparse and the animals more readily seen. But this does suit those who wish to enjoy the magnificent beaches.

EXCHANGE RATES PER US$1.00

	Currency	Symbol	2009[1]	2010[2]
Algeria	Dinar	DA	71.42	74.70
Angola	New Kwanza	Nkz	88.16	92.02
Benin	CFA Franc	CFAF	434.75	495.40
Botswana	Pula	P	6.51	6.64
Burkina Faso	CFA Franc	CFAF	434.75	495.40
Burundi	Burundi Franc	FBu	1,220	1,217
Cameroon	CFA Franc	CFAF	434.75	495.40
Cape Verde	Escudo	C.V. Esc.	74.04	83.25
Cent. Afr. Rep.	CFA Franc	CFAF	434.75	495.40
Chad	CFA Franc	CFAF	434.754	495.40
Comoros	Com. Franc	CF	326.155	371.41
Congo, DR of	Cong. Franc	CDF	885.00	890.00
Congo, Rep.	CFA Franc	CFAF	434.75	495.40
Côte d'Ivoire	CFA Franc	CFAF	434.75	495.40
Djibouti	Djib. Franc	DF	162.55	175.75
Egypt	Eg. Pound	£E	5.47	5.79
Eq. Guinea	CFA Franc	CFAF	434.75	495.40
Eritrea	Nafka	Nfa	15.10	15.00
Ethiopia	Birr	Br	12.59	16.50
Gabon	CFA Franc	CFAF	434.75	495.40
Gambia, The	Dalasi	D	26.90	26.90
Ghana	Cedi	¢	1.4295	1.4550
Guinea	Guinea Franc	GNF	5,003.0	6,950.0
Guinea-Bissau	CFA Franc	CFAF	434.75	495.40
Kenya	Shilling	KSh	74.73	80.50
Lesotho	Loti	L	7.32	6.88
Liberia	Liberian dollar	L$	66.00	68.50
Libya	Libyan Dinar	LD	1.20	1.24
Madagascar	Ariary	MGA	1,932.00	2,090.00
Malawi	Kwacha	MK	142.00	150.00
Mali	CFA Franc	CFAF	434.75	495.40
Mauritania	Ouguiyas	UM	261.50	284.50
Mauritius	Rupee	MauR	28.25	30.20
Morocco	Dirham	DH	7.56	8.41
Mozambique	Metical	Mt	30.58	34.15
Namibia	Namib.dollar	N$	7.32	6.88
Niger	CFA Franc	CFAF	434.75	495.40
Nigeria	Naira	N	148.41	151.76
Rwanda	Rw. Franc	RF	569.40	588.00
São Tomé & P.	Dobra	Db	15,560	18,615
Senegal	CFA Franc	CFAF	434.75	495.40
Seychelles	Rupee	SR	10.50	12.08
Sierra Leone	Leones	Le	3,879	4,175
Somalia	Shilling	SoSh	1,400	1,600
South Africa	Rand	ZAR	7.32	6.88
Sudan	Pounds	SDG	2.23	2.49
Swaziland	Lilangeni	SZL	7.32	6.88
Tanzania	Shilling	TSh	1,337.40	1,475.50
Togo	CFA Franc	CFAF	434.75	495.40
Tunisia	Dinar	TD	1.27	1.44
Uganda	Shilling	USh	1,868.00	2,308.00
Zambia	Kwacha	ZK	4,694.99	4,765.00
Zimbabwe	Zimb. Dollar	Z$	361.90[3]	361.90

1. Exchange rate on December 2, 2009. 2. Exchange rate on December 9, 2010
3. Zimbabwe redenominated old currency to new at a rate of 1 trillion for 1 new Zimdollar.

African Time Zones

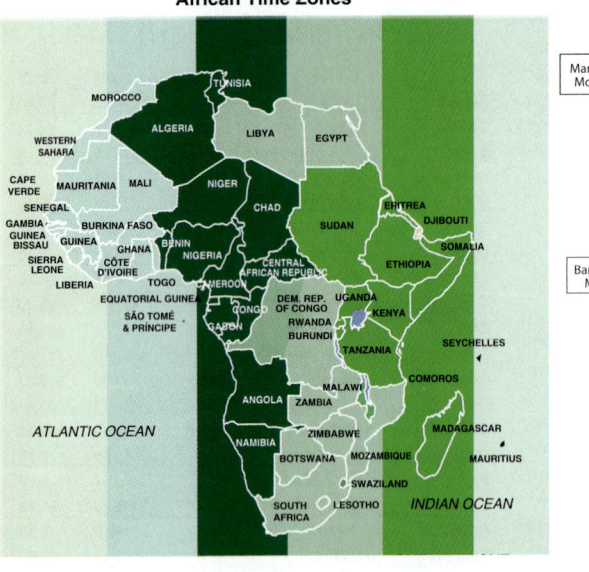

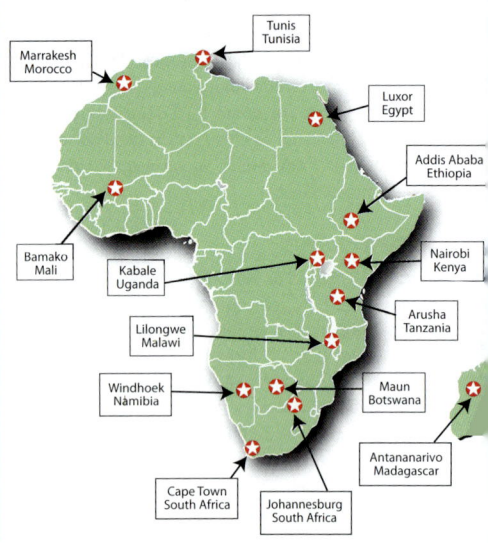

CALLING CODES

COUNTRY	TO[1]	FROM[2]
Algeria	213	00
Angola	244	00
Benin	229	00
Botswana	267	00
Burkina Faso	226	00
Burundi	257	90
Cameroon	237	00
Cape Verde Islands	238	0
Central African Republic	236	19
Chad	235	15
Comoros	269	10
Congo (Brazzaville)	242	00
Congo (Kinshasa)	243	00
Côte d'Ivoire	225	00
Djibouti	253	00
Egypt	20	00
Equatorial Guinea	240	00
Eritrea	291	00
Ethiopia	251	00
Gabon	241	00
Gambia	220	00
Ghana	233	00
Guinea-Bissau	245	00
Guinea	224	00
Kenya	254	000
Lesotho	266	00
Liberia	231	00
Libya	218	00
Madagascar	261	00
Malawi	265	101
Mali	223	00
Mauritania	222	00
Mauritius	230	00

COUNTRY	TO	FROM
Morocco	212	00
Mozambique	258	00
Namibia	264	09
Niger	227	00
Nigeria	234	009
Rwanda	250	00
São Tomé and Principe	239	00
Senegal	221	00
Seychelles	248	00
Sierra Leone	232	00
Somalia	252	19
South Africa	27	00
Sudan	249	00
Swaziland	268	00
Tanzania & Zanzibar	255	000
Togo	228	00
Tunisia	216	00
Uganda	256	000
Zambia	260	00
Zimbabwe	263	00

OTHER TERRITORIES

Diego Garcia	246	00
Mayotte Island	269	10
Réunion Island	262	00
St. Helena	290	01

Source: AT&T

1. The country code to be used when making international calls to a particular African country before dialing the city area code and number. 2. The access code needed to make an outgoing international call from a specific African country or territory before dialing another country and city code and telephone number.

388

African Weather - °Fahrenheit and rain days per month

		JAN	FEB	MAR	APR	MAY	JUN	JUL	AUG	SEP	OCT	NOV	DEC
EGYPT	Max	73	78	84	95	104	106	106	106	104	95	84	77
LUXOR	Min	41	45	52	61	70	73	75	75	72	64	54	46
	Rain	-	-	-	-	-	-	-	-	-	-	-	-
ETHIOPIA	Max	75	75	77	77	77	73	70	70	72	75	73	73
ADDIS ABAB	Min	43	46	48	50	50	48	50	50	48	45	43	41
	Rain	2	5	8	10	10	20	28	27	21	3	2	2
MALI	Max	91	97	102	102	102	93	90	88	90	93	93	91
BAMAKO	Min	60	66	72	75	75	73	72	72	72	72	64	63
	Rain	-	-	-	2	5	10	16	17	12	6	1	-
MOROCCO	Max	64	68	73	78	84	91	100	100	91	82	73	66
MARAKESH	Min	39	43	48	52	57	63	66	68	63	57	48	43
	Rain	7	5	6	6	2	1	1	1	3	4	3	7
TUNISIA	Max	57	61	64	70	75	84	90	91	88	77	68	61
TUNIS	Min	43	45	46	52	55	63	68	70	66	59	52	45
	Rain	8	7	5	2	1	-	-	-	1	3	5	7
BOTSWANA	Max	89	88	88	88	82	77	77	84	90	95	93	90
MAUN	Min	66	66	64	59	50	43	43	48	57	66	66	66
	Rain	8	7	5	2	1	-	-	-	1	3	5	7
KENYA	Max	77	78	77	75	72	70	70	70	75	75	73	73
NAIROBI	Min	53	55	57	57	55	54	52	52	52	55	55	55
	Rain	5	6	11	16	17	9	6	7	6	8	15	11
MADAGASCAR	Max	78	78	78	75	73	70	68	70	73	81	81	81
ANTANANARIVO	Min	61	61	61	57	54	50	48	48	52	54	57	61
	Rain	21	20	17	11	9	9	10	9	7	9	13	20
MALAWI	Max	81	81	81	81	77	73	73	77	81	86	84	82
LILONGWE	Min	63	63	61	57	52	46	45	46	54	59	63	64
	Rain	19	18	13	5	1	-	-	1	1	1	7	15
NAMIBIA	Max	84	82	81	77	72	68	68	73	77	84	84	86
WINDHOEK	Min	63	61	59	55	48	45	43	46	54	59	59	63
	Rain	8	8	8	4	1	-	-	-	-	2	3	6
SOUTH AFRICA	Max	78	78	77	72	66	64	63	64	64	70	73	75
CAPE TOWN	Min	61	61	57	54	48	46	45	46	48	52	55	57
	Rain	3	2	3	6	9	9	10	9	7	5	3	3
SOUTH AFRICA	Max	78	77	75	72	66	63	63	68	73	77	77	79
JO'BURG	Min	57	57	55	50	43	39	39	43	48	54	55	57
	Rain	8	7	5	2	1	-	-	-	1	3	5	7
TANZANIA	Max	82	82	81	77	73	72	72	73	77	81	81	81
ARUSHA	Min	55	57	59	61	59	55	54	54	55	57	57	57
	Rain	12	9	11	7	2	-	-	-	-	1	4	9
UGANDA	Max	75	75	73	73	73	73	73	73	73	75	73	73
KABALE	Min	48	52	52	52	52	48	46	48	52	50	52	50
	Rain	11	13	16	20	16	5	3	8	15	18	19	15

Dr. Livingstone, I presume...

Ask anyone to name an explorer and the name David Livingstone jumps to the fore. Even that other famous explorer, Henry Stanley, was in such awe when he caught up with the famous Scottish missionary at Ujiji in darkest Africa that he lost his eloquence and muttered: "Dr. Livingstone, I presume?"

But few know that it was Verney Lovett Cameron who first crossed the continent from east to west. This accomplished British officer was doomed to obscurity much in the same way as Norwegian Roald Amundsen who beat Captain Robert Scott to the South Pole.

Fame

Before Livingstone there were Scottish, English, French and German explorers such as Brue, Bruce, Park, Clapperton, Caillie, Krapf and Rebmann, and after him came the Grants and Brazzas. Few of them were humanitarians like David Livingstone. Most were in it for fame and other more selfish reasons. There was Baker the hunter, Burton the intellectual and writer, and Henry Stanley, writer-adventurer and colonial agent.

Even though the search for the source of the Nile and the course of the Niger were major themes for early exploration, Africa is hardly a continent of waterways. With the exception of these two major rivers and a few other partly navigable ones such as the Senegal, Gambia, and Zambezi, most consist of forbidding swamps or seasonal swirling waters.

Few explorers could claim that they "discovered" new territory. Friendly local folks often served as guides and facilitators while hostile tribesmen at times added to the dangers already posed by wildlife and debilitating tropical diseases.

Ripping

But by "ripping Africa open," as Englishman John Speke dramatically described the process, these explorers sparked in Europe an interest that turned into a scramble for land and the stripping of Africa's newly-discovered wealth. Some explorers actually became agents of imperialism. Stanley was employed by Belgian King Leopold as his agent in the Congo while De Brazza helped found the French Congo, and Karl Peters helped launch the German Protectorate of East Africa.

- Andre Brue (French) 1698
- James Bruce (Scottish) 1769-72
- Mungo Park (Scottish) 1795-97
- Mungo Park (Scottish) 1805-06
- Dixon Denham & Hugh Clapperton (English) 1823-25
- Gordon Laing (Scottish) 1825
- Clapperton & Richard Lander (English) 1825-27
- Rene Caillie (French) 1827-28
- Richard Lander (English) 1830
- Ludwig Krapf & Johann Rebmann (German) 1848-49
- David Livingstone (Scottish) 1849
- Heinrich Barth (German) 1850-55
- Gerhard Rohlfs (German) 1861-69/1873-80
- David Livingstone (Scottish) 1853-56
- David Livingstone (Scottish) 1858-63
- David Livingstone (Scottish) 1866-73
- Richard Burton (English) 1857-58
- James Grant (Scottish) & John Speke (English) 1859-63
- Verney Lovett Cameron (English) 1873-76
- Henry M. Stanley (American) 1874-77
- Joseph Thomson (English) 1884-85
- Savorgnan de Brazza (French) 1875-79

Diplomatic Addresses

AFRICAN EMBASSIES IN THE US

ALGERIA
Embassy of the Republic of Algeria
2118 Kalorama Road NW
Washington, DC, 20008
Tel: 202-265-2800 Fax: 202-667-2174

ANGOLA
Embassy of the Republic of Angola
1615 M Street NW, Suite 900
Washington, DC, 20036
Tel: 202-785-1156 Fax: 202-785-1258

BENIN
Embassy of the Republic of Benin
2737 Cathedral Avenue NW
Washington, DC, 20008
Tel: 202-232-6656 Fax: 202-265-1996

BOTSWANA
Embassy of the Republic of Botswana
1533 New Hampshire Ave NW
Washington, DC, 20036
Tel: 202-244-4990 Fax: 202-244-4164

BURKINA FASO
Embassy of Burkina Faso
2340 Massachusetts Avenue NW
Washington, DC, 20008
Tel: 202-332-5577 Fax: 202-667-1882

BURUNDI
Embassy of the Republic of Burundi
2233 Wisconsin Avenue NW, Suite 212
Washington, DC, 20007
Tel: 202-342-2574 Fax: 202-342-2578

CAMEROON
Embassy of the Republic of Cameroon
2349 Massachusetts Ave NW
Washington, DC, 20008
Tel: 202-265-8790 Fax: 202-387-3826

CAPE VERDE
Embassy of the Republic of Cape Verde
3415 Massachusetts Avenue NW
Washington, DC, 20007
Tel: 202-965-6820 Fax: 202-965-1207

CENTRAL AFRICAN REPUBLIC
Embassy of Central African Republic
1618 22nd Street NW
Washington, DC, 20008
Tel: 202-483-7800 Fax: 202-332-9893

CHAD
Embassy of the Republic of Chad
2002 R Street NW
Washington, DC, 20009
Tel: 202-462-4009 Fax: 202-265-1937

COMOROS
Embassy of the Republic of Comoros
420 E. 50th St.
New York, NY, 10022
Tel: 212-972-8010 Fax: 212-983-4712

CONGO [KINSHASA]
Embassy of the Dem. Republic of Congo
1800 New Hampshire Ave NW
Washington, DC, 20009
Tel: 202-234-7690 Fax: 202-234-2609

CONGO [BRAZZAVILLE]
Embassy of the Republic of the Congo
4891 Colorado Avenue NW
Washington, DC, 20011
Tel: 202-726-0825 Fax: 202-726-1860

CÔTE D'IVOIRE
Embassy of the Republic of Cote d'Ivoire
3421 Massachusetts Avenue NW
Washington, DC, 20008
Tel: 202-797-0300 Fax:202-462-9444

DJIBOUTI
Embassy of the Republic of Djibouti
1156 15th Street NW, Suite 515
Washington, DC, 20005
Tel: 202-331-0270 Fax: 202-331-0302

EGYPT
Embassy of the Arab Republic of Egypt
3521 International Court NW
Washington, DC, 20008
Tel: 202-895-5400 Fax: 202-244-5131

EQUATORIAL GUINEA
Embassy of the Republic of Equatorial Guinea
2020 16th Street NW
Washington, DC, 20009
Tel: 202-518-5700 Fax: 202-518-5252

ERITREA
Embassy of the State of Eritrea
1708 New Hampshire Ave NW
Washington, DC, 20009
Tel: 202-319-1991 Fax: 202-319-1304

ETHIOPIA
Embassy of the Fed. Dem. Rep. of Ethiopia
2134 Kalorama Road NW
Washington, DC, 20008
Tel: 202-364-1200 Fax: 202-686-9857

GABON
Embassy of the Gabonese Republic
2034 20th Street NW, Suite 200
Washington, DC, 20009
Tel: 202-797-1000 Fax: 202-332-0668

GAMBIA
Embassy of The Gambia
1155 15th Street NW, Suite 1000
Washington, DC, 20005
Tel: 202-785-1399 Fax: 202-785-1430

GHANA
Embassy of the Republic of Ghana
3512 International Drive NW
Washington, DC, 20008
Tel: 202-686-4520 Fax: 202- 686-4527

GUINEA
Embassy of the Republic of Guinea
2112 Leroy Place NW
Washington, DC, 20008
Tel: 202-483-9420 Fax: 202-483-8688

GUINEA-BISSAU
Embassy of the Republic of Guinea-Bissau
15929 Yukon Lane
Rockville, MD, 20855
Tel: 301-947-3958 Fax: 301-947-3958

KENYA
Embassy of the Republic of Kenya
2249 R Street NW
Washington, DC, 20008
Tel:202-387-6101 Fax:202-462-3829

LESOTHO
Embassy of the Kingdom of Lesotho
2511 Massachusetts Ave NW
Washington, DC, 20008.
Tel: 202-797-5533 Fax: 202-234-6815

LIBERIA
Embassy of the Republic of Liberia
5303 Colorado Avenue NW
Washington, DC, 20011
Tel: 202-723-0437 Fax: 202-723-0436

LIBYA
Libyan Permanent Representative to the UN
309-315 East 48th St
New York, NY, 10017
Tel: 212-752-5775 Fax: 212-593-4787

MADAGASCAR
Embassy of the Republic of Madagascar
2374 Massachusetts Avenue NW
Washington, DC, 20008
Tel: 202-265-5525 Fax: 202-265-3034

MALAWI
Embassy of the Republic of Malawi
2408 Massachusetts Avenue NW
Washington, DC, 20008
Tel: 202-797-1007 Fax:202-265-0976

MALI
Embassy of the Republic of Mali
2130 R Street NW
Washington, DC, 20008
Tel: 202-332-2249 Fax: 202-332-6603

MAURITANIA
Embassy of the Islamic Rep. of Mauritania
2129 Leroy Place NW
Washington, DC, 20008
Tel: 202-232-5700 Fax: 202-319-2623

MAURITIUS
Embassy of Republic of Mauritius
4301 Connecticut Ave NW
Washington, DC, 20008
Tel: 202-244-1491 Fax: 202-966-0983

MOROCCO
Embassy of the Kingdom of Morocco
1601 21st Street NW
Washington, DC, 20009
Tel:202-462-7979 Fax:202-265-0161

MOZAMBIQUE
Embassy of the Republic of Mozambique
1990 M Street NW, Suite 570
Washington, DC, 20036
Tel: 202-293-7146 Fax: 202-835-0245

NAMIBIA
Embassy of the Republic of Namibia
1605 New Hampshire Ave NW
Washington, DC, 20009
Tel: 202-986-0540 Fax: 202-986-0443

NIGER
Embassy of the Republic of Niger
C2204 R Street NW
Washington, DC, 20008
Tel: 202-483-4224

NIGERIA
Embassy of the Federal Rep. of Nigeria
1333 16th Street NW
Washington, DC, 20036
Tel: 202-986-8400 Fax: 202-986-8449

RWANDA
Embassy of the Republic of Rwanda
1714 New Hampshire Ave NW
Washington, DC, 20009
Tel: 202-232-2882 Fax: 202-232-4544

SÃO TOMÉ & PRÍNCIPE
UN Mission of São Tomé & Príncipe
400 Park Ave, 17th Floor
New York, NY, 10022
Tel:212-317-0533 Fax: 212-317-0580

SENEGAL
Embassy of the Republic of Senegal
2112 Wyoming Ave NW
Washington, DC, 20008
Tel: 202-234-0540 Fax: 202-332-6315

SEYCHELLES
UN Mission of the Republic of Seychelles
820 Second Avenue, Suite 900F
New York, NY, 10017
Tel: 212-687-9766 Fax: 212-922-9177

SIERRA LEONE
Embassy of the Republic of Sierra Leone
1701 19th Street NW
Washington, DC, 20009
Tel: 202-939-9261 Fax: 202-483-1793

SOUTH AFRICA
Embassy of the Republic of South Africa
3051 Massachusetts Ave NW
Washington, DC, 20008
Tel: 202-232-4400 Fax: 202-265-1607

SUDAN
Embassy of the Republic of the Sudan
2210 Massachusetts Ave NW
Washington, DC, 20008
Tel: 202-338-8565 Fax: 202-667-2406

SWAZILAND
Embassy of the Kingdom of Swaziland
3400 International Drive NW
Washington, DC, 20008
Tel: 202-234-5002 Fax: 202-234-8254

TANZANIA
Embassy of the United Republic of Tanzania
2139 R Street NW
Washington, DC, 20008
Tel: 202-939-6125 Fax: 202-797-7408

TOGO
Embassy of the Republic of Togo
2208 Massachusetts Avenue NW
Washington, DC, 20008
Tel: 202-234-4212 Fax: 202-232-3190

TUNISIA
Embassy of the Republic of Tunisia
1515 Massachusetts Ave NW
Washington, DC, 20005
Tel: 202-862-1850 Fax: 202-862-1858

UGANDA
Embassy of the Republic of Uganda
5911 16th Street NW
Washington, DC, 20011
Tel: 202-726-7100 Fax: 202-726-1727

ZAMBIA
Embassy of the Republic of Zambia
2419 Massachusetts Ave NW
Washington, DC, 20008
Tel: 202-265-9717 Fax: 202-332-0826

ZIMBABWE
Embassy of the Republic of Zimbabwe
1608 New Hampshire Ave NW
Washington, DC, 20009
Tel: 202-332-7100 Fax: 202-483-9326

US EMBASSIES IN AFRICA

ALGERIA
4 Chemin Cheikh Bachir El-Ibrahimi, Algiers 16000
Tel: [213] (2) 69-12-55 Fax: 69-39-79
Web: us-embassy.eldjazair.net.dz.

ANGOLA
Rua Houari Boumedienne No. 32, Luanda
Tel: [244] (2) 347-028/345-481 Fax: 346-924

BENIN
rue Caporal Bernard Anani, Cotonou 2012
Tel: [229] 30-06-50 Fax: 30-14-39
Web: amemb.coo@intnet.bj.

BOTSWANA
P.O. Box 90, Gaborone
Tel: [267] 353-982 Fax: 356-947
E-mail: usembgab@global.co.za

BURKINA FASO
602 Avenue Raoul Follerau, Ouagadougou 01 B.P. 35
Tel: (226) 30-67-23 Fax: (226) 30-38-90
Web: amembouaga@ouagadougb.us-state.gov/

BURUNDI
Avenue Des Etas-Unis , Bujumbura B.P. 1720
Tel: [257] 22-34-54 Fax: 22-29-26
E-mail: @bujumburab.us-state.gov.

CAMEROON
rue Nachtigal, Yaounde B.P. 817
Tel: (237) 23-40-14 Fax: 23-07-53
Web: yaounde@youndeb.us-state.gov.

CAPE VERDE
Rua Abilio Macedo 81, Praia, C.P. 201
Tel: [238] 61-56-16 Fax: 61-13-55

CENTRAL AFRICAN REPUBLIC
Avenue David Dacko, Bangui B.P. 924
Tel: [236] 61-02-00 Fax: 61-44-94

CHAD
Ave. Felix Eboue, N'Djamena B.P. 413
Tel: [235] (51) 70-09 Fax: 51-56-54
Web: paschallrc@ndjamenab.us-state.gov.

DEM. REPUBLIC OF THE CONGO
310 Avenue des Aviateurs, Kinshasa
Tel: [243] (12) 21804 Fax: (88) 43805

REPUBLIC OF THE CONGO
The Brazzaville Embassy Office
is co-located in Kinshasa
Tel: [243] (88) 43608 Fax: (88) 41036

COTE D'IVOIRE
5 rue Jesse Owens, Abidjan 01 B.P. 1712
Tel: [225] 20-21-09-79 Fax: 20-22-32-59

DJIBOUTI
Plateau du Serpent, Blvd, Djibouti B.P. 185
Tel: [253] 35-39-95 Fax: 35-39-40

EGYPT
8 Kamal el-Din Salah St., Garden City Cairo
Tel: [20] (2) 355-7371 Fax: 357-3200

ERITREA
Franklin D. Roosevelt St, Asmara
Tel: [291] (1) 120004 Fax: 127584

ETHIOPIA
Entoto St. P.O. Box 1014, Addis Ababa
Tel: [251] (1) 550-666 Fax: 551-328
Email: usembassy@telecom.net.et.

GABON
Blvd. de la Mer, Libreville B.P. 4000
Tel: [241] 762-003/4 Fax: 745-507

THE GAMBIA
Fajara, Kairaba Ave, Banjul P.M.B. 19
Tel: (220) 392-856 Fax: 392-475

GHANA
Ring Road East - P.O. Box 194, Accra
Tel: [233] (21) 775-348 Fax: 776-008
Web: http:www.usembassy.org.gh.

GUINEA
rue KA 038, Conakry B.P. 603
Tel: [224] 41-15-20 Fax: 41-15-22
Web: www.eti-bull.net/usembassy

KENYA
Mombasa Road
Nairobi
Tel: [254] (2) 537-800 Fax: 537-810

LESOTHO
P.O. Box 333 , Maseru 100
Tel: [266] 312-666
310-116 Fax: E-mail: amles@lesoff.co.za.

LIBERIA
111 United Nations Dr., Mamba Point Monrovia
Tel: [231] 226-370-380 Fax: 226-148

MADAGASCAR
14 & 16, rue Rainitovo Antsahavola, Antananarivo 101
Tel: [261] (20) 22 21257 Fax: (20) 22 34539

MALAWI
P.O. Box 30016, Lilongwe 3
Tel: [265] 783-166 Fax: 780-471

MALI
rue Rochester NY
Bamako B.P. 34
Tel: [223] 22-54-70 Fax: 223712
Web: ipc@usa.org.ml.

MAURITANIA
rue Abdallaye, Nouakchott B.P. 222
Tel: (222) 25-26-60 Fax: 25-15-92
Web: aemnouak@opt.mr.

MAURITIUS
(Also COMOROS & SEYCHELLES)
Rogers House (4th Fl.) John Kennedy St, Port Louis
Tel: [230] 208-2347 Fax: 208-9534

MOROCCO
2 Ave. de Marrakech , Rabat PSC 74
Tel: [212] (7) 76-22-65 Fax: 76-56-61
Web: http://www.usembassy-morocco.org.ma.

MOZAMBIQUE
Avenida Kenneth Kaunda 193, Maputo
Tel: [258] (1) 49-27-97 Fax: 49-01-14
Web: usacomm@mail.tropical.co.mz

NAMIBIA
Ausplan Building 14 Lossen St. , Windhoek
Tel: [264] (61) 221-601 Fax: 229-792
Web: www.usemb.org.na.

NIGER
rue Des Ambassades, Niamey B.P. 11201
Tel: [227] 72-26-61 Fax: 73-31-67
Email: usemb@intnet.ne.

NIGERIA
2 Walter Carrington Crescent, Victoria Island, Lagos
Tel: [234] (1) 261-0050 Fax: 261-9856

RWANDA
Blvd. de la Revolution, Kigali B.P. 28
Tel: [250] 75601/2/3 Fax: 419-710-9346
Email: amembkigali@hotmail.com.

SIERRA LEONE
Walpole and Siaka Stevens Sts, Freetown
Tel: [232] (22) 226-481 Fax: 225-471

SOUTH AFRICA
877 Pretorius St., Arcadia Pretoria 0083
Tel: [27] (12) 342-1048 Fax: 342-2244

SUDAN
Sharia Ali Abdul Latif, Khartoum
Tel: [249] (11) 774611 Fax: [249] (11) 774137

TANZANIA
140 Msese Road, Kinondoni District, Dar Es Salaam
Tel: [255] (51) 666010-5 Fax: 666701
Web: usembassy-dar2@cats-net.com.

TOGO
rue Pelletier Caventou & rue Vauban, Lome B.P. 852
Tel: [228] 21-29-91 Fax: 21-79-52
Web: ustogo1#cafŽ.tg.

TUNISIA
144 Ave. de la Liberte, Tunis-Belvedere 1002
Tel: [216] (1) 782-566 Fax: 789-719

UGANDA
Parliament Ave, Kampala
Tel: [256] (41) 259792/3/5 Fax: 259794

ZAMBIA
Independence & United Nations Aves, Lusaka
Tel: [260] (1) 250-955 Fax: 252-225

ZIMBABWE
172 Herbert Chitepo Ave, Harare
Tel: [263] (4) 250-593 Fax: 796487
Email: amembzim@africaonline.co.zw.

INDEX

A

Abidjan Stock Exchange 70
Acrow Bridges 109, 110
AES 90, 91
Topography 34
Africa Measured 32
African Continent 33
African Convention on Preventing and
  Combating Corruption 167
African Development Bank (ADB) 56, 120, 116
African Embassies in the US 391
African Growth and Opportunity Act (AGOA) 65
African Information Society Initiative (AISI) 105
African milestones 25
African Peer Review Mechanism (APRM) 46
African Stock Exchange Association (ASEA) 69
African Telecommunications Union (ATU) 100
African Union (AU) 29, 46
Africa Project Development Facility (APDF) 116
Africa's Nations 173
  Map and Flags 174
Afwerki, Isaias 243
AGOA (See African Growth and Opportunity Act)
Agriculture 110, 112
  Environment Map 155
Ahmed, Sheikh Sharif 342
AIDS (See HIV/AIDS) 158
Airports 108
Akosombo Dam 164
Al Amoudi, Mohammed 23
Al-Bashir, Omer Hassan 20, 350
Algeria 27, 28, 29, 177
  Doing Business With 180
  Fast Facts 178
  Profile 177
American Depositary Receipts (ADRs) 71
Amundsen, Roald 390
Angola 26, 28, 29, 181
  Doing Business Wiith 184
  Fast Facts 182
  Profile 181
Annan, Kofi 29, 31
Arab Bank for Economic Development
  in Africa (ABED) 56
Arab Maghreb Union (AM 56
Armed Conflict (See Wars) 152
Assoumani, Azali 218
Aswan Dam 42,164
Atbara River 41
Atlas Mountains 34
Australapithecus africanus 25
Aziz, Ould Abdel 297

B

Banda, Rupiah 374
Bani River 44
Banking 118
  Top Banks by Region 118
  Top Fifty Banks 119
Bartholomeu Dias 26
Batoka Gorge 45
Bechuanaland 29
Bédié, Henri Konan 18

Bemba, Jean-Pierre 221
Ben Ali, Zine El Abidine 366
Benin 26,28,185
  Doing Business With 188
  Fast Facts 186
  Profile 185
Bine El Ouidane Dam 164
Biya, Paul 201
Blatter, Sepp 16
Blue Nile 41,42
Boni, Thomas Yayi 186
Bono 171
Botswana 29, 189
  Doing Business With 192
  Fast Facts 190
  Profile 189
Botswana Stock Exchange 69
Bourse Régionale des Valeurs Mobilières (BRVM) 70
Bouteflika, Abdelaziz 178
Boyoma Falls 43
Bozizé, François 211
Bribe Payers Index 168
Burkina Faso 28, 193
  Doing Business With 196
  Fast Facts 194
  Profile 193
Burundi 29, 197
  Doing Business With 199
  Fast Facts 198
  Profile 197

C

Cahora Bassa dam 45, 92, 165
Cameroon 29, 200
  Doing Business With 204
  Fast Facts 201
  Profile 200
Cape Mesurado 27
Cape of Good Hope 26
Cape Verde 29, 206
  Doing Business With 209
  Fast Facts 207
  Profile 206
Capital Outflows 68
Casablanca Stock Exchange 69
Central African Republic 210
  Doing Business With 212
  Fast Facts 211
  Profile 210
Central African States Development Bank (BDEAC) 56
Chad 29, 213
  Doing Business With 216
  Fast Facts 214
  Profile 213
Challenges of Africa 151
  Corruption 167
  Diseases
    Bilharziasis 157
    Dengue 157
    Ebola 157
    HIV/AIDS 156, 158
    Malaria 156
    River Blindness 157
    Sleeping sickness 156
    Tropical 156
    Yellow Fever 157
  Foreign Debt 170

Illiteracy 169
  Statistcal Overview 166
  Water 161
China in Africa 76
Chissano, Joaquim Alberto 309
Chobe River 45
Christianity 36
Clinton Global Initiative 23
Clooney, George 21
Coal 78
Coca-Cola 18, 148, 149
Coetzee, John Maxwell (JM) 31
Colonialism 38
Commission for East African Co-operation (EAC) 58
Common Market for Eastern and Southern Africa (COMESA) 57, 66, 120
Commonwealth (CWLTH) 57
Comoros 29, 217
  Doing Business With 219
  Fast Facts 218
  Profile 217
Compaoré, Blaise 194
Computers in Africa
  Statistics 105
Condé, Alpha 19, 262
Congo, Democratic Republic of 220
  Doing Business With 223
  Fast Facts 221
  Profile 220
Congo, Republic of 224
  Doing Business With 226
  Fast Facts 225
  Profile 224
Congo River 40, 42
Conté, Lansana 261
Corporate Council on Africa, The (CCA) 145
Corruption 167, 168
Côte d'Ivoire 227
  Doing Business With 230
  Fast Facts 228
  Profile 227
Country profiles 175
Credit Ratings (See Sovereign Credit Ratings) 142
Cultures of Africa 46
Customs and Economic Union of Central Africa (CEMAC) 57

D

Dams in Africa 164
Dangote, Aliko 23
Dar es Salaam Exchange 69
Darfur 20, 153
Debt Burden 48, 52, 72, 97, 158, 169
Debt, Foreign
  Statistics 170
Debt Relief 49
Debt Services Map 171
Déby, Idriss 214
de Klerk, FW 31
de Menezes, Fradique 328
Diplomatic addresses 391
Djibo, Salou 317
Djibouti 29, 231
  Doing Business With 233
  Fast Facts 232
  Profile 231

Doing Business with Africa
  Advice 145
  Assistance 146
  Ease comparison 135
  Licenses 136
  Setting Up 134
  Starting a Business 136
dos Santos, José Eduardo 182

E

East African Development Bank (EADB) 58
Economic Commission for Africa (ECA) 52
Economic Community for West African States (ECOWAS) 19, 58, 66, 120, 153
Economic Indicators Table 176
Economic Social and Cultural Council (ECOSOCC) 46
Economy 47
Egypt 26, 27, 28, 234
  Doing Business With 237
  Fast facts 235
  Profile 234
Egyptian Exchange 69
El Baradei, Mohamed 29, 31
Electricity 89
  Statistics 88
Energy 78
Equatorial Guinea 29, 238
  Doing Business With 241
  Fast Facts 239
  Profile 238
Eritrea 28, 29, 242
  Doing Business With 245
  Fast Facts 243
  Profile 242
Ethiopia 26, 28, 246
  Doing Business With 249
  Fast Facts 247
  Profile 246
European Union 39,66
Exchange rates 387
Export-Import Bank of the US (Eximbank) 147

F

Famine 154
  Hunger Map 154
FDI (See Foreign Direct Investment) 50
Fédération Internationale de Football Association (FIFA) 17
Fisher, Angela 122
Fitch 142
Food and Agriculture Organization (FAO) 52, 112
Food shortages (See also Famine) 113
Forcados river 44
Foreign Debt (Also see Debt, Foreign) 49, 170
Foreign Direct Investment (FDI) 50, 67, 116
Foreign Direct Investment Statistics 68
Foreign Investors, Major 67
Franc Zone (CFA) 58

G

Gabon 29, 250
  Doing Business With 253
  Fast Facts 251
  Profile 250

Gambia, The 29, 254
  Doing Business With 256
  Fast Facts 255
  Profile 254
Gbagbo, Laurent 18, 228
GDP Growth 48
Geldof, Bob 171
General Electric (GE) 89
Gezira Irrigation Project 162
Ghana 25, 28, 257
  Doing Business With 260
  Fast Facts 258
  Profile 257
Ghana Stock Exchange 69
Global Business Coalition on HIV/AIDS 160
Global Crisis 15, 48, 66
Global Depositary Receipts (GDRs) 71
Gnassingbé, Faure 362
Gordimer, Nadine 31
Goree Island 125
Grand Inga 165
Great Man-Made River Project 163
Gross Domestic Product (GDP)
  Share by Sector Statistics 114
Guebuza, Armando 309
Guinea 27, 28, 261
  Doing Business With 264
  Fast Facts 262
  Profile 261
Guinea-Bissau 29, 265
  Doing Business With 267
  Fast Facts 266
  Profile 265
Gwembe Valley 45

H

Harbors 108
Hassan 1 Dam 164
Hayes, Stephen 11
Heavily Indebted Poor Countries (HIPC) 170, 171
Hindu 36
HIPC Initiative 171
HIV/AIDS 50, 112, 158
Horn of Africa 35, 162
Human Indicators Table 172

I

Ibrahim, Mo 23
Illiteracy
  Statistics 169
Illiteracy Map 171
Indian Ocean Commission (IOC) 60
Indian Ocean Rim Association for
  Regional Cooperation 60
Information and Communication
  Technology (ICT) in Africa 97
Inga Rapids Project 164
Intergovernmental Authority for Development (IGAD) 59
Interim Economic Partnership Agreements (IEPAs) 66
International Arrivals 2002 121
International Atomic Energy Agency 52
International Chamber of Commerce (ICC) 59
International Confederation of Free Trade Unions 59
International Criminal Police Organization 59
International Development Association (IDA) 52, 146, 171
International Finance Corporation (IFC) 53, 116,146

International Labour Organization (ILO) 53
International Maritime Organization (IMO) 53
International Mobile Satellite Organization (Inmarsat) 60
International Monetary Fund (IMF) 53, 145
International Organization for Migration (IOM) 59
International Telecommunications Union (ITU) 53, 97,100
Internet 103
  Africa Compared to World 104
  African Statistics 102
  Broadband 103
  Circuits 105
  Cost 104
  E-Mail 104
Investment 63
Investment, Indirect 69
Islam 36

J

Jammeh, Yaya 254
Johannesburg Securities Exchange 69, 70
Johnson-Sirleaf, Ellen 29, 277
Jonathan, Goodluck 321
Jugnauth, Sir Aneerood 300

K

Kabila, Joseph 221
Kagame, Paul 325
Kagera River 41
Kalahari Desert 32, 34
Kariba Dam 45, 164
Katse Dam 164
Kenya 29, 268
  Doing Business With 271
  Fast Facts 269
  Profile 268
Kérékou, Mathieu 186
Key Sectors 77
Khama, Seretse Ian 189
Khartoum Stock Exchange 69
Kibaki, Mwai 269
Kiir, Salva 20
Kikwete, Jakaya 358
Ki-moon, Ban 15, 19, 46
King Letsie III 273
King Mohammed VI 305
King Mswati III 354
Koeberg 89
Konate, Sekouba 262
Koroma Ernest Bai 338
Kossou Dam 164
Kufuor, John Agyekum 258

L

Lake Chad 26, 162
Lake Kyoga 41
Lake Mweru 43
Lake Nasser 42
Lake Tanganyika 27, 32
Lake Victoria 32, 41, 125
Languages of Africa 35, 173
Lesotho 272
  Doing Business With 275
  Fast Facts 273
  Profile 272
Lesotho Highlands Project 89, 91, 164, 165

Liberia 27, 276
  Doing Business With 279
  Fast Facts 277
  Profile 276
Libya 28, 29, 280
  Doing Business With 283
  Fast Facts 281
  Profile 280
Libya Stock Market 69
Livingstone, David 27, 37, 43, 45, 390
Logone River 162
Lovett, Verney Cameron 390
Lualaba River 43
Luthuli, Albert John 31
Luyt, Louis 16

M

Maathai, Wangari 29, 31
Madagascar 26, 29, 32, 284
  Doing Business With 287
  Fast Facts 285
  Profile 284
Mahfouz, Naguib 31
Makuza, Bernard 325
Malaria 156
Malawi 29, 288
  Doing Business With 291
  Fast Facts 289
  Profile 288
Malawi Stock Exchange 69
Mali 26, 29, 292
  Doing Business With 295
  Fast Facts 293
  Profile 292
Mandela, Nelson 27, 29, 122, 344
Manufacturing 50, 115
Markala Dam 44
Masire, Ketumile 189
Mau-Mau 28
Mauritania 29, 296
  Doing Business With 299
  Fast Facts 297
  Profile 296
Mauritius 29, 300
  Doing Business With 303
  Fast Facts 301
  Profile 300
Mauritius Stock Exchange 69
Mbasogo, Teodoro Obiang Nguema 239
Mbeki, Thabo 16, 344
McKinsey 48
Michel, James 335
Mills, John Evans Atta 258
Mineral Production Statistics 95
Minerals 93
Minierals Map of Africa 94
Mogae, Festus 189
Mo Ibrahim Foundation 23, 137
Moody's 142
Morocco 26, 28, 304
  Doing Business With 307
  Fast Facts 305
  Profile 304
Mosisili, Pakalitha 273
Motlanthe, Kgalema 345
Motsepe, Patrice 23
Mount Elgon 34

Mount Kenya 34, 40, 128
Mount Kilimanjaro 32, 33, 40, 125
Mount Stanley 40
Mozambique 26, 28, 29, 308
  Doing Business With 311
  Fast Facts 309
  Profile 308
Mubarak, Hosni 234
Mugabe, Robert 29, 378
Multilateral Insurance Guarantee Agency (MIGA) 94, 146
Muluzi, Bakili 289
Murchison Falls 41
Museveni, Yoweri 370
Muslim 26

N

Nairobi Stock Exchange 69
Namibia 312
  Doing Business With 315
  Fast Facts 313
  Profile 312
Namibian Stock Exchange 69
Natural Gas 78
Ndayizeye, Domitien 198
Neto, Agostinho 182
Neves, José Maria Pereira 207
New Partnership for African
  Development (NEPAD) 29, 46, 112
Ngorongoro Crater 125
Niger 27, 28, 29, 316
  Doing Business With 319
  Fast Facts 317
  Profile 316
Niger Delta 44
Nigeria 26, 29, 320
  Doing Business With 323
  Fast Facts 321
  Profile 320
Nigerian Stock Exchange 69
Nile River 32,33, 40, 41, 43, 163
Nkoana-Mashabane, Maite 53
Nkurunziza, Pierre 198
Nobel Laureates 31
Nuclear Power 89
Nun River 44

O

Obama, Barack 27, 29, 54
Obasanjo, Olusegun 321
Obiang, Teodoro (a.k.a. Mbasogo) 239
Odinga, Raila Amolo 269
  Vegetation 35
Oil in Africa
  Major Producers 80
  Reserves 78
  Regions 79
Oil River 28
Olduvai Gorge 36
Omar, Ismail Guelleh 232
Ondimba, Ali Bongo 251
Oppenheimer, Nicky 23
Organization for Economic Cooperation
  and Development (OECD) 104,167
Organization of African Unity (OAU) 29, 46
Organization of Petroleum Exporting
  Countries (OPEC) 61

Ouattara, Alassane 19, 228
Overseas Private Investment Corporation (OPIC) 147
Owen Falls 42

P

Pan African Parliament (PAP) 29, 30
Pan-African Telecommunications (Panaftel) 100
Peacekeeping 153
   African Union 153
   United Nations 153
   UN Missions 153
Petroleum 78
Ping, Jean 46
Pires, Pedro 207
Pohamba, Hifikepunye 313
Population of Africa 51
Population, Urban 51
PPP Method (Purchasing Power Parity) 175
PricewaterhouseCoopers (PwC) 132, 138, 140
Privatization 72
Puntland 341
Purchasing Power Parity (PPP) 175

Q

Qaddafi, Muammar 29, 281

R

Rajoelina, Andry 285
Ramgoolam, Navinchandra 301
Ras ben Sekka 33
Ras Dashen Terara 40
Ras Hafun Peninsula 33
Ravalomanana, Marc 285
Refugees 152
Regional African Satellite
   Communications (RASCOM) 100
Regional markets 66
Religions of Africa 36
Rhodes, Cecil 28
River blindness 157
Rivers, Lakes and Mountains 40
Robben Island, 29
Roosevelt, Theodore 125, 128
Roseires Dam 42
Rupert, Johann 23
Rwanda 29, 324
   Doing Business With 326
   Fast Facts 325
   Profile 324

S

Sahara Desert 32, 33, 44, 125
Sambi, Ahmed Abdallah 218
Sanhá, Malam Bacai 266
São Tomé & Príncipé 29, 327
   Doing Business With 329
   Fast Facts 328
   Profile 327
Sappi 74, 116, 347
Sassou-Nguesso, Denis 224
Sawiris, Naguib 23
Sawiris, Nassef 23
Sawiris, Onsi 23

Senegal 26, 27, 29, 330
   Doing Business With 333
   Fast Facts 331
   Profile 330
Sennar Dam 42
Seychelles 29, 334
   Doing Business With 336
   Fast Facts 335
   Profile 334
Sierra Leone 27, 29, 337
   Doing Business With 339
   Fast Facts 338
   Profile 337
Slavery 28, 37
Sleeping sickness 156
Soccer World Cup 13, 15, 18, 27, 29, 17
Somalia 340
   Doing Business With 342
   Fast Facts 341
   Profile 340
Somaliland 28, 341
South Africa 27, 28, 29, 343
   Doing Business With 348
   Fast Facts 344
   Profile 343
Southern African Customs Union (SACU) 61
Southern African Development
   Community (SADC) 61, 66, 91
Sovereign Credit Ratings 142, 143
Soyinka, Wole 31
Standard & Poor's 142
Stanley, Henry 43, 390
Stock Exchanges, Africa 69
Stock Exchanges, African Performance Statistics 71
Sudan 26, 27, 28, 350
   Doing Business With 352
   Fast Facts 351
   Profile 350
Sudd swamps 41
Swaziland 29, 353
   Doing Business With 356
   Fast Facts 354
   Profile 353
Swaziland Stock Exchange 69
Symbion 92

T

Tanzania 26, 29, 357
   Doing Business With 360
   Fast Facts 358
   Profile 357
Taxes 132, 138
   Country Summary 138
Telecommunications
   African Statistics 99
   Business Potential 101
   Competition 100
   Fixed Lines 97
   Mobile Phones 98
   Privatization 101
   Rates 100
Togo 28, 29, 361
   Doing Business With 364
   Fast Facts 362
   Profile 361
Touré, Amadou 293

399

Tourism 121
  Foreign Investment 129
  International Arrivals 123
  Safari 126
Trade 63, 64
Trade Statistics 65
Transparency International (TI) 167
Transport 107
  Air 108, 126
  Airports Map 108
  Facilities Statistics 106
  Map 107
  Rail 107
  Road 107
Travel Tips 383, 384
  Accommodation 384
  Air Travel 384
  Business Hours 384
  Car Rental 384
  Climate 384
  Clothes 384
  Credit Cards 384
  Electricity 385
  Email 385
  Food 385
  Health 385
  Media 385
  Medical Services 385
  Money Matters 385
  Photography 385
  Public Holidays 386
  Public Transport 386
  Security 386
  Shopping 386
  Sport 386
  Telecommunications 386
  Trains 386
  Travel Insurance 387
  Visas 387
  Water 387
  When to Go 387
Tsvangirai, Morgan 378
Tudor Jones, Paul 129
Tunisia 27, 28, 365
  Doing Business With 368
  Fast Facts 366
  Profile 365
Tunis Stock Exchange 69
Tutu, Desmond 31

U

Uganda 29, 369
  Doing Business With 372
  Fast Facts 370
  Profile 369
Uganda Securities Exchange 69
Ujiji 27
UNAIDS 158
UN Development Program (UNDP) 145, 147
UN Economic Commission for Africa (ECA) 105
UN Food and Agriculture Administration (FAO) 160
UN High Commissioner for Refugees (UNHCR) 152
UN Industrial Development Organization (UNIDO) 49, 146
United Nations 52
United Nations Conference on Trade and Development (UNCTAD) 54

United Nations Development Programme (UNDP) 116
United Nations High Commissioner for Refugees (UNHCR) 54
United Nations Industrial Development Organization (UNIDA) 54
UN World Tourism Organization (UNWTO) 121
US Agency for International Aid and Development (USAID) 147
US Embassies in Africa 393
US Exports to Africa 64
US Imports from Africa 64
US Small Business Administration (SBA) 147
US Trade and Development Agency (TDA) 147

V

Veiga, Carlos 207
Victoria Falls 44
Victoria Falls, 125
Vieira, João Bernardo 266
Vuvuzela 18

W

Wade, Abdoulaye 21, 56, 331
wa Mutharika, Bingu 23, 46, 54, 289
Wars 152
Water Wars 161
Weah, George 277
Weather Chart 389
West African Development Bank (WADB) 62
West African Economic and Monetary Union (WAEMU) 62
Western Sahara 381
  Profile 381
White Nile 41
Wolde-Giyorgis, Girma 247
World Bank 54, 146
World Health Organization (WHO) 55, 158
World Intellectual Property Organization (WIPO) 55
World Meteorological Organization (WMO) 55
World Tourism Organization (UNWTO) 55
World Trade Organization (WTO) 55

Y

Yar'Adua Umaru Musa 321
Year in Review 15
Yellow Fever 157
Yoruba 25, 27

Z

Zaire 29
Zaïre River 42
Zambezi River 40, 44
Zambia 29, 373
  Doing Business With 376
  Fast Facts 374
  Profile 373
Zanj 25
Zanzibar 27, 28, 29
Zenawi, Meles 57, 247
Zimbabwe 25, 29, 377
  Doing Business With 380
  Fast Facts 378
  Profile 377
Zuma, Jacob 345